WRISTWATCH ANNUAL 2005

THE CATALOG

of

PRODUCERS, MODELS,

and

SPECIFICATIONS

by

PETER BRAUN

ABBEVILLE PRESS PUBLISHERS
New York London

Dear Readers,

In our industry, it seems that no watch can be sold without a discount. But does this "common" practice really reflect what the high-quality mechanical watch is all about? If you ask me, it is more about the love of precision mechanics and the passionate feeling that overcomes us as we place one of these ticking beauties housed in a precious metal on our wrists. The price is secondary; and if it's not, then there are a few things that should be remembered. One is certainly the extreme amount of love and attention to detail that went into making any of the outstanding works of art shown in this publication. If you have ever visited a watchmaker's workshop, then you will know exactly what it is that I am talking about. Rich watchmakers do not exist; they do this for the love of the art. And this is something that all of us should remember when we are squeezing the last cent out of the local jeweler down the street or threatening to turn to the Internet for a better deal (something I would strongly advise against).

As always, I would like to remind our readers that the prices shown in *Wristwatch Annual 2005* are the official retail prices given out by the manufacturers and distributors at press time (fall 2004). These prices are certainly subject to change throughout the year and should be used as a guideline only. They also do not reflect any discounts you may or may not be able to wrangle for yourself (while keeping the above-mentioned in mind). Due to certain companies' policies, some prices are listed in euros. And in some very rare cases, prices for brand-new watches were not available at press time. Your friendly neighborhood jeweler or watchmaker will certainly be more than happy to provide you with official current pricing.

And, finally, I do want to mention that in the past year, we lost a valuable member of the watchmaking community: Steven Phillips, inventor of the eternal winding system (EWS) and the first American candidate member of the A.H.C.I., passed away on February 27, 2004. May his handmade, innovative style be long remembered.

And may your hours reading *Wristwatch Annual 2005* be enjoyable.

Thomas Kretschmann. Actor.
Stays out of the limelight.

MASTERPIECE
DOUBLE RÉTROGRADE
Passion for Details: retrograde 24-h indicator for a second time zone, retrograde date indicator, power reserve indicator, small seconds, hand-decorated hand-wound movement.
TIME IS PRECIOUS. TREAT IT ACCORDINGLY.

The completion of a Langematik Perpetual requires several months of precision craftsmanship.

The making of the movement of the Langematik Perpetual.
The master watchmakers at Lange assemble each movement twice – part by part, with the utmost concentration. The enormous amount of additional work involved in the disassembly and reassembly processes is necessary to guarantee the absolutely flawless functionality of this highly complicated timekeeping mechanism. The same meticulous care is applied to the micron-accurate production of the 478 individual parts and the time-consuming artistic decoration of their surfaces, even on those sides that later remain concealed to the eye of the beholder.

In 1845, Adolph Lange gave up his privileged position as the watchmaker to the royal Saxon court and ventured into the impoverished mining town of Glashütte in the Ore Mountains to establish the German precision watchmaking industry. He developed totally new precision tools, invented innovative mechanisms and manufacturing methods, and began to craft watches for perpetuity. In the course of time, he created unique masterpieces of inestimable value, many of which today can be admired in prestigious public and private collections. Subsequently, for 100 years the watches of "A. Lange & Söhne" were among th most sought-after in the world, until the division o Germany eradicated the proud company's name o timepiece dials. "A. Lange & Söhne" became a legend

In the United States and Canada Lange watches can be found exclusively at the following locations: In Boston: Alpha Omega, Harvard Square, Prudential Center, phone (617) 864 12 27 • **Cambridge** • **Las Vegas:** Tesorini at Bellagio, 3600 Las Vegas Blvd South, phone (702) 693 79 24 • **McLean:** Liljenquist & Beckstead, 2001 International Drive, phone (703) 448 67 31 • **New Orleans:** ADLER'S, 722 Canal Street Avenue, phone (212) 888 05 05. **New York:** Wempe, 700 Fifth Avenue, phone (212) 397 90 00 • **Palm Beach:** Hamilton Jewelers, 215 Worth Avenue, phone (561) 659 67 88 • **San Francisco:** Shreve & Co.

Piaget, jardin secret

TOURBILLON MARINE
The TOURBILLON D'ART COLLECTION comprises watches which can be worn every day, in the city or at the beach.
These Tourbillon movement watches, either manual or automatic, harmonize metallic colours with traditional materials such as Alligator skin, Galuchat and mother of pearl. A unique opportunity to choose an exceptional watch perfectly matching your tastes: exceptional!
Limited edition of 500 numbered watches. Automatic movement with a flying tourbillon (ASC 1.2). Stainless steel case (316 L). Antiglare sapphire crystal. Water resistant to 200 m / 650 feet. Rubber strap and steel bracelet.
Alain Silberstein®
ARCHITECTE HORLOGER
GALERIE ALAIN SILBERSTEIN - 200 Boulevard Saint-Germain - 75007 Paris - Tél +33 (0)1 45 44 10 10 - paris@a-silberstein.fr - www.a-silberstein.fr

JACOB & Co.
JACOB & Co.
789

PARMIGIANI
FLEURIER
12
9
3
5·7

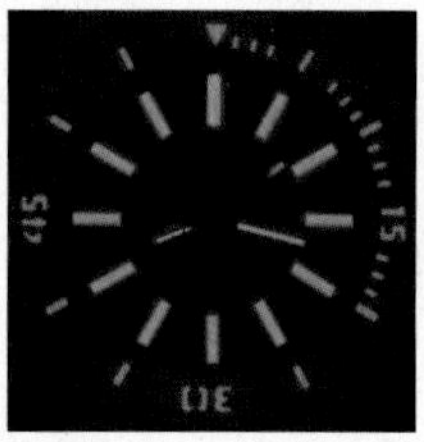

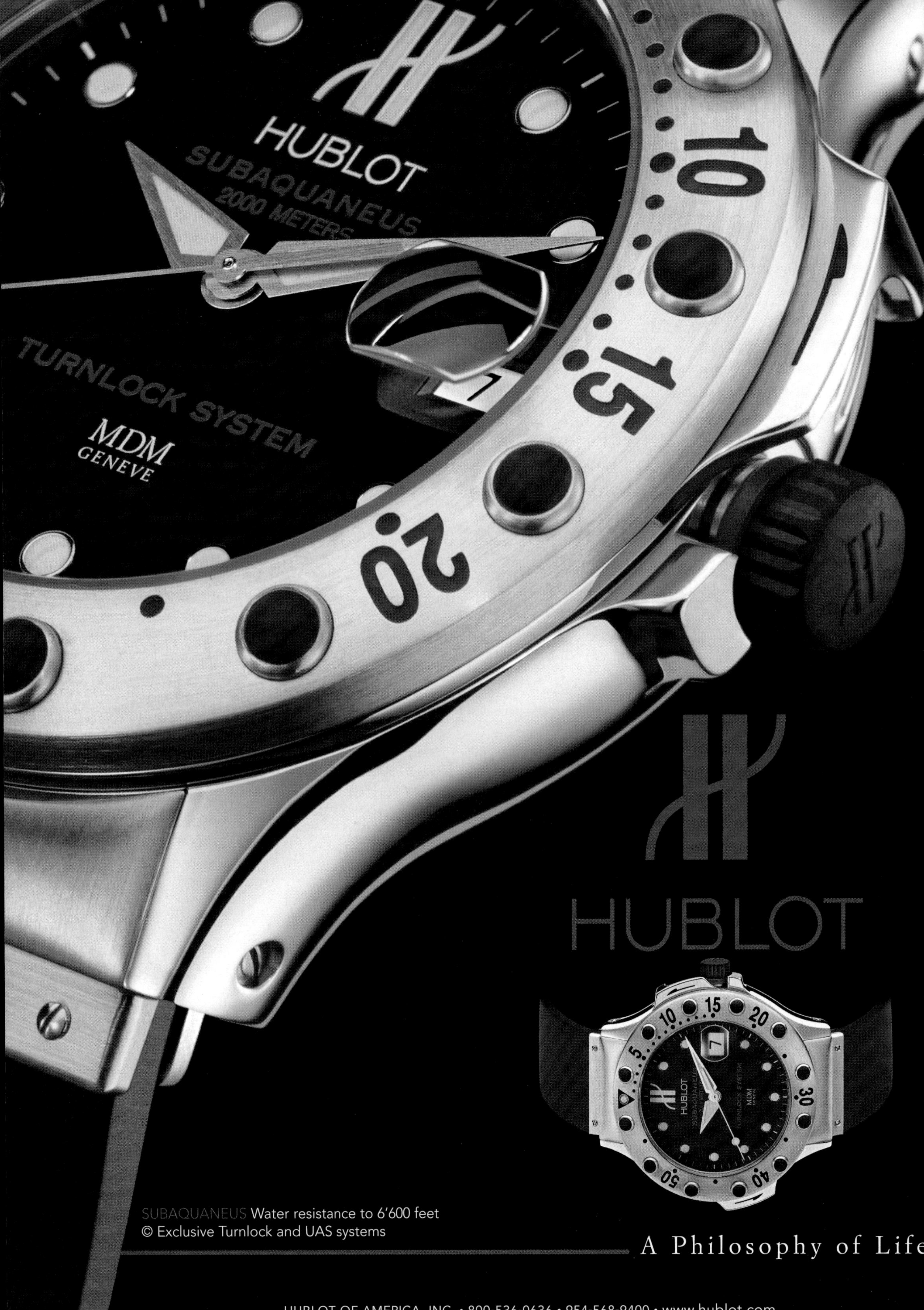
HUBLOT
SUBAQUANEUS
2000 METERS
TURNLOCK SYSTEM
MDM
GENEVE
10
15
20
HUBLOT
SUBAQUANEUS Water resistance to 6'600 feet
© Exclusive Turnlock and UAS systems
A Philosophy of Life
HUBLOT OF AMERICA, INC. • 800-536-0636 • 954-568-9400 • www.hublot.com

SWISS
MADE

F.P. Journe

Inventing and Making

by Elizabeth Doerr

This exceptional watchmaker was born in 1957 in Marseilles, France. By 1977 he had graduated from Paris's School of Watchmaking, after which he began working at his uncle's Parisian workshop. Remarkably, in that same year he constructed his own pocket watch outfitted with a tourbillon. François-Paul Journe was just twenty years of age.

This is the stuff legends are made of – just think of fourteen-year-old Daniel JeanRichard, for example (see page 218). Journe, certainly aware of his exceptional talent, decided to make a go of creating and marketing his own watches and opened his own workshops on Paris's rue de Verneuil in 1985. He joined the newly founded A.H.C.I. in 1986, finding a group of like-minded individuals with similar wills to create and the talent to match. The late eighties did a great deal to solidify Journe's reputation as an individual with a great sense of traditional watchmaking and more than enough talent to make things happen. His work brought him a number of awards, a few of them certainly based on the unique clock he constructed for Asprey's of London in 1986. The Sympathique, as it was named, is a pendulum clock outfitted with a *remontoir d'égalité*. A remontoire, as it is called in English, is a constant-force device that maintains a continuous transmission of the movement's driving power to the escape wheel, thereby stabilizing the rate. The Sympathique had a number of unusual features, the most striking certainly being the minute-repeater pocket watch placed in the recess at the top of the clock. The two movements run in a synchronized manner when the watch is placed on its base. The clock's case is crafted in the finest 18-karat gold, rock crystal, and more than three thousand pieces of coral in ten different colors.

Following this, a number of handmade, unique pocket watches outfitted with rare, traditional devices brought him the interest of both collectors and the Swiss watchmaking industry. In 1994 he was awarded the prestigious Gaia by La Chaux-de-Fonds's legendary museum.

Getting serious about grabbing hold of the industry, he moved to Geneva in 1996 and opened a workshop he called TIM SA. During this time he cooperated with some of the industry's biggest names, producing alarm mechanisms, mystery clocks, and watches for other exclusive companies. Feeling it was time to use his own name as a brand itself, Journe opened a new workshop in 1999, establishing F.P. Journe – Invenit et Fecit – at the same time. Suddenly, his production was altered. From creating and manufacturing one-of-a-kind pieces with all parts made by hand, he now had to hire other watchmakers and set up for serial production. Although his intellectual approach has remained identical, the actual manufacturing process has changed a bit. From creating just a few pieces a year, he has now gone to producing almost 600 annually, about 150 of which make it to the United States.

His premiere serial collection was based on two principles: the remontoire discussed above and the concept of resonance. The latter phenomenon uses two separate balance wheels that move in a synchronized manner, vibrating at the same frequency, to maintain a common, constant rate. In 1999 he introduced two limited models of ninety-nine pieces, each featuring devices according to this principle.

The Tourbillon Souverain was the premiere piece, and the world's only timepiece to combine a tourbillon with a constant-force remontoire. In the same year he introduced his Chronomètre à Résonance, a chronometer that incorporated the principle of resonance. Journe explains why he finds this phenomenon so interesting, "With the invention of the pendulum, watchmakers noticed that their beat often interfered with their

Journe's first women's watch, Octa Divine

The Octa Zodiaque from 2004

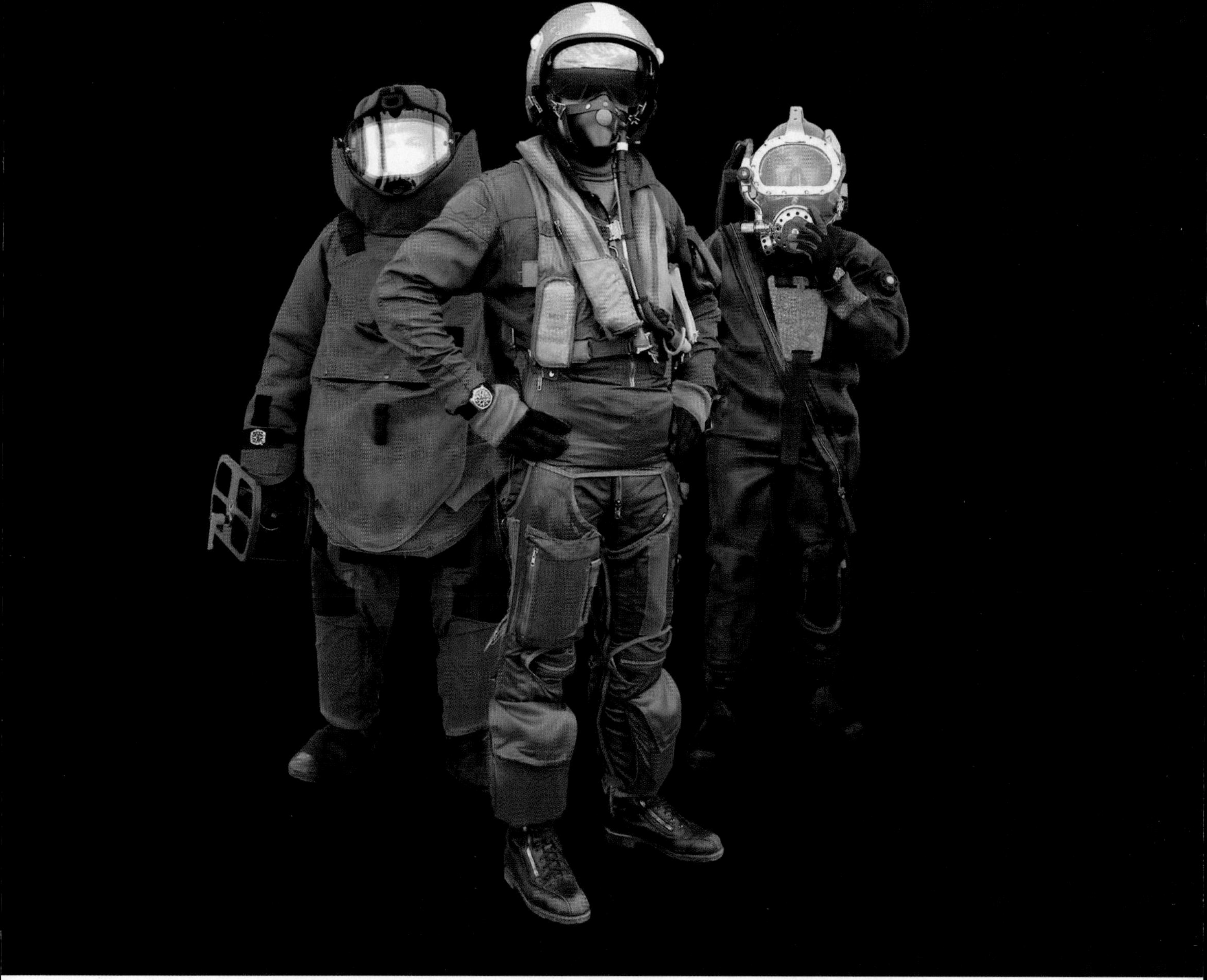

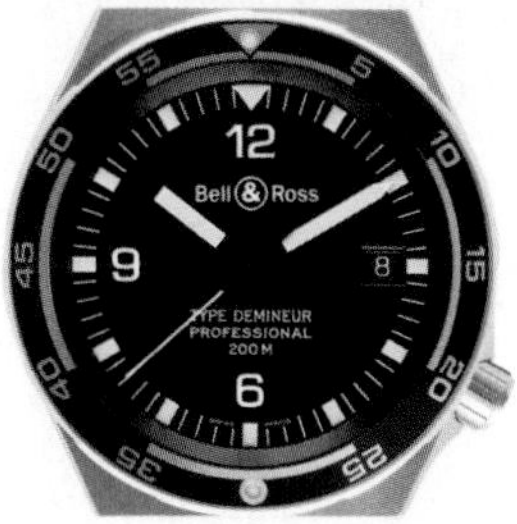

Type Demineur Black

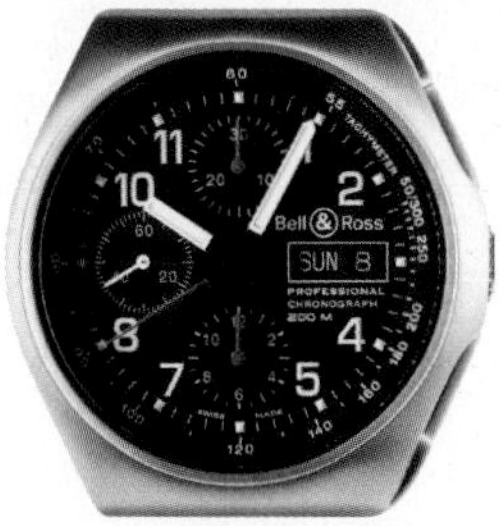

Space 3 Metal Black

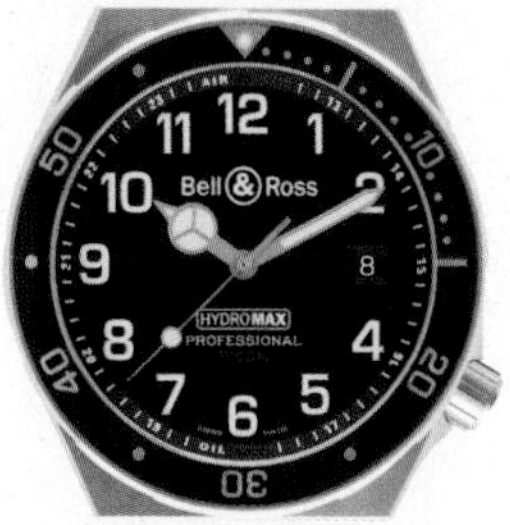

Hydromax 11 100M Black

2003's Octa Lune

environment, and it was not unusual for a pendulum clock to stop of its own accord when it entered into resonance with the driving-weight suspended from its cords. Antide Janvier was the first to have the feeling that one might turn this disadvantage into an asset. His idea was to build two complete movements with two precision escapements and to place them close to each other, ensuring that the two pendulums were hanging from the same construction. Just as he imagined, the pendulums recovered the energy dissipated by each other and began to beat together, thus entering into resonance." Journe's resonant chronometer also features twin independent dials, each driven by one of the separate twin movements. The movements are both wound by one crown, and the dial also features a power reserve indicator.

In 2001 Journe proved his extraordinary sense of spatial conception when he introduced the Octa caliber. This is an automatic caliber that was entirely conceived by Journe. Although this doesn't sound like anything extraordinary, the fact that Journe planned it so that complications could later be added without changing the measurements of the mechanism is actually quite remarkable. Three years in research and two years in development, Journe says of his first serial caliber, "The construction of the Octa caliber has less powerful ties with the history of watchmaking than do the remontoire or the resonance models, but it nonetheless symbolizes a horological ideal of giving timekeepers the highest possible degree of precision and autonomy!" Another remarkable feature of the movement 30 mm in diameter and 5.7 mm in height is the fact that it has an incredible five days of power reserve. To offset the classic problem of the balance representing the weak point within a movement with long power reserves, Journe created an overly large balance with a 10.1-mm diameter.

Journe's Tourbillon Souverain combining a tourbillon with a remontoire for the first time

The automatic Octa Réserve de Marche model with date from 2001 was followed by the Octa Chronograph, whose functions are naturally arranged in characteristic Journe manner on the dial – everything off-center – and the Octa Calendrier in 2002. The year 2003 saw the introduction of the Octa Lune, adding a moon phase model to the young brand's repertoire, as well as its first purpose-built women's watch, albeit one with a case diameter of 36 mm. Octa Divine also premieres both a gem-set bezel and a more conventional display of the hours and minutes. Since Divine is also outfitted with the Octa caliber, its subsidiary seconds, moon phase, and date displays have all remained in the same location as on the other models. The latest addition to the Octa family is of a highly celestial nature: Octa Zodiaque. This characteristic Journe timepiece is highlighted by a scale around the outside of the dial that shows both the current sign of the zodiac and the current month.

There is no doubt that pieces made by F.P. Journe are collectible, but just how collectible they are was illustrated clearly in 2004. This is the year Journe stopped making brass movements entirely, turning to 18-karat rose gold instead as his primary material. This means that even though the brass movements might be less valuable in a purely financial sense, they will become even more sought-after as rare collector's pieces.

A world premiere: wristwatch with resonance technology

No built in mp3 players.
No gps system.
No plasma screens.

Isn't life complicated
enough already?

The Tage Olson From Angular Momentum. Nickel-finished lever mechanical movement, caliber ETA 7001. 10,500 lines, 17 rubies. Curved silvered matte dial with applied batons in rhodium diamantée, polished rhodium dauphine hands, subsidiary seconds. 3 ATM water resistant polished stainless steel case with snap back, down-turned lugs, single curved sapphire crystal.
Learn more about this instant classic at www.angularmomentum.com or www.angularmomentum.us in the U.S.

One Hundred Years...
ARMAND NICOLET
TRAMELAN
CHRONOGRAPH
AUTOMATIC
TACHYMETER
SWISS MADE
ARMAND NICOLET
TRAMELAN
www.armandnicolet.com
Fifth Avenue Luxury Group
590 Fifth Avenue, 2nd Floor, New York, NY 10036 Tel 212.398.4440

GRANDE SECONDE
HOMMAGE GENÈVE 1784
JAQUET DROZ
JAQUET DROZ
ART HORLOGER DEPUIS 1738

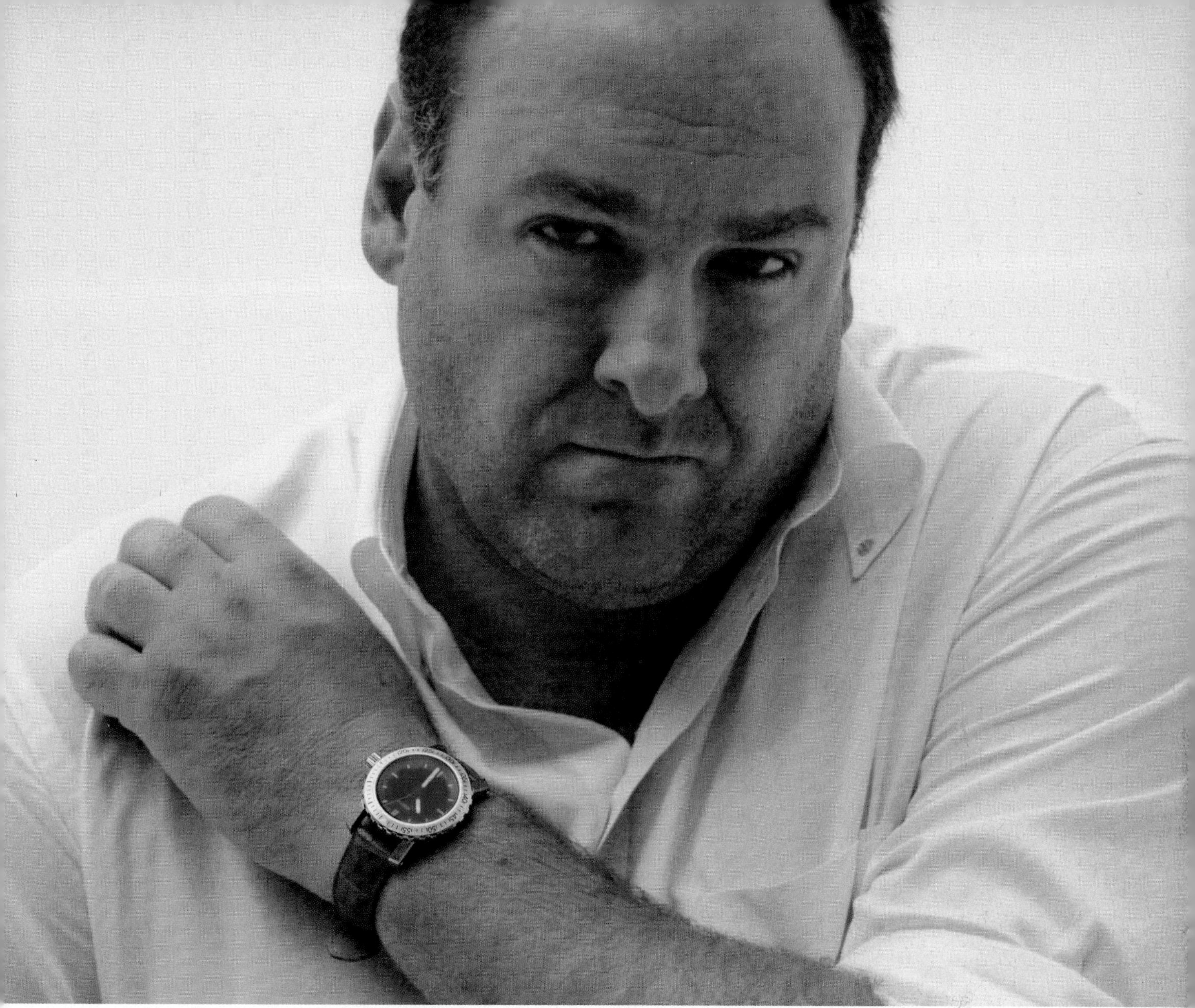

Actor and Kobold client James Gandolfini. Pictured here with his Soarway Diver №1049.

The watch alone won't make you tough.

The best thing about wearing a Kobold?
Suddenly you think you're tough.
We'll do our part. The rest is up to you.

KOBOLD Watch Company 1-877-SOARWAY www.koboldwatch.com

Svend Andersen

The international greats of the watchmaking scene seem to congregate in Geneva to find the horological rush they need to keep their creative juices flowing. One such creative opportunity was without a doubt the founding of the A.H.C.I. (Horological Academy of Independent Creators) in the middle of the 1980s in Geneva — by an Italian and a Dane living in the heart of Switzerland's watchmaking region: Vincent Calabrese and Svend Andersen. Inventor and watchmaker Svend Andersen spent his formative years at the Danish School of Watchmaking, a school integrated into the Royal Technological Institute of Copenhagen. In 1963, at the age of twenty-one, he went to Switzerland to learn more about the world's finest timepieces. His first job was with Swiss luxury jeweler Gübelin in Lucerne where he worked in after-sales service. Recognizing Andersen's talent for languages, the company sent him to Geneva in 1965 to help out in the store, a gig that ended abruptly in 1969 when Andersen presented a clock in a bottle on television that he had constructed after working hours. This project served its purpose, however, and Andersen was from then on known as the "watchmaker of the impossible," earning him a job on the Mount Olympus of watchmaking — in one of Patek Philippe's complication ateliers.

In the year 1979, Andersen founded his own workshop in Geneva, notably working on his perpetual flyback. In 1989 Andersen created his first world time watch and christened it Communication. This was followed by the subscription series Communication 24, of which Prince Consort Henrik of Denmark wears number one. Also in 1989 Andersen created the world's smallest calendar watch, a timepiece that was entered into the *Guinness Book of World Records* that year. Nineteen ninety-three saw the advent of Andersen's Perpetual 2000, as he puts it, "the only readable perpetual calendar on the market." The Mundus, a series of twenty-four numbered pieces from 1994, still counts as the thinnest automatic watch available (4.2 mm) and displays world time, various automata (some of them erotic), and some intricate designs based on vintage pocket and wristwatch movements incorporating every complication imaginable.

That time does not focus on just one moment is demonstrated by Andersen's Perpetual Secular Calendar, created in 1996, whose complicated gear train is crowned by a small pinion that turns once every 400 years in order to take into account the suppression of the leap year required to bring the Gregorian calendar in line with the solar year. Allowing precious moments to be documented discretely is the domain of a watch created in 1998 appropriately named Montre à Tact. Here the time is not indicated on the dial, but changes in increments shown in a window placed between the strap lugs. Just how difficult this apparently simple task turned out to be can only be appreciated by a glance inside the movement. The display drum surrounding the movement made winding by crown impossible, which is why Andersen decided to simply move the winding mechanism to the back of the case. He also used this same principle for his Montre avec Date Discrète where the drum features date divisions instead of hours. Due to the absence of a manual winding mechanism, the watch is supplied with a Scatola del Tempo watch winder. The case front, where the dial would normally be located, is available with individual hand engraving upon request.

The current season saw the great Dane introduce a watch in homage to the standardized world time created by Sir Sandford Fleming. Fleming originally presented his concept to twenty-five participating nations at the Prime Meridian Conference in Washington, D.C., in 1884. Appropriately, Andersen has named his new masterpiece 1884, dedicating the gold rotor to Fleming and including his name, years of birth and death, bust, and the words "inventor of world time." Andersen's 1884 world time watch is available in both white and yellow gold cases.

Grand Jour et Nuit

Reference number: KW1000SA
Movement: manual winding, Frédéric Piguet 15, ø 35.64 mm, height 1.90 mm; 20 jewels; 21,600 vph, ultra-flat jump hour module added to base movement
Functions: hours, minutes, subsidiary seconds; day/night indication
Case: white gold, ø 42 mm, height 8 mm; sapphire crystal, anti-reflective; transparent case back; water-resistant to 30 m
Band: reptile skin, buckle
Remarks: silver dial with guilloché
Price: $29,000
Variations: in white and rose gold, with black or white dial

Orbita Lunae

Reference number: KW1010SA
Movement: automatic, AS 1147, ø 29.45 mm, height 4.60 mm; 17 jewels; 21,600 vph
Functions: hours, minutes, sweep seconds; date, moon phase
Case: white gold, ø 38 mm, height 10 mm; sapphire crystal; transparent case back; water-resistant to 30 m
Band: reptile skin, buckle
Remarks: dial made of blue gold
Price: $16,800
Variations: in rose gold and in two-tone (all $16,800)

Communication

Movement: automatic, Frédéric Piguet 953 (base Frédéric Piguet 950) ø 21 mm, height 3.25 mm; 21 jewels; 21,600 vph, world time module added to base movement
Functions: hours, minutes; world time
Case: yellow gold, ø 32 mm, height 6.4 mm; bidirectionally rotating yellow gold bezel; sapphire crystal; water-resistant to 30 m
Band: reptile skin, buckle
Remarks: flattest world time watch
Price: $9,500

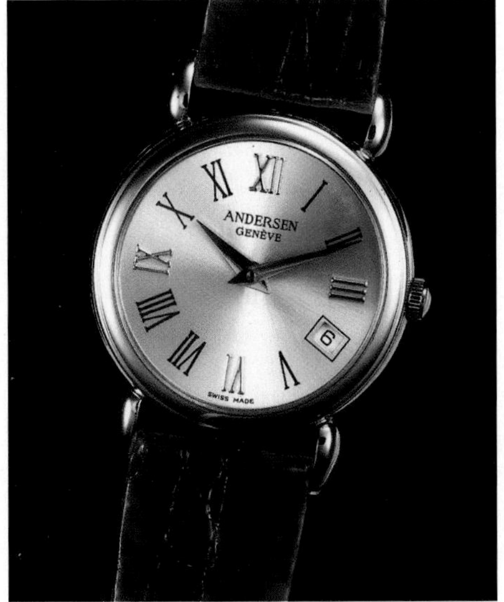

Maya

Movement: automatic, Frédéric Piguet 951, ø 21 mm, height 3.25 mm; 21 jewels; 21,600 vph
Functions: hours, minutes; date
Case: red gold, ø 25.5 mm, height 6.4 mm; sapphire crystal; transparent case back; water-resistant to 30 m
Band: reptile skin, buckle
Price: $6,800

Golden Reminder

Reference number: KW1040SAWGLD
Movement: automatic, Svend Andersen, ø 26 mm, height 5.50 mm; 27 jewels; 28,800 vph
Functions: hours, minutes
Case: white gold, ø 36.6 mm, height 10.9 mm; bidirectionally winding white gold bezel with one diamond as reminder; sapphire crystal; water-resistant to 30 m
Band: stingray, buckle
Remarks: blue gold dial with 12 diamond markers
Price: $14,500
Variations: in yellow gold ($14,500)

Montre à Tact

Reference number: KW1020SA
Movement: automatic, AS 1147C, ø 25.80 mm, height 4.10 mm; 17 jewels; 21,600 vph, time display is also found in window on side of case
Functions: hours, minutes
Case: white gold, ø 43 mm, height 9.8 mm; two correctors for time-setting mechanism on case back; sapphire crystals; water-resistant to 30 m
Band: reptile skin, buckle
Remarks: blue gold "dial" with guilloché
Price: $29,000
Variations: also available with rose gold guilloché "dial"

Angular Momentum

This name suggests dynamics — the dynamics of a rotational movement to be more precise. The great astronomer and physicist Johannes Kepler (1571-1630) was the first to construe an interrelation between a moment of inertia and angular velocity when he formulated his theory about the creation of the universe. He described the rotational inertia of an object or a system of objects in motion, using it to illustrate the movement of the earth around the sun in combination with our planet's alignment with its satellite, the rotating moon. With a sarcastic wink of the eye, Angular Momentum is also alluding to the system of the contemporary Swiss watchmaking industry — a system where many small bodies rotate around one large body. In reality, this small Swiss brand revolves around the improvement of a watch dial's legibility, without turning conventional reading habits completely upside down. A small rotating disk containing an hour scale, which is located underneath the hand arbors, and a reference point underneath the 12 support the display of the time shown by the hands, and could even replace it: Revolving Disk is the name of the simple system that marks the hour — clean, clear, and unmistakable.

In the new Tec & Art Collection, the fully disk-shaped hour hand offers a peaceful and large-surfaced presentation platform for different surface treatments against the wonderful backdrops of the artful dials. Here a stainless steel model illustrates a dial in "cat scratch," an artistic stone polishing. There are also various paints that cause other effects and mirror-polished surfaces, which can be applied to the dial or the "hour hand dial" as the client wishes. All Tec & Art watches are thus artistically unique. Parallel to these two design collections, Angular Momentum also offers a decidedly classic watch line called Tage Olsen, named for an ancestor of owner and creator Martin Pauli. Although Tage Olsen might interest a broader audience, the brand's trademark models utilizing the Revolving Disk system represent a more classic direction for the company and will surely create far more recognition value.

Illum / VI Chronograph

Reference number: IL 6.50.0000.AT.AC.RU
Movement: automatic, ETA 7750, ø 30 mm, height 7.9 mm; 25 jewels; 28,800 vph
Functions: hours, minutes, subsidiary seconds; chronograph; date
Case: stainless steel, ø 42 mm, height 16 mm; sapphire crystal; transparent case back; screw-in crown
Band: stainless steel, folding clasp
Price: $2,275
Variations: with rubber strap ($2,000); dial in six SuperLumiNova colors

AXIS / I Navigator

Reference number: AX 6.10.0000.AT.AC.L
Movement: automatic, ETA 2824-2, ø 25.6 mm, height 4.6 mm; 25 jewels; 28,800 vph
Functions: hours ("Revolving Disk"), minutes, sweep seconds; date
Case: stainless steel, ø 42 mm, height 14 mm; sapphire crystal; transparent case back; screw-in crown
Band: stainless steel, folding clasp
Price: $1,525
Variations: with leather strap ($1,250)

AXIS / III Handwinder

Reference number: AX 6.10.0000.HW.AC.L
Movement: manual winding, ETA 6497-1, ø 36.6 mm, height 4.5 mm; 17 jewels; 21,600 vph, finely decorated with côtes de Genève and blued screws
Functions: hours ("Revolving Disk"), minutes, subsidiary seconds ("Revolving Disk")
Case: stainless steel, ø 42 mm, height 14 mm; sapphire crystal; transparent case back; screw-in crown
Band: stainless steel, folding clasp
Price: $1,825
Variations: with leather strap ($1,550)

AXIS / VII Worldtimer

Reference number: AX 6.30.0000.AT.AC.L
Movement: automatic, ETA 2893-2, ø 25.6 mm, height 4.1 mm; 21 jewels; 28,800 vph
Functions: hours, minutes, sweep seconds; date; world time display (second time zone) via "Revolving Disk"
Case: stainless steel, ø 42 mm, height 14 mm; sapphire crystal; transparent case back; screw-in crown
Band: stainless steel, folding clasp
Price: $2,125
Variations: with leather strap ($1,850)

Tec & Art Cat-Scratch

Reference number: TA 6.10.CS-L.AT.AC.L
Movement: automatic, ETA 2824-2, ø 25.6 mm, height 4.6 mm; 25 jewels; 28,800 vph
Functions: hours ("Revolving Disk"), minutes, sweep seconds; date
Case: stainless steel, ø 41 mm, height 14 mm; sapphire crystal; transparent case back; screw-in crown
Band: stainless steel, folding clasp
Remarks: dial individually made by hand in various surface finishing techniques
Price: $2,275
Variations: leather strap; with gold or rhodium-plated case

Tage Olsen

Reference number: TO 3.10.0000.HW.AC.L
Movement: manual winding, ETA 7001, ø 23.3 mm, height 2.5 mm; 17 jewels; 21,600 vph
Functions: hours, minutes, subsidiary seconds
Case: stainless steel, ø 36 mm, height 12 mm; sapphire crystal
Band: leather, buckle
Price: $950

Anonimo

Florentine horological tradition? Watchmaking for the Italian military? Starting to sound familiar? It might to a whole lot of people interested in another brand also rooted in Florence, Italy, but connoisseurs know that outside of these items, there are very few similarities between these two brands known for the very large dimensions of their watches. One may have kicked off a trend with its timepieces, practically achieving cult status, but the other is not so far behind — and doing things its own way. A different way, however intertwined the roots may be.

The former is Panerai, which in 1993 released its first modern watch, becoming a hot tip for the trendy connoisseur. It wasn't long until 1997 when it was taken over by the Vendôme group (now Richemont) and the brand's production was moved to Switzerland, leaving a group of creative Italian watchmakers, case makers, and designers on the Swiss-Italian border without occupation.

The same year, designer and entrepreneur Federico Massacesi founded the other enterprise, using this very team of veteran horological specialists, to continue manufacturing watches in tasteful Florentine tradition. He named his brand Anonimo, Italian for anonymous, to emphasize the fact that these watches are about the individual wearing them — not about the watches as an end in themselves.

Massacesi's distinct design and demands on quality for Anonimo are based on two elements: The unique case production and the patented Kodiak strap. The case, made of AISI 316L surgical stainless steel is manufactured in a much different way than most cases. It is "scooped out" on a lathe and turned from the inside, rather than stamped as conventional cases are, to prevent the case from experiencing too much stress. Massacesi's firm belief is that when metal is struck, the molecules are largely restructured, making the metal brittle. The Anonimo style of manufacture results in a case with a more organic feel to it, almost like salt water hitting rocks. The smooth, satinated case sides do not scratch as easily as conventional steel, and they have a truly individualistic appearance.

Massacesi introduced another interesting aspect to cases in 2004: the Ox-Pro surface treatment. Ox-Pro is an oxidation process performed on the case's surface to turn it black. It is used by Anonimo in place of PVD coating, for example. In fourteen individual steps, the Ox-Pro process modifies the surface molecules of the stainless steel causing them to become darker, obtaining a deep, warm black tone. It is a process that has, until now, been used for military instruments and small weapons and was created by a company in — where else? — Florence.

The Kodiak process for the straps is equally as interesting as that of the cases. These straps, originally chosen by Panerai, are created by a patented process that allows leather to be continuously immersed in fresh- or seawater for up to twenty-four hours. No wonder, then, that Panerai was interested. Anonimo SpA now holds the sole patent to the Kodiak process, one that basically makes leather water-resistant. This is an advantage not only in the water, but also in hot, tropical climates where conventional leather is almost uncomfortable when worn for too long — not to mention what it generally looks like after being subjected to water or moist air for extended periods. The Kodiak strap, in comparison, looks fresh as a daisy.

Anonimo's first watch, the Millimetri, was released in 1998 to great critical acclaim from watch buyers and professional divers alike in Italy. A cooperation with one of the most important deep-sea diving industrial companies in the world, C.N.S. Cooperativa Nazionale Subacquei, allows the Italian brand to have its watches tested firsthand by professionals under real conditions. Anonimo, with its annual production of about 4,000 watches, successfully entered the American market a few years ago when Scott Moskovitz, a brand-new watch fan, acquired shares in the factory. Now positioned at fifty of America's high-end retail shops, the brand is often proudly located next to its countryman, Panerai. But no worries, these watches can truly stand up to any scrutiny that dyed-in-the-wool Paneristi can dish out.

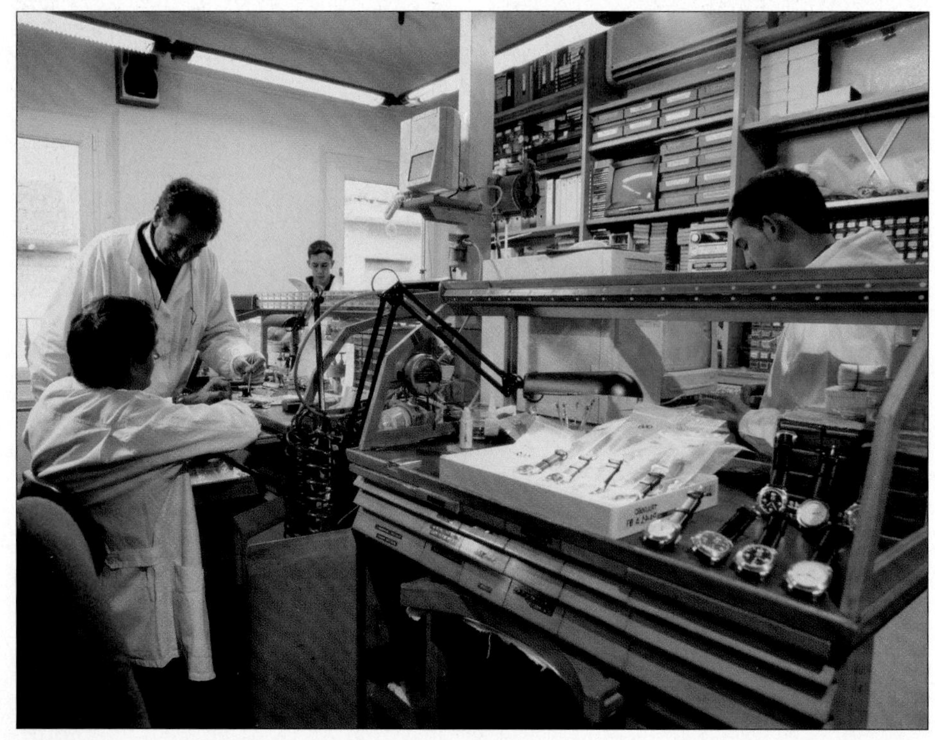

Militare Crono

Reference number: 2007 Black Dial
Movement: automatic, Dubois-Dépraz 2035 (base ETA 2892-A2); ø 26 mm, height 5.05 mm; 21 jewels; 28,800 vph, modified chronograph module
Functions: hours, minutes, subsidiary seconds; date; chronograph
Case: stainless steel, ø 43.4 mm, height 15.10 mm; sapphire crystal, shaped buttons on left side of case for protection; water-resistant to 120 m
Band: Kodiak leather, buckle
Remarks: patented crown vanishing locking device
Price: $4,300

Firenze Dual Time

Reference number: 2009 Silver Dial
Movement: automatic, Anonimo 02.1 (base ETA 2678); two movements with 25 jewels and 28,000 vph, soigné finish, adjusted in four positions
Functions: hours, minutes; date, day; second time zone
Case: stainless steel, ø 43.4 mm, height 14.5 mm; sapphire crystal; transparent case back; water-resistant to 120 m
Band: Kodiak leather, buckle
Remarks: patented crown vanishing locking device for double crowns at 6 and 12 o'clock
Price: $3,900

Militare Automatico

Reference number: 2010 Black Dial
Movement: automatic, Anonimo 03.1(base ETA 7750); ø 30 mm, height 7.9 mm; 25 jewels; 28,800 vph, colimassoné finish, adjusted in four positions
Functions: hours, minutes, subsidiary seconds; date; chronograph
Case: blackened stainless steel, ø 43.4 mm, height 14.4 mm; screw-locked bezel with 60-minute scale; sapphire crystal; transparent case back; water-resistant to 120 m
Band: Dinex fabric with Lorica lining, buckle
Remarks: ox-pro blackening treatment; patented crown
Price: $3,400

Hi-Dive

Reference number: 2011 Black Dial
Movement: automatic, Anonimo 01.0 (base ETA 2824-2); ø 26 mm, height 4.6 mm; 21 jewels; 28,800 vph, colimassoné finish, adjusted in four positions, rotor manufactured according to Anonimo's specifications
Functions: hours, minutes, sweep seconds; date
Case: blackened stainless steel, ø 45.6 mm, height 14.8 mm; automatic helium valve,bezel with 60-minute scale; sapphire crystal; screw-in crown; water-resistant to 120 m
Band: rubber, buckle
Remarks: limited edition of 500 pieces, ox-pro blackening
Price: $2,600

Match Racing Valencia

Reference number: 2012 Black Dial
Movement: automatic, Dubois-Dépraz 2073 (base ETA 2892-A2); ø 26 mm, height 5.05 mm; 46 jewels; 28,800 vph, colimassoné and soigné finish, adjusted in four positions
Functions: hours, minutes, subsidiary seconds; chronograph, countdown function, 24-hour counter, day/night indication
Case: blackened stainless steel, ø 45.6 mm, height 14.5 mm; bezel secured with four screws; sapphire crystal; screw-in crown and buttons; water-resistant to 120 m
Band: Kodiak sharkskin, buckle
Remarks: limited edition of 250 pieces, ox-pro blackening
Price: $3,400

Professionale Evolution

Reference number: 6000 Black Dial
Movement: automatic, Anonimo 01.0 (base ETA 2824-A2); ø 26 mm, height 4.6 mm; 21 jewels; 28,800 vph, colimassoné finish, adjusted in four positions
Functions: hours, minutes, sweep seconds; date
Case: stainless steel, ø 49.1 mm, height 15.7 mm; automatic helium valve, bezel and back locking system; sapphire crystal with magnifying lens above the date display; screw-in crown; water-resistant to 2000 m
Band: rubber, buckle
Remarks: limited edition of 250 pieces
Price: $5,400

Arnold & Son

The Swiss watch group The British Masters has resuscitated one of the greatest names in horology with Arnold & Son, and this interesting brand is finally finding its way to the world's various markets, including the United States.

The Englishman John Arnold was a contemporary of Abraham-Louis Breguet, sharing time with him that is documented by a lively correspondence. They were also united by a tourbillon that Breguet later presented the late master watchmaker's son: Breguet had mounted his first functioning tourbillon onto a chronometer made by John Arnold and had the following phrase engraved onto its movement: *This combines the first Breguet tourbillon escapement with one of Arnold's earliest movements. It is presented to Arnold's son by Breguet as a tribute to the memory of his beloved father in the year 1808.*

Arnold had a special place among the British watchmakers of his time, for he produced his chronometers on an almost industrial basis, developing standards and hiring numerous other watchmakers. During his lifetime, he is said to have manufactured something like 5,000 marine chronometers, selling them at reasonable prices to the British Royal Navy and the West Indies merchant fleet. Arnold chronometers were included in the traveling trunks of great discoverers such as Sir John Franklin, Captain Phipps, Sir Ernest Shackleton, Captain Cook, George Vancouver, Captain W. R. Broughton, Matthew Flinders, George Holbrook, and Dr. Livingstone.

The *manufacture* was known as Arnold & Son from 1787, after John Arnold took his son John Roger into the company. Until the middle of the nineteenth century, the historical brand remained in the possession of two generations of the great name, after which it was carried on by two further generations of nonrelated great master watchmakers.

The contributions to British seafaring and navigation made by John Arnold and his sons are the subject of the wristwatch collection presently being issued under the name of Arnold & Son. The Longitude II is characteristic of the brand's modern image: Outfitted like a contemporary navigational instrument, this timepiece possesses a rotating bezel, which can be set by the crown and is printed with a longitudinal scale, as well as an additional 24-hour scale in the center of the dial. Underneath the hinged lid on the back of the case, there is a small disk that indicates the equation of time, showing the difference between solar and mean time. Studying the instruction booklet can easily occupy an entire evening: Arnold & Son produces entertaining *and* educational watches!

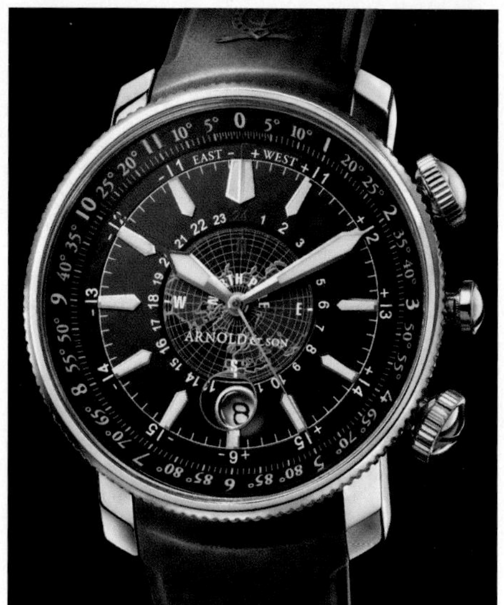

Longitude II

Reference number: 1L2AS.B02A.K02B
Movement: automatic, Arnold & Son 714 (base ETA 2892-A2); ø 25.6 mm, height 3.6 mm; 21 jewels; 28,800 vph, certified chronometer (C.O.S.C.)
Functions: hours, minutes, sweep seconds; date; 24-hour display/sun compass; numeral ring for current longitude; hinged case back with indication for equation of time
Case: stainless steel, ø 44.5 mm, height 15 mm; bidirectionally rotating bezel under crystal with longitudinal scale; sapphire crystal; screw-in crowns; water-resistant to 100 m
Band: rubber, buckle
Price: $7,000

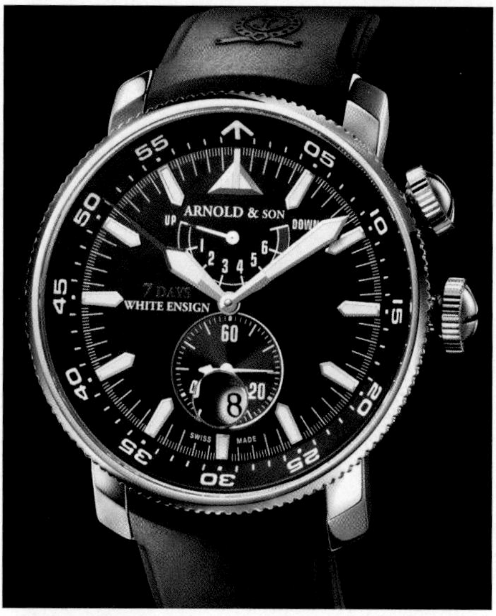

White Ensign

Reference number: 1WEBS.B01.K02B
Movement: manual winding, Arnold & Son 294E, ø 25.6 mm, height 4.3 mm; 20 jewels; 21,600 vph, power reserve 7 days
Functions: hours, minutes, subsidiary seconds; date; power reserve display
Case: stainless steel, ø 44.5 mm, height 12 mm; bidirectionally rotating bezel with 60-minute scale under crystal settable via crown; sapphire crystal; transparent case back; screw-in crown; water-resistant to 200 m
Band: rubber, buckle
Price: $8,500

GMT II Compass Rose

Reference number: 1G2AS.B03.C01B
Movement: automatic, Arnold & Son 788 (base ETA 2892-A2); ø 25.6 mm, height 3.6 mm; 21 jewels; 28,800 vph
Functions: hours, minutes, sweep seconds; date; 24-hour display, second time zone (settable via button)
Case: stainless steel, ø 42 mm, height 12 mm; sapphire crystal; screw-in crown; water-resistant to 50 m
Band: reptile skin, buckle
Price: $7,750

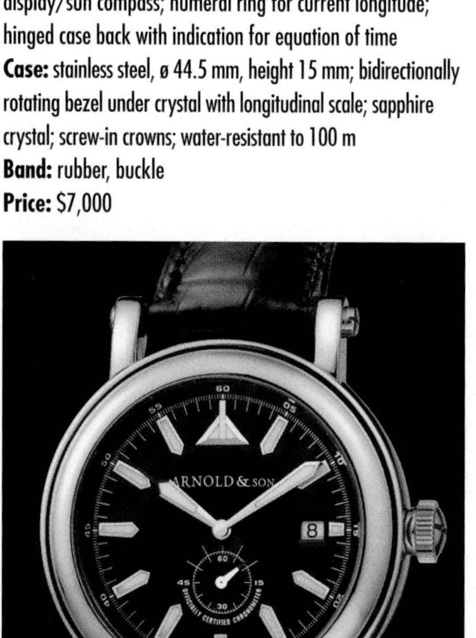

HMS

Reference number: 1H2AS.B01A.C03B
Movement: automatic, Arnold & Son 295 (base ETA 2892-A2); ø 25.6 mm, height 3.6 mm; 21 jewels; 28,800 vph, certified chronometer (C.O.S.C.)
Functions: hours, minutes, subsidiary seconds; date
Case: stainless steel, ø 42 mm, height 12 mm; sapphire crystal; screw-in crown; water-resistant to 50 m
Band: reptile skin, buckle
Price: $4,800

Tourbillon

Reference number: 1T1AW.S04.C01B
Movement: manual winding, Arnold & Son 1736, ø 25.6 mm, height 3.6 mm; 21 jewels; 21,600 vph, one-minute tourbillon; power reserve 110 hours
Functions: hours, minutes, subsidiary seconds (on tourbillon cage); 24-hour display; second time zone (settable via button)
Case: white gold, ø 42 mm, height 14 mm; sapphire crystal; transparent case back; screw-in crown; water-resistant to 50 m
Band: reptile skin, buckle
Price: $169,000

True North

Reference number: 1QPAW.S01A.C40B
Movement: manual winding, Arnold & Son 1794 (base Jaquet 7050); ø 40 mm, height 9.4 mm; 41 jewels; 21,600 vph, power reserve 7 days; côtes de Genève
Functions: hours, minutes; perpetual calendar (date, month, moon phase, leap year); double equation of time; display of true solar time, true direction, longitude; power reserve
Case: white gold, ø 42.5 mm, height 14.63 mm; bidirectionally rotating bezel under crystal with longitudinal scale and compass; sapphire crystal; screw-in crown; water-resistant to 50 m
Band: reptile skin, buckle
Price: $56,000

Audemars Piguet

In just about 130 years, Audemars Piguet has written watch history more than once. The brand hailing from Le Brassus was one of the few companies largely responsible for the renaissance of the mechanical watch at the end of the 1980s, but it was in 1972 — more than thirty years ago — that the Royal Oak delivered the premiere definition of a prestigious sports watch. Everything about the Royal Oak was new: the octagonal shape, the use of steel as a precious metal, the difficult construction of the case with eight screws going right through it, and the introduction of a band integrated right into the case.

It's no wonder, then, that this year the Royal Oak is again the brand's focus, as it has developed into a cult watch for the prominent and famous of this world. Former Mr. Universe and current governor of California Arnold Schwarzenegger even had a special edition of the Royal Oak Offshore Chronograph in a gold case dedicated to him. The striking watch is also the base of a special edition model honoring Columbian Formula 1 driver Juan Pablo Montoya. This watch possesses a bezel and crown protection made of carbon fiber that are secured with double hexagonal screws — in reverence to racing motors. The crown is shaped like a leaf shutter wheel nut from a Formula 1 racing car.

Alongside numerous technical highlights such as the Concept Watch and the new Cabinet 4, the *manufacture* from Le Brassus is turning strongly to the woman — the sporty woman, to be precise. The new Royal Oak Lady remains loyal to the spirit of the archetypal timepiece, playing with precious materials and maintaining an aristocratic aura. Softly rounded edges lend the octagonal bezel a feminine touch, and the partially polished and partially satin-finished surfaces create fascinating light effects. The Royal Oak Lady can also thank the many refined details such as the domed crystal, which continues in the contours of the bezel without influencing the legibility of the dial, or the eight hexagonal screws that fit perfectly and seamlessly into the domed surface of the bezel for its overall grace.

Audemars Piguet is meanwhile the oldest watch *manufacture* still owned by its founding family. In 1875 Jules-Louis Audemars and Edward-Auguste Piguet together founded a company "for the manufacture of fine and complicated watches using the most modern of production methods." To commemorate these founding fathers, today's owners have created the model lines Jules Audemars and Edward Piguet.

The elegant rectangular chronograph Edward Piguet has been gracefully reworked for the new season. The case and its lugs have grown somewhat, receiving a stronger curve when observed from the side. Additionally, there are now two new dial variations. And in the Jules Audemars collection, a tourbillon with a chronograph premiered that is outfitted with a fully new *manufacture* movement.

Royal Oak Automatic

Reference number: 14790ST.00.0789ST.10
Movement: automatic, Audemars Piguet 2225, ø 26 mm, height 3.25 mm; 35 jewels; 28,800 vph
Functions: hours, minutes, sweep seconds; date
Case: stainless steel, ø 36 mm, height 8.2 mm; bezel screwed through to case back with eight white gold screws; sapphire crystal; screw-in crown; water-resistant to 50 m
Band: stainless steel, folding clasp
Price: $8,900
Variations: in stainless steel/yellow gold; in yellow gold; diverse dial variations

Royal Oak Jumbo

Reference number: 15202ST.00.0944ST.01
Movement: automatic, Audemars Piguet 2121, ø 28 mm, height 3.05 mm; 36 jewels; 19,800 vph
Functions: hours, minutes; date
Case: stainless steel, ø 38.7 mm, height 8 mm; bezel screwed through to case back with eight white gold screws; sapphire crystal; water-resistant to 50 m
Band: stainless steel, folding clasp
Price: $14,700
Variations: in yellow gold; diverse dial variations

Royal Oak Dual Time

Reference number: 25730ST.00.0789ST.06
Movement: automatic, Audemars Piguet 2229/2845 (base AP 2224); ø 26 mm, height 4.85 mm; 37 jewels; 28,800 vph
Functions: hours, minutes, second time zone; power reserve display
Case: stainless steel, ø 36 mm, height 9.9 mm; bezel screwed through to case back with eight white gold screws; sapphire crystal; screw-in crown; water-resistant to 50 m
Band: stainless steel, folding clasp
Price: $13,800
Variations: in stainless steel/yellow gold; in yellow gold

Royal Oak Tourbillon Chronograph

Reference number: 25977BA.00.1205BA.01
Movement: manual winding, Audemars Piguet 2889, ø 29.3 mm, height 7.65 mm; 25 jewels; 21,600 vph, one-minute tourbillon
Functions: hours, minutes, subsidiary seconds; chronograph
Case: yellow gold, ø 44 mm, height 12.85 mm; bezel screwed through to case back with eight white gold screws; sapphire crystal; transparent case back; screw-in crown
Band: yellow gold, folding clasp
Price: $167,200
Variations: in stainless steel

Royal Oak Chronograph

Reference number: 25860ST.00.1110ST.03
Movement: automatic, Audemars Piguet 2385, ø 25.6 mm, height 5.5 mm; 37 jewels; 21,600 vph
Functions: hours, minutes, subsidiary seconds; chronograph; date
Case: stainless steel, ø 40 mm, height 11.3 mm; bezel screwed through to case back with eight white gold screws; sapphire crystal; screw-in crown and buttons; water-resistant to 50 m
Band: stainless steel, folding clasp
Price: $15,200
Variations: in yellow gold; in white gold; diverse dial variations

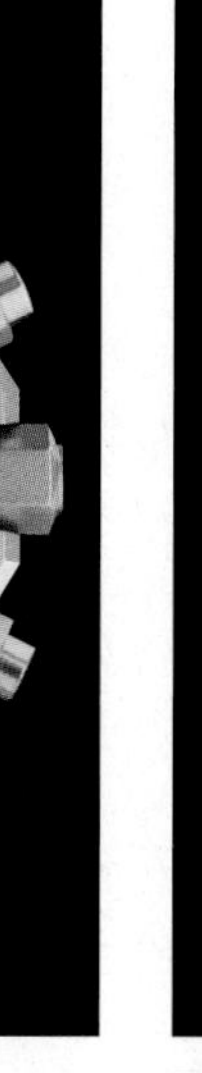

Royal Oak Quantième Perpétuel

Reference number: 25820SP.00.0944SP.02
Movement: automatic, Audemars Piguet 2120/2802, ø 28 mm, height 4.05 mm; 38 jewels; 19,800 vph
Functions: hours, minutes, perpetual calendar with date, day, month, moon phase, leap year
Case: stainless steel, ø 38.7 mm, height 9.5 mm; bezel in platinum screwed through to case back with eight white gold screws; sapphire crystal
Band: stainless steel/platinum, folding clasp
Price: $46,800
Variations: in stainless steel; in yellow gold; in platinum

Royal Oak Offshore Chronograph

Reference number: 25940OK.OO.D002CA.01
Movement: automatic, Audemars Piguet 2226/2840, ø 30 mm, height 6.15 mm; 54 jewels; 28,800 vph, with soft iron core for magnetic field protection
Functions: hours, minutes, subsidiary seconds; chronograph; date
Case: red gold, ø 44 mm, height 14.4 mm; bezel with rubber coating, screwed to case back with eight white gold screws; sapphire crystal; screw-in crown; water-resistant to 100 m
Band: rubber, folding clasp
Price: $33,300
Variations: in stainless steel/rubber

Royal Oak Offshore Chronograph Montoya

Reference number: 26030RO.OO.D001IN.01
Movement: automatic, Audemars Piguet 2226/2840, ø 30 mm, height 6.15 mm; 54 jewels; 28,800 vph
Functions: hours, minutes, subsidiary seconds; chronograph; date
Case: red gold, ø 42 mm, height 14.4 mm; bezel and button protection, screwed to case back with 8 screws; sapphire crystal; transparent case back and engraving "Juan Pablo Montoya"; screw-in crown in wheel bolt design; water-resistant to 100 m
Band: Ingrassato leather, folding clasp
Price: $37,500

Royal Oak Offshore Chronograph

Reference number: 26020ST.OO.D001IN.01
Movement: automatic, Audemars Piguet 2226/2840, ø 30 mm, height 6.15 mm; 54 jewels; 28,800 vph
Functions: hours, minutes, subsidiary seconds; chronograph; date
Case: stainless steel, ø 42 mm, height 14.4 mm; bezel screwed through to case back with eight white gold screws; sapphire crystal; screw-in crown with rubber cap; water-resistant to 100 m
Band: Ingrassato leather, folding clasp
Price: $16,600

Lady Royal Oak

Reference number: 67600BA.OO.D090CR.01
Movement: quartz, Audemars Piguet 2712
Functions: hours, minutes; date
Case: yellow gold, ø 33 mm, height 9.15 mm; bezel, screwed through to case back with eight white gold screws; sapphire crystal; screw-in crown; water-resistant to 50 m
Band: reptile skin, folding clasp
Price: $10,500
Variations: with yellow gold link bracelet; in stainless steel with leather or link bracelet; with diamonds

Royal Oak Offshore Chronograph Safari

Reference number: 26020ST.OO.D001IN.01
Movement: automatic, Audemars Piguet 2226/2840, ø 30 mm, height 6.15 mm; 54 jewels; 28,800 vph
Functions: hours, minutes, subsidiary seconds; chronograph; date
Case: stainless steel, ø 42 mm, height 14.4 mm; bezel screwed to case back with eight white gold screws; sapphire crystal; screw-in crown with rubber cap; water-resistant to 100 m
Band: Ingrassato leather, folding clasp
Price: $16,600
Variations: with blue leather strap

Royal Oak Chronograph

Reference number: 26022OR.OO.D088CR.01
Movement: automatic, Audemars Piguet 2385, ø 25.6 mm, height 5.5 mm; 37 jewels; 21,600 vph
Functions: hours, minutes, subsidiary seconds; chronograph; date
Case: red gold, ø 38.7 mm, height 10,95 mm; bezel screwed through to case back with eight red gold screws; sapphire crystal; screw-in crown and buttons; water-resistant to 50 m
Band: reptile skin, folding clasp
Price: $25,500
Variations: in yellow gold; in white gold

Jules Audemars 3120 Globe

Reference number: 15120OR.00.A088CR.02
Movement: automatic, Audemars Piguet 3120, ø 26.6 mm, height 4.25 mm; 40 jewels; 21,600 vph, power reserve appx. 60 hours
Functions: hours, minutes, sweep seconds; date
Case: red gold, ø 38.7 mm, height 9.5 mm; sapphire crystal; transparent case back
Band: reptile skin, buckle
Price: $13,800
Variations: in white gold

Jules Audemars 3120 Classic

Reference number: 15120BC.00.A002CR.01
Movement: automatic, Audemars Piguet 3120, ø 26.6 mm, height 4.25 mm; 40 jewels; 21,600 vph, power reserve appx. 60 hours
Functions: hours, minutes, sweep seconds; date
Case: white gold, ø 38.7 mm, height 9.5 mm; sapphire crystal; transparent case back
Band: reptile skin, buckle
Price: $14,800
Variations: in red gold

Jules Audemars Metropolis

Reference number: 25919OR.00.D002CR.01
Movement: automatic, Audemars Piguet 2120/2804, ø 28 mm, height 4 mm; 40 jewels; 19,800 vph
Functions: hours, minutes; perpetual calendar with date, day, month, leap year; world time display
Case: red gold, ø 39 mm, height 9.8 mm; sapphire crystal; transparent case back
Band: reptile skin, folding clasp
Price: $47,900
Variations: in platinum

Jules Audemars Équation du Temps

Reference number: 25934BA.00.D001CR.01
Movement: automatic, Audemars Piguet 2120/2808, ø 28 mm, height 5.35 mm; 41 jewels; 19,800 vph
Functions: hours, minutes, subsidiary seconds, perpetual calendar with date, day, month, moon phase, leap year; times of sunrise and sunset; equation of time
Case: yellow gold, ø 37 mm, height 10.2 mm; bezel with scale for equation of time; sapphire crystal; transparent case back
Band: reptile skin, folding clasp
Price: $68,000
Variations: in red gold; in white gold

Jules Audemars Dynamographe

Reference number: 25945BC.00.D001CR.01
Movement: manual winding, Audemars Piguet 2891, ø 29.3 mm, height 5.8 mm; 57 jewels; 21,600 vph, large and small strike train with three gongs (carillon)
Functions: hours, minutes, subsidiary seconds, power reserve for movement (dependent on torque) and strike train; minute repeater, grande sonnerie
Case: white gold, ø 39 mm, height 13.4 mm; sapphire crystal
Band: reptile skin, folding clasp
Price: $317,700
Variations: in platinum

Jules Audemars Tourbillon Minute Repeater

Reference number: 25858BC.00.D002CR.02
Movement: manual winding, Audemars Piguet 2872, 27 x 21.2 mm, height 6.1 mm; 32 jewels; 21,600 vph, one-minute tourbillon
Functions: hours, minutes, subsidiary seconds (on tourbillon cage); hour, quarter hour and minute repeater
Case: white gold, ø 40 mm, height 10.25 mm; sapphire crystal; transparent case back
Band: reptile skin, folding clasp
Price: $240,000

Edward Piguet Automatic

Reference number: 15121OR.OO.A002CR.02
Movement: automatic, Audemars Piguet 2140, ø 20 mm, height 4 mm; 31 jewels; 28,800 vph
Functions: hours, minutes, sweep seconds; date
Case: red gold, 29 x 46 mm, height 9.7 mm; sapphire crystal
Band: reptile skin, folding clasp
Price: $13,900
Variations: in white gold

Edward Piguet Chronograph

Reference number: 25987BC.OO.D002CR.01
Movement: automatic, Audemars Piguet 2385, ø 25.6 mm, height 5.5 mm; 37 jewels; 21,600 vph
Functions: hours, minutes, subsidiary seconds; chronograph; date
Case: white gold, 29 x 48.7 mm, height 11.9 mm; sapphire crystal
Band: reptile skin, folding clasp
Price: $22,600
Variations: in red gold

Edward Piguet Tourbillon

Reference number: 26006BC.OO.D002CR.01
Movement: manual winding, Audemars Piguet 2878, 27 x 20.3 mm, height 6.1 mm; 21 jewels; 21,600 vph, one-minute tourbillon, shaped movement, limited production of 40 movements per year
Functions: hours, minutes, subsidiary seconds (on tourbillon cage); power reserve display
Case: white gold, 29 x 48.7 mm, height 12.3 mm; sapphire crystal; transparent case back
Band: reptile skin, folding clasp
Price: $109,400
Variations: in red gold; in platinum

Canapé Tourbillon

Reference number: 25942BC.OO.D002CR.02
Movement: manual winding, Audemars Piguet 2878, 27 x 20.3 mm, height 6.1 mm; 21 jewels; 21,600 vph, one-minute tourbillon, shaped movement
Functions: hours, minutes, subsidiary seconds (on tourbillon cage); power reserve display
Case: white gold, 28 x 41 mm, height 12.7 mm; sapphire crystal; transparent case back
Band: reptile skin, folding clasp
Price: $129,400
Variations: in platinum

Promesse

Reference number: 67361BA.ZZ.1180BA.03
Movement: quartz, Audemars Piguet 2508, ø 17.2 mm, height 1.6 mm; 7 jewels
Functions: hours, minutes
Case: yellow gold, 18 x 32.5 mm, height 6.5 mm; bezel set with brilliant-cut diamonds; sapphire crystal; crown with cabochon
Band: yellow gold, folding clasp
Price: $16,500
Variations: in white gold

Royal Oak Offshore

Reference number: 67450BA.OO.1108BA.01
Movement: quartz, Audemars Piguet 2710, ø 16.2 mm, height 3.1 mm; 8 jewels
Functions: hours, minutes; date
Case: yellow gold, ø 28 mm, height 7.3 mm; bezel with eight gold claws; sapphire crystal; water-resistant to 50 m
Band: yellow gold, folding clasp
Price: $16,700
Variations: in stainless steel; diverse dial variations

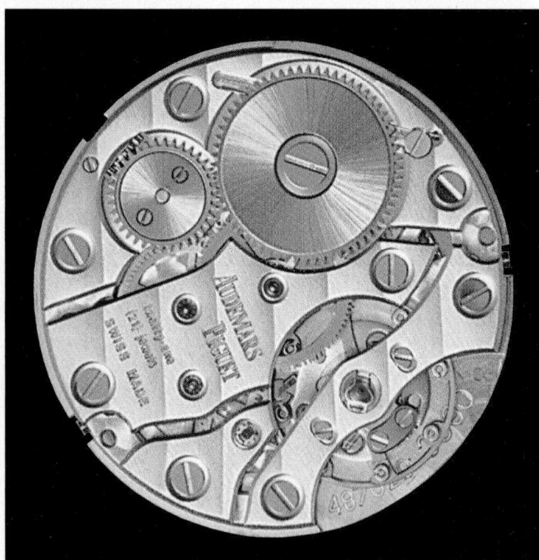

Caliber 3090-3900

Mechanical with manual winding, power reserve 48 hours
Functions: hours, minutes, subsidiary seconds; date; power reserve display
Diameter: 20.8 mm (9'''); **Height:** 4.1 mm; **Jewels:** 24
Balance: Cube (copper-beryllium) with adjustable eccentric weights; **Frequency:** 21,600 vph
Balance spring: flat hairspring with cemented balance spring stud; **Shock protection:** Kif Elastor
Number of individual parts: 177
Remarks: balance bridge; steel parts beveled and polished; base plate with perlage, bridges with côtes de Genève
Related calibers: 3090 (subsidiary seconds, height 2.8 mm, 21 jewels); 3091 (hours and minutes only); 3091 SQ (skeletonized)

Caliber 3120

Mechanical with automatic winding, rotor bilaterally winding; power reserve 60 hours
Functions: hours, minutes, sweep seconds; date
Diameter: 26.6 mm
Height: 4.25 mm
Jewels: 40
Balance: Cube (copper-beryllium) with adjustable eccentric weights
Frequency: 21,600 vph
Balance spring: flat hairspring
Shock protection: Kif Elastor
Remarks: balance bridge; rotor made of 22-karat gold; steel parts beveled and polished; base plate with perlage, bridges with côtes de Genève

Caliber 2873

Mechanical with manual winding, power reserve 48 hours
Functions: hours, minutes, subsidiary seconds; hour, quarter-hour, and minute repeater with carillon (three gongs)
Diameter: 22.3 mm (10''')
Height: 5 mm
Jewels: 34
Balance: glucydur with compensation screws
Frequency: 21,600 vph
Balance spring: flat hairspring
Shock protection: Kif Elastor
Number of individual parts: 337
Remarks: steel parts beveled and polished; base plate with perlage, bridges with côtes de Genève

Caliber 2878

Mechanical with manual winding, one-minute tourbillon; power reserve 78 hours
Functions: hours, minutes; power reserve display
Diameter: 27 x 20.3 mm
Height: 6.1 mm
Jewels: 21
Balance: glucydur with four gold screws
Frequency: 21,600 vph
Balance spring: with Breguet terminal curve
Shock protection: Kif Elastor
Number of individual parts: 168
Remarks: steel parts beveled and polished; base plate with perlage, bridges with côtes de Genève

Caliber 2879-1

Mechanical with manual winding, one-minute tourbillon; power reserve 70 hours
Functions: hours, minutes, subsidiary seconds; chronograph
Diameter: 29.3mm (12 1/2''')
Height: 7.65 mm
Jewels: 25
Balance: glucydur with four gold screws
Frequency: 21,600 vph
Balance spring: with Breguet terminal curve
Shock protection: Kif Elastor
Number of individual parts: 234
Remarks: steel parts beveled and polished; base plate with perlage, bridges with côtes de Genève

Caliber 2885

Mechanical with automatic winding, power reserve 48 hours
Functions: hours, minutes, subsidiary seconds; perpetual calendar (date, day, month, moon phase, leap year indication); hour, quarter-hour, and minute repeater; split-seconds chronograph
Diameter: 31 mm (13 1/2''')
Height: 8.55 mm; **Jewels:** 52
Balance: glucydur with four gold screws
Frequency: 19,800 vph
Balance spring: with Breguet terminal curve
Shock protection: Kif Elastor
Number of individual parts: 648
Remarks: steel parts beveled and polished; base plate with perlage, bridges with côtes de Genève

Caliber 2888

Mechanical with manual winding, one-minute tourbillon, power reserve 48 hours
Functions: hours, minutes
Dimensions: 21.8 x 28
Height: 6.05 mm
Jewels: 19
Balance: glucydur with four gold screws
Frequency: 21,600 vph
Balance spring: with Breguet terminal curve
Shock protection: Kif Elastor
Number of individual parts: 134
Remarks: base plate made of naturally grown quartz crystal; bridges decorated with special AP pattern

Caliber 2891

Mechanical with manual winding, power reserve 48 hours
Functions: hours, minutes, subsidiary seconds; grande sonnerie with hour, quarter-hour, and minute repeater, carillon (three gongs) with power reserve display for torque and strike train
Diameter: 29.3 mm (12 1/2''')
Height: 5.8 mm
Jewels: 57
Balance: glucydur with compensation screws
Frequency: 21,600 vph
Balance spring: flat hairspring
Number of individual parts: 490
Remarks: steel parts beveled and polished; base plate with perlage, bridges with côtes de Genève

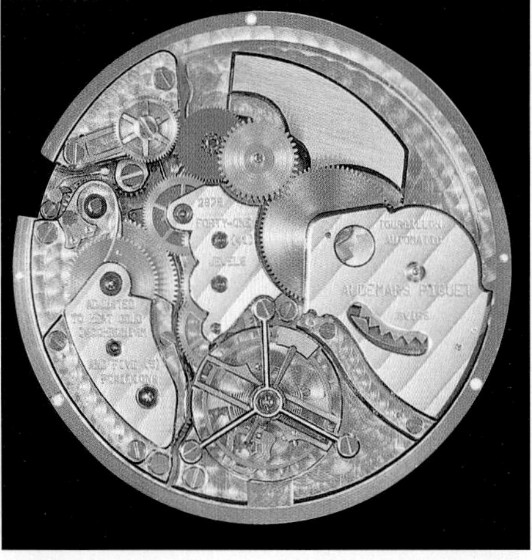

Caliber 2875

Mechanical with automatic winding, one-minute tourbillon; power reserve 50 hours
Functions: hours, minutes; date, day; power reserve display
Diameter: 30 mm (13''')
Height: 5.7 mm
Jewels: 41
Balance: glucydur with compensation screws
Frequency: 21,600 vph
Balance spring: flat hairspring
Number of individual parts: 268
Remarks: steel parts beveled and polished; base plate with perlage, bridges with côtes de Genève

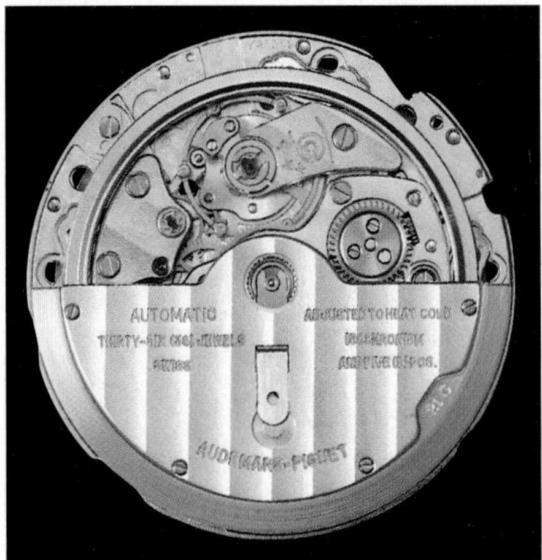

Caliber 2120-21

Mechanical with automatic winding; extra-flat rotor with side support rollers and 21-karat gold segment, power reserve 48 hours
Functions: hours, minutes; date, day (2121 with sweep seconds and day)
Diameter: 28 mm (12 1/2''')
Height: 2.45 mm (2121: 3,05 mm), **Jewels:** 36
Balance: Cube (copper-beryllium) with six weights
Frequency: 19,800 vph
Balance spring: flat hairspring
Shock protection: Kif Elastor
Number of individual parts: 214
Remarks: steel parts beveled and polished; base plate with perlage, bridges with côtes de Genève

Caliber 2120-2808

Mechanical with automatic winding; extra-flat rotor with side support rollers and 21-kt gold segment, power reserve 48 hours
Functions: hours, minutes; perpetual calendar (date, day, month, moon phase, leap year indication); sunrise/sunset times, equation of time
Diameter: 28 mm (12 1/2'''); **Height:** 5.35 mm
Jewels: 41;**Balance:** Cube (copper-beryllium) with six weights
Frequency: 19,800 vph; **Balance spring:** flat hairspring
Shock protection: Kif Elastor
Number of individual parts: 423
Remarks: steel parts beveled and polished; base plate with perlage, bridges with côtes de Genève
Related calibers: 2120-2801 (perp. cal. with calendar week); 2120-2804 (perp. cal. with world time instead of equation)

Caliber 2141-2806

Mechanical with automatic winding; rotor with 21-karat gold segment, power reserve 48 hours
Functions: hours, minutes; perpetual calendar (date, day, month, moon phase)
Diameter: 20 mm (9''')
Height: 5.55 mm
Jewels: 33
Balance: glucydur
Frequency: 28,800 vph
Balance spring: flat hairspring
Shock protection: Kif Elastor
Number of individual parts: appx. 305
Remarks: steel parts beveled and polished; base plate with perlage, bridges with côtes de Genève

Ball Watch Company

The pocket watch and ensuing wristwatch industry that sprang up in America had a lot to do with the increasing popularity of trains and their need for precise timing. If an engineer's watch was off, people's lives could be in great danger. A need for great precision was recognized, and all of America's eastern railroad companies agreed upon a uniform time, including dividing the country into time zones, long before this was officially recognized or introduced by the government.

By 1893 many companies had adopted the General Railroad Timepiece Standards. Although they changed from year to year, the Standards included many characteristics of a high-quality Swiss watch: regulated in at least five positions, precision to within thirty seconds in a week, Breguet balance spring, and so on. And an American pocket watch industry emerged that was able to meet these qualifications.

One of the chief players in developing these standards, and thus the industry, was Webster Clay Ball, or Webb C. Ball as he preferred to be known. Born in Fredericktown, Ohio, in 1847, Ball grew up on a farm. As a young man, he cast about for a new career and became an apprentice to watchmaker George Lewin, the town's jeweler.

From there he moved on to a sales position for John Dueber, a manufacturer of watch cases. After purchasing an interest in the firm of Whitcomb and Metten in 1879, he was quick to buy out Metten, then founded the Whitcomb and Ball Jewelry Store with his new partner. Later the same year, he bought out Whitcomb and established the Webb C. Ball Company in Clevelend, Ohio. The enterprising Ball was the first jeweler to use the time signals of the Naval Observatory in Washington after Standard Time was adopted in 1883, thus bringing precise time to Cleveland. Legend has it that he also imported the first chronometer to Ohio, which he put on display in his store window.

On July 19, 1891, Ball was appointed chief inspector for the Lake Shore Lines. He invented a watch inspection system and a set of timepiece guidelines that most American manufacturers set out to meet. Ball ended up being in charge of governing the precision of at least 175,000 miles of railroad, and he also extended his system into Mexico and Canada.

His inspection system was set up to keep records of a watch's performance using standard forms and uniform regulations, carefully supervising railroad time service with the aid of competent watchmakers. His system called for four standard watches to be present on every train, regardless of whether it was the passenger or freight variety. These timepieces were in the possession of the conductor, engineer, fireman, and rear brakeman. The watches were tested every two weeks and compared to standard Washington time. A variation of more than thirty seconds caused a watch to be sent in and repaired or regulated where necessary.

Ball Watch has now successfully been reintroduced to the U.S. and is embarking on a few innovative sponsoring activities along the way. Jim Whittaker, one of the new spokesmen, was the first American to climb Mount Everest in 1963.

"Accuracy is everything when you climb Mount Everest," the now seventy-five-year-old mountaineer reports of his cooperation with Ball. The company's second ambassador, Richard Limeburner, is a senior research specialist with the U.S. Global Ocean Ecosystems Dynamics. Precise timepieces are crucial for his scientific experiments in Antarctica, which include the study of predicting how populations of marine animal species respond to climactic changes. These adventurous men are helping to prove that Ball's tagline "since 1891, accuracy under adverse conditions" is not all marketing.

Engineer Hydrocarbon

Reference number: DM1016A-SIJ-WH
Movement: automatic, ETA 2892-2, ø 25.6 mm, height 3.6 mm; 21 jewels; 28,800 vph, constant rate up to -40°C
Functions: hours, minutes, sweep seconds; date
Case: stainless steel, ø 40 mm, height 14.1 mm; unidirectionally rotating bezel with 60-minute scale, safety crown locking system; sapphire crystal, anti-reflective; screw-in crown; water-resistant to 300 m
Band: stainless steel, double folding clasp
Remarks: 15 self-powered micro gas lights for night reading
Price: $1,250
Variations: available with black, white, and blue dials

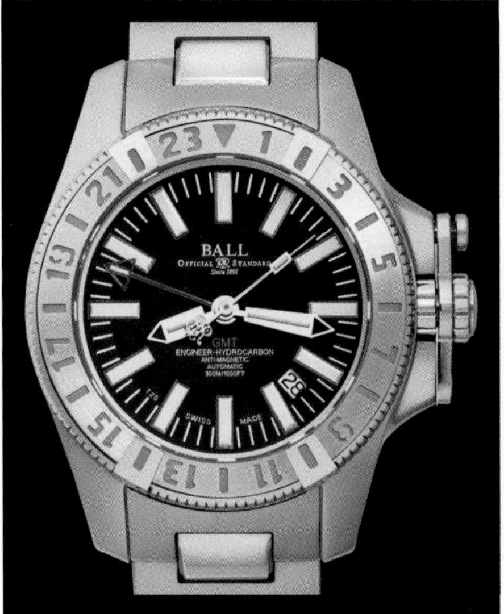

Engineer Hydrocarbon GMT

Reference number: DG1016A-SIJ-BK
Movement: automatic, ETA 2893-2, ø 25.6 mm, height 4.10 mm; 21 jewels; 28,800 vph, constant rate up to -40°C
Functions: hours, minutes, sweep seconds; date, 2nd time zone
Case: stainless steel, ø 40 mm, height 14.1 mm; unidirectionally rotating bezel, safety crown locking system; sapphire crystal, anti-reflective; screw-in crown; water-resistant to 300 m
Band: stainless steel, double folding clasp
Remarks: 16 self-powered micro gas lights for night reading capability
Price: $1,500
Variations: available with black, white, and blue dials

Engineer Arabic

Reference number: NM1016C-SAJ-BK
Movement: automatic, ETA 2836-2, ø 25.6 mm, height 5.05 mm; 25 jewels; 28,800 vph
Functions: hours, minutes, sweep seconds; date, day
Case: stainless steel, ø 38 mm, height 13 mm; sapphire crystal, anti-reflective; screw-in crown; water-resistant to 100 m
Band: stainless steel, double folding clasp
Remarks: 27 self-powered micro gas lights for night reading capability
Price: $840
Variations: with crocodile skin strap ($790); available with black, white, and blue dials

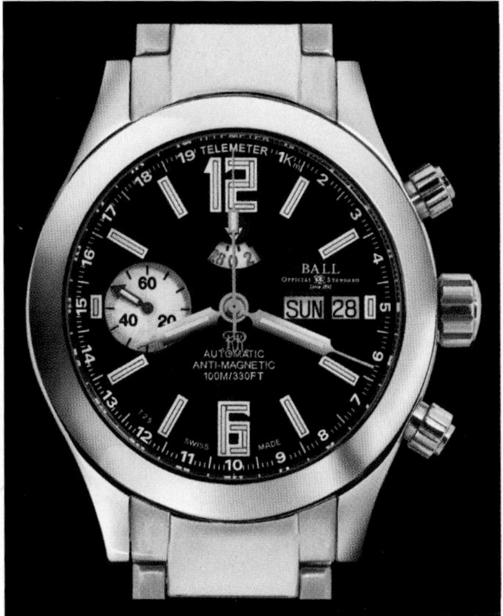

Engineer Master Telemeter

Reference number: CM1020C-S-BK
Movement: automatic, ETA 7750, ø 30 mm, height 7.90 mm; 25 jewels; 28,800 vph
Functions: hours, minutes, subsidiary seconds; date, day; chronograph
Case: stainless steel, ø 41 mm, height 16.2 mm; telemeter scale; sapphire crystal, anti-reflective; screw-in crown; water-resistant to 100 m
Band: stainless steel, double folding clasp
Remarks: 27 self-powered micro gas lights for night reading
Price: $1,670
Variations: with calfskin strap; black and white dials

Engineer Master Chronometer Limited Edition

Reference number: NM1020C-SCJ-SL
Movement: automatic, ETA 2836-2, ø 25.6 mm, height 5.05 mm; 25 jewels; 28,800 vph, C.O.S.C. certified
Remarks: hours, minutes, sweep seconds; date, day
Case: stainless steel, ø 40 mm, height 13 mm; sapphire crystal, anti-reflective; screw-in crown; water-resistant to 100 m
Band: stainless steel, double folding clasp
Remarks: 32 self-powered micro gas lights for night reading
Price: $1,250
Variations: with crocodile skin strap ($1,250); available with silver, gold, and black dials

Inspector

Reference number: DM1018B-SIJ-BK
Movement: automatic, ETA 2824-2, ø 25.6 mm, height 4.60 mm; 25 jewels; 28,800 vph
Functions: hours, minutes, sweep seconds; date, day
Case: stainless steel, 38.5 x 46.5 mm, height 13.5 mm; unidirectionally rotating bezel with 60-minute scale; sapphire crystal, anti-reflective; screw-in crown; water-resistant to 200 m
Band: stainless steel, folding clasp
Remarks: 19 self-powered micro gas lights for night reading capability
Price: $1,075
Variations: available with black, white, and blue dials

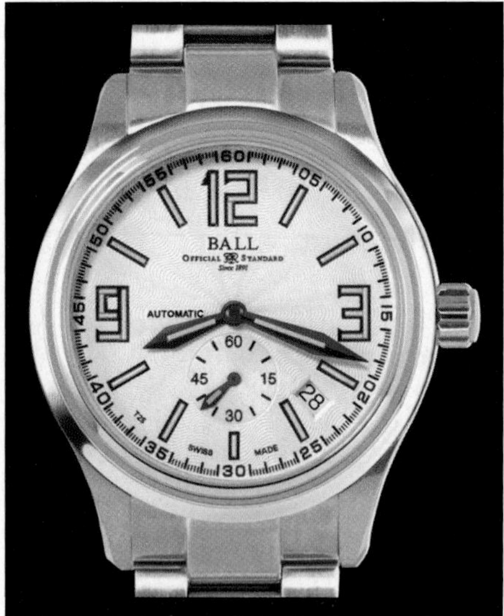

TrainMaster Small Seconds

Reference number: NM1050D-SAJ-WH
Movement: automatic, ETA 2895-2, ø 25.6 mm, height 4.35 mm; 30 jewels; 28,800 vph
Functions: hours, minutes, subsidiary seconds; date
Case: stainless steel, ø 38.3 mm, height 11.4 mm; sapphire crystal, anti-reflective; transparent case back; screw-in crown; water-resistant to 50 m
Band: stainless steel, double folding clasp
Remarks: 26 self-powered micro gas lights for night reading
Price: $1,030
Variations: with calfskin strap ($1,030); available with black, blue, and white dials

TrainMaster 60 Seconds

Reference number: NM1038-SJ-WH
Movement: automatic, ETA 2892-A2, ø 25.6 mm, height 3.6 mm; 21 jewels; 28,800 vph
Functions: hours, minutes, sweep seconds; date
Case: stainless steel, ø 38.3 mm, height 10.6 mm; sapphire crystal, anti-reflective; transparent case back; screw-in crown; water-resistant to 30 m
Band: stainless steel, double folding clasp
Remarks: 15 self-powered micro gas lights for night reading
Price: $930
Variations: with calfskin strap ($880); available with black and white dials

TrainMaster GMT

Reference number: GM1038C-SJ-BK
Movement: automatic, ETA 2893-2, ø 25.6 mm, height 4.10 mm; 21 jewels; 28,800 vph
Functions: hours, minutes, sweep seconds; date, second time zone
Case: stainless steel, ø 38.3 mm, height 10.5 mm; sapphire crystal, anti-reflective; transparent case back; screw-in crown; water-resistant to 30 m
Band: reptile skin, double folding clasp
Remarks: 24 self-powered micro gas lights for night reading
Price: $1,150
Variations: available with black and white dials

TrainMaster Pulse Meter

Reference number: CM1010D-SJ-WH
Movement: automatic, ETA 7750, ø 30 mm, height 7.90 mm; 25 jewels; 28,800 vph
Functions: hours, minutes, sweep seconds; date, day; chronograph, power reserve display
Case: stainless steel, ø 41 mm, height 14 mm; sapphire crystal, anti-reflective; transparent case back; screw-in crown; water-resistant to 50 m
Band: stainless steel, double folding clasp
Remarks: 18 self-powered micro gas lights for night reading
Price: $1,450
Variations: with calfskin strap; black, white, and blue dials

Conductor Power Reserve Limited Edition

Reference number: GM1068-W-BK
Movement: automatic, ETA 9035, ø 25.6 mm, height 5.10 mm; 28,800 vph, power reserve 48 hours
Functions: hours, minutes, sweep seconds; date; second time zone, power reserve display
Case: stainless steel, 35.5 x 47.5 mm, height 14.5 mm; sapphire crystal; transparent case back; screw-in crown; water-resistant to 50 m
Band: reptile skin, buckle
Remarks: 16 self-powered micro gas lights for night reading
Price: $2,310

Conductor Arabic Limited Edition

Reference number: NM1068D-LAJ-BK
Movement: automatic, ETA 2892-2, ø 25.6 mm, height 3.6 mm; 21 jewels; 28,800 vph
Functions: hours, minutes, sweep seconds; date
Case: stainless steel, 35.5 x 47.5 mm, height 13.2 mm; sapphire crystal; transparent case back; screw-in crown; water-resistant to 50 m
Band: reptile skin, buckle
Remarks: 24 self-powered micro gas lights for night reading
Price: $1,410
Variations: available with black, white, and gold dials; in women's size ($1,210)

Baume & Mercier

This company of long standing was founded by the Baume family in the western part of Switzerland in 1830. After merging with Genevan jeweler Paul Mercier in 1918, Baume & Mercier made a name for itself as a manufacturer of sporty chronographs.

Together with luxury brands Cartier and Piaget, Baume & Mercier forms the original core of the watch sector in the Richemont group. Today, this enterprise is represented in seventy-five countries and produces approximately 200,000 watches yearly. Its most important markets are found in Europe, particularly Italy, Spain, and France. In Germany, the Baume & Mercier brand is distributed by 220 exclusive watch retailers. Last September, Baume & Mercier opened new production buildings in Switzerland's Les Brenets. Within the last few years, Baume & Mercier has made a name for itself as a trendsetter, and by no means was this done solely on the strength of characteristically fashionable watches. Models such as the Riviera and the Hampton, named for the stylish resorts and high-society meeting places of the U.S. east coast, defined a new watch style in the 1980s and '90s for both him and her, calling a great deal of imitators into the market.

Baume & Mercier's watches most giftedly play with extroverted shapes and the large surfaces of '70s fashion trends. The perfect surface finish, the tangible quality of the material, and finally the security of style with regard to dimensions and proportions never emanate a feeling of nostalgia. These watches are as modern and fresh as the break of the new day.

A daring new interpretation of the TV Screen topic caused Baume & Mercier to courageously go to the front of the class a few years ago. After the edgy, provoking Hampton Spirit of the previous year presented the watch world with its first level of evolution, the Hampton City is clearly more obliging, showing an edge only at places where it neither rubs the wrong way nor fights the cufflink.

There are not many watch shapes that are accepted right from the beginning. Timepieces that stray too far from the normed circle or even square quickly leave an unserious aftertaste. The slim, well-proportioned shape of the Hampton City finds the border without crossing it.

For those who haven't (yet) embarked upon the adventure of a rectangular watch, Baume & Mercier has introduced a new collection of simple, round watches in European dimensions this year at the S.I.H.H. called Executives. Sometimes even trendsetters can fall back on old traditions ...

Hampton Milleis

Reference number: MOA08245
Movement: automatic, BM 8395-1 (base ETA 2000-1); ø 20 mm, height 3.6 mm; 20 jewels; 28,800 vph
Functions: hours, minutes; date
Case: yellow gold, 26 x 40 mm, height 9 mm; sapphire crystal
Band: reptile skin, folding clasp
Price: $3,395
Variations: with quartz movement; small model

Hampton Classic

Reference number: MOA08436
Movement: quartz, BM 5001 (base ETA 901.001)
Functions: hours, minutes
Case: yellow gold, 20 x 32 mm, height 7 mm; sapphire crystal
Band: reptile skin, buckle
Price: $2,195
Variations: large model

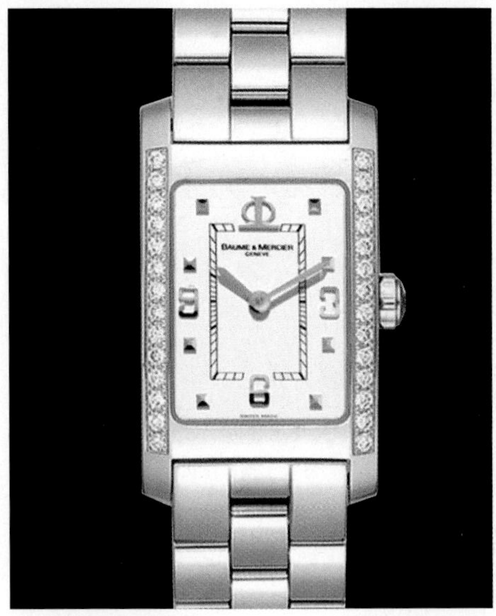

Hampton Classic

Reference number: MOA08407
Movement: quartz, BM 5001 (base ETA 901.001)
Functions: hours, minutes
Case: stainless steel, 20 x 32 mm, height 7 mm; bezel set with 28 brilliant-cut diamonds; sapphire crystal
Band: stainless steel, folding clasp
Price: $2,995

Hampton Milleis Chronograph

Reference number: MOA08484
Movement: quartz, BM 10471 (base ETA 251.471)
Functions: hours, minutes, subsidiary seconds; date; chronograph
Case: stainless steel, 30 x 46.5 mm, height 10.5 mm; sapphire crystal; water-resistant to 50 m
Band: reptile skin, folding clasp
Price: $1,895
Variations: with silver-plated dial and stainless steel bracelet

Hampton Milleis

Reference number: MOA08442
Movement: automatic, BM 11892/2A (base ETA 2892-A2); ø 26.2 mm, height 3.6 mm; 21 jewels; 28,800 vph
Functions: hours, minutes, sweep seconds; date
Case: stainless steel, 30 x 46.5 mm, height 10.5 mm; sapphire crystal; water-resistant to 50 m
Band: reptile skin, folding clasp
Price: $1,895
Variations: with silver-plated dial and stainless steel bracelet

Hampton Classic

Reference number: MOA08440
Movement: quartz, BM 5001 (base ETA 901.001)
Functions: hours, minutes
Case: stainless steel, 20 x 32 mm, height 7 mm; sapphire crystal; case back with engraving "Hampton 10 ans"
Band: reptile skin, buckle
Remarks: special edition 10 Years of Hampton
Price: $1,295
Variations: as special edition Hampton Milleis, Hampton City, and Hampton Spirit

Hampton City Chronograph

Reference number: MOA08345
Movement: automatic, BM 122894 (base ETA 2894-2); ø 28.6 mm, height 6.1 mm; 37 jewels; 28,800 vph
Functions: hours, minutes, subsidiary seconds; chronograph
Case: stainless steel, 42.4 x 46 mm, height 14.15 mm; sapphire crystal
Band: reptile skin, buckle
Price: $3,295
Variations: with silver-plated dial

Hampton City

Reference number: MOA08342
Movement: automatic, BM 72671 (base ETA 2671); ø 17.5 mm, height 4.8 mm; 25 jewels; 28,800 vph
Functions: hours, minutes, sweep seconds
Case: stainless steel, 39.2 x 42.2 mm, height 12.3 mm; sapphire crystal
Band: reptile skin, buckle
Price: $1,895
Variations: with stainless steel Milanaise-style bracelet; in yellow gold with leather strap

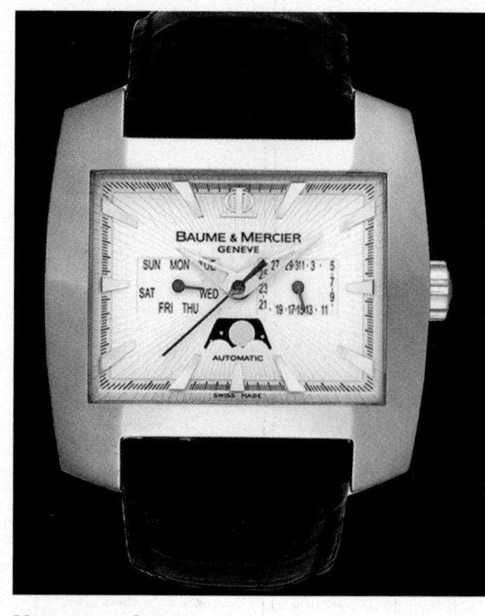

Hampton Spirit

Reference number: MOA08487
Movement: automatic, BM 11600 (base Dubois-Dépraz 5600); ø 26.2 mm, height 5.2 mm; 21 jewels; 28,800 vph
Functions: hours, minutes, subsidiary seconds; date, day, moon phase
Case: stainless steel, 42.1 x 43.4 mm, height 14 mm; sapphire crystal; transparent case back; water-resistant to 50 m
Band: reptile skin, buckle
Price: $3,495
Variations: in yellow or rose gold

CapeLand S Chronograph

Reference number: MOA08502
Movement: automatic, BM 13750 (base ETA 7750); ø 30.4 mm, height 7.9 mm; 25 jewels; 28,800 vph, certified chronometer (C.O.S.C.)
Functions: hours, minutes, subsidiary seconds; chronograph; date
Case: stainless steel, ø 41 mm, height 16.85 mm; unidirectionally rotating bezel with 60-minute scale; sapphire crystal; screw-in crown; water-resistant to 200 m
Band: stainless steel, double folding clasp
Price: $2,995
Variations: with rubber strap; in two-tone

CapeLand S Ladies

Reference number: MOA08325
Movement: quartz, BM 10425 (base ETA 955.412)
Functions: hours, minutes, sweep seconds; date
Case: stainless steel, ø 36 mm, height 13.5 mm; unidirectionally rotating bezel with 60-minute scale; sapphire crystal; screw-in crown; water-resistant to 100 m
Band: stainless steel, double folding clasp
Price: $1,795
Variations: with rubber strap

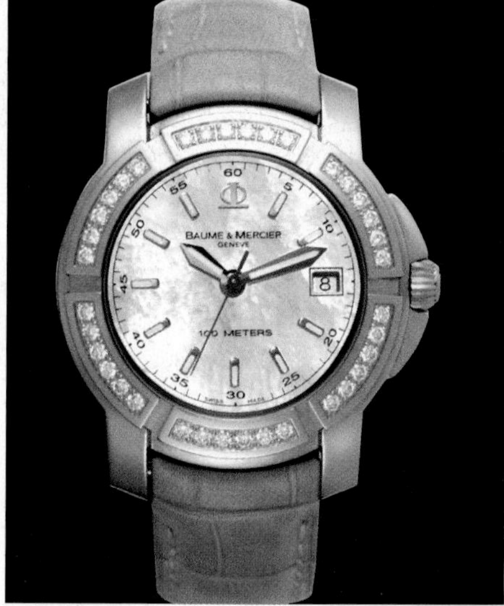

CapeLand S Ladies

Reference number: MOA08381
Movement: quartz, BM 10425 (base ETA 955.412)
Functions: hours, minutes, sweep seconds; date
Case: stainless steel, ø 36 mm, height 13.5 mm; bezel set with 36 brilliant-cut diamonds; sapphire crystal; screw-in crown; water-resistant to 100 m
Band: reptile skin, folding clasp
Price: $4,795
Variations: with stainless steel bracelet

Classima Executives XL Dual Time

Reference number: MOA08462
Movement: automatic, BM 11893-2 (base ETA 2893-2); ø 26.2 mm, height 3.6 mm; 21 jewels; 28,800 vph
Functions: hours, minutes, sweep seconds; date; 24-hour display (second time zone)
Case: stainless steel, ø 42 mm, height 9 mm; sapphire crystal
Band: reptile skin, buckle
Price: $1,595

Classima Executives XL Small Seconds

Reference number: MOA08461
Movement: manual winding, BM 16498 (base ETA 6498-2); ø 37.2 mm, height 4.2 mm; 17 jewels; 21,600 vph
Functions: hours, minutes, subsidiary seconds
Case: stainless steel, ø 42 mm, height 9 mm; sapphire crystal; transparent case back
Band: reptile skin, buckle
Price: $1,795

Classima Executives

Reference number: MOA08547
Movement: quartz, BM 11425 (base ETA 955.112)
Functions: hours, minutes; date
Case: stainless steel, ø 42 mm, height 7.5 mm; sapphire crystal
Band: reptile skin, buckle
Price: $1,295
Variations: with white dial and black leather strap

Classima Executives

Reference number: MOA08460
Movement: quartz, BM 11425 (base ETA 955.112)
Functions: hours, minutes, sweep seconds; date
Case: stainless steel, ø 33.5 mm, height 7 mm; sapphire crystal
Band: reptile skin, buckle
Price: $995

Classima

Reference number: MOA08160
Movement: automatic, BM 11892/2A (base ETA 2892-A2); ø 26.2 mm, height 3.6 mm; 21 jewels; 28,800 vph
Functions: hours, minutes, sweep seconds; date
Case: yellow gold, ø 33 mm, height 7 mm; sapphire crystal
Band: reptile skin, buckle
Price: $2,495

Classima

Reference number: MOA08230
Movement: manual winding, BM 10001 (base ETA 7001); ø 23.7 mm, height 2.5 mm; 17 jewels; 21,600 vph
Functions: hours, minutes, subsidiary seconds
Case: yellow gold, ø 33 mm, height 7 mm; sapphire crystal
Band: reptile skin, buckle
Price: $2,100

Bell & Ross

When founding his company, Carlos A. Rosillo was well aware of the risks of an entrepreneurial solo run, particularly since he had a clear idea of what "his" watch collection should be: The best materials, high-quality workmanship, and unconditional reliability and precision pretty much outlined Bell & Ross's fundamentals, and nothing less would do for the brand with the stylized ampersand (&) as its trademark. The short English-language name perfectly expressed the professional, instrument-like character of the watches that had until then existed only in technical drawings. It was not Rosillo's intention to revolutionize the watch world. His goal was perfection.

Bell & Ross has managed to get a foot in the door of the crowded, mid-priced sporty steel watch market in a relatively short amount of time. The brand has become more successful than it could ever have dreamed at the time of its market introduction back in the 1990s.

In just a few short years, the brand has been successful in setting up an individualistic image and creating an independent product palette that contains both mechanical and quartz timepieces coexisting peacefully side by side.

The watches are available with dials that are mostly designed in black or a specific shade of beige that Bell & Ross practically invented, forming a charming complement to the unimaginative, technical supply of "instrument watches" that are available today. With the product line Vintage, the company offers chronographs that are inspired by timekeepers of the same category that were modern at the beginning of the 1960s.

The latest products, two models featuring jump hour and power reserve displays, were created in cooperation with master watch-maker Vincent Calabrese, who adds the corresponding module to the reliable ETA Caliber 2892. With these models, the young brand is building a bridge between modern design and traditional craft. The limited platinum version disposes of a grey, hand-guilloché dial with an unusual power reserve display in the shape of a disk with an arrow marker that moves within an arced window.

Vintage 123 Jumping Hour

Movement: automatic, ETA 2892, modified, ø 25.6 mm, height 3.6 mm; 30 jewels; 28,800 vph; power reserve 40 h
Functions: hours (digital, jump), minutes; power reserve display
Case: platinum, ø 37.5 mm, height 12 mm; sapphire crystal, anti-reflective; transparent case back; screw-in crown; water-resistant to 100 m
Band: alligator skin, buckle
Remarks: limited to 99 pieces; 18-karat gold guilloché dial
Price: $27,000

Vintage 123 Jumping Hour

Movement: automatic, ETA 2892, modified, ø 25.6 mm, height 3.6 mm; 30 jewels; 28,800 vph; power reserve 40 h
Functions: hours (digital, jump), minutes; power reserve display
Case: rose gold, ø 37.5 mm, height 12 mm; anti-reflective sapphire crystal; transparent case back; screw-in crown; water-resistant to 100 m
Band: alligator skin, buckle
Remarks: limited to 99 pieces; 18-karat gold guilloché dial
Price: $11,900

Vintage 126 Big Date

Movement: automatic, ETA 2894-2; ø 28.6 mm, height 6.1 mm; 49 jewels; 28,800 vph; power reserve 40 h
Functions: hours, minutes, subsidiary seconds; chronograph; annual calendar with large date and month
Case: rose gold, ø 39 mm, height 15 mm; anti-reflective sapphire crystal; transparent case back; screw-in crown; water-resistant to 200 m
Band: alligator skin, buckle
Remarks: limited to 99 pieces
Price: $12,900

Geneva 123 White

Movement: automatic, ETA 2895-1, ø 26.2 mm, height 4.35 mm; 30 jewels; 28,800 vph; power reserve 42 h
Functions: hours, minutes, subsidiary seconds; date
Case: stainless steel, ø 37.5 mm, height 11.5 mm; anti-reflective sapphire crystal; engraved case back with small exhibition window; screw-in crown; water-resistant to 100 m
Band: stainless steel, double folding clasp
Price: $2,500
Variations: with alligator strap and stainless steel folding clasp ($2,100)

Geneva 126 Black

Movement: automatic, ETA 2894-2, ø 28.6 mm, height 6.1 mm; 28 jewels; 28,800 vph; power reserve 42 h
Functions: hours, minutes, subsidiary seconds; chronograph; date
Case: stainless steel, ø 39 mm, height 15 mm; anti-reflective sapphire crystal; transparent case back; screw-in crown; water-resistant to 200 m
Band: alligator skin, folding clasp
Price: $3,300
Variations: with stainless steel bracelet ($3,700)

Military Type 126

Movement: automatic, ETA 2894-2, ø 28.6 mm, height 6.1 mm; 28 jewels; 28,800 vph; power reserve 42 h
Functions: hours, minutes, subsidiary seconds; chronograph; date
Case: stainless steel, ø 39 mm, height 15 mm; anti-reflective sapphire crystal; transparent case back; screw-in crown; water-resistant to 100 m
Band: leather, folding clasp
Remarks: limited to 999 pieces
Price: $3,250

Classic Pilot Acrylic

Movement: automatic, ETA 2894-2, ø 28.6 mm, height 6.1 mm; 28 jewels; 28,800 vph; power reserve 42 h
Functions: hours, minutes, subsidiary seconds; chronograph; date
Case: stainless steel, ø 40 mm, height 14 mm; bidirectionally rotating bezel with 60-minute graduated scale; ultra-domed acrylic crystal; screw-in crown; water-resistant to 100 m
Band: leather, folding clasp
Price: $2,200
Variations: with stainless steel bracelet ($2,700)

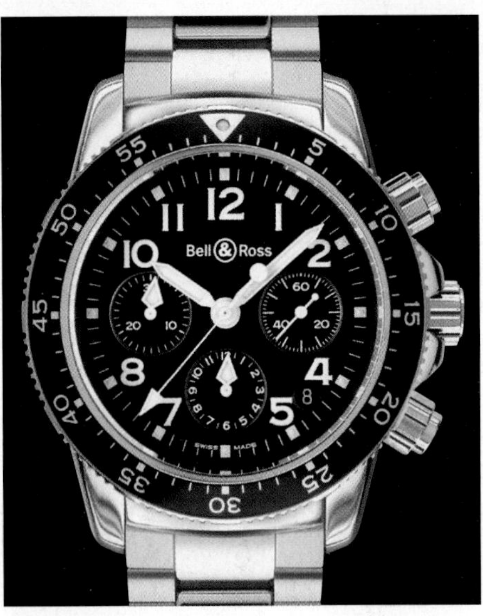

Classic Pilot Sapphire

Movement: automatic, ETA 2894-2, ø 28.6 mm, height 6.1 mm; 28 jewels; 28,800 vph; power reserve 42 h
Functions: hours, minutes, subsidiary seconds; chronograph; date
Case: stainless steel, ø 40 mm, height 13.8 mm; bidirectionally rotating bezel with graduated 60-minute scale; anti-reflective sapphire crystal; transparent case back; screw-in crown and buttons; water-resistant to 200 m
Band: stainless steel, double folding clasp
Price: $3,850
Variations: with leather strap and folding clasp ($3,350)

Classic Diver 300

Movement: automatic, ETA 2894-2, ø 28.6 mm, height 6.1 mm; 28 jewels; 28,800 vph; power reserve 42 h
Functions: hours, minutes, subsidiary seconds; chronograph; date
Case: stainless steel, ø 40 mm, height 13.5 mm; unidirectionally rotating bezel with graduated 60-minute scale; anti-reflective sapphire crystal; screw-in crown and buttons; water-resistant to 300 m
Band: water-resistant synthetic, folding clasp
Price: $2,950
Variations: with stainless steel bracelet ($3,450)

Function Index Black

Movement: quartz, ETA 988.431/988.432, multifunctional electronic module with LCD display integrated into dial
Functions: hours, minutes; chronograph, perpetual calendar with date, day, calendar week, month, leap year, second time zone, alarm and countdown in LCD display
Case: stainless steel, ø 37.5 mm, height 11.5 mm; anti-reflective sapphire crystal; screw-in crown; water-resistant to 100 m
Band: rubber, folding clasp
Price: $1,850
Variations: with alligator skin strap ($1,950); with stainless steel bracelet ($2,350)

Hydromax Black

Movement: quartz, ETA 955.612, case completely filled with liquid (Hydroil); volume adjustment via rubber membrane in case back; long-lasting battery (four years)
Functions: hours, minutes, subsidiary seconds; date
Case: stainless steel, ø 39 mm, height 11 mm; unidirectionally rotating bezel with 60-minute scale; sapphire crystal; screw-in crown; water-resistant to 11,100 m
Band: comes in set with three bands (rubber, synthetic, steel)
Price: $2,400
Variations: with white dial

Space 3 Day-Date

Movement: automatic, ETA 7750, ø 30 mm, height 7.9 mm; 25 jewels; 28,800 vph; power reserve 42 h
Functions: hours, minutes, subsidiary seconds; chronograph; date and day
Case: titanium, ø 41 mm, height 16 mm; sapphire crystal; screw-in crown, flat buttons; water-resistant to 200 m
Band: titanium, double folding clasp
Price: $3,150
Variations: with rubber strap ($2,750); in stainless steel on rubber strap ($2,500); in stainless steel with stainless steel bracelet ($2,600)

Annual calendar
The automatic allowances for the different lengths of each month of a year in the calendar module of a watch. This type of watch also usually shows the date and month, and most of the time the phases of the moon.

Anti reflection
A film created by steaming the crystal to eliminate light reflection and to improve legibility. Anti reflection functions best when applied to both sides of the crystal, but because it scratches, some producers prefer to have it only on the interior of the crystal. It is mainly used on synthetic sapphire crystals.

Automatic winding
A rotating weight, set into motion by moving the wrist, winds the spring barrel via the gear train of a mechanical watch movement. Automatic winding was invented during the pocket watch era in 1770 by Abraham-Louis Perrelet, who created a timepiece with a weight swinging to and fro (when carried in a vest pocket, a pocket watch usually makes vertical movements). The first automatic-winding wrist-watches, invented by John Harwood in the 1920s, utilized so-called hammer winding, whereby a weight swung in an arc between two banking pins. The breakthrough automatic winding movement via rotor began with the ball bearing Eterna-Matic in the late 1940s, and the workings of such a watch haven't changed fundamentally since. Today we speak of unidirectional winding and bidirectionally winding rotors, depending on the type of gear train used.

Balance
The heart of a mechanical watch movement is the balance. Fed by the energy of the mainspring, a tirelessly oscillating little wheel, just a few millimeters in diameter and possessing a spiral-shaped balance spring, sets the rhythm for the escape wheel and lever with its vibration frequency. Today the balance is usually made of one piece of anti-magnetic glucydur, which expands very little when exposed to heat.

Bar/Cock
A metal plate fastened at one point to the main plate, leaving room for a gear wheel or pinion. The balance is usually stored in a bar called the balance cock.

Bevel
To grind down the sharp edges of a plate, bridge, or bar and give it a high polish.

Bridge
A metal plate fastened at two points to the main plate leaving room for a gear wheel or pinion.

Caliber
A term, similar to type or model, that refers to different watch movements.

Chronograph
From the Greek *chronos* (time) and *graphein* (to write). Originally a chronograph literally wrote, inscribing the time elapsed on a piece of paper with the help of a pencil attached to a type of hand. Today this term is used for watches that show not only the time of day, but also certain time intervals via independent hands that may be started or stopped at will. So-called stopwatches differ from chronographs because they do not show the time of day. Not be mistaken for a chronometer.

Chronometer
Literally, "measurer of time." As the term is used today, a chronometer denotes an especially accurate watch (one with a deviation of no more than five seconds a day for mechanical movements). Chronometers are usually supplied with an official certificate from an independent office such as the C.O.S.C.

Circular graining/Perlage
Surface decoration comprising an even pattern of partially overlapping dots, applied with a quickly rotating plastic or wooden peg. Also called *perlage.*

Cloisonné enamel
Whisper-thin gold threads with a diameter of less than a tenth of a millimeter divide a motif swimming in colored enamel paste into separate segments (*cloisons*) and prohibit the enamels from running. The intricate crafting and the tricky firing procedures (many losses occur due to burn spots and warping) raise this type of enameling to an art form all its own.

C.O.S.C.
The Contrôle Officiel Suisse de Chronometrage, the official Swiss testing office for chronometers. The C.O.S.C. is the world's largest issuer of so-called chronometer certificates, which are only otherwise given out individually by certain observatories (such as those in Neuchâtel, Switzerland). For a fee, the C.O.S.C. tests the rate of movements that have been adjusted by watchmakers. These are usually mechanical movements, but the office also tests some high precision quartz movements. Those that pass the specifications for being a chronometer are awarded a certificate.

Côtes de Genève
Also called *vagues de Genève.* Surface decoration comprising an even pattern of parallel stripes, applied with a quickly rotating plastic or wooden peg.

Escapement
The combined mechanism of balance, lever, and escape wheel, which divides the impulses coming from the spring barrel into small, accurately portioned doses.

Flange
The usually inclined ring that separates the crystal from the dial. The flange is sometimes equipped with features such as tachymetric scales and pulsometers.

Flyback Chronograph
A chronograph with a special dial train switch that makes the immediate re-use of the chronograph movement possible after resetting the hands. It was developed for special timekeeping duties (such as found in aviation), which require the measurement of time intervals in quick succession. A flyback may also be called a *retour en vol.*

Glucydur
An antimagnetic metal alloy comprising beryllium, nickel, and copper that expands very little when exposed to heat. This quality makes glucydur useful in making balances.

Guilloché
Surface decoration, normally on the dial, whereby a grooving tool with a sharp tip is used to cut an even pattern onto a level surface. The exact adjustment of the tool for each new path is controlled by a device similar to a pantograph, and the movement of the tool can be controlled either manually or mechanically. Real *guillochis* (the correct term used by a master of guilloché) are very intricate and expensive to produce, which is why most of the dials decorated in this fashion are produced by stamping machines.

Jewel
To minimize friction, the hardened steel tips of the axles of the rotating gear wheels (pinions) of a movement are lodged in synthetic rubies (fashioned as

.... continued on page 69

Ernst Benz

Ernst Benz Limited entered the North American market in 2001 with the introduction of a line of largely dimensioned watches. Benz's name may be familiar to some readers, but not from the wristwatch industry. He is a Swiss engineer who made quite a name for himself in the audio industry. Beginning his career in the 1960s, Benz went to California to work at Consolidated Electrodynamics developing accelerometers and pressure transducers for the aircraft industry. After many years in the United States, he returned to Switzerland to develop a patented process for producing diamond styli for hi-fi cartridges. This was the basis for the company he founded, and he was soon able to acquire one of his customers, Empire Scientific, a renowned American cartridge and turntable producer. A later cartridge, the Benz Micro, became the ultimate moving coil cartridge in the 1970s and '80s and is still in demand today by discerning audio buffs and deejays who work with vinyl.

In the 1980s, as cassette tapes and CDs began to displace records, Benz refocused his energies, developing an innovative aircraft instrument chronograph. As a pilot and gliding enthusiast, he was well aware of the necessity for accurate and instantly legible instruments while in the air. This was also a successful instrument, and his Benz Micro aircraft chronograph is presently standard equipment in many single-engine planes, military trainers, jets, and sailplanes, with more than one thousand in daily use globally.

As the cockpit of a glider or sailplane is limited in space, but the need for accurate timekeeping remains critical, Benz decided to design a large-format, automatic-winding chronograph after receiving many inquiries from fellow pilots. Previously relying on ETA to supply him with the trustworthy movements to power his navigational instruments, he once again turned to the world's largest supplier of mechanical movements to furnish the energy for these instruments for the wrist. Being both Swiss and a pilot, he knows how important precision timing is. At the beginning, he produced some watches in very limited quantities, noticing that Swiss and German pilots, yachtsmen, and rally and race car drivers were utilizing them more than anyone else.

The decision to enter the North American arena was actually a fluke. Benz winters in Boca Raton, Florida, where Charles Agnoff, president of Orbita Corporation, also keeps his boat. As their docks are neighboring, it was obvious that it wouldn't be long before the two met. Agnoff was very impressed by the large size of the sapphire crystal exhibition window on the case back of Benz's watches and bought six of the timepieces in order to show the winding action of Orbita's watch winders at the next trade show he was attending. Much to his surprise, many Orbita dealers were fascinated with the new watch and asked Agnoff where they could be found. The decision was ultimately made to set up an American-based operation to inventory and market the pieces with Orbita providing assistance.

Two thousand five marks the year of Ernst Benz downsizing! While these anything but modest timekeepers are well-known for their size, Ernst Benz is following the general trend in the industry toward reviving smaller sizes so that they may function as unisex watches. In addition to the gargantuan 47-mm pieces that have made up the collection until now, the company has added a host of 40-mm variations to please both men and women. Add a diamond bezel to one of these babies, and it becomes a high-end fashion statement par excellence.

Chronojewel 47 mm

Reference number: GC5520

Movement: automatic, ETA 7750, ø 29 mm, height 10 mm; 25 jewels; 28,800 vph

Functions: hours, minutes, subsidiary seconds; date, day; chronograph

Case: stainless steel, ø 47 mm, height 16 mm; bezel set with 64 diamonds and flange set with 48 diamonds for a total of 5 carats; sapphire crystal; transparent case back; double-sealed crown; water-resistant to 50 m

Band: crocodile skin, double folding clasp

Price: $10,995

Variations: with stainless steel bracelet ($10,995)

Chronojewel 47 mm

Reference number: GC5502

Movement: automatic, ETA 7750, ø 29 mm, height 10 mm; 25 jewels; 28,800 vph

Functions: hours, minutes, subisidiary seconds; date, day; chronograph

Case: stainless steel, ø 47 mm, height 16 mm; sapphire crystal; transparent case back; double-sealed crown; water-resistant to 50 m

Band: stainless steel, folding clasp

Price: $2,395

Variations: with leather strap ($2,195); black or white dial

Chronolunar 47 mm

Reference number: GC4002

Movement: automatic, ETA 7751, ø 30 mm, height 7.9 mm; 25 jewels; 28,800 vph

Functions: hours, minutes, sweep seconds; date, day, month; moon phase

Case: stainless steel, ø 47 mm, height 16 mm; sapphire crystal; transparent case back; double-sealed crown; water-resistant to 50 m

Band: leather, folding clasp

Price: $2,595

Variations: with stainless steel bracelet ($2,795); with diamond bezel ($8,795 with leather strap and $8,995 on steel)

Chronoscope 47 mm

Reference number: GC1102

Movement: automatic, ETA 7750, ø 29 mm, height 10 mm; 25 jewels; 28,800 vph

Functions: hours, minutes, subsidiary seconds; date, day

Case: stainless steel, ø 47 mm, height 16 mm; sapphire crystal; transparent case back; double-sealed crown; water-resistant to 50 m

Band: stainless steel, folding clasp

Price: $1,995

Variations: with diamond bezel ($7,995 with leather strap and $8,195 on steel); on leather strap

Diamond Millenium Limited Edition

Reference number: GC5000

Movement: automatic, ETA 2836-2, ø 25.6 mm, height 5.05 mm; 25 jewels; 28,800 vph, gold-plated and decorated movement

Functions: hours, minutes, sweep seconds; date, day

Case: stainless steel/yellow gold, ø 47 mm, height 16 mm; 18-karat gold bezel set with 48 diamonds (3.5 carats); sapphire crystal; transparent case back; double-sealed crown; water-resistant to 50 m

Band: crocodile skin, yellow gold folding clasp

Remarks: limited edition of 100 pieces

Price: $12,995

Chronosport 47 mm

Reference number: GC2000

Movement: automatic, ETA 2836-2, ø 25.6 mm, height 5.05 mm; 25 jewels; 28,800 vph

Functions: hours, minutes, sweep seconds; date, day

Case: stainless steel, ø 47 mm, height 16 mm; sapphire crystal; transparent case back; double-sealed crown; water-resistant to 50 m

Band: leather, buckle

Price: $995

Variations: with stainless steel bracelet ($1,195); with black, white, or copper-colored dial

Chronojewel 40 mm

Reference number: GC8002
Movement: automatic, ETA 7750, ø 29 mm, height 10 mm; 25 jewels; 28,800 vph, engraved rotor
Functions: hours, minutes, subsidiary seconds; date, day; chronograph
Case: stainless steel, ø 40 mm, height 16 mm; sapphire crystal; transparent case back; double-sealed crown; water-resistant to 50 m
Band: leather, folding clasp
Price: $2,095
Variations: with stainless steel bracelet ($2,295); with black or white dial

Chronojewel 40 mm

Reference number: GC8020
Movement: automatic, ETA 7750, ø 29 mm, height 10 mm; 25 jewels; 28,800 vph, engraved rotor
Functions: hours, minutes, subsidiary seconds; date, day; chronograph
Case: stainless steel, ø 40 mm, height 16 mm; bezel set with 54 diamonds and flange set with 52 diamonds; sapphire crystal; transparent case back; double-sealed crown; water-resistant to 50 m
Band: crocodile skin, folding clasp
Price: $6,495
Variations: with stainless steel bracelet; black or white dial

Chronojewel 40 mm

Reference number: GC8012
Movement: automatic, ETA 7750, ø 29 mm, height 10 mm; 25 jewels; 28,800 vph, engraved rotor
Functions: hours, minutes, subsidiary seconds; date, day; chronograph
Case: stainless steel, ø 40 mm, height 16 mm; bezel set with 54 diamonds totaling 1.25 ct.; sapphire crystal; transparent case back; double-sealed crown; water-resistant to 50 m
Band: crocodile skin, folding clasp
Price: $4,995
Variations: with stainless steel bracelet ($4,995); with black or white dial

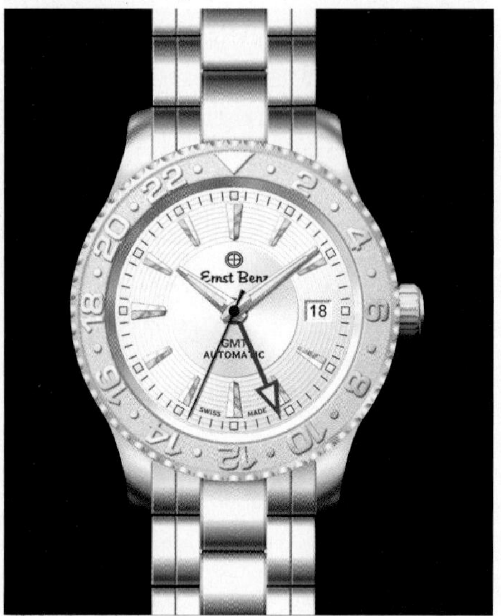

GMT 40 mm

Reference number: GC6602
Movement: automatic, ETA 2893-2, ø 25.6 mm, height 4.1 mm; 21 jewels; 28,800 vph, engraved rotor
Functions: hours, minutes, sweep seconds; date; second time zone
Case: stainless steel, ø 40 mm, height 16 mm; sapphire crystal; transparent case back; double-sealed crown; water-resistant to 50 m
Band: stainless steel, folding clasp
Price: $1,495
Variations: with leather strap ($1,295); black or white dial

Chronosport 40 mm

Reference number: GC6002
Movement: automatic, ETA 2836-2, ø 25.6 mm, height 5.05 mm; 25 jewels; 28,800 vph, engraved rotor
Functions: hours, minutes, sweep seconds; date, day
Case: stainless steel, ø 40 mm, height 16 mm; sapphire crystal; transparent case back; double-sealed crown; water-resistant to 50 m
Band: leather, buckle
Price: $895
Variations: with stainless steel bracelet ($1,095); with black or white dial

Chronolunar 40 mm

Reference number: GC7100
Movement: automatic, ETA 7751, ø 30 mm, height 7.9 mm; 25 jewels; 28,800 vph, engraved rotor
Functions: hours, minutes, sweep seconds; date, day, month, moon phase
Case: stainless steel, ø 40 mm, height 16 mm; sapphire crystal; transparent case back; double-sealed crown; water-resistant to 50 m
Band: leather, folding clasp
Price: $2,495
Variations: with stainless steel bracelet ($2,695), white dial

.... continued from page 65

stones with a hole) and lubricated with a very thin layer of special oil. During the pocket watch era, real rubies with hand-drilled holes were still used, but because of the high costs, only in movements with especially quickly rotating gears.

Manufacture

A watch company that uses a movement in at least one of its models that it has manufactured itself on its own premises.

Minute Repeater

A striking mechanism with hammers and gongs for acoustically signalling the hours, quarter hours, and minutes elapsed since noon or midnight. The wearer pushes a slide, which winds the spring. Normally a repeater uses two different gongs to signal hours (low tone), quarter hours (high and low tones in succession), and minutes (high tone). Some watches have three gongs, called a carillon.

Perpetual Calendar

The calendar module for this watch type automatically makes allowances for the different lengths of each month as well as leap years. A perpetual calendar also usually shows the date, month, and four-year cycle, and may show the day of the week and moon phase as well.

Plate

A metal platform having several tiers for the gear train. The main plate of a movement usually incorporates the dial and carries the bearings for the primary pinions of the "first floor" of a gear train. The gear wheels are made complete by tightly fitting screw-mounted bridges and bars on the back side of the plate. A specialty of the so-called Glashütte school, as opposed to the Swiss school, is the reverse completion of a movement not via different bridges and bars, but rather a three-quarter plate.

Pulsometer

Scale on the dial, flange, or bezel that, in conjunction with the second hand, may be used to measure a pulse rate. A pulsometer is always marked with a reference number; if it is marked, for example *gradué pour 15 pulsations* then the wearer counts 15 beats of a pulse. At the last beat, the second hand will show what the pulse rate is in beats per minute on the pulsometer scale.

Quartz

Timekeeping's technical revolution found its way to the world's wrists in the late 1960s. This was a principally Swiss invention: The first functioning quartz wrist-watches were manufactured by Girard-Perregaux and Piaget as the result of an early joint venture within the Swiss watch industry, but the Japanese (primarily Seiko) came to dominate the market with new technology. The quartz movement uses the famously stable vibration frequency of a quartz crystal subjected to electronic tension (usually 32,868 Hz) as its norm. The fact that a quartz-controlled second hand jumps to the tact of each second is a concession to the use of outside energy.

Screw Balance

Before the invention of the perfectly weighted balance by use of a smooth ring, balances were fitted with weighted screws to get the exact impetus desired. Today a screw balance is a subtle sign of quality in a movement due to its costly construction.

Sonnerie

A variety of minute repeater that – like a tower clock – sounds the time not at the will of the wearer, but rather automatically (*en passant*) every hour (*petite sonnerie*) or quarter hour (*grande sonnerie*).

Split-Seconds Chronograph Rattrapante

A watch with two second hands, one of which can be stopped with a special dial train lever to indicate an intermediate time while the other continues to run. When released, the split-seconds hand jumps ahead to the position of the other second hand. This type of chronograph is also called a *rattrapante*.

Tachymeter

A scale on the dial, flange, or bezel of a chronograph that, in conjunction with the second hand, gives the speed of a moving object. A tachymeter takes a value determined in less than a minute and converts it into miles per hour. For example, a wearer could measure the time it takes a car to pass between two mile markers on the highway. When the car passes the second marker, the second hand will be pointing to the car's speed in miles per hour on the tachymetric scale.

Tourbillon

A technically demanding device to compensate for the interference of gravity on the balance and thus improve a watch's rate. In a tourbillon (from the French word for *whirlwind*), the entire escapement is mounted on an epicyclic train in a "cage" and rotated completely on its axis over regular periods of time, usually once a minute. Today this superb technical delicatesse is a sign of the highest quality.

Tritium

Slightly radioactive material that collects light energy and is sometime still used to coat hands, numerals, and hour markers on watch dials in order to make reading the time in the dark possible. Watches bearing tritium must be marked as such, with the letter T on the dial near 6 o'clock. It is gradually being replaced by non-radioactive materials such as SuperLumiNova and Traser due to medical misgivings and expected governmental regulation of its use.

Vibration Frequency (vph)

The ring-shaped balance swings around its own axis and acts as the ruling organ of the movement's escapement. The amplitude (normally about 300 degrees) is restricted by the very thin balance spring, which also provides for the reversing of the direction of rotation. The frequency of the alternating vibrations is measured in Hertz (Hz) or in the more usual vibrations per hour (vph), which is also sometimes written as A/h, the A standing for the French *alternance* (change). Most of today's wristwatches tick at frequencies of 28,800 vph (4 Hz) or 21,600 vph (3 Hz). Less usual, but still found in certain models, are vibration frequencies of 18,000 vph (2.5 Hz) and 36,000 vph (5 Hz).

Blancpain

Blancpain celebrated its refounding in 1982 with a small collection of complicated watches in a classically round case. Currently, the *manufacture* is taking up this tradition once again with its top new product: the Equation Marchante, a wristwatch that displays a running equation of time. An explanation of this complication is based in the fact that watches don't show that which a sundial does: true solar time. Instead, a mean time was developed from the varying lengths of the true solar day, meaning that a watch's minute hand can deviate from true solar time by

up to sixteen minutes over the course of a year. This, known as the equation of time, is shown very graphically on the new Blancpain watch. Alongside the classic minute hand, there is a second gold hand that culminates in a small sun to illustrate true solar time. Thus, the deviation between solar time and mean time is visible right at first glance.

The new Caliber 3863 is the result of many years of developmental work. It comprises about 400 components and has a power reserve of seventy-two hours. The exclusive running equation of time system was integrated into an automatic watch movement that is already outfitted with the world's flattest perpetual calendar module and another module for a retrograde moon phase display. The clever watchmakers working for Blancpain were able to correctly adjust the old caliber to make adding the new complication possible. Caliber 3863 is housed in a traditional round case; the dial is white, and it is framed by a characteristic stepped bezel.

The Equation Marchante and other complicated Blancpain watches are manufactured in the tranquil atmosphere of an old farmhouse in Le Brassus, based on movements produced by the movement factory Frédéric Piguet. This company, like Blancpain, belongs to the Swatch Group and manufactures its products almost exclusively for the high-class brand.

In the last couple of years, Blancpain has undergone a change of leadership with a clear course set for expansion in the firm's second location in Paudex near Lausanne, where the administration and sales departments are located. Alongside a careful restoration of model policies, new boss Marc Hayek has put special emphasis on improving service and introducing a contemporary system for stocking watches and replacement parts.

Blancpain takes care of its select clientele with the continuous introduction of top performances in watchmaking, achieving a true highlight in the model named for the year of Blancpain's original founding, 1735. This model contains a tourbillon, a perpetual calendar, a rattrapante chronograph, and a minute repeater.

However, sports watches also have tradition at Blancpain. In 1953 these specialists introduced the first diver's watch that was water-resistant to

almost 100 meters, or more precisely 91.45 meters, better known as 50 fathoms. This unit of measurement dating from early Christian seafaring also gave the watch its name: 50 Fathoms. The timepiece was originally developed in cooperation with Captain Robert (Bob) Maloubier for the French navy and for many, many years represented the epitome of diver's watches.

Equation Marchante Le Brassus

Reference number: 4238-344255B
Movement: automatic, Blancpain 3863, ø 26.8 mm, height 5.25 mm; 39 jewels; 21,600 vph
Functions: hours, minutes, subsidiary seconds; perpetual calendar (date, day, month, moon phase, leap year); indirect and running display of equation of time via additional minute hand
Case: platinum, ø 42 mm, height 12.3 mm; sapphire crystal; transparent case back
Band: reptile skin, folding clasp
Remarks: limited to 50 pieces
Price: $119,300

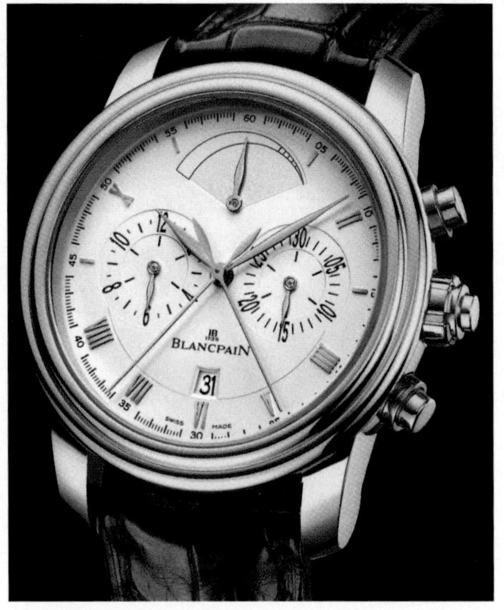

Flyback Rattrapante Le Brassus

Reference number: 4246F-364255B
Movement: automatic, Blancpain 40F6, ø 26.2 mm, height 8 mm; 37 jewels; 21,600 vph
Functions: hours, minutes; split seconds chronograph with flyback function; date; power reserve display
Case: red gold, ø 42 mm, height 15.1 mm; sapphire crystal; transparent case back
Band: reptile skin, folding clasp
Price: $35,800

Flyback Rattrapante Perpetual Calendar Le Brassus

Reference number: 4286P-3642A55B
Movement: automatic, Blancpain 56F9A, ø 26.2 mm, height 8.1 mm; 38 jewels; 21,600 vph
Functions: hours, minutes; split seconds chronograph with flyback function; perpetual calendar with date, day, month, moon phase, leap year
Case: red gold, ø 42 mm, height 15 mm; sapphire crystal; transparent case back
Band: reptile skin, folding clasp
Price: $43,800

Grande Complication Le Brassus

Reference number: 1735-342755
Movement: automatic, Blancpain 1735, ø 31.5 mm, height 11 mm; 44 jewels; 21,600 vph, one-minute tourbillon; power reserve 80 hours: 740 individual components
Functions: hours, minutes; hour, quarter hour, and minute repeater; split seconds chronograph; perpetual calendar with date, day, month, moon phase
Case: platinum, ø 42 mm, height 16.5 mm; sapphire crystal; transparent case back
Band: reptile skin, folding clasp
Remarks: limited to 30 pieces
Price: $731,900

GMT Le Brassus

Reference number: 4276-3642A55B
Movement: automatic, Blancpain 67A6 (base 1150); ø 27 mm, height 6 mm; 30 jewels; 21,600 vph, two spring barrels, power reserve 100 hours
Functions: hours, minutes, subsidiary seconds; date, day, month, moon phase, 24-hour display (second time zone)
Case: red gold, ø 42 mm, height 13.3 mm; sapphire crystal; water-resistant to 50 m
Band: reptile skin, folding clasp
Price: $23,000
Variations: in platinum

Flyback Rattrapante Tourbillon Le Brassus

Reference number: 4289Q-344255B
Movement: automatic, Blancpain 56F9U, ø 27.6 mm, height 7.7 mm; 39 jewels; 21,600 vph, one-minute tourbillon
Functions: hours, minutes, subsidiary seconds; split seconds chronograph with flyback function; perpetual calendar with date, day, month, moon phase, leap year
Case: platinum, ø 42 mm, height 17.4 mm; sapphire crystal; transparent case back; water-resistant to 50 m
Band: reptile skin, folding clasp
Price: $180,800
Variations: with brilliant-cut diamonds

Villeret Chronograph Monopoussoir

Reference number: 6185-112755
Movement: automatic, Blancpain M185, ø 31.8 mm, height 5.5 mm; 37 jewels; 21,600 vph, control of chronograph functions via single button in crown
Functions: hours, minutes, subsidiary seconds; chronograph; date
Case: stainless steel, ø 38 mm, height 11.4 mm; sapphire crystal; transparent case back
Band: reptile skin, buckle
Price: $9,800
Variations: in white or red gold

Villeret Ultraflat

Reference number: 6223-112755
Movement: automatic, Blancpain 1153, ø 26.2 mm, height 3.25 mm; 28 jewels; 21,600 vph, two spring barrels, power reserve 100 hours
Functions: hours, minutes, sweep seconds; date
Case: stainless steel, ø 38 mm, height 9.2 mm; sapphire crystal
Band: reptile skin, buckle
Price: $5,100
Variations: in white or red gold

Villeret Moon Phase

Reference number: 6263-3642A55
Movement: automatic, Blancpain 6763, ø 27 mm, height 4.9 mm; 30 jewels; 21,600 vph
Functions: hours, minutes, subsidiary seconds; date, day, month, moon phase
Case: red gold, ø 38 mm, height 10.7 mm; sapphire crystal
Band: reptile skin, buckle
Price: $12,400
Variations: in white gold; in stainless steel

Villeret Time Zone

Reference number: 6260-154255
Movement: automatic, Blancpain 5L60, ø 26.2 mm, height 3.25 mm; 30 jewels; 21,600 vph
Functions: hours, minutes, subsidiary seconds; date; second time zone; day/night indication
Case: white gold, ø 37.6 mm, height 10.1 mm; sapphire crystal
Band: reptile skin, buckle
Price: $13,500
Variations: in red gold

Villeret Ultraflat Women's Watch

Reference number: 6102-112795
Movement: automatic, Blancpain 953, ø 21 mm, height 3.25 mm; 21 jewels; 21,600 vph
Functions: hours, minutes, sweep seconds
Case: stainless steel, ø 29 mm, height 8.7 mm; sapphire crystal
Band: reptile skin, buckle
Price: $6,000
Variations: in red gold; with diamonds on the bezel

Villeret Ultraflat Women's Watch

Reference number: 6102-462895
Movement: automatic, Blancpain 953, ø 21 mm, height 3.25 mm; 21 jewels; 21,600 vph
Functions: hours, minutes, sweep seconds
Case: stainless steel, ø 29 mm, height 8.7 mm; bezel, set with brilliant-cut diamonds; sapphire crystal
Band: reptile skin (set with 5 colored leather straps), buckle
Remarks: dial with 12 diamond markers
Price: $8,700
Variations: in red gold

Tourbillon Large Date Léman

Reference number: 2825A-364253B
Movement: automatic, Blancpain 6925, ø 27.6 mm, height 6.35 mm; 35 jewels; 21,600 vph, one-minute tourbillon; power reserve 7 days
Functions: hours, minutes, subsidiary seconds (on tourbillon cage); large date; power reserve display
Case: red gold, ø 38 mm, height 12.4 mm; sapphire crystal; transparent case back
Band: reptile skin, folding clasp
Price: $69,000
Variations: in white gold

Large Date Léman

Reference number: 2850-113053
Movement: automatic, Blancpain 6950, ø 32 mm, height 4.75 mm; 35 jewels; 21,600 vph, two spring barrels, power reserve 70 hours
Functions: hours, minutes, sweep seconds; large date
Case: stainless steel, ø 40 mm, height 11.4 mm; sapphire crystal; transparent case back
Band: reptile skin, buckle
Price: $6,900
Variations: with white dial

Large Date Léman limited

Reference number: 2850A-363064B
Movement: automatic, Blancpain 6950, ø 32 mm, height 4.75 mm; 35 jewels; 21,600 vph, two spring barrels, power reserve 70 hours
Functions: hours, minutes, sweep seconds; large date
Case: red gold, ø 40 mm, height 11.4 mm; sapphire crystal; transparent case back
Band: rubber, folding clasp
Remarks: limited to 333 pieces
Price: $12,300

Tourbillon Léman

Reference number: 2125-152753
Movement: automatic, Blancpain 25, ø 26.2 mm, height 6.35 mm; 29 jewels; 21,600 vph, one-minute tourbillon; power reserve 168 hours
Functions: hours, minutes, subsidiary seconds (on tourbillon cage); date; power reserve display
Case: white gold, ø 38 mm, height 10.7 mm; sapphire crystal; transparent case back; water-resistant to 100 m
Band: reptile skin, buckle
Price: $69,000
Variations: in yellow or red gold

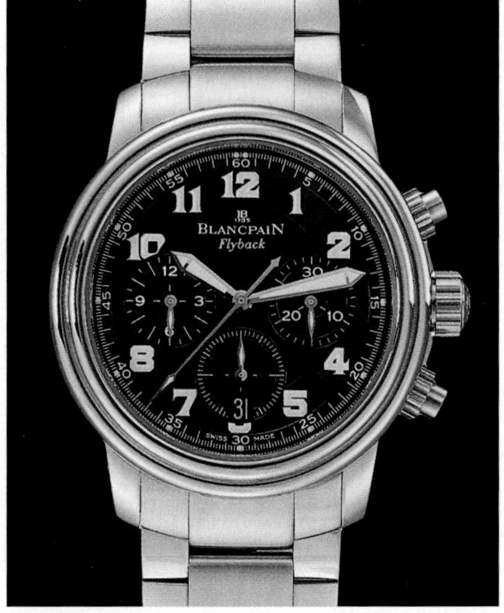

Chronograph Flyback Léman

Reference number: 2185F-113071
Movement: automatic, Blancpain F185, ø 26.2 mm, height 5.5 mm; 37 jewels; 21,600 vph
Functions: hours, minutes, subsidiary seconds; chronograph with flyback function; date
Case: stainless steel, ø 38 mm, height 11.7 mm; sapphire crystal; water-resistant to 100 m
Band: stainless steel, double folding clasp
Price: $9,200

Moon Phase Léman

Reference number: 2360-3691A55
Movement: automatic, Blancpain 6763, ø 27 mm, height 4.9 mm; 30 jewels; 21,600 vph
Functions: hours, minutes, subsidiary seconds; date, day, month, moon phase
Case: red gold, ø 33.5 mm, height 11.4 mm; sapphire crystal
Band: reptile skin, buckle
Price: $11,500

Alarm Léman

Reference number: 2041-1542M53B
Movement: automatic, Blancpain 1241, ø 31.7 mm, height 6.2 mm; 38 jewels; 21,600 vph, alarm movement with automatic winding
Functions: hours, minutes, subsidiary seconds; date; 24-hour display (second time zone); alarm time display, display of alarm's power reserve, alarm function indication
Case: white gold, ø 40 mm, height 13.3 mm; sapphire crystal; transparent case back; water-resistant to 100 m
Band: reptile skin, folding clasp
Price: $23,900
Variations: in red gold

Women's Chronograph Flyback Léman

Reference number: 2385F-463071
Movement: automatic, Blancpain F185, ø 26.2 mm, height 5.5 mm; 37 jewels; 21,600 vph
Functions: hours, minutes, subsidiary seconds; chronograph with flyback function; date
Case: stainless steel, ø 36 mm, height 11.4 mm; bezel set with brilliant-cut diamonds; sapphire crystal; water-resistant to 100 m
Band: stainless steel, double folding clasp
Price: $14,000

Flyback Rattrapante Léman

Reference number: 2086F-1130M53B
Movement: automatic, Blancpain F186, ø 26.2 mm, height 6.9 mm; 38 jewels; 21,600 vph
Functions: hours, minutes, subsidiary seconds; split seconds chronograph with flyback function; date
Case: stainless steel, ø 40 mm, height 13.7 mm; sapphire crystal; transparent case back; water-resistant to 100 m
Band: reptile skin, folding clasp
Price: $19,900

Fifty Fathoms

Reference number: 220-113071
Movement: automatic, Blancpain 1151, ø 26.2 mm, height 3.25 mm; 28 jewels; 21,600 vph, two spring barrels, power reserve 100 hours
Functions: hours, minutes, sweep seconds; date
Case: stainless steel, ø 40.5 mm, height 13 mm; unidirectionally rotating bezel with 60-minute scale; sapphire crystal; water-resistant to 300 m
Band: leather, double folding clasp
Price: $7,500

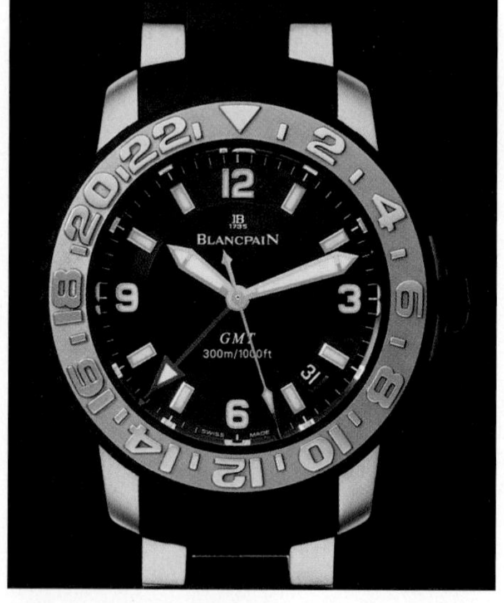

Diver's Watch GMT

Reference number: 2250-653066
Movement: automatic, Blancpain 5A50, ø 26.2 mm, height 4.35 mm; 28 jewels; 21,600 vph, two spring barrels, power reserve 100 hours
Functions: hours, minutes, sweep seconds; date; 24-hour display (second time zone)
Case: stainless steel/rubber, ø 40.5 mm, height 13 mm; bidirectionally rotating bezel with 24-hour scale; sapphire crystal; water-resistant to 300 m
Band: stainless steel/rubber, double folding clasp
Price: $9,000

Diver's Watch Air Command

Reference number: 2285F-653066
Movement: automatic, Blancpain F185, ø 26.2 mm, height 5.5 mm; 37 jewels; 21,600 vph
Functions: hours, minutes, subsidiary seconds; chronograph with flyback function; date
Case: stainless steel/rubber, ø 40.5 mm, height 13.3 mm; unidirectionally rotating bezel with 60-minute scale; sapphire crystal; water-resistant to 200 m
Band: stainless steel/rubber, double folding clasp
Price: $10,700

Caliber 1151

Mechanical with automatic winding, twin spring barrels, power reserve to 100 hours
Functions: hours, minutes, sweep seconds; date
Diameter: 26.8 mm (12''')
Height: extra-flat, 3.25 mm; **Jewels:** 29
Balance: beryllium copper
Frequency: 21,600 vph
Balance spring: flat hairspring with fine adjustment via micrometer screw
Shock protection: Kif
Remarks: regulation in five positions; base plate and rotor decorated with côtes de Genève; 185 individual parts
Related calibers: 1161 (with subsidiary seconds); 1106 (manually wound, subsidiary seconds, date, power reserve)

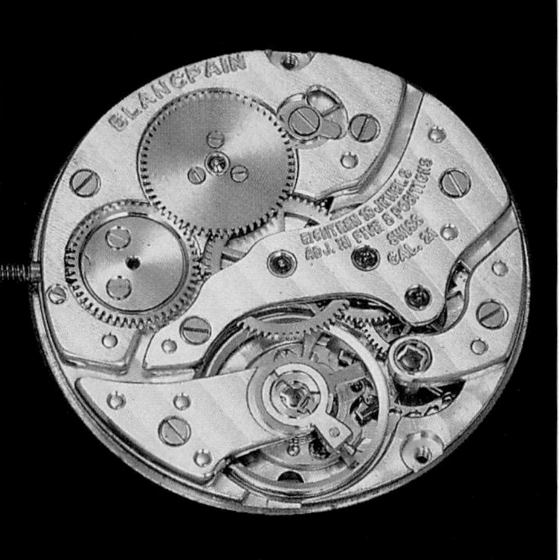

Caliber 21

Mechanical with manual winding, power reserve 40 hours
Functions: hours, minutes
Diameter: 20.4 mm (9''')
Height: extra-flat, 1.73 mm
Jewels: 18
Balance: beryllium copper
Frequency: 21,600 vph
Balance spring: flat hairspring
Shock protection: Kif (balance), Duofix (escape wheel)
Remarks: regulation in five positions; base plate decorated with perlage, bridges with côtes de Genève; 132 individual parts
Related caliber: 21 S (skeletonized)

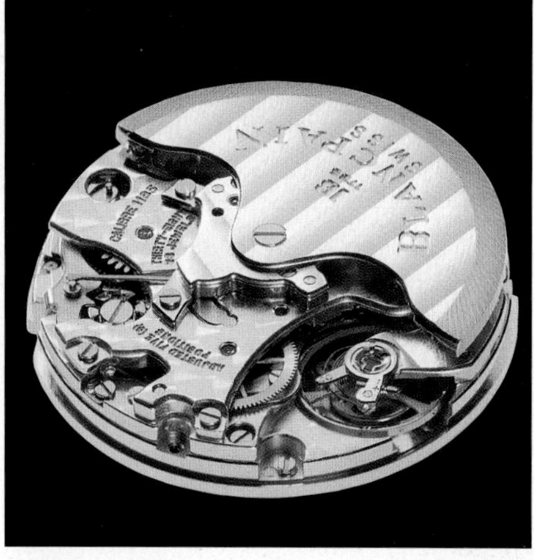

Caliber 1185

Mechanical with automatic winding, power reserve 40 hours; rotor in 18-karat gold
Functions: hours, minutes; date, chronograph
Diameter: 25.6 mm (12'''); **Height:** 5.5 mm; **Jewels:** 37
Balance: beryllium copper; **Frequency:** 21,600 vph
Shock protection: Kif
Remarks: regulation in five positions; 304 individual parts
Related calibers: 1186 (with rattrapante), F185 (with flyback function), F585 (flyback with perpetual calendar), 1180 (manual winding), 1181 (manual winding with rattrapante), 5580 (manual winding with perpetual calendar), 5581 (with perpetual calendar and rattrapante), 5585 (with perpetual calendar), 23F9A (flyback with rattrapante and tourbillon)

Caliber 23

Mechanical with manual winding, tourbillon, power reserve 8 days
Functions: hours, minutes, subsidiary seconds (above tourbillon cage); date, power reserve display
Diameter: 25.6 mm
Height: 3.5 mm
Jewels: 19
Balance: monometallic with regulating screws
Frequency: 21,600 vph
Shock protection: Kif
Remarks: regulation in five positions; 195 individual parts
Related caliber: 25 (mechanical with automatic winding)

Caliber 33

Mechanical with manual winding, power reserve 44 hours
Functions: hours, minutes, subsidiary seconds; minute repeater
Diameter: 23.6 mm (10 1/2'''); **Height:** 3.3 mm
Jewels: 31
Frequency: 21,600 vph
Balance: monometallic with masselotte and regulating screws
Balance spring: Breguet
Shock protection: Kif
Remarks: regulation in five positions; base plate decorated with perlage, bridges (beveled) with côtes de Genève; 320 individual parts; fourth wheel, escape wheel, and balance under separate bridge
Related caliber: 35 (automatic winding)

Caliber 6.15

Mechanical with automatic winding, power reserve 42 hours
Functions: hours, minutes
Diameter: 15.3 mm
Height: 3.9 mm
Jewels: 29
Frequency: 21,600 vph
Balance: beryllium copper
Balance spring: flat hairspring
Shock protection: Kif
Remarks: regulation in five positions; base plate and rotor decorated with perlage; 152 individual parts; rotor in platinum

blu-source du temps

blu — source du temps, "source of time," is the brand named by a German master watchmaker who is certainly not unknown to our readers. For his brand, Bernhard Lederer has moved to Switzerland — to the source of the art of watchmaking. The combination of traditional watch know-how and innovative display technology Lederer is so famous for harmonizes wonderfully, producing exotic-looking timepieces of the best quality.

This brand has not just come out of the blue: Lederer, who is responsible for the technical and design side of the brand, has made a name for himself over more than twenty years of unconventional constructions and interpretations of adventurous displays and designs of time. In *blu — source du temps* this tradition of innovation continues.

The unusual watches represent a new concept that leaves room for the philosophical contemplation of time and its perspectives. This is especially clear in the continual rotation of the dials on the Planet models with their off-center subsidiary minutes that rotate with the rest, seeming to say, "It's not time that is at the center of our lives. We are." In order to create this amazing impression, ingenious technology is necessary under the dial: A tiny differential continually keeps the subsidiary minute dial in a "vertical" or "correct" position with respect to the dial's imaginary 12 as it travels around the larger hour disc.

The same technology is used to keep the small subdial on the Lady-blu in position while the base plate that functions as a "date hand" moves forward every night at midnight. Thus, the watch shows a somewhat different "face" every day, and the jeweled motifs that are available on request — such as the Cherry Blossom shown on this page made of diamonds and pink sapphires — can be experienced anew again and again.

Alongside the Planet, a second model line has emerged that juggles conventional and retrograde dial trains and whose models bear the name Duett, Terzett, or Quintett, depending on the amount of displays shown on the dial.

The blu Terzett model has its three displays (hours, minutes, and date) arranged in strictly separated spheres, although the individual circles of numerals intertwine. Different from a classic regulator arrangement, the minute circle cuts through the hour circle. By arranging the hands and scale circles on two different levels, the smaller hour hand runs underneath the scale ring for the minute display, lending the dial an unusual spatiality. The blu Quartett model is also outfitted with an off-center hour hand, while its minute hand jumps back to the beginning upon reaching the end of its half-circle. Not only does blu Quintett's minute hand move with the help of the lower arbor, but also a sweet little retrograde month hand, which forms the calendar together with the window displays of date and day.

blu Terzett

Reference number: G13/241.50.9/L
Movement: automatic, blu-Orbit (base ETA 2892-A2); ø 25.6 mm, height 3.6 mm; 25 jewels; 28,800 vph, autonomous automatic module with fine côtes de Genève
Functions: hours (off-center), minutes; date
Case: rose gold, ø 39 mm, height 13 mm; case with movable lugs; sapphire crystal; transparent case back
Band: reptile skin, buckle
Remarks: minute scale dial with nine diamond markers
Price: $17,500
Variations: in stainless steel without diamonds; with stainless steel bracelet; silver-colored dial

blu Quartett

Reference number: G14/740.50.9/L
Movement: automatic, blu-Orbit (base ETA 2892-A3); ø 25.6 mm, height 3.6 mm; 25 jewels; 28,800 vph, autonomous automatic module with fine côtes de Genève
Functions: hours (off-center), minutes (off-center, retrograde), sweep seconds; date
Case: rose gold, ø 39 mm, height 13 mm; case with movable lugs; sapphire crystal; transparent case back
Band: reptile skin, buckle
Price: $15,900
Variations: with anthracite-colored dial; in stainless steel; in white gold with leather strap

blu Quintett

Reference number: G15/710.50.9/L
Movement: automatic, blu-Orbit (base ETA 2892-A4); ø 25.6 mm, height 3.6 mm; 25 jewels; 28,800 vph, autonomous automatic module with fine côtes de Genève
Functions: hours (off-center), minutes; date, day, month (retrograde)
Case: rose gold, ø 39 mm, height 13 mm; case with movable lugs; sapphire crystal; transparent case back
Band: reptile skin, buckle
Price: $16,900
Variations: with anthracite-colored dial; in stainless steel; in white gold with leather strap

blu Paris

Reference number: G21/544.50.9/L
Movement: automatic, blu-Orbit (base ETA 2892-A2); ø 25.6 mm, height 3.6 mm; 31 jewels; 28,800 vph, autonomous automatic module with fine côtes de Genève
Functions: hours (rotating dial with sapphire marker), minutes (hand in rotating circle, watch shows 3:50)
Case: rose gold, ø 39 mm, height 13 mm; case with movable lugs; sapphire crystal; transparent case back; recessed crown
Band: reptile skin, buckle
Price: $16,500
Variations: in stainless steel; in white gold with leather strap; as Atoll with diamonds on minute disk ($21,900)

blu Moonlight

Reference number: G41/271.10.9/L
Movement: automatic, blu-Orbit (base ETA 2892-A2); ø 25.6 mm, height 3.6 mm; 31 jewels; 28,800 vph, autonomous automatic module with fine côtes de Genève
Functions: hours (rotating dial with sapphire marker), minutes (hand in rotating circle, watch shows 2:00)
Case: stainless steel, ø 39 mm, height 13 mm; case with movable lugs; sapphire crystal; transparent case back; recessed crown
Band: reptile skin, buckle
Remarks: mother-of-pearl, diamonds and 5 sapphire markers
Price: $20,900

blu Galaxy

Reference number: G62/281.50.9/T
Movement: automatic, blu-Orbit (base ETA 2892-A2); ø 25.6 mm, height 3.6 mm; 25 jewels; 28,800 vph, autonomous automatic module with fine côtes de Genève
Functions: hours, minutes and seconds displayed by three concentric aventurine disks with diamond markers
Case: rose gold, ø 39 mm, height 13 mm; case with movable lugs; sapphire crystal; transparent case back; recessed crown
Band: reptile skin, buckle
Price: $16,900
Variations: in stainless steel with aventurine and mother-of-pearl dial and leather strap; in white gold with leather strap

Rainer Brand

In the heart of Germany, geographically located exactly between the watch *manufactures* of the Swiss Jura and Germany's new, yet traditional watchmaking stronghold Glashütte, Rainer and Petra Brand find the peace and quiet that are needed to pursue Rainer's craft in his studio and workshop. Brand, who rose from the ranks learning his craft from the base up, is also in charge of the design of his watches. This man of few words loves harmonious proportions. The simple shapes of his watches culminate in exacting attention to detail. True to his motto, "style is the product of quality and consciousness," precision, perfection, beauty, and understatement have top priority.
It all began in 1993 with the Havanna model that was renamed Panama in 1996 on the order of a resourceful patent lawyer working for the Cuban tobacco industry. It represents both the collection's entry-level model and bestseller. Panama Dualtime is the variation designed for globe-trotters at home in the different time zones of the world. In the area of mechanical women's watches, the Sybaris model has caught the public's attention. The watch, named for a symbol of fine living, is both an eye-catcher and a technical delicacy.
Brand's new leading model for sporty, ambitious chronograph fans is the Kerala. It boasts somewhat more robust dimensions and striking luminous hands, driving it toward the edge of the brand's established style.
The brand's first square-shaped model, the reversible Giro, is more than just a timepiece. It is at once both a beautiful piece of jewelry and an eternally interesting toy. Because of the limited supply of the rare, hand-wound caliber FEF 170 used in this model, an interested buyer needs a lot of luck to find one of these sold-out watches. Part of the Giro — namely, the rectangular, perfectly proportioned case that turns and rotates in its frame — lives on in the quadrate women's watch Pezzo. Since the success of this watch became so apparent, Brand has become much more adventurous in his design while simultaneously remaining true to himself, as the newest creations of the house of Brand illustrate. A logical companion to the successful Pezzo is the rectangular men's watch Ecco, a timepiece that also displays new perspectives. The strict case design and its narrow strap lugs build the simple frame for a dial feelingly reduced to only that which is necessary. It becomes more impressive with each glance and is irreplaceable in the Rainer Brand collection.

Panama Gold

Reference number: RB 11 KX
Movement: automatic, ETA 2892-A2, modified, ø 25.6 mm, height 3.6 mm; 21 jewels; 28,800 vph, finely decorated with côtes de Genève
Functions: hours, minutes, sweep seconds; date hand
Case: yellow gold, polished and satin-finished, individually numbered, ø 36 mm, height 11 mm; sapphire crystal; transparent case back
Band: leather, buckle
Price: $5,900

Panama Classic

Reference number: RB 11 KS
Movement: automatic, ETA 2892-A2, modified, ø 25.6 mm, height 3.6 mm; 21 jewels; 28,800 vph, finely decorated with côtes de Genève
Functions: hours, minutes, sweep seconds; date hand
Case: stainless steel, polished and satin-finished, serially numbered, ø 36 mm, height 11 mm; sapphire crystal; transparent case back
Band: leather, buckle
Price: $2,100
Variations: as chronometer with black dial

Panama Dualtime

Reference number: RB 11 DS
Movement: automatic, ETA 2892-A2, modified, ø 25.6 mm, height 3.6 mm; 21 jewels; 28,800 vph, finely decorated with côtes de Genève
Functions: hours, minutes, sweep seconds; date hand; second time zone
Case: stainless steel, polished and satin-finished, serially numbered, ø 36 mm, height 11 mm; sapphire crystal; transparent case back
Band: leather, buckle
Price: $2,500
Variations: as chronometer with black dial

Kerala

Reference number: RB 10 S
Movement: automatic, ETA/Valjoux 7750 Tricompax, ø 30 mm, height 7.9 mm; 25 jewels; 28,800 vph, finely decorated with côtes de Genève and blued screws
Functions: hours, minutes, subsidiary seconds; chronograph
Case: stainless steel, polished and satin-finished, serially numbered, ø 40.5 mm, height 15 mm; sapphire crystal; transparent case back; water-resistant to 50 m
Band: leather, buckle
Price: $3,500
Variations: as chronometer with black dial

Ecco

Reference number: RB 02 S
Movement: automatic, ETA 2892-A2, modified, ø 25.6 mm, height 3.6 mm; 21 jewels; 28,800 vph
Functions: hours, minutes, sweep seconds; date
Case: stainless steel, polished, serially numbered, 36 x 31 mm, height 8 mm; sapphire crystal; transparent case back
Band: leather, buckle
Price: $2,200

Ecco Chronometer

Reference number: RB 02 SC
Movement: automatic, ETA 2892-A2, modified, ø 25.6 mm, height 3.6 mm; 21 jewels; 28,800 vph, certified chronometer (C.O.S.C.)
Functions: hours, minutes, sweep seconds; date
Case: stainless steel, polished, serially numbered, 36 x 31 mm, height 8 mm; sapphire crystal; transparent case back
Band: leather, buckle
Price: $2,500

Martin Braun

A good name needs to be chosen deliberately. Black Forest master watchmaker Martin Braun likes to name his watches after figures from Greek mythology — at least this was the case with the Eos, a wristwatch featuring the display of sunrise and sunset times, which he introduced in 2000. The very fitting choice of name represents the goddess of the dawn. Boreas, as it stands in Martin Braun's catalogue, was one of Eos's sons. As the Greeks described him, he was the god of the North Wind and rather rough company. When looking at the family ties, it becomes clear that the youngest offspring inherited quite a bit from his mother.

Eos set the watch world in an uproar at its introduction with its remarkable display of sunrise and sunset by means of two long, crossed hands and short arched scales. A specialty of the Eos technology is the index cams of the crossed hands visible at the bottom of the dial, which, along with the scale segments, can be replaced to fit the various geographical degrees of latitude. Boreas has in a sense inherited the Eos module, including its index cams and crossed hands, but also brings an additional astronomical complication into the game: the equation of time. A slender hand sweeping from the center of the dial displays the deviation of our mean time from the reality of the time that the sun keeps in minutes on a small scale segment.

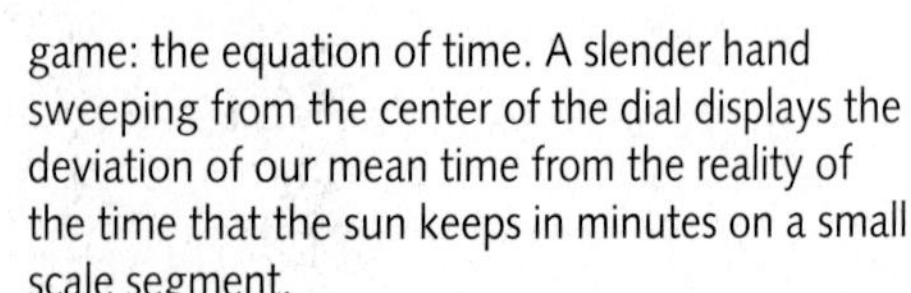

This predilection for constellations is also expressed in Martin Braun's latest creation: The Heliozentric has the sun placed in the middle of its dial, around which circles an amazingly three-dimensional looking earth on an elliptical path — almost like in our actual solar system, in which everything revolves around the sun. The mechanics powering this display are astonishingly simple; it was just a matter of coming up with the idea.

Naturally, the rest of Martin Braun's watch collection languishes in the shadow of these famous complicated timepieces. But in the end, it is the neoclassics constructed with care and expertise from remnants of vintage *manufacture* movements that form the basis for the ambitious creations, including the Korona line of sporty models featuring a striking case and dial design. Fundamentally it is this, old and new side by side, classic yet innovative, that makes Martin Braun's watches so attractive.

Boreas

Reference number: MB161S
Movement: automatic, ETA 2892-A2, modified, ø 25.6 mm, height 3.6 mm; 21 jewels; 28,800 vph, autonomous module MAB 2; movement finely finished; gold rotor
Functions: hours, minutes; date; times of sunrise/sunset; equation of time
Case: stainless steel, ø 42 mm, height 12.5 mm; sapphire crystal; transparent case back
Band: reptile skin, buckle
Price: $14,275
Variations: different dial variations; with 39 mm case diameter; with gold case

EOS

Reference number: MB001B
Movement: automatic, ETA 2892-A2, modified, ø 25.6 mm, height 3.6 mm; 21 jewels; 28,800 vph, autonomous module MAB 1; movement finely finished; gold rotor
Functions: hours, minutes; date; times of sunrise/sunset
Case: stainless steel, ø 39 mm, height 12.5 mm; sapphire crystal; transparent case back
Band: reptile skin, buckle
Price: $7,950
Variations: different dial variations; with 42 mm case diameter; with gold case

Boreas

Reference number: MB
Movement: automatic, ETA 2892-A2, modified, ø 25.6 mm, height 3.6 mm; 21 jewels; 28,800 vph, autonomous module MAB 2; movement finely finished; gold rotor
Functions: hours, minutes; date; times of sunrise/sunset; equation of time
Case: platinum, ø 42 mm, height 12.7 mm; bezel set with 64 diamonds; sapphire crystal; transparent case back
Band: reptile skin, buckle
Price: $50,700
Variations: with diamond markers ($51,245); in 39 mm case diameter; with gold or stainless steel case

La Sonnerie II

Reference number: MB191
Movement: automatic, AS 5008, ø 30.5 mm, height 7.5 mm; 17 jewels; 28,800 vph, movement finely finished, hand-guilloché blued steel rotor
Functions: hours, minutes, sweep seconds; date; alarm
Case: stainless steel, ø 42 mm, height 14 mm; sapphire crystal
Band: reptile skin, buckle
Remarks: limited to 100 pieces
Price: $6,950
Variations: with white dial

Bigdate

Reference number: MB251SG
Movement: automatic, TT 651 (base ETA 2892-A2); ø 25.6 mm, height 3.6 mm; 21 jewels; 28,800 vph
Functions: hours, minutes, sweep seconds; large date; second time zone
Case: red gold, ø 39 mm, height 11 mm; sapphire crystal
Band: reptile skin, buckle
Remarks: hand-guilloché silver dial
Price: $13,850
Variations: different dial variations

Heliozentric

Reference number: MB252B
Movement: automatic, ETA 2892-A2, modified, ø 25.6 mm, height 3.6 mm; 21 jewels; 28,800 vph, power reserve 42 h, autonomous module MAB 3; finely finished; gold rotor
Functions: hours, minutes; date, month, sign of the zodiac, position of earth in relation to orbit around sun
Case: stainless steel, ø 42 mm, height 13 mm; sapphire crystal
Band: reptile skin, buckle
Remarks: constellations Orion and Big Dipper comprise diamonds on blued steel
Price: $15,800
Variations: with silver-colored dial; in red gold

Breguet

In commemoration of the centuries-old tie that was forged between Breguet and Russia, this watch *manufacture* began an unusual partnership with the estimable State Hermitage Museum in St. Petersburg: From June 10 until September 26, 2004, a remarkable exhibition of antique Breguet watches took place with the support of the museum's general director and curator, Dr. Mikhail Borisovitch Piotrovski. St. Petersburg was the ideal place for the exhibition, for Abraham-Louis Breguet once maintained the first and only foreign branch of his business at the court of the Russian czars.
Among the pieces on exhibition were numerous loans, from both private collectors and large international museums such as the Musée des Arts et Métiers and the Louvre in Paris, the Moscow Kremlin Museum, and the British Museum in London.
Alongside an unusually full glass case with early subscription watches (only outfitted with one hand), it was naturally the highly complicated pocket watches that chiefly captured visitors' interest. For example, the Breguet watches bearing the numbers 42 and 92 from the Kremlin Museum and the Musée des Arts et Métiers, respectively, whose myriad of displays and functions are only superseded by the legendary Marie Antoinette watch (no. 160), a timepiece that since its theft more than twenty years ago has disappeared without a trace. Two original *montres sympathiques* (astronomical table clocks with clever winding and setting devices for pocket watches that rest above the dial) from the personal possessions of Czar Alexander I and Carlos V of Spain, as well as an experimental tourbillon (no. 1252) and a double-pendulum grandfather clock containing two escapements that influence each other, are only arbitrarily chosen examples of the opulent compilation of unique timepieces from the high point of genius watchmaker Abraham-Louis Breguet's career.
The old ideals of the brand will continue to be the new ones: exclusivity, innovation, and lasting value. Watches made by Breguet have always represented the pinnacle of an entire group, and they still do — maybe even more so today than before.
The Swatch Group and its president took the special opportunity in 2002 to respectfully celebrate the two hundredth anniversary of one of the many inventions of Abraham-Louis Breguet: The tourbillon, also implemented as the highest expression of horological skill by many other top companies, is indisputably associated with the name of Breguet. Nicolas G. Hayek cares for the fortunes of Breguet himself: The successful and, by employees and opponents alike, highly respected manager has found in Abraham-Louis Breguet his alter ego. "Not in watchmaking, for in that Breguet was without equal," qualifies Hayek, "but as a businessman and visionary." In fact, the memory of Breguet would not be nearly as vivid if he hadn't been so versed in lucratively applying his inventions and patents.

In order to close the 200-year-old gap between then and now, the Swatch Group has invested a great deal in renovating the movement factory Nouvelle Lémania, christening it the new Breguet Manufacture. From the concept and manufacture of components all the way to the fabrication of entire movements, Breguet disposes of a wide range of knowledge, paired with the most modern in technology, guaranteeing the high quality of its products.
But even in a *manufacture* that occupies itself with top technology, there are individual workshops in which the master watchmakers cloak themselves in silence and concentration. Only now and then do the characteristic whistles of the spirit lamps with which Breguet hands are blued or the discreet rubbing sound of the diamond files with which a fine piece of a tourbillon is minutely polished dare to make a noise.
This is where time in its purest form ticks and ticks ...

Tourbillon Régulateur Automatique

Reference number: 5307 BA 12 9V6
Movement: automatic, Breguet 587, ø 27.6 mm; 31 jewels; 21,600 vph, one-minute tourbillon; power reserve 120 hours
Functions: hours (off-center), minutes, subsidiary seconds (on tourbillon cage)
Case: yellow gold, ø 39 mm, height 10.75 mm; sapphire crystal; transparent case back
Band: reptile skin, folding clasp
Price: $85,000
Variations: in platinum

Tourbillon with Perpetual Calendar

Reference number: 3757 BA 1E 9V6
Movement: manual winding, Breguet 558QPT, ø 30.5 mm, height 6.45 mm; 21 jewels; 18,000 vph, one-minute tourbillon, hand-engraved movement
Functions: hours, minutes (off-center), subsidiary seconds (on tourbillon cage); perpetual calendar with date, day, month, leap year indication
Case: yellow gold, ø 39 mm, height 10.25 mm; sapphire crystal; transparent case back
Band: reptile skin, folding clasp
Price: $104,400
Variations: in platinum

Tourbillon with Power Reserve

Reference number: 3657 BA 12 9V6
Movement: manual winding, Breguet 560T, ø 30.5 mm, height 6 mm; 18,000 vph, one-minute tourbillon
Functions: hours, minutes, subsidiary seconds (on tourbillon cage), 24-hour display (retrograde); power reserve display
Case: yellow gold, ø 39 mm, height 10.2 mm; sapphire crystal; transparent case back
Band: reptile skin, folding clasp
Price: $88,900
Variations: in platinum

Tourbillon Jewellery

Reference number: 3358 BB 52 986 DD00
Movement: manual winding, Breguet 558.1, ø 30.5 mm, height 4.8 mm; 21 jewels; 18,000 vph, one-minute tourbillon, hand-engraved movement
Functions: hours, minutes (off-center), subsidiary seconds (on tourbillon cage)
Case: white gold, ø 35 mm, height 9.15 mm; bezel and lugs set with 73 diamonds; sapphire crystal; transparent case back
Band: reptile skin, folding clasp
Price: $82,000

Tourbillon Squelette

Reference number: 3355 PT 00 986
Movement: manual winding, Breguet 558SQ.1, ø 30.5 mm, height 4.8 mm; 21 jewels; 18,000 vph, one-minute tourbillon, hand-skeletonized and engraved movement
Functions: hours, minutes (off-center), subsidiary seconds (on tourbillon cage)
Case: platinum, ø 35 mm, height 8.9 mm; sapphire crystal; transparent case back
Band: reptile skin, folding clasp
Price: $110,800

Perpetual Calendar Power Reserve

Reference number: 5327 BA 1E 9V6
Movement: automatic, Breguet 502.3.DRP.1, ø 27.9 mm, height 2.62 mm (base movement); 37 jewels; 18,000 vph
Functions: hours, minutes; perpetual calendar with date, day, month, true moon phase, leap year; power reserve display
Case: yellow gold, ø 39 mm, height 9.05 mm; sapphire crystal; transparent case back
Band: reptile skin, folding clasp
Price: $53,000
Variations: in white gold

GMT Alarm Watch

Reference number: 5707 BA 12 9V6
Movement: automatic, Breguet 519F, ø 27.6 mm, height 6.2 mm; 38 jewels; 28,800 vph, alarm movement with automatic winding
Functions: hours, minutes, subsidiary seconds; date; 24-hour display (second time zone); alarm time, display of alarm mechanism power reserve, indication of alarm function
Case: yellow gold, ø 39 mm, height 11.35 mm; sapphire crystal
Band: reptile skin, folding clasp
Price: $27,300
Variations: in white gold

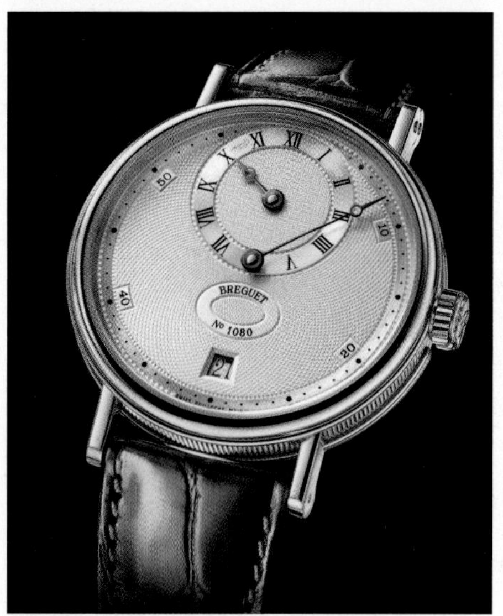

Régulateur Automatique

Reference number: 5187 BR 15 986
Movement: automatic, Breguet 591QSHD, ø 26.2 mm, height 2.95 mm; 25 jewels; 28,800 vph, hand-guilloché rotor
Functions: hours (off-center), minutes; date
Case: rose gold, ø 35.5 mm, height 8.47 mm; sapphire crystal; transparent case back
Band: reptile skin, buckle
Price: $15,100
Variations: in platinum

Retrograde Seconds

Reference number: 5207 BA 12 9V6
Movement: automatic, Breguet 516DRSR, ø 32 mm, height 4.62 mm; 34 jewels; 28,800 vph,
Functions: hours, minutes, subsidiary retrograde seconds; power reserve display
Case: yellow gold, ø 39 mm, height 9.85 mm; sapphire crystal
Band: reptile skin, folding clasp
Price: $15,800
Variations: in white gold

Manual Winding

Reference number: 5907 BA 12 984
Movement: manual winding, Breguet 510DR, ø 26.8 mm, height 2.8 mm; 23 jewels; 21,600 vph, two spring barrels, power reserve appx. 95 hours
Functions: hours, minutes, subsidiary seconds; power reserve display on the back
Case: yellow gold, ø 34 mm, height 7.5 mm; sapphire crystal; transparent case back
Band: reptile skin, buckle
Price: $9,700
Variations: in white gold; in rose gold

Moon Phases

Reference number: 3130 BA 11 986
Movement: automatic, Breguet 502DR, ø 27.9 mm, height 2.62 mm (base movement); 37 jewels; 18,000 vph
Functions: hours, minutes, date; moon phase; power reserve display
Case: yellow gold, ø 35.5 mm, height 7.35 mm; sapphire crystal; crown with double o-ring; water-resistant to 50 m
Band: reptile skin, folding clasp
Price: $26,400
Variations: in white gold; in rose gold; with gold link bracelet; with sapphire crystal case back

Classique Jewellery

Reference number: 8068 BB 52 964 D000
Movement: automatic, Breguet 537.1, ø 20 mm, height 3.6 mm; 20 jewels; 21,600 vph
Functions: hours, minutes, sweep seconds
Case: white gold, ø 30 mm, height 7.7 mm; bezel set with 48 diamonds; sapphire crystal; crown with sapphire cabochon
Band: reptile skin, buckle
Remarks: dial hand-guilloché, natural mother-of-pearl
Price: $14,250
Variations: in yellow gold

Reine de Naples

Reference number: 8908 BB V2 864 D00D
Movement: automatic, Breguet 537 DRL1, ø 20 mm, height 5 mm; 23 jewels; 21,600 vph
Functions: hours, minutes, subsidiary seconds; moon phase; power reserve display
Case: white gold, 28.45 x 36.5 mm, height 10.5 mm; bezel set with 128 diamonds; sapphire crystal; transparent case back; crown with diamond cabochon
Band: satin, folding clasp
Remarks: genuine mother-of-pearl dial
Price: $26,900

Reine de Naples

Reference number: 8918 BB 58 864 D00D
Movement: automatic, Breguet 537.1, ø 20 mm, height 3.6 mm; 20 jewels; 21,600 vph
Functions: hours, minutes
Case: white gold, 30.45 x 38.5 mm, height 10 mm; bezel set with 117 diamonds; sapphire crystal; crown with diamond cabochon
Band: satin, folding clasp
Remarks: dial with teardrop diamond marker
Price: $26,900
Variations: in yellow gold

Heritage Large Date

Reference number: 5480 BB 12 996
Movement: automatic, Breguet 516GG, ø 26.2 mm, height 3.37 mm; 30 jewels; 28,800 vph, two spring barrels, power reserve appx. 95 hours
Functions: hours, minutes, subsidiary seconds; large date
Case: white gold, 40.4 x 34 mm, height 9.25 mm; sapphire crystal
Band: reptile skin, buckle
Price: $18,600
Variations: in yellow gold

Heritage Chronograph

Reference number: 5460 BB 12 996
Movement: automatic, Breguet 550, ø 23.9 mm, height 6.9 mm; 38 jewels; 21,600 vph, column-wheel control of chronograph functions
Functions: hours, minutes, subsidiary seconds; chronograph; date
Case: white gold, 38.7 x 32.8 mm, height 10.65 mm; sapphire crystal
Band: reptile skin, folding clasp in white gold
Price: $23,500
Variations: in yellow gold; in platinum

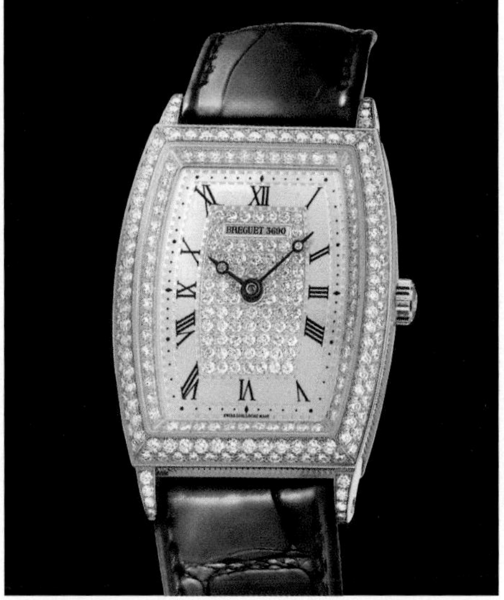

Ladies' Heritage Jewellery Collection

Reference number: 8671 BA 61 964 D000
Movement: automatic, Breguet 532SP, ø 20 mm, height 3.5 mm; 25 jewels; 21,600 vph
Functions: hours, minutes
Case: yellow gold, 29.2 x 24.4 mm, height 7.9 mm; bezel and lugs set with 204 diamonds; sapphire crystal
Band: reptile skin, buckle
Remarks: dial set with 77 diamonds
Price: $26,500
Variations: in white gold, with white gold bracelet, without diamonds

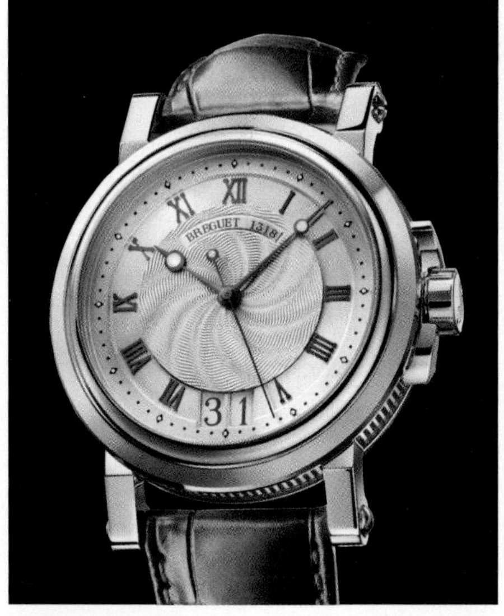

Marine Automatic

Reference number: 5817 BA 12 9V6
Movement: automatic, Breguet 517GG, ø 26.2 mm, height 3.37 mm; 28 jewels; 28,800 vph, power reserve appx. 65 hours
Functions: hours, minutes, sweep seconds; large date
Case: yellow gold, ø 39 mm, height 11.85 mm; sapphire crystal; transparent case back; screw-in crown; water-resistant to 100 m
Band: reptile skin, folding clasp
Price: $16,300

Marine Chronograph

Reference number: 3460 BB 12 996
Movement: automatic, Breguet 576, ø 26.2 mm, height 5.4 mm; 21,600 vph, column-wheel control of chronograph functions
Functions: hours, minutes, subsidiary seconds, chronograph; date
Case: white gold, ø 35.5 mm, height 9.9 mm; sapphire crystal; crown with double o-ring; water-resistant to 50 m
Band: reptile skin, folding clasp in white gold
Price: $20,700
Variations: with white gold bracelet; in yellow gold, with yellow gold bracelet; in platinum, with platinum bracelet

Ladies' Marine Chronograph

Reference number: 8491 BB 52 964
Movement: automatic, Breguet 550, ø 23.9 mm, height 6 mm; 38 jewels; 21,600 vph, column-wheel control of chronograph functions
Functions: hours, minutes, subsidiary seconds, chronograph; date
Case: white gold, ø 38 mm, height 10.4 mm; bezel set with 48 diamonds; sapphire crystal
Band: reptile skin, folding clasp
Price: $20,500
Variations: with white gold bracelet; in yellow gold, with yellow gold bracelet

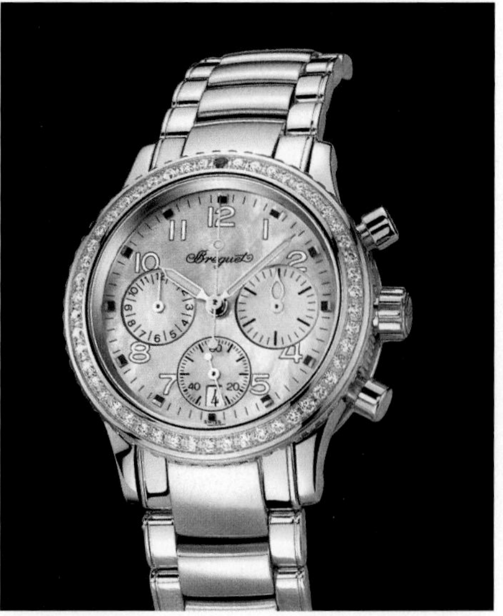

Ladies' Type XX Collection

Reference number: 4821 ST 59 576
Movement: automatic, Breguet 550, ø 23.9 mm, height 6.4 mm; 38 jewels; 28,800 vph, column-wheel control of chronograph functions
Functions: hours, minutes, subsidiary seconds, chronograph, date
Case: stainless steel, ø 32.5 mm, height 12.5 mm; unidirectionally rotating bezel set with 48 diamonds and one sapphire; sapphire crystal; screw-in crown; water-resistant to 100 m
Band: stainless steel, folding clasp
Remarks: mother-of-pearl dial
Price: $13,600

Type XX Aeronavale

Reference number: 3800 ST 92 SW9
Movement: automatic, Breguet 582, ø 31 mm, height 6.4 mm; 25 jewels; 28,800 vph, column-wheel control of chronograph functions
Functions: hours, minutes, subsidiary seconds, chronograph with flyback function
Case: stainless steel, ø 39 mm, height 14.4 mm; unidirectionally rotating bezel with 60-minute scale; sapphire crystal; screw-in crown; water-resistant to 100 m
Band: stainless steel, folding clasp
Price: $7,100
Variations: with leather strap

Type XX Transatlantique

Reference number: 3820 ST H2 SW9
Movement: automatic, Breguet 582Q, ø 31 mm, height 6.4 mm; 25 jewels; 28,800 vph, column-wheel control of chronograph functions
Functions: hours, minutes, subsidiary seconds; chronograph with flyback function; date
Case: stainless steel, ø 39 mm, height 14.4 mm; unidirectionally rotating bezel with 60-minute scale; sapphire crystal; screw-in crown; water-resistant to 100 m
Band: stainless steel, folding clasp
Price: $7,950
Variations: with leather strap

Type XX Transatlantique

Reference number: 3820 BR M2 9W6
Movement: automatic, Breguet 582Q, ø 31 mm, height 6.4 mm; 25 jewels; 28,800 vph, column-wheel control of chronograph functions
Functions: hours, minutes, subsidiary seconds; chronograph with flyback function; date
Case: rose gold, ø 39 mm, height 14.4 mm; unidirectionally rotating bezel with 60-minute scale; sapphire crystal; screw-in crown; water-resistant to 100 m
Band: reptile skin, folding clasp
Price: $14,900
Variations: in white or yellow gold

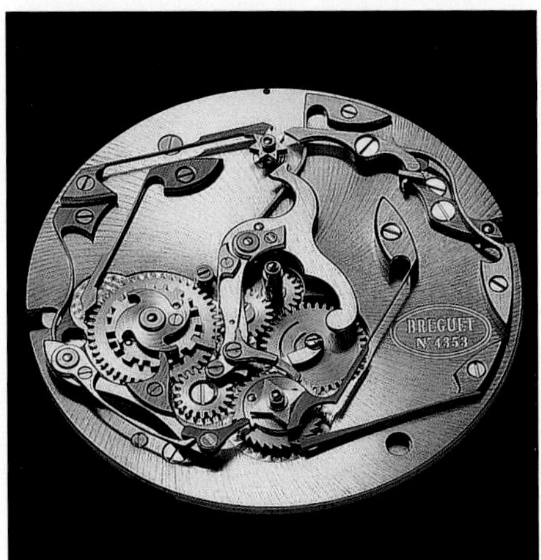

Caliber 502 QPLT

Mechanical with automatic winding, power reserve 45 hours
Functions: hours, minutes; perpetual calendar (date, day, month, leap year), linearly arranged displays with direct year change (Breguet patent 1997)
Diameter: 32.4 mm
Height: 5.07 mm
Jewels: 35
Balance: glucydur
Frequency: 18,000 vph
Balance spring: Nivarox flat hairspring
Shock protection: Kif
Remarks: escapement with straight pallets

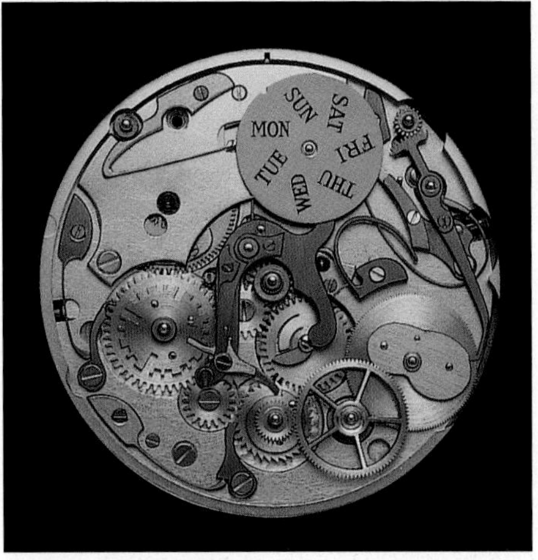

Caliber 502 DPET

Mechanical with automatic winding, power reserve 45 hours
Functions: hours, minutes; perpetual calendar (date, day, month, leap year, moon phase), power reserve display; equation of time (combination of equation and perpetual calendar, patented in 1992)
Diameter: 32.4 mm
Height: 5.07 mm
Jewels: 35
Balance: glucydur
Frequency: 18,000 vph
Balance spring: Nivarox flat hairspring
Shock protection: Kif

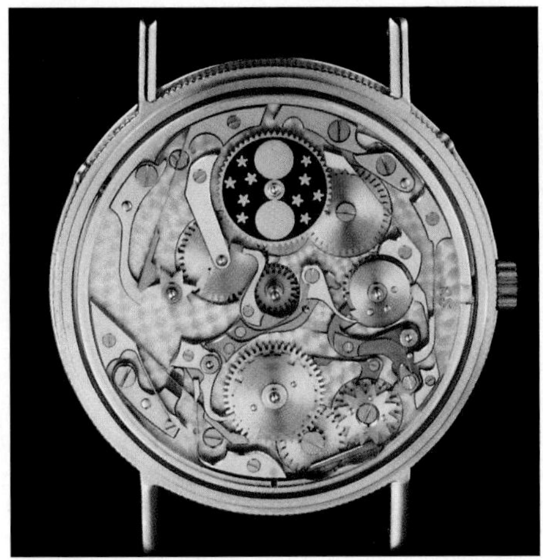

Caliber 502 QSE

Mechanical with automatic winding, power reserve 45 hours
Functions: hours, minutes (off-center); date, day, moon phase
Diameter: 32.4 mm
Height: 5.07 mm
Jewels: 35
Balance: glucydur
Frequency: 18,000 vph
Balance spring: Nivarox flat hairspring
Shock protection: Kif

Caliber 533 NT

Mechanical with manual winding, power reserve 47 hours
Functions: hours, minutes, subsidiary seconds; split-seconds chronograph
Diameter: 27.5 mm
Height: 7.1 mm
Jewels: 23
Balance: glucydur with weighted screws
Frequency: 18,000 vph
Balance spring: Breguet
Shock protection: Incabloc
Remarks: two column wheels to control the chronograph functions

Breitling

Fans of classic chronographs are in just the right place when they turn to Breitling in Grenchen. After all, the company founded by Leon Breitling in 1864 has specialized in stopwatch timing right from the beginning. In the 1960s, Breitling cooperated with Heuer, Hamilton-Büren, and the movement specialist Dubois-Dépraz in order to breathe life into the first chronograph movement outfitted with automatic winding. The jointly developed product lost the race to be first by a hair as Zenith introduced its El Primero to the public just a few weeks earlier, but Caliber 11's success remains the stuff of legends. The Breitling chronographs outfitted with it were called Chrono-Matic, recognizable by the crown on the left side, and experienced a renaissance at the beginning of 2004.

One year earlier, two new Breitling watches were presented in Geneva — not at a watch show, but at the Geneva International Motorshow. There was good reason for this unusual premiere celebration for a watch brand: This chronograph specialist from Grenchen had contributed a stylish clock to the dashboard of the new Bentley showpiece, Continental GT, whose design and choice of materials were oriented on the charac-teristic vent openings of the car's interior as well as the chrome-plated settings of the dashboard's round instruments. The second above-mention-ed Breitling-Bentley timepiece is one for the wrist: A special edition of the Navitimer in a completely new case designed in titanic propor-tions, naturally including a rotating bezel and a slide rule scale.

Both of these timepieces highly recommended Breitling for the job of sponsoring the Bentley team for the 2003 24-hour Le Mans race. As in the wild '20s and '30s, when the daring Bentley Boys ruled the racetracks of Europe, both of the modern racing-green sports cars dominated this traditional long-distance race and rocketed to a perfectly well-deserved win — also scoring for the proud watchmaker.

After that, Breitling proudly presented — this time, as it should be, at Baselworld — two new Bentley editions that are dedicated to the Continental GT and 6.75 models. Even though both of these watch giants, measuring 45 and 49 mm in diameter, respectively, display a number of typical Bentley design elements, they can in no way deny their derivation from the Navitimer.

The Navitimer — a word created by combining navigation and timing — is the most striking and well-known chronograph made by this sports and pilot's watch brand. It is the most important image-bearer for Breitling and has remained part of the unofficial basic equipment of pilots, board engineers, and aviation personnel for more than half a century.

Navitimer Heritage

Reference number: J35350-017
Movement: automatic, Breitling 35 (base ETA 2892-A2); ø 25.6 mm, height 3.6 mm (base movement); 38 jewels; 28,800 vph, certified chronometer (C.O.S.C.)
Functions: hours, minutes, subsidiary seconds; chronograph; date
Case: white gold, ø 43 mm, height 15.4 mm; bidirectionally rotating bezel with integrated slide rule and tachymeter scale; sapphire crystal
Band: white gold, folding clasp
Price: $25,000
Variations: in stainless steel; in yellow gold; various dial colors

Navitimer Montbrillant Datora

Reference number: A21330-045
Movement: automatic, Breitling 21 (base ETA 7751); ø 30 mm, height 7.9 mm; 25 jewels; 28,800 vph, certified chronometer (C.O.S.C.)
Functions: hours, minutes, subsidiary seconds; chronograph; date, day, month, 24-hour display
Case: stainless steel, ø 43 mm, height 14.1 mm; bidirectionally rotating bezel with integrated slide rule and tachymeter scale; sapphire crystal
Band: stainless steel, folding clasp
Price: $5,450
Variations: with leather strap

Navitimer World

Reference number: A24322-101
Movement: automatic, Breitling 24 (base ETA 7754); ø 30 mm, height 7.9 mm; 25 jewels; 28,800 vph, certified chronometer (C.O.S.C.)
Functions: hours, minutes, subsidiary seconds; chronograph; date; 24-hour display (second time zone)
Case: stainless steel, ø 46 mm, height 15.6 mm; bidirectionally rotating bezel with integrated slide rule and 60-minute scale; sapphire crystal
Band: leather, buckle
Price: $4,430
Variations: in red gold (from $14,280); in white gold

Navitimer

Reference number: A23322-161
Movement: automatic, Breitling 23 (base ETA 7750); ø 30 mm, height 7.9 mm; 25 jewels; 28,800 vph, certified chronometer (C.O.S.C.)
Functions: hours, minutes, subsidiary seconds; chronograph; date
Case: stainless steel, ø 41.8 mm, height 14.6 mm; bidirectionally rotating bezel with integrated slide rule and tachymeter scale; sapphire crystal
Band: leather, buckle
Price: $4,130
Variations: with stainless steel bracelet; in yellow gold

Navitimer Montbrillant

Reference number: A41330-101
Movement: automatic, Breitling 41 (base ETA 2892-2); ø 25.6 mm, height 3.6 mm (base movement); 38 jewels; 28,800 vph, certified chronometer (C.O.S.C.)
Functions: hours, minutes, subsidiary seconds; chronograph; date
Case: stainless steel, ø 38 mm, height 13 mm; bidirectionally rotating bezel with tachymeter scale; mineral crystal
Band: leather, buckle
Price: $3,580
Variations: with stainless steel bracelet; in rose gold with leather strap

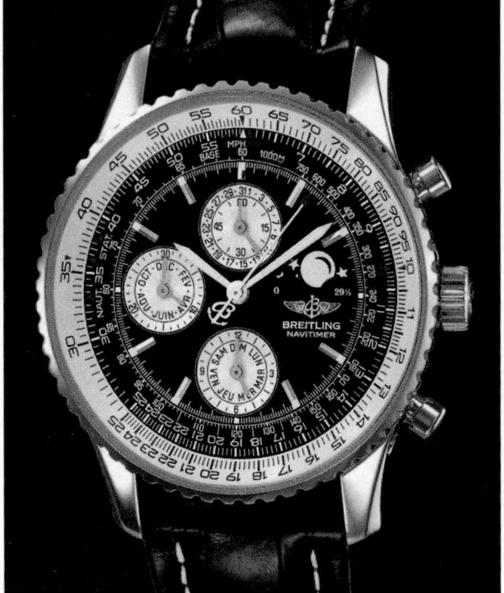

Navitimer Olympus

Reference number: A19340-011
Movement: automatic, Breitling 19 (base ETA 2892-A2); ø 25.6 mm, height 3.6 mm (base movement); 38 jewels; 28,800 vph, certified chronometer (C.O.S.C.)
Functions: hours, minutes, subsidiary seconds; chronograph; four-year calendar with date, day, month, moon phase
Case: stainless steel, ø 43 mm, height 15.3 mm; bidirectionally rotating bezel with integrated slide rule and tachymeter scale; sapphire crystal
Band: leather, buckle
Price: $5,530
Variations: with stainless steel bracelet

Emergency Mission

Reference number: A73321-018
Movement: quartz, Breitling 73 (base ETA 251.262); certified chronometer (C.O.S.C.)
Functions: hours, minutes, subsidiary seconds; chronograph; date; micro antenna with aviation emergency frequency 121.5 MHz
Case: stainless steel, ø 45 mm, height 19.2 mm; bidirectionally rotating bezel with 60-minute scale; sapphire crystal; screw-in crown; water-resistant to 100 m
Band: stainless steel, folding clasp
Remarks: extendable emergency antenna
Price: $4,850

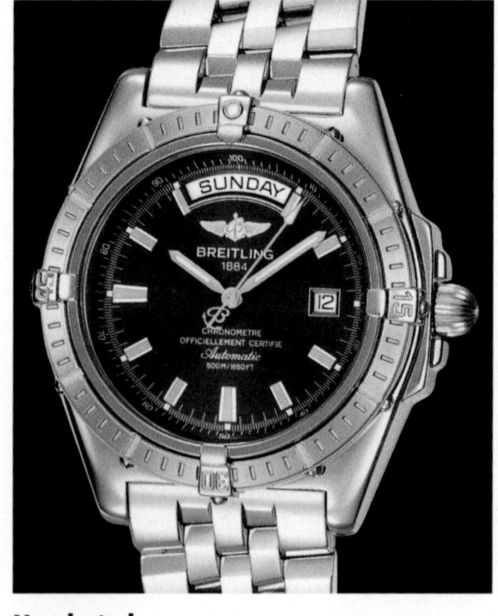

Headwind

Reference number: A45355-075
Movement: automatic, Breitling 45 (base ETA 2836-2); ø 25.6 mm, height 4.6 mm; 21 jewels; 28,800 vph, certified chronometer (C.O.S.C.)
Functions: hours, minutes, sweep seconds; date and day
Case: stainless steel, ø 43.7 mm, height 15.3 mm; unidirectionally rotating bezel with 60-minute scale; sapphire crystal; screw-in crown; water-resistant to 500 m
Band: stainless steel, folding clasp
Price: $3,500
Variations: with leather strap; in yellow gold

Chrono Cockpit

Reference number: A13357-011
Movement: automatic, Breitling 13 (base ETA 7750); ø 30 mm, height 7.9 mm; 25 jewels; 28,800 vph, certified chronometer (C.O.S.C.)
Functions: hours, minutes, subsidiary seconds; chronograph; date
Case: stainless steel, ø 39 mm, height 16.2 mm; unidirectionally rotating bezel with 60-minute scale; sapphire crystal; screw-in crown; water-resistant to 100 m
Band: leather, buckle
Price: $3,730
Variations: in stainless steel/gold; in yellow gold

Super Avenger

Reference number: A13370-168
Movement: automatic, Breitling 13 (base ETA 7750); ø 30 mm, height 7.9 mm; 25 jewels; 28,800 vph, certified chronometer (C.O.S.C.)
Functions: hours, minutes, subsidiary seconds; chronograph; date
Case: stainless steel, ø 48.4 mm, height 18.6 mm; unidirectionally rotating bezel with 60-minute scale; sapphire crystal; screw-in crown; water-resistant to 300 m
Band: stainless steel, buckle
Price: $3,550
Variations: with leather strap; with reptile skin strap

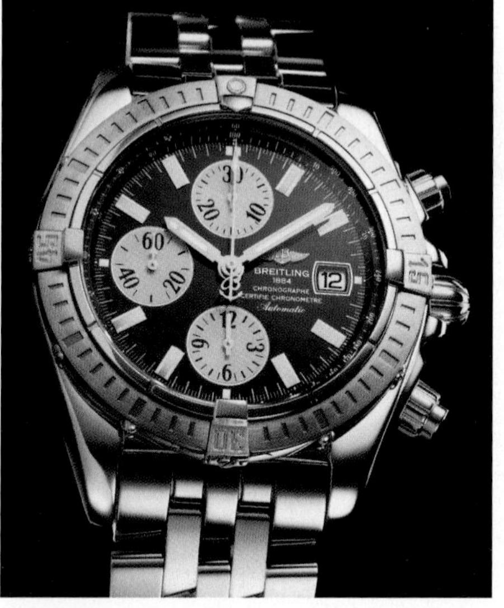

Chronomat Evolution

Reference number: B13356-086
Movement: automatic, Breitling 13 (base ETA 7750); ø 30 mm, height 7.9 mm; 25 jewels; 28,800 vph, certified chronometer (C.O.S.C.)
Functions: hours, minutes, subsidiary seconds; chronograph; date
Case: stainless steel, ø 40.5 mm, height 14.7 mm; unidirectionally rotating bezel with gold claws and 60-minute scale; sapphire crystal; crown and buttons in gold, screw-in; water-resistant to 300 m
Band: stainless steel/yellow gold, folding clasp
Price: $6,200

Colt GMT

Reference number: A32350-301
Movement: automatic, Breitling 32 (base ETA 2893-2); ø 25.6 mm, height 4.1 mm; 21 jewels; 28,800 vph, certified chronometer (C.O.S.C.)
Functions: hours, minutes, subsidiary seconds; date; 24-hour display (second time zone)
Case: stainless steel, ø 40.5 mm, height 13.2 mm; unidirectionally rotating bezel with 60-minute scale; sapphire crystal; screw-in crown; water-resistant to 500 m
Band: leather, buckle
Price: $1,980
Variations: with stainless steel bracelet

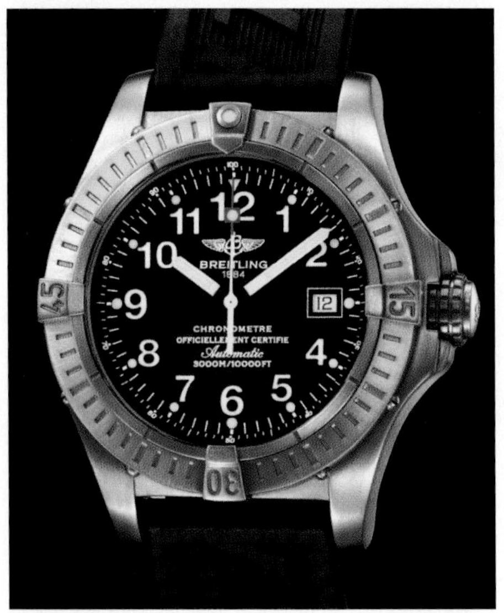

Avenger Seawolf

Reference number: E17370-1014
Movement: automatic, Breitling 44 (base ETA 2892-A2); ø 25.6 mm, height 3.6 mm; 21 jewels; 28,800 vph, certified chronometer (C.O.S.C.)
Functions: hours, minutes, sweep seconds; date
Case: titanium, ø 44 mm, height 18.4 mm; unidirectionally rotating bezel with 60-minute scale; sapphire crystal; screw-in crown; water-resistant to 300 m
Band: rubber, buckle
Price: $2,375
Variations: with titanium bracelet

Chrono Avenger M1

Reference number: E73360-2014
Movement: quartz, Breitling 73 (base ETA 251.262); certified chronometer (C.O.S.C.)
Functions: hours, minutes, subsidiary seconds; chronograph; regatta function (10-minute countdown); date
Case: titanium, ø 44 mm, height 17.2 mm; unidirectionally rotating bezel with 60-minute scale; sapphire crystal; screw-in crown; water-resistant to 1000 m
Band: rubber, buckle
Price: $2,725
Variations: with titanium bracelet

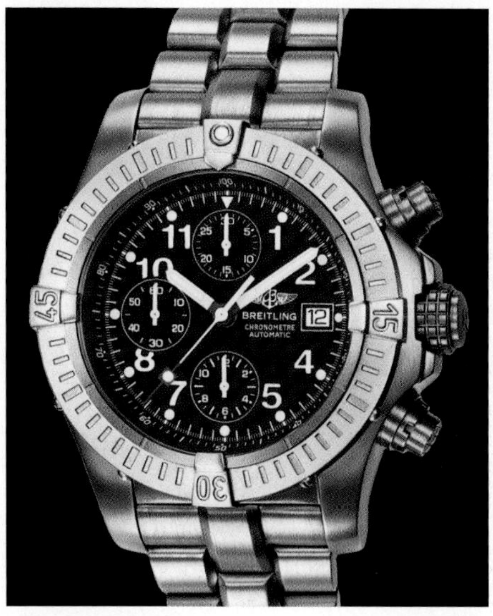

Chrono Avenger

Reference number: E13360-308
Movement: automatic, Breitling 13 (base ETA 7750); ø 30 mm, height 7.9 mm; 25 jewels; 28,800 vph, certified chronometer (C.O.S.C.)
Functions: hours, minutes, subsidiary seconds; chronograph; date
Case: titanium, ø 44 mm, height 17.6 mm; unidirectionally rotating bezel with 60-minute scale; sapphire crystal; screw-in crown; water-resistant to 300 m
Band: titanium, folding clasp
Price: $3,025
Variations: with Diver Pro bracelet

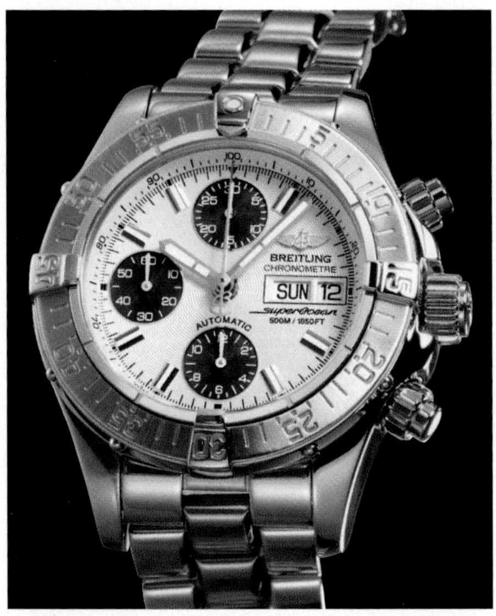

Chrono Superocean

Reference number: A13340-018
Movement: automatic, Breitling 13 (base ETA 7750); ø 30 mm, height 7.9 mm; 25 jewels; 28,800 vph, certified chronometer (C.O.S.C.)
Functions: hours, minutes, subsidiary seconds; chronograph; date, day
Case: stainless steel, ø 42 mm, height 15.1 mm; unidirectionally rotating bezel with 60-minute scale; sapphire crystal; screw-in crown and buttons; water-resistant to 500 m
Band: stainless steel, folding clasp
Price: $3,250
Variations: with leather strap; different dial colors

B - One

Reference number: A78362-101U
Movement: quartz, Breitling 78, certified chronometer
Functions: hours, minutes, sweep seconds (analogue); chronograph with digital display for interval and addition timing as well as countdown, perpetual calendar with digital display for date, day, month, year, second time zone, world time display; alarm timer; additional analogue 24-hour watch
Case: stainless steel, ø 43.2 mm, height 16.5 mm; bidirectionally rotating bezel with 60-minute scale; sapphire crystal; water-resistant to 50 m
Band: leather, buckle
Price: $3,130

B - Two

Reference number: A42362-118
Movement: automatic, Breitling 42 (base ETA 2892-A2); ø 25.6 mm, height 3.6 mm (base movement); 38 jewels; 28,800 vph, certified chronometer (C.O.S.C.)
Functions: hours, minutes, subsidiary seconds; chronograph; date
Case: stainless steel, ø 44.8 mm, height 15.7 mm; bidirectionally rotating bezel with 360° scale; sapphire crystal; water-resistant to 100 m
Band: stainless steel, folding clasp
Price: $3,400
Variations: in yellow gold; in white gold

Carl F. Bucherer

The Carl F. Bucherer watch brand represents a small empire in itself within the Bucherer group, totally individual and with a strong identity — there is certainly a reason that it bears the entire name of the company founder.
Carl F. Bucherer can rely on competence gathered in the more than eighty years of its existence. During its long history, Carl F. Bucherer has been able to assert itself successfully, winning international fame and recognition for the technical and aesthetic quality of its products, under difficult circumstances. In 1919 the visionary entrepreneur Bucherer introduced his first watch collection, into which he poured not only his knowledge of watchmaking, but also his special feel for the needs of his demanding clientele.
Carl Friedrich Bucherer was an exceptional man, and he possessed the courage to veer off of the beaten path. With creativity and wild enthusiasm, both he and the ensuing two generations of his family created a very successful company, displaying a special talent for uniting traditional values with new ideas.
In harmony with the values of its visionary company founder, the Carl F. Bucherer brand has consciously decided to avoid following short-lived trends, making its dedication to authentic products the center of its brand philosophy.
However, continuity alone isn't what counts: The use of long years of experience and traditional talents as well as the very Swiss passion for the art of watchmaking is also the basis for utilizing the newest in technical developments.
Proof of this brand's technical competence is well represented by the Patravi Chronograph GMT model, whose hour hand can be quick-set simply by manipulating the crown — independent of the minute hand — in increments of one hour, backward and forward. The date goes back and forth as necessary along with the hour hand.
The highest quality demands, attention to detail, and individual design characterize all of Carl F. Bucherer's watches. A good example of these is represented by the Patravi Chronograph with perpetual calendar and moon phase display, which is limited to 125 pieces. Here, the entire potential of Caliber CFB 1959 is used, which, despite its high complexity, even fulfills the strict demands of the C.O.S.C. (Contrôle Officiel de Chronomètrage).
The 2004/2005 collection has received various line extensions for the Patravi and Alacria families. The Tonneau Chronograph with large date, chronograph, and power reserve display brings a new feel to the men's collection. The large, new Alacria comes across like a diva due to its excellent mixture of grace and opulence.

After opening branches in Hong Kong and Munich, a Carl. F. Bucherer subsidiary was launched in the United States in May 2004. Carl F. Bucherer North America Inc. is headquartered in Dayton, Ohio, and will be individually responsible for all activities in the U.S.

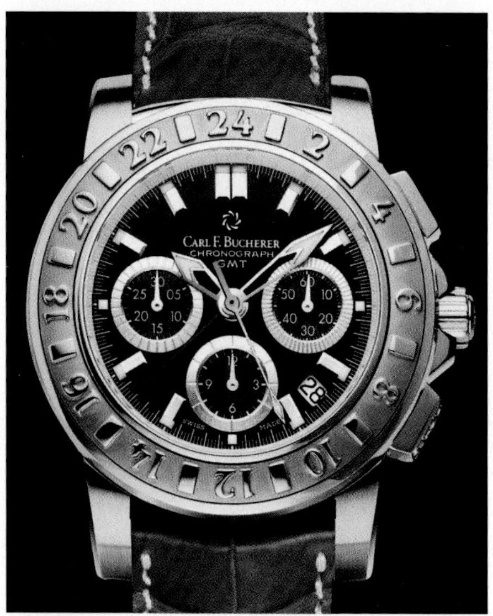

Patravi Chronograph GMT

Reference number: 00.10610.08.33.01
Movement: automatic, CFB 1901 (base ETA 2894-2); ø 28.6 mm, height 7.3 mm; 39 jewels; 28,800 vph,
Functions: hours, minutes, subsidiary seconds; chronograph; date; 24-hour display (second time zone)
Case: stainless steel, ø 40 mm, height 13 mm; bidirectionally rotating bezel with 24-hour scale; sapphire crystal; transparent case back; screw-in crown; water-resistant to 50 m
Band: reptile skin, folding clasp
Price: $4,900
Variations: with stainless steel bracelet; in yellow gold

Patravi Tribute to Fritz Brun

Reference number: 00.10614.02.33.01
Movement: automatic, CFB 1959 (base ETA 2892-A2); ø 30 mm, height 7.7 mm; 38 jewels; 28,800 vph, certified chronometer (C.O.S.C.)
Functions: hours, minutes, subsidiary seconds; chronograph; perp. calendar with date, day, month, moon phase, leap year
Case: white gold, ø 42 mm, height 14.7 mm; sapphire crystal; screw-in crown; water-resistant to 50 m
Band: reptile skin, folding clasp
Remarks: limited to 50 pieces
Price: $39,900
Variations: in red gold, limited to 75 pieces

Patravi Chronograph Large Date Annual Calendar

Reference number: 169-241-1
Movement: automatic, CFB 1957 (base ETA 2892-A2); ø 30 mm, height 7.3 mm; 49 jewels; 28,800 vph,
Functions: hours, minutes, subsidiary seconds; chronograph; annual calendar with large date and month
Case: yellow gold, ø 40 mm, height 13.5 mm; sapphire crystal; transparent case back; screw-in crown
Band: reptile skin, folding clasp
Price: $15,900

Patravi Tonneaugraph

Reference number: 00.10615.08.33.01
Movement: automatic, CFB 1960 (base ETA 2892-A2); ø 30 mm, height 7.3 mm; 47 jewels; 28,800 vph
Functions: hours, minutes, subsidiary seconds; chronograph; large date; power reserve display
Case: stainless steel, 39 x 52 mm, height 13.8 mm; sapphire crystal; screw-in crown
Band: reptile skin, folding clasp
Price: $4,500
Variations: with stainless steel bracelet

Alacria Diva

Reference number: 369.394.4
Movement: quartz, ETA 256.031 5 jewels,
Functions: hours, minutes
Case: white gold, 45.1 x 31.35 mm; sapphire crystal; screw-down case back; water-resistant to 30 m
Band: textile, folding clasp
Remarks: case set with 128 diamonds (2.5 carats)
Price: $25,900
Variations: with 46 diamonds ($18,400); with 46 black sapphires and 36 diamonds ($43,000)

Pathos Diva

Reference number: 369.204.2
Movement: quartz, ETA 976.001 6 jewels
Functions: hours, minutes
Case: white gold, ø 32 mm, ; sapphire crystal; screw-down case back
Band: textile, folding clasp
Remarks: case set with 116 diamonds (2.2 carats)
Price: $20,900
Variations: in yellow gold with 116 diamonds (2.2 carats), $19,500

Bvlgari

Bvlgari S.p.A. is a worldwide operating concern listed on the London and Milan stock markets, possessing branches in twenty-three countries that employ 1,827 employees and comprise a total of forty individual companies.

Even though Bvlgari is the world's third-largest jewelry producer after Cartier and Tiffany, watches play an important role in the company's portfolio. Its own watch brand, Bvlgari, naturally plays the main role, but the purchase of Daniel Roth and Gérald Genta, including their production centers and highly specialized workforce in the Vallée de Joux, has opened up new perspectives for Bvlgari — especially where complicated watches are concerned.

While the design of Bvlgari's watches is chiefly done in Rome, the development and production are done solely in Switzerland. Since the beginning of the 1980s, Bvlgari watches have been produced in Neuchâtel, close to the charming little lake of the same name. Almost 440 employees work in the spacious factory, which was acquired in 1990. Extensive modernization and renovation incorporating a rare combination of wood, natural stone, glass, and warm color tones has transformed the old factory building into a contemporary place of business.

Even Bvlgari's watches embody a clear, "architectonic" style. The timeless case shapes are striking in their underscored simplicity, reminding one of the classic architectural masterpieces of the Hellenic era — which is no wonder, for the Bulgari family is originally from Greece.

With designer pieces, jeweled watches, sports models, and veritable mechanical masterpieces, Bvlgari can draw on a considerable repertoire of models, from outrageously expensive individual pieces to timepieces in the price range of fine steel watches. With reasonably priced new models, Bvlgari is increasingly giving those who are perhaps a little less well-heeled than others access to its exclusive boutiques, which in addition to watches and jewelry also increasingly sell fashion accessories such as silk scarves, eyeglass frames, porcelain, leather goods, perfumes, eau de toilette, and bath salts.

Bvlgari-Bvlgari Tourbillon

Reference number: BB 38 GLTB
Movement: manual winding, Daniel Roth R&G 052, ø 28 mm, height 4.4 mm; 20 jewels; 21,600 vph, one-minute tourbillon; power reserve 64 hours
Functions: hours, minutes; subsidiary seconds (on tourbillon cage); power reserve display (on back)
Case: yellow gold, ø 38 mm, height 9.4 mm; engraved bezel; sapphire crystal; transparent case back
Band: reptile skin, folding clasp
Remarks: limited to 25 pieces, numbered
Price: $73,800
Variations: in white gold

Bvlgari-Bvlgari Tourbillon

Reference number: BB 38 GLTB
Movement: Not only does the Bvlgari Group profit from the purchase of the Daniel Roth Manufacture, the watch brand Bvlgari also finds many advantages in this rather new family situation. The technology available in Daniel Roth's movement factory in Le Sentier makes the conception, design, and manufacture of the most complicated calibers possible – such as this impressive new toubillon.

Bvlgari-Bvlgari Chrono

Reference number: BB 38 SLD CH
Movement: automatic, Bvlgari MVA 080 (base ETA 2894-2); ø 28.6 mm, height 6.1 mm; 37 jewels; 28,800 vph, certified chronometer (C.O.S.C.)
Functions: hours, minutes, subsidiary seconds; chronograph; date
Case: stainless steel, ø 38 mm, height 10.5 mm; engraved bezel; sapphire crystal; screw-in crown
Band: pork leather, buckle
Price: $4,200
Variations: with stainless steel bracelet; in yellow gold, with white dial, with reptile skin strap

Bvlgari-Bvlgari Moon Phases

Reference number: BBW 38 GLMP/C5
Movement: automatic, Jaquet 3103 (base ETA 2892-A2); ø 27 mm, height 5.35 mm; 26 jewels; 28,800 vph; power reserve 42 h
Functions: hours, minutes, subsidiary seconds; date; moon phase
Case: white gold, ø 38 mm, height 9.2 mm; engraved bezel; sapphire crystal
Band: reptile skin, buckle
Price: $15,100
Variations: in yellow gold; in limited edition of 99 pieces, also available with green or light blue dial

Bvlgari-Bvlgari Annual Calendar

Reference number: BB 38 GLAC 4/C5
Movement: automatic, Dubois-Dépraz 5733 (base ETA 2892-A2); ø 25.6 mm, height 5.2 mm; 21 jewels; 28,800 vph; power reserve 42 h
Functions: hours, minutes, sweep seconds; annual calendar with date, month
Case: yellow gold, ø 38 mm, height 9.8 mm; engraved bezel; sapphire crystal
Band: reptile skin, buckle
Price: $15,100
Variations: white gold; limited edition of 99 pieces; in yellow gold with brown or in white gold with bordeaux-colored dial

Bvlgari-Bvlgari Squelette

Reference number: BBW 33 GLSK/PA
Movement: automatic, Parmigiani (base ETA 2892-A2); ø 25.6 mm, height 3.6 mm; 21 jewels; 28,800 vph; power reserve 42 h, movement completely skeletonized and hand-engraved
Functions: hours, minutes
Case: white gold, ø 33 mm, height 7.95 mm; engraved bezel; sapphire crystal; transparent case back
Band: reptile skin, buckle
Price: $9,000
Variations: in yellow gold

Diagono Professional GMT Flyback

Reference number: GMT 40 SVD/FB
Movement: automatic, Dubois-Dépraz 21340 (developed exclusively for Bvlgari) (base ETA 2892-A2); ø 31.4 mm, height 6.8 mm; 53 jewels; 28,800 vph, certified chronometer (C.O.S.C.)
Functions: hours, minutes, sweep seconds; chronograph with flyback function; date, 24-hour display (second time zone)
Case: stainless steel, ø 40 mm, height 13.95 mm; bidirectionally rotating bezel with 24-hour scale; sapphire crystal; screw-in crown and buttons; water-resistant to 100 m
Band: rubber/stainless steel, double folding clasp
Price: $6,300

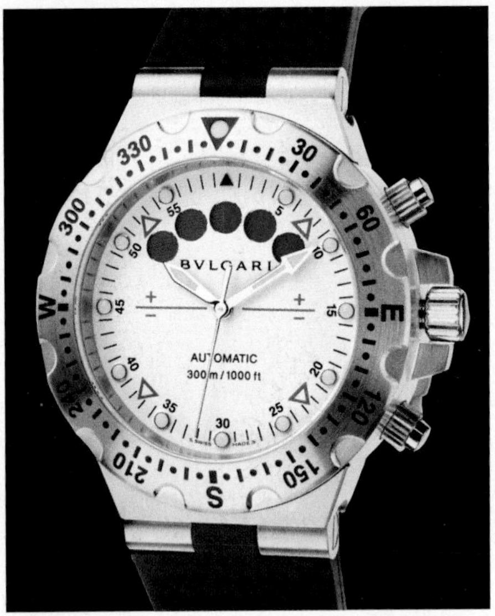

Diagono Professional Regatta

Reference number: SD 40 SV/RE
Movement: automatic, Dubois-Dépraz 42028 (modified for Bvlgari) (base ETA 2892-A2); ø 30 mm, height 7.6 mm; 39 jewels; 28,800 vph
Functions: hours, minutes, sweep seconds; chronograph with flyback function and countdown display
Case: stainless steel, ø 40 mm, height 15.6 mm; bidirectionally rotating bezel with 360° scale/compass directions; sapphire crystal; screw-in crown and buttons
Band: rubber/stainless steel, double folding clasp
Remarks: lines and arrows on dial as course aid at a regatta
Price: $5,800

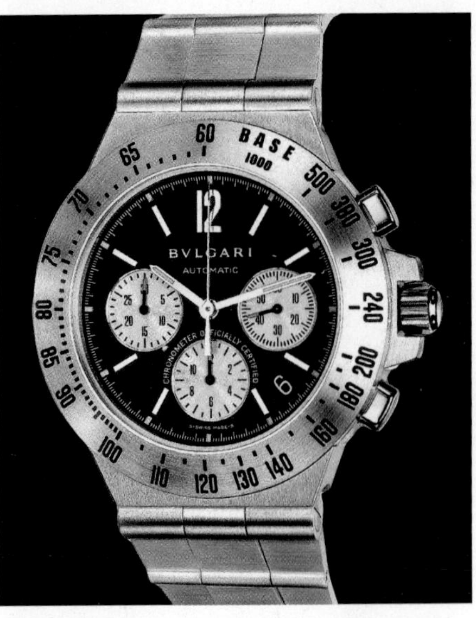

Diagono Professional Tachymeter Chronograph

Reference number: CH 40 SSDTA
Movement: automatic, Bvlgari MVA 080 (base ETA 2894-2); ø 28.6 mm, height 6.1 mm; 37 jewels; 28,800 vph, certified chronometer (C.O.S.C.)
Functions: hours, minutes, subsidiary seconds; chronograph; date
Case: stainless steel, ø 40 mm, height 11.1 mm; engraved bezel with tachymeter scale; sapphire crystal; screw-in crown; water-resistant to 100 m
Band: stainless steel, folding clasp
Price: $5,850

Diagono Professional Tachymeter Chronograph Rattrapante

Reference number: CHW 40 GLTARA
Movement: automatic, Jaquet 8601 (modified by Bvlgari) (base ETA 7750); ø 30.4 mm, height 8.4 mm; 31 jewels; 28,800 vph, certified chronometer (C.O.S.C.)
Functions: hours, minutes, subsidiary seconds; split-seconds chronograph
Case: white gold, ø 40 mm, height 11.1 mm; engraved bezel with tachymeter scale; sapphire crystal; transparent case back; screw-in crown; water-resistant to 100 m
Band: reptile skin, folding clasp
Price: $27,900

Diagono Professional Scuba Diving 2000m

Reference number: SD 42 SVDAUTO
Movement: automatic, ETA 2892-A2, ø 25.6 mm, height 3.6 mm; 21 jewels; 28,800 vph. power reserve 42 h, certified chronometer (C.O.S.C.)
Functions: hours, minutes, sweep seconds; date
Case: stainless steel, ø 42 mm, height 17.1 mm; unidirectionally rotating bezel with 60-minute scale; sapphire crystal; transparent case back; screw-in crown; water-resistant to 2000 m
Band: rubber/stainless steel, double folding clasp
Remarks: helium valve
Price: $4,250

Diagono Chrono Amplificator

Reference number: CHW 40 GL/AMPLI
Movement: automatic, ETA 2892-A2 with chronograph module 2027 by Dubois-Dépraz, ø 27 mm, height 6.6 mm; 47 jewels; 28,800 vph, certified chronometer (C.O.S.C.)
Functions: hours, minutes, subsidiary seconds; chronograph with countdown display
Case: white gold, ø 40 mm, height 12.75 mm; engraved bezel; sapphire crystal; screw-in crown and buttons; water-resistant to 50 m
Band: reptile skin, folding clasp
Price: $17,900

Rettangolo Réserve de Marche

Reference number: RT 49 PLD
Movement: manual winding, Parmigiani 115, 29.3 x 23.6 mm, height 6.55 mm; 28 jewels; 28,800 vph, power reserve 8 days
Functions: hours, minutes, subsidiary seconds; date; power reserve display
Case: platinum, 47.65 x 29 mm, height 10.35 mm; sapphire crystal; transparent case back
Band: reptile skin, double folding clasp
Remarks: limited to 99 pieces
Price: upon request

Rettangolo Tourbillon

Reference number: RT 49 PLTB
Movement: manual winding, Claret 97, 37.5 x 27.3 mm, height 7.04 mm; 19 jewels, one-minute tourbillon; power reserve 100 hours
Functions: hours, minutes
Case: platinum, 48.65 x 30.5 mm, height 11.5 mm; sapphire crystal; transparent case back
Band: reptile skin, folding clasp
Remarks: limited to 20 pieces, numbered
Price: upon request

Anfiteatro Tourbillon

Reference number: AT 40 GLTB
Movement: manual winding, Bvlgari MVT 9902 TB (base GP 9902); ø 28.8 mm, height 6.75 mm; 20 jewels; 21,600 vph, one-minute tourbillon; completely hand-finished and engraved
Functions: hours, minutes
Case: yellow gold, ø 40 mm, height 10.6 mm; engraved flange; sapphire crystal
Band: reptile skin, buckle
Price: $77,600
Variations: in platinum

Anfiteatro Répétition Minutes

Reference number: AT 40 PLRM
Movement: manual winding, GP 9950, ø 28.8 mm, height 6.75 mm; 45 jewels; 28,800 vph, completely hand-finished and engraved
Functions: hours, minutes, subsidiary seconds; hour, quarter hour, and minute repeater
Case: platinum, ø 40 mm, height 11.25 mm; engraved flange; sapphire crystal; transparent case back
Band: reptile skin, buckle
Price: $124,000
Variations: in yellow gold

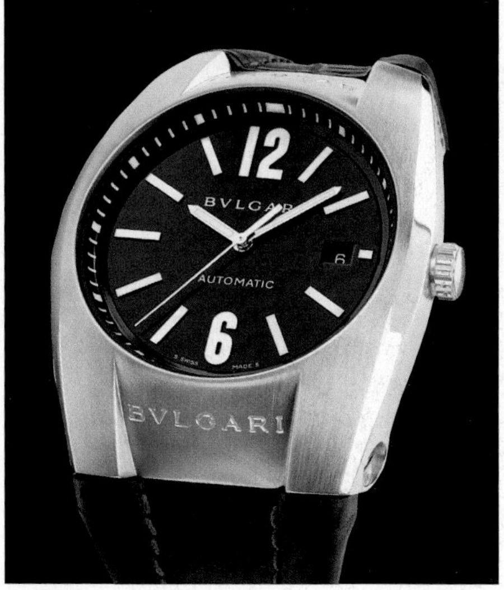

Ergon

Reference number: EG 35 BSLD
Movement: automatic, ETA 2892-A2, ø 26.2 mm, height 3.6 mm; 21 jewels; 28,800 vph
Functions: hours, minutes, sweep seconds; date
Case: stainless steel, 35 x 43.9 mm, height 9.85 mm; sapphire crystal
Band: reptile skin, folding clasp
Price: $2,600
Variations: with stainless steel bracelet

Ergon Chrono

Reference number: EGW 40 C5 GLD CH
Movement: automatic, ETA 2894-2, ø 28.6 mm, height 6.1 mm; 37 jewels; 28,800 vph
Functions: hours, minutes, sweep seconds; chronograph; date
Case: white gold, 40.4 x 51 mm, height 12.3 mm; sapphire crystal
Band: reptile skin, folding clasp
Price: $12,100

Cartier

Big events are celebrated accordingly at Cartier. For this reason, 2004 is not just any year, but rather the stage for an event of the century: The hundredth anniversary of the first wristwatch issuing from the workshops of the Parisian jeweler, conceived and realized as a gift for a good friend. This friend was Alberto Santos-Dumont, and the stainless steel watch was known as the Santos. The anniversary edition is called Santos 100 and represents the end to a moving century, characterized by the fashion of wearing a clock on the wrist. And it opens a new chapter in the history of the wristwatches by Cartier.

Innumerable legends have been called to life in the last hundred years regarding the story of the birth of this unusually sober wristwatch, practical and technical in appearance, called the Santos. This is no wonder when you think about the enigmatic main character of this story: Alberto Santos-Dumont was a very rich Brazilian roué, an exotic bird in turn-of-the-century Parisian society, causing excitement with his escapades, fashion, and quirks. Santos-Dumont dedicated his life to aviation, and he asked Louis Cartier, whom he had met at one of the innumerable Parisian society parties that he attended, to build him a watch that he did not need to first pull out of his vest pocket to read in the cockpit of his flying machine.

The fact that Louis Cartier thought up something special for the pilot speaks volumes not only for the degree of their friendship, but also for the creative strength of the designer, as Cartier would be termed today. The coolness and strength of the stainless steel case with the characteristic screws on the bezel lent the watch a very professional appearance. Alberto Santos-Dumont did not wear a special flight suit in the cockpit, but always took to the skies in an elegant street suit with a stiff collar and a hat. The timekeeper on a strap must have appeared that much more obvious underneath the starched cuffs, which Santos-Dumont loved to push back for admirers.

The new Santos 100 is so large that it hardly fits underneath the cuffs of a shirt. The successful transformation of the Santos shape to a larger dimension lays a cornerstone for the new interpretation of numerous other Cartier designs from the founding years of the previous century. Until now, new issues of great Cartier classics have been kept loyal to the historical models. The Santos 100 definitely goes down a new path.

Sabot PM – Collection Cartier Libre

Reference number: WJ302550
Movement: quartz, Cartier 58
Functions: hours, minutes
Case: white gold, set with baguette-cut diamonds; sapphire crystal
Band: textile (toile brossée), buckle set with baguette-cut diamonds
Remarks: limited to 50 pieces
Price: $58,400

Tortue XL - Collection Privée

Reference number: W1542851
Movement: automatic, Cartier 9421 MC (base GP 3300 with module by Dubois-Dépraz); ø 25.6 mm, height 4.8 mm; 27 jewels; 28,800 vph
Functions: hours, minutes; perpetual calendar with date, day, month, leap year; 24-hour display (second time zone)
Case: red gold, 48 x 38 mm, height 11.65 mm; mineral crystal; transparent case back; crown with sapphire cabochon
Band: reptile skin, folding clasp
Price: $44,900
Variations: in platinum

Tortue Chronograph GM

Reference number: WA506351
Movement: manual winding, Cartier 045 MC, ø 25.2 mm, height 3.8 mm; 22 jewels; 21,600 vph, chronograph control via single button in crown
Functions: hours, minutes, subsidiary seconds; chronograph
Case: white gold, 43 x 34 mm, height 10.2 mm; case set with diamonds; mineral crystal; transparent case back; crown with diamond cabochon
Band: reptile skin, folding clasp
Price: $38,000
Variations: in red gold

Tank Chinoise GM

Reference number: WE300251
Movement: manual winding, Cartier 430 MC (base Piaget 430 P); ø 20.5 mm, height 2.1 mm; 21 jewels; 21,600 vph
Functions: hours, minutes
Case: platinum, 37.15 x 30.6 mm, height 7.7 mm; case sides and lugs set with diamonds; mineral crystal; crown with diamond cabochon
Band: reptile skin, folding clasp
Price: $28,500
Variations: small model (PM) in red gold with quartz movement

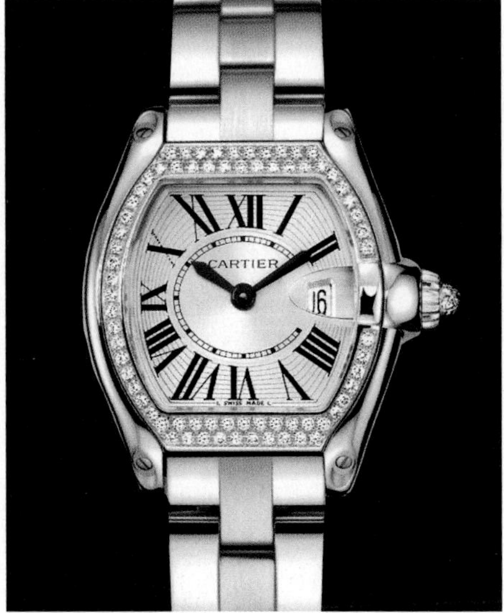

Roadster PM

Reference number: WE5002X2
Movement: quartz, Cartier 688 H3
Functions: hours, minutes; date
Case: white gold, 37 x 36.75 mm, height 8.9 mm; bezel set with diamonds; sapphire crystal with magnifying lens; crown with diamond cabochon
Band: white gold, folding clasp
Remarks: band quick-change system, delivered with changeable bands
Price: $23,500
Variations: in yellow gold; with leather strap

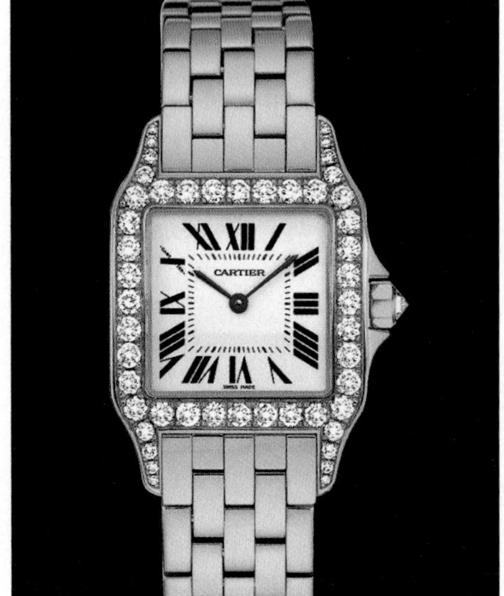

Santos Demoiselle GM

Reference number: WF9002Y7
Movement: quartz, Cartier 690
Functions: hours, minutes
Case: yellow gold, 36.7 x 26 mm, height 7 mm; bezel and lugs set with diamonds; sapphire crystal; crown with diamond cabochon
Band: yellow gold, folding clasp
Price: $27,900
Variations: small model (PM); in white gold

Tortue GM - Collection Privée

Reference number: W1539851
Movement: manual winding, Cartier 9750 MC (base Piaget 430 P); ø 20.5 mm, height 3.7 mm; 20 jewels; 21,600 vph
Functions: hours, minutes; date; power reserve display
Case: red gold, 43 x 34 mm, height 10.8 mm; sapphire crystal; transparent case back; crown with sapphire cabochon
Band: reptile skin, folding clasp
Remarks: limited to 150 pieces
Price: $13,600
Variations: in white gold

Tonneau GM

Reference number: WE400251
Movement: manual winding, Cartier 8970 MC (base JLC 846)
Functions: hours, minutes
Case: white gold; bezel set with diamonds; sapphire crystal; crown with diamond cabochon
Band: reptile skin, folding clasp
Price: $20,400
Variations: small model (PM)

Tank Cintrée - Collection Privée

Reference number: W1544451
Movement: manual winding, Cartier 9780 MC (base JLC 849)
Functions: hours, minutes
Case: yellow gold, 46.3 x 23 mm, height 6.4 mm; sapphire crystal; crown with sapphire cabochon
Band: reptile skin, folding clasp
Price: $15,000

Pasha

Reference number: WJ117736
Movement: automatic, Cartier 500 MC (base Piaget 500); ø 20.5 mm, height 3.4 mm; 26 jewels; 21,600 vph
Functions: hours, minutes; date
Case: red gold, ø 32.3 mm, height 3.4 mm; sapphire crystal; transparent case back; crown under screw cap with diamond cabochon
Band: textile (toile brossée), folding clasp
Remarks: dial with eight diamond markers
Price: $10,900
Variations: in yellow gold; in white gold

Santos-Dumont

Reference number: W2006851
Movement: manual winding, Cartier 430 MC (base Piaget 430 P); ø 20.5 mm, height 2.1 mm; 18 jewels; 21,600 vph
Functions: hours, minutes
Case: yellow gold, 44 x 36 mm, height 5.6 mm; sapphire crystal; crown with sapphire cabochon
Band: reptile skin, folding clasp
Price: $9,500
Variations: in white gold; in red gold

Déclaration

Reference number: WT000550
Movement: quartz, Cartier 56
Functions: hours, minutes
Case: titanium, 38.1 x 16.2 mm, height 5.7 mm; sapphire crystal
Band: textile (toile brossée), folding clasp
Remarks: movable rings made of ceramic and white gold (with diamonds), case set with four diamonds
Price: $9,300

Pasha

Reference number: W31037H3
Movement: automatic, Cartier 480 (base GP 3100); ø 26 mm, height 3.28 mm; 27 jewels; 28,800 vph
Functions: hours, minutes, sweep seconds; date; 24-hour display (second time zone); power reserve display
Case: stainless steel, ø 38 mm, height 10 mm; unidirectionally rotating bezel with 60-minute scale; sapphire crystal; transparent case back; crown under screw cap with spinel cabochon
Band: stainless steel, folding clasp
Price: $7,275
Variations: in yellow gold

Tank Louis Cartier GM

Reference number: W1529756
Movement: quartz, Cartier 687
Functions: hours, minutes, sweep seconds; date
Case: yellow gold, 33.7 x 25.5 mm, height 6.35 mm; mineral crystal; crown with sapphire cabochon
Band: reptile skin, buckle
Price: $5,250
Variations: small model (PM); in white gold

Baignoire 1920

Reference number: W1506056
Movement: quartz, Cartier 57
Functions: hours, minutes
Case: yellow gold; sapphire crystal; crown with sapphire cabochon
Band: reptile skin, buckle
Price: $5,800
Variations: Mini version; in white gold

Tank Américaine PM

Reference number: W2601956
Movement: quartz, Cartier 157
Functions: hours, minutes
Case: white gold, 34.8 x 19 mm, height 7.3 mm; mineral crystal; crown with sapphire cabochon
Band: reptile skin, buckle
Price: $5,900
Variations: in yellow gold, with metal bracelet

Santos 100

Reference number: W20076X8
Movement: automatic, Cartier 49 (base ETA 2892-A2); ø 25.6 mm, height 3.6 mm; 21 jewels; 28,800 vph
Functions: hours, minutes, sweep seconds
Case: stainless steel, 51 x 42 mm, height 10.3 mm; sapphire crystal; crown with spinel cabochon
Band: reptile skin, folding clasp
Remarks: case back with engraving "Santos 100 1904-2004"
Price: $4,200
Variations: in stainless steel/gold; in yellow gold

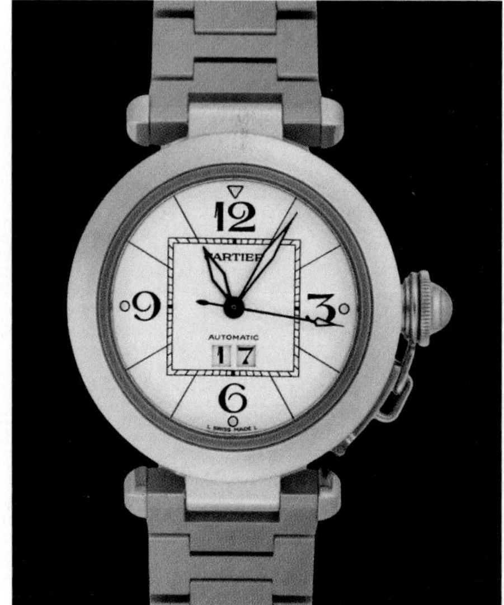

Pasha C

Reference number: W31055M7
Movement: automatic, Cartier 052 (base TIM 052/ETA 2982-A2); ø 25.6 mm, height 4.6 mm; 21 jewels; 28,800 vph
Functions: hours, minutes, sweep seconds; large date
Case: stainless steel, ø 35.3 mm, height 9.8 mm; sapphire crystal; crown under screw cap
Band: stainless steel, folding clasp
Price: $3,725

Roadster PM

Reference number: W62017V3
Movement: quartz, Cartier 688
Functions: hours, minutes; date
Case: stainless steel, 37 x 36.75 mm, height 8.9 mm; sapphire crystal with magnifying lens; crown with steel cabochon
Band: stainless steel, folding clasp
Remarks: band quick-change system, delivered with changeable bands
Price: $3,450
Variations: with white dial; large model (GM)

Must 21 XXL Chronoscaph

Reference number: W10172T2
Movement: quartz, Cartier 272
Functions: hours, minutes, sweep seconds; chronograph; date
Case: stainless steel, ø 38.5 mm; engraved bezel; sapphire crystal with magnifying lens; crown with rubber cabochon
Band: stainless steel, folding clasp
Price: $3,475
Variations: with stainless steel/rubber band

Mini Tank Divan

Reference number: W6300255
Movement: quartz, Cartier 157
Functions: hours, minutes
Case: stainless steel, 25.6 x 31.5 mm, height 6.22 mm; sapphire crystal; crown with sapphire cabochon
Band: reptile skin, buckle
Price: $2,600
Variations: in yellow gold; large model (GM)

Tank Francaise MM

Reference number: W51011Q3
Movement: quartz, Cartier 175 A
Functions: hours, minutes; date
Case: stainless steel, 32 x 25 mm, height 8 mm; sapphire crystal; crown with spinel cabochon
Band: stainless steel, folding clasp
Price: $3,000
Variations: small model (PM) and large model (GM)

Tank Solo GM

Reference number: W1018355
Movement: quartz, Cartier 690
Functions: hours, minutes
Case: stainless steel, 27.4 x 34.8 mm, height 5.6 mm; sapphire crystal; crown with spinel cabochon
Band: reptile skin, folding clasp
Price: $1,750
Variations: small model (PM)

Tank Must Vermeil GM

Reference number: W1017454
Movement: quartz, Cartier 687
Functions: hours, minutes, sweep seconds; date
Case: gold-plated silver, 33.7 x 25.5 mm, height 6.1 mm; mineral crystal; crown with spinel cabochon
Band: reptile skin, folding clasp
Price: $1,925
Variations: small model (PM)

Abyss 1000 Professional Diving Automatic

Reference number: CD225.2LX1
Movement: automatic, ETA 2824-2, ø 25.6 mm, height 4.6 mm; 25 jewels; 28,800 vph; special movement finish
Functions: hours, minutes, sweep seconds; date
Case: stainless steel, ø 44 mm, height 11 mm; sapphire crystal; transparent case back; screw-in crown; water-resistant to 300 m
Band: stainless steel, folding clasp
Remarks: limited to 999 pieces
Price: $995
Variations: with silver, blue, black, or rose gold dial

Combat Command Automatic

Reference number: CD250.1LL2-BRO6
Movement: automatic, ETA 7750, ø 30 mm, height 7.9 mm; 25 jewels; 28,800 vph
Functions: hours, minutes, subsidiary seconds; date, day; chronograph
Case: stainless steel, ø 40 mm, height 15 mm; unidirectionally rotating bezelwith 60-minute scale; sapphire crystal; transparent case back; screw-in crown; water-resistant to 100 m
Band: stainless steel, folding double-lock security clasp
Price: $1,195
Variations: with black, blue, yellow, red, or white dial

Couture Collection Automatic Chrono

Reference number: CD298.80WE-AALN-AA
Movement: automatic, ETA 7750, ø 30 mm, height 7.9 mm; 25 jewels; 28,800 vph
Functions: hours, minutes, subsidiary seconds; date, day; chronograph
Case: yellow gold, ø 40 mm, height 14 mm; bezel set with diamonds; sapphire crystal; transparent case back; screw-in crown with gemstone cabochon
Band: reptile skin, buckle
Remarks: mother-of-pearl dial set with diamonds around totalizers; limited edition of 99 per color
Price: $12,950

Fighter Command Gold Automatic

Reference number: CD262.8WOX-ALLN
Movement: automatic, ETA 7750, ø 30 mm, height 7.9 mm; 25 jewels; 28,800 vph
Functions: hours, minutes, subsidiary seconds; date, day; chronograph
Case: yellow gold, ø 40 mm, height 13 mm; fluted bezel; sapphire crystal; screw-in crown and buttons; water-resistant to 30 m
Band: yellow gold, folding clasp
Remarks: mother-of-pearl subdials; limited ed. 250 pieces
Price: $4,950
Variations: on reptile skin strap

Combat Command GMT Automatic

Reference number: CD251.9BBS
Movement: automatic, ETA 7750, ø 30 mm, height 7.9 mm; 25 jewels; 28,800 vph
Functions: hours, minutes, subsidiary seconds; date, day; chronograph
Case: stainless steel, ø 40 mm, height 15 mm; bidirectionally rotating bezelwith 24-hour scale; sapphire crystal; transparent case back; screw-in crown and buttons; water-resistant to 100 m
Band: stainless steel, folding double-lock security clasp
Remarks: serially numbered, limited edition
Price: $1,995

Tattico Automatic

Reference number: CD255.2BBX
Movement: automatic, ETA 2824-2, ø 25.6 mm, height 4.6 mm; 25 jewels; 28,800 vph
Functions: hours, minutes, sweep seconds; date
Case: stainless steel, 45 x 46 mm, height 12 mm; sapphire crystal, anti-reflective; transparent case back; water-resistant to 50 m
Band: reptile skin, folding clasp
Price: $895

Chopard

While the seventh year of a marriage often seems to be the most difficult one, Chopard and its movement factory in Fleurier seem to be absolutely inspired by their situation. In September 2003, vice president Karl-Friedrich Scheufele and his management team decided to produce a brand-new tourbillon, and in March 2004 it was already done. Steel Wings is the name of the watch hulled in purist steel whose tourbillon bridge has the shape of a wing. Only thirty pieces of the limited, numbered complications will be manufactured.

The changeover from being exclusively the manufacturer of jeweled and luxury timepieces to a true *manufacture* was achieved by Chopard with its Caliber L.U.C. 1.96, completely developed and manufactured on premises and named using the initials of company founder Louis Ulysse Chopard as well as the developmental line and the year of its introduction. The caliber's interesting design, including a microrotor and stacked spring barrels, was even recognized for its rate precision with a chronometer certificate awarded by the C.O.S.C. Because some of the company's watches and movements are assembled in Chopard's Genevan headquarters, they are also allowed to carry the Seal of Geneva.

In the meantime, the L.U.C. collection, which occupies an absolute and well-cared-for special position within the Chopard palette, includes three base calibers with a total of eight variations, from an elegant three-hand watch with subsidiary seconds to a robust sporty diver's watch with sweep seconds to the collection's "evergreen" L.U.C. Quattro featuring a manually wound movement with more than eight days of power reserve thanks to four serially operating, yet space-saving spring barrels. This technology has served the young *manufacture* well as a basis for the next design and production challenge it had set for itself: its own tourbillon.

The model, naturally named L.U.C. Quattro 4T, displays a continuously rotating carriage underneath a striking bridge in a cutaway on the dial at 6 o'clock. Very obvious are the unusually large dimensions of the tourbillon cage, bounded only by the axis of the hands and the diameter of the watch's movement. It was unavoidable that a part of the minute wheel peeks into the dial's cutaway.

The balance contains weighted screws with eccentrics that are integrated into the spokes, a construction with patent pending, as well as a freely swinging balance spring with a Breguet terminal curve. The Chopard caliber L.U.C. 1.02 contains 224 individual parts, all of which are especially finely finished and decorated — there were, of course, no corners cut on a masterpiece of this format and range. Only 100 pieces each in rose gold and platinum have been planned for a production period of several years, making the Quattro 4T a rare sight, indeed.

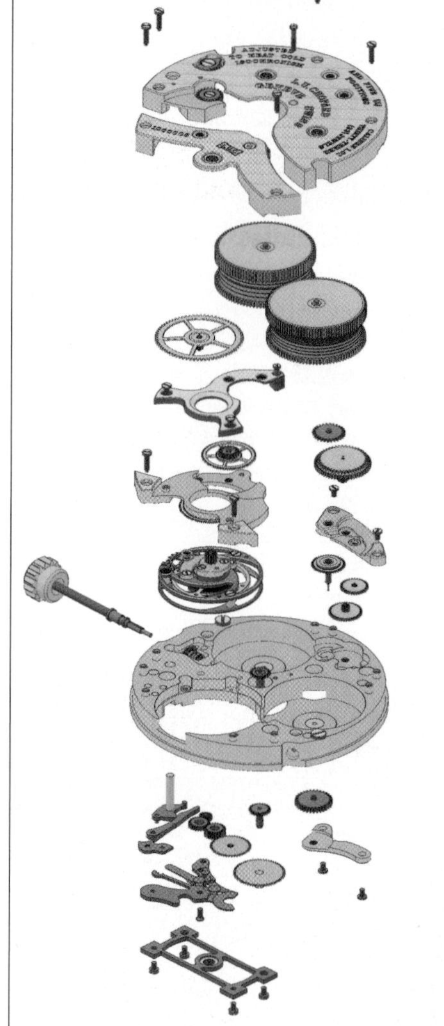

This is also true of the limited series Eszeha by Chopard. This watch series commemorates the 100-year anniversary of the Pforzheim-based company Eszeha, which was owned and run by the Scheufele family before it took over Chopard. The Scheufeles have resuscitated the typical Pforzheim tradition of housing a fine Swiss movement in a precious gold case manufactured in Germany's famed jewelry city. The movement in question is none other than L.U.C. 3.96.

L.U.C. 3.97 Tonneau

Reference number: 16/2267
Movement: automatic, L.U.C. 3.97, 27.4 x 23 mm, height 3.3 mm; 32 jewels; 28,800 vph, shaped movement with microrotor; 2 spring barrels
Functions: hours, minutes, subsidiary seconds; date
Case: yellow gold, 37 x 41 mm, height 8.5 mm; sapphire crystal; transparent case back
Band: reptile skin, buckle
Remarks: limited to 1,860 pieces
Price: $15,360
Variations: in white gold ($16,230)

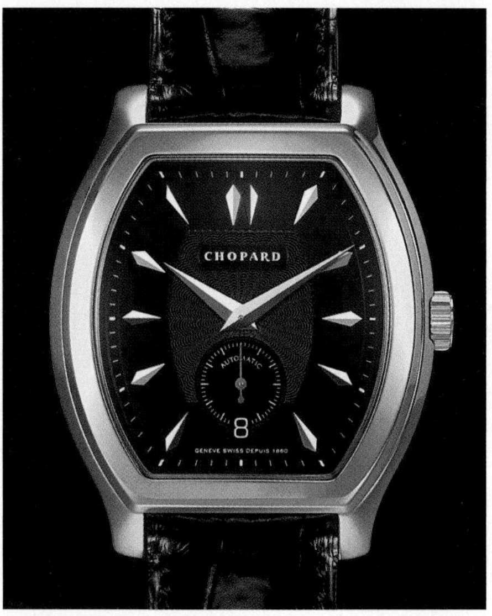

L.U.C. 3.97 Tonneau

Reference number: 16/92267
Movement: automatic, L.U.C. 3.97, 27.4 x 23 mm, height 3.3 mm; 32 jewels; 28,800 vph, shaped movement with microrotor; 2 spring barrels
Functions: hours, minutes, subsidiary seconds; date
Case: platinum, 37 x 41 mm, height 8.5 mm; sapphire crystal; transparent case back
Band: reptile skin, buckle
Remarks: limited to 1,860 pieces
Price: $25,460

Chronograph Jacky Ickx

Reference number: 16/8934
Movement: automatic, ETA 2894, ø 25.6 mm, height 7.3 mm; 49 jewels; 28,800 vph, modified with 24-hour counter and large date; certified chronometer (C.O.S.C.)
Functions: hours, minutes, subsidiary seconds; chronograph; large date
Case: stainless steel, ø 40.5 mm, height 13.4 mm; bezel with tachymeter scale; sapphire crystal
Band: leather, buckle
Remarks: special edition model in honor of Jacky Ickx's six wins at the 24 Hours of Le Mans race
Price: $6,095

L.U.C. GMT

Reference number: 16/1867
Movement: automatic, L.U.C. 4.96/1-H1 (base L.U.C. 4.96); ø 27.4 mm, height 4.15 mm; 34 jewels; 28,800 vph, 2 spring barrels; microrotor; certified chronometer (C.O.S.C.)
Functions: hours, minutes, sweep seconds; date; 24-hour display (second time zone)
Case: white gold, ø 38 mm, height 9.5 mm; sapphire crystal; transparent case back
Band: reptile skin, buckle
Price: $10,920
Variations: in yellow gold ($10,300)

L.U.C. 4R Quattro Régulateur

Reference number: 16/1874
Movement: manual winding, L.U.C. 1.3789 (base L.U.C. 1.98 Quattro); ø 28 mm, height 4.9 mm; 39 jewels; 28,800 vph, 4 spring barrels, power reserve more than 200 hours; certified chronometer (C.O.S.C.)
Functions: hours (off-center), minutes, subsidiary seconds; date; 24-hour display (second time zone); power reserve display
Case: yellow gold, ø 39.5 mm, height 11 mm; sapphire crystal; transparent case back
Band: reptile skin, folding clasp
Remarks: limited to 250 pieces
Price: $29,100

L.U.C. Quattro

Reference number: 16/91863
Movement: manual winding, L.U.C. 1.98, ø 28.6 mm, height 3.7 mm; 39 jewels; 28,800 vph, 4 spring barrels, power reserve more than 200 hours; certified chronometer (C.O.S.C.)
Functions: hours, minutes, subsidiary seconds; date
Case: platinum, ø 38 mm, height 10 mm; sapphire crystal; transparent case back
Band: reptile skin, buckle
Price: $28,270
Variations: in rose or yellow gold; in white gold

L.U.C. 1.96

Reference number: 16/1860/2
Movement: automatic, L.U.C. 1.96, ø 27.4 mm, height 3.3 mm; 32 jewels; 28,800 vph, certified chronometer (C.O.S.C.); 2 spring barrels; microrotor
Functions: hours, minutes, subsidiary seconds; date
Case: yellow gold, ø 36.4 mm, height 7.75 mm; sapphire crystal; transparent case back
Band: reptile skin, buckle
Remarks: limited to 1,860 pieces; delivered with additional case back with honeycomb logo
Price: $11,790
Variations: in white gold ($12,290); in platinum

L.U.C. 4T Quattro Tourbillon

Reference number: 16/1869
Movement: manual winding, L.U.C. 1.02, ø 29.1 mm, height 6.5 mm; 33 jewels; 28,800 vph, one-minute tourbillon; weighted balance with eccentrics; 4 spring barrels, power reserve more than 200 hours; certified chronometer (C.O.S.C.)
Functions: hours, minutes, subsidiary seconds (on tourbillon cage); power reserve display
Case: rose gold, ø 36.4 mm, height 11 mm; sapphire crystal; transparent case back
Band: reptile skin, folding clasp
Remarks: limited to 100 pieces
Price: $87,760

Steel Wings Tourbillon

Reference number: 16/8963
Movement: manual winding, L.U.C. 1.02, ø 29.1 mm, height 6.5 mm; 33 jewels; 28,800 vph, one-minute tourbillon; weighted balance with eccentrics; 4 spring barrels, power reserve more than 216 hours; certified chronometer (C.O.S.C.)
Functions: hours, minutes, subsidiary seconds (on tourbillon cage); power reserve display
Case: stainless steel, ø 40.5 mm, height 11 mm; sapphire crystal; transparent case back
Band: reptile skin, folding clasp
Price: $96,450

L.U.C. Sweep Seconds

Reference number: 16/1862
Movement: automatic, L.U.C. 4.96, ø 27.4 mm, height 3.3 mm; 34 jewels; 28,800 vph, 2 spring barrels; microrotor; certified chronometer (C.O.S.C.)
Functions: hours, minutes, sweep seconds; date
Case: yellow gold, ø 36.4 mm, height 7.75 mm; sapphire crystal; transparent case back
Band: reptile skin, buckle
Remarks: limited to 1,860 pieces; delivered with additional case back with honeycomb logo
Price: $7,200
Variations: in white gold ($8,100)

L.U.C. Sport 2000

Reference number: 16/2000
Movement: automatic, L.U.C. 4.96, ø 27.4 mm, height 3.3 mm; 34 jewels; 28,800 vph, 2 spring barrels; microrotor; certified chronometer (C.O.S.C.)
Functions: hours, minutes, sweep seconds; date
Case: yellow gold, ø 40 mm, height 10.1 mm; sapphire crystal; transparent case back; screw-in crown; water-resistant to 100 m
Band: reptile skin, buckle
Remarks: limited to 2,000 pieces
Price: $11,000
Variations: in white gold ($11,670)

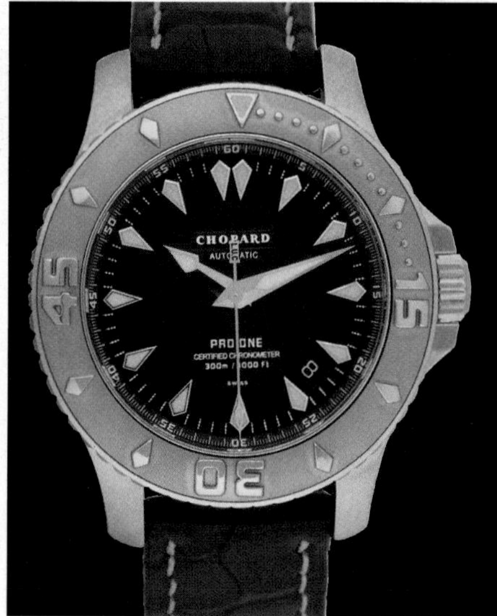

L.U.C. Pro One

Reference number: 16/8912/1
Movement: automatic, L.U.C. 4.96 Pro One, ø 27.4 mm, height 3.5 mm; 34 jewels; 28,800 vph, 2 spring barrels; movement finished with black microrotor; certified chronometer (C.O.S.C.)
Functions: hours, minutes, sweep seconds; date
Case: stainless steel, ø 42 mm, height 13 mm; unidirectionally rotating bezel with 60-minute scale; sapphire crystal; transparent case back; screw-in crown; water-resistant to 300 m
Band: rubber, folding clasp
Price: $6,800
Variations: with silver, blue or black dial

Chronograph Perpetual Calendar

Reference number: 36/1224
Movement: automatic, base caliber JLC 889/2, ø 26 mm, height 3.25 mm; 36 jewels; 28,800 vph, cadrature for perpetual calendar by Chopard
Functions: hours, minutes, subsidiary seconds; chronograph; perpetual calendar with date, day, month, moon phase, seasons, year, calendar week; 24-hour display
Case: yellow gold, ø 40.8 mm, height 12.5 mm; sapphire crystal; transparent case back
Band: reptile skin, buckle
Remarks: limited to 50 pieces
Price: $42,000

Perpetual Calendar Tonneau

Reference number: 36/2249
Movement: automatic, base caliber JLC 888, cadrature for perpetual calendar by Chopard
Functions: hours, minutes; perpetual calendar with date (retrograde), day, month, moon phase, year; 24-hour display
Case: white gold, 34.5 x 36.5 mm, height 9.1 mm; sapphire crystal
Band: reptile skin, buckle
Remarks: limited to 50 pieces
Price: $35,820
Variations: in yellow gold ($35,220)

Dual Tec

Reference number: 16/2274
Movement: automatic ETA 2671 and quartz ETA Caliber 952
Functions: hours, minutes (twice)
Case: yellow gold, 36 x 49 mm, height 8.9 mm; sapphire crystal
Band: reptile skin, folding clasp
Price: $11,740
Variations: in white gold ($11,910)

Chronograph Mille Miglia

Reference number: 16/8331
Movement: automatic, ETA 2894-2, ø 28.6 mm, height 6.1 mm; 37 jewels; 28,800 vph, certified chronometer (C.O.S.C.)
Functions: hours, minutes, subsidiary seconds; chronograph; date
Case: stainless steel, ø 40.5 mm, height 12.7 mm; sapphire crystal
Band: rubber mit Dunlop tire tracks, buckle
Price: $3,220
Variations: in yellow gold; in white gold

Chronograph Mille Miglia GMT 2004

Reference number: 16/8954
Movement: automatic, ETA 7754, ø 30 mm, height 7.9 mm; 29 jewels; 28,800 vph, certified chronometer (C.O.S.C.)
Functions: hours, minutes, subsidiary seconds; chronograph; 24-hour display (second time zone); date
Case: stainless steel, ø 42.5 mm, height 14.8 mm; engraved bezel with 24-hour scale; sapphire crystal
Band: leather, buckle
Remarks: limited to 2,004 pieces
Price: $4,050
Variations: in red gold

Chronograph Mille Miglia

Reference number: 16/8920
Movement: automatic, ETA 2894-2, ø 28.6 mm, height 6.1 mm; 37 jewels; 28,800 vph, certified chronometer (C.O.S.C.)
Functions: hours, minutes, subsidiary seconds; chronograph; date
Case: stainless steel, ø 40.5 mm, height 12.7 mm; bezel with tachymeter scale; sapphire crystal; case back with Mille Miglia course in relief
Band: rubber mit Dunlop tire tracks, buckle
Remarks: limited to 1000 pieces with year, then unlimited
Price: $3,700
Variations: in white gold; in yellow gold

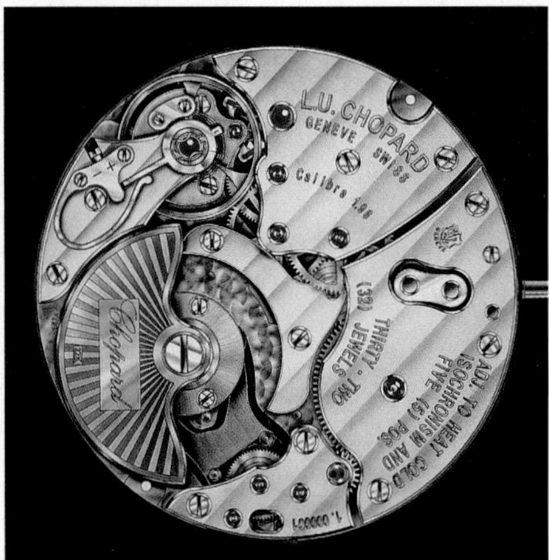

L.U.C. 1.96

Mechanical with automatic winding, power reserve 65 hours
Functions: hours, minutes, subsidiary seconds; date
Diameter: 27.4 mm
Height: 3.3 mm
Jewels: 32
Balance: glucydur
Frequency: 28,800 vph
Balance spring: Breguet
Index system: swan-neck fine adjustment
Remarks: two stacked, serially operating spring barrels, micro-rotor in 22-karat gold; base plate with perlage; beveled bridges with côtes de Genève, polished steel parts and screw heads; Seal of Geneva; official chronometer with C.O.S.C. certificate

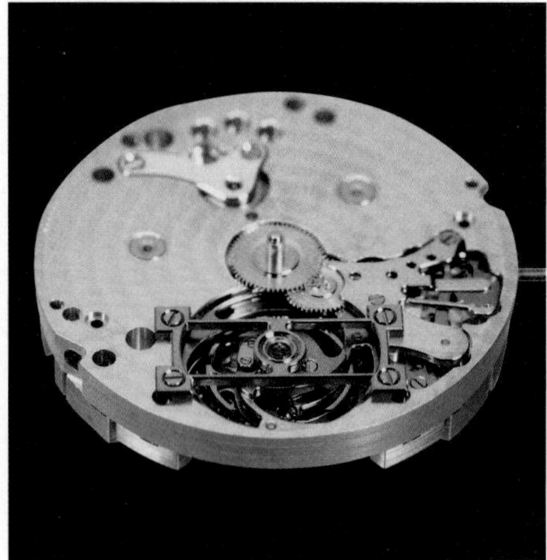

L.U.C. 1.02

Mechanical with manual winding, one-minute tourbillon; power reserve appx. 200 hours
Functions: hours, minutes, subsidiary seconds; power reserve display
Diameter: 29.1 mm
Height: 6.1 mm
Jewels: 33
Balance: Variner with adjustable eccentric weights
Frequency: 28,800 vph
Individual components: 224
Remarks: two stacked, serially operating spring barrels; base plate with perlage; beveled bridges with côtes de Genève, polished steel parts and screw heads; Seal of Geneva; official chronometer with C.O.S.C. certificate

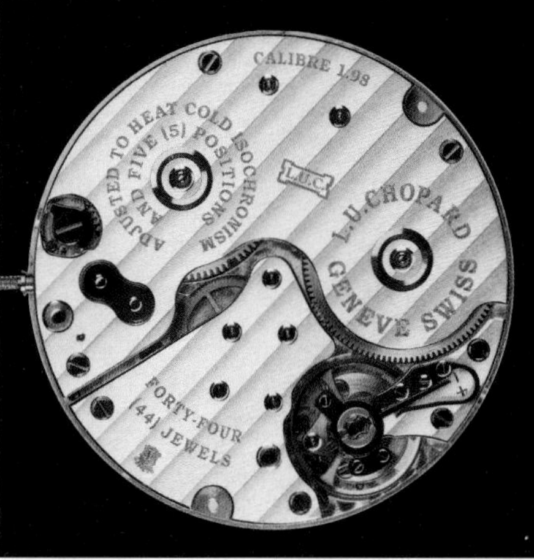

L.U.C. 1.98

Mechanical with manual winding, power reserve appx. 200 hours
Functions: hours, minutes, subsidiary seconds; date; power reserve display
Diameter: 28.6 mm; **Height:** 3.7 mm; **Jewels:** 39
Balance: Glucydur
Frequency: 28,800 vph
Balance spring: Breguet
Index system: swan-neck fine adjustment
Remarks: two stacked, serially operating spring barrels, micro-rotor in 22-karat gold; base plate with perlage; beveled bridges with côtes de Genève, polished steel parts and screw heads; Seal of Geneva; official chronometer with C.O.S.C. certificate

L.U.C. 4.96

Mechanical with automatic winding, power reserve 65 hours
Functions: hours, minutes, sweep seconds; date
Diameter: 27.4 mm
Height: 3.3 mm
Jewels: 34
Balance: glucydur
Frequency: 28,800 vph
Balance spring: flat hairspring, Nivarox I
Index system: micrometer screw
Remarks: two stacked, serially operating spring barrels, micro-rotor in 18-karat gold; base plate with perlage; beveled bridges with côtes de Genève, polished steel parts and screw heads; official chronometer with C.O.S.C. certificate

L.U.C. 4.96

The dial side of Caliber 4.96 from the Chopard L.U.C. 2000 Sport model.

L.U.C. 3.96

Mechanical with automatic winding, power reserve 65 hours
Functions: hours, minutes, subsidiary seconds; date
Diameter: 27.4 mm
Height: 3.3 mm
Jewels: 32
Balance: glucydur
Frequency: 28,800 vph
Balance spring: flat hairspring, Nivarox I
Index system: micrometer screw
Remarks: two stacked, serially operating spring barrels, micro-rotor in 18-karat gold; base plate with perlage; beveled bridges with côtes de Genève, polished steel parts and screw heads; official chronometer with C.O.S.C. certificate

Chronoswiss

Gerd-Rüdiger Lang has been Chronoswiss's owner since its founding in 1983. In times of shareholder value and corporate concentration, companies still managed by their owners have become increasingly rare — especially in the watch industry.

The brand name Chronoswiss is artificial, uniting the most important elements for Lang in one word. One is the Greek word for time, *chronos*, while the other, *swiss*, refers to the motherland of mechanical watchmaking. This is so important because Lang only uses components in his watches that have been manufactured in Switzerland — for him a symbol of longevity in our fast-paced times. "For many, we are a brand that is already very old," Lang ponders, wondering why his brand would ever be mentioned in the same breath as centuries-old traditional Swiss watch companies.

Actually, Chronoswiss has only been in existence for the past twenty-one years. At the time the company was founded, the future looked dismal for mechanical watches and for Lang's beloved profession of watchmaking. Quartz watches were in, and mechanical watches and movements were literally dumped by the ton into the garbage.

Back then, Lang, who was running a special workshop for the repair of chronographs, was already feeling the "Fascination of Mechanics" that would coin his future, making this a slogan that has today become his brand's motto. The logo and corporate identity, also unmistakable hallmarks of the brand, were created at this early point in time. "I have been lucky, and I have often done the right thing, without knowing exactly at that moment that it was the right thing to do," says the modest chronograph expert in a quiet manner that radiates a great deal of composure. It is also the inner attitude of the company's boss, who still confirms the authenticity of each Chronoswiss watch with a hand-signed certificate, which differentiates Chronoswiss from other companies within the watch industry.

The unmistakable look of the typical voluminous Chronoswiss case with its large crystals and onion-shaped crown, fluted edges, and strong,

curved strap lugs were laughed about by the brand's competitors twenty years ago. The beginning of the 1990s brought with it a number of imitators, however, and today Chronoswiss watches are absolutely in fashion. Chronoswiss acted as a bridge builder between horological traditions of the past and modern watch creations, consequently introducing the case back made of sapphire glass for all of its models, which has almost become standard in the industry today.

One of Chronoswiss's youngest offspring and the company founder's "favorite child" is the Chronoscope, developed entirely by Chronoswiss, a model that combines modern watch technology with an admiring look to the beginnings of stopwatch construction. It is outfitted with the Enicar 165 caliber, a movement exclusively used by Chronoswiss, into whose base caliber the stop mechanism, controlled by a column wheel, was integrated during extensive reconstruction.

At the same time, Lang's next watch concept to be executed is now ready for delivery: The Repetition à Quarts (15-minute repeater) model deviates in both form and function from the numerous models developed before it by Chronoswiss, fascinating the observer with the soft sound of its strike train.

In the future, a woman will also help in determining the destiny of Chronoswiss: Natalie Lang, daughter of the company head, has completed her watchmaker education in Switzerland as well as ensuing training in management, preparing her optimally for the position of junior president.

Cabrio

Reference number: CH 2673 CO
Movement: automatic, ETA 2670, ø 17.2 mm, height 4.8 mm; 25 jewels; 28,800 vph
Functions: hours, minutes, sweep seconds
Case: stainless steel, 35 x 27 mm, height 9 mm; case can be turned and rotated 360°; two sapphire crystals
Band: reptile skin, buckle
Price: $4,950
Variations: diverse dial variations; in yellow gold; in red gold/stainless steel; various bands, also with folding clasp

Chronograph Rattrapante

Reference number: CH 7321
Movement: automatic, Chronoswiss C.732 (base ETA 7750); ø 30 mm, height 8.3 mm; 28 jewels; 28,800 vph, split-seconds mechanism patented; movement finished with côtes de Genève; individually numbered
Functions: hours, minutes; (off-center), subsidiary seconds; split-seconds chronograph
Case: yellow gold, ø 38 mm, height 15.25 mm; sapphire crystal; transparent case back
Band: reptile skin, buckle
Price: $16,900
Variations: in two-tone; in white gold; in platinum (limited)

Répétition à quarts

Reference number: CH 1641 R
Movement: automatic, Chronoswiss C.126 (base Enicar with strike train module E 94 by Dubois-Dépraz); ø 26.8 mm, height 8.35 mm; 30 jewels; 21,600 vph
Functions: hours, minutes, subsidiary seconds; quarter-hour repeater
Case: red gold, ø 40 mm, height 13.8 mm; sapphire crystal; transparent case back
Band: reptile skin, buckle
Price: $29,500
Variations: in stainless steel; in yellow or white gold; in yellow or red gold/stainless steel; in platinum (limited)

Chronoscope

Reference number: CH 1521 R
Movement: automatic, Chronoswiss C.125 (base Enicar); ø 26.8 mm, height 7.85 mm; 30 jewels; 21,600 vph, chronograph integrated into base movement with column-wheel control of the three functions (start-stop-reset)
Functions: hours (off-center), minutes, subsidiary seconds; chronograph
Case: red gold, ø 38 mm, height 12 mm; sapphire crystal; transparent case back
Band: reptile skin, buckle
Price: $13,500
Variations: in white or yellow gold; in two-tone; in platinum

Delphis

Reference number: CH 1422
Movement: automatic, Chronoswiss C.124 (base Enicar); ø 26.8 mm, height 6.9 mm; 32 jewels; 21,600 vph, côtes de Genève
Functions: hours (digital, jump), minutes (retrograde), subsidiary seconds (analog)
Case: yellow gold/stainless steel, ø 38 mm, height 11 mm; sapphire crystal; transparent case back
Band: reptile skin, buckle
Price: $8,950
Variations: in stainless steel; in yellow, white or red gold; in platinum (limited edition), diverse dial variations and bands

Kairos Medium Diamonds

Reference number: CH 2823 K M D
Movement: automatic, ETA 2892-A2, ø 25.6 mm, height 3.6 mm; 21 jewels; 28,800 vph, côtes de Genève
Functions: hours, minutes, sweep seconds; date
Case: stainless steel, ø 34 mm, height 8.3 mm; bezel set with 60 brilliant-cut diamonds; sapphire crystal; transparent case back
Band: reptile skin, buckle
Price: $8,750
Variations: without diamonds; with black dial; various bands, also with folding clasp

Klassik Chronograph Turtle

Reference number: CH 7404
Movement: automatic, Chronoswiss C.741 (base ETA 7750); ø 30 mm, height 7.9 mm; 25 jewels; 28,800 vph
Functions: hours, minutes, subsidiary seconds; chronograph; date
Case: rose gold/stainless steel, ø 37 mm, height 13.9 mm; sapphire crystal; transparent case back
Band: reptile skin, buckle
Price: $7,600
Variations: with tachymeter or pulsometer scale; in red gold, red gold/stainless steel and stainless steel; different dials, various bands, also with folding clasp

Lunar Complete Calendar

Reference number: CH 9321 R
Movement: automatic, Chronoswiss C.931 (base ETA 2892-A2); ø 25.6 mm, height 5.75 mm; 21 jewels; 28,800 vph, calendar cadrature by Dubois-Dépraz
Functions: hours, minutes, sweep seconds; date, day, month, moon phase
Case: red gold, ø 38 mm, height 10.65 mm; sapphire crystal; transparent case back
Band: reptile skin, buckle
Price: $12,700
Variations: in yellow or white gold; in platinum (limited); in two-tone; in stainless steel; different dials and bands

Lunar Chronograph

Reference number: CH 7520 L
Movement: automatic, Chronoswiss C.755 (base ETA 7750); ø 30 mm, height 7.9 mm; 25 jewels; 28,800 vph
Functions: hours, minutes, subsidiary seconds; chronograph; date, moon phase
Case: platinum, ø 38 mm, height 15 mm; sapphire crystal; transparent case back
Band: reptile skin, buckle
Remarks: limited to 99 pieces
Price: $37,500
Variations: in yellow, red or white gold; in two-tone; in stainless steel; different dials and bands

Opus

Reference number: CH 7521 S R
Movement: automatic, Chronoswiss C.741 S (base ETA 7750); ø 30 mm, height 7.9 mm; 25 jewels; 28,800 vph, movement completely skeletonized; dials individually numbered
Functions: hours (off-center), minutes, subsidiary seconds; chronograph
Case: red gold, ø 38 mm, height 15 mm; sapphire crystal; transparent case back
Band: reptile skin, buckle
Price: $16,950
Variations: in yellow or white gold; in two-tone; in stainless steel; in platinum (limited to 99 pieces); different bands

Orea Manual Winding

Reference number: CH 1163
Movement: manual winding, Chronoswiss C.111 (base Marvin 700); ø 29.4 mm, height 3.3 mm; 17 jewels, 21,600 vph
Functions: hours, minutes, subsidiary seconds
Case: stainless steel, ø 36.5 mm, height 8.4 mm; sapphire crystal; transparent case back
Band: reptile skin, buckle
Remarks: genuine enamel dial
Price: $4,200
Variations: in gold, red gold, gold/steel, various bands, also with folding clasp, also as Orea Automatic and Orea Lady

Pathos

Reference number: CH 7323 S
Movement: automatic, Chronoswiss C.732 S (base ETA 7750); ø 30 mm, height 8.3 mm; 28 jewels; 28,800 vph, movement completely skeletonized; dials individually numbered
Functions: hours, minutes; (off-center), subsidiary seconds; split seconds chronograph
Case: stainless steel, ø 38 mm, height 15.25 mm; sapphire crystal; transparent case back
Band: reptile skin, buckle
Price: $14,500
Variations: in yellow or red gold; in two-tone; in platinum (limited edition); various bands, also with folding clasp

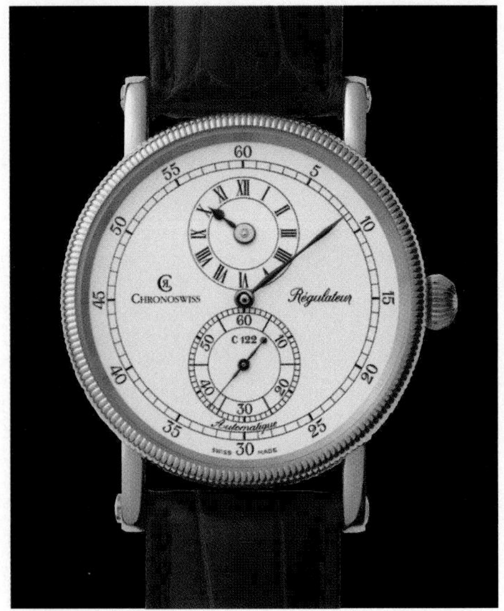

Régulateur

Reference number: CH 1221 R
Movement: automatic, Chronoswiss C.122 (base Enicar); ø 26.8 mm, height 5.3 mm; 30 jewels; 21,600 vph
Functions: hours (off-center), minutes, subsidiary seconds
Case: red gold, ø 38 mm, height 10.5 mm; sapphire crystal; transparent case back
Band: reptile skin, buckle
Price: $10,200
Variations: in white or yellow gold; in yellow or red gold/stainless steel; in stainless steel; different dials, various bands, also with folding clasp; medium-sized case

Timemaster 24 Hours

Reference number: CH 6433 bk
Movement: manual winding, Chronoswiss C.672 (base ETA 6497-1); ø 36.6 mm, height 5.4 mm; 18 jewels; 18,000 vph
Functions: hours (24 hours), minutes, sweep seconds
Case: stainless steel, ø 44 mm, height 12.3 mm; bidirectionally rotating bezel with reference marker; sapphire crystal; transparent case back; extra-large crown, screw-in; water-resistant to 100 m
Band: reptile skin including extendable leather strap, buckle
Price: $6,450
Variations: dial completely inlaid with luminous substance

Timemaster Automatic

Reference number: CH 2833 lu
Movement: automatic, Chronoswiss ETA 2892-A2, ø 25.60 mm, height 3.6mm, 21 jewels. 28,800 vph
Functions: hours, minutes, sweep seconds; date
Case: stainless steel, ø 40 mm, height 12.5 mm; bidirectionally rotating bezel with reference marker; sapphire crystal; transparent case back; extra-large screw-in crown; water-resistant to 100 m
Band: water-resistant leather strap, buckle
Price: $3,800
Variations: with black dial, crown at left

Timemaster Flyback

Reference number: CH 7633 LE lu MB-S
Movement: automatic, Chronoswiss C.763 (base ETA 7750); ø 30 mm, height 7.9 mm; 29 jewels; 28,800 vph
Functions: hours, minutes, subsidiary seconds; chronograph with flyback function
Case: stainless steel, ø 40 mm, height 16 mm; bidirectionally rotating bezel with reference marker; sapphire crystal; transparent case back; extra-large screw-in crown (on left side); water-resistant to 100 m
Band: stainless steel, folding clasp
Price: $8,150
Variations: for left- and right-handers; luminous dial

Tora Chronograph

Reference number: CH 7423 bk
Movement: automatic, Chronoswiss C.743 (base ETA 7750); ø 30 mm, height 8.1 mm; 25 jewels; 28,800 vph
Functions: hours, minutes, subsidiary seconds, chronograph; date; 24-hour display (second time zone)
Case: stainless steel, ø 38 mm, height 15.1 mm; sapphire crystal; transparent case back
Band: reptile skin, buckle
Price: $7,600
Variations: in yellow, red or white gold; in yellow or red gold/stainless steel; in stainless steel; in platinum (limited edition); various bands also with folding clasp

Régulateur à Tourbillon

Reference number: CH 3123
Movement: manual winding, Chronoswiss C.361 (base STT); ø 30 mm, height 5.4 mm; 23 jewels; power reserve appx. 72 h, flying one-minute tourbillon; two spring barrels
Functions: hours (off-center), minutes, seconds
Case: stainless steel, ø 38 mm, height 10.6 mm; sapphire crystal; transparent case back
Band: reptile skin, buckle
Price: $29,500
Variations: in yellow, red or white gold; in yellow gold/stainless steel; in platinum (limited edition); various bands, also with folding clasp

Caliber C.126 (dial side)

Base caliber: C.122 (Enicar 165) with strike train module E 94 by Dubois-Dépraz
Mechanical with automatic winding, power reserve 35 hours; ball-bearing rotor in platinum, skeletonized and gold-plated
Functions: hours, minutes, subsidiary seconds; quarter-hour repeater
Diameter: 28 mm; **Height:** 8.35 mm; **Jewels:** 38
Balance: glucydur, three-legged
Frequency: 21,600 vph; **Shock protection:** Incabloc
Balance spring: Nivarox I flat hairspring, with fine adjustment via eccentric screw
Remarks: all-or-nothing strike train; two gongs; base plate with perlage; beveled bridges with perlage; côtes de Genève; rotor with côtes de Genève

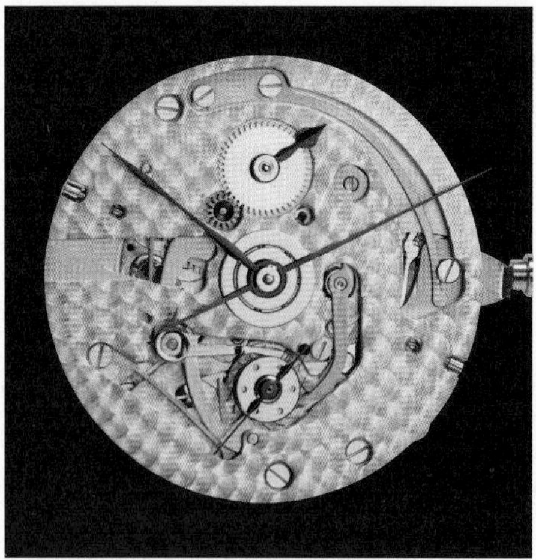

Caliber C.125 (dial side)

Base caliber: C.122 (Enicar 165)
Mechanical with automatic winding, power reserve 35 hours; ball-bearing rotor in platinum, skeletonized and gold-plated
Functions: hours (off-center), minutes, subsidiary seconds; chronograph
Diameter: 26.8 mm (11 '''); **Height:** 7.85 mm
Jewels: 30; **Balance:** glucydur, three-legged
Frequency: 21,600 vph; **Shock protection:** Incabloc
Balance spring: Nivarox I flat hairspring, with fine adjustment via eccentric screw
Remarks: column wheel chrono mechanism integrated into base movement; crown button for start-stop-reset; ball-bearing chronograph center wheel; base plate with perlage; beveled bridges with perlage; côtes de Genève

Caliber C.111

Base caliber: Marvin 700
Mechanical with manual winding, power reserve 46 hours
Functions: hours, minutes, subsidiary seconds
Diameter: 29.4 mm (13 ''')
Height: 3.3 mm
Jewels: 17
Balance: glucydur, three-legged
Frequency: 21,600 vph
Shock protection: Incabloc
Balance spring: Nivarox I flat hairspring
Remarks: bridges with perlage; polished pallet fork, escape wheel, and screws

Caliber C.122

Base caliber: Enicar 165
Mechanical with automatic winding, power reserve 40 hours; ball-bearing rotor, skeletonized and gold-plated
Functions: hours, minutes, subsidiary seconds
Diameter: 26.8 mm (11 ''')
Height: 5.3 mm
Jewels: 30
Balance: glucydur, three-legged
Frequency: 21,600 vph
Shock protection: Incabloc
Balance spring: Nivarox I flat hairspring
Remarks: base plate with perlage; beveled bridges with perlage and côtes de Genève; rotor with côtes de Genève; polished pallet fork, escape wheel, and screws

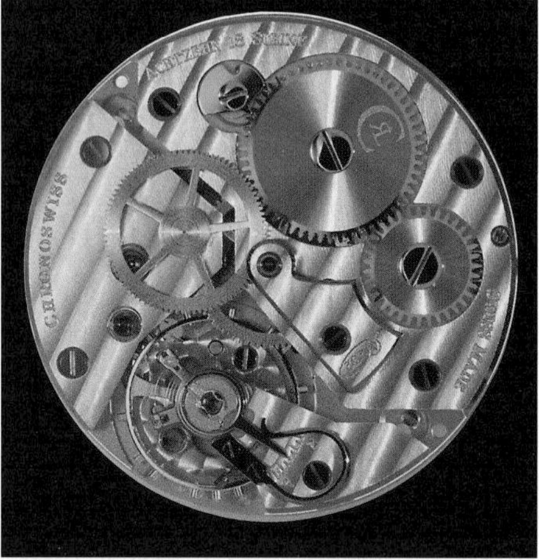

Caliber C.672

Base caliber: ETA 6497-1
Mechanical with manual winding, power reserve appx. 50 hours; stop-seconds (balance stop)
Functions: hours, minutes, sweep seconds
Diameter: 36.6 mm (16 1/2 ''')
Height: 5.4 mm; **Jewels:** 18
Balance: glucydur, three-legged
Frequency: 18,000 vph
Shock protection: Incabloc
Balance spring: Nivarox I flat hairspring, swan-neck fine adjustment
Remarks: beveled bridges with côtes de Genève; polished pallet fork, escape wheel, and screws; escape bridge with perlage

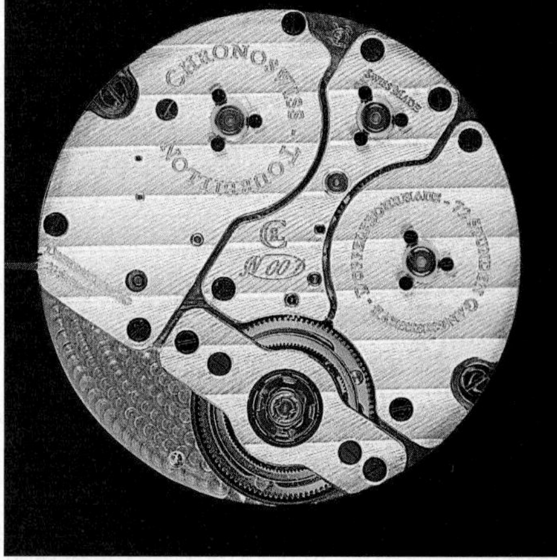

Caliber C.361

Base caliber: STT 6361
Mechanical with manual winding, power reserve 72 hours; twin spring barrels; one-minute tourbillon, ruby ball bearing
Functions: hours (off-center), minutes
Diameter: 30 mm (13 ''')
Height: 5.4 mm
Jewels: 23, three of which are embedded in gold chatons
Balance: glucydur, with weighted screws
Frequency: 28,800 vph
Shock protection: Incabloc
Balance spring: Nivarox I flat hairspring
Remarks: bridges with côtes de Genève

CHRONOSWISS
TOURBILLON
SWISS
MADE

Frédérique Constant

In Geneva, the city of watch dreams and dreamers, Aletta Bax and Peter Stas founded Frédérique Constant S.A. in a back-alley building on rue Vautier in the middle of the Carouge business quarter. Attractively priced watches with a characteristic "peephole" on the dial for the balance magically helped to win over the hearts of watch fans during the 1990s, and the Genevan brand has seen large turnover growth every year. Definitely a good time to cultivate the collection and increase production. The jump from being simply a producer (buying parts like movements, cases, dials, crystals, and bands from different suppliers and having them put together to form whole watches by assembly ateliers well known within the trade) to an autonomous manufacturer was greater than company owner and managing director Peter Stas had initially believed. Even finding the right employees turned out to be a difficult task: In a city like Geneva, where the watch industry is buzzing, good help isn't so easy to find. Frédérique Constant (Peter Stas admits, "In reality these are two first names: My great-grandmother was named Frédérique, and my great-grandfather Constant.") now lodges in large, modern factory buildings on the edge of the Genevan watch quarter Plan-les-Ouates, and the collection continues to grow by leaps and bounds.

Inspired by the success of the Heart Beat models, which allow a look at the ticking heart of the watch in a cutaway underneath the 12, the company's engineers and watchmakers have concentrated their efforts on perfecting this popular "peep show."

An eight-man team of specialists at Frédérique Constant developed a new, fully autonomous, manually-wound movement in cooperation with the Genevan School of Watchmaking, the Genevan School of Engineering, and the Dutch watchmaker trade school Zadkine in which various design principles were literally turned upside down.

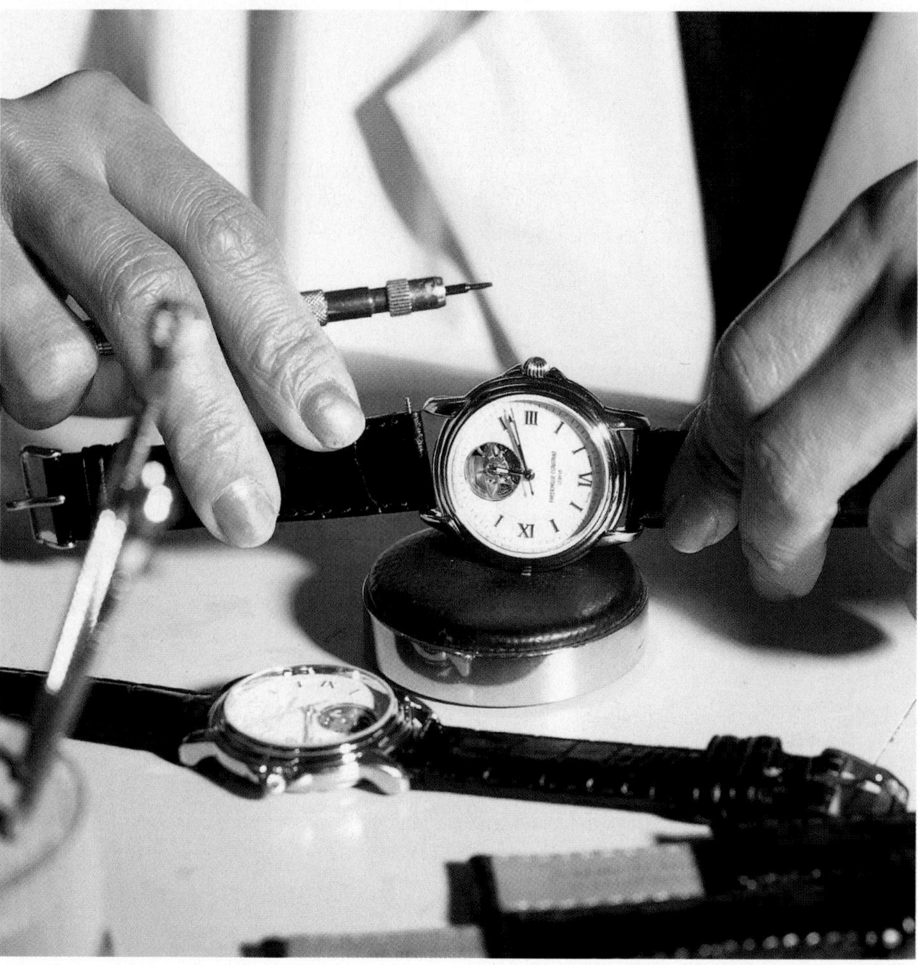

The old Heart Beat watches were outfitted with only slightly modified automatic movements, which, because of their conventional designs, only allow a partial look at the balance: The peephole in the dial was somewhat blocked by part of the base plate — unfortunately, it's not possible to cut any more away from the plate without damaging its stability.

The design team was clever: It simply changed the position of the balance in the newly developed Caliber FC 910. The filigreed balance cock and fine adjustment were moved to the dial side of the movement, graphically presented in a large opening. This innovatively positioned balance is integrated into a large and complexly shaped "half-plate" on the back of the movement. The area surrounding the balance itself is skeletonized to the borders of stability in order to guarantee the most unobstructed view possible.

The most remarkable thing about the completely new caliber is that, according to Frédérique Constant, all components not manufactured in-house are delivered solely by Swiss suppliers. Since the entire manufacturing process is concentrated in the canton of Geneva, with the necessary quality and design prerequisites being fulfilled, Caliber FC 910 is even able to carry the sought-after Seal of Geneva.

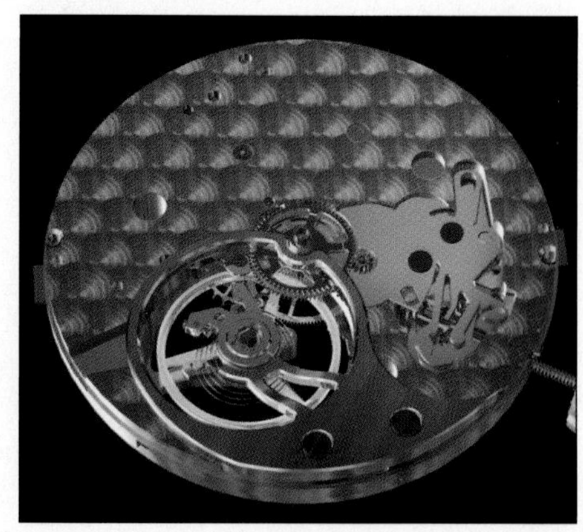

Classics Automatic Chronometer

Reference number: FC-303CA3P5
Movement: automatic, Frédérique Constant FC 303 (base ETA 2824); ø 25.6 mm, height 4.6 mm; 25 jewels; 28,800 vph, certified chronometer (C.O.S.C.)
Functions: hours, minutes, sweep seconds; date
Case: stainless steel (gold-plated PVD), ø 38 mm, height 10 mm; sapphire crystal
Band: leather, buckle
Price: $1,100
Variations: in stainless steel

Persuasion Automatic

Reference number: FC-303M3P6B
Movement: automatic, Frédérique Constant FC 303 (base ETA 2824); ø 25.6 mm, height 4.6 mm; 25 jewels; 28,800 vph
Functions: hours, minutes, sweep seconds; date
Case: stainless steel, ø 38 mm, height 10 mm; sapphire crystal
Band: stainless steel, folding clasp
Price: $900
Variations: with leather strap; in gold-plated PVD

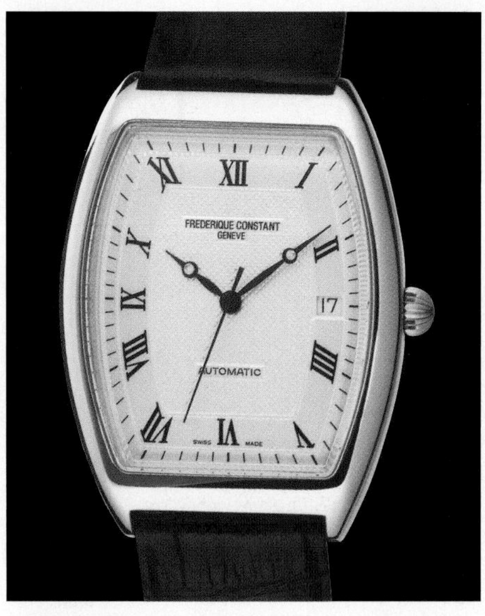

Classics Tonneau Automatic

Reference number: FC-303M4T6
Movement: automatic, Frédérique Constant FC 303 (base ETA 2824); ø 25.6 mm, height 4.6 mm; 25 jewels; 28,800 vph
Functions: hours, minutes, sweep seconds; date
Case: stainless steel, 47 x 36 mm, height 11.2 mm; sapphire crystal
Band: leather, buckle
Price: $1,100
Variations: in gold-plated PVD

Classics Automatic

Reference number: FC-303MC3P5
Movement: automatic, Frédérique Constant FC 303 (base ETA 2824); ø 25.6 mm, height 4.6 mm; 25 jewels; 28,800 vph
Functions: hours, minutes, sweep seconds; date
Case: stainless steel (gold-plated PVD), ø 38 mm, height 10 mm; sapphire crystal
Band: leather, buckle
Price: $900
Variations: in stainless steel

Classics Automatic

Reference number: FC-303V4B4
Movement: automatic, Frédérique Constant FC 303 (base ETA 2824); ø 25.6 mm, height 4.6 mm; 25 jewels; 28,800 vph
Functions: hours, minutes, sweep seconds; date
Case: stainless steel (gold-plated PVD), ø 38 mm, height 10 mm; sapphire crystal
Band: leather, buckle
Price: $1,000
Variations: in stainless steel

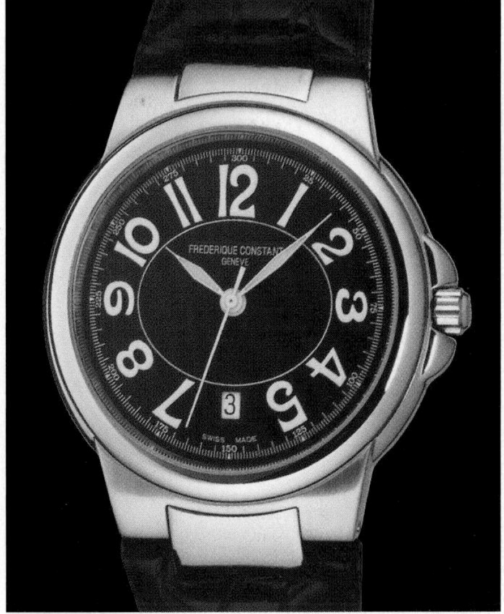

Highlife Slim Line Automatic

Reference number: FC-305AB4H6
Movement: automatic, Frédérique Constant FC 305 (base ETA 2892-A2); ø 25.6 mm, height 3.6 mm; 21 jewels; 28,800 vph
Functions: hours, minutes, sweep seconds; date
Case: stainless steel, ø 42 mm, height 9 mm; sapphire crystal; screw-in crown
Band: reptile skin, buckle
Price: $1,650
Variations: with stainless steel bracelet

Persuasion Automatic

Reference number: FC-310M3P6
Movement: automatic, Frédérique Constant FC 310 (base ETA 2824); ø 25.6 mm, height 4.6 mm; 25 jewels; 28,800 vph, modified with partial skeletonizing
Functions: hours, minutes, sweep seconds
Case: stainless steel, ø 38 mm, height 10 mm; sapphire crystal; transparent case back
Band: leather, buckle
Price: $1,000
Variations: with stainless steel bracelet; with gold-plated case; with black dial

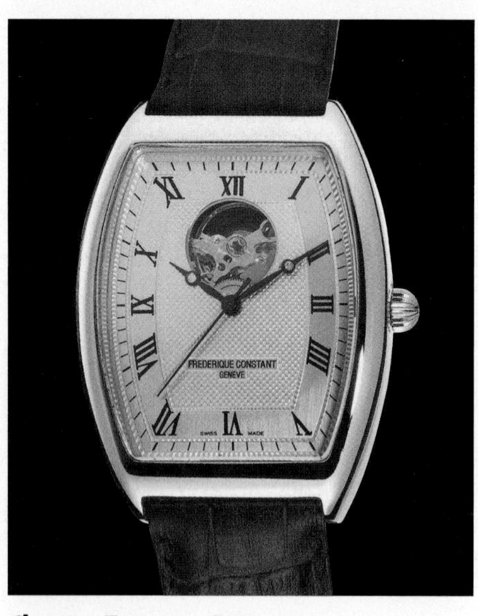

Classics Tonneau Automatic

Reference number: FC-310M4T5
Movement: automatic, Frédérique Constant FC 310-3 (base ETA 2824); ø 25.6 mm, height 4.6 mm; 25 jewels; 28,800 vph, modified with partial skeletonizing
Functions: hours, minutes, sweep seconds
Case: stainless steel (gold-plated PVD), 47 x 36 mm, height 11.2 mm; sapphire crystal; transparent case back
Band: leather, buckle
Price: $1,150
Variations: in stainless steel

Classics Big Date Dual Time

Reference number: FC-325MC3P6
Movement: automatic, Frédérique Constant FC 325 (base ETA 2892); ø 25.6 mm, height 3.6 mm; 21 jewels; 28,800 vph
Functions: hours, minutes, sweep seconds; large date; second time zone
Case: stainless steel, ø 38 mm, height 10.9 mm; sapphire crystal; transparent case back
Band: leather, buckle
Price: $1,850
Variations: in gold-plated PVD

Persuasion Automatic Moonphase

Reference number: FC-360M4P6
Movement: automatic, Frédérique Constant FC 360 (base ETA 2892); ø 25.6 mm, height 3.6 mm; 21 jewels; 28,800 vph
Functions: hours, minutes, sweep seconds; date, day, month, moon phase
Case: stainless steel, ø 40 mm, height 11 mm; sapphire crystal; transparent case back
Band: leather, buckle
Price: $1,450
Variations: with silver-plated dial; in gold-plated PVD

Persuasion Moonphase Carree

Reference number: FC-365B4C6
Movement: automatic, Frédérique Constant FC 365 (base ETA 2892); ø 25.6 mm, height 3.6 mm; 21 jewels; 28,800 vph
Functions: hours, minutes, sweep seconds; date, day, month, moon phase
Case: stainless steel, 39.5 x 36.5 mm, height 11.3 mm; sapphire crystal; transparent case back
Band: leather, buckle
Price: $1,650
Variations: with silver-plated dial; in gold-plated PVD

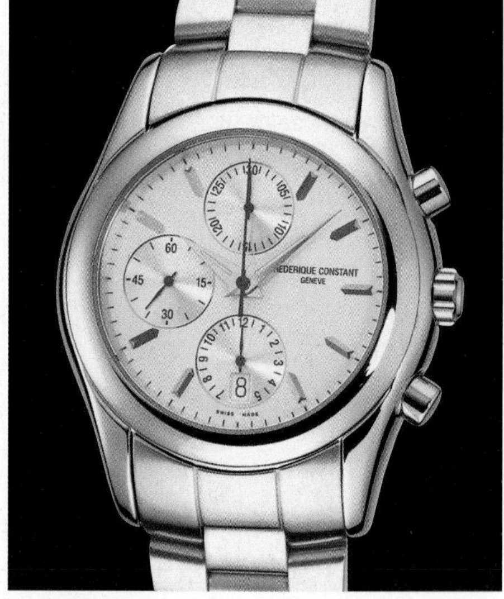

Classics Index Chronograph

Reference number: FC-392S5B6B
Movement: automatic, Frédérique Constant FC 392 (base ETA 7750); ø 30 mm, height 7.9 mm; 25 jewels; 28,800 vph
Functions: hours, minutes, subsidiary seconds; chronograph; date
Case: stainless steel, ø 42 mm, height 14.1 mm; sapphire crystal; transparent case back
Band: stainless steel, folding clasp
Price: $1,950
Variations: rose gold-plated PVD; leather strap; black dial

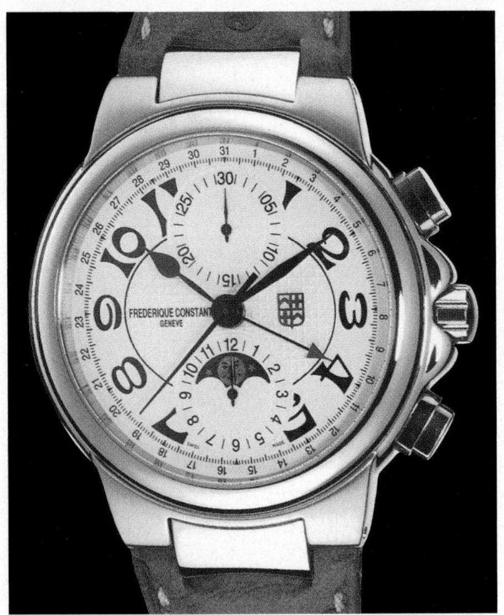

Highlife Moonphase Chronograph

Reference number: FC-395AS4H6
Movement: automatic, Frédérique Constant FC 395 (base ETA 7751); ø 30 mm, height 7.9 mm; 25 jewels; 28,800 vph
Functions: hours, minutes, subsidiary seconds; chronograph; date; moon phase display
Case: stainless steel, ø 42 mm, height 14.8 mm; sapphire crystal; screw-in crown
Band: leather, buckle
Price: $4,950
Variations: with stainless steel bracelet; with black dial

Classics Manually Wound Limited Edition

Reference number: FC-445M4S9
Movement: manual winding, Frédérique Constant FC 445 (base ETA 7001); ø 23.3 mm, height 2.3 mm; 17 jewels; 21,600 vph, modified with date display
Functions: hours, minutes, subsidiary seconds; date
Case: rose gold, ø 37 mm, height 8 mm; sapphire crystal
Band: leather, buckle
Remarks: limited to 99 pieces
Price: upon request
Variations: in stainless steel

Highlife Heart Beat Day-Date

Reference number: FC-610M3A6
Movement: automatic, Frédérique Constant FC 610 (base ETA 2892); ø 25.6 mm, height 3.6 mm; 21 jewels; 28,800 vph, developed with Dubois-Dépraz, modified with partial skeletonizing
Functions: hours, minutes, sweep seconds; date, day
Case: stainless steel, ø 39 mm, height 10.5 mm; sapphire crystal; transparent case back
Band: leather, buckle
Price: $3,800
Variations: in gold-plated PVD

Highlife Heart Beat Retrograde

Reference number: FC-680AB3H6
Movement: automatic, Frédérique Constant FC 680 (base ETA 2892-A2); ø 25.6 mm, height 3.6 mm; 21 jewels; 28,800 vph, modified with partial skeletonizing
Functions: hours, minutes, subsidiary seconds (retrograde)
Case: stainless steel, ø 38 mm, height 10.5 mm; sapphire crystal; transparent case back; screw-in crown
Band: leather, buckle
Price: $4,950
Variations: with stainless steel bracelet; with white dial

Highlife Heart Beat Retrograde Platinum

Reference number: FC-680AS3HP
Movement: automatic, Frédérique Constant FC 680 (base ETA 2892-A2); ø 25.6 mm, height 3.6 mm; 21 jewels; 28,800 vph, modified with partial skeletonizing
Functions: hours, minutes, subsidiary seconds (retrograde)
Case: platinum, ø 39 mm, height 10.5 mm; sapphire crystal; transparent case back
Band: reptile skin, folding clasp
Price: $18,500
Variations: in stainless steel; in rose gold

Classics Heart Beat Manufacture

Reference number: FC-910MC3H6
Movement: manual winding, Frédérique Constant Manufakturkaliber FC 910, ø 30.5 mm, height 3.3 mm; 17 jewels; 28,800 vph, manufacture caliber with "backward" positionioning of the balance and escapement on the dial side
Functions: hours, minutes
Case: stainless steel, ø 39.5 mm, height 8.5 mm; sapphire crystal; transparent case back
Band: leather, buckle
Price: $3,500
Variations: in rose gold

Corum

Founded in 1955 in La Chaux-de-Fonds, this brand became a symbol of avant-garde watches within just a few years. What differentiated Corum from other high-class brands right from the beginning was its desire to present the unusual and the extravagant. This watch brand has always possessed a special creativity, earmarked by its untiring search for that which is new and original. Additionally, the name Corum also stands for creations that pay homage to the great art of watchmaking.
This was what finally enticed the successful watch creator and manager Severin Wunderman into taking over Corum in 2000 after the company had run into some financial trouble. He found his own special predilections mirrored in the creative potential, dominated by the unusual. "The watch world is not waiting for yet another round or square watch," Wunderman knows. "It really wants something new. Everything that we make is innovative. I love challenges. I want to do things that others do not dare to do."
Above all, watch lovers reward Wunderman's unusual designs paired with the high-quality materials and technology used exclusively by Corum. Connoisseurs are aware of the value of Corum's continually developing classics, many of which are currently experiencing a true renaissance. They are being taken out of the vaults, thoroughly dusted, and resuscitated with modified designs.
One such example is the Admiral's Cup: Forty years after its debut, it is conquering watch lovers' hearts anew with highly innovative ideas. The Admiral's Cup Marées is one of just a very few watches that can predict and display the tides with its patented mechanism. Another example is the Classical line with its off-center spheres, which stand for a completely new way to read the time.
In 2005 Corum celebrates its fiftieth anniversary, which will be cause for the introduction of many new surprises.

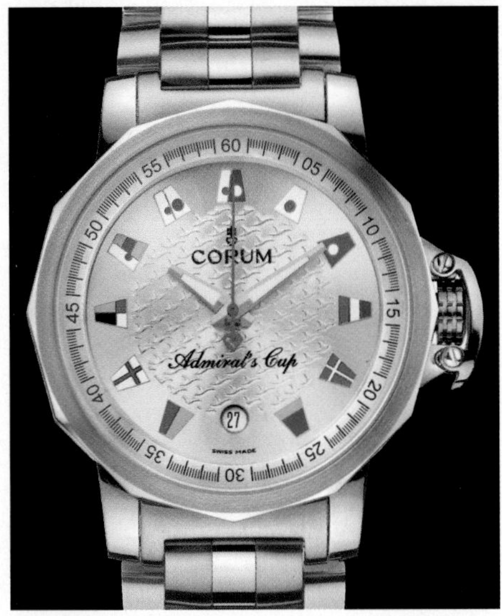

Admiral's Cup Trophy 41

Reference number: 082.830.20 V786 AA52
Movement: automatic, ETA 2892-A2, ø 25.6 mm, height 3.6 mm; 21 jewels; 28,800 vph
Functions: hours, minutes, sweep seconds; date
Case: stainless steel, ø 41 mm, height 10 mm; sapphire crystal; crown with security device; water-resistant to 100 m
Band: stainless steel, folding clasp
Price: $2,495
Variations: with rubber strap; with blue dial

Admiral's Cup Tides 44

Reference number: 977.630.20 V785 AB32
Movement: automatic, Corum Co 277 (base ETA 2892-A2 with exclusive tide module by Dubois-Dépraz); certified chronometer (C.O.S.C.)
Functions: hours, minutes, sweep seconds; date; moon phase; tides and strength of tides
Case: stainless steel, ø 44 mm, height 12 mm; bezel with nautical flag numerals and 360° scale; sapphire crystal; transparent case back; screw-in crown; water-resistant to 50 m
Band: stainless steel, folding clasp
Price: $5,495
Variations: with leather strap

Admiral's Cup 44

Reference number: 982.630.20 F603 AA32
Movement: automatic, Corum SW 003 (base ETA 2892-A2); ø 25.6 mm, height 3.6 mm; 21 jewels; 28,800 vph, certified chronometer (C.O.S.C.)
Functions: hours, minutes, sweep seconds; date
Case: stainless steel, ø 44 mm, height 12 mm; bidirectionally rotating bezel with nautical flag numerals and 360° scale; sapphire crystal; transparent case back; screw-in crown; water-resistant to 50 m
Band: high-tech fiber strap, folding clasp
Price: $3,395
Variations: with stainless steel bracelet

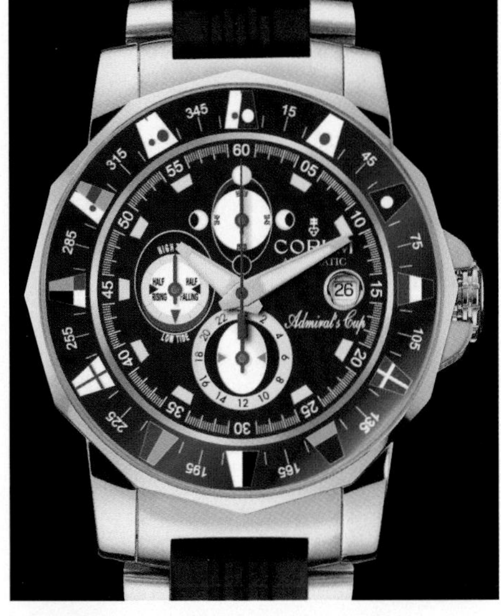

Admiral's Cup Tides 44 Regatta

Reference number: 977.633.55 V793 AB33
Movement: automatic, Corum Co 277 (base ETA 2892-A2 with exclusive tide module by Dubois-Dépraz); certified chronometer (C.O.S.C.)
Functions: hours, minutes, sweep seconds; date; moon phase; tides and strength of tides
Case: rose gold, ø 44 mm, height 12 mm; bezel with nautical flag numerals and 360° scale; sapphire crystal; transparent case back; screw-in crown; water-resistant to 50 m
Band: rose gold/rubber, folding clasp
Remarks: limited to 250 pieces
Price: $22,000

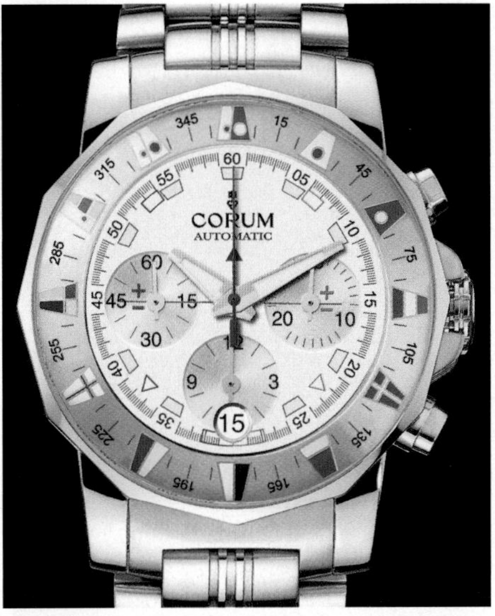

Admiral's Cup Chronograph

Reference number: 285.630.20 V785 AA32
Movement: automatic, Corum SW 002/CO 285 COSC (base ETA 2892-A2 with chrono module by Dubois-Dépraz); ø 30 mm, height 6.9 mm; 57 jewels; 28,800 vph, C.O.S.C certified
Functions: hours, minutes, subsidiary seconds; chronograph; date
Case: stainless steel, ø 45 mm, height 12 mm; bidirectionally rotating bezel with nautical flag numerals and 360° scale; sapphire crystal; transparent case back; screw-in crown; water-resistant to 50 m
Band: stainless steel, folding clasp
Price: $4,895

Classical GMT

Reference number: 983.201.20 0F03 FB24
Movement: automatic, Corum Co 983.GMT (base ETA 2892-A2 with module 313 by Dubois-Dépraz); ø 26.2 mm, height 4.65 mm; 21 jewels; 28,800 vph, certified chronometer (C.O.S.C.); GMT hour hand settable by button
Functions: hours, minutes, sweep seconds; date; 24-hour display (second time zone)
Case: stainless steel, ø 42 mm, height 11 mm; bidirectionally rotating bezel with the names of the time zone reference cities; sapphire crystal; screw-in crown; water-resistant to 50 m
Band: crocodile skin, folding clasp
Price: $3,995

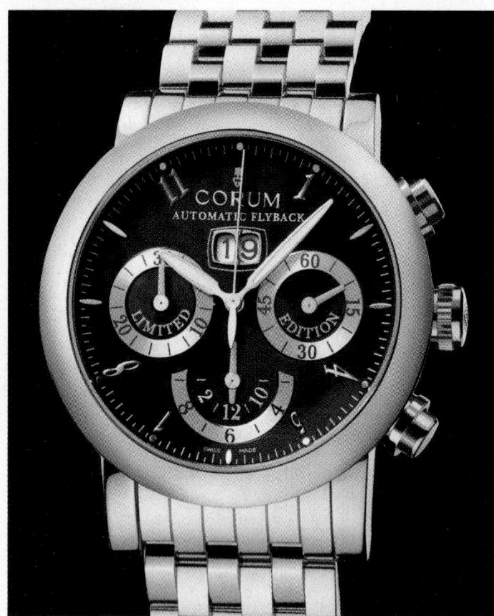

Classical Flyback Large Date

Reference number: 996.201.20 M400 BN06
Movement: automatic, Dubois-Dépraz 44500 (base ETA 2892-A2); ø 25.6 mm, height 3.6 mm (base movement); 21 jewels; 28,800 vph, certified chronometer (C.O.S.C.)
Functions: hours, minutes, subsidiary seconds; chronograph; large date
Case: stainless steel, ø 43 mm, height 14 mm; sapphire crystal; transp. case back; screw-in crown; water-resistant to 50 m
Band: stainless steel, folding clasp
Remarks: limited edition
Price: $5,795
Variations: with leather strap

Classical Grande Date

Reference number: 922.201.20 0F01 CR12
Movement: automatic, Corum Co 922.GD COSC (base ETA 2824 with large date module by Jaquet); ø 26.2 mm, height 4.9 mm; 26 jewels; 28,800 vph, certified chronometer (C.O.S.C.)
Functions: hours, minutes, subsidiary seconds; large date
Case: stainless steel, ø 42 mm, height 11 mm; sapphire crystal; screw-in crown; water-resistant to 50 m
Band: crocodile skin, folding clasp
Price: $3,600
Variations: in different dial variations; in yellow gold

Classical Power Reserve

Reference number: 973.201.20 0F02 BA 12
Movement: automatic, Corum Co 973.PW (base ETA 2892-A2 with module by Jaquet); ø 26.2 mm, height 4.3 mm; 22 jewels; 28,800 vph, certified chronometer (C.O.S.C.)
Functions: hours, minutes; date; power reserve display
Case: stainless steel, ø 42 mm, height 11 mm; sapphire crystal; screw-in crown; water-resistant to 50 m
Band: crocodile skin, folding clasp
Price: $3,000
Variations: with stainless steel bracelet

Bubble Skeleton

Reference number: 082.150.20 0F01
Movement: automatic, ETA 2892-A2, ø 25.6 mm, height 3.6 mm; 21 jewels; 28,800 vph, completely skeletonized and PVD-coated black
Functions: hours, minutes, sweep seconds
Case: stainless steel, ø 45 mm, height 19 mm; massive domed sapphire crystal; screw-in crown; water-resistant to 200 m
Band: crocodile skin, folding clasp
Price: $4,495

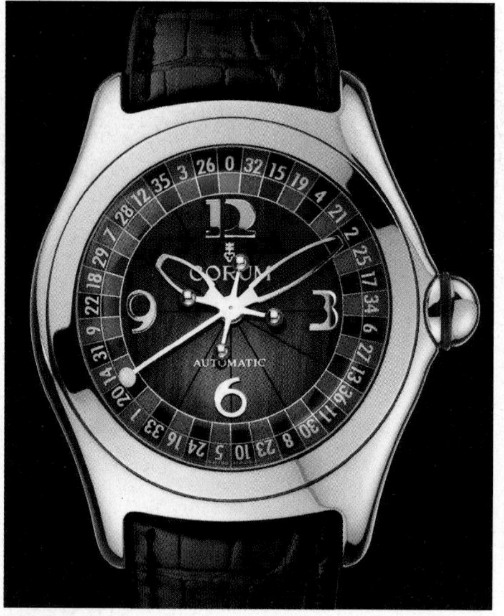

Bubble Casino

Reference number: 082.150.20 0F01 FB 36
Movement: automatic, ETA 2892-A2, ø 25.6 mm, height 3.6 mm; 21 jewels; 28,800 vph
Functions: hours, minutes, sweep seconds
Case: stainless steel, ø 45 mm, height 19 mm; massive domed sapphire crystal; screw-in crown; water-resistant to 200 m
Band: crocodile skin, folding clasp
Remarks: Bubble of the Year 2003 (only manufactured in 2003)
Price: $2,695
Variations: in yellow gold

Bubble Dive Bomber

Reference number: 082.181.20 F732
Movement: automatic, ETA 2892-A2, ø 25.6 mm, height 3.6 mm; 21 jewels; 28,800 vph
Functions: hours, minutes, propeller-shaped sweep seconds; date
Case: stainless steel, ø 45 mm, height 19 mm; massive domed sapphire crystal; screw-in crown; water-resistant to 200 m
Band: leather, folding clasp
Remarks: Bubble of the Year 2004 (only manufactured 2004)
Price: $2,995
Variations: with dial motif "shark mouth"; as chronograph

d.freemont

David Freemont McCready was first introduced to watchmaking about fifty years ago. Raised in Altoona, Pennsylvania, an area that houses more clock- and watchmaking than any other in the United States, McCready came in contact with the micromechanical art form at the tender age of fifteen as the result of an agreement between his father, a man also fascinated by mechanics and electronics, and a local watchmaker. After a number of months occupied with this learning experience, the teenaged McCready's technical mind turned to more pressing matters: motorcycles and automobiles, a love of which would also accompany him throughout his life. Twenty-five years later, the early activity became a hobby, and the previous experience in watchmaking manifested itself in the restoration and repair of wristwatches.

In the early 1990s, this rekindled interest coupled with the maturity necessary to own a business led to the establishment of d.freemont, Inc. Having spent the greater part of three decades as a technical sales engineer, McCready's instincts and unspent creativity guided him in creating his own wristwatches. His company philosophy stresses the importance of customer satisfaction and the development of consumer loyalty. d.freemont watches are offered exclusively via McCready's own Internet website both to assure the consumer of the timepieces' source and as a way to cut the retail cost by forgoing the middleman.

Functionality and attention to detail are the typical characteristics of d.freemont watches. When designing his watches, it is not McCready's intent to latch on to a current trend, but rather to make his timepieces classic and collectible. His goal is to keep the concentration on the real purpose of the watch — telling time — all the while attempting to incorporate an enduring presence binding the timepiece to the owner.

d.freemont's original mechanical collection was inspired by well-known locations in North America and Europe, with McCready striving to capture their essence and flavor in the design. Famous names such as Barcelona, Rockefeller Center, Miami, Niagara, 90212 Rodeo Drive, and even Basel adorn the watches ranging in price from $280 to $1,850.

McCready considers his best work to be the Acugraph line, the leading model of which, Acugraph 7750, is a chronograph whose honest intent is to tell the time clearly without forcing the wearer to first wade through many other visual displays before finally getting to the meat. The Acugraph's features are much simpler than those of other chronographs. There is, for example, only one chapter ring for the combined functions of tachymeter, telemeter, and pulsometer. This eliminates the superfluous ranges of these timing parameters in favor of the ranges most commonly used.

Proving that McCready's creative mind isn't only technical, 2002 saw the release the Ancyent Marinere model. This piece was inspired by the 1798 poem *The Rime of the Ancient Mariner* by Samuel Taylor Coleridge. McCready endeavored to capture the ballad's message in the watch's design, subtly reminding man that it is his duty to be kind.

McCready's main interest lies in supplying his customers with the best quality he can. Each of

the watches, even those that sell for under $300, is timed in two positions just before shipping and delivered with a computer-aided certificate bearing the owner's name and the watch's precise rate.

Semi Skeleton

Reference number: DSCF00 25
Movement: automatic, 28E (base ETA 2824); ø 26 mm, height 5 mm; 25 jewels; 28,800 vph, partially engraved and skeletonized movement
Functions: hours, minutes, sweep seconds
Case: stainless steel, ø 36.5 mm, height 9 mm; tachymetric and telemetric scale; sapphire crystal; transparent case back
Band: leather, buckle
Price: $450

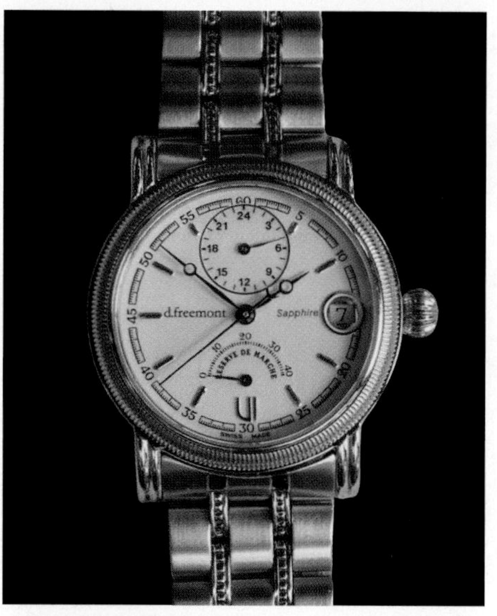

Sapphire Power Reserve

Reference number: DSCF00 43
Movement: automatic, GMT 92 (base ETA 2892-A2); ø 26 mm, height 7 mm; 21 jewels; 28,800 vph
Functions: hours, minutes, sweep seconds; date; power reserve display; second time zone
Case: stainless steel, ø 33.5 mm, height 9 mm; sapphire crystal; transparent case back
Band: stainless steel, folding clasp
Price: $750

Precision Automatic

Reference number: DSCF00 39
Movement: automatic, PA 28 (base ETA 2824); ø 26 mm, height 5 mm; 25 jewels; 28,800 vph
Functions: hours, minutes, sweep seconds; date
Case: stainless steel, ø 36 mm, height 9.5 mm; tachymetric scale; sapphire crystal; transparent case back
Band: leather, buckle
Price: $350

Basel

Reference number: DSCF00 40
Movement: automatic, B750 (baseETA 7750); ø 27 mm, height 7 mm; 25 jewels; 28,800 vph
Functions: hours, minutes, subsidiary seconds; date; chronograph
Case: stainless steel, ø 38 mm, height 13 mm; sapphire crystal; screw-down case back; screw-in crown and buttons
Band: polymer, double folding clasp
Price: $1,250

Acugraph 14 K

Reference number: DSCF00 41
Movement: automatic, A 750 (baseETA 7750); ø 27 mm, height 7 mm; 25 jewels; 28,800 vph
Functions: hours, minutes, subsidiary seconds; date; chronograph
Case: white gold, ø 40 mm, height 12.5 mm; sapphire crystal; transparent case back
Band: leather, folding clasp
Price: $2,500

Rodeo Drive

Reference number: DSCF00 42
Movement: quartz, 980 (base ETA); ø 18 mm; 15 jewels
Functions: hours, minutes, subsidiary seconds
Case: stainless steel, 31 x 35 mm, height 7 mm; mineral crystal
Band: stainless steel, folding clasp
Price: $175

Davosa

The mechanical collection of the Davosa brand has been characterized in recent years by technical, mainly masculine watches with sporty qualities — such as the successful series Ternos and Simplex, as well as the Centum Edition, limited to 400 pieces.
For the fall of 2004, Davosa is chiming in somewhat quieter, though fully ringing tones. The watches of the new Pares line — including an automatic, a chronograph, and two manually wound models with small complications – glow with harmony and inner balance. The combination of tradition, style, and technology are especially obvious in the models pictured on this page, both of which are based on the reliable hand-wound caliber 6498 (Unitas).
The origins of the Davosa brand can be traced back to the year 1861 when the farmer Abel Frédéric Hasler began manufacturing silver cases for pocket watches in the long winter months in his hometown of Tramelan in the Swiss Jura. Two of his brothers found their way to the big

city and opened a watch factory in Geneva. A third brother moved to Biel and also began to work in the watch industry. The next Hasler generation was completely involved in the watch industry, and it was, above all, Paul Hasler who excelled with a flourishing assembly and finishing workshop that was able to call the biggest and most noted brands its customers. Paul and his brother David, who had meanwhile joined him, began making their own watches after World War II, even though the name Hasler & Co. showed up only on the mail and overseas packages that left the small company. As modest private-label manufacturers, the Haslers let their customers in Europe and the United States garner the laurels.
Only in 1987 did they develop their own collection and distribute it under the name Davosa. Today's success in the trade and an impressive model palette, especially in the area of mechanical watches, confirm the brothers' courageous decision.

Vireo Day-Date Automatic

Reference number: 161.443.15
Movement: automatic, ETA 2834-2, ø 29 mm, height 5.05 mm; 25 jewels; 28,800 vph
Functions: hours, minutes, sweep seconds; date, day
Case: stainless steel, ø 42.7 mm, height 10.2 mm; mineral crystal; water-resistant to 50 m
Band: leather, buckle
Price: $425
Variations: with stainless steel bracelet; with black dial; chronograph version

Centum Limited Edition

Reference number: 161.002.56
Movement: automatic, ETA 7750, ø 30 mm, height 7.9 mm; 25 jewels; 28,800 vph, rhodium-plated, perlage, blued screws, decoration
Functions: hours, minutes, subsidiary seconds; chronograph; date and day
Case: stainless steel, ø 42.2 mm, height 15.7 mm; bidirectionally rotating bezel, with reference marker; sapphire crystal; transparent case back; water-resistant to 100 m
Band: leather, buckle
Remarks: limited edition
Price: $1,495

Selente Manual Winding

Reference number: 160.398.16
Movement: manual winding, ETA 7001, ø 23.3 mm, height 2.5 mm; 17 jewels; 21,600 vph
Functions: hours, minutes, subsidiary seconds
Case: stainless steel, ø 40 mm, height 7.4 mm; sapphire crystal; transparent case back; water-resistant to 50 m
Band: leather, buckle
Price: $595
Variations: with black dial

Insight Automatic

Reference number: 161.441.56
Movement: automatic, ETA 2824-2, ø 25.6 mm, height 4.6 mm; 25 jewels; 28,800 vph
Functions: hours, minutes, sweep seconds; date
Case: stainless steel, ø 48 mm, height 14.7 mm; bezel under crystal with 60-minute scale, settable via crown; sapphire crystal; transparent case back; water-resistant to 50 m
Band: leather, buckle
Price: $595
Variations: as chronograph

Simplex Chronograph

Reference number: 161.432.20
Movement: automatic, ETA 7750, ø 30 mm, height 7.9 mm; 25 jewels; 28,800 vph
Functions: hours, minutes, subsidiary seconds; chronograph; date
Case: stainless steel, ø 44.2 mm, height 14.5 mm; sapphire crystal; transparent case back; water-resistant to 50 m
Band: stainless steel, folding clasp
Price: $1,325
Variations: with leather strap

Outback Chronograph

Reference number: 161.438.25
Movement: automatic, ETA 7750, ø 30 mm, height 7.9 mm; 25 jewels; 28,800 vph
Functions: hours, minutes, subsidiary seconds; chronograph; date
Case: stainless steel, ø 48 mm, height 16.4 mm; unidirectionally rotating bezel with 60-minute scale, settable via crown; sapphire crystal; transparent case back; screw-in crown; water-resistant to 100 m
Band: leather, buckle
Price: $1,395
Variations: as three-hand watch

De Grisogono

In the eyes of dyed-in-the-wool watch fans, it is often a handicap for a jewelry producer to change over to the discipline of watches, especially if that jeweler has often stood in the limelight with his shimmering creations and extravagant productions. It was for this reason that Instrumento No. Uno was received with half-hearted applause in 2000, regardless of the fact that the watch disposed of a complete second time zone display, separately settable via the single crown, a slightly domed case with movable lugs, and a mechanical automatic movement that leaves quite a good impression. The measuring stick, however, was high for De Grisogono mastermind Fawaz Gruosi: A few years ago the Oriental fairy prince with Italian passport and Swiss residence found his fairy princess in Caroline Scheufele, junior boss of the Chopard dynasty. Her brother Karl-Friedrich didn't waste much time explaining the quality demands of Swiss *haute horlogerie*, for the maxim of jewelry producer De Grisogono doesn't leave a whole lot of room for disdainful technology with no soul.

However, the above-mentioned handicap remained, at least in the puritanical minds of the European watchmaking public, and Gruosi was forced to act. Earlier than planned, a staff of technicians unveiled Instrumento Doppio in the spring of 2002. The "double instrument" truly earns its name as it not only offers the functions of a chronograph with large date on one side, but also a second time zone on the other. In order to put hands on the "back" of the watch, the automatic movement needed to be completely reworked (extended dial train,

separate setting of the hands on the back and the front) and several modules added on.

Now, Instrumento Doppio Tre has followed as a logical development on the theme: Instead of a chronograph, the new timepiece offers the dial visuals of the Instrumento No. Uno with two full sets of hands to display dual time zones. Together with the set of hands on the back of the watch, Instrumento Doppio Tre offers three perfectly legible and cleanly separated displays of time, making it more than just a watch — Instrumento Doppio Tre is actually three watches in one.

And this is also obvious in its dimensions: With a length of 60 mm, a width of 36 mm, and a height of 18 mm, Instrumento Doppio Tre is really almost as big as three watches put together.

Instrumento No. Uno

Reference number: UNO DF/N1
Movement: automatic, ETA 2892-A2 with module for second time zone and large date, ø 25.6 mm, height 5.75 mm; 21 jewels; 28,800 vph, black movement finish with blued screws
Functions: hours, minutes; large date; second time zone
Case: stainless steel, 53 x 33 mm, height 10.8 mm; sapphire crystal; transparent case back
Band: reptile skin, double folding clasp
Price: $9,900
Variations: in different dial versions, case materials and bands

Instrumento Tondo

Reference number: TONDO
Movement: automatic, RM 14-899 (base ETA 2892-A2 with module for second time zone and power reserve display); ø 25.6 mm, height 5.75 mm; 21 jewels; 28,800 vph, black movement finish with blued screws
Functions: hours, minutes; date; 24-hour display (second time zone); power reserve display
Case: stainless steel, ø 38.5 mm, height 10.5 mm; sapphire crystal; transparent case back
Band: reptile skin, double folding clasp
Price: $9,100
Variations: in red or white gold

Instrumento Doppio

Reference number: DOPPIO/CR N1
Movement: automatic, ETA 2892-A2, modified with dial train on back, large date and chronograph module, 30 x 30 mm, height 8.8 mm; 28,800 vph, black movement finish with blued screws
Functions: hours, minutes; large date; chronograph (front); second time zone (back)
Case: stainless steel, 60 x 36 mm, height 18 mm; case can be turned and rotated 180°, opened and closed via screw on case; movable lugs; 2 sapphire crystals
Band: reptile skin, double folding clasp
Price: $25,000

Instrumentino

Reference number: TINO S10
Movement: automatic, ETA 2892-A2 with module for second time zone, ø 25.6 mm, height 5.75 mm; 21 jewels; 28,800 vph
Functions: hours, minutes; second time zone
Case: white gold, 49 x 29 mm, height 10 mm; case and lugs completely set with diamonds; sapphire crystal; transparent case back; crown with sapphire cabochon
Band: stingray, double folding clasp
Remarks: dial with diamond pavé
Price: $70,000

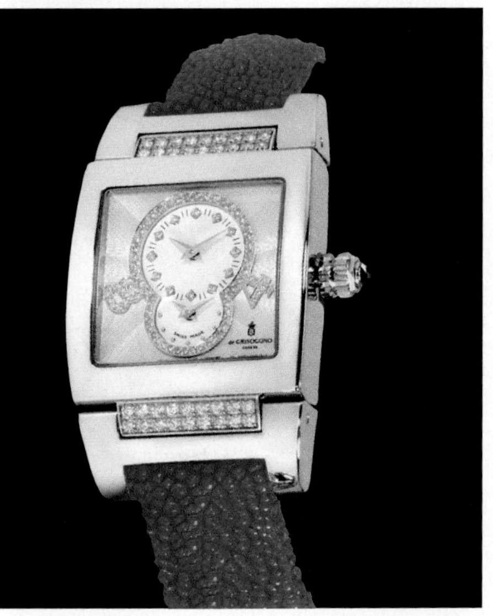

Instrumentino

Reference number: TINO S2
Movement: automatic, ETA 2892-A2 with module for second time zone, ø 25.6 mm, height 5.75 mm; 21 jewels; 28,800 vph
Functions: hours, minutes; second time zone
Case: white gold, 49 x 29 mm, height 10 mm; lugs set with diamonds; sapphire crystal; transparent case back; crown with sapphire cabochon
Band: stingray, double folding clasp
Remarks: dial set with diamonds
Price: $28,000

Instrumentino Acier

Reference number: N05/B
Movement: quartz, ETA with module für second time zone,
Functions: hours, minutes; second time zone
Case: stainless steel, 49 x 29 mm, height 9.6 mm; lugs set with 36 diamonds; sapphire crystal
Band: stainless steel, double folding clasp
Remarks: dial with diamond markers
Price: $8,100
Variations: with black or copper-colored dial

Doxa

In 1889 Georges Ducommun, at barely the age of twenty, founded his own reassembly atelier in Le Locle. It was the stepping-stone to a career which might be termed typically American by a European in this day and age. Within just a few years, Ducommun's backyard workshop had been turned into a veritable factory, over whose door the proud brand name Doxa was emblazoned.

The industrious craftsman obviously knew how to enjoy the good things in life as well, for he made his home in the idyllic Château des Monts castle high above Le Locle, where today the world-famous watch museum is housed. He managed the steep path to the factory in the mornings and evenings by horse-drawn buggy — it's no wonder that the talented designer showed a very early interest in automobiles. Ducommun was one of the first to possess an "iron carriage" in the entire canton of Neuchâtel.

It was his car that led him to one of his most successful business ideas: Doxa was soon manufacturing large numbers of clocks for automobile dashboards, outfitted with eight-day movements that Ducommun patented in 1908. Very clever.

These historical anecdotes were very important for the new launch of the traditional Doxa brand, thus there exists once again a pocket watch with an eight-day movement at Doxa. And there is also a sporty chronograph named for the legendary automobile race: The Coppa Milano-San Remo, which was attended by Europe's racing elite in the years between the two world wars.

A further highlight of the company's history, also commemorated by the contemporary owners, was the success of the diver's watch Sub 300T. When this watch was issued in 1967, it was clearly very different from most of the other so-called professional diver's watches. The U.S. Diving Association turned out to be a valuable consultant, and the American frogmen obviously knew exactly what they needed: a light-colored dial for mid-range diving depths, where it is not yet dark enough for luminous numerals, and a wide case base that lays securely on the arm. The special feature of this watch, however, is the two rows of numerals found on the unidirectionally rotating bezel: The inner ring of numbers is a conventional *minuterie*, but the outer set constitutes a display of depth in meters. When used with the minute display found on the inner half of the bezel, it is a functional decompression table: When, at the beginning of the dive, both markers are set to the top of the minute display, it is possible to read from the bezel that at a diving depth of 30 meters it is about time to think about slowly getting back to the surface after about 25 minutes; at 40 meters, after 15 minutes; and, correspondingly, at 20 meters, only after 50 minutes. Very, very clever.

The contemporary Doxa product developers who pulled the striking '60s design of the Sub 300T out of the drawer and are now offering it to watch collectors and traditionally minded divers in various limited editions were also very clever. These watches are only offered via the Internet, while the rest of the collection is traditionally sold by jewelers. The limited edition Sub 300T is delivered with a certificate signed by Clive Cussler, author of the Dirk Pitt series, whose hero of the same name wears a Doxa diving watch during his fictitious adventures in paperback form. Cinematic fans will be able to experience both Dirk Pitt and his Doxa live when Cussler's *Sahara* opens on the big screen in 2005, starring Matthew McConnaughey as the legendary NUMA agent.

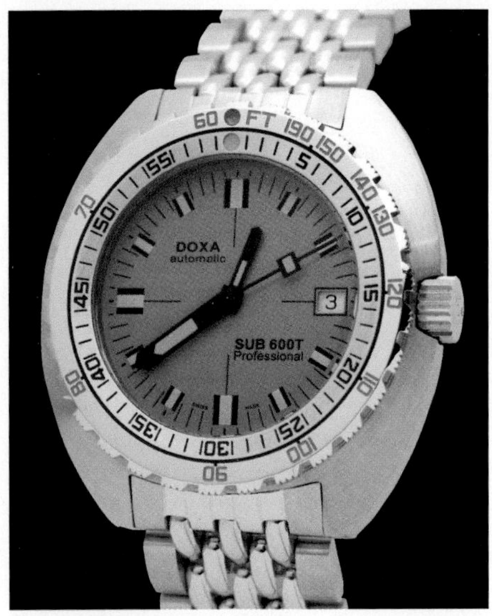

SUB 600T Professional

Reference number: 6000330001
Movement: automatic, ETA 2824-2, ø 25.6 mm, height 4.6 mm; 25 jewels; 28,800 vph
Functions: hours, minutes, sweep seconds; date
Case: stainless steel, ø 42.5 mm, height 14 mm; unidirectionally rotating bezel with engraved decompression table (patented); sapphire crystal; screw-in crown; water-resistant to 600 m
Band: stainless steel, folding clasp
Remarks: new edition of original from 1968, lim. to 3000 pcs
Price: $1,149
Variations: with rubber strap

SUB 600T Sharkhunter

Reference number: 6000330002
Movement: automatic, ETA 2824-2, ø 25.6 mm, height 4.6 mm; 25 jewels; 28,800 vph
Functions: hours, minutes, sweep seconds; date
Case: stainless steel, ø 43 mm, height 14 mm; unidirectionally rotating bezel with engraved decompression table (patented); sapphire crystal; screw-in crown; water-resistant to 600 m
Band: stainless steel, folding clasp
Remarks: new edition of the original from 1968, limited to 3000 pieces
Price: $1,149
Variations: with rubber strap

Chronograph Coppa Milano Sanremo

Reference number: CMS2003250
Movement: automatic, ETA 2898-2 with chronograph module 283 by Lemania, ø 30 mm, height 6.5 mm; 40 jewels; 28,800 vph
Functions: hours, minutes, subsidiary seconds; chronograph; date
Case: stainless steel, ø 41.2 mm, height 13.5 mm; unidirectionally rotating bezel with 12-hour scale; sapphire crystal; screw-in crown; water-resistant to 100 m
Band: leather, buckle
Remarks: limited to 250 pieces
Price: $1,590

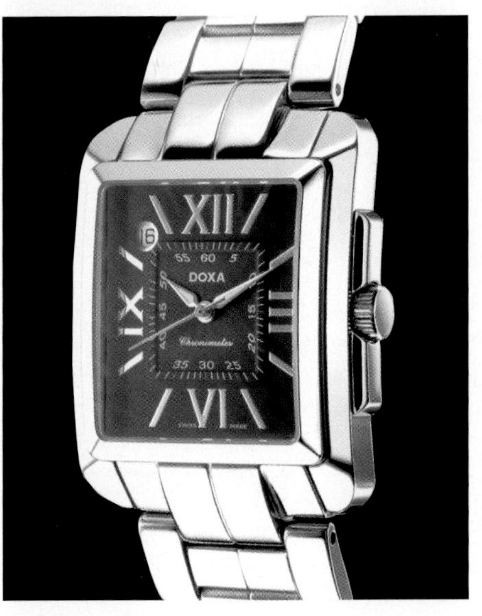

Quadro

Reference number: 251.10.012.02
Movement: automatic, ETA 2824-2, ø 25.6 mm, height 4.6 mm; 25 jewels; 28,800 vph, certified chronometer (C.O.S.C.)
Functions: hours, minutes, sweep seconds; date
Case: stainless steel, 36 x 36 mm, height 8 mm; sapphire crystal; transparent case back
Band: stainless steel, folding clasp
Remarks: new edition of the Doxa Grafic from 1956
Price: $990
Variations: with leather strap

Flieger II

Reference number: 600.10.101.01
Movement: manual winding, ETA 2804, ø 25.6 mm, height 3.35 mm; 17 jewels; 28,800 vph
Functions: hours, minutes, sweep seconds; date
Case: stainless steel, ø 34 mm, height 7 mm; Hesalite crystal
Band: leather, buckle
Remarks: new edition of the Doxa pilot's watch from 1948
Price: $499

8 Days

Reference number: 1889.15
Movement: manual winding, Doxa 11.B, ø 50.6 mm, height 9 mm; 15 jewels; 18,000 vph, skeletonized and decorated, 8 days power reserve
Functions: hours, minutes, subsidiary seconds
Case: stainless steel, palladium-coated, ø 66 mm, height 18.5 mm; sapphire crystal; transparent case back
Band:
Remarks: new edition of an original from 1910
Price: $1,890
Variations: with gold-plated case

Dubey & Schaldenbrand

Among the lesser known dynamic duos of watch history, one pair occupies a special place: Georges Dubey, in his day a teacher at the reputable school of watchmaking in La Chaux-de-Fonds, and master watchmaker René Schaldenbrand. These two men registered a mechanism for a patent on March 12, 1946, that was basically made up of one little spring. This little spring was spiral in shape, winding around the stem of the sweep second hand of a Landeron chronograph, and was part of a simplified version of a split-seconds chronograph. The less expensive to manufacture "people's rattrapante" took the hearts of watch fans by storm, and its official name, Index Mobile, became synonymous with that of the Dubey & Schaldenbrand brand, making the company famous almost overnight.

Today the Dubey & Schaldenbrand philosophy is not only cemented in the genius of its founding fathers, but rests also in the anachronistic, affectionate care for production found in the principles of the classic art of making beautiful watches. The owner of the company, Cinette Robert, a daughter of the watchmaker dynasty Meylan-LeCoultre and an absolute expert in early watch masterpieces, has an impressive talent for combining the technology of modern mechanical movements with timeless and classic lines.

On the leading models of the new collections, the spiral-shaped springs located on the second hand once again play an important role — even if it is more aesthetic than technical these days. Genuine Isoval springs from Dubey & Schaldenbrand's original stock are placed on the models Spiral Cap, Spiral VIP, and Spiral Venus. Mounted at the foot of the second hand — without a function — they lend the dial a very special and technical appearance.

The movements of the designated collectors' pieces have also received special attention from the skilled hand of an engraver. Every watch thus decorated becomes in effect an individual work

of art since the prescribed patterns are always slightly different, determined as they are by the imagination of the artist, and as a result contribute to the exclusive quality of each piece. The Venus calibers 220 and 277 used in the Spiral Venus model — which are already rarities as they are literally few and far between forty years after their production ended — become true treasures after they have been engraved and decorated.

Aerodyn Date

Movement: automatic, ETA 2892 modified, ø 25.6 mm, height 4.9 mm; 26 jewels; 28,800 vph
Functions: hours, minutes, subsidiary seconds; large date
Case: stainless steel, domed, 33 x 44 mm, height 11.8 mm; sapphire crystal
Band: alligator skin, buckle
Price: $4,250
Variations: with stainless steel bracelet ($4,700); in rose gold ($9,950)

Aerodyn Elegance

Movement: automatic, ETA 2895, ø 25.6 mm, height 4.35 mm; 30 jewels; 28,800 vph
Functions: hours, minutes, subsidiary seconds; date
Case: stainless steel, domed, 33 x 44 mm, height 11.5 mm; sapphire crystal
Band: alligator skin, folding clasp
Price: $3,950
Variations: with stainless steel bracelet ($4,400)

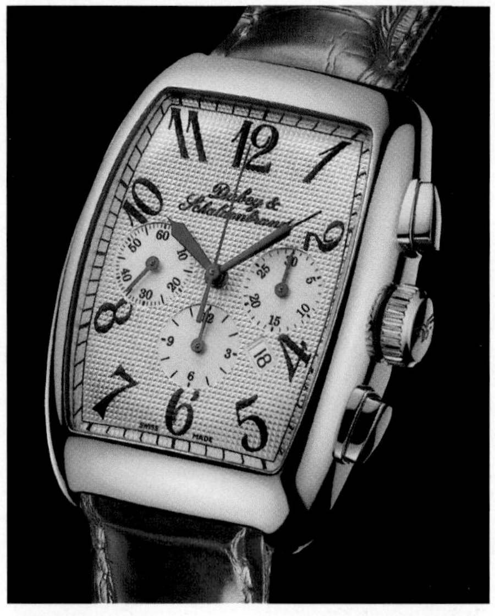

Aerochrono

Movement: automatic, ETA 2094, ø 23.9 mm, height 5.5 mm; 33 jewels; 28,800 vph
Functions: hours, minutes, subsidiary seconds; chronograph; date
Case: stainless steel, domed, 33 x 44 mm, height 12.2 mm; sapphire crystal; transparent case back
Band: alligator skin, folding clasp
Price: $5,950
Variations: with stainless steel bracelet ($6,400); in rose gold ($11,950)

Sonnerie GMT

Movement: automatic, Jaquet 5900 (base AS 5008); ø 30 mm, height 7.75 mm; 31 jewels; 28,800 vph, two spring barrels for movement and alarm
Functions: hours, minutes, sweep seconds; date; 24-hour display (second time zone); alarm
Case: stainless steel, domed, 38 x 50 mm, height 15.5 mm; sapphire crystal; transparent case back
Band: stainless steel, folding clasp
Price: $6,950
Variations: with alligator skin strap ($6,500)

Aquadyn

Movement: automatic, ETA 2892 modified, ø 25.6 mm, height 4.9 mm; 26 jewels; 28,800 vph
Functions: hours, minutes, subsidiary seconds; large date
Case: stainless steel, domed, 37 x 47 mm, height 14.1 mm; sapphire crystal; screw-in crown; water-resistant to 100 m
Band: rubber/stainless steel, folding clasp
Price: $5,450
Variations: with stainless steel bracelet ($5,900); in rose gold ($15,950 on strap and $26,950 on bracelet)

Gran' Chrono Astro

Movement: automatic, ETA 7751 modified, ø 30 mm, height 7.9 mm; 25 jewels; 28,800 vph, bridges hand-engraved, rotor skeletonized with company logo
Functions: hours, minutes; chronograph; date, day, month, moon phase
Case: rose gold, 38 x 50 mm, height 15.5 mm; sapphire crystal; transparent case back
Band: alligator skin, folding clasp
Price: $15,950
Variations: with rose gold bracelet ($26,950); in stainless steel ($6,950)

Antica

Movement: manual winding, AS 1727, ø 19.4 mm, height 3.55 mm, 17 jewels; 21,600 vph, finely decorated and engraved
Functions: hours, minutes, subsidiary seconds
Case: rose gold, 27 x 37 mm, height 8.9 mm; case completely set with 173 brilliant-cut diamonds; sapphire crystal; transparent case back; crown with sapphire cabochon
Band: alligator skin, folding clasp
Remarks: limited edition of 100 pieces
Price: $17,900
Variations: with rose gold bracelet ($24,900); without diamonds in rose gold (limited edition of 75, $8,950)

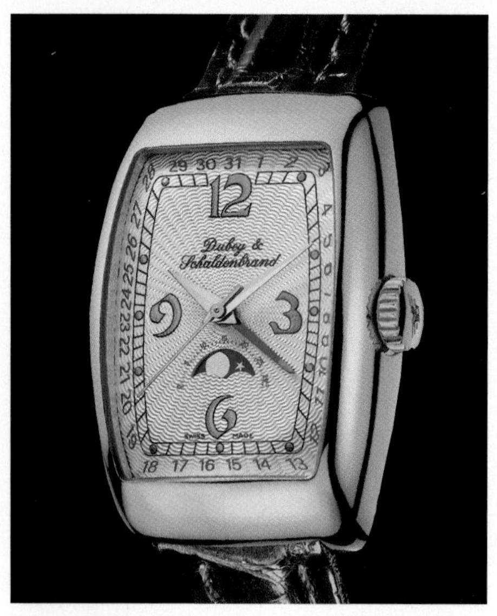

Lady Star

Movement: automatic, ETA 2685, ø 19.4 mm, height 5.35 mm; 25 jewels; 28,800 vph
Functions: hours, minutes, sweep seconds; date; moon phase
Case: rose gold, 37 x 27 mm, height 10.7 mm; sapphire crystal
Band: alligator skin, folding clasp
Remarks: limited edition
Price: sold out
Variations: in stainless steel (sold out)

Spiral VIP

Movement: The Spiral VIP's movement is based on a very modified ETA chronograph Caliber 7751, upon which the watchmakers, skeletonizers, and engravers in Dubey & Schaldenbrand's workshops were able to show their stuff. Not only did the aesthetics, but also the technology, profit from the special treatment: the movement is officially certified according to the C.O.S.C. chronometer norm.

Spiral Rattrapante

Movement: automatic, ETA 7750 modified, ø 30 mm, height 8 mm; 30 jewels; 28,800 vph, hand-engraved; chronograph second hand with a visibly added (though functionless) spring from the legendary Index Mobile split-seconds chronograph
Functions: hours, minutes, subsidiary seconds; split-seconds chronograph; date
Case: stainless steel, with movable lugs, ø 40 mm, height 14.7 mm; sapphire crystal; transparent case back; crown with sapphire cabochon
Band: alligator skin, folding clasp
Price: $9,500

Spiral Cap

Movement: automatic, ETA 2892-A2, modified, ø 25.6 mm, height 4.95 mm; 22 jewels; 28,800 vph, visibly added (though functionless) spring on second hand
Functions: hours, minutes, sweep seconds; large date; power reserve display
Case: stainless steel, with movable lugs, ø 35.5 mm, height 10.7 mm; sapphire crystal; transparent case back; crown with sapphire cabochon
Band: alligator skin, buckle
Remarks: limited edition of 300 pieces
Price: $4,500

Spiral VIP

Movement: automatic, ETA 7751, modified, ø 30 mm, height 7.9 mm; 25 jewels; 28,800 vph, hand-engraved; chronograph second hand with a visibly added (though functionless) spring from the legendary Index Mobile split seconds chronograph
Functions: hours, minutes, subsidiary seconds; chronograph; date, day, month, moon phase; 24-hour display
Case: stainless steel, with movable lugs, ø 40 mm, height 14.3 mm; sapphire crystal; transparent case back; crown with sapphire cabochon
Band: alligator skin, buckle
Price: $6,950
Variations: stainless steel bracelet; in rose gold ($15,950)

Dubey &
Schaldenbrand
SWISS
MADE
Dubey &
Schaldenbrand

Roger Dubuis

Roger Dubuis

Carlos Dias

Roger Dubuis's skill as a watchmaker has been undisputed for decades. However, translating that into the successful watch brand Roger Dubuis, a marque that has fans of *haute horlogerie* swooning, has taken until recently — just shortly before the talented master watchmaker himself retired.

In 1980 he ventured out on his own by opening a small repair and restoration workshop, and he immediately received his first contracts for construction and detail development at the same time. Soon, Dubuis was known as a specialist in unusual problem solving, and designers for all the great Genevan brands, whenever they happened to be at a loss for a good solution, came knocking at his door. Dubuis would probably still be doing this today for comparatively modest fees if destiny hadn't led Carlos Dias to walk through the door of his workshop in the same year. Dias, a passionate lover of fine watches, actually only wanted Dubuis to repair one of his timepieces. But this first visit turned into regular meetings and, later, a business partnership.

In the eight years since it was founded, the *manufacture* has designed and constructed eight base movements and a total of fourteen variations that tick their way through six watch lines. And now Carlos Dias has created a completely new watch genre — following the idea of the motorized all-rounder sport utility vehicle (SUV), his creation is called the Sports Activity Watch (SAW). With three lines — the round Easy Diver, the square Sea More, and the rectangular AquaMare — the project includes sporty yet precious tickers, powered of course by *manufacture* movements that were created on-premises.

From the very beginning, Dubuis's own contribution to the movements' production was large enough to allow him to put the desirable Seal of Geneva on them. The strict rules applying to the use of the seal secured him not only the admiration of his colleagues but also the support of the customers who had gotten to know the young brand, so demanding of itself. As a member of the Groupement Genevois de Cabinotiers, a loose organization of quality- and status-conscious Genevan watchmakers and engineers, Dubuis today feels even more obliged to work according to Geneva's "watch purity law."

The wondrous, airy construction housing the *manufacture* in the industrial quarter of Meyrin-Satigny became too small after only two years of use and has been expanded by yet another building. The great amount of energy put into this expansion serves the goal of achieving the greatest amount of production freedom possible: Except for just a small amount of parts supplied, almost all of the components that make up Roger Dubuis watches are constructed on machines located here. Even if the number of pieces in each series is not that large, the technical energy put into constructing the filigreed components is immense.

Judging by the impressive set of machines, Dias still has quite a few plans for the Roger Dubuis brand.

S.A.W. EasyDiver

Reference number: SE46 56 9/0
Movement: manual winding, RD 56, ø 25.6 mm, height 5.05 mm; 25 jewels; 21,600 vph, Seal of Geneva
Functions: hours, minutes, subsidiary seconds; chronograph
Case: stainless steel, ø 46 mm, height 17 mm; unidirectionally rotating bezel in white gold with 60-minute scale; sapphire crystal; screw-in crown and buttons; water-resistant to 300 m
Band: reptile skin, buckle
Remarks: limited to 280 pieces
Price: upon request
Variations: in stainless steel, limited to 888 pieces; in yellow, red or white gold, limited to 28 pieces each

S.A.W. SeaMore

Reference number:
Movement: automatic, RD 14, ø 25.6 mm, height 3.43 mm; 31 jewels; 28,800 vph, Seal of Geneva
Functions: hours, minutes
Case: stainless steel, domed, 43 x 43 mm, height 15 mm; white gold bezel with 60-minute scale; sapphire crystal; screw-in crown; water-resistant to 300 m
Band: reptile skin, buckle
Remarks: limited to 280 pieces
Price: upon request
Variations: in stainless steel, limited to 888 pieces

S.A.W. AcquaMare

Reference number: G41 57 9/0
Movement: automatic, RD 14, ø 25.6 mm, height 3.43 mm; 31 jewels; 28,800 vph, Seal of Geneva
Functions: hours, minutes
Case: stainless steel, domed, 56 x 34 mm, height 15 mm; white gold bezel with 60-minute scale; sapphire crystal; screw-in crown; water-resistant to 300 m
Band: reptile skin, buckle
Remarks: limited to 280 pieces
Price: upon request
Variations: in stainless steel, limited to 888 pieces

Much More Minute Repeater

Reference number: M34 26 0/9.63
Movement: manual winding, RD 26, 30 jewels; 21,600 vph, Seal of Geneva
Functions: hours, minutes, subsidiary seconds; hour, quarter hour, and minute repeater
Case: white gold, domed, 34 x 45 mm, height 13 mm; sapphire crystal; transparent case back
Band: reptile skin, buckle
Remarks: limited to 28 pieces
Price: upon request

MuchMore

Reference number: M34 57 0/3.73/01
Movement: automatic, RD 57, ø 25.6 mm, height 2.95 mm; 25 jewels; 21,600 vph, Seal of Geneva
Functions: hours, minutes
Case: white gold, domed, 56 x 34 mm, height 11 mm; sapphire crystal; transparent case back
Band: reptile skin, buckle in white gold
Remarks: limited to 28 pieces
Price: upon request
Variations: in rose gold; in different dial variations

MuchMore Bi-Retrograde

Reference number: M34 5740 5/3.6
Movement: automatic, RD 5740, ø 25.6 mm, height 4.8 mm; 29 jewels; 21,600 vph, Seal of Geneva
Functions: hours, minutes; date and day (retrograde), moon phase
Case: rose gold, domed, 34 x 45 mm, height 11 mm; sapphire crystal; transparent case back
Band: reptile skin, buckle
Remarks: limited to 28 pieces
Price: upon request
Variations: in white gold; in different dial variations

Golden Square Flying Tourbillon

Reference number: G40 035/N1.52
Movement: manual winding, RD 03, 33.8 x 33. 8 mm; 27 jewels; 21,600 vph, flying one-minute tourbillon; crown button for date correction
Functions: hours, minutes (off-center), subsidiary seconds (on tourbillon cage); large date; power reserve display
Case: rose gold, domed, 40 x 40 mm, height 12 mm; sapphire crystal; transparent case back
Band: reptile skin, buckle
Remarks: limited to 28 pieces
Price: upon request

Golden Square Perpetual Calendar

Reference number: G40 5739 5/5.7A
Movement: automatic, RD 5739, ø 25.6 mm, height 4.8 mm; 25 jewels; 21,600 vph, exactly jumping displays
Functions: hours, minutes; perpetual calendar with date, day, month, moon phase, leap year
Case: rose gold, domed, 40 x 40 mm, height 11.5 mm; sapphire crystal; transparent case back
Band: reptile skin, buckle
Remarks: limited to 28 pieces
Price: upon request
Variations: in white gold

Golden Square Dual Time

Reference number: G43 5747 5N 37.56DT
Movement: manual winding, RD 5747, ø 25.6 mm, height 4.8 mm; 25 jewels; 21,600 vph, module for two time zones with jump hour display
Functions: hours (double, jump), minutes
Case: rose gold, domed, 43 x 43 mm, height 11.8 mm; sapphire crystal; transparent case back
Band: reptile skin, buckle
Remarks: limited to 28 pieces
Price: upon request
Variations: in white gold

Golden Square Perpetual Calendar

Reference number: G43 5729 5/5.7
Movement: automatic, RD 57, ø 25.6 mm, height 5.95 mm; 25 jewels; 21,600 vph, five jump window displays; Seal of Geneva
Functions: hours, minutes; perpetual calendar with date, day, month, moon phase, leap year, 24-hour display (second time zone)
Case: rose gold, domed, 43 x 43 mm, height 12 mm; sapphire crystal; transparent case back
Band: reptile skin, buckle
Remarks: limited to 28 pieces
Price: upon request
Variations: in white gold ($77.700,-)

Golden Square

Reference number: G34 985/3.73
Movement: manual winding, RD 98, ø 23.3 mm, height 3.8 mm; 19 jewels; 21,600 vph, Seal of Geneva; chronometer with observatory certificate
Functions: hours, minutes, subsidiary seconds
Case: rose gold, domed, 34 x 34 mm, height 9 mm; sapphire crystal; transparent case back
Band: reptile skin, buckle
Remarks: limited to 28 pieces
Price: upon request
Variations: in white gold; in different dial variations

Hommage Bi-Retrograde Chronograph

Reference number: H40 5630 0/5.6
Movement: manual winding, RD 5630, ø 27.5 mm, height 7.42 mm; 25 jewels; 21,600 vph, column-wheel control of the chronograph functions; Seal of Geneva
Functions: hours, minutes, subsidiary seconds; chronograph; date and day (retrograde)
Case: white gold, ø 40 mm, height 11 mm; sapphire crystal; transparent case back
Band: reptile skin, buckle
Remarks: limited to 28 pieces
Price: upon request

Sympathie Tourbillon

Reference number: S40 1102 0/N96.5
Movement: manual winding, RD 1102, ø 28 mm, height 5.96 mm; 9 jewels; 21,600 vph, one-minute tourbillon; Seal of Geneva
Functions: hours, minutes, subsidiary seconds; perpetual calendar with date and day (both retrograde), month, moon phase, leap year
Case: white gold, 40 x 40 mm, height 14 mm; sapphire crystal; transparent case back
Band: reptile skin, buckle in white gold
Remarks: limited to 28 pieces
Price: upon request

Sympathie Bi-Retrograde Perp. Cal.

Reference number: S37 5772 5/6.3
Movement: automatic, RD 5772, ø 25.6 mm, height 4.8 mm; 29 jewels; 21,600 vph, patented double retrograde mechanism; Seal of Geneva
Functions: hours, minutes, sweep seconds; perpetual calendar with date and day (retrograde), month, moon phase, leap year
Case: rose gold, 37 x 37 mm, height 11 mm; sapphire crystal; transparent case back
Band: reptile skin, buckle
Remarks: limited to 28 pieces
Price: upon request

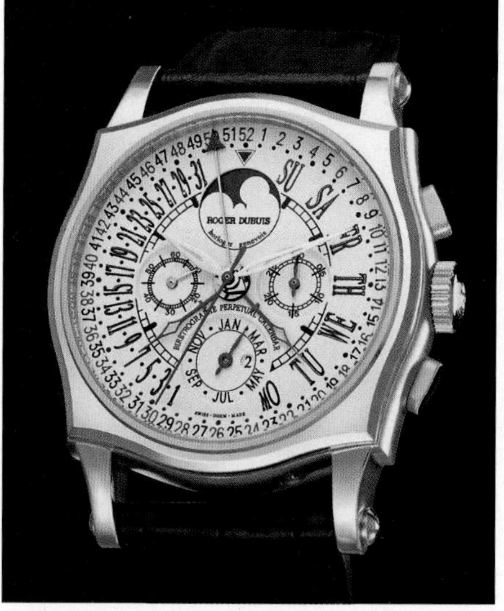

Sympathie Chronographe QP Bi-Retrograde par le Centre

Reference number: S43 5610 0/5.0
Movement: manual winding, RD 5610, ø 27.5 mm, height 8.07 mm; 21 jewels; 21,600 vph, column-wheel control of the chronograph functions; Seal of Geneva
Functions: hours, minutes, subsidiary seconds; chronograph; perpetual calendar with date and day (retrograde), calendar week, month, moon phase, leap year
Case: white gold, 43 x 43 mm, height 12 mm; sapphire crystal; transparent case back
Band: reptile skin, folding clasp in white gold
Price: upon request

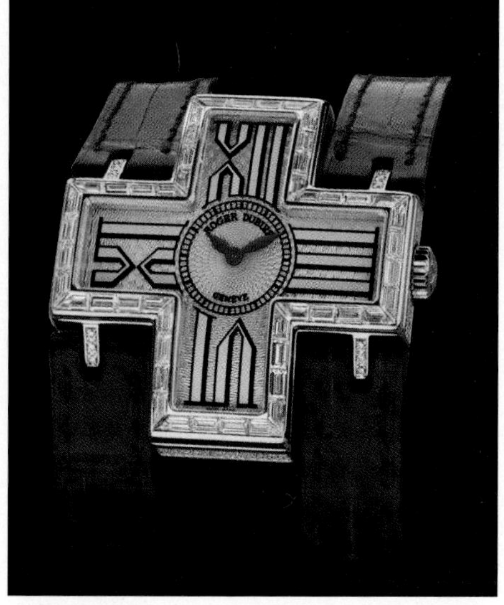

Follow Me

Reference number: F17 540/FBD F2.7A
Movement: manual winding, RD 54, ø 18 mm, height 2.5 mm; 19 jewels; 21,600 vph
Functions: hours, minutes
Case: white gold, cross-shaped, domed, 40 x 40 mm, height 10 mm; bezel and lugs set with 48 baguette-cut diamonds and 115 brilliant-cut diamonds; sapphire crystal
Band: double reptile skin strap, double buckle
Remarks: limited to 28 pieces
Price: upon request
Variations: different dial variations

Lady TooMuch

Reference number: T22 18 0-D/ND6.3 & T22 18 0FD/NDG.3
Movement: manual winding, RD 18, ø 17.5 mm, height 2 mm; 20 jewels; 21,600 vph, Seal of Geneva
Functions: hours, minutes
Case: white gold, domed, 22 x 34 mm, height 7 mm; bezel set with brilliant-cut diamonds; sapphire crystal; transparent case back
Band: double reptile skin strap, double buckle
Remarks: limited to 28 pieces each
Price: upon request
Variations: in red gold

Lady MuchMore

Reference number: M22 18 5/1.62
Movement: manual winding, RD 18, ø 17.5 mm, height 2 mm; 20 jewels; 21,600 vph, Seal of Geneva
Functions: hours, minutes
Case: rose gold, domed, 39 x 22 mm, height 8 mm; sapphire crystal; transparent case back
Band: yellow gold, folding clasp
Remarks: limited to 28 pieces
Price: upon request
Variations: with leather strap; in white gold with white gold bracelet; in different dial variations

Caliber RD 28

Mechanical with manual winding, column-wheel control of chronograph functions, manipulated by one single button on crown
Functions: hours, minutes, subsidiary seconds; chronograph
Diameter: 25.6 mm (10 ''')
Height: 5.05 mm
Jewels: 25
Balance: glucydur, three-legged
Frequency: 21,600 vph
Balance spring: Breguet, swan-neck fine adjustment
Remarks: 224 individual components; rhodium-plated plates; côtes de Genève; Seal of Geneva

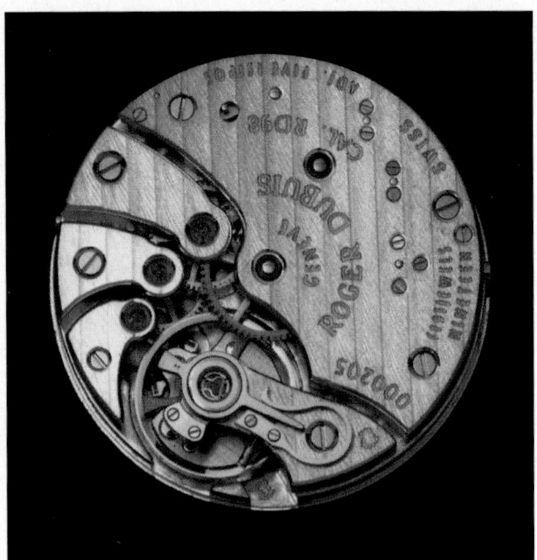

Caliber RD 98

Mechanical with manual winding
Functions: hours, minutes, subsidiary seconds
Diameter: 25.6 mm (10 ''')
Height: 3.8 mm
Jewels: 19
Balance: glucydur, three-legged
Frequency: 21,600 vph
Balance spring: flat hairspring, swan-neck fine adjustment
Remarks: 134 individual components; rhodium-plated plates; côtes de Genève; Seal of Geneva

Caliber RD 8230

Mechanical with manual winding, column-wheel control of chronograph functions, manipulated by one single button on crown; twin spring barrels, power reserve appx. eight days
Functions: hours, minutes, subsidiary seconds; chronograph; power reserve display
Dimensions: 31 x 28 mm (13 1/2''')
Height: 7.6 mm; **Jewels:** 25
Balance: glucydur, three-legged
Frequency: 21,600 vph
Balance spring: flat hairspring, swan-neck fine adjustment
Remarks: 315 individual components; rhodium-plated plates; côtes de Genève; Seal of Geneva
Related calibers: RD 8231 (without power reserve display); RD 82 (without chronograph, 21 jewels, 4.1 mm high)

Caliber RD 54

Mechanical with manual winding
Functions: hours, minutes
Diameter: 18 mm (8''')
Height: 2.5 mm
Jewels: 19
Balance: glucydur, three-legged
Frequency: 21,600 vph
Balance spring: flat hairspring, swan-neck fine adjustment
Remarks: 105 individual components; rhodium-plated plates; côtes de Genève; Seal of Geneva

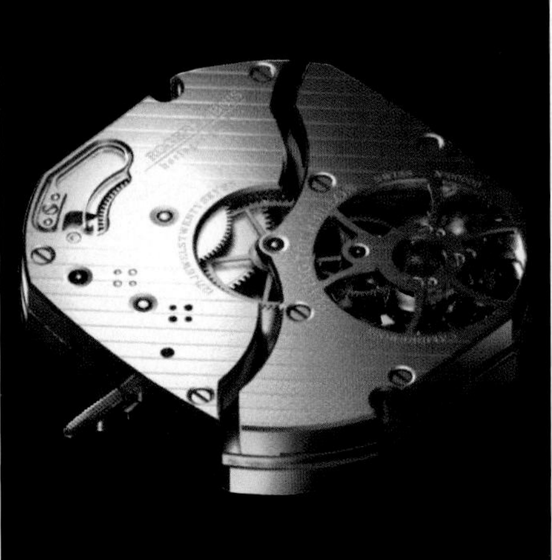

Caliber RD 03

Mechanical with manual winding; one-minute tourbillon
Functions: hours, minutes; large date; power reserve display
Dimensions: 33.8 x 33.8 mm (15''')
Height: 5.7 mm
Jewels: 27
Frequency: 21,600 vph
Balance spring: flat hairspring
Remarks: flying one-minute tourbillon; precisely jumping large date; 270 individual components; rhodium-plated plates; côtes de Genève; Seal of Geneva

Caliber RD 03

The dial side of the shaped tourbillon movement from the Roger Dubuis *manufacture.*

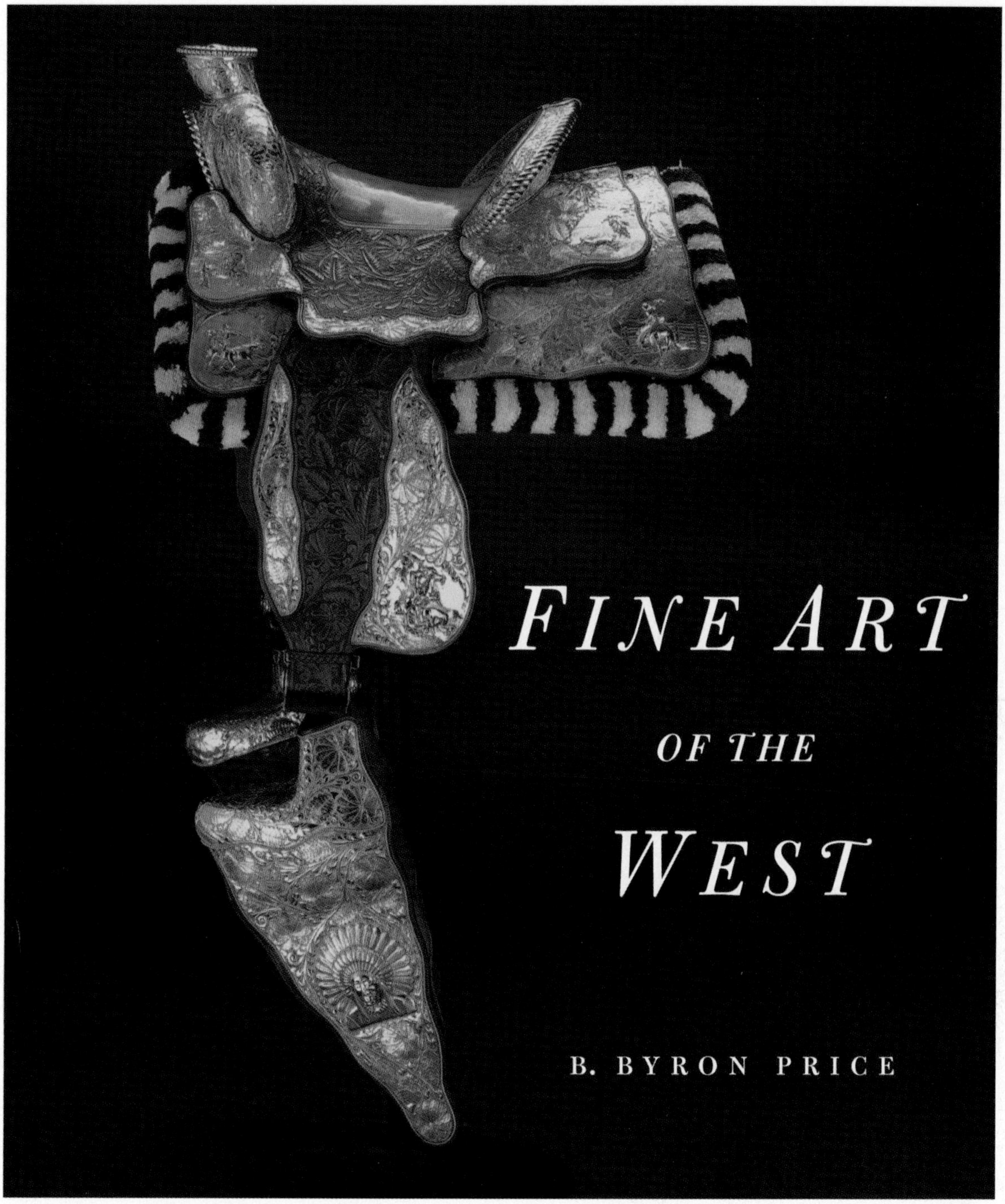

This landmark study delves into the traditional arts and crafts of the wild American West and their lasting effects on contemporary design.

By B. Byron Price
Approximately 275 illustrations, 250 in full color
276 pages • 10 × 12 in. • Cloth
ISBN 0-7892-0659-5 • $75.00

Published by ABBEVILLE PRESS
116 West 23rd Street, New York, N.Y. 10011
1-800-ARTBOOK (in U.S. only)
Also available wherever fine books are sold
Visit us at www.abbeville.com

Dunhill

The watch collection that Dunhill debuted this year at the S.I.H.H. in Geneva no longer had much in common with the classic, almost nostalgically designed wristwatches that have borne the A. Dunhill Ltd., London logo in recent years. Those represented more charming accessories than serious watches.

Dunhill Motorities was founded in the year 1884. Alfred Dunhill had developed the company from his father's saddlery, and the modern man of the world could find everything here to warm the heart of any automobile enthusiast, making transportation on four wheels an absolute joy: from newly developed signal horns and goggles to clothing providing protection against the elements. After all, the street mongrels of the time didn't show any respect for the strange new vehicles; the streets themselves were unsurfaced and accordingly dusty; and the new means of transportation did not for the most part feature a sensible chassis. In 1906 Alfred Dunhill offered his customers a watch for the first time — as the *dernier cri*, so to speak — which was, of course, tailored to the needs of the motor car enthusiast. It contained a stopwatch with whose help it was possible to time laps during increasingly popular automobile races. Dunhill, who had in the meantime established himself as a tobacco specialist in the fashionable St. James quarter, subsequently built his watches into artistically decorated cigarette lighters, ashtrays, pipe accessories, and even into belt buckles and brooches. In line with the current trend, his first wristwatches were introduced in the middle of the 1930s, among which was the Faceted Watch.

After the takeover by the Richemont luxury group, the classic Dunhill watch models were at the forefront of the line for quite a while again, but now the traditional brand is radically breaking with nostalgia.

The new collection is the creation of designer Tom Bolt, better known as the founder of the online watch company WatchGuru Ltd. Cutting edge facets, exciting arcs, and breaking light dominate the new creations City Tamer and City Fighter who wear their gaskets on the outside. A special element of the City Fighter is the attachable magnifying lens that protects the faceted crystal, simultaneously giving the watch a very special look.

A very technical solution was to move the crown to the front of the X-Centric: Only after loosening the screw and sliding it toward the lugs is the crown connected to the dial train and winding mechanism. Just as remarkable is the mechanism for protecting the chronograph buttons on the Bobby Finder model: By rotating the bezel, the buttons are recessed into the case and completely hidden by a slide.

The new functions and features of the Dunhill watches are incredible, unusual, and realized with a large portion of British outrageousness. Not much should stand in the way of their success in the stores when they hit the retail markets this fall.

X-Centric

Reference number: DCX 201 AL
Movement: automatic, Dubois-Dépraz 9031, ø 26.2 mm; 21 jewels; 28,800 vph
Functions: hours, minutes, sweep seconds; date
Case: stainless steel, ø 40 mm; sapphire crystal; screw-in crown engages the movement by being slid to the side ("Twist & Slide," patented)
Band: reptile skin, folding clasp
Price: appx. $3,500
Variations: in rose or white gold

Citytamer

Reference number: DCX 901 AM
Movement: automatic, ETA 2671, ø 17.2 mm, height 4.8 mm; 25 jewels; 28,800 vph
Functions: hours, minutes, sweep seconds; date
Case: stainless steel, domed, 26 x 49 mm, height 15 mm; sapphire crystal, faceted; screw-in crown
Band: reptile skin, folding clasp
Remarks: comes with additional steel bracelet
Price: appx. $3,200
Variations: in rose or white gold

Cityfighter

Reference number: DCX 991 AM
Movement: automatic, ETA 2671, ø 17.2 mm, height 4.8 mm; 25 jewels; 28,800 vph
Functions: hours, minutes, sweep seconds
Case: stainless steel, domed, 28 x 44 mm, height 15 mm; bezel under crystal with 60-minute scale settable via crown; sapphire crystal, faceted
Band: water buffalo/rubber, folding clasp
Remarks: clip-on crystal protection with integrated magnifying lens
Price: appx. $3,500

Bobby Finder SP 30

Reference number: DCX 551 AL
Movement: automatic, Dubois-Dépraz 2030, ø 30 mm; 45 jewels; 28,800 vph
Functions: hours, minutes, subsidiary seconds; chronograph
Case: stainless steel, ø 42 mm; rotating bezel, activates button functions and recesses them in case (patented); sapphire crystal; crown and buttons made of ceramic
Band: leather, folding clasp
Price: appx. $4,800

Car Watch

Reference number: DCX 300 AM
Movement: automatic, ETA 2671, ø 17.2 mm, height 4.8 mm; 25 jewels; 28,800 vph
Functions: hours, minutes, sweep seconds; date
Case: stainless steel, domed, 27 x 45 mm; sapphire crystal
Band: leather, folding clasp
Remarks: comes with additional steel bracelet; exchangeable "license plate" on case
Price: appx. $3,200
Variations: in ceramic and titanium

Facet 1936

Reference number: DUX 180 AM
Movement: manual winding, ETA 2660, ø 17.2 mm, height 3.5 mm; 17 jewels; 28,800 vph
Functions: hours, minutes
Case: rose gold, domed and faceted, 26 x 41 mm, height 12 mm; sapphire crystal, faceted
Band: reptile skin, folding clasp
Price: appx. $5,700

Ebel

After an intermezzo in the portfolio of the LVMH group (Louis Vuitton, Moet & Hennessy), the traditional brand Ebel (a name created from the first initials of "**E**ugène **B**lum **E**t **L**évy") surprisingly changed owners: Just before Christmas 2003 it was announced that the Movado Group Inc., headquartered in Paramus, NJ, had reached an agreement with LVMH regarding the takeover of the watch brand Ebel.

Efraim Grinberg, president of the Movado Group, explained: "The takeover of Ebel represents a unique strategic opportunity for Movado. At the same time, it is our first takeover since the purchase of the Movado brand in 1983. Ebel will contribute considerably in building upon our presence at the upper end of the luxury wristwatch market segment."

The Ebel and Movado brands are actually a good fit with regard to their company histories. At the very least, the destinies of these two Swiss brands situated in La Chaux-de-Fonds and Le Locle, respectively, have crossed more than one time in the last hundred years.

Movado was founded in 1881 by a young watchmaker, Achille Ditesheim, in La Chaux-de-Fonds. Ebel was founded in 1911 by Eugène Blum and Alice Lévy and made a name for itself above all as a manufacturing and assembly plant for other reputable watch manufacturers. Perfect quality and high flexibility secured quick success for the company. A lucrative partnership with Cartier catapulted its development into a new dimension in 1972. Under the management of Pierre-Alain Blum, grandson of the company's founder, a new collection was developed, which established the company on international ground as a luxury watch brand with a high demand on design ("Architects of Time").

At this point in time, Movado was already entrenched in the holding group Mondia-Zenith-Movado (1970/1971) and shortly thereafter was sold together with Zenith to the American Zenith Radio Corporation. Movado's factory was moved to Le Locle; the Ditesheim family lost all influence. In 1978 the Zenith group was bought back by Swiss industrial magnate Paul Castella, and the Movado brand was purchased by the North American Watch Corp. in 1984. The NAWC belonged to the Grinberg family, who had already bought the Swiss watch brand Concord in 1969 and developed it very successfully.

While Movado prospered overseas, Ebel slid into dangerous territory in the '80s due to Blum's less successful attempts at diversification. The new president, Sandro Ahrabian, sold the watch brand to Investcorp in 1994, a group of investors whose interests mainly involved short-lived increase in value and resale. Blum left the company two years later with a "golden handshake." In 1999 Ebel was sold to the luxury goods concern LVMH, which also purchased the brands TAG Heuer, Zenith, and Chaumet at the same time.

The period of time since Movado's takeover is too short to be able to see anything new in Ebel's collection. During the transitory phase, various restructuring measures are planned to define and establish the complex brand and collection appearances of Ebel and Movado.

1911 Carrée

Reference number: 8120I40/16530134
Movement: automatic, Ebel 120 (base ETA 2892-A2); ø 25.6 mm, height 3.6 mm; 21 jewels; 28,800 vph, rotor with côtes de Genève, blued screws
Functions: hours, minutes, sweep seconds; date
Case: yellow gold, 39.5 x 40 mm, height 9.7 mm; sapphire crystal; transparent case back
Band: reptile skin, buckle
Price: $7,000
Variations: with link bracelet; different dials

1911 Carrée

Reference number: 9120I43/16535217
Movement: automatic, Ebel 120 (base ETA 2892-A2); ø 25.6 mm, height 3.6 mm; 21 jewels; 28,800 vph, rotor with côtes de Genève, blued screws
Functions: hours, minutes, sweep seconds; date
Case: stainless steel, 39.5 x 40 mm, height 9.7 mm; sapphire crystal; transparent case back
Band: reptile skin, folding clasp
Price: $2,550
Variations: with link bracelet; different dials

1911 XL Large Date

Reference number: 9125250/15567
Movement: automatic, Ebel 125 (base ETA 2892-A2 + Jaquet module); ø 25.6 mm, height 4.9 mm; 21 jewels; 28,800 vph, rotor with côtes de Genève, blued screws
Functions: hours, minutes, sweep seconds; large date
Case: stainless steel, ø 40 mm, height 10 mm; sapphire crystal; water-resistant to 100 m
Band: stainless steel, folding clasp
Price: $2,950
Variations: with leather strap; different dials

1911 Chronograph XXL

Reference number: 9137260/26535136
Movement: automatic, Ebel 137, ø 30 mm, height 6.4 mm; 27 jewels; 28,800 vph, certified chronometer (C.O.S.C.)
Functions: hours, minutes, subsidiary seconds; chronograph; date
Case: stainless steel, ø 42.8 mm, height 14.5 mm; sapphire crystal; transparent case back; water-resistant to 100 m
Band: reptile skin, folding clasp
Price: $4,350
Variations: with link bracelet; different dials

Tarawa Chronograph

Reference number: 9137J40/6435136
Movement: automatic, Ebel 137, ø 30 mm, height 6.4 mm; 27 jewels; 28,800 vph, certified chronometer (C.O.S.C.)
Functions: hours, minutes, subsidiary seconds; chronograph; date
Case: stainless steel, 44.5 x 49.5 mm, height 16 mm; case and crystal triple domed; sapphire crystal; transparent case back
Band: reptile skin, folding clasp
Price: $5,500
Variations: different band and dial variations

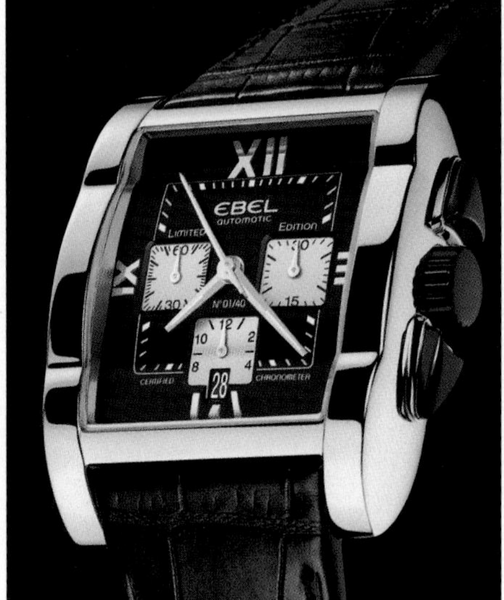

Tarawa Chronograph Limited Edition

Reference number: 8137J40/5435136
Movement: automatic, Ebel 137, ø 30 mm, height 6.4 mm; 27 jewels; 28,800 vph, certified chronometer (C.O.S.C.)
Functions: hours, minutes, subsidiary seconds; chronograph; date
Case: yellow gold, 44.5 x 49.5 mm, height 16 mm; case and crystal triple domed; sapphire crystal; transparent case back; crown and buttons in onyx
Band: reptile skin, folding clasp
Remarks: limited to 40 pieces
Price: $17,200

Tarawa Gent

Reference number: 9127J48/983035217
Movement: automatic, Ebel 127 (base ETA 2895-1); ø 25.6 mm, height 4.35 mm; 30 jewels; 28,800 vph, rotor with côtes de Genève
Functions: hours, minutes, subsidiary seconds; date
Case: stainless steel, 37 x 45.1 mm, height 11.7 mm; case and crystal triple domed, set with 22 diamonds; sapphire crystal
Band: reptile skin, folding clasp
Price: $5,000
Variations: different band variations; without diamonds

Tarawa Gent

Reference number: 9127J40/5486
Movement: automatic, Ebel 127 (base ETA 2895-1); ø 25.6 mm, height 4.35 mm; 30 jewels; 28,800 vph, rotor with côtes de Genève
Functions: hours, minutes, subsidiary seconds; date
Case: stainless steel, 37 x 45.1 mm, height 11.7 mm; case and crystal triple domed; sapphire crystal
Band: stainless steel, folding clasp
Price: $3,200
Variations: with leather strap; different dials

Tarawa Gent Haute Joallerie

Reference number: 3120J49/552030136
Movement: automatic, Ebel 120 (base ETA 2892-A2); ø 25.6 mm, height 3.6 mm; 21 jewels; 28,800 vph, rotor with côtes de Genève
Functions: hours, minutes, sweep seconds; date
Case: white gold, 37 x 45.1 mm, height 11.7 mm; case and crystal triple domed, set with 310 diamonds (including dial); sapphire crystal
Band: reptile skin, buckle
Price: $28,000
Variations: different variations (case material, dial, diamonds, etc.)

Classic Wave Chronograph Automatic

Reference number: 9126F41/6335134
Movement: automatic, Ebel 126 (base ETA 2894-2); ø 28 mm, height 6.1 mm; 37 jewels; 28,800 vph, rotor with côtes de Genève
Functions: hours, minutes, subsidiary seconds; chronograph; date
Case: stainless steel, ø 39.6 mm, height 12 mm; sapphire crystal; water-resistant to 50 m
Band: reptile skin, folding clasp
Price: $2,950
Variations: different dial variations

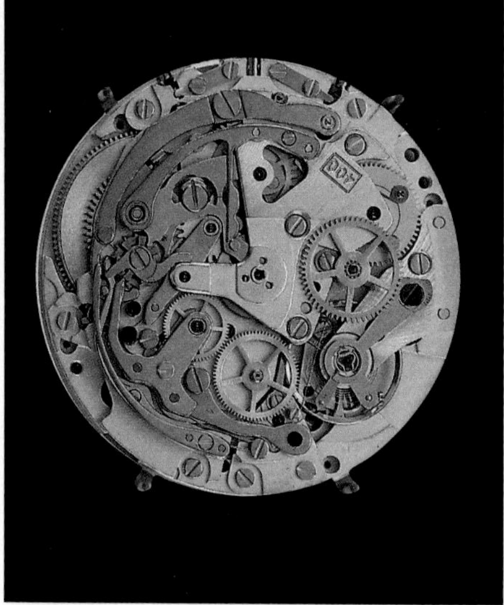

Caliber 136

Base caliber: Zenith 400 El Primero
Mechanical with automatic winding, power reserve 50 hours, ball-bearing rotor
Functions: hours, minutes, subsidiary seconds; chronograph (hours, minutes, sweep seconds); perpetual calendar (date, day, month, leap year, moon phase)
Diameter: 30 mm; **Height:** 8.1 mm; **Jewels:** 31
Balance: glucydur; **Frequency:** 36,000 vph
Balance spring: flat hairspring with fine adjustment via eccentric screw; **Shock protection:** Kif
Remarks: rotor with côtes circulaires, calendar module with perlage

Caliber 137

Mechanical with automatic winding, power reserve more than 48 hours, ball-bearing rotor
Functions: hours, minutes, subsidiary seconds; date (quick-set); chronograph with three counters (hours, minutes, subsidiary seconds)
Diameter: 31 mm (13 '''); **Height:** 6.4 mm; **Jewels:** 27
Balance: glucydur, three-legged
Frequency: 28,800 vph
Balance spring: Nivarox I flat hairspring with fine adjustment via micrometer screw (Triovis)
Shock protection: Incabloc
Remarks: officially certified C.O.S.C. chronometer

What's in a Name?

A Pronunciation Guide by Elizabeth Doerr

The editors of *Wristwatch Annual* have often been asked to include a pronunciation guide for the names of the brands we list to aid those English speakers who do not have command of another language such as French or German, the most important languages in watchmaking. Along with the pronunciation guide, we have also included a brief summary of the origin of the company's name.

Pronunciation Key:

ä = short a, as in the standard American pronunciation of father

ā = long a, as in day or date

ə = short French e, as in the u in the English word hurry

ē = long e, as in see

ī = long i, as in fine

ō = long o, as in bone

ö = French and German sound as found in French word *boeuf* or German *Söhne*

ū = long u, as in dune

ü = French or German pinched u sound, as in the French word *rue*, almost sounding like the English word you

n̲ = nasal, French n as in the French word *bonjour*

Svend Andersen svend ändersen
Svend Andersen is a Danish watchmaker living in Geneva.

Angular Momentum pronounced as in English
Named for a concept taken from astrophysics that combines a moment of inertia with an angular velocity.

Anonimo änonīmō
Anonimo is the Italian word for anonymous, chosen by the brand's owners to depict the fact that good watchmaking is not contingent upon the names the watches bear.

Arnold & Sons pronounced as in English
A brand named for famed British watchmaker John Arnold.

Audemars Piguet ōdəmär pēgā
Two French-language proper names taken from the Swiss founders watchmaker Jules Audemars and financial expert Jules Piguet.

Ball pronounced as in English
The last name of Ohio's Webb C. Ball.

Baume & Mercier bōm ā mersēä
Two French-language proper names taken from the Swiss Baume family and Genevan jeweler Paul Mercier.

Bell & Ross pronounced as in English
A fictional English-language name chosen for the French company.

Ernst Benz ernst bents
Name of the company's Swiss-born founder.

Blancpain blänkpan
The French-language last name of founding Swiss businessman Jean Jacques Blancpain.

blu blü
Fictional French word chosen for this Swiss company by its German founder, watchmaker Bernhard Lederer.

Rainer Brand rīner bränt
This is German-born watchmaker Rainer Brand's name.

Martin Braun martēn broun
This is German-born watchmaker Martin Braun's name.

Breguet brəgā
The last name of Swiss-born watchmaker Abraham-Louis Breguet.

Breitling brītling
The German-language last name of Swiss-born company founder Leon Breitling.

Carl F. Bucherer kärl f būcherer
The name of the company's Swiss-born founder, jeweler Carl F. Bucherer.

Bvlgari bulgärē
Derivative of the last name of the Italian Bulgari family.

Cartier kärtēä
Last name of French-born Louis Cartier.

Chase-Durer pronounced as in English
The name of this American company is a combination of founding Chase family and Swiss watchmaker Maximilian Durer.

Chopard shōpär
This is the French-language last name of Swiss-born founder Louis-Ulysse Chopard.

Chronoswiss krōnōswis
A fictional name chosen by German watchmaker Gerd-Rüdiger Lang for his Munich-based company.

Frédérique Constant frederīk kōnstän̲
The names of owner and founder Peter Stas's great-grandmother Frédérique and great-grandfather Constant.

Corum korūm
Swiss founding partners Gaston Ries & René Bannwart chose the Latin word *quorum* as the name of their company and simplified its spelling.

d.freemont pronounced as in English
Taken from American founder and owner David Freemont McCready's name.

Davosa dävōsä
Name that Swiss founding brothers Paul and David Hasler chose for their brand.

De Bethune də bətūn
Taken from a Swiss watchmaker known as Monsieur le Chevalier de Bethune.

De Grisogono dā grisōgōnō
The maiden name of an associate's mother who worked with Italian-born founder Fawaz Gruosi when he opened his first boutique in Geneva.

Doxa pronounced as in English
Name chosen by Swiss-born company founder Georges Ducommun for his brand.

Dubey & Schaldenbrand dübā ā shäldənbränt
The last names of founding Swiss watchmakers René Schaldenbrand and Georges Dubey.

Roger Dubuis rōjā dübwē
Swiss-born Roger Dubuis's French-language name.

Dunhill pronounced as in English
Last name of London-born Alfred Dunhill.

Ebel ābəl
Name taken from first letters of Eugene Blum et Levy, Levy being the maiden name of Swiss Eugene Blum's wife.

Eberhard āberhärd
Last name of Swiss founder Georges-Emile Eberhard.

Epos āpōs
Name chosen by Swiss company founder Peter Hofer.

Eterna āternä
Name chosen by Swiss company founders Urs Schild and Dr. Josef Girard.

Jacques Etoile jäk ātwäl
Francophone moniker taken from the names of master watchmaker and owner Klaus Jakob's last name and wife Yildiz Jakob's first name (*Yildiz* is Turkish for star and *etoile* is French for star).

Carlo Ferrara cärlō fərärä
Name chosen by Swiss company founders Urs Schild and Dr. Josef Girard.

Fortis fortis
Name chosen by Swiss founder Walter Vogt. It is Latin and means strong.

Gérald Genta jeräl jən̲tä
Name of Swiss-born watchmaker Gérald Genta, a man of Italian descent.

Gevril jəvril
French-language last name of Swiss watchmaker Jacques Gévril.

Girard-Perregaux jirär perəgō
French proper names derived from the company that was eventually owned by Swiss countryman Constant Girard-Perregaux.

Glashütte Original gläshütə originäl
Taken from Germany's historical watch city Glashütte.

Glycine glicēn
A glycine is a type of climbing plant indigenous to Switzerland. The founders of the Glycine watch brand, Switzerland's Charles Hertig and Sam Glur, named their brand for this plant that now graces the entire facade of the factory.

Graham pronounced as in English
Named for British watchmaker George Graham.

Hanhart hänhärt
Named for German founder Willy Hanhart.

Harwood pronounced as in English
Taken from English watchmaker John Harwood's last name.

Hermès erməz
Last name of founder Thierry Hermès, a man of French origin, though a German citizen.

Hublot üblō
French word meaning "porthole" that Swiss founder Carlo Crocco chose for his watches, as they reminded him of a ship's porthole.

IWC pronounced as in English
Stands for International Watch Company, founded in Switzerland by American Florentine Ariosto Jones.

Jacob jākəb
Russian-born American Jacob Arabo's first name, company founder and owner.

Jaeger-LeCoultre yāgər ləkūltr
Taken from the last names of Swiss founders Pierre Jaeger and Charles-Antoine LeCoultre.

Jaquet Droz jäkā drō
Taken from Swiss Pierre Jaquet Droz's last name.

... continued on page 153

Eberhard & Co.

The name Eberhard has been inseparably linked with sports timekeeping from its early days. Just a few years after the company was founded in the Swiss mountain town of La Chaux-de-Fonds in 1887, Eberhard was commissioned to time one of the first competitive motor races with the result that the chronograph specialists soon earned an excellent reputation among motor enthusiasts as well as watch connoisseurs.

Special models have recently strengthened this reputation for connoisseurs. One example is the Tazio Nuvolari, a chronograph that the founder's successor, a motor sport enthusiast, named after the wiry race driver from Mantua in 1992. The watches of this collection commemorate this popular Italian hero, known as the Flying Mantuan, a driver who piloted his car to numerous successes in the 1930s.

New developments such as the Traversetolo, a very large hand-wound watch outfitted with a vintage *manufacture* caliber, demonstrate that Eberhard not only preserves a sense of tradition, but also has a soft spot for collectors with limited financial resources.

One of the brand's latest innovations may seem like a stylistic gag, but it has an astounding effect. The counters of the new chronograph module, arranged in a straight line via an ingenious gear train under the dial, lend the Eberhard Chrono 4 such an unforgettable "face" that it is bound to cause more of a stir when worn than many very expensive *manufacture* products, much to the joy of its wearer. The new arrangement of the hand arbors make an additional thin module plate necessary — developed and produced in-house at Eberhard & Co. — that is placed upon the base chronograph movement, ETA Caliber 2894. Since Caliber 2894 is also built in modular fashion, using the base plate of Caliber 2892-A2 and its gear train, automatic winding device, and fine adjustment as its "motor," a large number of jewels were used to ensure that the complex mechanics could move without experiencing friction. There are a total of fifty-three jewels, thirty-seven of which can already be found in the base chronograph movement. Skeletonized hands facilitate reading the stopped time during the problematic periods between 7:15 and 7:45 when the linearly arranged counters (including the subsidiary seconds and twenty-four-hour display) would otherwise be covered.

The company's product developers, although always looking for innovation, remain true to their own tradition. The latest example of this is the chronograph Tazio Nuvolari Vanderbilt Cup. Expressed here are both the company's enthusiasm for technical progress and its exquisite love of historical detail — in the chronograph buttons arranged coaxially to the crown.

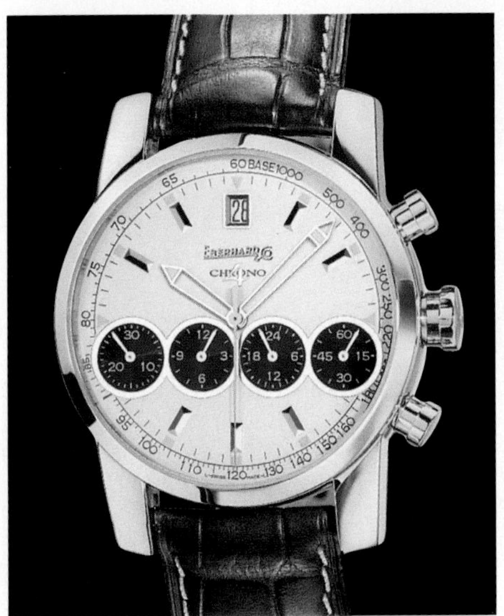

Chrono 4

Reference number: 31041
Movement: automatic, Eberhard EB 200 (base ETA 2894-2); ø 33 mm, height 7.5 mm; 53 jewels; 28,800 vph, four counters in a row
Functions: hours, minutes, subsidiary seconds; chronograph; date; 24-hour display
Case: stainless steel, ø 40 mm, height 13.8 mm; sapphire crystal; screw-in crown; water-resistant to 50 m
Band: reptile skin, buckle
Price: $4,290
Variations: with stainless steel link bracelet ($4,990); in rose gold

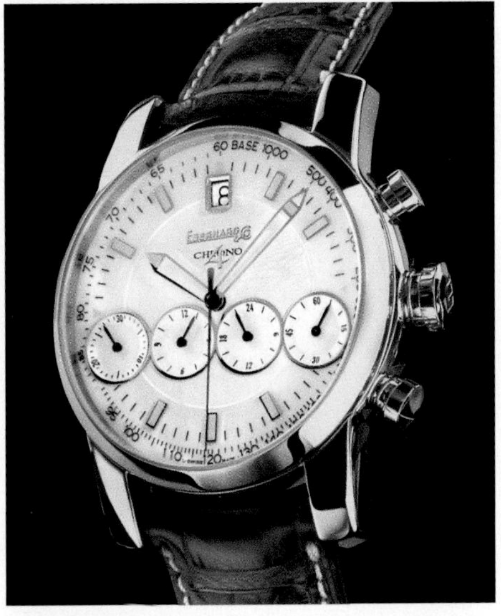

Chrono 4

Reference number: 31041
Movement: automatic, Eberhard EB 200 (base ETA 2894-2); ø 33 mm, height 7.5 mm; 53 jewels; 28,800 vph, four counters in a row
Functions: hours, minutes, subsidiary seconds; chronograph; date; 24-hour display
Case: stainless steel, ø 40 mm, height 13.8 mm; sapphire crystal; screw-in crown; water-resistant to 50 m
Band: reptile skin, buckle
Price: $4,290
Variations: with stainless steel link bracelet ($4,990)

Chrono 4 Bellissimo Coeur Vitré Abricot

Reference number: 31043
Movement: automatic, Eberhard EB 200 (base ETA 2894-2); ø 33 mm, height 7.5 mm; 53 jewels; 28,800 vph, four counters in a row; movement finely finished with blued screws, rotor with côtes de Genève
Functions: hours, minutes, subsidiary seconds; chronograph; date; 24-hour display
Case: stainless steel, ø 40 mm, height 14 mm; sapphire crystal; transparent case back; screw-in crown; water-resistant to 50 m
Band: reptile skin, buckle
Price: upon request
Variations: with stainless steel link bracelet

Chrono 4 Bellissimo

Reference number: 39060
Movement: automatic, Eberhard EB 200 (base ETA 2894-2); ø 33 mm, height 7.5 mm; 53 jewels; 28,800 vph, four counters in a row; movement finely finished with blued screws, rotor with côtes de Genève
Functions: hours, minutes, subsidiary seconds; chronograph; date; 24-hour display
Case: stainless steel, ø 40 mm, height 14 mm; sapphire crystal; transparent case back; screw-in crown
Band: reptile skin, buckle
Price: $4,490
Variations: with stainless steel link bracelet ($5,190)

Tazio Nuvolari Vanderbilt Cup

Reference number: 30061
Movement: automatic, Eberhard 8102 (base ETA 7750); ø 30 mm, height 7.9 mm; 25 jewels; 28,800 vph, chronograph reset function via crown button
Functions: hours, minutes, subsidiary seconds; chronograph
Case: rose gold, ø 42 mm, height 16.3 mm; sapphire crystal; transparent case back
Band: reptile skin, buckle
Price: upon request
Variations: in stainless steel ($5,500) with leather strap or stainless steel bracelet

Champion Schwarz

Reference number: 31044
Movement: automatic, ETA 7750, ø 30 mm, height 7.9 mm; 25 jewels; 28,800 vph
Functions: hours, minutes, subsidiary seconds; chronograph; date
Case: stainless steel, ø 39.5 mm, height 14.45 mm; engraved bezel with tachymeter scale; sapphire crystal; screw-in crown; water-resistant to 50 m
Band: stainless steel, folding clasp
Price: upon request
Variations: with leather strap, different dial variations

Extra Fort Grande Date Réserve de Marche

Reference number: 40036
Movement: automatic, Eberhard 3531 (base ETA 2892-A2); ø 25.6 mm, height 5.1 mm; 22 jewels; 28,800 vph
Functions: hours, minutes, sweep seconds; large date; power reserve display
Case: rose gold, ø 37.5 mm, height 10.8 mm; sapphire crystal; transparent case back; screw-in crown; water-resistant to 50 m
Band: reptile skin, buckle
Price: upon request
Variations: in white gold; in stainless steel

Extra Fort Grande Date

Reference number: 41024
Movement: automatic, Eberhard 3532 (base ETA 2892-A2); ø 25.6 mm, height 5.1 mm; 26 jewels; 28,800 vph
Functions: hours, minutes, subsidiary seconds; large date
Case: stainless steel, ø 37.5 mm, height 10.25 mm; sapphire crystal; transparent case back; screw-in crown; water-resistant to 50 m
Band: reptile skin, buckle
Price: $2,950
Variations: with stainless steel link bracelet; in rose gold ($5,700); different dial variations

Les Grandes Courbées

Reference number: 41022
Movement: automatic, ETA 2824-2, ø 25.6 mm, height 4.6 mm; 25 jewels; 28,800 vph
Functions: hours, minutes, sweep seconds; date
Case: stainless steel, domed, 30.6 x 45.1 mm, height 10.3 mm; sapphire crystal
Band: reptile skin, buckle
Price: $1,990
Variations: with stainless steel bracelet ($2,690); different dials

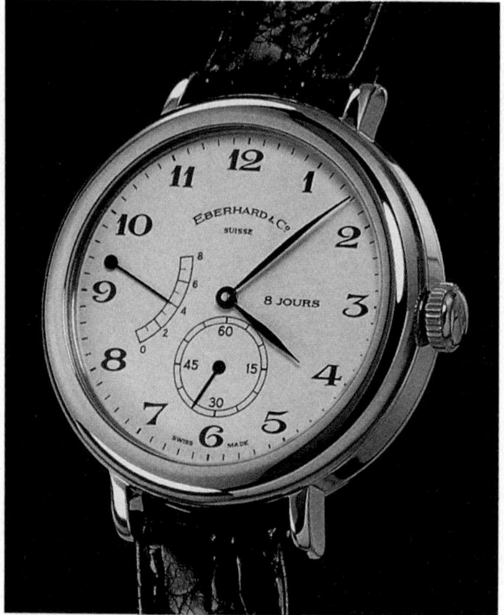

Traversetolo Vitré

Reference number: 20020
Movement: manual winding, ETA 6498, ø 36.6 mm, height 4.5 mm; 17 jewels; 21,600 vph, movement gold-plated, with blued screws and perlage
Functions: hours, minutes, subsidiary seconds
Case: rose gold, ø 43 mm, height 11.4 mm; sapphire crystal; transparent case back
Band: leather, buckle
Price: upon request
Variations: in stainless steel with leather strap ($1,650) or stainless steel bracelet

8 Days

Reference number: 21017
Movement: manual winding, ETA 7001, modified by Jaquet, ø 34 mm, height 5 mm; 25 jewels; 21,600 vph, two mainsprings; power reserve 192 hours (8 days)
Functions: hours, minutes, subsidiary seconds; power reserve display
Case: stainless steel, ø 39.4 mm, height 11.55 mm; sapphire crystal
Band: reptile skin, buckle
Price: $2,190
Variations: with stainless steel link bracelet ($2,790); in yellow gold

8 Days Postillon

Reference number: 21022
Movement: manual winding, ETA 7001, modified by Jaquet, ø 34 mm, height 5 mm; 25 jewels; 21,600 vph, two mainsprings; power reserve 192 hours (8 days)
Functions: hours, minutes, subsidiary seconds; power reserve display
Case: stainless steel, ø 39 mm, height 9.9 mm; sapphire crystal
Band: reptile skin, buckle
Price: $2,390
Variations: with stainless steel link bracelet; in yellow gold

... continued from page 149

JeanRichard jänrichär
Taken from Swiss watchmaker Daniel JeanRichard's name.

Journe jurn
French master watchmaker Francois-Paul Journe's name.

Kobold kōbolt
Taken from American founder and president Michael Kobold's last name, a man of German descent.

Maurice Lacroix morēs läkwä
Fictional francophone name chosen for brand by Swiss parent company Desco von Schulthess.

A. Lange & Söhne ä längə ünt sönə
Taken from German founding watchmaker Ferdinand Adolph Lange's name.

Limes lēməs
Brand name fabricated by the German Ickler family.

Longines lonjēn
Swiss founder Ernest Francillon bought a property by the name of Longines, built a factory there, and named his brand after it.

Marcello C. märchelō c
Derivative of German owner and founder Marcel Kainz's name.

Mido mēdō
Name chosen by Swiss founder Georges Schaeren for his brand. The word is derived from the name of a former Spanish-language trade fair, as Schaeren's company did most of its business in South America at the beginning.

Daniel Mink dänyel mink
Play on founder Aaron Minkowitz's last name.

Montblanc mōnblänk
Name of the German-based famed writing instrument company derived from the Swiss/French mountain Mont Blanc.

Movado mōvädō
A name originating in the synthetic world language Esperanto and meaning «constantly in motion.»

Mühle mülə
Last name of German founder Robert Mühle.

Franck Muller fränk mülər
Name of Swiss-born watchmaker Franck Muller.

Ulysse Nardin ūlis närdən
French-language name of Swiss founder Ulysse Nardin.

NBY pronounced as in English
No Barriers Yäeger, a name constructed by German master watchmaker Martin Braun, loosely inspired by pilot Chuck Yeager's name.

Armand Nicolet ärmänd nēkōlā
A Swiss watchmaker.

Nivrel nēvrel
A registered Swiss name acquired by German Gerd Hofer for his company.

Nomos nōmōs
The name of an historical Glashütte watch company. German owner and founder of the modern Nomos company, Roland Schwertner, acquired the name after the fall of the Berlin Wall.

Omega ōmāgä
Name chosen for the company by Swiss founder Louis Brandt's sons, Louis Paul and César.

Oris oris
Named by Swiss founders Paul Cattin and Georges Christian for the small stream that runs near the factory.

Panerai päneri
The Italian word *officine* (previously included in the brand's name) means workshops, and Panerai is taken from the name of the Italian founder, Guido Panerai.

Parmigiani pärmijänē
Last name of Swiss founder watchmaker Michel Parmigiani.

Patek Philippe pätek filēp
Last names of founding Polish immigrant to Switzerland, entrepreneur Antoine Norbert de Patek, and French watchmaker Adrien Philippe.

Piaget pēäjā
French-language last name of Swiss founder Georges Piaget.

Paul Picot pol pēkō
Name chosen by Italian entrepreneur Mario Boiocchi for his com-pany.

Poljot polyot
Name of Russian brand manufactured by the First Moscow Watch Factory.

Porsche Design porshə dəsīn
Taken from German owner and founder Ferdinand A. Porsche's last name.

Rado rädō
Later director Paul Lüthi christened the Swiss company Schlup & Co. Rado in the mid 1950s.

Auguste Reymond augüst rāmōn
Taken from Swiss founder Auguste Reymond's name.

RGM pronounced as in English
Taken from American founder and owner Roland G. Murphy's initials.

Rolex rōlex
German-born founder Hans Wildorf took the name from a combination of the Spanish words *relojes excelentes* (excellent watches) and modified it.

Daniel Roth dänyel rōt
Taken from Swiss founding watchmaker Daniel Roth's name.

Scalfaro skälfärō
Name invented by German founding brothers Kuhnle.

Jörg Schauer yörg shauər
Taken from German-born goldsmith, founder, and owner Jörg Schauer's name.

Alain Silberstein älən silbərstīn
Taken from French-born architect, founder, and owner Alain Silberstein's name.

Sinn zin
Taken from German-born founder Helmut Sinn's last name.

Sothis zōtis
German-born founder and owner Wolfgang Steinkrüger chose this name from Egyptian mythology for his brand.

Stowa shtōvä
Derived from the name of German founder **Wal**ter **Sto**rz.

Swiss Army pronounced as in English
Brand name used by Karl Elsener and his ensuing family members for the U.S. version of the Swiss brand Victorinox.

TAG Heuer täg hoiər
Taken from Swiss founding watchmaker Edouard Heuer's last name and the TAG group, who bought the brand in 1985.

Temption temptsēōn
Name chosen by German founder and owner Klaus Ulbrich combining *temp*us and func*tion*.

Tissot tisō
French-language last name of Swiss founders Charles-Félicien and Charles-Emile Tissot (father and son respectively).

Tudor pronounced as in English
Name chosen by Rolex for its second brand.

Tutima tūtēmä
Brand name derived from Latin word *tutus*, meaning certain or protected, by German-born founder Dr. Ernst Kurtz.

Union ūnēōn
The name German-born Johannes Dürrstein gave to his Glashütte-based company.

Vacheron Constantin väshərōn cōnstäntən
French-language last names of Swiss founders Jean-Marc Vacheron and Francois Constantin.

Ventura pronounced as in English
Swiss-born founder and owner Pierre Nobs named his company after Ventura, California

Harry Winston pronounced as in English
The name of prominent New Yorker jeweler Harry Winston, born in 1896.

Xemex zəməx
Name invented by Swiss founders and owners, designer Ruedi Külling and businessman Hans-Peter Hanschick.

Zenith pronounced as in English
Swiss-born founder Georges Favre-Jacot gave this name to his company.

Zeno pronounced as in English
André-Charles Eigeldinger, son of the second owner of the parent company, introduced the Zeno brand, the name of which is derived from the Greek word *zenodopolus*, meaning "gift of Zeus" or "divine offering."

Epos

Epos in Biel was founded in 1983 by Peter Hofer. This company has been one of the most active manufacturers of private label watches for many years and has until now sold very little under its own brand name. This is to change in the near future: Under new management since the beginning of the year, the company's distribution structures in the most important European watch markets are being built up little by little. The U.S. also counts as one of the more active markets for the brand. Since 2002 the brand has been owned by Tamdi Chonge and his wife Ursula after the original, but childless, owner put Epos up for sale. This watch expert born in Tibet has lived in Switzerland since 1966 and can look back on a long career with various Swatch Group brands. In the coming months, Epos will certainly develop its own strong personality under Tamdi Chonge's management.

These watches have proven their quality and honorable pricing policy a thousand times over — under foreign names, of course. Epos's leading models are in a somewhat higher market segment, both in quality and price. The brand sets itself apart from continuous comparisons with famous faces made by other brands with its unique cases, dials, and hands as well as perfect quality to the smallest detail, of course.

Small complications such as jump hours, power reserve displays, regulator underdials, calendars, and flyback chronographs are created in cooperation with reputable specialists such as Dubois-Dépraz and Jaquet. The legendary Eight Day watch — only currently available in the Epos line — which is based on an old manually wound Hebdomas pocket watch caliber, is just one of the highlights in the collection.

The company usually makes its turnover with more unspectacularly outfitted manually wound and automatic models in pleasing round and rectangular cases as well as convincing chronograph classics in a 1940s style.

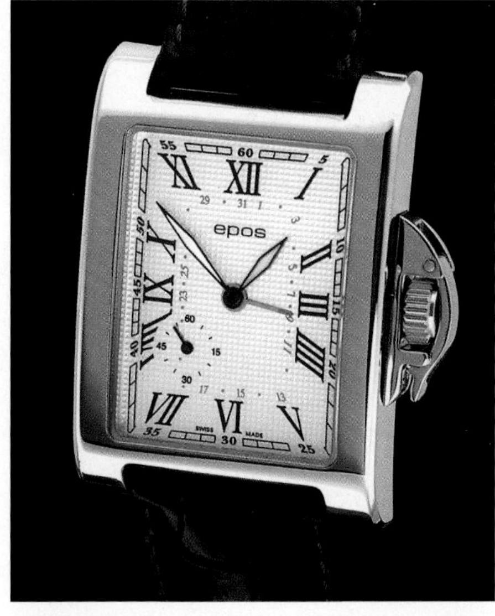

Edition Antiquité

Reference number: 3340
Movement: manual winding, Hebdomas 15, 17 jewels, movement according to historic models from the 19th century; 8 days power reserve; visible balance cock decorated
Functions: hours, minutes
Case: stainless steel, ø 42 mm, height 14 mm; sapphire crystal
Band: leather, buckle
Remarks: enamel dial
Price: $2,950
Variations: with gold-plated case; with white or black dial

Edition Antiquité Duograph

Reference number: 3364
Movement: automatic, ETA 7750, ø 30 mm, height 7.9 mm; 25 jewels; 28,800 vph, with côtes de Genève and blued screws
Functions: hours, minutes, subsidiary seconds; chronograph; date
Case: stainless steel, ø 42 mm, height 14 mm; sapphire crystal; transparent case back
Band: leather, buckle
Price: $2,150
Variations: different dials

Bellagio

Reference number: 3349
Movement: automatic, ETA 2824-2 QPS EPOS, ø 25.6 mm, height 4.6 mm; 25 jewels; 28,800 vph, protected movement module with off-center seconds and date hand
Functions: hours, minutes, subsidiary seconds; date
Case: stainless steel, 39.2 x 33.5 mm, height 9.8 mm; sapphire crystal; transparent case back; crown with crown guard device; water-resistant to 50 m
Band: leather, buckle
Price: $1,295
Variations: with black dial

Emotion

Reference number: 3167
Movement: manual winding, Epos P 7046 power reserve (base Peseux 7046); 17 jewels; 21,600 vph, protected movement module; decorated with côtes de Genève
Functions: hours, minutes, subsidiary seconds; date; power reserve display
Case: stainless steel, ø 37.5 mm, height 8.5 mm; sapphire crystal; transparent case back; water-resistant to 50 m
Band: leather, buckle
Price: $1,650
Variations: with gold-plated bezel

Action Team

Reference number: 3341
Movement: automatic, ETA 7751 (modified), ø 30 mm, height 7.9 mm; 25 jewels; 28,800 vph, with côtes de Genève and blued screws
Functions: hours, minutes; chronograph; date, day, month, moon phase
Case: stainless steel, ø 42.5 mm, height 15.5 mm; sapphire crystal; transparent case back; water-resistant to 50 m
Band: leather, buckle
Price: $2,750
Variations: with gold-plated case; with silver dial

Action Team

Reference number: 4314 OH
Movement: automatic, ETA 2824 (partially skeletonized), ø 25.6 mm, height 4.6 mm; 25 jewels; 28,800 vph
Functions: hours, minutes, sweep seconds
Case: stainless steel, ø 32 mm, height 9.4 mm; sapphire crystal; transparent case back
Band: leather, buckle
Price: $695
Variations: with round or heart-shaped dial cutaway; different strap colors

Eterna

Things are happening at Eterna: This traditional Swiss brand is working very hard at once again becoming a true *manufacture*. Even though its R&D capacity has at least partially been zapped in the past few years for the ambitious and recently introduced Indicator project by sister brand Porsche Design, now the technicians at Eterna can fully concentrate on their own complete watch movement. It needs to be done at the latest by 2006, for during that year the brand will be celebrating a big anniversary.

Eterna can proudly look back on a long history as one of the leading Swiss watch brands. In the year 1876 the first watch bearing this name appeared on the market: Eterna was the new brand name for the watches coming from a factory that had been founded in 1856. Since then, the brand has proved its technical competence again and again.

Eterna's trademark illustrates the brand's importance: five dots in the shape of a pentagon. This symbol represents the five tiny steel balls in the ball bearing that Eterna's engineers invented in 1948 — the one that rocketed the brand to worldwide fame in one fell swoop. This trail-blazing invention in micromechanics represents still today a worldwide watchmaking standard and is utilized by countless watch companies.

The positioning of the watch families 1948 and the evergreen KonTiki are proof positive that Eterna is careful to keep its great past in the conscious memory of the watch fan. This is not to say that the company would like to be regarded as old-fashioned, but the return to old values does fit into the horological world's contemporary frame of mind.

For Eterna this is all part of the corporate objective for the future — a very promising future as the year 1995 proved, when Eterna went into the hands of no less than Professor Ferdinand Alexander Porsche. Since the takeover by F. A. P. Beteiligung GmbH, not only has Eterna produced Porsche Design's watches, but a positive side effect has emerged in the form of the developmental support, innovative talent, and creativity emanating in Eterna's direction from F. A. Porsche's design office.

It was a good two years ago that the company took another step in bringing the old brand back to its earlier successful path. Company president Ernst F. Seyr, who came on board then, has lots of plans racing around his head, and it's not hard to believe that he can make Eterna into what it once was: a watch brand with its own movement production, a genuine *manufacture*.

In 2006, Eterna will celebrate its 150th anniversary. Perhaps Eterna's great past will be part of its future by then. At any rate, this is more than enough reason to look forward to this jubilee year!

1935 Grande Automatic

Reference number: 8492.41.40
Movement: automatic, Eterna 633 (base ETA 2824-2); ø 25.6 mm, height 4.6 mm; 25 jewels; 28,800 vph
Functions: hours, minutes, sweep seconds; date
Case: stainless steel, 42 x 26.4 mm, height 9.7 mm; sapphire crystal; transparent case back
Band: stainless steel, folding clasp
Price: $2,150
Variations: with ostrich leather strap; with reptile skin strap

KonTiki Chronograph

Reference number: 1591.41.40
Movement: automatic, Eterna 674 (base ETA 7750); ø 30 mm, height 7.9 mm; 25 jewels; 28,800 vph
Functions: hours, minutes, subsidiary seconds; chronograph; date
Case: stainless steel, ø 42 mm, height 15 mm; sapphire crystal; case back with medallion
Band: leather, buckle
Price: $3,000
Variations: with stainless steel bracelet ($3,300)

Kontiki Four-Hand Watch

Reference number: 1592.41
Movement: automatic, Eterna 636 (base ETA 2836-2 H6); ø 25.6 mm, height 5.05 mm; 25 jewels; 28,800 vph, date hand module by Eterna
Functions: hours, minutes, sweep seconds; date
Case: stainless steel, ø 40 mm, height 11.7 mm; sapphire crystal; case back with medallion
Band: stainless steel, folding clasp
Price: $2,250
Variations: with leather or rubber strap ($1,950)

1948 Grande Date

Reference number: 8425.41.10
Movement: automatic, Eterna 608 (base ETA 2892-A2); ø 25.6 mm, height 3.6 mm; 25 jewels; 28,800 vph, certified chronometer (C.O.S.C.)
Functions: hours, minutes, sweep seconds; large date
Case: stainless steel, ø 40 mm, height 11 mm; sapphire crystal; transparent case back
Band: reptile skin, folding clasp
Price: $3,000
Variations: with matching metal bracelet ($3,500); in rose gold

1948 Moon Phase Chronograph

Reference number: 8515.41.10
Movement: automatic, ETA 7751, ø 30 mm, height 7.9 mm; 25 jewels; 28,800 vph, certified chronometer (C.O.S.C.); case designed exactly according to original plans of first Eterna-Matic from 1948
Functions: hours, minutes, subsidiary seconds; chronograph; date, day, month, moon phase
Case: stainless steel, ø 39 mm, height 14 mm; sapphire crystal; transparent case back
Band: reptile skin, folding clasp
Remarks: numbered edition
Price: $3,500

1948 Alarm

Reference number: 8510.69.41
Movement: automatic, AS 5008, ø 30 mm, height 7.6 mm; 31 jewels; 28,800 vph, case designed exactly according to original plans of first Eterna-Matic from 1948
Functions: hours, minutes, sweep seconds; alarm; date, day
Case: rose gold, ø 39 mm, height 14.2 mm; sapphire crystal; transparent case back
Band: reptile skin, folding clasp
Remarks: numbered edition
Price: $7,900
Variations: in stainless steel

Jacques Etoile

Klaus Jakob, owner of the Jacques Etoile brand, is a passionate diver. For this reason, he has now added a diver's watch to his collection that is professional in both equipment and quality, doing justice to true divers' needs. A unilaterally rotating bezel with minute markings, a large red minute hand, inlaid with plenty of luminous substance, as are the hour hand and markers, and integrated magnetic field protection all belong to the equipment found therein. Additionally, the watch is water-resistant to 500 meters' depth.

However, master watchmaker Jakob's heart beats above all for old traditions — and vintage movements that are no longer in production. This tireless collector somehow always manages to unearth old hand-assembled calibers or perhaps only parts of them on remote dusty shelves or in some forgotten box on his extensive travels through the Swiss watchmaking countryside. Then he lovingly reworks and places them in attractive, classic cases. Thanks to a respectable pricing policy, these limited editions of exceptional watches are snapped up immediately by interested buyers.

In the last few years Jakob has established himself as one of the leading specialists in the working and finishing of the legendary column-wheel chronograph movement caliber Venus 175, causing a loyal following to flock to his company. The technical beauty and spectacular finish of his Venus movements hold a special place of honor in collectors' circles.

Jakob also has somewhat of a monopoly on the use of the Unitas caliber 6300, no longer in production. Outside of Jacques Etoile, there is no company with watches utilizing this movement in its program, although the 6300 has proved its qualities a thousand times over. After Jakob's finishing touches, the movement appears in a splendor that the original watchmakers of the Unitas movement *manufacture* could probably only have dreamed of.

Since Jacques Etoile's clientele has always been very receptive to unique things, special constructions in Jakob's contemporary models and patented plans have begun to play a much larger role. Jakob has maintained good relations with movement manufacturer Swiss Time Technology (STT, formerly Progress) for quite a while. This small factory supplied the movement for Jacques Etoile's first tourbillon, and the 11-line automatic movement by STT will also be included in the ever-growing collection.

The industrious watchmaker also invests well in the "packaging" of his ticking jewels. All of the cases used on Jacques Etoile watches come from the Sächsische Uhrgehäuse-Manufaktur Glashütte (Saxon Watch Case Manufacture Glashütte), better known as SUG, and are remarkable in their excellent craftsmanship and brilliant surface finish. Most of the chronograph models with round cases are manufactured according to a clever modular construction system that makes changing the bezel — even after the fact — possible. In addition, the interested party has a wide assortment of stylistically matching dials to choose from. Although it may be hard to choose, it certainly is a pleasant decision to have to make!

Maximat

Movement: automatic, ETA 2824-2, ø 25.6 mm, height 4.6 mm; 25 jewels; 28,800 vph
Functions: hours, minutes, sweep seconds
Case: stainless steel, ø 42 mm, height 11.6 mm; sapphire crystal
Band: leather, buckle
Price: $750

Atlantis

Movement: automatic, ETA 2824-2, ø 25.6 mm, height 4.6 mm; 25 jewels; 28,800 vph, magnetic field protection
Functions: hours, minutes, sweep seconds; date
Case: stainless steel, ø 43 mm, height 13.3 mm; unidirectionally rotating bezel with 60-minute scale; sapphire crystal; screw-in crown; water-resistant to 500 m
Band: reptile skin, buckle
Price: $1,350
Variations: with rubber strap; with stainless steel link bracelet

Unitas 6300 Monte Carlo

Movement: manual winding, Unitas 6300, ø 29.4 mm, height 4.62 mm; 19 jewels; 18,000 vph, rare vintage manufacture movement, thoroughly reworked
Functions: hours, minutes, sweep seconds
Case: stainless steel, ø 38 mm, height 10 mm; sapphire crystal; transparent case back
Band: leather, buckle
Price: $1,950
Variations: dial versions Metropolis, Medicus or Primus

Chronograph Valjoux Imperial

Movement: automatic, ETA 7750, ø 30 mm, height 7.9 mm; 25 jewels; 28,800 vph
Functions: hours, minutes, subsidiary seconds; chronograph
Case: stainless steel, ø 42 mm, height 13 mm; sapphire crystal; transparent case back; water-resistant to 100 m
Band: leather, buckle
Price: $3,250
Variations: with stainless steel bracelet

Chronograph Venus Monte Carlo

Movement: manual winding, Venus 175, ø 31.25 mm, height 5.7 mm; 23 jewels; 18,000 vph, column-wheel control of the chronograph functions
Functions: hours, minutes, subsidiary seconds; chronograph
Case: stainless steel, ø 40 mm, height 10.5 mm; sapphire crystal; transparent case back; water-resistant to 100 m
Band: leather, buckle
Price: $8,975
Variations: in 18-karat gold ($12,950); different dial variations

Saximus

Movement: manual winding, ETA 6498, ø 37.2 mm, height 4.5 mm; 17 jewels; 18,000 vph
Functions: hours, minutes, subsidiary seconds
Case: stainless steel, ø 42 mm, height 10.3 mm; sapphire crystal; transparent case back
Band: leather, buckle
Price: $1,550
Variations: upon request with elements of fine finishing such as a swan-neck fine adjustment

Carlo Ferrara

When in Rome, do as the Romans do. If this saying were always true, then the horological world would be deprived of a truly unusual watch, and Carlo Ferrara would probably be more involved in jewelry than the watch business.

Ferrara's only model to date, albeit in several different variations, is a modified regulator. Regulators first appeared on the scene in the late seventeenth century and were used as precision clocks by watchmakers to verify rates. In those days, they were regarded as the most accurate of timepieces, since neither quartz nor atomic clocks had yet been invented. The catch was the coaxial arrangement of the hands to enable a precise glance at the seconds, which were supremely legible when arranged in this fashion. Visually speaking, someone not familiar with watchmaking practices might actually think that there is a hand missing on a regulator dial.

Ferrara is an Italian watchmaker following in a family tradition. His father was also a watchmaker, though neither he nor Carlo ever attended watchmaking school. Both men autodidactically honed their talents, learning the basics from their respective fathers. Carlo worked as a watchmaker in a little atelier for thirty years. Day in, day out, he saw different watches come into the workshop that were all basically the same. They had different cases, different dials, and different shapes, but they all shared one trait: The hands were placed in the center of the dial, eternally sweeping the outer ring, just like every other watch. He felt the need to create something else, something unique, something that "cannot be considered boring," as he puts it.

In 1991 he finally made a prototype of his novel watch idea, using it to learn how to perfect all the details of the regulator. With the help of Swiss designers, the prototype was miniaturized and the "only wristwatch regulator equipped with dancing hours" was born.

The watch owes its nickname to the movement of the hands as the day progresses. The hour hand on the right side of the dial and the minute hand on the left side of the dial appear to do a slow dance as they mark the passage of time, moving up and down in their tracks and rotating 180 degrees at each end of the track.

The movement used in all these unusual watches is a patented, modified ETA 2892-A2 and possesses an Etachron fine adjustment, a glucydur balance wheel, a Nivarox 1 balance spring, and Incabloc shock protection. All of the models are water-resistant to at least three atmospheres and outfitted with sapphire crystals. The cases are manufactured in stainless steel or 18-karat yellow, rose, or white gold. As is plain to see, there is no lack of quality on any of these timepieces.

Production of Carlo Ferrara watches is quite limited as every piece is finished by hand in Switzerland. At the moment, only a total of 1,500 pieces are being produced per year, but the small family-owned company would like to raise this number to 2,500 per year in the near future. Sergio Ferrara, Carlo's son and a law graduate, is the man in charge of the non-technical side of the business. He stresses that production is so difficult because of the high amount of work done by hand on these watches. The watches are now distributed in many countries, including the United States, Italy, Japan, Hong Kong, and the Saudi Emirates. Plans for the future also include employing more watchmakers, both in Rome and Switzerland.

Zaffiro

Movement: automatic, CF 100 (base ETA 2892-A2); ø 34 mm; 32 jewels; 28,800 vph, sapphire crystal bridge, côtes de Genève on base plate
Functions: hours, minutes, sweep seconds; date
Case: rose gold, ø 39.5 mm, height 10.9 mm; sapphire crystal; transparent case back; water-resistant to 30 m
Band: crocodile skin, buckle
Remarks: skeletonized dial
Price: $18,120
Variations: in white gold

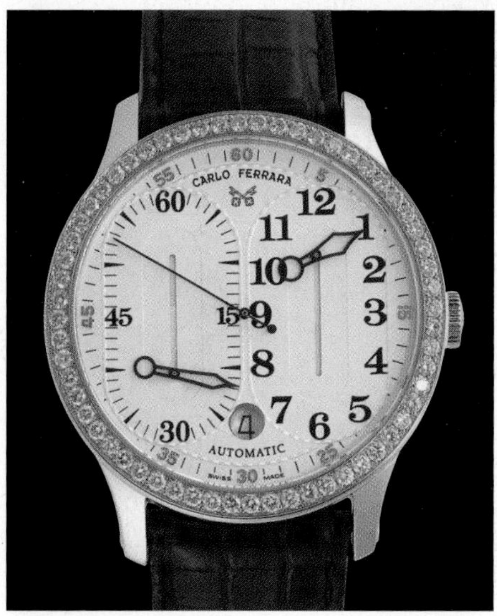

Diamond Collection

Reference number: 131.411/110
Movement: automatic, CF 100 (base ETA 2892-A2); ø 34 mm; 32 jewels; 28,800 vph
Functions: hours, minutes, sweep seconds; date
Case: rose gold, ø 39.5 mm, height 10.9 mm; diamond-set bezel; sapphire crystal; transparent case back; water-resistant to 30 m
Band: crocodile skin, buckle
Price: $17,920
Variations: in white gold

Jockey Collection

Reference number: 110.392/110
Movement: automatic, CF 100 (base ETA 2892-A2); ø 34 mm; 32 jewels; 28,800 vph
Functions: hours, minutes, sweep seconds; date
Case: stainless steel, ø 39.5 mm, height 10.9 mm; sapphire crystal; transparent case back; water-resistant to 30 m
Band: crocodile skin, buckle
Price: $5,310
Variations: three different dial variations

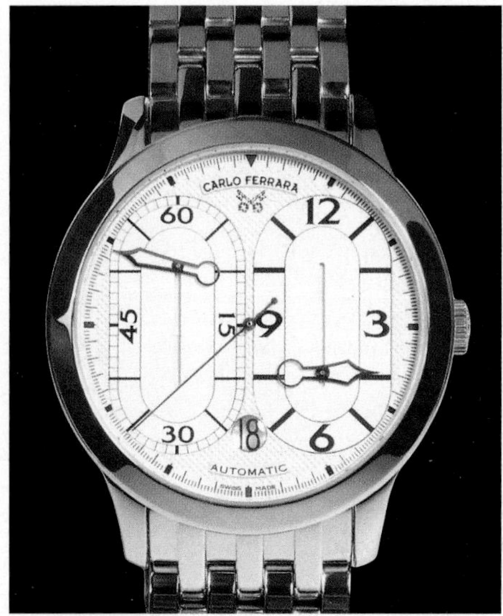

Sport Collection

Reference number: 110.211/300
Movement: automatic, CF 100 (base ETA 2892-A2); ø 34 mm; 32 jewels; 28,800 vph
Functions: hours, minutes, sweep seconds; date
Case: stainless steel, ø 39.5 mm, height 10.9 mm; sapphire crystal; transparent case back; water-resistant to 30 m
Band: stainless steel, folding clasp
Price: $6,100
Variations: with white, blue, grey, or black dial

Quadro Collection

Reference number: 510.362/110
Movement: automatic, CF 100 (base ETA 2892-A2); ø 34 mm; 32 jewels; 28,800 vph
Functions: hours, minutes, sweep seconds; date
Case: stainless steel, 36 x 41 mm, height 11.9 mm; sapphire crystal; transparent case back; water-resistant to 30 m
Band: crocodile skin, buckle
Price: $6,300
Variations: in rose gold; different dial variations

Jockey Collection

Reference number: 110.362/110
Movement: automatic, CF 100 (base ETA 2892-A2); ø 34 mm; 32 jewels; 28,800 vph
Functions:
Case: stainless steel, ø 39.5 mm,height 10.9 mm; sapphire crystal; transparent case back; water-resistant to 30 m
Band: crocodile skin, buckle
Price: $5,310
Variations: three different dial variations

Fortis

Fortis means *strong* in Latin, and strength is certainly something that this watch brand has truly shown time and again for more than ninety years. The power of innovation with which company founder Walter Vogt continued to drive the brand during the entire span of his life represents both an example and motivation for the current company management.
More than once Fortis has written watch history: At the beginning of the 1920s with the world's first serial production of wristwatches with automatic winding and again in the middle of the 1980s — already outfitted with new management — with its clear dedication to the renaissance of the mechanical watch.
Fortis is one of the few Swiss watch manufacturers to remain independent and to continue to manufacture watches in its own company headquarters since its founding, taking part in creating the worldwide reputation of Swiss quality watches. This down-to-earth attitude is certainly necessary to deserve the trust of space specialists. At the beginning of the 1990s, the Russian space program chose Fortis as its partner for the development of automatic wristwatches for use on research and reconnaissance flights to space. In 1994 a Fortis automatic chronograph was chosen for the first time for an official mission after being tested under extreme conditions both in a laboratory and during actual space walk missions. The majority of the tests were completed at the boundaries of physics. Also extraordinary is the award for the development of mechanical chronographs for space travel: The Star of the Blue Planet from the Russian space agency Rosaviakosmos was awarded to Peter Peter, Fortis's managing director and head designer, for his commitment and consistency in developing timekeepers to be used in space. Under his direction, Fortis has developed a new movement in conjunction with the best specialists Switzerland has to offer.
For the first time, the three base functions needed to keep the passing of time were united in the microcosm of a watch, and, of course, powered by automatic winding: the passing of hours, minutes, and seconds, as well as the measurement made possible by the stopping of time (chronograph) and the interruption of time by an alarm signal that serves to remind one of a certain event. Even though this watch was escorted by functional aspects, aesthetics were not forgotten in the model development. The clean design of Fortis chronographs has achieved something of a normed status in the meantime, and many international flying squadron pilots can confirm the high quality and functionality of their choice.

FORTIS WANDFLUH CHRONOGRAPH
The history of the wristwatch is hardly one hundred years old. Fortis was already manufacturing complex movements with stop functions in 1937, on its 25th anniversary.

FORTIS FLIEGER CHRONOGRAPH
Operation Enduring Freedom is an international cooperative serving the fight against worldwide terrorism and searching to uphold freedom and the continuation of democratic values. The dial of this Fortis classic bears the operation's logo and is dedicated to those who risk their lives in dangerous situations for these goals.

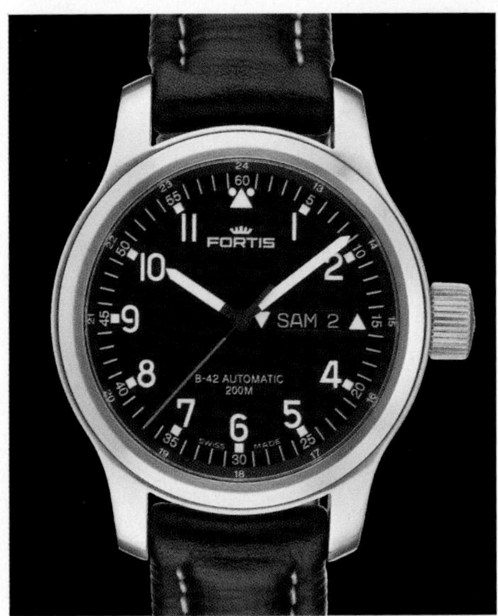

B-42 Pilot Professional Day/Date

Reference number: 645.10.11
Movement: automatic, ETA 2836-2, ø 25.6 mm, height 5.05 mm; 25 jewels; 28,800 vph
Functions: hours, minutes, sweep seconds; date and day
Case: stainless steel, brushed, ø 42 mm, height 15 mm; sapphire crystal; transparent case back; screw-in crown; water-resistant to 200 m
Band: leather, buckle
Price: $1,000
Variations: with stainless steel bracelet or rubber strap

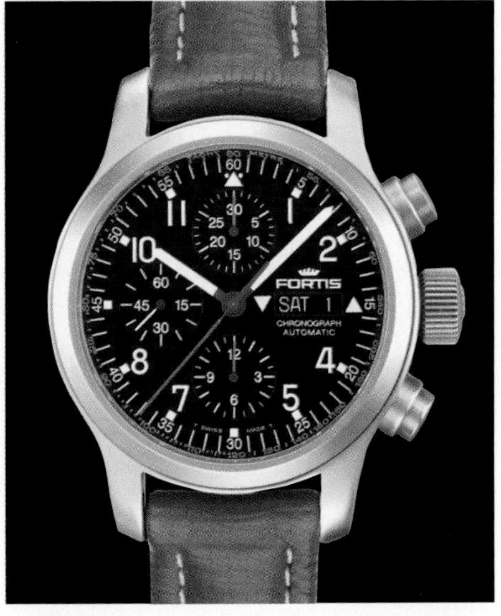

B-42 Pilot Professional Chronograph

Reference number: 635.22.11
Movement: automatic, ETA 7750, ø 30 mm, height 7.9 mm; 25 jewels; 28,800 vph
Functions: hours, minutes, subsidiary seconds; chronograph; date, day
Case: stainless steel, microsandblasted, ø 42 mm, height 15 mm; sapphire crystal; transparent case back; screw-in crown; water-resistant to 200 m
Band: leather, buckle
Price: $2,100
Variations: with stainless steel bracelet or rubber strap; as GMT model with second time zone

B-42 Pilot Professional Chronograph Alarm

Reference number: 636.22.11
Movement: automatic, Fortis F2001 (base ETA 7750); ø 30 mm, height 7.9 mm; 32 jewels; 28,800 vph, integrated alarm movement with automatic winding
Functions: hours, minutes, subsidiary seconds; chronograph; date; alarm
Case: stainless steel, microsandblasted, ø 42 mm, height 15 mm; sapphire crystal; screw-in crown; water-resistant to 200 m
Band: leather, buckle
Price: $5,650
Variations: with stainless steel bracelet or rubber strap

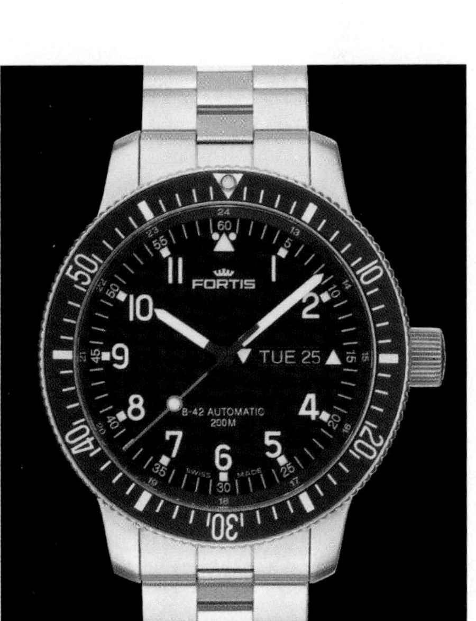

B-42 Official Cosmonauts Day/Date

Reference number: 647.10.11 M
Movement: automatic, ETA 2836-2, ø 25.6 mm, height 5.05 mm; 25 jewels; 28,800 vph
Functions: hours, minutes, sweep seconds; date and day
Case: stainless steel, brushed, ø 42 mm, height 15 mm; unidirectionally rotating bezel with 60-minute scale; sapphire crystal; case back with the official logo of the Russian space agency; screw-in crown; water-resistant to 200 m
Band: stainless steel, folding clasp with extension
Price: $1,400
Variations: with leather or rubber strap

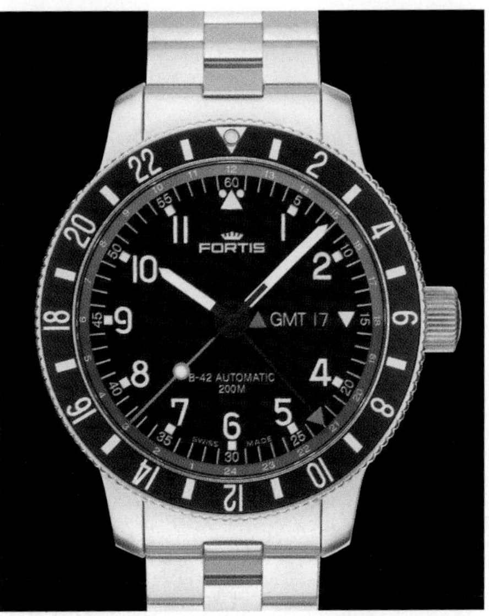

B-42 Official Cosmonauts GMT

Reference number: 649.10.11 M
Movement: automatic, ETA 2893-2, ø 25.6 mm, height 4.1 mm; 21 jewels; 28,800 vph
Functions: hours, minutes, sweep seconds; date; 24-hour display (second time zone)
Case: stainless steel, brushed, ø 42 mm, height 15 mm; bidirectionally rotating bezel with 24-hour scale; sapphire crystal; case back with the official logo of the Russian space agency; screw-in crown; water-resistant to 200 m
Band: stainless steel, folding clasp with extension
Price: $1,700
Variations: as chronograph GMT; in set

B-42 Cosmonaut Chronograph Alarm

Reference number: 639.22.11 M
Movement: automatic, Fortis F2001 (base ETA 7750); ø 30 mm, height 7.9 mm; 32 jewels; 28,800 vph, integrated alarm movement with automatic winding
Functions: hours, minutes, subsidiary seconds; chronograph; date; alarm
Case: stainless steel, microsandblasted, ø 42 mm, height 17 mm; unidirectionally rotating bezel with 60-minute scale; sapphire crystal; screw-in crown; water-resistant to 200 m
Band: leather, buckle
Price: $6,300
Variations: with stainless steel bracelet

Flieger Automatic

Reference number: 595.10.41
Movement: automatic, ETA 2824-2, ø 25.6 mm, height 4.6 mm; 25 jewels; 28,800 vph
Functions: hours, minutes, sweep seconds; date
Case: stainless steel, microsandblasted, ø 40 mm, height 11 mm; mineral crystal; screw-in crown; water-resistant to 200 m
Band: leather, buckle
Price: $625
Variations: with sapphire crystal, anti-reflective on both side; with transparent case back; with stainless steel bracelet; diverse dial variations; in 34 mm case diameter

Flieger 24h

Reference number: 596.10.11 M
Movement: automatic, Fortis 2893-2, ø 25.6 mm, height 4.1 mm; 21 jewels; 28,800 vph
Functions: hours, minutes, sweep seconds; date; 24-hour display (second time zone)
Case: stainless steel, microsandblasted, ø 40 mm, height 11 mm; mineral crystal; screw-in crown; water-resistant to 200 m
Band: stainless steel, folding clasp with extension
Price: $1,040
Variations: with sapphire crystal, anti-reflective on both side; with transparent case back; with leather strap

Flieger Chronograph Automatic

Reference number: 597.10.11
Movement: automatic, ETA 7750, ø 30 mm, height 7.9 mm; 25 jewels; 28,800 vph
Functions: hours, minutes, subsidiary seconds; chronograph; date, day
Case: stainless steel, microsandblasted, ø 40 mm, height 15 mm; mineral crystal; water-resistant to 100 m
Band: leather, buckle
Price: $1,600
Variations: with sapphire crystal, anti-reflective on both side; with transparent case back; with stainless steel bracelet; in 35 mm case diameter

B-42 Pilot Day/Date

Reference number: 645.10.12
Movement: automatic, ETA 2836-2, ø 25.6 mm, height 5.05 mm; 25 jewels; 28,800 vph
Functions: hours, minutes, sweep seconds; date and day
Case: stainless steel, brushed, ø 42 mm, height 15 mm; sapphire crystal; transparent case back; screw-in crown; water-resistant to 200 m
Band: leather, buckle
Price: $1,100
Variations: with stainless steel bracelet or rubber strap

B-42 Pilot Chronograph GMT

Reference number: 637.10.12 M
Movement: automatic, ETA 7750, ø 30 mm, height 7.9 mm; 25 jewels; 28,800 vph
Functions: hours, minutes, subsidiary seconds; chronograph; date; 24-hour display (second time zone)
Case: stainless steel, microsandblasted, ø 42 mm, height 15 mm; sapphire crystal; transparent case back; screw-in crown; water-resistant to 200 m
Band: stainless steel, folding clasp with extension
Price: $3,400
Variations: with leather or rubber strap

B-42 Pilot Chronograph Alarm

Reference number: 636.10.12 C
Movement: automatic, Fortis F2001 (base ETA 7750); ø 30 mm, height 7.9 mm; 32 jewels; 28,800 vph, integrated alarm movement with automatic winding
Functions: hours, minutes, subsidiary seconds; chronograph; date; alarm
Case: stainless steel, microsandblasted, ø 42 mm, height 17 mm; sapphire crystal; transparent case back; screw-in crown; water-resistant to 200 m
Band: reptile skin, buckle
Price: $6,150
Variations: with stainless steel bracelet

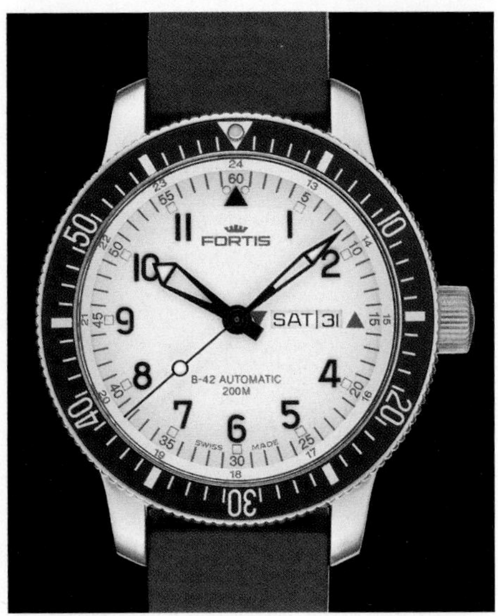

B-42 Diver Day/Date

Reference number: 648.10.12
Movement: automatic, ETA 2836-2, ø 25.6 mm, height 5.05 mm; 25 jewels; 28,800 vph
Functions: hours, minutes, sweep seconds; date and day
Case: stainless steel, brushed, ø 42 mm, height 15 mm; unidirectionally rotating bezel with 60-minute scale; sapphire crystal; screw-in crown; water-resistant to 200 m
Band: leather, buckle
Price: $1,200
Variations: with stainless steel bracelet

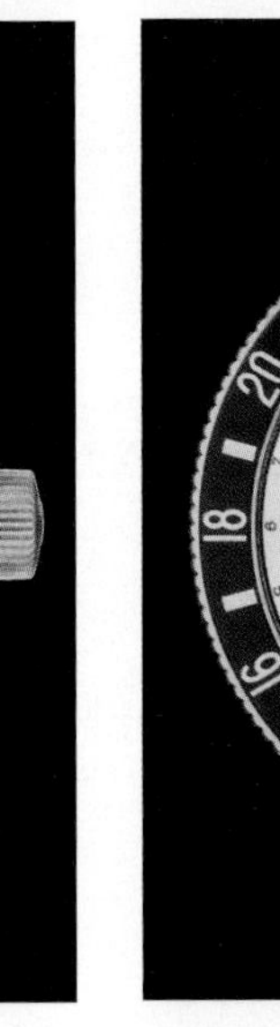

B-42 Diver GMT

Reference number: 650.10.12 M
Movement: automatic, ETA 2893-2, ø 25.6 mm, height 4.1 mm; 21 jewels; 28,800 vph
Functions: hours, minutes, sweep seconds; date; 24-hour display (second time zone)
Case: stainless steel, brushed, ø 42 mm, height 15 mm; bidirectionally rotating bezel with 24-hour scale; sapphire crystal; transparent case back; screw-in crown; water-resistant to 200 m
Band: stainless steel, folding clasp with extension
Price: $1,800
Variations: with leather or rubber strap

B-42 Diver Chronograph Alarm

Reference number: 641.10.12 C
Movement: automatic, Fortis F2001 (base ETA 7750); ø 30 mm, height 7.9 mm; 32 jewels; 28,800 vph, integrated alarm movement with automatic winding
Functions: hours, minutes, subsidiary seconds; chronograph; date; alarm
Case: stainless steel, brushed, ø 42 mm, height 17 mm; unidirectionally rotating bezel with 60-minute scale; sapphire crystal; transparent case back; screw-in crown; water-resistant to 200 m
Band: reptile skin, buckle
Price: $6,500

Official Cosmonauts Chronograph Alarm Platinum

Reference number: 607.70.12
Movement: automatic, Fortis F2001 (base ETA 7750); ø 30 mm, height 7.9 mm; 32 jewels; 28,800 vph, integrated alarm movement with automatic winding
Functions: hours, minutes, subsidiary seconds; chronograph; date; alarm
Case: platinum, ø 38 mm, height 16 mm; bezel with tachymeter scale; sapphire crystal; screw-in crown and buttons; water-resistant to 100 m
Band: reptile skin, buckle in platinum
Price: $19,000

Official Cosmonauts Chronograph Gold

Reference number: 630.50.12
Movement: automatic, ETA 7750, ø 30 mm, height 7.9 mm; 25 jewels; 28,800 vph
Functions: hours, minutes, subsidiary seconds; chronograph; date, day
Case: yellow gold, ø 38 mm, height 15 mm; engraved bezel with tachymeter scale; sapphire crystal; case back with the official logo of the Russian space agency; screw-in crown and buttons; water-resistant to 200 m
Band: reptile skin, buckle
Price: $9,250
Variations: with black dial

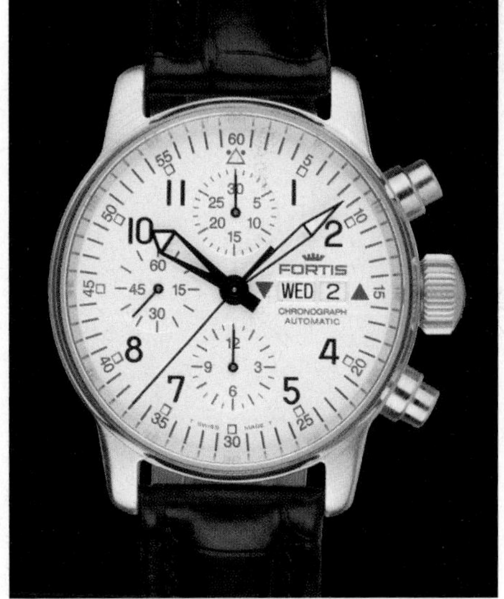

Flieger Chronograph Gold

Reference number: 597.50.12
Movement: automatic, ETA 7750, ø 30 mm, height 7.9 mm; 25 jewels; 28,800 vph
Functions: hours, minutes, subsidiary seconds; chronograph; date, day
Case: yellow gold, ø 40 mm, height 15 mm; sapphire crystal; water-resistant to 100 m
Band: reptile skin, buckle
Price: $9,850

Gérald Genta

Consistently modern, consistently unusual, and consistently different: The Gérald Genta brand has developed its own dynamic after the departure of its founder and namesake, which is rather comparable to the famous designer's creative genius. Retrograde displays, jumping numerals in windows, unusual dial materials and structures, daring colors, printed crystals, geometric case shapes — among the ranks of noble watch brands, Gérald Genta sticks out like an exotic bird of paradise. Some models are outfitted with a skeletonized dial along with diverse retrograde displays, allowing a view of the disks of a jump hour display, date, or weekday. With half-circle scale segments, psychedelic "dancing" numerals, and a window display for the hours, all similarities with a normal wristwatch are rather accidental ... The new owners of the brand have a difficult inheritance to follow: For a number of decades this descendant of Italian ancestors born in Geneva was the designer to set the tone in noble Swiss watchmaking with his creativity — even if it wasn't always under his own name. Genta only founded his own brand at the beginning of the 1990s. Before that, he worked as a stylist for such famous houses as Audemars Piguet, Patek Philippe, and Omega, influencing an entire epoch of Swiss watchmaking with his *lignes douces* style.

Even if the *grandseigneur* no longer personally directs the business of the brand named for him (after an intermezzo under the wings of the Singaporean Hour Glass company, it has now been incorporated into the expanding Bvlgari group), his successors at the drawing board still feel obligated to express his special feeling for style. Gérald Genta watches today still display

the characteristic soft curves, but the playful details have given way to the more modern and striking use of shapes and functional elements. Gérald Genta shares the development and manufacture of complicated watch movements with the individualist brand Daniel Roth, also a member of the Bvlgari group — just as it shares its company headquarters in the Genevan quarter Pâquis as well as the production factories in the Vallée de Joux's Le Sentier.

Both of these brands have no problem existing alongside the Bvlgari brand, as each has its own market segment to cover. Bvlgari embodies the modern, sporty style; Daniel Roth stands for more classical watches with complications; and Gérald Genta chiefly represents the avant-garde in design and function.

Basically, this is how it has always been.

Grande Sonnerie

Reference number: GS 1.X.

Movement: manual winding, Gérald Genta 30, ø 31.5 mm, height 7.3 mm; 56 jewels; 21,600 vph, one-minute tourbillon; strike train with four hammers, Westminster gong

Functions: hours, minutes; large and small strike train, minute repeater; two power reserve displays movement and strike train)

Case: white gold, ø 41 mm, height 12 mm; sapphire crystal; transparent case back

Band: reptile skin, buckle

Price: $688,100

Octo Bi Retro

Reference number: OBR.Y.50.510.CN.BD

Movement: automatic, Gérald Genta 7722, ø 26.2 mm, height 5.28 mm; 27 jewels; 28,800 vph

Functions: hours (jump), minutes (retrograde); date (retrograde)

Case: red gold, ø 42.5 mm, height 11.9 mm; sapphire crystal; transparent case back; crown with onyx cabochon; water-resistant to 100 m

Band: reptile skin, folding clasp

Price: $28,800

Variations: in white gold

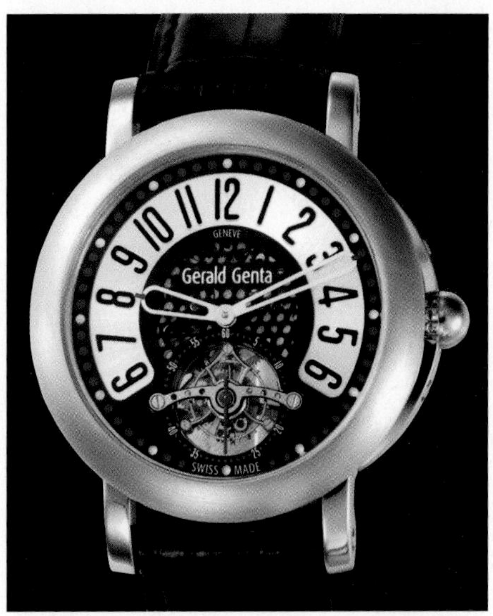

Arena Tourbillon Retrograde Hours

Reference number: ATR.X.75.911.CN.BD

Movement: automatic, Gérald Genta 9053, ø 29 mm, height 5.9 mm; 54 jewels; 21,600 vph, one-minute tourbillon; two spring barrels, power reserve 64 hours; movement completely gold-plated and decorated

Functions: hours (retrograde), minutes, subsidiary seconds (on tourbillon cage)

Case: platinum, ø 41 mm, height 13.15 mm; bezel made of palladium; sapphire crystal; water-resistant to 100 m

Band: reptile skin, folding clasp

Price: $106,000

Variations: with diamonds on the bezel

Arena GMT Perpetual Calendar

Reference number: AQG.Y.87.129.CM.BD

Movement: automatic, Gérald Genta 7044, ø 30 mm, height 4.98 mm; 27 jewels; 28,800 vph, movement completely gold-plated and decorated

Functions: hours, minutes, sweep seconds; perpetual calendar with date, day, month, leap year; 24-hour display (second time zone)

Case: titanium, ø 45 mm, height 13.9 mm; bezel made of platinum; sapphire crystal; water-resistant to 100 m

Band: reptile skin, folding clasp

Price: $55,500

Variations: in white gold with rubber bezel and strap

Arena Tourbillon Perpetual Calendar Moon Phase

Reference number: ATM.X.75.860.CN.BD

Movement: automatic, Gérald Genta 12110, ø 31 mm, height 7.4 mm; 43 jewels; 21,600 vph, one-minute tourbillon; two spring barrels, power reserve 64 hours; movement completely gold-plated and decorated

Functions: hours, minutes; perpetual calendar with date, day, month, leap year, moon phase; power reserve display

Case: platinum, ø 41 mm, height 14.3 mm; bezel made of palladium; sapphire crystal; water-resistant to 100 m

Band: reptile skin, folding clasp

Price: $146,300

Sport Bi Retro

Reference number: BSP.Y.10.125.LN.BD

Movement: automatic, Gérald Genta 7710, ø 26 mm, height 5.93 mm; 21 jewels; 28,800 vph

Functions: hours (jump), minutes (retrograde); date (retrograde)

Case: stainless steel, ø 45 mm, height 10.2 mm; sapphire crystal

Band: leather, folding clasp

Price: $8,800

Variations: with rubber strap; with diamonds

Gevril

The idyllically forested and equally peaceful highs and lows of the Swiss Jura mountains have traditionally been a mecca of watchmaking creativity. It was here that many world-famous names cultivated their talents and lay down the foundations for companies and legacies that would survive both the ravages of time and the quartz boom of the 1970s. Jacques Gévril certainly numbered as one of the gifted watchmakers of the eighteenth century to make a name for himself here.

Born in 1722 in La Chaux-de-Fonds, Gévril began his career as a restorer of timepieces, creating his first chronometer in 1743. He invented many watch and clock movements, and in the year 1744 he made horological history by creating a repetition dial. In 1758 he became the first Swiss watchmaker to ever export a timepiece, together with Pierre Jaquet Droz, and the recipient of this original work was the king of Spain. He was subsequently named watchmaker to the Spanish crown, remaining behind when Jaquet Droz returned to Switzerland. Gévril's family continued in the watchmaking tradition for a few generations, creating many fine and unique timepieces along the way that may still be found in the world's best watch museums. Eventually, however, the company closed, becoming another historic name lying dormant for a modern entrepreneur to reawaken like Sleeping Beauty.

This happened in the early 1990s when Switzerland's UTime, an international distribution conglomerate handling some of the most prestigious names in the business, purchased the rights to the Gevril name and created a high-end line with some interesting characteristics — such as the unlocked crown indicator and the exchangeable bezel system. In the late '90s, UTime disbanded and sold the rights to all of the brands it owned. After a brief stint with an American jeweler, in 2001 Gevril was bought by First SBF Holding, spearheaded and masterminded by Samuel Friedmann.

Friedmann, born in 1970 in Lugano, Switzerland, is a man with a long history in the watch business. His lifelong dream was to own his own watch brand, and he patiently waited for many years until the right brand name came along. Although he possessed the know-how and connections to have created his own brand at any time, he was painfully aware of the advantages of a name with a certain history, and when the Gevril name once again became available, he lost no time in fulfilling his destiny. His was a passion that was awakened for the first time at age seventeen. The youth, wanting to buy a watch for his brother, noticed that the particular Swiss city he was in contained a myriad of watch stores. He became fascinated by the ticking timepieces and their fine blend of art and science and immediately decided to enter the watch business, bucking a career in his family's upscale clothing boutiques. After graduating from college, Friedmann opened a sales office in Lugano that sold complicated pieces to collectors and also dealt in liquidation of overstocked watches. His later move to the United States had more to do with the love for his American wife than for watches, and today Friedmann is headquartered in New York, although he is more often than not to be found at the workshop in Tramelan, Switzerland, rather than the 6,000-square-foot villa that he has made into Gevril's head office.

Well equipped to lead his company into the new century, Friedmann has set his sights on quality and building the brand. In just four years, the collection has grown to encompass seven watch families and more than seventy models. The standout timepiece for the 2004/2005 season is the new Serenade. Housed in a characteristically large rectangular Avenue of Americas case, the Serenade is run by a movement designed by Gevril in cooperation with Swiss movement specialists. This movement powers the unique displays that illustrate two separate time zones and their accompanying day/night indicators. The Serenade is available only in a very limited edition of fifty pieces each of 18-karat rose gold, 18-karat white gold, and platinum.

Avenue of Americas Chronograph

Reference number: 5111
Movement: automatic, GV AOAWZ1(baseDubois-Dépraz 2020/ETA 2824); ø 30 mm, height 7.5 mm; 51 jewels; 28,800 vph
Functions: hours, minutes, subsidiary seconds; chronograph
Case: rose gold, 44 x 34 mm, height 12.25 mm; sapphire crystal; transparent case back; water-resistant to 50 m
Band: crocodile skin, buckle
Remarks: limited edition of 100 pieces
Price: $10,995

Avenue of Americas Day-Date-Moon Phase

Reference number: 5034
Movement: automatic, GV AOA71L(baseDubois-Dépraz 9319/ETA 2824); ø 25.98 mm, height 6.2 mm; 25 jewels; 28,800 vph
Functions: hours, minutes, sweep seconds; day, date, month; moon phase
Case: stainless steel, 44 x 34 mm, height 12.25 mm; sapphire crystal; transparent case back; water-resistant to 50 m
Band: crocodile skin, buckle
Remarks: limited edition of 500 pieces
Price: $15,995

Avenue of Americas GMT Power Reserve

Reference number: 5022
Movement: automatic, GV AOAX32(baseETA 2892-A2); ø 26 mm, height 5.2 mm; 25 jewels; 28,800 vph
Functions: hours, minutes, sweep seconds; date; power reserve display, GMT
Case: stainless steel, 44 x 34 mm, height 12.25 mm; sapphire crystal; transparent case back; water-resistant to 50 m
Band: crocodile skin, buckle
Remarks: limited edition of 500 pieces
Price: $7,995

Avenue of Americas GMT Power Reserve

Reference number: 5025
Movement: automatic, GV AOAX32(baseETA2892-A2); ø 26 mm, height 5.2 mm; 25 jewels; 28,800 vph
Functions: hours, minutes, sweep seconds; date; power reserve display, GMT
Case: stainless steel, 44 x 34 mm, height 12.25 mm; sapphire crystal; transparent case back; water-resistant to 50 m
Band: crocodile skin, buckle
Remarks: limited edition of 500 pieces
Price: $7,995

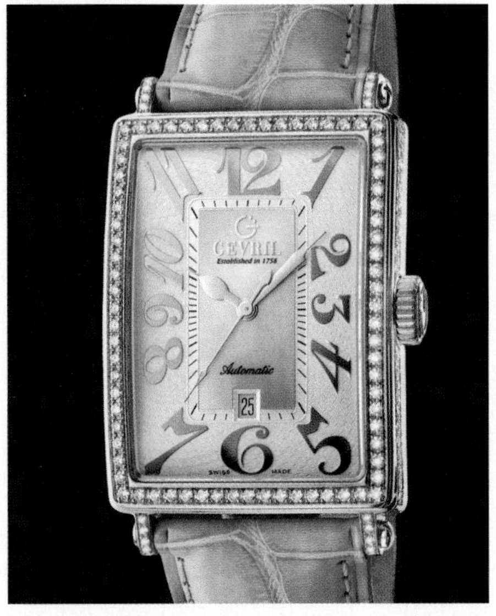

Avenue of Americas Glamour Collection

Reference number: 6207NV
Movement: automatic, GV AOA3J1(baseETA 2892-A2); ø 26 mm, height 4.6 mm; 25 jewels; 28,800 vph
Functions: hours, minutes, sweep seconds; date
Case: stainless steel, 44 x 34 mm, height 12.25 mm; case, bezel, lugs, and buckle set with 2.25 ct. diamonds; sapphire crystal; transparent case back; water-resistant to 50 m
Band: crocodile skin, buckle
Remarks: limited edition of 100 pieces
Price: $14,995
Variations: available with various combinations of diamonds ($8,495 to $15,995)

Lafayette

Reference number: 2912
Movement: automatic,GV 993(baseDubois-Dépraz 2020/ETA 2824); ø 30 mm, height 7.5 mm; 51 jewels; 28,800 vph
Functions: hours, minutes, subsidiary seconds; chronograph
Case: stainless steel, ø 37 mm, height 14.25 mm; bezel set with 1 ct. diamonds; Hesalite crystal; water-resistant to 100 m
Band: crocodile skin, buckle
Remarks: limited edition of 500 pieces
Price: $8,495
Variations: available without diamonds on the bezel ($5,295)

Madison

Reference number: 2502L
Movement: automatic, GV 834(baseETA 2895); ø 25.98 mm, height 6.2 mm; 30 jewels; 28,800 vph
Functions: hours, minutes, subsidiary seconds; date
Case: stainless steel, ø 39 mm, height 12.4 mm; sapphire crystal; transparent case back; water-resistant to 50 m
Band: crocodile skin, buckle
Remarks: limited edition of 500 pieces
Price: $2,495

Gramercy

Reference number: 2401
Movement: automatic, GV 182(baseJB 876/ETA 2824); ø 26 mm, height 6 mm; 31 jewels; 28,800 vph, regulator arrangement
Functions: hours, mintues, seconds
Case: stainless steel, ø 39 mm, height 11.65 mm; sapphire crystal; transparent case back; water-resistant to 50 m
Band: stainless steel, folding clasp
Remarks: limited edition of 500 pieces
Price: $3,995

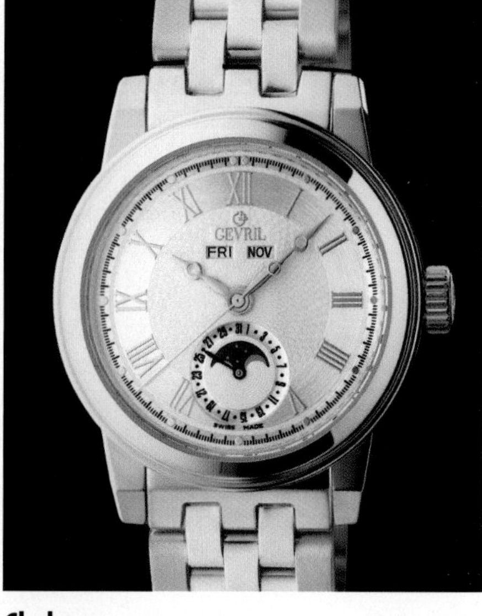

Chelsea

Reference number: 2305L
Movement: automatic, GV 934(baseDubois-Dépraz 9310/ETA 2824); ø 25.98 mm, height 6.2 mm; 25 jewels; 28,800 vph
Functions: hours, minutes, sweep seconds; date, day, month; moon phase
Case: yellow gold, ø 39 mm, height 12.4 mm; sapphire crystal; transparent case back; water-resistant to 50 m
Band: yellow gold, folding clasp
Remarks: limited edition of 100 pieces
Price: $15,995

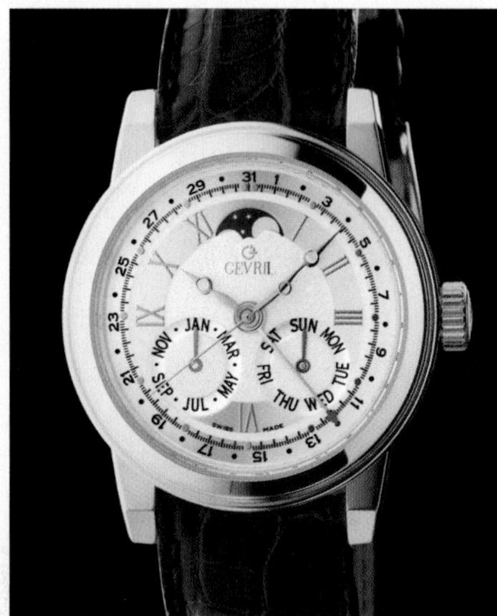

Soho Deluxe

Reference number: 2605L
Movement: automatic, GV 6113(baseDubois-Dépraz 9200/ETA 2824); ø 25.98 mm, height 6.2 mm; 25 jewels; 28,800 vph
Functions: hours, minutes, sweep seconds; date, day, month; moon phase
Case: yellow gold, ø 39 mm, height 12.4 mm; sapphire crystal; transparent case back; water-resistant to 50 m
Band: crocodile skin, buckle
Remarks: limited edition of 100 pieces
Price: $17,495

Sea Cloud

Reference number: 3107
Movement: automatic, GV 7B89(baseDubois-Dépraz 2020/ETA 2824); ø 30 mm, height 7.5 mm; 51 jewels; 28,800 vph
Functions: hours, minutes, subsidiary seconds; chronograph
Case: stainless steel, ø 40 mm, height 14.1 mm; unidirectionally rotating bezel in 18-kt. gold embossed with minute scale; sapphire crystal, anti-reflective; scewed-down case back; screw-in crown and buttons; water-resistant to 200 m
Band: stainless steel, folding clasp
Remarks: limited edition of 500 pieces
Price: $5,995

Mini Collection

Reference number: 7249NV
Movement: quartz, ETA 956 612, ø 19 mm, height 4 mm; 7 jewels
Functions: hours, mintues, sweep seconds
Case: stainless steel, 25 x 33 mm, height 9 mm; diamond-set bezel; sapphire crystal, anti-reflective; water-resistant to 50 m
Band: leather, buckle
Remarks: diamonds on buckle
Price: $9,995
Variations: with bracelet ($10,495) or rubber strap ($9,995); available with pink, green or blue mother-of-pearl dials and a variety of leather straps

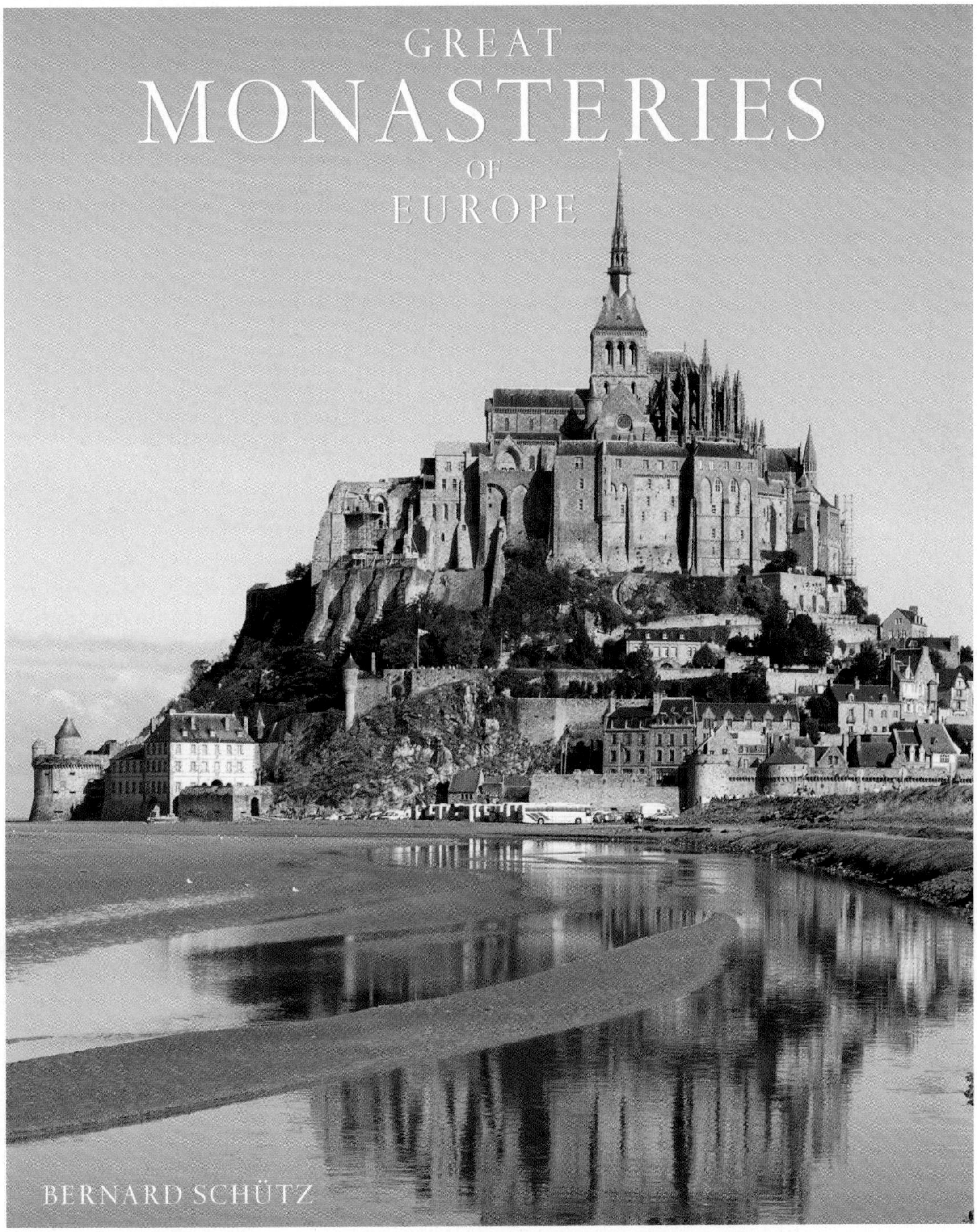
GREAT
MONASTERIES
OF
EUROPE
BERNARD SCHÜTZ

Girard-Perregaux

Moving in and opening the new *manufacture* building a year ago in upper La Chaux-de-Fonds fulfilled a longtime dream for the president of the SoWind Group and GP captain Dr. Luigi Macaluso. In 1992 the engineer took over the somewhat dusty traditional brand, and as fast as you can say "tourbillon" made it into one of the leading watch *manufactures* for complicated timepieces. The brand already had the prerequisites: A more than 200-year-old history rich in records and spectacular designs and spatial conditions that weren't all that bad.

But it was only through the systematic acquisition of property and empty buildings around the main factory located on Place Girardet that it became possible to cleanly separate production workshops, representation space, and management offices for the two watch brands Girard-Perregaux and JeanRichard from each other while keeping them connected by short pathways. Villa JeanRichard and its museum for tools and tooling machines is located just a few steps away from the Girard-Perregaux Museum within Villa Marguerite, and in between them the main factory and manufacturing buildings pretty much take up the rest of the block.

New editions of the legendary tourbillon models with gold bridges, enchanting minute repeaters, and chronograph specialties ensure that this company will retain its prominent position among the genuine Swiss *manufactures*.

This year, the relaunch of the Laureato was on center stage. In the 1970s, this noble sports watch took its place in history when the case, which features a striking screwed-down hexagonal bezel, housed a highly precise quartz caliber of the company's own production (Girard-Perregaux was in fact a pioneer in this technology, establishing today's valid oscillation frequency of 32,768 Hz). In the eighties, the model disappeared from the collection, but was dusted off once again in 1995, stylistically reworked, and outfitted with the *manufacture* caliber GP 3100. A chronograph version was even introduced, as well as a variation containing the legendary Tourbillon under Three Gold Bridges, causing quite an uproar in the industry.

Another revamped model has now been introduced: The third generation is called Laureato EVO 3 and (at first) will concentrate on an automatic chronograph whose movement comprises extra-flat Caliber 3300 and a module powering the chronograph functions. Like its predecessors, this third level of evolution is housed in a solid stainless steel case of the best craftsmanship that shows its special charm in the interplay between the satin-finished and polished surfaces. The striking hexagonal bezel on the EVO 3 is matte, highlighted by the buttons, crown, totalizers on the dial, and the middle links of the new bracelet.

Girard-Perregaux's ties to the Italian race and sports car manufacturer Ferrari is currently manifested in the form of a tourbillon chronograph with perpetual calendar. Honoring Enzo Ferrari, who lends the masterpiece his name, it is being manufactured in a limited edition as is the powerful sports car from Maranello of the same name. In addition, new annual chronograph editions have been issued to commemorate races and championships that have been won. And as long as the red racers continue winning on the racetracks of this world, the new timepiece editions will certainly keep coming.

Tribute to Enzo Ferrari

Reference number: 99190.0.71.6156
Movement: manual winding, GP 9982, ø 29.4 mm; 46 jewels; 21,600 vph, one-minute tourbillon under three gold bridges
Functions: hours, minutes, subsidiary seconds; chronograph; perpetual calendar with date, day, month, moon phase, leap year
Case: platinum, ø 43 mm, height 11 mm; sapphire crystal; transparent case back
Band: reptile skin, folding clasp
Price: $220,000

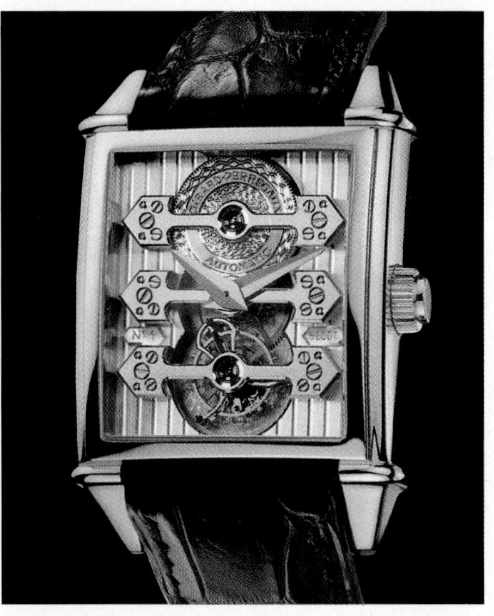

Vintage Tourbillon with 3 Gold Bridges

Reference number: 99870.0.52.000
Movement: automatic, GP 9600C, 32 jewels; 21,600 vph, one-minute tourbillon; microrotor
Functions: hours, minutes
Case: red gold, 32 x 32 mm, height 11.95 mm; sapphire crystal
Band: reptile skin, folding clasp
Price: $110,000
Variations: in yellow, white or red gold; in platinum

Vintage 1945 Tourbillon with 1 Gold Bridge

Reference number: 99850.0.52.815
Movement: automatic, GP 9610C, 32 jewels; 21,600 vph, one-minute tourbillon; microrotor
Functions: hours, minutes
Case: red gold, 32 x 32 mm, height 11.95 mm; sapphire crystal
Band: reptile skin, folding clasp
Price: $95,000
Variations: in yellow, rose or white gold; in platinum

Sea Hawk II PRO

Reference number: 49940.0.21.6117
Movement: automatic, GP 33RO (base GP 3300); ø 25.6 mm, height 4.55 mm; 27 jewels; 28,800 vph
Functions: hours, minutes, sweep seconds; date; power reserve display
Case: titanium, ø 44 mm; unidirectionally rotating bezel with 60-minute scale; sapphire crystal (4.85 mm thick); screw-in crown; water-resistant to 3000 m
Band: rubber, folding clasp
Remarks: case with helium valve
Price: $7,250
Variations: with titanium bracelet

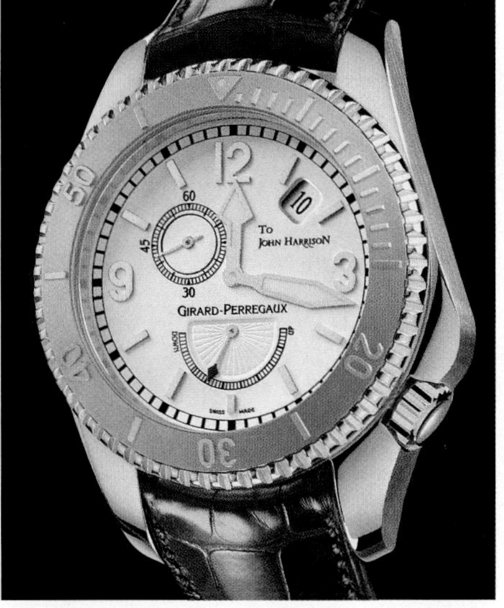

Sea Hawk II John Harrison

Reference number: 49910.0.51.7147
Movement: automatic, GP 33RO (base GP 3300); ø 25.6 mm, height 4.55 mm; 27 jewels; 28,800 vph, certified chronometer (C.O.S.C.)
Functions: hours, minutes, subsidiary seconds; date; power reserve display
Case: yellow gold, ø 42 mm; unidirectionally rotating bezel with 60-minute scale; sapphire crystal; screw-in crown; water-resistant to 300 m
Band: reptile skin, folding clasp
Price: $18,500
Variations: in rose gold; in stainless steel with white gold bezel

Sea Hawk II

Reference number: 49900.1.11.6146
Movement: automatic, GP 33RO (base GP 3300); ø 25.6 mm, height 4.55 mm; 27 jewels; 28,800 vph
Functions: hours, minutes, sweep seconds; date; power reserve display
Case: stainless steel, ø 42 mm; unidirectionally rotating bezel with 60-minute scale; sapphire crystal; screw-in crown; water-resistant to 300 m
Band: stainless steel, folding clasp
Price: $5,950
Variations: with rubber strap/folding clasp; in titanium, with rubber strap, with titanium bracelet

Vintage XXL Perpetual Calendar

Reference number: 90270.0.52.6175
Movement: automatic, GP 3170, ø 30 mm; 44 jewels; 28,800 vph
Functions: hours, minutes, subsidiary seconds; chronograph; perpetual calendar with date, day, month, moon phase, leap year
Case: rose gold, 36 x 37 mm, height 14.9 mm; sapphire crystal; transparent case back
Band: reptile skin, folding clasp
Price: $42,500
Variations: in white gold

Vintage Foudroyante XXL

Reference number: 90210.0.53.6046
Movement: automatic, GP E04C0 (base ETA 7750); ø 30 mm; 40 jewels; 28,800 vph, mechanism for foudroyante 1/8 seconds with its own spring barrel
Functions: hours, minutes, subsidiary seconds; split seconds chronograph with foudroyante seconds (1/8-seconds counter)
Case: white gold, 37 x 37 mm, height 8.7 mm; sapphire crystal
Band: reptile skin, folding clasp
Price: $29,500
Variations: in yellow or rose gold

Vintage 1945 Large Date Moon Phase

Reference number: 25800.0.52.815
Movement: automatic, GP 3330 (base GP 3300); ø 28.6 mm, height 4.9 mm; 32 jewels; 28,800 vph
Functions: hours, minutes, subsidiary seconds; large date; moon phase
Case: red gold, 32 x 32 mm, height 11.2 mm; sapphire crystal; transparent case back
Band: reptile skin, folding clasp
Price: $13,500
Variations: in yellow gold; in white gold

Vintage 1945 Power Reserve

Reference number: 25850.0.52.6456
Movement: automatic, GP 33R0 (base GP 3300); ø 25.6 mm, height 4.55 mm; 27 jewels; 28,800 vph
Functions: hours, minutes, subsidiary seconds; date; power reserve display
Case: red gold, 32 x 32 mm, height 11.2 mm; sapphire crystal; transparent case back
Band: reptile skin, folding clasp
Price: $12,500
Variations: in yellow gold; in white gold

Vintage 1945 King Size

Reference number: 25830.0.11.1141
Movement: automatic, GP 3300, ø 25.6 mm, height 3.28 mm; 28 jewels; 28,800 vph
Functions: hours, minutes, subsidiary seconds; date
Case: stainless steel, 32 x 32 mm, height 11 mm; sapphire crystal; transparent case back
Band: reptile skin, buckle
Price: $5,250
Variations: with stainless steel bracelet

Vintage 1945 Automatic

Reference number: 25960.0.52.1161
Movement: automatic, GP 3200, 22 x 23.1 mm, height 3.2 mm; 28 jewels; 28,800 vph
Functions: hours, minutes, subsidiary seconds; date
Case: red gold, 29 x 28 mm; sapphire crystal; transparent case back
Band: reptile skin, buckle
Price: $8,500
Variations: with red gold bracelet; in white gold with leather strap; in yellow gold with leather strap

Cat's Eye Power Reserve

Reference number: 08048D0A53.22L2
Movement: automatic, GP 33R0 (base GP 3300); ø 25.6 mm, height 4.55 mm; 27 jewels; 28,800 vph
Functions: hours, minutes, subsidiary seconds; power reserve display
Case: white gold, 35.24 x 30.24 mm, height 10.45 mm; bezel set with 68 diamonds; sapphire crystal; transparent case back
Band: satin, folding clasp
Price: $18,500

Cat's Eye Moon Phase

Reference number: 08049D0A51.72L7
Movement: automatic, GP 33R0 (base GP 3300); ø 25.6 mm, height 4.55 mm; 27 jewels; 28,800 vph
Functions: hours, minutes, subsidiary seconds; moon phase
Case: yellow gold, 30.24 x 35.24 mm, height 10.45 mm; bezel set with 68 diamonds; sapphire crystal; transparent case back
Band: satin, folding clasp
Price: $17,500

Richeville Lady Chronograph Joaillerie

Reference number: 02650B0R53.7287
Movement: automatic, GP 3080 (base GP 3000); ø 23.3 mm, height 6.28 mm; 38 jewels; 28,800 vph, column-wheel control of the chronograph functions
Functions: hours, minutes, subsidiary seconds; chronograph
Case: white gold, 29.8 x 30 mm, height 12 mm; bezel and case sides set with 44 baguette-cut diamonds and 214 brilliant-cut diamonds; sapphire crystal
Band: satin, folding clasp
Price: $75,000
Variations: different gemstones

Richeville Lady Chronograph

Reference number: 26500.0.51.72M7
Movement: automatic, GP 30CG, ø 23.3 mm, height 6.28 mm; 38 jewels; 28,800 vph
Functions: hours, minutes, subsidiary seconds; chronograph
Case: yellow gold, 29.8 x 30 mm, height 11.9 mm; sapphire crystal; transparent case back
Band: reptile skin, buckle
Price: $12,500
Variations: in red gold, in white gold

Richeville Large Date Moon Phase

Reference number: 27600.0.52.6151
Movement: automatic, GP 3330 (base GP 3300); ø 28.6 mm, height 4.9 mm; 32 jewels; 28,800 vph
Functions: hours, minutes, subsidiary seconds; large date; moon phase
Case: rose gold, 37 x 37 mm, height 10.5 mm; sapphire crystal
Band: reptile skin, folding clasp
Price: $15,000
Variations: in yellow gold; in white gold

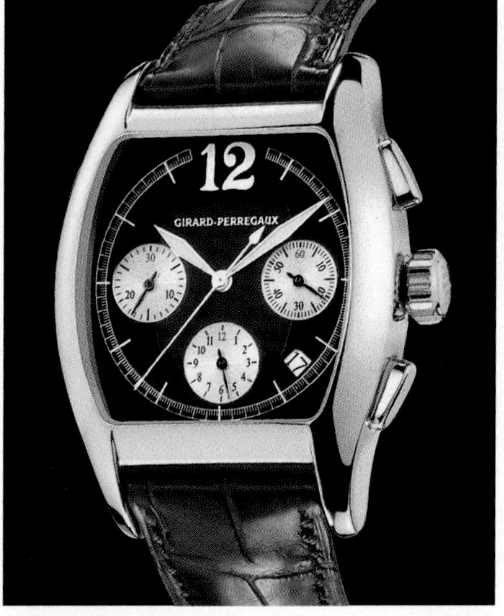

Richeville Chronograph

Reference number: 27650.0.52.6151
Movement: automatic, GP 3370 (base GP 3300 with module Dubois-Depraz 2021); ø 25.6/30 mm, height 6.5 mm; 63 jewels; 28,800 vph
Functions: hours, minutes, subsidiary seconds; chronograph; date
Case: red gold, 37 x 37 mm, height 12.5 mm; sapphire crystal; transparent case back
Band: reptile skin, folding clasp
Price: $15,000
Variations: in yellow gold, in white gold, in stainless steel

Large Date with Moon Phase

Reference number: 49530.0.53.4124
Movement: automatic, GP 3330 (base GP 3300); ø 28.6 mm, height 4.9 mm; 32 jewels; 28,800 vph
Functions: hours, minutes, subsidiary seconds; large date; moon phase
Case: white gold, ø 40 mm; sapphire crystal; transparent case back
Band: reptile skin, buckle
Price: $14,500
Variations: in yellow or red gold

ww.tc World Time Chronograph

Reference number: 49800.0.53.6146A
Movement: automatic, GP 3387 (base GP 3300 with chronograph module by Dubois-Dépraz and 24-hour module by GP); ø 30 mm, height 8 mm; 63 jewels; 28,800 vph
Functions: hours, minutes, subsidiary seconds; chronograph; date; world time (24-hour display)
Case: white gold, ø 43 mm, height 13.4 mm; bidirectionally rotating bezel with 24-hour scale under crystal; sapphire crystal; transparent case back; screw-in crown
Band: reptile skin, buckle
Price: $22,500
Variations: in titanium; in yellow or rose gold; in platinum

Traveller II

Reference number: 49350.0.11.614
Movement: automatic, GP 3387 (base AS 5008 with 24-h display by Dubois-Dépraz); ø 30 mm, height 7.75 mm; 31 jewels; 28,800 vph
Functions: hours, minutes, sweep seconds; date; 24-hour display (second time zone); alarm
Case: stainless steel, ø 40 mm, height 13.2 mm; sapphire crystal
Band: reptile skin, buckle
Price: $5,250
Variations: with stainless steel bracelet; in yellow or rose gold; in white gold

Laureato EVO3

Reference number: 80180.1.11.6516
Movement: automatic, GP 33CO-AOVAA, ø 26.2 mm; 52 jewels; 28,800 vph, sweep chronograph minute counter
Functions: hours, minutes, subsidiary seconds; chronograph; date; 24-hour display (second time zone)
Case: stainless steel, ø 44 mm, height 15.1 mm; sapphire crystal; transparent case back; screw-in crown; water-resistant to 50 m
Band: stainless steel, folding clasp
Price: $9,950
Variations: with light-colored dial

Vintage 1945 Lady Souveraine

Reference number: 25730.0.51.11M
Movement: automatic, GP 3200T (base GP 3200); 22 x 23.1 mm, height 3.28 mm; 27 jewels; 28,800 vph
Functions: hours, minutes, sweep seconds
Case: yellow gold, 26.5 x 26 mm; sapphire crystal
Band: reptile skin, buckle
Price: $9,250
Variations: in yellow or red gold, with leather strap; in white gold, with leather strap, with white gold bracelet

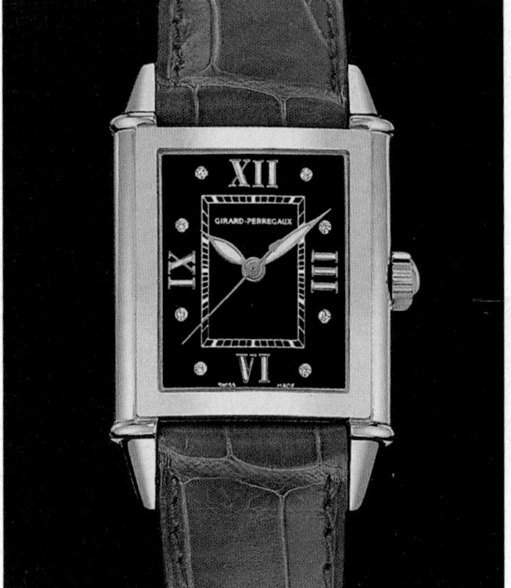

Vintage 1945 Lady Souveraine

Reference number: 25740.0.11.61M
Movement: quartz, GP 1310
Functions: hours, minutes, sweep seconds
Case: stainless steel, 26.5 x 26 mm; sapphire crystal
Band: reptile skin, buckle
Price: $4,250
Variations: in yellow or rose gold; in white gold; with stainless steel bracelet; with diamond bezel and stainless steel bracelet

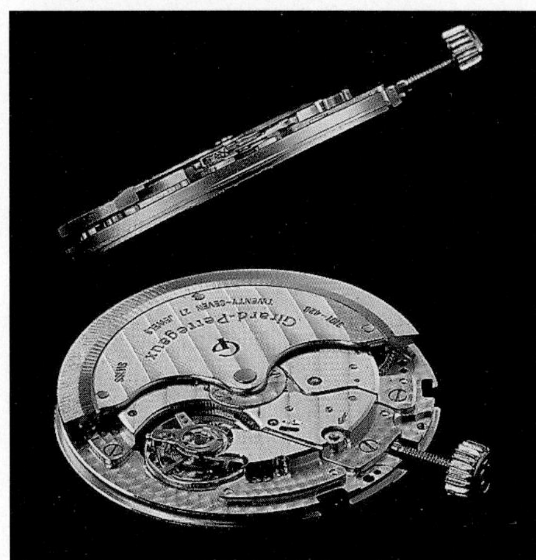

Caliber 3100

Mechanical with automatic winding, power reserve 42 hours
Functions: hours, minutes, sweep seconds; date
Diameter: 11‴ (26 mm)
Height: 2.98 mm
Jewels: 27
Balance: glucydur
Frequency: 28,800 vph
Balance spring: Nivarox 1 flat hairspring, fine adjustment via micrometer screw
Shock protection: Kif
Related caliber: 3000 (diameter 23.9 mm)

Caliber 3300

Base caliber: 3000/3100
Mechanical with automatic winding, power reserve 42 hours
Functions: hours, minutes, sweep seconds
Diameter: 11‴ (26 mm)
Height: 3.28 mm
Jewels: 27
Balance: glucydur
Frequency: 28,800 vph
Balance spring: Nivarox
Shock protection: Kif
Related calibers: 3200 (with date); 3320 (with date and power reserve display); 3330 (with large date and moon phase); 3370 (chronograph module); 3387 (chronograph module with world time indication)

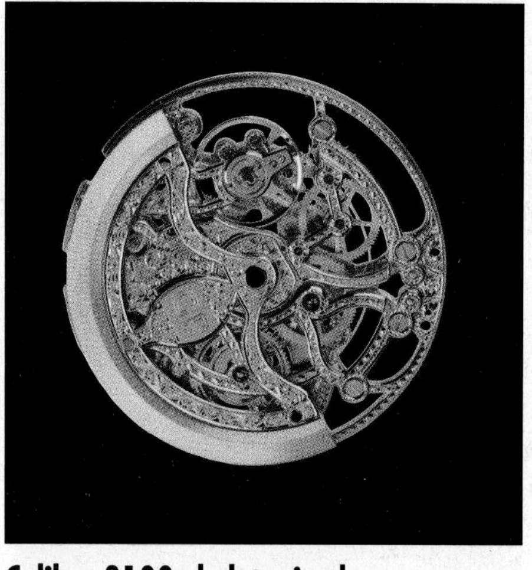

Caliber 3100 skeletonized

Mechanical with automatic winding, power reserve 42 hours
Functions: hours, minutes, sweep seconds
Diameter: 11 ‴ (26 mm)
Height: 2.98 mm
Jewels: 27
Balance: glucydur
Frequency: 28,800 vph
Balance spring: Nivarox
Shock protection: Kif
Remarks: movement completely skeletonized and engraved by hand

Caliber 3080 (dial side)

Mechanical with automatic winding, power reserve 42 hours
Functions: hours, minutes, subsidiary seconds; chronograph; date
Diameter: 10 ‴ (23.9 mm)
Height: 6.28 mm
Jewels: 38
Balance: glucydur
Frequency: 28,800 vph
Balance spring: Nivarox
Shock protection: Kif
Remarks: column-wheel control of chronograph functions

Caliber 9600

Mechanical with automatic winding; one-minute tourbillon; power reserve 48 hours
Functions: hours, minutes, subsidiary seconds (on tourbillon cage)
Diameter: 28.6 mm
Height: 6.22 mm
Jewels: 30
Frequency: 21,600 vph
Remarks: patented design of the tourbillon under three gold bridges; automatic winding with micro-rotor made of platinum

Glashütte Original

For more than 150 years, fine German watchmaking has been at home in Germany's Erzgebirge mountains. The precision watches made by Julius Assmann, F. A. Lange, and Alfred Helwig made Glashütter Uhrenbetriebe, located in the picturesque Müglitz Valley, famous far beyond Germany's borders. This watch *manufacture* continues in the tradition of these old masters by combining the most modern production technology with traditional craft, resulting in an above-average depth of production: From the smallest screw to the most complicated caliber, the lion's share of the parts needed for a watch is produced on-premises.

The new factory building allows an extra-ordinarily transparent view into all of the production areas of watchmaking, from the manufacture and finishing of the most miniscule parts to the assembly of complete watches. This modern production building stands for the virtues that have determined the actions of Glashütte's master watchmakers since 1845: precision, reliability, functionality, and aesthetics. A learning path leads interested visitors through three floors, making a unique look into the fascinating world of fine German watchmaking possible. In this way, guests are able to experience firsthand the character of an authentic and complete *manufacture*.

The newest technologies are used where precision and functionality are called for. In the spirit of the tradition they represent, the tiny components are finely finished and decorated by hand according to processes that have been handed down through generations. Even the outer appearance of mechanical timekeepers made by Glashütte Original communicate a "practical luxury" in form and design as it is traditionally executed in Germany: not superficial, but substantial.

Against this background so rich in tradition, another horological highlight of the Glashütte Original collection was presented in 2004: the automatic chronograph *PanoMaticChrono*. This new product combines the finest watchmaking with a unique aesthetic experience. Caliber 95, especially developed for the *PanoMaticChrono*, is a masterpiece in watchmaking that includes a great deal of technical innovation. The winding mechanism has been outfitted with a rotor that winds bilaterally, as well as a stepped gear that transmits its energy to two serially operating spring barrels. The stepped gear adjusts itself to the movement behavior of its wearer, thus making a targeted transmission of winding energy to the barrels possible and switching to unilateral winding when necessary. In this way, wear and tear to components are reduced to a minimum.

PanoMaticChrono

Reference number: 95-01-03-03-04
Movement: automatic, Glashütte Original 95-01, ø 32.2 mm, height 7.3 mm; 41 jewels; 28,800 vph, bilaterally winding centered rotor via step gears
Functions: hours, minutes, subsidiary seconds; chronograph with flyback function; panorama date
Case: platinum, ø 39.4 mm, height 12.3 mm; sapphire crystal; transparent case back
Band: reptile skin, buckle
Remarks: limited to 200 pieces
Price: $44,500

PanoMaticChrono

Reference number: 95-01-01-01-04
Movement: automatic, Glashütte Original 95-01, ø 32.2 mm, height 7.3 mm; 41 jewels; 28,800 vph, bilaterally winding centered rotor via step gears
Functions: hours, minutes, subsidiary seconds; chronograph with flyback function; panorama date
Case: rose gold, ø 39.4 mm, height 12.3 mm; sapphire crystal; transparent case back
Band: reptile skin, double folding clasp
Price: $37,250

PanoMaticTourbillon

Reference number: 93-01-03-03-04
Movement: automatic, Glashütte Original 93, ø 32.2 mm, height 7.65 mm; 40 jewels plus two diamond endstones; 21,600 vph, flying one-minute tourbillon
Functions: hours, minutes (off-center), subsidiary seconds (on tourbillon cage); panorama date
Case: platinum, ø 39.4 mm, height 12.3 mm; sapphire crystal; transparent case back
Band: reptile skin, buckle
Remarks: limited to 50 pieces
Price: $88,000

PanoRetroGraph

Reference number: 60-01-04-03-04
Movement: manual winding, Glashütte Original 60, ø 32.2 mm, height 7.2 mm; 54 jewels; 28,800 vph
Functions: hours, minutes, subsidiary seconds; chronograph with flyback and countdown functions with acoustic signal; panorama date
Case: rose gold, ø 39.4 mm, height 13.3 mm; sapphire crystal; transparent case back
Band: reptile skin, double folding clasp
Price: $49,000
Variations: in platinum, limited to 50 pieces; in white gold, limited to 150 pieces

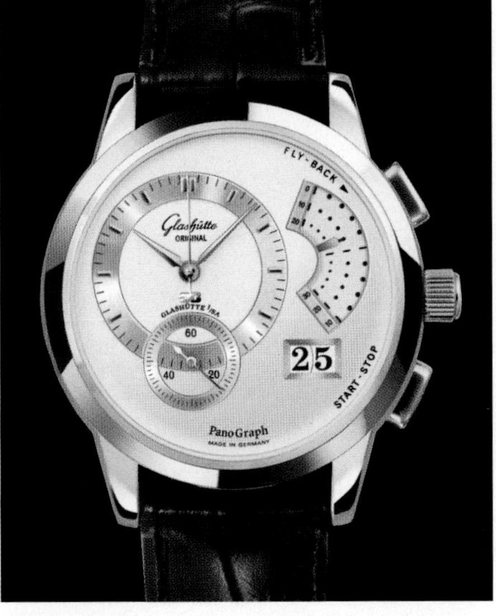

PanoGraph

Reference number: 61-01-02-02-04
Movement: manual winding, Glashütte Original 61, ø 32.2 mm, height 7.2 mm; 41 jewels; 28,800 vph
Functions: hours, minutes, subsidiary seconds; chronograph with flyback function; panorama date
Case: stainless steel, ø 39.4 mm, height 13.3 mm; sapphire crystal; transparent case back
Band: reptile skin, double folding clasp
Price: $11,300
Variations: in rose gold; in platinum, limited to 200 pieces

PanoReserve

Reference number: 65-01-01-01-04
Movement: manual winding, Glashütte Original 65-01, ø 32.2 mm, height 6.1 mm; 48 jewels; 28,800 vph
Functions: hours, minutes, subsidiary seconds; panorama date; power reserve display
Case: rose gold, ø 39.4 mm, height 11 mm; sapphire crystal; transparent case back
Band: reptile skin, double folding clasp
Price: $13,700
Variations: in stainless steel; in platinum, limited to 200 pieces

PanoMaticDate

Reference number: 90-01-02-02-04
Movement: automatic, Glashütte Original 90-01, ø 32.6 mm, height 7 mm; 47 jewels; 28,800 vph, off-center rotor; duplex swan-neck fine adjustment
Functions: hours, minutes, subsidiary seconds; panorama date
Case: stainless steel, ø 39.4 mm, height 11.9 mm; sapphire crystal; transparent case back
Band: reptile skin, buckle
Price: $6,950
Variations: in rose gold; in platinum, limited to 200 pieces

PanoMaticDate

Reference number: 90-01-01-01-04
Movement: automatic, Glashütte Original 90-01, ø 32.6 mm, height 7 mm; 47 jewels; 28,800 vph, off-center rotor; duplex swan-neck fine adjustment
Functions: hours, minutes, subsidiary seconds; panorama date
Case: rose gold, ø 39.4 mm, height 11.9 mm; sapphire crystal; transparent case back
Band: reptile skin, buckle
Price: $12,350
Variations: in stainless steel; in platinum, limited to 200 pieces

Senator Perpetual Calendar

Reference number: 39-50-08-15-04
Movement: automatic, Glashütte Original 39-50, ø 31.15 mm, height 7.2 mm; 48 jewels; 28,800 vph
Functions: hours, minutes, sweep seconds; perpetual calendar with panorama date, day, month, moon phase, leap year
Case: platinum, ø 39.3 mm, height 12.8 mm; sapphire crystal; transparent case back; water-resistant to 50 m
Band: reptile skin, buckle
Price: $23,750
Variations: in stainless steel; in rose gold

PanoMaticLunar

Reference number: 90-02-02-02-04
Movement: automatic, Glashütte Original 90-02, ø 32.6 mm, height 7 mm; 47 jewels; 28,800 vph, off-center rotor; duplex swan-neck fine adjustment
Functions: hours, minutes, subsidiary seconds; panorama date; moon phase
Case: stainless steel, ø 39.4 mm, height 11.9 mm; sapphire crystal; transparent case back
Band: reptile skin, double folding clasp
Price: $8,000
Variations: in rose gold; in platinum, limited to 200 pieces

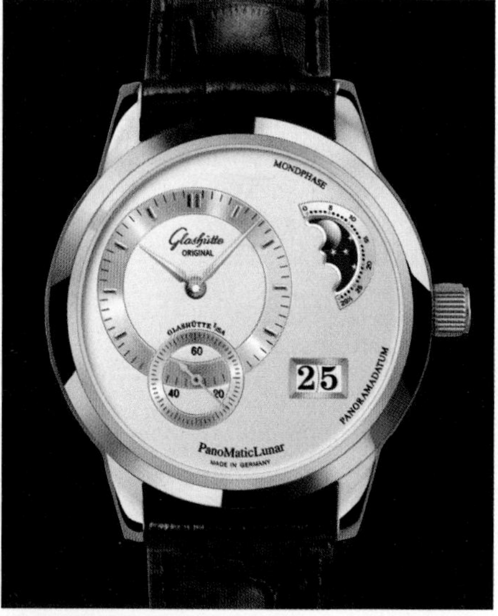

PanoMaticLunar

Reference number: 90-02-01-01-04
Movement: automatic, Glashütte Original 90-02, ø 32.6 mm, height 7 mm; 47 jewels; 28,800 vph, off-center rotor; duplex swan-neck fine adjustment
Functions: hours, minutes, subsidiary seconds; panorama date; moon phase
Case: rose gold, ø 39.4 mm, height 11.9 mm; sapphire crystal; transparent case back
Band: reptile skin, double folding clasp
Price: $13,350
Variations: in stainless steel; in platinum, limited to 200 pieces

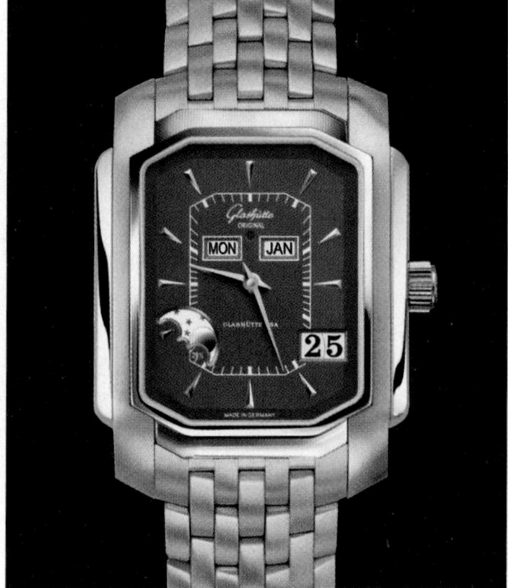

Karree Perpetual Calendar

Reference number: 39-51-14-02-14
Movement: automatic, Glashütte Original 39-51, ø 31.15 mm, height 7.2 mm; 48 jewels; 28,800 vph
Functions: hours, minutes; perpetual calendar with panorama date, day, month, moon phase, leap year
Case: stainless steel, 34.8 x 37.5 mm, height 12.5 mm; sapphire crystal; transparent case back
Band: stainless steel, double folding clasp
Price: $14,150
Variations: in rose gold

Senator Up and Down

Reference number: 39-44-16-22-04
Movement: automatic, Glashütte Original 39-44, ø 30.95 mm, height 5.9 mm; 36 jewels; 28,800 vph
Functions: hours, minutes, sweep seconds; date; moon phase; power reserve display
Case: stainless steel, ø 39.3 mm, height 11.4 mm; sapphire crystal; transparent case back; water-resistant to 50 m
Band: reptile skin, double folding clasp
Price: $4,500
Variations: in rose gold

Senator Panorama Date

Reference number: 39-42-14-24-04
Movement: automatic, Glashütte Original 39-42, ø 30.95 mm, height 5.9 mm; 44 jewels; 28,800 vph
Functions: hours, minutes, sweep seconds; panorama date
Case: stainless steel, ø 38.8 mm, height 11.8 mm; sapphire crystal; transparent case back; water-resistant to 50 m
Band: reptile skin, double folding clasp
Price: $6,100
Variations: in rose gold

Senator Panorama Date with Moon Phase

Reference number: 39-41-15-21-04
Movement: automatic, Glashütte Original 39-41, ø 30.95 mm, height 5.9 mm; 44 jewels; 28,800 vph
Functions: hours, minutes, sweep seconds; panorama date; moon phase
Case: rose gold, ø 38.8 mm, height 11.8 mm; sapphire crystal; transparent case back; water-resistant to 50 m
Band: reptile skin, double folding clasp
Price: $11,750
Variations: in stainless steel

Karree Panorama Date with Moon Phase

Reference number: 39-43-07-05-04
Movement: automatic, Glashütte Original 39-43, ø 30.95 mm, height 5.9 mm; 44 jewels; 28,800 vph
Functions: hours, minutes; panorama date; moon phase
Case: rose gold, 34.8 x 37.5 mm, height 11.3 mm; sapphire crystal; transparent case back
Band: reptile skin, double folding clasp
Price: $12,650
Variations: in stainless steel

Karree Chronograph

Reference number: 39-31-09-05-04
Movement: automatic, Glashütte Original 39-31, ø 31.15 mm, height 7.2 mm; 51 jewels; 28,800 vph
Functions: hours, minutes, subsidiary seconds; chronograph
Case: rose gold, 34.8 x 37.5 mm, height 12.5 mm; sapphire crystal; transparent case back
Band: reptile skin, double folding clasp
Price: $9,950
Variations: in stainless steel

Karree Small Seconds

Reference number: 42-05-11-11-04
Movement: manual winding, Glashütte Original 42-05, 26 x 20.5 mm, height 5.9 mm; 24 jewels; 28,800 vph
Functions: hours, minutes, subsidiary seconds
Case: stainless steel, 34.8 x 37.5 mm, height 12.5 mm; sapphire crystal; transparent case back
Band: reptile skin, double folding clasp
Price: $6,650
Variations: in rose gold

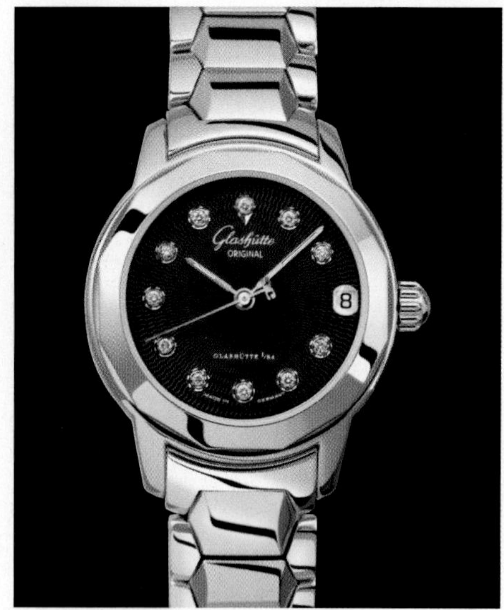

Lady Sport Automatic

Reference number: 39-11-15-41-16
Movement: automatic, Glashütte Original 39-11, ø 26.2 mm, height 4.3 mm; 25 jewels; 28,800 vph
Functions: hours, minutes, sweep seconds; date
Case: stainless steel, ø 31 mm, height 10.5 mm; sapphire crystal with magnifying lens, anti-reflective; transparent case back; screw-in crown; water-resistant to 100 m
Band: stainless steel, double folding clasp
Price: $4,400
Variations: in rose gold

Lady Sport Chronograph

Reference number: 39-31-44-36-06
Movement: automatic, Glashütte Original 39-31, ø 31.15 mm, height 7.2 mm; 51 jewels; 28,800 vph
Functions: hours, minutes, subsidiary seconds; chronograph
Case: rose gold, ø 38 mm, height 13.5 mm; bezel set with 72 brilliant-cut diamonds; sapphire crystal; transparent case back; water-resistant to 100 m
Band: reptile skin, buckle in rose gold
Remarks: dial with nine diamond markers
Price: $17,200
Variations: in stainless steel

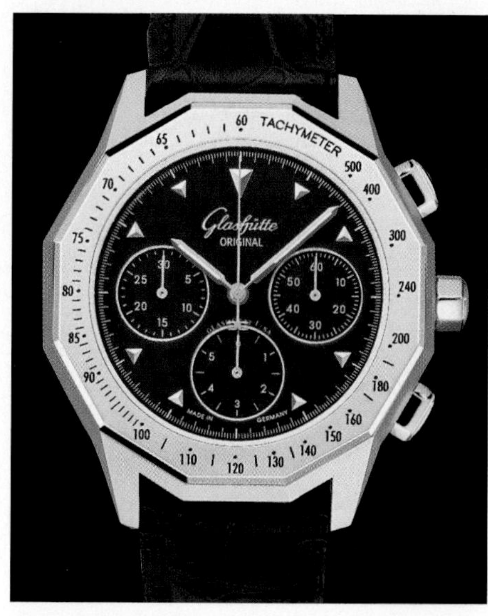

Sport Chrono

Reference number: 10-66-17-10-04
Movement: automatic, Glashütte Original 39-31, ø 31.15 mm, height 7.2 mm; 51 jewels; 28,800 vph
Functions: hours, minutes, subsidiary seconds; chronograph
Case: stainless steel, ø 41.5 mm, height 13.5 mm; engraved bezel with tachymeter scale; sapphire crystal; transparent case back; water-resistant to 100 m
Band: reptile skin, double folding clasp
Price: $4,100
Variations: in rose gold

Lady Karree Manually Wound

Reference number: 21-01-03-98-04
Movement: manual winding, Glashütte Original 21, 17.5 x 13.8 mm, height 3.7 mm; 17 jewels; 28,800 vph
Functions: hours, minutes
Case: stainless steel, 23.5 x 24.5 mm, height 8 mm; case flanks in white gold, set with 88 brilliant-cut diamonds; sapphire crystal; transparent case back
Band: stainless steel, double folding clasp
Price: $8,450
Variations: in rose gold, without diamonds

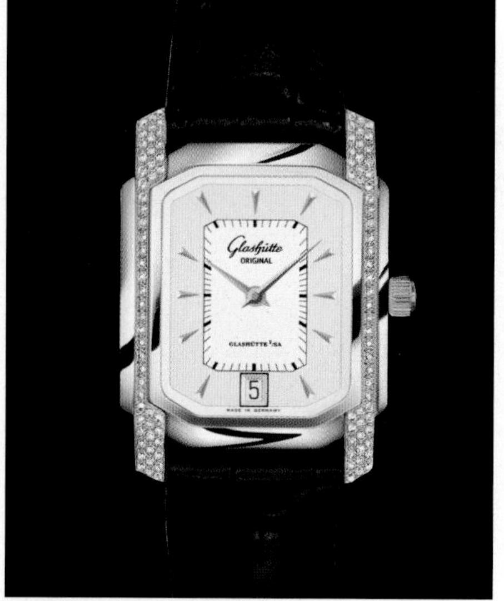

Lady Karree Automatic

Reference number: 39-20-02-62-04
Movement: automatic, Glashütte Original 39-20, ø 26.2 mm, height 4.3 mm; 25 jewels; 28,800 vph
Functions: hours, minutes; date
Case: rose gold, 30.5 x 33 mm, height 9.5 mm; case flanks set with brilliant-cut diamonds; sapphire crystal; transparent case back
Band: reptile skin, buckle in rose gold
Price: $12,300
Variations: without diamonds; in stainless steel

Sport Automatic Evolution

Reference number: 10-33-40-80-04
Movement: automatic, Glashütte Original 39-11, ø 26.2 mm, height 4.3 mm; 25 jewels; 28,800 vph
Functions: hours, minutes, sweep seconds; date
Case: stainless steel, ø 41.5 mm, height 11.3 mm; unidirectionally rotating bezel with 60-minute scale; sapphire crystal; transparent case back; screw-in crown; water-resistant to 200 m
Band: reptile skin, double folding clasp
Price: $3,000
Variations: with stainless steel bracelet

Caliber 95

Mechanical with automatic winding, twin spring barrels with step gear, bilateral winding in two speeds
Functions: hours, minutes (off-center), subsidiary seconds; chronograph with flyback function; panorama date
Diameter: 32.2 mm; **Height:** 7.3 mm ; **Jewels:** 41
Balance: screw balance with 18 gold balance screws
Frequency: 28,800 vph
Balance spring: Breguet, swan-neck fine adjustment
Remarks: separate wheel bridges for winding and chronograph; immaculately finished movement, beveled edges, polished steel parts, screw-mounted gold chatons, blued screws, winding wheels with double sunburst decoration, bridges and cocks with Glashütte ribbing, hand-engraved balance cock

Caliber 93

Mechanical with automatic winding, flying one-minute tourbillon; off-center rotor; power reserve 48 hours
Functions: hours, minutes (off-center), subsidiary seconds (on tourbillon cage); panorama date
Diameter: 32.2 mm; **Height:** 7.65 mm (without tourbillon cage); **Jewels:** 46 plus two diamond endstones
Balance: screw balance with 18 gold balance screws in tourbillon carriage, one revolution per minute
Frequency: 21,600 vph; **Balance spring:** Breguet
Remarks: flying one-minute tourbillon on dial side, immaculately finished movement; beveled edges, polished steel parts, screw-mounted gold chatons, blued screws, winding wheels with double sunburst decoration, bridges and cocks with Glashütte ribbing; hand-engraved balance cock

Caliber 90

Mechanical with automatic winding; power reserve 42 hours
Functions: hours, minutes (off-center), sweep seconds; panorama date, moon phase
Diameter: 32.6 mm; Height: 7 mm;
Jewels: 41
Balance: screw balance with 18 gold balance screws
Frequency: 28,800 vph
Balance spring: flat hairspring, duplex swan-neck fine adjustment (for rate and beat)
Shock protection: Incabloc
Remarks: immaculately finished movement; beveled edges, polished steel parts ; hand-engraved balance cock; three-quarter plate with Glashütte ribbing; off-center skeletonized rotor with 21-karat gold oscillating weight

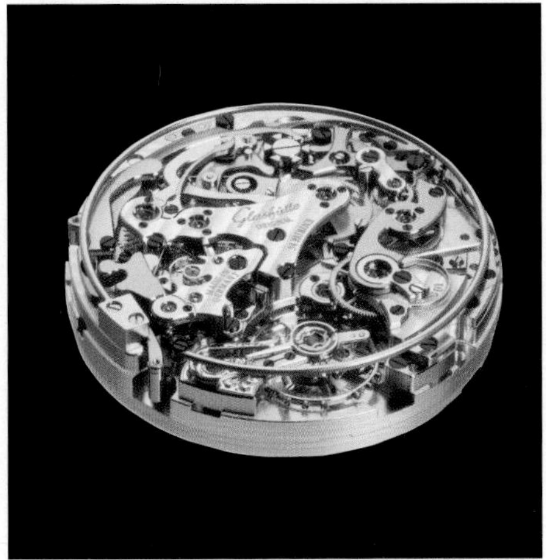

Caliber 60

Mechanical with manual winding, power reserve 42 hours
Functions: hours, minutes, subsidiary seconds; panorama date; chronograph with flyback and countdown functions (30 minutes, acoustic signal via gong)
Diameter: 32.2 mm; Height: 7.2 mm
Jewels: 54
Balance: screw balance with 18 gold balance screws
Frequency: 28,800 vph
Balance spring: flat hairspring, swan-neck fine adjustment
Remarks: immaculately finished movement, beveled edges, polished steel parts, screw-mounted gold chatons, blued screws, winding wheels with double sunburst pattern, bridges and cocks decorated with Glashütte ribbing, balance cock engraved by hand

Caliber 61

Mechanical with manual winding, power reserve 42 hours
Functions: hours, minutes, subsidiary seconds; chronograph with flyback function
Diameter: 32.2 mm
Height: 7.2 mm
Jewels: 41
Balance: screw balance with 18 gold balance screws
Frequency: 28,800 vph
Balance spring: flat hairspring, swan-neck fine adjustment
Remarks: immaculately finished movement, beveled edges, polished steel parts, blued screws, screw-mounted gold chatons, winding wheels with double sunburst pattern, bridges and cocks with Glashütte ribbing; balance cock engraved by hand

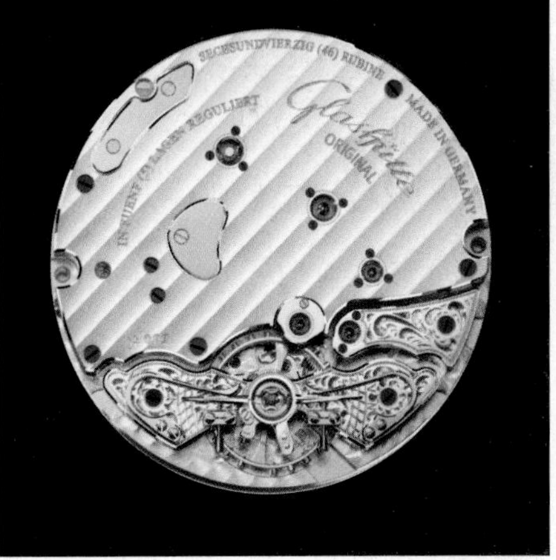

Caliber 65

Mechanical with manual winding, power reserve 42 hours
Functions: hours, minutes, subsidiary seconds; power reserve display
Diameter: 32.2 mm; **Height:** 6.1 mm
Jewels: 48
Balance: screw balance with 18 gold balance screws
Frequency: 28,800 vph
Balance spring: flat hairspring, duplex swan-neck fine adjustment (for rate and beat)
Remarks: immaculately finished movement, beveled edges, polished steel parts, blued screws, screw-mounted gold chatons, three-quarter plate decorated with Glashütte ribbing; winding wheels with double sunburst pattern; balance cock engraved by hand

Caliber 39

Mechanical with automatic winding, power reserve 40 hours
Functions: hours, minutes, sweep seconds
Diameter: 26 mm
Height: 4.3 mm
Jewels: 25
Frequency: 28,800 vph
Balance spring: flat hairspring, swan-neck fine adjustment
Shock protection: Incabloc
Remarks: immaculately finished movement, beveled edges, polished steel parts, winding wheels with sunburst decoration, three-quarter plate with Glashütte ribbing, skeletonized rotor with 21-karat gold oscillating weight

Caliber 39-50 (dial side)

Mechanical with automatic winding, power reserve 40 hours, stop-seconds
Functions: hours, minutes, sweep seconds; perpetual calendar with panorama date, day, month, moon phase, leap year indication
Diameter: 31.15 mm; **Height:** 7.2 mm
Jewels: 48
Frequency: 28,800 vph
Balance spring: flat hairspring, swan-neck fine adjustment
Shock protection: Incabloc
Remarks: immaculately finished movement, beveled edges, polished steel parts, winding wheels with sunburst decoration, three-quarter plate with Glashütte ribbing, skeletonized rotor with 21-karat gold oscillating weight

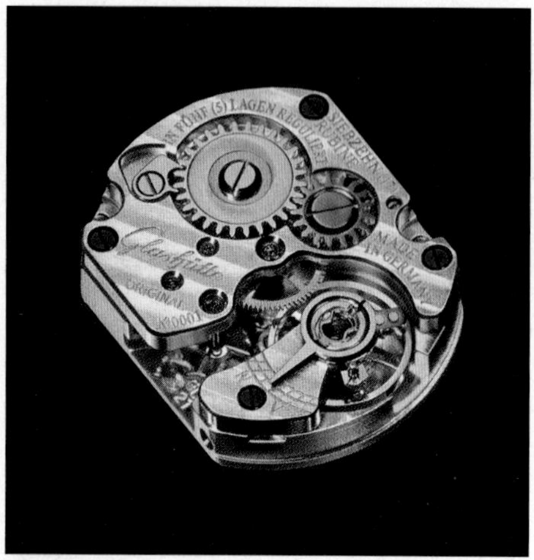

Caliber 21

Mechanical with manual winding, power reserve 38 hours
Functions: hours, minutes
Dimensions: 17.5 x 13.8 mm
Height: 3.7 mm
Jewels: 17
Frequency: 28,800 vph
Balance spring: flat hairspring
Remarks: immaculately finished movement, beveled edges, polished steel parts, blued screws, three-quarter plate decorated with Glashütte ribbing, winding wheels with sunburst decoration

Caliber 42

Mechanical with manual winding, power reserve 40 hours
Functions: hours, minutes
Dimensions: 26 x 20.5 mm
Height: 4.3 mm
Balance: screw balance with 18 gold balance screws
Frequency: 28,800 vph
Balance spring: flat hairspring, swan-neck fine adjustment
Remarks: immaculately finished movement, beveled edges, polished steel parts, blued screws, screwed-mounted gold chatons, three-quarter plate decorated with Glashütte ribbing, winding wheels with double sunburst decoration

J. ASSMANN 3
TOURBILLON
1 • 3 • 5 • 7 • 9 • 11 • 13 • 15 • 17 • 19 • 21 • 23 • 25 • 27 • 29 • 31
AUF
AB
GLASHÜTTE i./Sa.

Glycine

Glycine is taking off. This doesn't mean that the brand hailing from Biel has become arrogant in the ninetieth year of its existence. The fact is that it is sending a charming messenger for its watches to the skies: Pascale Alajouaine, European champion in motorized aerobatic flight. At Baselworld 2004, this master of the skies presented the latest pilot's and world time watch, Airman 9, together with Glycine's director Katharina Brechbühler.

The Airman 9 shows three time zones, two on the dial and one on the bezel, and additionally disposes of a chronograph mechanism. With a diameter of 44 mm, it is still one of the larger high-performance timepieces for the wrist, even if it is a bit smaller than the Airman 7 that was introduced two years ago. However, that is a timepiece that contains three independent automatic movements and therefore measures a remarkable 53 mm in diameter.

Large watches have always been one of the specialties of this watch brand. Founded in the year 1914, the brand at first produced voluminous watches with gold and platinum cases for solvent men. The production of watches containing mechanical movements was continued into the 1970s, even though the consumer was by then almost exclusively demanding quartz watches.

Glycine has always been one of the front-runners of new trends in mechanical watches. For example, in 1938 Glycine was one of the twenty-nine exhibitors at the first Basel fair after the Great Depression and ensuing world economic crisis in the early 1930s. Since then, Glycine hasn't missed a single Basel fair.

After the war, Glycine was one of the first Swiss brands to put its money on the automatic movement. In 1948 the company was already able to show an entire range of automatic watches. In 1952 Glycine introduced the renowned vacuum chronometers that became very famous for their incredible water and shock resistance.

In the year 1996 the company once again took up designing large-formatted watches, something that represented one of the traditional firm's most important production arms in the '50s and '60s. On the American and, especially, the Italian markets, Glycine has been strongly represented since the middle of the 1990s with oversized chronographs and sports watches.

By creating a detailed replica of the first Glycine automatic model from the year 1931, the brand is now turning a little further back in its history for inspiration. Along with a special automatic edition named for founder Eugène Meylan, there is also a large wristwatch with a transparent savonnette hinged lid in front of the dial, also known as a half hunter in English.

Airman 7

Reference number: 3829.19-LB9
Movement: automatic, ETA 1 x 2893-2, 2 x 2671-2, three independent ETA automatic movements, one with display of world time
Functions: hours, minutes, sweep seconds; date; three time zones; additional 24-hour display (fourth time zone)
Case: stainless steel, ø 53 mm, height 12.3 mm; sapphire crystal; transparent case back; crowns at 3, 8 and 10 o'clock
Band: leather, buckle
Price: $3,475
Variations: with rubber strap; in different dial variations

Airman 9

Reference number: 3840.191-LB9
Movement: automatic, ETA 7754, ø 30 mm, height 7.9 mm; 25 jewels; 28,800 vph, rose gold-plated rotor with côtes de Genève and engraving
Functions: hours, minutes; chronograph; date; 24-hour display (second time zone)
Case: stainless steel, ø 44 mm, height 15 mm; bidirectionally rotating bezel with 24-hour scale; sapphire crystal; transparent case back; screw-in crown
Band: leather, double folding clasp
Price: $3,675
Variations: with rubber strap; different dial colors

Incursore Half-Hunter

Reference number: 3843.19-LB9
Movement: manual winding, ETA 6498, ø 36.6 mm, height 4.5 mm; 17 jewels; 18,000 vph, bridges with chess-board decoration, blued screws
Functions: hours, minutes, subsidiary seconds
Case: stainless steel, ø 46 mm, height 14 mm; transparent protective lid with hinge; sapphire crystal; transparent case back; screw-in crown
Band: leather, buckle
Remarks: limited to 999 pieces
Price: $1,375
Variations: with green or yellow dial

Eugène Meylan

Reference number: 3835.19AT-LB7
Movement: automatic, ETA 2895-2, ø 25.6 mm, height 4.35 mm; 27 jewels; 28,800 vph, rhodium-plated, rotor with côtes de Genève, blued screws
Functions: hours, minutes, subsidiary seconds
Case: stainless steel, ø 42 mm, height 11.75 mm; sapphire crystal; transparent case back
Band: leather, double folding clasp
Price: $1,750
Variations: in a gold-plated case

Lagunare Chronograph

Reference number: 3837.19-1
Movement: automatic, ETA 7750, ø 30 mm, height 7.9 mm; 25 jewels; 28,800 vph, rhodium-plated, rotor with côtes de Genève, blued screws
Functions: hours, minutes, subsidiary seconds; chronograph; date
Case: stainless steel, ø 46 mm, height 15.7 mm; unidirectionally rotating bezel with 60-minute scale; sapphire crystal; transparent case back; screw-in crown and buttons
Band: stainless steel, double folding clasp
Price: $2,600
Variations: with leather or rubber strap ($2,350)

Combat Chronograph

Reference number: 3838.19AT8-LB9R
Movement: automatic, ETA 7750, ø 30 mm, height 7.9 mm; 25 jewels; 28,800 vph
Functions: hours, minutes, subsidiary seconds; chronograph; date
Case: stainless steel, ø 43 mm, height 14.5 mm; mineral crystal; transparent case back
Band: leather, buckle
Price: $1,400
Variations: with stainless steel bracelet

Graham

"Drive left" is the slogan of the martially designed Graham Chronofighter. This could be interpreted either as driving on the left side of the road or as something being powered from the left. At any rate, the slogan, the name of the brand, and the watch all leave an unmistakably British taste on the tongue. The somewhat old-fashioned chronograph, simultaneously quite technical in appearance, is without a doubt the brand's leading product and looks as if it came directly from the story of Captain Nemo in *20,000 Leagues under the Sea* — an effect that is certainly purposeful.

The Swiss group The British Masters has breathed new life into the old name Graham with such unusual watch creations. The moniker is derived from one of the most important figures in the history of watchmaking: The great George Graham is not only the namesake of the cylinder escapement from the eighteenth century, but is also said to be the inventor of the chronograph.

Graham began working for the famous Thomas Tompion in 1695, but soon started his own business — with the ambition of outdoing his master. Most of the watches that were built at this time deviated in rate precision by up to ten minutes per day. Graham was one of the first whose watches didn't deviate more than one second per day. Graham even received the contract from the Greenwich Royal Observatory to build its master clock. He was inducted into the Royal Society, an organization that was originally reserved for scientists and astronomers only.

His inventions made Graham famous throughout Europe, even if he had none of them patented — his moral ideals did not allow him to! He preferred to share his knowledge with his colleagues. Because of his great deeds performed in the name of his homeland, the English Parliament agreed on interring his earthly remains in Westminster Abbey's nave, where they still reside today.

Since then, chronographs have played an important role in Graham's brand philosophy, from flyback and split-seconds versions all the way to chronographs featuring a *seconde foudroyante*, a lightning-fast display of an eighth of a second whose mechanical realization makes the addition of a second spring barrel and escapement necessary.

Historical models always figure into the design of the brand's contemporary ones. The Chronofighter and its unusual thumb lever to start and stop the chronograph are derived from a prototype that British bomber pilots tried out during World War II. By positioning the striking mechanism on the left side of the case, it may even be hidden under a shirt sleeve — if that is so desired.

Chronofighter

Reference number: 2CFAS.B01A.L31B
Movement: automatic, Graham 1722 (base ETA 7750); ø 30.5 mm, height 8.75 mm; 30 jewels; 28,800 vph, chronograph control (start/stop) above crown button; certified chronometer (C.O.S.C.); movement finish with côtes de Genève
Functions: hours, minutes, subsidiary seconds; chronograph
Case: stainless steel, ø 43 mm, height 16 mm; sapphire crystal; crown button with security device; water-resistant to 50 m
Band: leather, buckle
Price: $7,450
Variations: with polished case and bezel

Chronofighter

Reference number: 2CFAR.B05A.C54B
Movement: automatic, Graham 1722 (base ETA 7750); ø 30.5 mm, height 8.75 mm; 30 jewels; 28,800 vph, chronograph control (start/stop) above crown button; certified chronometer (C.O.S.C.); movement finish with côtes de Genève
Functions: hours, minutes, subsidiary seconds; chronograph
Case: red gold, ø 43 mm, height 16 mm; sapphire crystal; crown button with security device; water-resistant to 50 m
Band: reptile skin, buckle
Price: $21,900

Swordfish

Reference number: 2SWAS.B01A.K06B
Movement: automatic, Graham 1726 (base ETA 7750); ø 30.5 mm, height 8.75 mm; 30 jewels; 28,800 vph, movement finish with côtes de Genève
Functions: hours, minutes, subsidiary seconds; chronograph
Case: stainless steel, ø 46.2 mm, height 16 mm; sapphire crystal with magnifying lenses above the totalizers; screw-in crown; water-resistant to 50 m
Band: rubber, buckle
Price: $7,000
Variations: also for right-handers (crown and buttons on left side of case)

Silverstone

Reference number: 2SIAS.B01A.C01B
Movement: automatic, Graham 1721 (base ETA 7750); ø 30.5 mm, height 8.75 mm; 30 jewels; 28,800 vph, movement finish with côtes de Genève
Functions: hours, minutes, subsidiary seconds; chronograph with flyback function; large date; 24-hour display (second time zone)
Case: stainless steel, ø 42 mm, height 15 mm; sapphire crystal; screw-in crown; water-resistant to 50 m
Band: reptile skin, buckle
Price: $6,990
Variations: in red gold ($18,900)

Aeroflyback

Reference number: 2AFAS.B05A.C01B
Movement: automatic, Graham 1723 (base ETA 7750); ø 30.5 mm, height 8.75 mm; 30 jewels; 28,800 vph, movement finish with côtes de Genève
Functions: hours, minutes, subsidiary seconds; chronograph with flyback function; date
Case: stainless steel, ø 42 mm, height 15 mm; sapphire crystal; screw-in crown; water-resistant to 50 m
Band: reptile skin, buckle
Price: $5,700

Foudroyante

Reference number: 2LIAS.B04A.C01B
Movement: automatic, Graham 1695 (base ETA 7750); ø 30.5 mm, height 8.75 mm; 40 jewels; 28,800 vph, mechanism for foudroyante 1/8 seconds with its own spring barrel
Functions: hours, minutes; split seconds chronograph with foudroyante seconds (1/8-second counter)
Case: stainless steel, ø 42 mm, height 16 mm; sapphire crystal; water-resistant to 50 m
Band: reptile skin, buckle
Price: $16,900
Variations: in rose gold ($27,000)

Hanhart

The Hanhart watch brand has traditional ties to aviation. Currently documenting this, the watch manufacturer hailing from Germany's Black Forest has just released the pilot's chronograph Dornier by Hanhart. The initiator of this watch is Irén Dornier, grandson of the legendary airplane designer Claude Dornier and a fan of classic mechanics. Thus, he had a chronograph manufactured at the factory in Gütenbach that is dedicated to the legendary flying boat Do-X, which will accompany him on a journey around the world of a special type: With the Hanhart chronograph strapped to his wrist, Irén Dornier is flying once around the globe in the historical water aircraft Do 24 ATT in 2004. Dornier not only wants to honor the work of his grandfather, but also to collect money for UNICEF. And in so doing, he has also achieved international attention for the otherwise rather introverted company Hanhart.
Connoisseurs of the logo and characteristic "Hanhart stud" on the leather strap have easily identified these symbols for quality and reliability for more than sixty years, even though the wristwatch section of this small company had been sorely neglected for a long time. But a good name will survive, and the widespread trend toward retro design has favored the return of a manufacturer with a proven and "evolved" tradition.
On the initiative of two enterprising product developers at Hanhart, wristwatches were once again added to the mechanical and electronic stopwatches and timers from Gütenbach, and with much care and attention to detail, the collection has been gradually expanded.
In 1997 two replicas of the military pilot's chronographs from World War II represented the starting point for the new Hanhart collection, and no effort was spared to reproduce them as accurately as possible. Dial details, hands, and the fluted bezel with a reference mark, originally laid down in the specifications of the military equipment supplier, are identical in every respect with the look of the original watch produced in 1939. Although Hanhart must now utilize purchased hand-wound Valjoux movements, the case specialists succeeded in duplicating the characteristic asymmetrical offset positioning of the buttons with respect to the crown by integrating a number of linkages. The company was also able to integrate a one-button mechanism (successively for start, stop, and reset) into the manually wound Valjoux movement, resulting in the awakening of a further classic Hanhart model.

The Minos and Sirius models have been removed a bit from the characteristic design originally stipulated in the "Description, Operation, and Maintenance Regulation for Air Force Watches" and break with the tradition of black dials, fluorescent hands, and fluorescent Arabic numerals. But unlike the remakes of the pilot's chronographs, there has been a certain amount of freedom taken in the design of these models, a fact that will move Hanhart out of the niche of military watch specialists sooner or later.
That certainly would have been in keeping with "stopwatch king" Willy Hanhart's philosophy as he developed a special enthusiasm for sports timing after the war. The chronograph Admiral and a chronograph with a gold case are dedicated to the founder and captain of the brand, both available with a choice of manually wound or automatic movements and — to offset the pilot's look — a matte white dial. The current chronograph, Dornier by Hanhart, extends this line of "civilian" timepieces in a consistent manner. The brand has, at any rate, potential, especially since plans for a historical column-wheel chronograph movement are stored in the Hanhart technicians' drawer, awaiting rebirth.

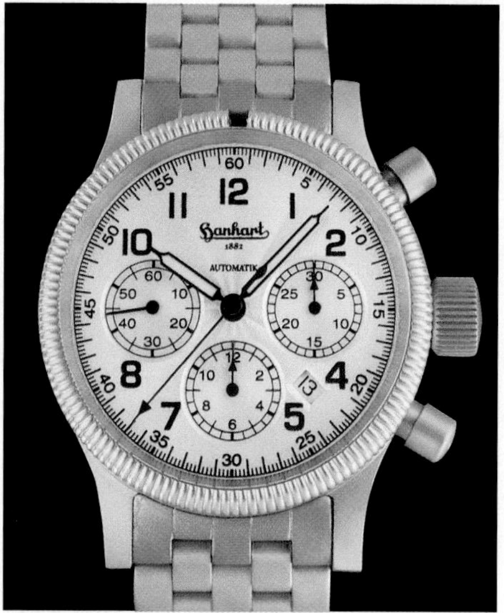

Fliegerchronograph Tachy-Tele Replica

Reference number: 702.1101-00
Movement: manual winding, ETA 7760, ø 30 mm, height 6.2 mm; 21 jewels; 28,800 vph, button positions modified
Functions: hours, minutes, subsidiary seconds; chronograph
Case: stainless steel, ø 40 mm, height 13.7 mm; bezel, bidirectionally rotating, with reference marker; sapphire crystal; water-resistant to 100 m
Band: leather, buckle
Price: $2,700
Variations: with brown leather strap

Sirius Chronograph

Reference number: 710.020A-00
Movement: automatic, ETA 7750, ø 30 mm, height 7.9 mm; 25 jewels; 28,800 vph, button positions modified
Functions: hours, minutes, subsidiary seconds; chronograph; date
Case: stainless steel, ø 40 mm, height 15.4 mm; bidirectionally rotating bezel with reference marker; sapphire crystal; transparent case back; screw-in crown; water-resistant to 100 m
Band: stainless steel, folding clasp
Price: $3,600
Variations: with black dial; with leather strap

Admiral Chronograph

Reference number: 715.0001-00
Movement: automatic, ETA 7750, ø 30 mm, height 7.9 mm; 25 jewels; 28,800 vph, button positions modified
Functions: hours, minutes, subsidiary seconds; chronograph
Case: stainless steel, ø 40 mm, height 15 mm; bidirectionally rotating bezel with reference marker; sapphire crystal; transparent case back; water-resistant to 100 m
Band: leather, buckle
Price: $3,100
Variations: with black dial

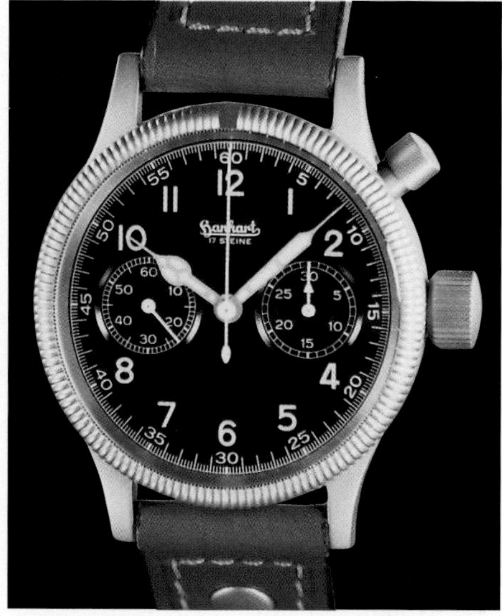

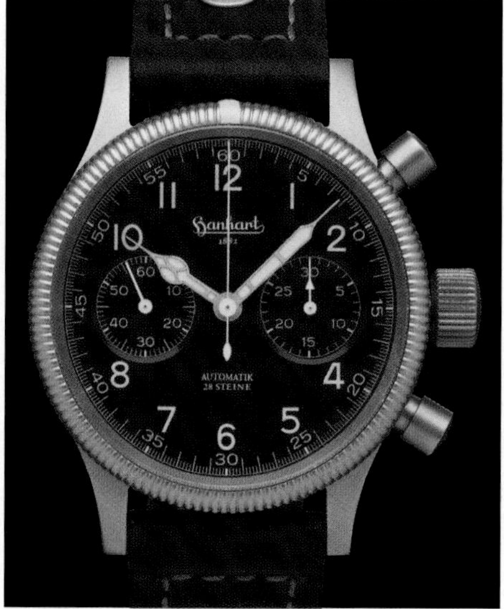

Primus One-Button Chronograph

Reference number: 704.0100-00
Movement: manual winding, Hanhart 704 (base ETA 7760); ø 30 mm, height 6.2 mm; 21 jewels; 28,800 vph, movement umkonstruiert auf einen individual button (start-stop-reset)
Functions: hours, minutes, subsidiary seconds; chronograph
Case: stainless steel, ø 40 mm, height 13.7 mm; bidirectionally rotating bezel with reference marker; sapphire crystal
Band: leather, buckle
Price: $2,900
Variations: as an automatic, with leather or stainless steel bracelet

Pioneer Caliber II

Reference number: 716.0100-00
Movement: automatic, Hanhart 716 (base ETA 7750); ø 30 mm, height 7.9 mm; 28 jewels; 28,800 vph, button positions modified
Functions: hours, minutes, subsidiary seconds; chronograph
Case: stainless steel, ø 40 mm, height 15 mm; bidirectionally rotating bezel with reference marker; sapphire crystal; transparent case back
Band: leather, buckle
Price: $3,100
Variations: different leather straps; with stainless steel bracelet

Dornier by Hanhart

Reference number: 790.0708-00
Movement: automatic, Hanhart 790 (base ETA 7750); ø 30 mm, height 7.9 mm; 28 jewels; 28,800 vph, gold-plated rotor
Functions: hours, minutes, subsidiary seconds; chronograph; date
Case: stainless steel, ø 42 mm, height 16.5 mm; sapphire crystal; transparent case back; crown with onyx cabochon
Band: reptile skin, buckle
Remarks: chronograph buttons specially shaped
Price: $5,700
Variations: with beige or copper-colored dial

Harwood

The Harwood watch has cornered a spot in all the best watch museums in the world, for it is a timepiece inextricably intertwined with the origins of the automatic wristwatch.
It has only been a short one hundred years since watches, until then so well kept in the vest pockets of gentlemen, began to seek positions on their wrists. Ladies also preferred the practicality of learning the time with a quick glance at the pragmatic timekeepers, and from that point on watches were worn openly either around the neck or on the wrist. They were held by a chain or a strap attached to the timepiece by rings that had been soldered to the sides of the pocket watch case.
Watchmakers of this era eyed these developments with horror, for they feared for the sensitive mechanisms placed on such an open area as the wrist, exposed as they were to shocks and the wrath of all weather.

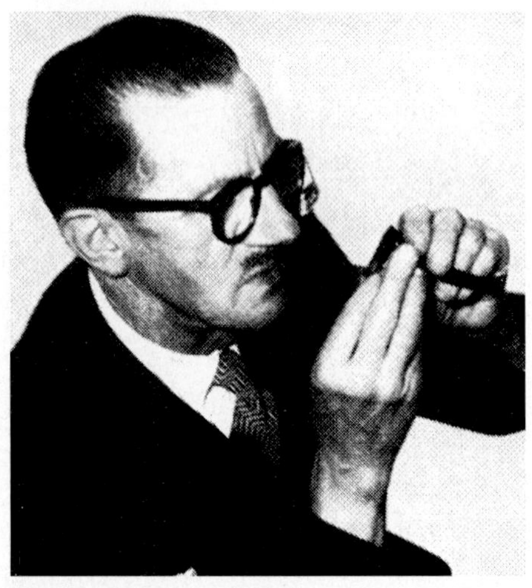

John Harwood had gotten to know these problems firsthand in his small watchmaker's atelier on the Isle of Man via numerous repairs and recognized that the opening in the case needed for the movement's winding mechanism was the weak link. Dust and moisture were finding their way into the interior of the case through the aperture created for the winding stem, which in the long run was damaging the movement. Harwood thought hard about a different type of winding system, one that would make an opening in the case's side obsolete, one that would tension the mainspring from the inside.
His forward-looking solution was a pendulum-type oscillating weight that took its energy from the movement made by the wrist of its wearer, which would tension the mainspring. And the automatic watch was born. Harwood registered his invention at the Federal Office of the Swiss Confederation for Intellectual Property in Bern, and on September 1, 1924, patent number 10 65 83 was issued to him for the first wristwatch with automatic winding worldwide.
Just two years later, the Harwood watch began its serial manufacture, creating a revolution on the watch market. A myriad of models were proof of the worldwide sales success, above all in the United States and Great Britain, and despite reports that might deem otherwise, this new technology proved reliable. These timepieces' faultless functionality even after eighty years is confirmed by vintage models still being sent to the Harwood Watch Co. by both collectors and auction houses.
Inventor John Harwood solved the problem of setting the hands with a special mechanism. Manufactured according to the original plans, every Harwood right up to today possesses the characteristic, fluted rotating bezel to set the time. The color of the window on the dial at 6 o'clock signals whether the watch is in the setting mode or if it is ready to tell time. (If the dot is colored, the watch is functioning; if it is not visible, then the watch is in setting mode.) In addition to setting the hands, when the bezel is turned counter-clockwise, it will tension the mainspring in order to ensure a stable starting rate after the movement has stopped.

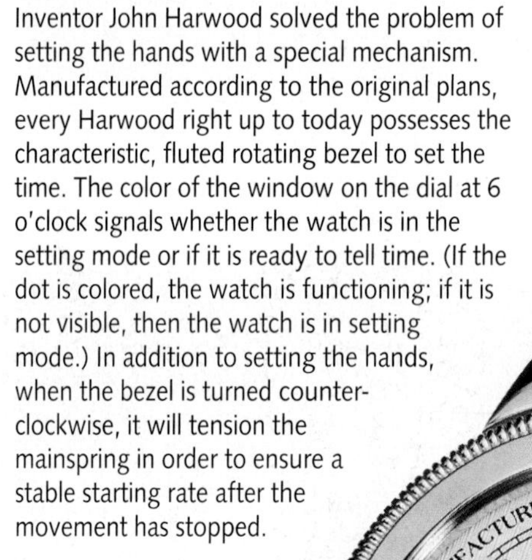

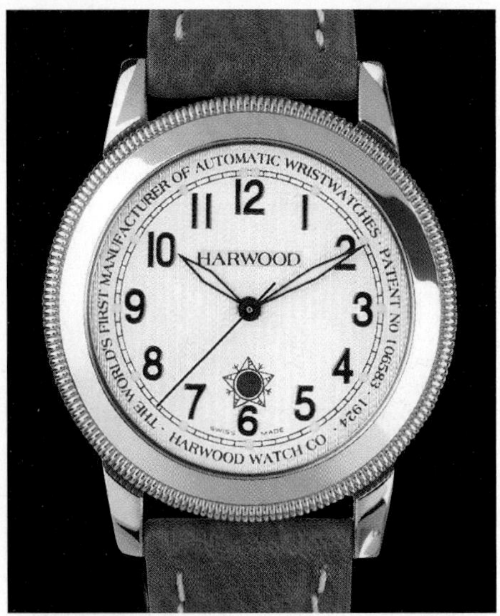

Automatic

Reference number: 516.10.15
Movement: automatic, ETA 2892-2, modified, ø 25.6 mm, height 3.6 mm; 21 jewels; 28,800 vph, hand-setting and winding via rotating bezel
Functions: hours, minutes, sweep seconds
Case: stainless steel, ø 39 mm, height 9.5 mm; bidirectionally rotating bezel to wind and set; sapphire crystal; transparent case back
Band: leather, folding clasp
Price: $3,150
Variations: with stainless steel bracelet; with reptile skin strap; as women's model (ø 35 mm)

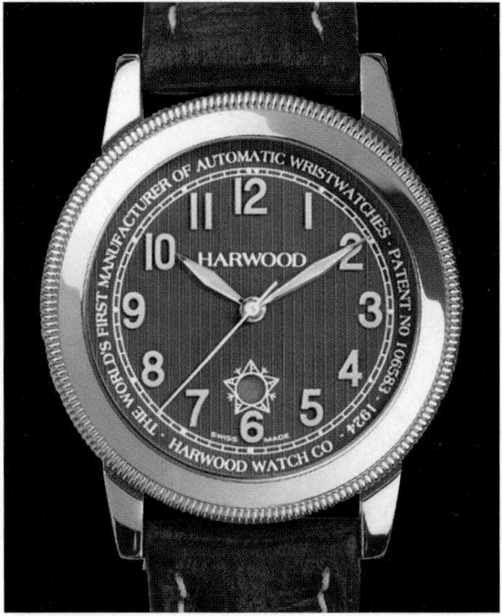

Automatic

Reference number: 516.10.11
Movement: automatic, ETA 2892-2, modified, ø 25.6 mm, height 3.6 mm; 21 jewels; 28,800 vph, hand-setting and winding via rotating bezel
Functions: hours, minutes, sweep seconds
Case: stainless steel, ø 39 mm, height 9.5 mm; bidirectionally rotating bezel to wind and set; sapphire crystal; transparent case back
Band: leather, folding clasp
Price: $3,150
Variations: with stainless steel bracelet; with reptile skin strap; as women's model (ø 35 mm)

Automatic

Reference number: 516.10.15 DM
Movement: automatic, ETA 2892-2, modified, ø 25.6 mm, height 3.6 mm; 21 jewels; 28,800 vph, hand-setting and winding via rotating bezel
Functions: hours, minutes, sweep seconds
Case: stainless steel, ø 39 mm, height 9.5 mm; bidirectionally rotating bezel to wind and set, set with diamonds; sapphire crystal; transparent case back
Band: stainless steel, folding clasp
Price: $7,300
Variations: with crocodile skin strap ($7,300); in yellow gold; as women's model (ø 35 mm)

Automatic

Reference number: 516.50.15 C
Movement: automatic, ETA 2892-2, modified, ø 25.6 mm, height 3.6 mm; 21 jewels; 28,800 vph, hand-setting and winding via rotating bezel
Functions: hours, minutes, sweep seconds
Case: yellow gold, ø 39 mm, height 9.5 mm; bidirectionally rotating bezel to wind and set; sapphire crystal; transparent case back
Band: reptile skin, buckle
Price: $12,800
Variations: as women's model (ø 35 mm)

Automatic

Reference number: 516.50.15 D C
Movement: automatic, ETA 2892-2, modified, ø 25.6 mm, height 3.6 mm; 21 jewels; 28,800 vph, hand-setting and winding via rotating bezel
Functions: hours, minutes, sweep seconds
Case: yellow gold, ø 39 mm, height 9.5 mm; bidirectionally rotating bezel to wind and set, set with diamonds; sapphire crystal; transparent case back
Band: reptile skin, buckle
Price: $16,900
Variations: as women's model (ø 35 mm)

Automatic Louis Reguin

Reference number: 517.10 LRC
Movement: automatic, ETA 2892-2, modified, ø 25.6 mm, height 3.6 mm; 21 jewels; 28,800 vph, hand-setting and winding via rotating bezel
Functions: hours, minutes, sweep seconds
Case: stainless steel, ø 39 mm, height 9.5 mm; bidirectionally rotating bezel to wind and set; sapphire crystal; transparent case back
Band: reptile skin, buckle
Remarks: enamel dial in honor of the artist Louis Réguin
Price: $4,600
Variations: with stainless steel bracelet ($4,600); in platinum

Hermès

Between Hermès and the horses found on its coat of arms, there has always been a concrete, yet tender and smooth relationship: leather. Horses, riding, and travel are themes that have dominated the history of the house since its founding in 1837 when Thierry Hermès (who was born in Germany's Krefeld) opened a little saddlery in Paris's Quartier de la Madeleine.

In 1928 Emile-Maurice Hermès began selling watches in his shop on the French metropolis's Faubourg Saint-Honoré. These were watches that he had had made by reputable Swiss manufactories according to his designs. To celebrate the seventy-fifth anniversary of the Hermès watch, the company — which is still independent today — has taken a remarkable initiative.

The new Dressage model (French for the training of animals, a word often used in equestrian sports) follows not only in the tradition of famous wristwatch creations by the company such as Kelly (1975), Arceau (1978), Harnais (1996), and Hour H (1997), but also continues in its old tradition of cooperating directly with exclusive movement manufacturers. The building in Biel housing La Montre Hermès is home to several assembly and tool-making workshops as well as production machines for various watch components on more than 3,800 square meters of floor. However, with only eighty-five employees it is just impossible to make one's own true watch movement production — and even putting them in only 140,000 watches per year would not be economical either.

Searching for an exclusive and qualitatively remarkable movement manufacturer, Hermès found what it was looking for in the dreamy little town of Fleurier — a town that used to be a flourishing bastion of the Swiss watchmaking industry. A few months ago, the movement *manufacture* Vaucher opened its doors, a subsidiary company of the watch manufacturer Parmigiani in charge of the development and production of the exquisite automatic and manually wound movements for the small noble brand.

Vaucher Caliber P1928, made exclusively for Hermès and used in the Dressage model, is based on Parmigiani's Caliber 331 with automatic winding. At 25.6 mm in diameter and 3.5 mm in height, it is one of the flattest movements around, although it offers a good fifty-five hours of power reserve thanks to its twin spring barrels. The shape and decoration of the bridges and cocks are personalized for Hermès, engraved with the characteristic Hermès H.

Along with the platinum version featuring a genuine mother-of-pearl dial limited to seventy-five pieces that comes with a C.O.S.C. chronometer certificate, there are unlimited versions in red, white, and yellow gold, with the dial either in mother-of-pearl or silver. The simple case shape is common to all of the versions as is the unmistakable dial design featuring twelve medallions as hour markers.

Dressage

Reference number: DR 1.770.213 M
Movement: automatic, Vaucher P 1928, ø 25.6 mm, height 3.5 mm; 32 jewels; 28,800 vph, oscillating weight in red gold
Functions: hours, minutes, sweep seconds; date
Case: red gold, 40 x 46 mm, height 9.72 mm; sapphire crystal; transparent case back; screw-in crown; water-resistant to 50 m
Band: reptile skin, folding clasp
Price: appx. $15,100
Variations: in yellow gold; in white gold; with mother-of-pearl dial

Dressage Moon Phase

Reference number: DR 2.765.712 M
Movement: automatic, Vaucher P 1929, ø 25.6 mm; 28,800 vph, oscillating weight in red gold
Functions: hours, minutes, sweep seconds; date (retrograde); moon phase
Case: platinum, 40 x 46 mm, height 9.72 mm; sapphire crystal; transparent case back; screw-in crown; water-resistant to 50 m
Band: reptile skin, folding clasp
Price: appx. $34,500
Variations: in rose gold; with mother-of-pearl dial

Arceau Automatic

Reference number: 4.810.130
Movement: automatic, ETA 2892-A2, ø 25.6 mm, height 3.6 mm; 21 jewels; 28,800 vph
Functions: hours, minutes, sweep seconds; date
Case: stainless steel, ø 41 mm, height 11 mm; sapphire crystal; water-resistant to 50 m
Band: leather, buckle
Price: appx. $1,700
Variations: with dark grey dial; different leather straps

Nomade Automatic

Reference number: NO 3.810.220 V
Movement: automatic, ETA 2892-A2, ø 25.6 mm, height 3.6 mm; 21 jewels; 28,800 vph
Functions: hours, minutes, sweep seconds; date
Case: stainless steel, ø 39 mm, height 10 mm; sapphire crystal; water-resistant to 50 m
Band: leather, buckle
Price: appx. $1,900
Variations: with silver-colored dial; with stainless steel bracelet; different leather straps

H-our

Reference number: HH 1.210.260. VDT
Movement: quartz, ETA 901.001
Functions: hours, minutes
Case: stainless steel, 21 x 21 mm, height 7 mm; sapphire crystal
Band: leather, double wrapped, buckle
Price: appx. $1,250
Variations: different leather straps

Barenia

Reference number: BA 1.510.130 V
Movement: quartz, ETA 956.412
Functions: hours, minutes
Case: stainless steel, 31.5 x 25 mm, height 7 mm; sapphire crystal
Band: Barenia calf skin, buckle
Price: appx. $1,450
Variations: different leather straps

Hublot

The Hublot (French for porthole) watch line resulted from a refusal to be like everyone else. Carlo Crocco, born into a Milanese watchmaking family, had the opportunity to study and compare the collections of countless brands for many years. He noticed that even among the more exclusive brands (or particularly so) caution and conformity were generally the rule. And so it was that the aesthete, beginning with the simple principle of "nothing unnecessary, no repetition, but beyond the fickle trends of fashion," started off on his quest. Crocco created a simple, clean shape, defining important quality criteria, and founded a brand with the meaningful name MDM – *Montre des Montres* (watch of all watches).

It was not easy to find a shape that, on the one hand, broke with old traditions, and on the other, would be seen in a favorable light when judged on the basis of classical criteria. The nature of the watch, after all, was to be unobtrusive and suitable for all occasions and any wardrobe.

In the end, the watch became a porthole; or did the porthole become the watch? Twelve screws through the bezel not only ensured that the watch was completely watertight, but they also replaced the need for hour markers on the dial,

which now stood out round and plain as the main focus of attention. The more the project took shape, the more it became clear that a watch of unparalleled aesthetic beauty had been created: the Hublot.

Luxury experienced a new dimension. The slightly vanilla-smelling rubber strap of his watches, with which Crocco truly worked as a pioneer in the 1980s, was fundamentally a high-tech material, flexible, and corrosion-, sweat-, abrasion-, and waterproof. In addition to all this, it was extremely tear-resistant because of the steel fibers woven into the material. Developing it took an entire three years.

The Hublot collection has been more consolidated than developed in the last few years. Even the new Régulateur does not step outside the box created by the Hublot Classic a full twenty-four years ago. At the same time, the unusual dial visuals of the Régulateur represent an additional attraction for fans of precision timekeeping. The numerous jeweled versions and limited series with hand-engraved motifs on the case backs and hinged lids have brought the Hublot brand a new clientele interested in jeweled watches.

In the summer of 2004, Crocco brought Jean-Claude Biver of Blancpain fame into Hublot's head managerial team. This creative and go-getting manager will certainly have his own ideas regarding the collection …

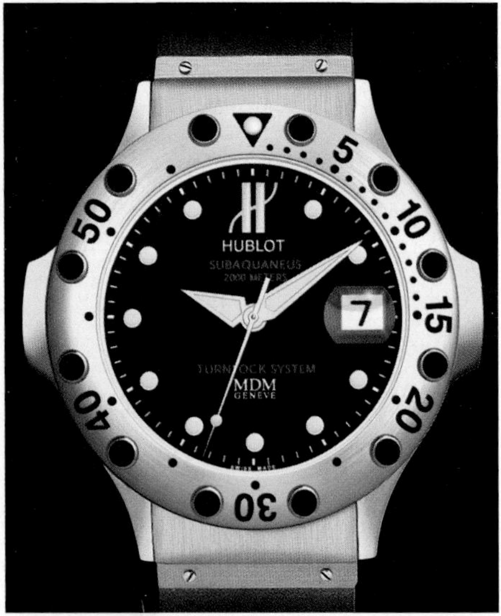

Subaquaneus Sport

Reference number: 1950.140.1
Movement: automatic, ETA 2892-A2, ø 25.6 mm, height 3.6 mm; 21 jewels; 28,800 vph
Functions: hours, minutes, sweep seconds; date
Case: stainless steel, ø 42 mm, height 13 mm; unidirectionally rotating bezel (security ratcheting "Turn Lock" system), with 60-minute scale and rubber elements; sapphire crystal; screw-in crown; water-resistant to 2000 m
Band: rubber, double folding clasp
Price: $4,600

Classic Regulateur

Reference number: 1860.135.3
Movement: automatic, Dubois-Dépraz 14070 (base ETA 2892-A2); ø 25.6 mm; 21 jewels; 28,800 vph
Functions: hours (off-center), minutes, subsidiary seconds; date
Case: yellow gold, ø 39 mm, height 9.5 mm; bezel with 12 screws; sapphire crystal; screw-in crown; water-resistant to 50 m
Band: rubber, double folding clasp
Price: $13,000
Variations: in white or red gold

Classic Regulateur

Reference number: 1860.135.1
Movement: automatic, Dubois-Dépraz 14070 (base ETA 2892-A2); ø 25.6 mm; 21 jewels; 28,800 vph
Functions: hours (off-center), minutes, subsidiary seconds; date
Case: stainless steel, ø 39 mm, height 9.5 mm; bezel with 12 screws; sapphire crystal; screw-in crown; water-resistant to 50 m
Band: rubber, double folding clasp
Price: $4,700

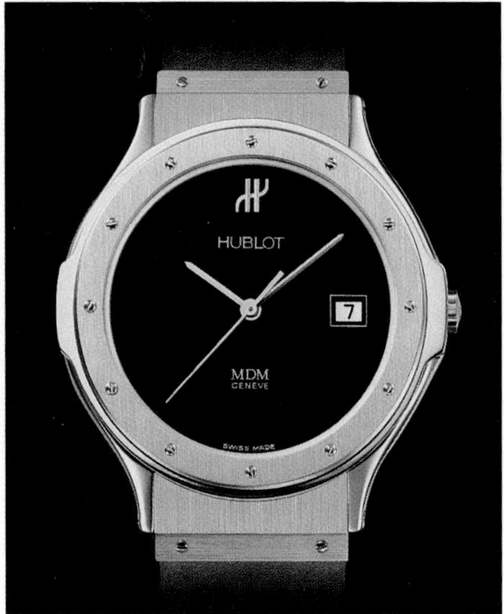

Classic Quarz

Reference number: 1520.100.3
Movement: quartz, ETA 955.412
Functions: hours, minutes, sweep seconds; date
Case: yellow gold, ø 36 mm, height 8 mm; bezel with 12 screws; sapphire crystal; screw-in crown; water-resistant to 50 m
Band: rubber, double folding clasp
Price: $8,800
Variations: available in different dial variations and case sizes

Grand Quantième

Reference number: 1840.100.1
Movement: automatic, ETA 2892 with Dubois-Dépraz module 14370
Functions: hours, minutes, sweep seconds; large date, day
Case: stainless steel, ø 38.4 mm, height 10.5 mm; bezel with 12 screws; sapphire crystal; screw-in crown; water-resistant to 50 m
Band: rubber, double folding clasp
Price: $4,600
Variations: different dial variations

Grand Quantième

Reference number: 1840.BUR.8
Movement: automatic, ETA 2892 with Dubois-Dépraz module 14370
Functions: hours, minutes, sweep seconds; large date, day
Case: red gold, ø 38.4 mm, height 10.5 mm; bezel with 12 screws; sapphire crystal; screw-in crown; water-resistant to 50 m
Band: rubber, double folding clasp
Price: $12,800
Variations: different dial variations

Elegant

Reference number: 1910.140.1
Movement: automatic, ETA 2892, ø 25.6 mm, height 3.6 mm; 21 jewels; 28,800 vph
Functions: hours, minutes, sweep seconds; date
Case: stainless steel, ø 41.6 mm, height 11.6 mm; sapphire crystal; screw-in crown; water-resistant to 50 m
Band: rubber, double folding clasp
Price: $3,600
Variations: with meteor-grey dial

Elegant

Reference number: 1910.Per10.1
Movement: automatic, ETA 2892, ø 25.6 mm, height 3.6 mm; 21 jewels; 28,800 vph
Functions: hours, minutes, sweep seconds; date
Case: stainless steel, ø 41.6 mm, height 11.6 mm; sapphire crystal; screw-in crown; water-resistant to 50 m
Band: rubber, double folding clasp
Price: $3,600

Elegant Power Reserve

Reference number: 1830.135.1
Movement: automatic, Soprod 9035 (base ETA 2892-A2); ø 25.6 mm; 21 jewels; 28,800 vph
Functions: hours, minutes, sweep seconds; date; power reserve display
Case: stainless steel, ø 40 mm, height 12 mm; sapphire crystal; screw-in crown; water-resistant to 50 m
Band: rubber, double folding clasp
Price: $4,100
Variations: different dial variations

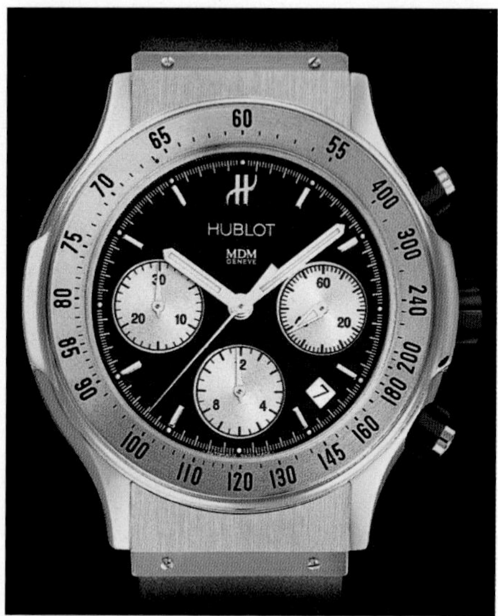

Chrono SuperB Sport

Reference number: 1920.110.1
Movement: automatic, Dubois-Dépraz 2021 (base ETA 2892-A2); ø 31.15 mm, height 7.2 mm; 48 jewels; 28,800 vph
Functions: hours, minutes, subsidiary seconds; chronograph; date
Case: stainless steel, ø 42.5 mm, height 13.1 mm; bezel with tachymeter scale; sapphire crystal; crown and buttons in natural rubber; water-resistant to 100 m
Band: rubber, double folding clasp
Price: $5,100
Variations: different dial variations

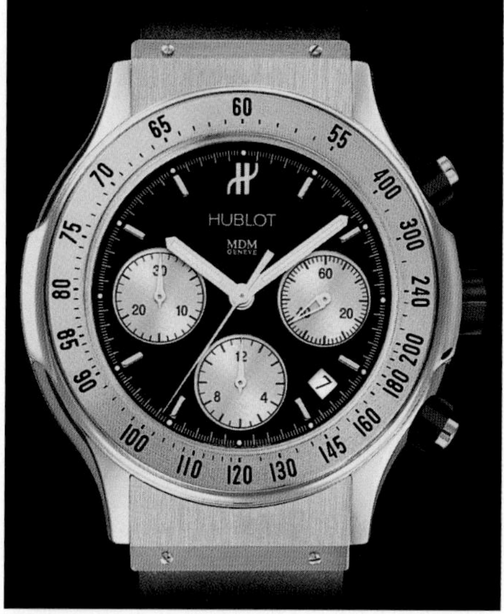

Chrono SuperB Sport

Reference number: 1920.110.7
Movement: automatic, Dubois-Dépraz 2021 (base ETA 2892-A2); ø 31.15 mm, height 7.2 mm; 48 jewels; 28,800 vph
Functions: hours, minutes, subsidiary seconds; chronograph; date
Case: stainless steel, ø 42.5 mm, height 13.1 mm; bezel in red gold with tachymeter scale; sapphire crystal; crown and buttons in natural rubber; water-resistant to 100 m
Band: rubber, double folding clasp
Price: $6,500

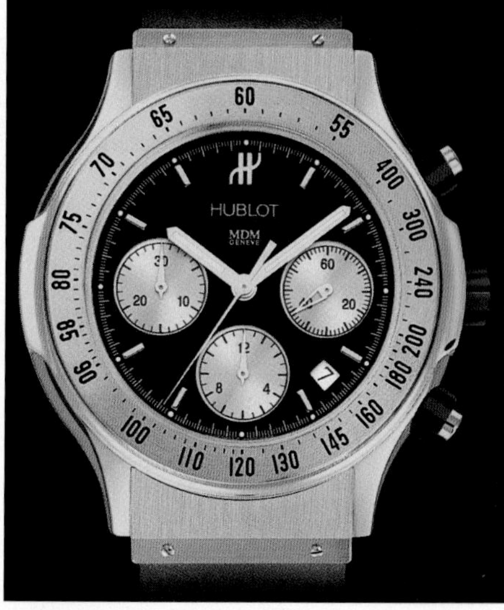

Chrono SuperB Sport

Reference number: 1920.110.8
Movement: automatic, Dubois-Dépraz 2021 (base ETA 2892-A2); ø 31.15 mm, height 7.2 mm; 48 jewels; 28,800 vph
Functions: hours, minutes, subsidiary seconds; chronograph; date
Case: red gold, ø 42.5 mm, height 13.1 mm; bezel with tachymeter scale; sapphire crystal; crown and buttons in natural rubber; water-resistant to 100 m
Band: rubber, double folding clasp
Price: $16,900

Chrono Joaillerie Elegant

Reference number: 1810.144.3.054
Movement: automatic, Dubois-Dépraz 2021 (base ETA 2892-A2); ø 31.15 mm, height 7.2 mm; 48 jewels; 28,800 vph
Functions: hours, minutes, subsidiary seconds; chronograph; date
Case: yellow gold, ø 40 mm, height 13.1 mm; bezel and lugs set with diamonds; sapphire crystal; screw-in crown; water-resistant to 100 m
Band: rubber, double folding clasp
Remarks: dial with diamond markers
Price: $22,500
Variations: different dial variations

Chrono Joaillerie Elegant

Reference number: 1640.144.1.024
Movement: quartz, Frédéric Piguet 1270
Functions: hours, minutes, subsidiary seconds; chronograph; date
Case: stainless steel, ø 37 mm, height 9.8 mm; bezel and case sides set with diamonds; sapphire crystal; screw-in crown; water-resistant to 50 m
Band: rubber, double folding clasp
Remarks: dial with diamond markers
Price: $13,400
Variations: different dial variations

Chrono Joaillerie Elegant

Reference number: 1810.444.1.024
Movement: automatic, Dubois-Dépraz 2021 (base ETA 2892-A2); ø 31.15 mm, height 7.2 mm; 48 jewels; 28,800 vph
Functions: hours, minutes, subsidiary seconds; chronograph; date
Case: stainless steel, ø 40 mm, height 13.1 mm; bezel and case sides set with diamonds; sapphire crystal; screw-in crown; water-resistant to 50 m
Band: rubber, double folding clasp
Remarks: dial with diamond markers
Price: $11,100
Variations: different dial variations

Joaillerie Elegant

Reference number: 1710.124.1.024
Movement: automatic, ETA 2892-A2, ø 25.6 mm, height 3.6 mm; 21 jewels; 28,800 vph
Functions: hours, minutes, sweep seconds; date
Case: stainless steel, ø 37 mm, height 9,8 mm; bezel and case sides, set with diamonds; sapphire crystal; screw-in crown; water-resistant to 50 m
Band: rubber, double folding clasp
Remarks: dial with diamond markers
Price: $8,800
Variations: different dial variations

Joaillerie Classic

Reference number: 1390.100.5.014
Movement: quartz, ETA 956.112,
Functions: hours, minutes, sweep seconds; date
Case: stainless steel, ø 28 mm, height 7 mm; bezel and lugs in white gold, set with 48 diamonds; sapphire crystal; screw-in crown; water-resistant to 50 m
Band: rubber, double folding clasp
Price: $6,400
Variations: in different case sizes and dial variations available

Joaillerie Classic

Reference number: 1390.124.3.054
Movement: quartz, ETA 956.112,
Functions: hours, minutes, sweep seconds; date
Case: yellow gold, ø 28 mm, height 7 mm; bezel, lugs and buckle, set with diamonds; sapphire crystal; screw-in crown; water-resistant to 50 m
Band: rubber, double folding clasp
Price: $16,300
Variations: in different case sizes and dial variations available

IWC

Geographically positioned outside the French-language region of the Jura, IWC has a special place among Swiss watch companies. Since the brand with the exceptional reputation for "engineering" was taken over by the prestigious Richemont group, along with Jaeger-LeCoultre and A. Lange & Söhne, its loyal following has increased markedly — as has its number of new models, from very complicated to completely neutral. The 2004/2005 watch season finds it communicating a new generation of diver's watches: the new Aquatimer.

This name is traditional. In 1967, IWC launched the first diver's watch under the name of Aquatimer. Jacques-Yves Cousteau contributed heavily to its success, increasing the demand for diver's watches as he popularized diving as a sport with his underwater films in the 1950s and '60s. He literally took people with him underwater in his moving documentary scenes and set off a true boom in diving, which indirectly helped the watch industry. Next to air tanks, the diver's watch is the most important piece of equipment to ensure the safety of a diver: The diver measures both dive and decompression times with it. This presented a challenge for the *manufacture* from Schaffhausen, which had made a name for itself in aviation until that point. Thus, the Aquatimer was born, IWC's first diver's watch, a simple, round timekeeper with two crowns. One of the crowns, located at 2 o'clock, was in charge of winding and setting; the second at 4 o'clock was used to move the rotating ring located underneath the sapphire crystal in a counterclockwise manner. An unusual answer: Normally the diver's ring is designed as a rotating bezel on the outside.

The new diver's family comprises four models, all of which have retained this rotating ring on the inside. Of course, the other details on the watches were improved: Alongside the display of the total dive time on the inner rotating ring, professional divers needed the possibility to make interval timings, such as for decompression stops. That would have been possible with a chronograph, but for one thing, the small totalizers are hard to read under water, and for another, divers are interested in the measure of minutes, not seconds. Thus, the Schaffhausen watchmakers designed a minute rattrapante ("split minutes"), which functions independently of the chronograph. With the aid of a pivoted detent control between 8 and 9 o'clock that is also easily activated while wearing gloves, the rattrapante is stopped while the minute hand keeps running. The difference is the desired interval or decompression time. Resetting the detent immediately resets the rattrapante and minute hands as well. And the watch also contains a normal chronograph function to boot. Alongside the Split Minute chrono, a conventional diver's chronograph as well as two versions of the Aquatimer Automatic, available in either 1000 or 2000 meters of water-resistance, make up the other members of the family.

Aquatimer Split Minute Chronograph

Reference number: 372301
Movement: automatic, IWC C.79470 (base ETA 7750); ø 30 mm, height 8.2 mm; 30 jewels; 28,800 vph
Functions: hours, minutes, subsidiary seconds; chronograph with additional separate stoppable minute hand (flyback)
Case: titanium, ø 44 mm, height 16.3 mm; unidirectionally rotating bezel under crystal with 60-minute scale, settable via crown; sapphire crystal; screw-in crown; water-resistant to 120 m
Band: titanium, folding clasp with security button
Price: $9,700
Variations: with rubber strap ($8,700)

Aquatimer Automatic 2000

Reference number: 353804
Movement: automatic, IWC C.30110 (base ETA 2892-A2); ø 25.6 mm, height 3.6 mm; 21 jewels; 28,800 vph
Functions: hours, minutes, sweep seconds; date
Case: titanium, ø 42 mm, height 14.8 mm; unidirectionally rotating bezel under crystal with 60-minute scale, settable via crown; sapphire crystal; screw-in crown; water-resistant to 2000 m
Band: rubber, folding clasp with security button
Price: $3,700
Variations: with titanium link bracelet ($4,700)

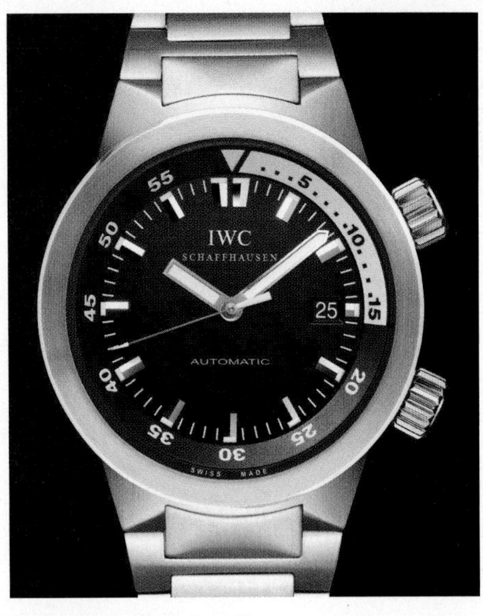

Aquatimer Automatic

Reference number: 354801
Movement: automatic, IWC C.30110 (base ETA 2892-A2); ø 25.6 mm, height 3.6 mm; 21 jewels; 28,800 vph
Functions: hours, minutes, sweep seconds; date
Case: stainless steel, ø 42 mm, height 12.8 mm; unidirectionally rotating bezel under crystal with 60-minute scale, settable via crown; sapphire crystal; screw-in crown; water-resistant to 1000 m
Band: stainless steel, folding clasp with security button
Price: $4,700
Variations: with rubber strap ($3,700)

Aquatimer Chrono-Automatic

Reference number: 371923
Movement: automatic, IWC C.79320 (base ETA 7750); ø 30 mm, height 7.9 mm; 25 jewels; 28,800 vph
Functions: hours, minutes, subsidiary seconds; chronograph; date, day
Case: stainless steel, ø 42 mm, height 13.4 mm; unidirectionally rotating bezel under crystal with 60-minute scale, settable via crown; sapphire crystal; screw-in crown; water-resistant to 120 m
Band: rubber, folding clasp with security button
Price: $4,200
Variations: with stainless steel bracelet ($5,200)

GST Perpetual Calendar

Reference number: 375617
Movement: automatic, IWC C.79261 (base ETA 7750 with module for perpetual calendar)
Functions: hours, minutes, subsidiary seconds; chronograph; perpetual calendar with date, day, month, four-digit year display, moon phase
Case: stainless steel, ø 43 mm, height 16 mm; sapphire crystal; screw-in crown; water-resistant to 120 m
Band: stainless steel, folding clasp with security button
Price: $14,700
Variations: different dial variations; in titanium ($14,700)

GST Chrono Rattrapante

Reference number: 371526
Movement: automatic, IWC C.79230 (base ETA 7750); ø 30 mm, height 7.9 mm; 25 jewels; 28,800 vph
Functions: hours, minutes, subsidiary seconds; split seconds chronograph; date, day
Case: stainless steel, ø 43 mm, height 16.9 mm; sapphire crystal; screw-in crown; water-resistant to 120 m
Band: stainless steel, folding clasp with security button
Price: $9,995
Variations: different dial variations; in titanium

Portuguese Minute Repeater Squelette

Reference number: 524102
Movement: manual winding, IWC C.95911, 54 jewels; 18,800 vph, movement completely skeletonized, beveled, and decorated
Functions: hours, minutes; hour, quarter hour, and minute repeater
Case: red gold, ø 42 mm, height 12.3 mm; sapphire crystal; transparent case back
Band: reptile skin, buckle
Remarks: limited to 50 pieces
Price: $89,000
Variations: in white gold ($97,000)

Portuguese Minute Repeater Squelette (back)

Reference number: 524102 (back)
Movement: The fine skeletonizing on this repeater mechanism looks fairly "technical," as is characteristic for the company's style. The Swiss-Germans from Schaffhausen do carry on in a certain "engineering" tradition that is retained throughout the collection, a tradition that does not harmonize well with floral engraving motifs and jewels. The fascination of this horological specialty remains right on track with the rest.

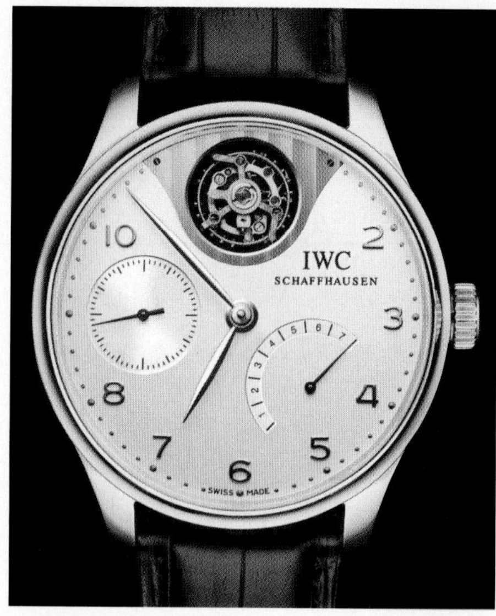

Portuguese Tourbillon

Reference number: 504204
Movement: manual winding, IWC C.50900, 44 jewels; 18,800 vph, flying one-minute tourbillon; Pellaton automatic winding (patented); theoretical power reserve 8 1/2 days, mechanically limited to 7 days
Functions: hours, minutes, subsidiary seconds; power reserve display
Case: platinum, ø 44.2 mm, height 14.2 mm; sapphire crystal
Band: reptile skin, buckle
Remarks: limited to 50 pieces
Price: $105,000
Variations: in rose gold ($89,000)

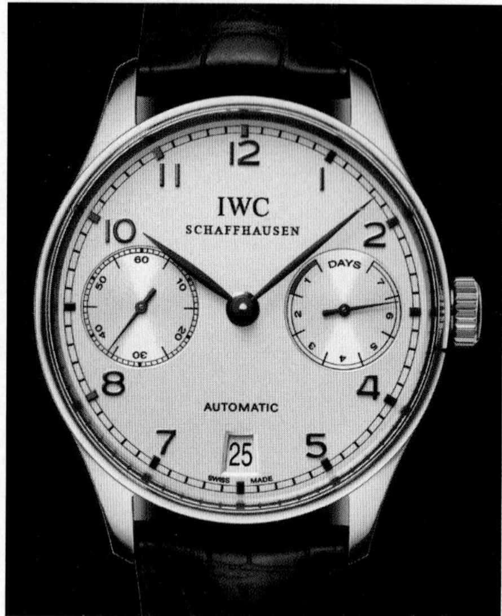

Portuguese Automatic

Reference number: 500107
Movement: manual winding, IWC C.50010, ø 38.2 mm, height 7.44 mm; 44 jewels; 18,000 vph, Pellaton automatic winding (patented); theoretical power reserve 8 1/2 days, mechanically limited to 7 days
Functions: hours, minutes, subsidiary seconds; date; power reserve display
Case: stainless steel, ø 42.3 mm, height 13.9 mm; sapphire crystal
Band: reptile skin, buckle
Price: $9,700
Variations: in rose gold ($13,700); in platinum ($31,000)

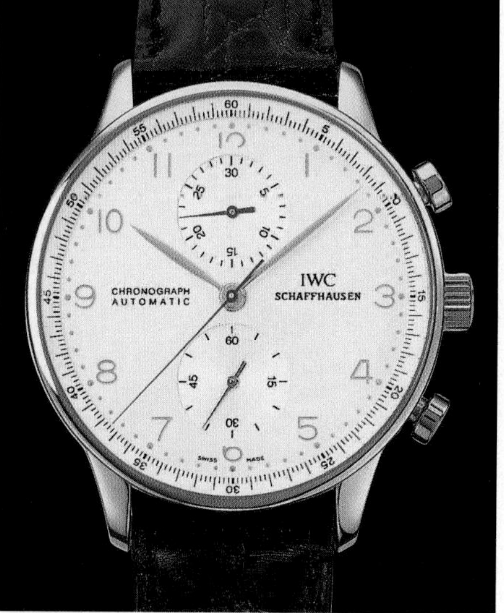

Portuguese Chrono Automatic

Reference number: 371401
Movement: automatic, IWC C.79240 (base ETA 7750); ø 30 mm, height 7.9 mm; 25 jewels; 28,800 vph
Functions: hours, minutes, subsidiary seconds; chronograph
Case: stainless steel, ø 40.9 mm, height 12.3 mm; sapphire crystal
Band: reptile skin, buckle
Price: $6,300
Variations: different dial-variations; in rose or yellow gold ($12,700); in white gold ($14,200)

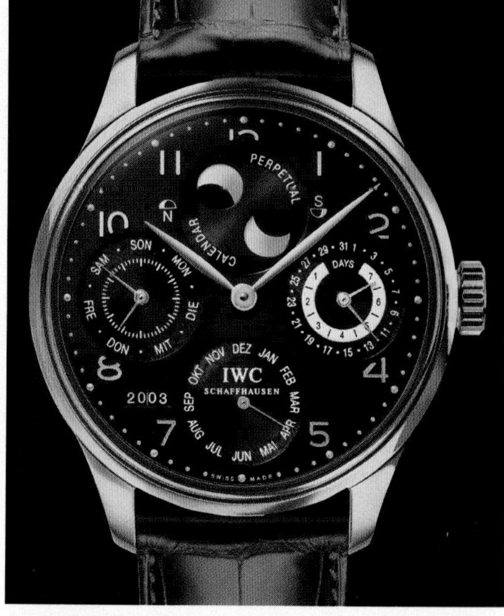

Portuguese Perpetual Calendar

Reference number: 502101
Movement: automatic, IWC C.50611, ø 38.2 mm; 66 jewels; 18,000 vph, Pellaton automatic winding (patented); theoretical power reserve 8 1/2 days, mechanically limited to 7 days
Functions: hours, minutes, subsidiary seconds; perpetual calendar with date, day, month, four-digit year display, double moon phase (for southern and northern hemispheres)
Case: rose gold, ø 44.2 mm, height 15.5 mm; sapphire crystal; transparent case back
Band: reptile skin, folding clasp
Price: $28,500
Variations: in yellow gold ($28,500)

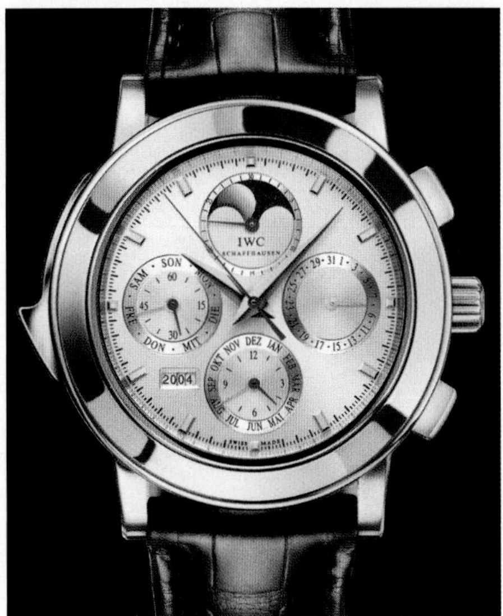

Grande Complication

Reference number: 377019
Movement: automatic, IWC C.79091
Functions: hours, minutes, subsidiary seconds; chronograph; perpetual calendar with date, day, month, year, moon phase; hour, quarter hour, and minute repeater
Case: yellow gold, ø 42.2 mm, height 16.3 mm; sapphire crystal; screw-in crown
Band: reptile skin, buckle
Price: $180,000
Variations: in limited-edition platinum ($200,000)

Da Vinci

Reference number: 375803
Movement: automatic, IWC C.79261 (base ETA 7750 with module for perpetual calendar)
Functions: hours, minutes, subsidiary seconds; chronograph; perpetual calendar with date, day, month, four-digit year display, moon phase
Case: stainless steel, ø 41.5 mm, height 16.4 mm; sapphire crystal; screw-in crown
Band: reptile skin, buckle
Price: $13,500
Variations: in yellow gold ($22,700)

Da Vinci Tourbillon

Reference number: 375201
Movement: manual winding, IWC C.76061, flying one-minute tourbillon
Functions: hours, minutes, subsidiary seconds; chronograph; perpetual calendar with date, day, month, four-digit year display, moon phase
Case: yellow gold, ø 39 mm, height 14.3 mm; sapphire crystal; transparent case back
Band: reptile skin, buckle
Remarks: limited to 200 pieces
Price: $65,000
Variations: gold bracelet, limited to 200 pieces ($74,000)

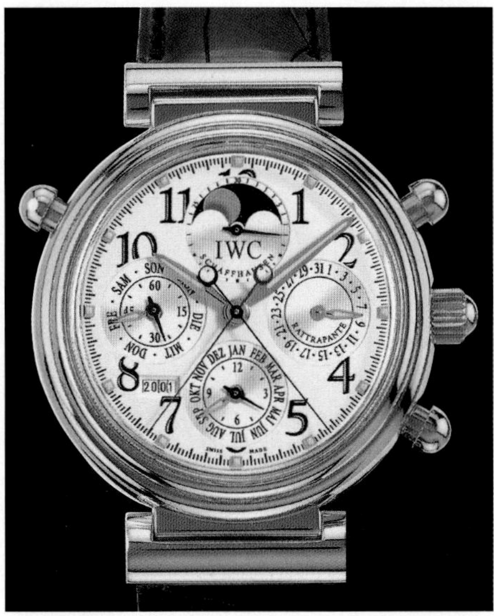

Da Vinci Rattrapante

Reference number: 375401
Movement: automatic, IWC C.79252,
Functions: hours, minutes, subsidiary seconds; split-seconds chronograph; perpetual calendar with date, day, month, four-digit year display, moon phase
Case: rose gold, ø 41.5 mm, height 16 mm; Plexiglas, on request sapphire crystal; screw-in crown
Band: reptile skin, buckle
Price: $24,900
Variations: in platinum ($38,000)

Da Vinci

Reference number: 375819
Movement: automatic, IWC C.79261 (base ETA 7750 with module for perpetual calendar)
Functions: hours, minutes, subsidiary seconds; chronograph; perpetual calendar with date, day, month, four-digit year display, moon phase
Case: yellow gold, ø 41.5 mm, height 16.4 mm; sapphire crystal; screw-in crown
Band: reptile skin, buckle
Price: $22,700
Variations: in stainless steel ($13,500)

Small Da Vinci

Reference number: 373605
Movement: quartz, IWC C.630, mechanical chronograph module
Functions: hours, minutes, subsidiary seconds; chronograph; date; moon phase
Case: stainless steel, ø 29 mm, height 8.3 mm; sapphire crystal; screw-in crown
Band: reptile skin, buckle
Price: $3,200
Variations: in yellow gold ($7,500)

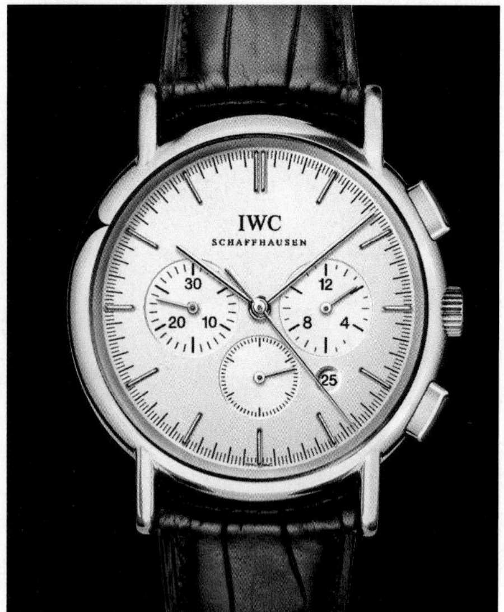

Portofino Chronograph

Reference number: 372403
Movement: quartz, IWC C.631, mechanical chronograph module
Functions: hours, minutes, subsidiary seconds; chronograph; date
Case:, ø 38 mm, height 8.6 mm; sapphire crystal
Band: reptile skin, buckle
Price: $3,200
Variations: with stainless steel bracelet ($3,700)

Portofino Automatic

Reference number: 353314
Movement: automatic, IWC C.30110 (base ETA 2892-A2); ø 25.6 mm, height 3.6 mm; 21 jewels; 28,800 vph
Functions: hours, minutes, sweep seconds; date
Case: yellow gold, ø 38 mm, height 8.6 mm; sapphire crystal
Band: reptile skin, buckle
Price: $6,200
Variations: with yellow gold bracelet ($16,200); stainless steel with alligator skin strap ($2,500); stainless steel with steel bracelet ($3,300)

Large Pilot's Watch

Reference number: 500201
Movement: automatic, IWC C. 5011, ø 38.2 mm, height 7.44 mm; 44 jewels; 18,000 vph, Pellaton automatic winding (patented); theoretical power reserve 8 1/2 days, mechanically limited to 7 days; soft iron core for magnetic protection
Functions: hours, minutes, sweep seconds; date; power reserve display
Case: stainless steel, ø 46.2 mm, height 15.8 mm; sapphire crystal; screw-in crown; water-resistant to 60 m
Band: buffalo leather, folding clasp
Price: $11,900
Variations: in platinum ($39,900)

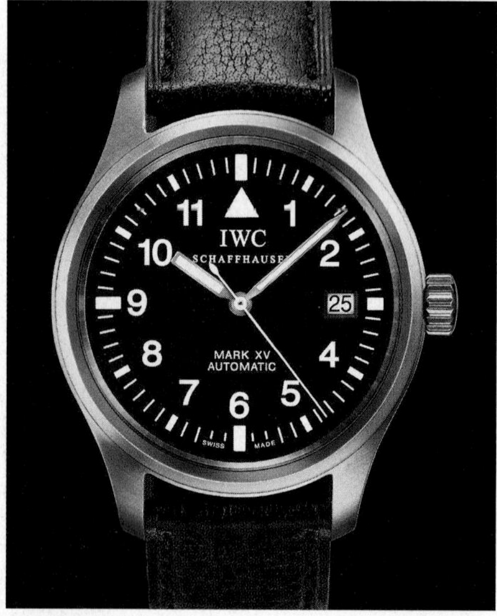

Mark XV

Reference number: 325301
Movement: automatic, IWC C.37524 (base ETA 2892-A2); ø 25.6 mm, height 3.6 mm; 21 jewels; 28,800 vph, soft iron core for magnetic protection
Functions: hours, minutes, sweep seconds; date
Case: stainless steel, ø 38 mm, height 10.5 mm; sapphire crystal; screw-in crown; water-resistant to 60 m
Band: buffalo leather, folding clasp
Price: $3,200
Variations: with stainless steel bracelet ($4,300)

Pilot's Double Chrono Spitfire

Reference number: 371341
Movement: automatic, IWC C.79230 (base ETA 7750); ø 30 mm, height 7.9 mm; 25 jewels; 28,800 vph, soft iron core for magnetic protection
Functions: hours, minutes, subsidiary seconds; split seconds chronograph; date, day
Case: stainless steel, ø 42 mm, height 16.2 mm; sapphire crystal; screw-in crown; water-resistant to 60 m
Band: reptile skin, buckle
Price: $8,600
Variations: with stainless steel bracelet ($9,800)

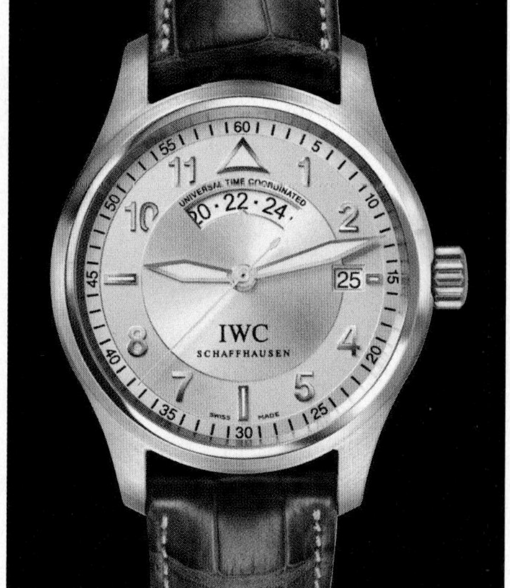

Pilot's Watch UTC Spitfire

Reference number: 325107
Movement: automatic, IWC C.37526 (base ETA 2892-A2); ø 25.6 mm, height 3.6 mm; 21 jewels (base movement); 28,800 vph, soft iron core for magnetic protection
Functions: hours, minutes, sweep seconds; date; 24-hour display (second time zone)
Case: stainless steel, ø 39 mm, height 12.5 mm; sapphire crystal; screw-in crown; water-resistant to 60 m
Band: reptile skin, buckle
Price: $3,900
Variations: with stainless steel bracelet ($5,100)

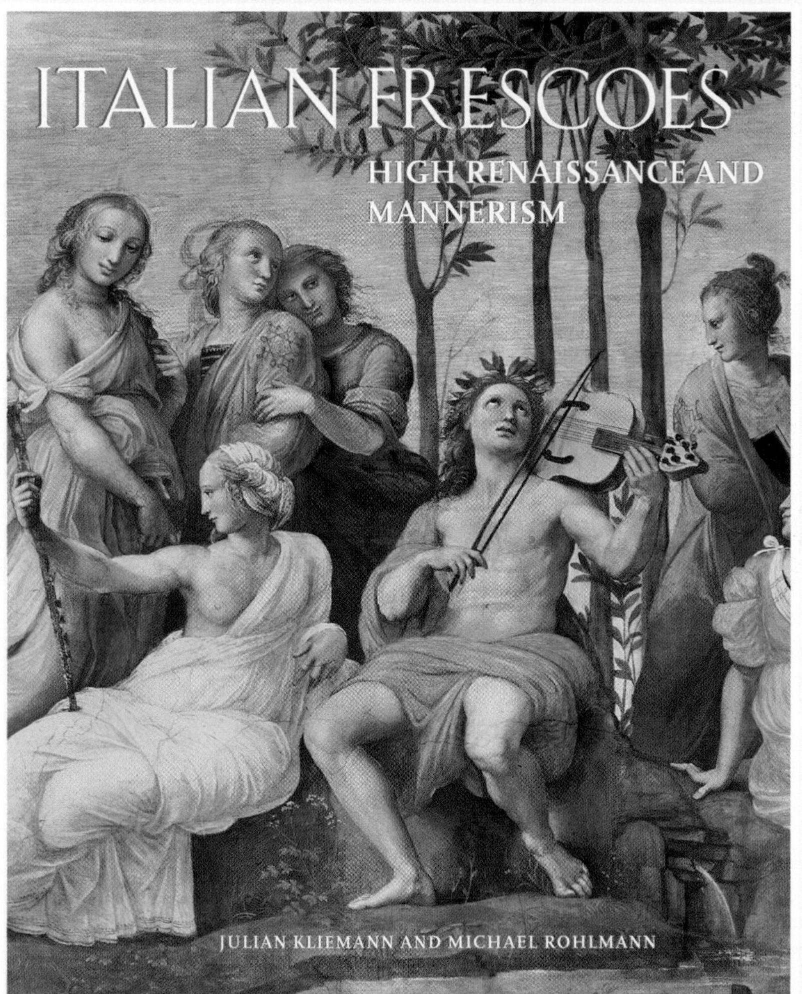

Italian Frescoes:
The High Renaissance to the Mannerism, 1510–1600
The third volume in the only comprehensive modern survey of the surviving frescoes created during the later years of the great Italian Renaissance to the Mannerist period.

By Julian Kliemann and Michael Rohlmann
Photography by Antonio Quattrone
and Ghigo Roli
360 full-color illustrations
464 pages • 11 × 13 in. • Cloth
ISBN 0-7892-0831-8 • $135.00

Italian Frescoes:
The Flowering of the Renaissance, 1470–1510
The second volume in the only comprehensive modern survey of Italian Renaissance frescoes focuses on the middle years of that glorious artistic milieu.

By Dr. Steffi Roettgen
Photography by Antonio Quattrone
384 illustrations, 314 in full color
464 pages • 11 × 13 in. • Cloth
ISBN 0-7892-0221-2 • $135.00

Italian Frescoes:
The Early Renaissance, 1400–1470
The first comprehensive survey in modern times of the surviving fresco cycles of the early Renaissance, this pathblazing work is an extraordinary achievement in scholarship and publishing.

By Dr. Steffi Roettgen
Photography by Antonio Quattrone
402 illustrations, 337 in full color
452 pages • 11 × 13 in. • Cloth
ISBN 0-7892-0139-9 • $135.00

Published by ABBEVILLE PRESS
116 West 23rd Street, New York, N.Y. 10011
1-800-ARTBOOK (in U.S. only)
Also available wherever fine books are sold
Visit us at www.abbeville.com

Jacob & Co.

American pop culture would currently be unthinkable without Jacob & Co. From hip-hop to mainstream, and from sportscaster to movie diva, anyone who's anyone is wearing a watch by "Jacob the Jeweler" these days.

This type of attention positively smacks of the short-lived and cheap. And even though Jacob's masterfully designed, overly large timepieces kicked off a trend all their own — even calling to life a great deal of "icy" copycats, certainly the purest form of flattery — they are anything but cheap and trendy.

Jacob Arabo grew up in Russia, where his passion for creating jewelry developed during his formative years. After immigrating to the United States as a teenager, Arabo enrolled in a jewelry design course with the intent of developing his natural talents. Showing exceptional aptitude, he was urged to begin his career in earnest and thus immediately began designing for a number of jewelry labels and private clients. In 1986, a short five years after that, Arabo opened his current company, Diamond Quasar, and from then on designed exclusively for his own label, Jacob & Co.

Arabo's signature timepiece, aptly dubbed the 5 Time Zone Watch, was inspired both by his jewelry creations and the jet-set lifestyle of so many of the celebrity clients that he had meanwhile amassed. This timepiece is, although quartz-driven, unique. The colorful dial is separated into four fields, each representing the glamour-puss time zones L.A., New York, Paris, and Tokyo. The main sweep hands are used for the wearer's local time. Jacob & Co. has extended this theme almost as far as it can go, and offers a veritable myriad of dial colors and materials (bling!) in precious metal cases. Although celebrities prefer to wear the in-your-face, 47-mm version, which is certainly visible at any distance and detectable by any TV camera, 40-mm versions do exist in all variations.

Despite the way the current models might appear to conservative watch fans, these timepieces are not cheap throwaways. Their bezels are interchangeable and screwed-down, and they even come in a set including straps of varying color (and a changing tool!) and bezels to match the dial. The non-jeweled 40-mm collection begins at $8,800 and continues on up to about $62,000 in the 47-mm case. The Diamond Collection can burn a hole of up to $155,000 in one's wallet for full pavé and a jeweled map of the world on the dial.

And soon, Jacob & Co. will be presenting an exciting addition to its line: A mechanical 5-time zone model! Little is known about the watch thus far, but a prototype is in existence that is dressed a little less flamboyantly than its bird of paradise siblings. Working with horological specialists in Switzerland, Jacob & Co. will hopefully be able to unveil this world-first during the course of 2005. It will join the automatic chronograph (powered by a Valjoux 7753) already ensconced in the collection, which features the dial design typical of Arabo minus the extra time zones.

Five Time Zone "The World is Yours"

Reference number: JC-47
Movement: quartz, 1 x ETA 956.112, 4 x ETA 280.002; a total of five ETA quartz movements
Functions: hours, minutes, sweep seconds; date; five time zones
Case: stainless steel, ø 47 mm, height 13.25 mm; paved with a total of 4 carats of natural and treated diamonds, interchangeable bezel; mineral crystal; water-resistant to 100 m
Band: stainless steel, folding clasp
Remarks: comes in a set with 4 colored polyurethane straps
Price: $114,000
Variations: various diamonds, from $24,000 to $125,000

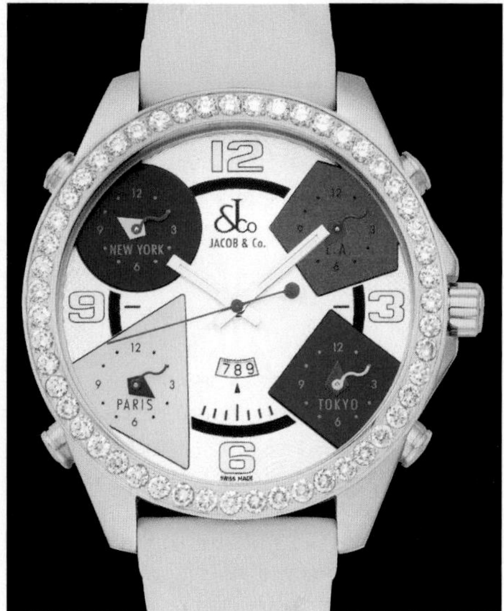

Five Time Zone Full Size

Reference number: JC-1
Movement: quartz, 1 x ETA 956.112, 4 x ETA 280.002; a total of five ETA quartz movements
Functions: hours, minutes, sweep seconds; date, five time zones
Case: stainless steel, ø 47 mm, height 13.25 mm; bezel paved with 3.25 ct of diamonds, interchangeable bezel; mineral crystal; water-resistant to 100 m
Band: polyurethane, folding clasp
Remarks: comes in a set with 4 colored polyurethane straps
Price: $12,100
Variations: from $6,600 (without diamonds) to $50,000

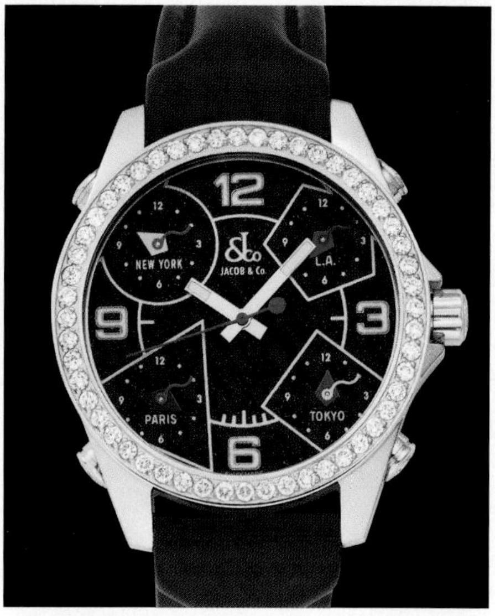

Five Time Zone Mid Size

Reference number: JC-M29
Movement: quartz, 1 x ETA 980.106, 4 x ETA 280.002; a total of five ETA quartz movements
Functions: hours, minutes, sweep seconds; date, five time zones
Case: stainless steel, ø 40 mm, height 12.3 mm; bezel paved with 2 ct of diamonds, interchangeable bezel, aventurine dial; mineral crystal; water-resistant to 100 m
Band: polyurethane, folding clasp
Remarks: comes in a set with 4 colored polyurethane straps
Price: $9,800
Variations: from $6,500 (without diamonds) to $44,000

Automatic Chronograph

Reference number: AC-2
Movement: automatic, ETA 7753 ø 30.40 mm, height 7.9 mm; 27 jewels; 28,800 vph, finely finished
Functions: hours, minutes, subsidiary seconds; date, chronograph
Case: stainless steel, ø 40 mm, height 14.95 mm; bezel paved with 2 carats of diamonds; interchangeable bezel; mineral crystal; water-resistant to 30 m
Band: polyurethane, folding clasp
Remarks: comes in a set with 4 colored polyurethane straps
Price: $9,800
Variations: with plain bezel ($6,500); with 3.2 ct diamonds

Five Time Zone Mid Size

Reference number: JC-M34
Movement: quartz, 1 x ETA 980.106, 4 x ETA 280.002 a total of five ETA quartz movements
Functions: hours, minutes, sweep seconds; five time zones
Case: stainless steel, ø 40 mm, height 12.3 mm; dial paved with one carat of diamonds, interchangeable bezel; mineral crystal; water-resistant to 100 m
Band: reptile skin, folding clasp
Remarks: comes in a set with 4 colored polyurethane straps
Price: $14,800
Variations: from $11,500 (without diamonds on bezel) to $44,000 (14.25 ct and JC bracelet); yellow, white, rose gold

Angel Collection Two Time Zone

Reference number: JC-A18
Movement: quartz, 1 x ETA 956.112, 1 x ETA E01.001; a total of two ETA quartz movements
Functions: hours, minutes, sweep seconds; date; second time zone
Case: stainless steel, 44.2 x 24.8 mm, height 8.9 mm; paved case and bracelet for a total of 10.5 carats of diamonds; mineral crystal; water-resistant to 30 m
Band: stainless steel, folding clasp
Remarks: aventurine dial with mother-of-pearl inlay
Price: $38,900
Variations: available in yellow, white, or rose gold

Jaeger-LeCoultre

The history of the Jaeger-LeCoultre *manufacture* is rich in horological top performances and works of art. But the Gyrotourbillon I that was presented this year at the S.I.H.H. beats everything that has come out until now: It combines a perpetual calendar with a double retrograde date display, a direct display of the equation of time, and a spherical tourbillon that rotates on a double axis. With this masterpiece, the company at home in the Vallée de Joux's Le Sentier has once again proven its skill in building watch movements.
And by the way, it is not only the company's own products that profit from this, for Jaeger-LeCoultre has discreetly supplied quality movements to other reputable watch manufacturers for decades. During the last few years, especially since the brand was sold to the Richemont luxury concern, Jaeger-LeCoultre has focused its attention on making its high technical competence more recognizable for the consumer. At the same time, the delivery of watch movements to competitors outside the Richemont group has been restricted even more. The design of new or strongly altered watch movements in past years has above all benefited the most well-known product made by Jaeger-LeCoultre: the Reverso model family. Although the *manufacture* generates the lion's share of its turnover with this line, it reflects only a part of the company's horological competence.
Now the fine, round automatic movements that are used as the "motors" for various complicated watches are being taken care of. Just recently the *manufacture* presented the first models of the new caliber family 970 (internally called the Autotractor), in which numerous modern technologies have been realized. These begin with the winding mechanism, whose rotor was outfitted with a ball bearing containing ceramic balls that function wonderfully without lubrication. The engineers even went down a new path with the escapement, positioning the large balance wheel underneath a balance cock that is attached to the plate at two different points. The watch's rate is not regulated by an index that moves the balance spring, which is, by the way, attached by its end points with a laser, but by four weighted screws on the balance wheel. Even the shape of the gear train's teeth was calculated anew and now functions more effectively.

This high-tech mechanical movement is being used first in the Master Hometime, a time zone watch that was created especially for globetrotters, but which is not necessarily recognizable as such at first glance. Only after the crown has been pulled and the hour hand set to the time of the new location does a second hour hand, hidden until that point, become visible to show home time. A small indicator between 9 and 11 o'clock shows whether it is currently day or night at home. It is hardly possible to present such functions in a more elegant or refined way.
Alongside the obvious joy in high-tech watchmaking, the specialists in Le Sentier are also careful with good old traditions. With the renewed interested in Caliber 101, found in timepieces such as the Joaillerie Rivière 101, watches have been presented that will certainly fascinate both men interested in technology and women who enjoy fine, delicate jewelry watches: In a tiny case, held to the wrist by a double-stranded band of leather or white gold, there ticks the smallest mechanical movement ever created, Caliber LeCoultre 101. It weighs a mere gram, was first constructed in 1929, and comprises ninety-eight individual components.

Reverso Grande GMT

Reference number: 302 84 20
Movement: manual winding, JLC 878, height 5.6 mm, 35 jewels; 28,800 vph, 2 spring barrels, power reserve 8 days
Functions: hours, minutes, subsidiary seconds; large date (front); hours, minutes (second time zone); power reserve display; day/night display, GMT synchronization (back)
Case: stainless steel, 46.5 x 28.5 mm, height 9.3 mm; case can be turned and rotated 180°; two sapphire crystals
Band: reptile skin, folding clasp
Price: $9,900
Variations: with link bracelet; in red gold with leather strap or link bracelet

Reverso Grande Réserve

Reference number: 301 24 20
Movement: manual winding, JLC 874, 25.2 x 31.2 mm, height 6.45 mm; 25 jewels; 28,800 vph, 2 spring barrels, power reserve 8 days
Functions: hours, minutes, subsidiary seconds; jump digital power reserve display in window on case back
Case: red gold, 46.5 x 29.25 mm, height 12 mm; case can be turned and rotated 180°; sapphire crystal
Band: reptile skin, folding clasp
Price: $6,800
Variations: with red gold bracelet; in stainless steel with leather strap or stainless steel bracelet

Reverso Grande Taille

Reference number: 270 14 10
Movement: manual winding, JLC 822, 22.6 x 17.2 mm, height 2.94 mm; 21 jewels; 21,600 vph
Functions: hours, minutes, subsidiary seconds
Case: yellow gold, 42.2 x 26.1 mm, height 9.5 mm; case can be turned and rotated 180°; sapphire crystal
Band: reptile skin, folding clasp
Price: $9,600
Variations: with yellow gold link bracelet; in stainless steel with leather strap or stainless steel bracelet; in stainless steel/yellow gold with leather strap or two-tone bracelet

Reverso Duoface

Reference number: 271 84 10
Movement: manual winding, JLC 854, 17.2 x 22 mm, height 3.8 mm; 21 jewels; 21,600 vph
Functions: hours, minutes, subsidiary seconds (front); hours, minutes (second time zone), 24-hours-display (back)
Case: stainless steel, 42.2 x 26.1 mm, height 9.5 mm; case can be turned and rotated 180°; two sapphire crystals
Band: reptile skin, folding clasp
Price: $6,500
Variations: with stainless steel bracelet; in red or yellow gold with leather strap or link bracelet

Reverso Gran'Sport Duo

Reference number: 294 16 01
Movement: manual winding, JLC 851, 22.6 x 17.2 mm, height 4.5 mm; 21 jewels; 21,600 vph
Functions: hours, minutes, subsidiary seconds; date; 24-hour display (second time zone)
Case: yellow gold, 42.2 x 26.1 mm, height 9.3 mm; case can be turned and rotated 180°, ergonomically optimized; sapphire crystal; water-resistant to 50 m
Band: rubber, double folding clasp with fine fit
Price: $15,300
Variations: with yellow gold bracelet; in stainless steel with rubber strap or stainless steel bracelet

Reverso Gran'Sport Automatique

Reference number: 290 84 10
Movement: automatic, JLC 960R, ø 21.3 mm, height 4.5 mm; 31 jewels; 28,800 vph
Functions: hours, minutes, sweep seconds; date
Case: stainless steel, 37 x 26 mm, height 9 mm; case can be turned and rotated 180°, ergonomically optimized; sapphire crystal; water-resistant to 50 m
Band: reptile skin, folding clasp
Price: $5,200

Reverso Gran'Sport Dame

Reference number: 296 84 01
Movement: manual winding, JLC 864, 18.4 x 17.2 mm, height 3.45 mm, 19 jewels; 21,600 vph
Functions: hours, minutes, subsidiary seconds (front); hours, minutes (second time zone); day/night display
Case: stainless steel, 38.7 x 24.83 mm, height 12.25 mm; case can be turned and rotated 180°, ergonomically optimized; two sapphire crystals; water-resistant to 50 m
Band: reptile skin, folding clasp
Price: $6,100

Reverso Duetto Classique

Reference number: 256 84 01
Movement: manual winding, JLC 865, 18.4 X 17.2 mm, height 3.45 mm; 19 jewels; 21,600 vph
Functions: hours, minutes, subsidiary seconds (front); hours, minutes (back)
Case: stainless steel, 38 x 23 mm; case can be turned and rotated 180°; two sapphire crystals
Band: satin, folding clasp in stainless steel
Remarks: case back set with 32 diamonds
Price: $5,800
Variations: with leather strap; with link bracelet; in red or yellow gold with leather or satin strap, with link bracelet

Reverso Duetto

Reference number: 266 51 20
Movement: manual winding, JLC 844, 15.2 x 13 mm, height 3.45 mm; 18 jewels; 21,600 vph
Functions: hours, minutes (front); hours, minutes (second time zone) (back)
Case: stainless steel/yellow gold, 28.6 x 20.7 mm; case can be turned and rotated 180°; two sapphire crystals
Band: stainless steel/yellow gold, folding clasp
Remarks: case back set with 32 diamonds; second dial with mother-of-pearl segment
Price: $9,350
Variations: with leather strap; in yellow gold

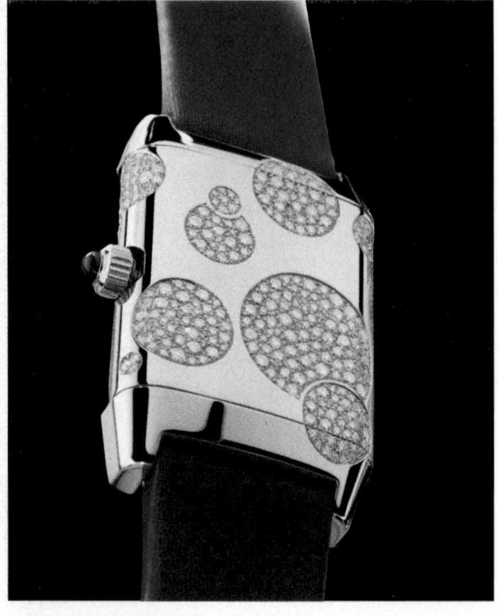

Reverso Volga

Reference number: 267 34 09
Movement: manual winding, JLC 846, 15.3 x 13 mm, height 2.9 mm; 18 jewels; 21,600 vph
Functions: hours, minutes
Case: white gold, 28.6 x 20.7 mm, height 7.5 mm; case can be turned and rotated 180°; sapphire crystal; crown with sapphire cabochon
Band: satin, folding clasp in white gold
Remarks: case and folding clasp decorated with about 425 snow-set diamonds
Price: $48,000
Variations: with quartz movement

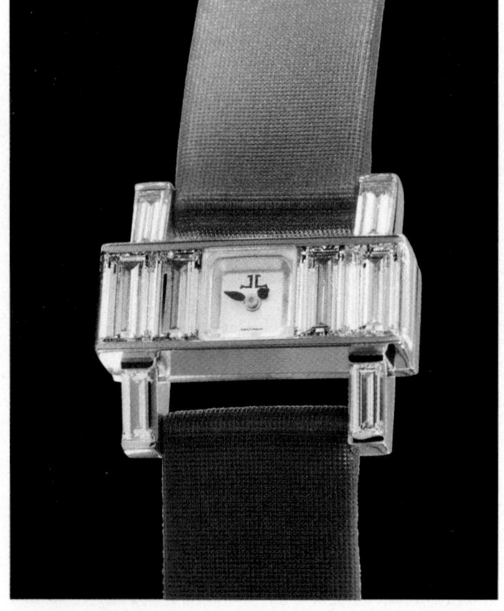

Reverso Joaillerie 101 Etrier

Reference number: 282 34 11
Movement: manual winding, JLC 101, 14 x 4.8 mm, height 3.4 mm; 19 jewels; 21,600 vph, world's smallest mechanical movement (baton movement)
Functions: hours, minutes
Case: white gold; case set with 10 baguette-cut diamonds; sapphire crystal
Band: satin, buckle
Price: $57,000
Variations: with white gold bracelet and 174 baguette-cut diamonds; in white gold with 6 baguette diamonds and 4 rubies; in white gold with 6 baguette diamonds and 4 sapphires

Reverso Grande Date

Reference number: 300 84 20
Movement: manual winding, JLC 875, 25.2 x 31.2 mm, height 5.3 mm; 25 jewels; 28,800 vph, 2 spring barrels, power reserve 8 days
Functions: hours, minutes, subsidiary seconds; large date; power reserve display
Case: stainless steel, 42.2 x 26.1 mm, height 9.5 mm; case can be turned and rotated 180°; sapphire crystal; transparent case back
Band: reptile skin, folding clasp
Price: $7,900
Variations: with stainless steel bracelet; in yellow gold

Master Gyrotourbillon

Reference number: 600 64 20

Movement: manual winding, JLC 177, ø 36.3 mm, height 10.85 mm; 77 jewels; 21,600 vph, spherical tourbillon with 2 axes, 2 spring barrels with sapphire lids, power reserve 150 h

Functions: hours, minutes, subsidiary seconds; direct equation of time; perpetual calendar with date (two retrograde hands), month (retrograde) and leap year (back); power reserve display

Case: platinum, ø 43 mm, height 14.9 mm; sapphire crystal; case back with small exhibition window; limited to 75 pieces

Band: reptile skin, folding clasp

Price: $275,000

Master Eight Days Perpetual

Reference number: 161 24 2D

Movement: manual winding, JLC 876, height 6.6 mm; 37 jewels; 28,800 vph, 2 spring barrels, power reserve 8 days

Functions: hours, minutes; perpetual calendar with date, day, month, year (four-digit); day/night display; power reserve display

Case: red gold, ø 41.5 mm, height 11 mm; sapphire crystal; transparent case back; water-resistant to 50 m

Band: reptile skin, folding clasp

Price: $36,000

Variations: with diamonds; in platinum with reptile skin strap; in platinum with baguette-cut diamonds on the bezel

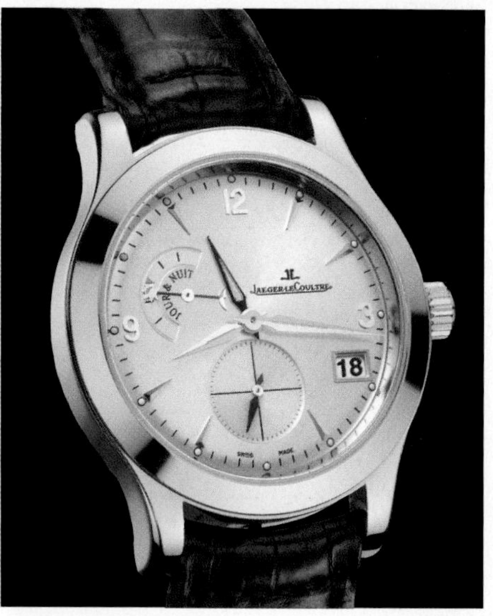

Master Hometime

Reference number: 162 84 20

Movement: automatic, JLC 975, ø 30 mm, height 5.7 mm; 29 jewels; 28,800 vph, ceramic ball bearings

Functions: hours, minutes, subsidiary seconds; separately settable hour hand (second time zone); day/night display (attached to local time); date

Case: stainless steel, ø 40 mm, height 10 mm; sapphire crystal; transparent case back; water-resistant to 50 m

Band: reptile skin, folding clasp

Price: $5,700

Variations: with stainless steel bracelet; in red gold with leather strap

Master Compressor Dualmatic

Reference number: 173 84 70

Movement: automatic, JLC 972, height 6.14 mm; 29 jewels; 28,800 vph

Functions: hours, minutes, subsidiary seconds; separately settable hour hand (second time zone); 24-hour display (attached to second time zone); date

Case: stainless steel, ø 41.5 mm, height 11 mm; bidirectionally rotating bezel under crystal, settable via crown; sapphire crystal; compression key system on crown (patented); water-resistant to 100 m

Band: leather, folding clasp

Price: $5,900

Master Eight Days

Reference number: 160 24 20

Movement: manual winding, JLC 877, ø 32 mm, height 5.3 mm; 25 jewels; 28,800 vph, 2 spring barrels, power reserve 8 days; movement decorated with côtes Soleillées

Functions: hours, minutes, subsidiary seconds; large date; day/night display; power reserve display

Case: red gold, ø 41.5 mm, height 10.9 mm; sapphire crystal; transparent case back; water-resistant to 50 m

Band: reptile skin, folding clasp

Price: $15,800

Master Grande Memovox

Reference number: 146 34 4D

Movement: automatic, JLC 909-440 (base JLC 918); ø 31 mm, height 8.3 mm; 36 jewels; 28,800 vph

Functions: hours, minutes, sweep seconds; perpetual calendar with date, day, month, moon phase, year; 24-hour display; alarm

Case: white gold, ø 41.5 mm, height 14 mm; sapphire crystal; water-resistant to 50 m

Band: reptile skin, folding clasp

Price: $32,700

Variations: in red gold with leather strap

Master Compressor Memovox

Reference number: 170 84 70
Movement: automatic, JLC 918 (base JLC 916); ø 30 mm, height 7.45 mm; 22 jewels; 28,800 vph
Functions: hours, minutes, sweep seconds; date; alarm
Case: stainless steel, ø 41.5 mm, height 12 mm; bidirectionally rotating bezel with 60-minute scale under crystal, settable via crown; sapphire crystal; compression key system on crown (patented); water-resistant to 50 m
Band: calfskin, folding clasp
Price: $6,950
Variations: stainless steel bracelet; red gold with leather strap or red gold bracelet; in white gold with strap or bracelet

Master Compressor Automatic

Reference number: 172 24 40
Movement: automatic, JLC 960M, ø 20.4 mm, height 4.2 mm; 31 jewels; 28,800 vph
Functions: hours, minutes, sweep seconds; date
Case: red gold, ø 36.8 mm, height 4.2 mm; bidirectionally rotating bezel with 60-minute scale under crystal, settable via crown; sapphire crystal; compression key system on crown (patented); water-resistant to 200 m
Band: reptile skin, folding clasp
Price: $11,500
Variations: with red gold bracelet; in stainless steel with calfskin strap or stainless steel bracelet

Master Compressor Geographic

Reference number: 171 84 70
Movement: automatic, JLC 923, ø 26 mm, height 4.9 mm; 31 jewels; 28,800 vph
Functions: hours, minutes, sweep seconds; date; second time zone, world time display with 24 time zones in window; AM/PM indication
Case: stainless steel, ø 41.5 mm, height 13.9 mm; sapphire crystal; compression key system on crown (patented); water-resistant to 100 m
Band: calfskin, folding clasp
Price: $8,200
Variations: with bracelet; in red or white gold

Master Moon

Reference number: 143 34 7D
Movement: automatic, JLC 891-448-2 (base JLC 889-1); ø 28.8 mm, height 5.53 mm; 36 jewels; 28,800 vph
Functions: hours, minutes, subsidiary seconds; date, day, month, moon phase
Case: white gold, ø 37.1 mm, height 10,2 mm; sapphire crystal; transparent case back; water-resistant to 50 m
Band: reptile skin, folding clasp
Price: $12,700
Variations: in red gold with leather strap; in stainless steel with leather strap

Master Control

Reference number: 140 24 20
Movement: automatic, JLC 889/2, ø 26 mm, height 3.25 mm; 36 jewels; 28,800 vph
Functions: hours, minutes, sweep seconds; date
Case: red gold, ø 37 mm, height 6.1 mm; sapphire crystal; water-resistant to 50 m
Band: reptile skin, folding clasp
Price: $9,600
Variations: in stainless steel with leather strap

Master Ultra-Thin

Reference number: 145 84 04
Movement: manual winding, JLC 849 (base JLC 839); ø 20.8 mm, height 1.85 mm; 19 jewels; 21,600 vph, ultraflat movement
Functions: hours, minutes
Case: stainless steel, ø 33.4 mm, height 4,2 mm; sapphire crystal; transparent case back; water-resistant to 50 m
Band: reptile skin, folding clasp
Price: $4,300
Variations: in red gold; in white gold, with grey dial; all models also with buckle

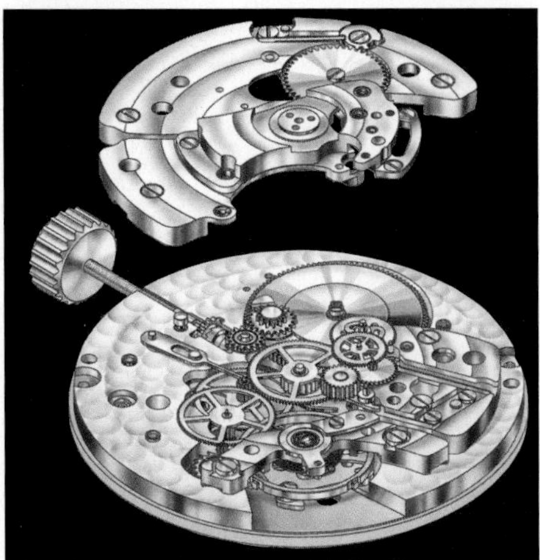

Caliber 975 "Autotractor"

Mechanical with automatic winding; lubrication-free central rotor on ceramic ball bearings (maintenance-free); power reserve 50 hours
Functions: hours, minutes, subsidiary seconds; separately adjustable hour hand (second time zone); day/night indication (attached to first time zone); date
Diameter: 30 mm; **Height:** 5.7 mm
Jewels: 29
Balance: screw balance with four weights
Frequency: 28,800 vph
Balance spring: flat hairspring
Shock protection: Kif
Remarks: base plate with perlage; bridges with côtes circulaires

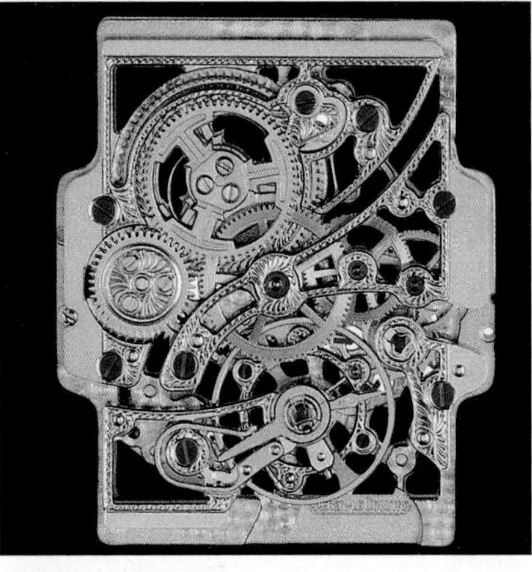

Caliber 849R-SQ

Mechanical with manual winding
Functions: hours, minutes
Dimensions: 16.4/20 x 23.5 mm
Height: 2.25 mm
Jewels: 19
Balance: glucydur
Frequency: 21,600 vph
Balance spring: flat hairspring
Shock protection: Kif
Remarks: skeletonized by hand and decorated with Greek motifs; 128 individual components; 35 hours power reserve

Caliber 828

Mechanical with manual winding, power reserve 45 hours
Functions: hours, minutes, subsidiary seconds; power reserve display
Dimensions: 23.4 x 28.9 mm (10 1/2''' x 12 3/4''')
Height: 4.79 mm
Jewels: 27
Balance: glucydur with compensation screws, one-minute tourbillon with steel cage
Frequency: 21,600 vph
Balance spring: Breguet
Shock protection: Kif
Remarks: base plate with perlage, bridges with côtes de Genève, dial segment hand-engraved

Caliber 943

Mechanical with manual winding, power reserve 35 hours
Functions: hours, minutes; minute repeater
Dimensions: 27.4 x 28.9 mm (12 x 12 3/4''')
Height: 4.85 mm
Jewels: 38
Balance: glucydur
Frequency: 21,600 vph
Balance spring: flat hairspring
Shock protection: Kif
Remarks: base plate with perlage, bridges with côtes de Genève

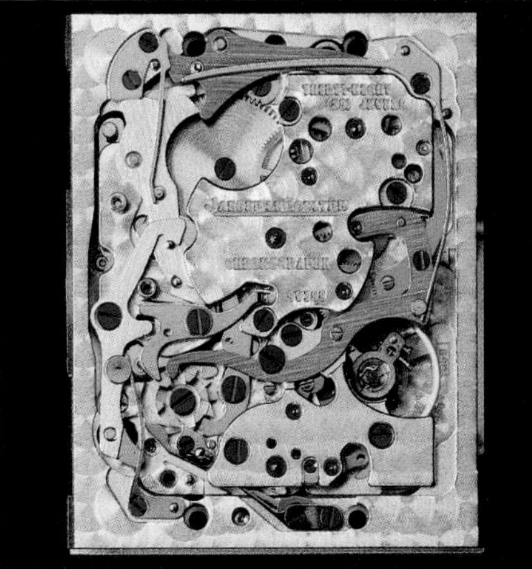

Caliber 859

Mechanical with manual winding; power reserve 45 hours
Functions: hours, minutes, sweep seconds (front); chronograph with second counter and retrograde minute counter (back)
Dimensions: 22.6 x 17.2 mm
Height: 4.5 mm
Jewels: 38
Balance: glucydur with compensation screws
Frequency: 28,800 vph
Balance spring: flat hairspring
Shock protection: Kif
Related caliber: 829

Caliber 878

Mechanical with manual winding; twin spring barrels, power reserve eight days
Functions: hours, minutes, subsidiary seconds; large date (front); hours, minutes (second time zone); power reserve display; day/night indication, GMT synchronization (back)
Dimensions: 25.2 x 31.2 mm
Height: 5.6 mm
Jewels: 35
Balance: glucydur with compensation screws
Frequency: 28,800 vph
Balance spring: flat hairspring
Shock protection: Kif

Caliber 879

Mechanical with manual winding; power reserve eight days
Functions: hours, minutes, subsidiary seconds; large date, day/night indication, power reserve display
Dimensions: 25.2 x 31.2 mm
Height: 5.3 mm
Jewels: 25
Balance: glucydur
Frequency: 28,800 vph
Balance spring: flat hairspring
Shock protection: Kif
Remarks: 224 individual parts, twin spring barrels

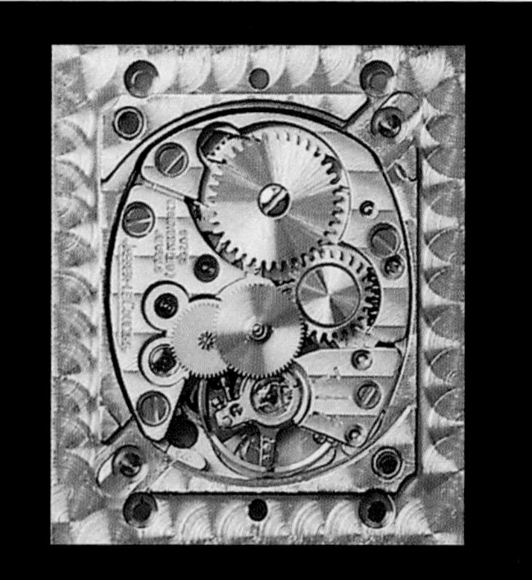

Caliber 101

Mechanical with manual winding
Functions: hours, minutes
Dimensions: 4.8 x 14 mm
Height: 3.4 mm
Jewels: 19
Balance: glucydur
Frequency: 21,600 vph
Balance spring: flat hairspring
Shock protection: Kif
Remarks: 98 individual parts, world's smallest mechanical watch movement

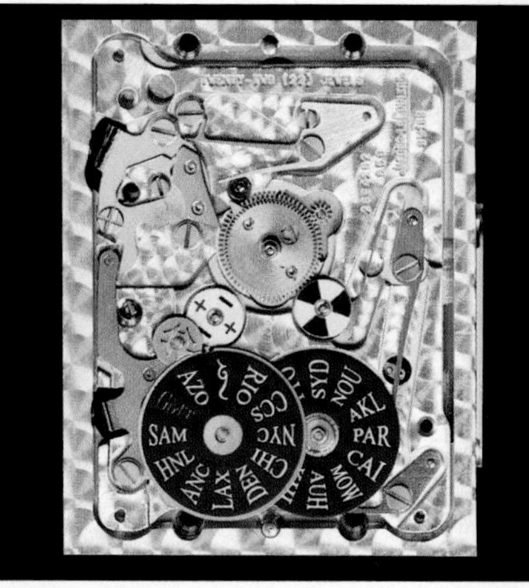

Caliber 858 (dial side)

Mechanical with manual winding, power reserve 45 hours
Functions: hours, minutes, seconds; day/night indication; second time zone in hours/minutes
Dimensions: 22.6 x 17.2 mm
Height: 3.8 mm
Jewels: 22
Balance: glucydur with compensation screws
Frequency: 21,600 vph
Balance spring: flat hairspring
Shock protection: Kif
Remarks: limited to 500 pieces

Caliber 854-J

Mechanical with manual winding
Functions: hours, minutes, subsidiary seconds, day/night indication (front); second time zone, day/night disk (back)
Dimensions: 17.2 x 22 mm
Height: 3.8 mm
Jewels: 22
Balance: glucydur
Frequency: 21,600 vph
Balance spring: flat hairspring
Shock protection: Kif
Remarks: 150 individual parts, power reserve 50 hours

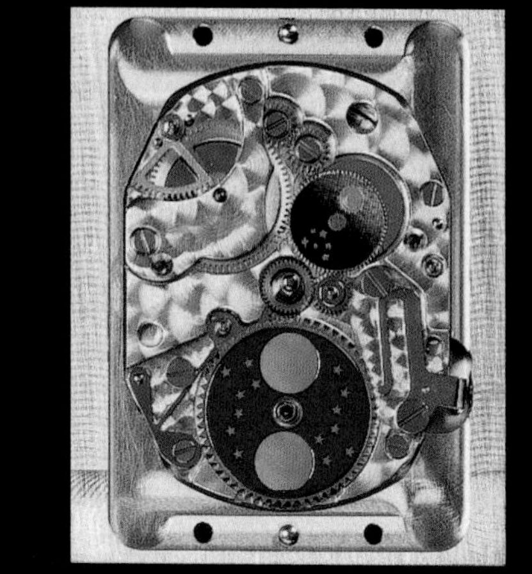

Caliber 823 (dial side)

Base caliber: 822
Mechanical with manual winding, power reserve 45 hours
Functions: hours, minutes, subsidiary seconds; day/night indication; power reserve; moon phase
Dimensions: 22.6 x 17.2 mm
Height: 4.14 mm
Jewels: 23
Balance: glucydur with compensation screws
Frequency: 21,600 vph
Balance spring: flat hairspring
Shock protection: Kif
Remarks: base plate on dial side with perlage, bridges with côtes de Genève

Caliber 835

Mechanical with manual winding, power reserve 45 hours
Functions: hours, minutes, subsidiary seconds; date, day, day/night indication
Dimensions: 22 x 17.2 mm
Height: 4.14 mm
Jewels: 21
Balance: glucydur
Frequency: 21,600 vph
Balance spring: flat hairspring
Shock protection: Kif
Remarks: 167 individual parts

Caliber 849

Mechanical with manual winding, power reserve 35 hours
Functions: hours, minutes
Diameter: 20.8 mm (9''')
Height: 1.85 mm
Jewels: 19
Balance: glucydur
Frequency: 21,600 vph
Balance spring: flat hairspring
Shock protection: Kif
Remarks: 123 individual parts, bridges with côtes de Genève

Caliber 891/448/2 (dial side)

Mechanical with automatic winding, power reserve 40 hours
Functions: hours, minutes, subsidiary seconds; complete calendar (date, day, month, moon phase)
Diameter: 28.8 mm
Height: 5.53 mm
Jewels: 36
Balance: glucydur
Frequency: 28,800 vph
Balance spring: flat hairspring with fine adjustment via micrometer screw
Shock protection: Kif
Related caliber: 891/447

Caliber 929/3

base caliber: 889/1
Mechanical with automatic winding, power reserve 42 hours; ball-bearing, two-part rotor with 21-karat yellow gold oscillating segment
Functions: hours, minutes, sweep seconds; sweep date, second time zone with reference cities, day/night indication; power reserve display
Diameter: 26 mm; **Height:** 4.85 mm, **Jewels:** 38
Balance: glucydur; **Frequency:** 28,800 vph
Balance spring: flat hairspring with fine adjustment via micrometer screw
Shock protection: Kif
Remarks: 293 individual parts; base plate with perlage, bridges with côtes de Genève, blued screws
Related calibers: 889, 928

Caliber 889/2

Mechanical with automatic winding, power reserve 38 hours
Functions: hours, minutes, calendar
Diameter: 26 mm (11 1/2''')
Height: 3.25 mm
Jewels: 36
Balance: glucydur
Frequency: 28,800 vph
Balance spring: flat hairspring with fine adjustment via micrometer screw
Shock protection: Kif
Remarks: 202 individual parts; base plate with perlage, bridges with côtes de Genève

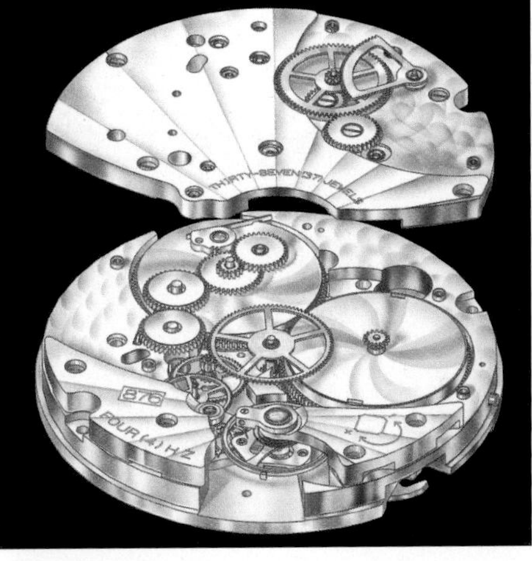

Caliber 876

Mechanical with manual winding; twin spring barrels, power reserve eight days
Functions: hours, minutes; perpetual calendar with date, day, month, year (four-digit), day/night indication; power reserve display
Diameter: 32 mm
Height: 6.6 mm
Jewels: 37
Balance: glucydur with compensation screws
Frequency: 28,800 vph
Balance spring: flat hairspring
Shock protection: Kif

Caliber 914

Base caliber: 911
Mechanical with manual winding, power reserve 45 hours
Functions: hours, minutes, sweep seconds; alarm
Diameter: 29.8 mm
Height: 5.15 mm
Jewels: 18
Balance: glucydur
Frequency: 28,800 vph
Balance spring: Nivarox
Shock protection: Kif
Remarks: 159 individual parts; base plate with perlage, bridges with côtes de Genève, blued screws

Jaquet Droz

In China, the number eight is a symbol for luck. Pierre Jaquet Droz had already adopted this figure for the design of one of the many pocket watches that his *manufactures* exported to the Far East at the end of the eighteenth century. Together with his son, he had built up a prosperous company whose products enjoyed a remarkable reputation in the parts of the world known to Europeans back then. Not only was he known at European courts, but also charmed Chinese mandarins, Indian maharajas, and Japanese rulers.

Pierre Jaquet Droz was born on July 28, 1721, of modest means. The town's preacher made a point of sending the young man to the theological faculty of the university in Neuchâtel. Obviously, little Pierre was not the same kind of child as others in the village.

It's not clear why Jaquet Droz turned his back to theology. The fact remains that he became a watchmaker — obviously his true vocation — and his early designs already awed his established colleagues. Jaquet Droz set new standards in micromechanics, and his interest soon led him past watch movements to other, more complicated mechanical mechanisms. During a journey to the Spanish royal court in 1758, his creations, including a small dog that barked, were received with great interest, and in the following years Jaquet Droz and his partner Jean-Frédéric Leschot dedicated themselves more often to the manufacture of complicated automated figures, also known as androids, than to watches.

More than once Jaquet Droz was suspected of witchcraft by his former master, the church, whose guardians of public morals had a hard time understanding the charming movements made by the drawing child, the young writer, and the finely chiseled pianist. Even today it is truly a special experience to observe the androids at work in the art and history museum of Neuchâtel where they are kept, admiring the sheer complexity of the mechanics hidden beneath the clothes, porcelain, and horsehair wigs. A small workshop in La Chaux-de-Fonds still produces such mechanisms and artful treasures today – the commonplace last name of Jaquet Droz is not forgotten in Neu-châtel's area of the Jura.

In the meantime, another tradition of the house of Jaquet Droz is also being revived: watchmaking. Under the roof of the Swatch Group, Jaquet Droz is to be built into a brand that orients itself toward more traditional values in watchmaking, stylistically kept more classical and elegant than sporty.

The new company's model palette is continually growing, showing the way to the future of the brand, which is to close the gap between the mid-level and top brands according to the wishes of the Swatch Group's directors.

Grande Seconde Marine

Reference number: J020034201
Movement: automatic, Jaquet Droz 2663.4 (base Frédéric Piguet 1150); ø 26,2 mm, height 4.52 mm; 30 jewels; 28,800 vph; twin spring barrels, power reserve 72 hours; certified chronometer (C.O.S.C.)
Functions: hours, minutes (off-center), large subsidiary seconds
Case: white gold, ø 43 mm, height 12 mm sapphire crystal; screw-in crown; water-resistant to 100 m
Band: reptile skin and rubber, buckle
Remarks: genuine Grand Feu enamel dial; limited to 88 pieces
Price: $17,900

Les Lunes Réhaut Ardoise

Reference number: J012624204
Movement: automatic, Jaquet Droz 6553.4 (base Frédéric Piguet 1150); ø 26.2 mm, height 4,9 mm; 28 jewels; 28.800 A/h; twin spring barrels, power reserve 72 hours
Functions: hours, minutes; date, day, month and moon phase
Case: white gold, ø 40.5 mm, height 11.85 mm; sapphire crystal
Band: reptile skin, buckle
Remarks: slate-colored, opalized dial
Price: $20,900

Grande Seconde Cerclée

Reference number: J003034204
Movement: automatic, Jaquet Droz 2663.4 (base Frédéric Piguet 1150); ø 26.2 mm, height 4.52 mm; 30 jewels; 28,800 vph; twin spring barrels, power reserve 72 hours
Functions: hours, minutes (off-center), large subsidiary seconds
Case: white gold, ø 43 mm, height 11.5 mm; sapphire crystal
Band: reptile skin, buckle
Remarks: slate-colored, opalized dial
Price: $13,900

Chrono Monopoussoir

Reference number: J007634202
Movement: automatic, Jaquet Droz 2688.M (base Frédéric Piguet 1180); ø 26.2 mm, height 6.6 mm; 30 jewels; 21,600 vph; column-wheel control of the chronograph functions
Functions: hours, minutes (off-center), subsidiary seconds; chronograph
Case: white gold, ø 43 mm, height 13,65 mm; sapphire crystal
Band: reptile skin, buckle
Remarks: slate-colored, opalized dial
Price: $21,400

Tourbillon Répétition Minutes

Reference number: J011834202
Movement: manual winding, Jaquet Droz 2692.T (base CL92); ø 26.2 mm; 36 jewels; 18,000 vph; one-minute tourbillon; strike train with two gongs and hammers
Functions: hours, minutes, subsidiary seconds; hour, quarter-hour, and minute repeater
Case: white gold, ø 43 mm, height 14.5 mm sapphire crystal
Band: reptile skin, buckle
Remarks: slate-colored, opalized dial; limited to 8 pieces
Price: $300,000

Les Douze Villes Emaille

Reference number: J009634202
Movement: automatic, Jaquet Droz 3663.4 (base Frédéric Piguet 1150); ø 26.2 mm, height 5.15 mm; 28 jewels; 28,800 vph; twin spring barrels, power reserve 72 hours
Functions: hours and time zone indication with twelve reference city names (jump, settable via button), minutes
Case: white gold, ø 40.5 mm, height 11.85 mm; sapphire crystal
Band: reptile skin, buckle
Remarks: genuine Grand Feu enamel dial; limited to 88 pieces
Price: $20,700

JeanRichard

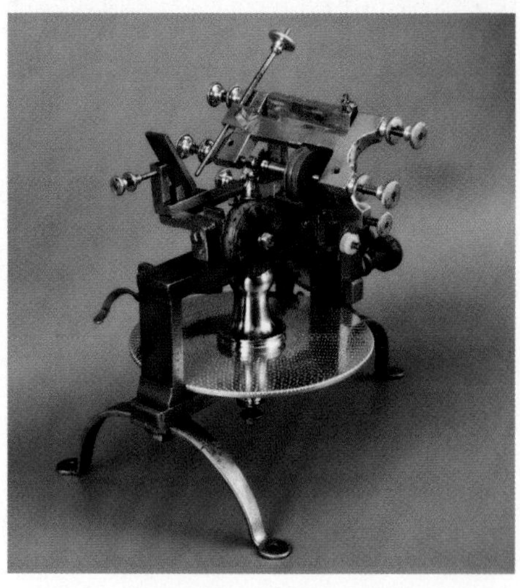

Daniel JeanRichard was born around the year 1665 in La Sagne, today a small farming village in a high valley of the mountain range that separates the plateau of La Chaux-de-Fonds and Le Locle from Neuchâtel on the quiet shores of the lake of the same name. In the seventeenth century La Sagne was larger than today's industrial cities on the plateau, or, perhaps better stated, not quite as small as the other unimportant places in the central Swiss Jura.

Daniel JeanRichard's father and grandfather were justices of the peace and smiths in La Sagne, which didn't actually mean that their lots in life were better than those of the rest of the farming folk. The JeanRichards had perhaps a few more visitors than those working in agricultural and forestry, and this was the reason that a horse dealer passing through noticed the filigreed iron wares and silver jewelry that young Daniel had created on long winter evenings. The dealer had an English pocket watch in his baggage that had stopped working some-where between London and Basel. The young JeanRichard with his obvious talent appeared trustworthy to him, and he gave Daniel the valu-able timepiece to repair. He wanted to pick it up again a few weeks later on his way home from Geneva.

Daniel JeanRichard repaired the watch with his primitive tools — and more. During the repair process he had memorized all of the details, allowing him to build an exact replica of the watch during the following winter. No one had been able to construct his own pocket watch in the entire canton of Neuchâtel up to that point. The year was 1679, and Daniel JeanRichard was just fourteen years of age.

Massimo Macaluso was a few years older than that when his father first introduced him to the watch business. After working for many years in an import business for Swiss watches, his father Luigi Macaluso bought his own Swiss watch brand. Using the Girard-Perregaux *manufacture* as a springboard, he created JeanRichard as a second brand and systematically extended the collection, becoming more upscale — and now it even includes a tourbillon.

The next big step was already taken under the aegis of Massimo: The introduction of an autonomous movement by the caliber name of JR 1000, produced exclusively for JeanRichard by GP Manufacture. We are not talking about a redecorated Girard-Perregaux caliber, which would have been far too expensive for what was intended. No, Caliber JR 1000 displays a number of unique characteristics, such as the subsidiary seconds, which is driven outside of the flow of energy by a micromodule gear wheel with a special tooth shape that can also double as the driving source for additional complications if necessary. Additionally, the use of a double third wheel makes it possible to arrange a direct sweep seconds display under its own power, which can make room for a larger spring barrel if necessary. But, as we know, technologies of the future are created by understanding traditions: last year, JeanRichard moved into the main building of Schwob Frères in La Chaux-de-Fonds, the founding place of the Cyma watch brand, and opened an interesting museum for tools and tooling machines in the building now known as Villa JeanRichard.

Paramount JR 1000

Reference number: 61108-11-60A-AA6
Movement: automatic, JR 1000; ø 25.6 mm, height 5.1 mm; 32 jewels; 28,800 vph
Functions: hours, minutes, subsidiary seconds; date
Case: stainless steel, 34.3 x 36.5 mm, height 11.15 mm; sapphire crystal
Band: reptile skin, buckle
Remarks: limited to 1000 pieces
Price: $4,250
Variations: in rose gold, limited to 25 pieces

Caliber JR 100

Movement: Girard-Perregaux's sister brand proudly presents its first autonomous movement, JR 1000. This movement has a modern design with an incredibly low amount of elements borrowed from the calibers of GP Manufacture, Girard-Perregaux's movement department – and now JeanRichard's as well.
Automatic winding, ø 25.6 mm, height 5,1 mm; 32 jewels, 28,800 vph.

TV Screen Grand Tourbillon

Reference number: 96016-49-10A-AAE
Movement:, JR 960 (base Christophe Claret); 33 x 33 mm; 30 jewels; 21,600 vph, one-minute tourbillon
Functions: hours, minutes, subsidiary seconds (on tourbillon cage)
Case: red gold, 39 x 41 mm, height 11.4 mm; sapphire crystal
Band: reptile skin, buckle
Price: $95,000
Variations: in white gold

Grand TV Screen Double Rétrograde

Reference number: 23116-49-10A-AAE
Movement: automatic, JR 23 (base ETA 2892-A2); ø 25.6 mm, height 4.35 mm; 30 jewels; 28,800 vph
Functions: hours, minutes, subsidiary seconds (retrograde); date (retrograde)
Case: rose gold, 39 x 41 mm, height 11 mm; sapphire crystal
Band: reptile skin, buckle
Price: $17,500

TV Screen Retrograde

Reference number: 45006-49-10A-AAE
Movement: automatic, JR 45 (base ETA 2892 with module AGH 2302); ø 29.2 mm; height 5.55 mm; 31 jewels; 28,800 vph
Functions: hours, minutes, subsidiary seconds (retrograde)
Case: rose gold, 35 x 37 mm, height 12.4 mm; sapphire crystal
Band: reptile skin, buckle
Price: $12,500
Variations: in stainless steel, with silver-grey dial

TV Screen Maxi Triple Date

Reference number: 52116-11-62B-AACD
Movement: automatic, JR 52 (base ETA 2892 with Jaquet module 3105); ø 27 mm, height 5.55 mm; 27 jewels; 28,800 vph
Functions: hours, minutes, subsidiary seconds; date, day, month
Case: stainless steel, 39 x 41 mm, height 12.79 mm; sapphire crystal
Band: reptile skin, folding clasp
Price: $3,750
Variations: with stainless steel bracelet; with cream-colored dial

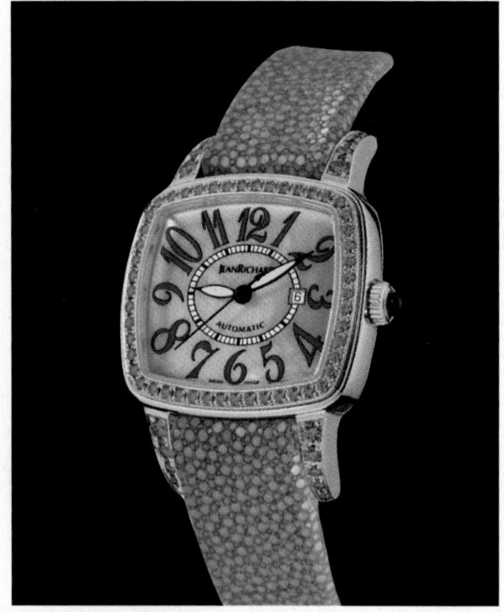

TV Screen Milady Joaillerie

Reference number: 26113 E 11B-A6A
Movement: automatic, JR 25 (base ETA 2671); ø 17.2 mm, height 4.8 mm; 25 jewels; 28,800 vph
Functions: hours, minutes, sweep seconds; date
Case: stainless steel, 31.7 x 28.7 mm, height 9.7 mm; bezel set with emeralds; sapphire crystal
Band: stingray, folding clasp
Price: $13,500
Variations: in different color variations

TV Screen Lady

Reference number: 26006 U 11A-91A-11A
Movement: automatic, JR 25 (base ETA 2671); ø 17.2 mm; height 4.8 mm; 25 jewels; 28,800 vph
Functions: hours, minutes, sweep seconds
Case: stainless steel, 28 x 29 mm, height 9.48 mm; bezel set with sapphires; sapphire crystal
Band: stainless steel, folding clasp
Price: $7,500
Variations: with leather strap; with light blue dial, with blue sapphires; without sapphires in different dial variations, with leather strap

Grand TV Screen Lady

Reference number: 24006 D 11A-11A-AACD
Movement: automatic, JR 24 (base ETA 2824-2); ø 25.6 mm, height 4.6 mm; 25 jewels; 28,800 vph
Functions: hours, minutes, sweep seconds
Case: stainless steel, 35 x 37 mm, height 12.3 mm; bezel set with brilliant-cut diamonds; sapphire crystal
Band: reptile skin, folding clasp
Price: $7,500
Variations: without brilliant-cut diamonds; in different dial variations

Diverscope

Reference number: 24120-11-62C-AC6
Movement: automatic, JR 24 (base ETA 2824-2); ø 25.6 mm, height 4.6 mm; 25 jewels; 28,800 vph
Functions: hours, minutes, sweep seconds; date
Case: stainless steel, ø 43 mm, height 13 mm; bidirectionally rotating bezel with 60-minute scale under crystal, settable via crown; mineral crystal; screw-in crown; water-resistant to 300 m
Band: rubber, buckle
Price: $1,950
Variations: diverse dial variations; with stainless steel bracelet; in titanium

Bressel Chronograph GMT

Reference number: 54112-11-11A-AAGD
Movement: automatic, JR 54 (base ETA 7750 with Jaquet module 8105); ø 30 mm, height 7.9 mm; 25 jewels (base movement); 28,800 vph
Functions: hours, minutes, subsidiary seconds; chronograph; date; 24-hour display (second time zone)
Case: stainless steel, ø 43 mm, height 15.4 mm; mineral crystal; water-resistant to 50 m
Band: reptile skin, folding clasp
Price: $2,950

TV Screen Chronoscope

Reference number: 25030-11-61A-AEE
Movement: automatic, JR 25 (base ETA 2824-2 with Dubois-Dépraz module 2020); ø 28.8 mm, height 6.9 mm; 51 jewels; 28,800 vph
Functions: hours, minutes, subsidiary seconds; chronograph
Case: stainless steel, 43.2 x 43.2 mm, height 14.5 mm; bidirectionally rotating bezel with 60-minute scale under crystal, settable via crown; sapphire crystal; screw-in crowns; water-resistant to 50 m
Band: leather, buckle
Price: $3,750
Variations: with light-colored dial

Kobold

The Kobold Watch Company specializes in precise wrist instruments for explorers and adventurers. Over the years, the small, family-owned company has concentrated on the manufacture of instrument watches, underscoring the association by making watches for polar explorers, a small but elite segment of the market. "In 2003 and 2004, the company's flagship watch, the Polar Surveyor Chronograph, was worn by more polar explorers and on more polar expeditions than any other watch," according to company president Michael Kobold. He continues by explaining, "There is a good reason for this: Kobold realizes that every watch is a potential lifeline, and therefore the company's production department takes special care to ensure the accuracy and uncompromising reliability of each Kobold watch." Indeed, at temperatures as low as minus 90 degrees Celsius, complete with whiteouts and fierce winds, a polar explorer's equipment can mean the difference between life and death. "My life depends on accurate timing and navigation," says legendary explorer Ben Saunders, who has been wearing a Kobold for years.

The Polar Surveyor Chronograph was released in 2002 after more than two years of continuous research and design. It premiered automatic winding with the functions of local time, second time zone (24-hour base), date, chronograph, and an AM/PM indicator for local time. The latter is actually a crucial function, allowing polar explorers to determine whether it is night or day during months of perpetual daylight. The Polar Surveyor Chronograph is housed in the so-called Soarway case, which consists of thirty-two individual parts. Its core is milled from a solid block of surgical stainless steel and features screwed-in strap bars, buttons, crown, and case back.

In 2005, Kobold is releasing several new versions of its unique Polar Surveyor Chronograph. The Sir Ranulph Fiennes Edition pays tribute to the man whom the *Guinness Book of World Records* describes as the "world's greatest living explorer." The watch features regal design cues, including a brushed and satin-finished stainless steel case, a navy-blue bezel with 24-hour scale, and a polished black dial with silver numerals and hands. The back of the watch displays an elaborate engraving of the Antarctic continent, which Sir Fiennes crossed unsupported on foot.

Instruments such as the Polar Surveyor Chronograph and other Kobold models are created in cooperation with a number of experts in the fields of metallurgy, watchmaking, mechanical engineering, and polar exploration. Kobold, also the company's founder, maintains close personal relationships with these professionals and draws on their expertise when designing new models. Despite the success of the brand, Kobold keeps a modest profile and relays all praise to his design team. Awarded the title "Mr. Chronograph 2003" by a small group of watch aficionados, the young entrepreneur said, "Of course, I am honored and a bit surprised, actually. I believe that I stand on the shoulders of giants, and I cannot give enough credit to my mentors and design consultants, who made all of this possible."

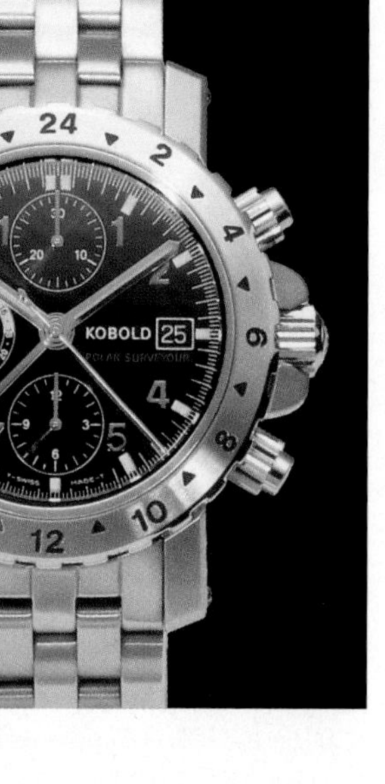

Polar Surveyor

Reference number: 915151
Movement: automatic, K. 751 (base ETA 7750); ø 30 mm, height 8.1 mm; 28 jewels; 28,800 vph, côtes de Genève, perlage, gold-plated rotor with engraving
Functions: hours, minutes, subsidiary seconds; date; chronograph, world time
Case: stainless steel, ø 42 mm, height 15.5 mm; sapphire crystal; transparent case back; screw-in crown and buttons; water-resistant to 300 m
Band: stainless steel, folding clasp
Price: $5,450
Variations: in 18-kt red gold ($12,500); in titanium ($6,250)

Polar Surveyor

Reference number: 915151
Movement: automatic, K. 751 (base ETA 7750); ø 30 mm, height 8.1 mm; 28 jewels; 28,800 vph, côtes de Genève, perlage, gold-plated rotor with engraving
Functions: hours, minutes, subsidiary seconds; date; chronograph, world time
Case: stainless steel, ø 42 mm, height 15.5 mm; sapphire crystal; transparent case back; screw-in crown and buttons, water-resistant to 300 m
Band: stainless steel, folding clasp
Price: $5,450
Variations: in 18-kt red gold ($12,500); in titanium ($6,250)

Polar Surveyor Ranulph Fiennes Edition

Reference number: 915261
Movement: automatic, K. 751 (base ETA 7750); ø 30 mm, height 8.1 mm; 28 jewels; 28,800 vph, côtes de Genève, perlage, gold-plated rotor with engraving
Functions: hours, minutes, subsidiary seconds; date; chronograph, world time
Case: stainless steel, ø 41 mm, height 15.5 mm; sapphire crystal; transparent case back; screw-in crown and buttons; water-resistant to 300 m
Band: stainless steel, folding clasp
Price: $5,450

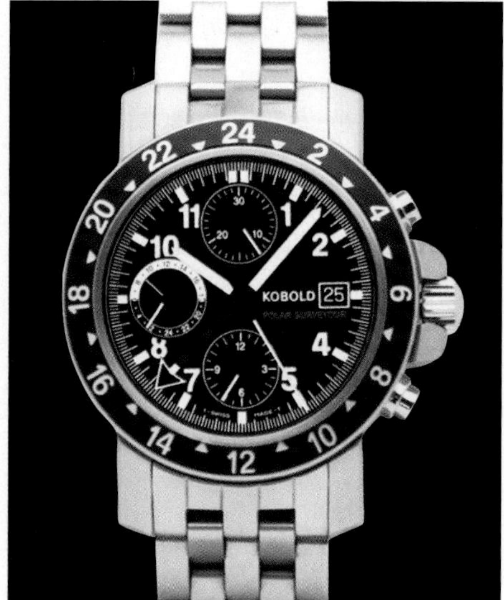

Polar Surveyor II

Reference number: 915461
Movement: automatic, K. 751 (base ETA 7750); ø 30 mm, height 8.1 mm; 28 jewels; 28,800 vph, côtes de Genève, perlage, gold-plated rotor with engraving
Functions: hours, minutes, subsidiary seconds; date; chronograph, world time
Case: stainless steel, ø 41 mm, height 15.5 mm; sapphire crystal; transparent case back; screw-in crown and buttons; water-resistant to 300 m
Band: stainless steel, folding clasp
Price: $5,850

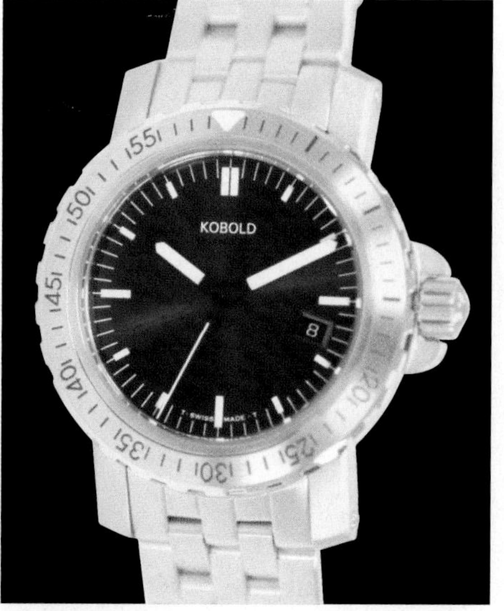

Soarway Diver

Reference number: 242121
Movement: automatic, ETA 2892-A2, ø 25.6 mm, height 4.35 mm; 22 jewels; 28,800 vph, côtes de Genève, perlage, gold-plated rotor with engraving
Functions: hours, minutes, sweep seconds; date
Case: stainless steel, ø 42 mm, height 12.5 mm; unidirectionally rotating bezel with 60-minute scale; sapphire crystal; transparent case back; screw-in crown; water-resistant to 300 m
Band: stainless steel, folding clasp
Price: $3,200
Variations: in 18-karat red gold ($8,500); in red gold with gold bracelet ($18,500)

Sir Ernest Shackleton

Reference number: 637121
Movement: manual winding, K. 348 (base Unitas 6497-1); ø 36.6 mm, height 5.4 mm; 18 jewels; 18,000 vph, côtes de Genève, perlage, engraving
Functions: hours, minutes, sweep seconds
Case: stainless steel, ø 44 mm, height 12 mm; sapphire crystal; transparent case back; screw-in crown; water-resistant to 100 m
Band: reptile skin, buckle
Price: $3,650

Maurice Lacroix

Since 1973, René Baumann has for the most part characterized the appearance of Maurice Lacroix as its product head, thus contributing heavily to the success of the young brand. Many of his models became popular bestsellers on the watch market, and numerous international awards were proof positive of his fine feeling for attractive design and unusual watches. With the Masterpiece Collection, Baumann has written an additional chapter in Swiss watch history. Fascinated by the long tradition of Switzerland's art of watchmaking and mechanical watches, in particular, it was his vision to create unique timekeepers that were able to inspire their wearers with their attractive additional functions and timeless design, optimally uniting classic and modern elements every time. "I was able to fulfill this dream with the Masterpiece Collection," the enthusiastic watch creator said at Baselworld, where he took his leave of the watch industry. Almost three decades had passed since the brand with the stylized M in its logo entered the watch market. The line's strength lay above all in the middle price range, where the exceptionally well-outfitted watches from Saignelégier in the Swiss Jura were quickly able to assert themselves against the competition.

A path right through the world of mechanical watches was thus the base of all concepts and ideas: Real values are not created by appearance alone. The "inner value" was still missing, the human countenance, the masterly touch. The basic idea for the concern's future top collection was born, and it even had a name: the Masterpiece Collection — a collection of masterpieces

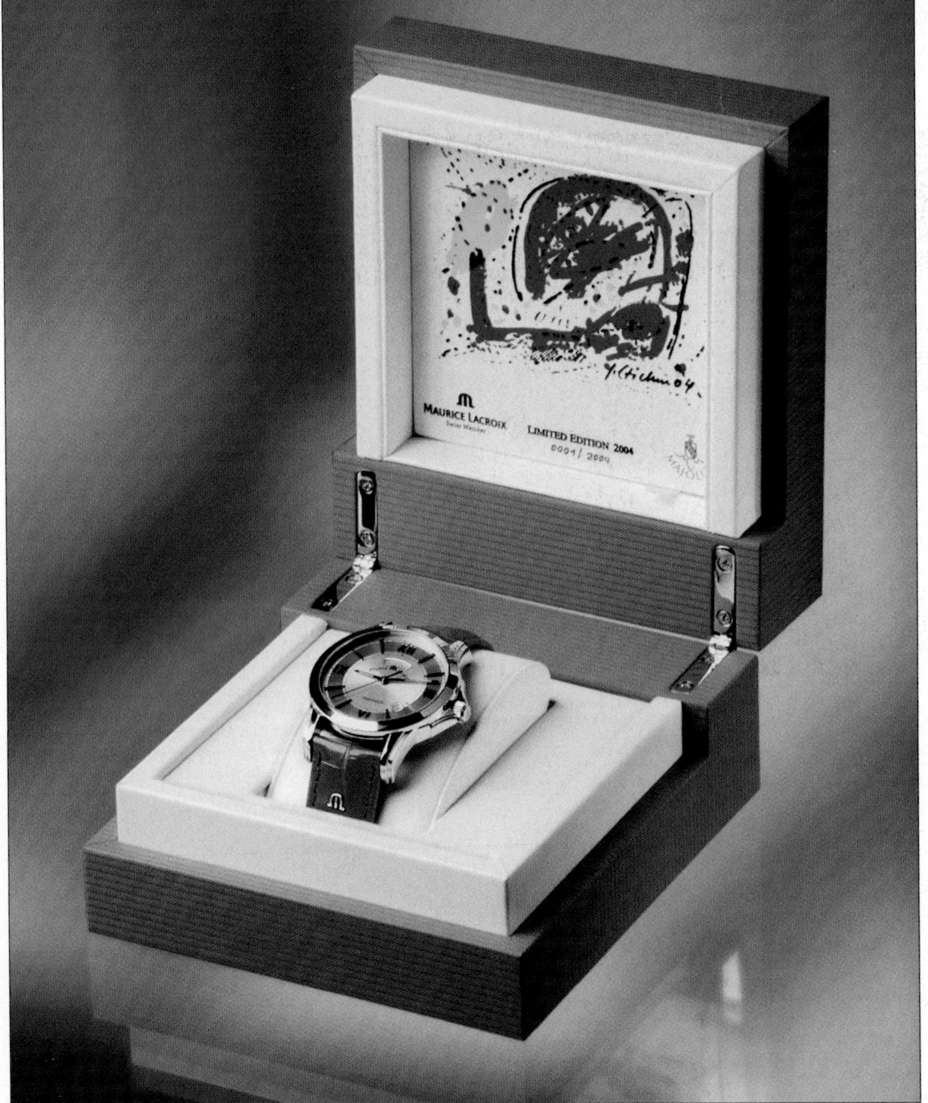

with technical innovation as its trademark. The Masterpiece Collection has in the meantime become so important for the company that it has been given its own product developers: Patrick Graells will take over this part, while his colleague Sandro Reginelli will care for the contemporary collection.

Both product managers have had the opportunity in the last few months to work closely with Baumann. Thus, the Masterpiece Vénus was created, whose design is clearly reminiscent of old times. Additionally, the elegant round case with its slightly curved lugs, small onion-shaped crown, and elongated chronograph buttons adds to the impression, also reinforced by a dial that is guilloché in the center, and above which blued Breguet hands make their rounds. A look through the transparent case back, though, where the legendary chronograph caliber Vénus 175 becomes visible, really brings on the history. Already rather aesthetic in its design, the quality of the movement is underscored by finishing that includes decoration, beveled edges, and blued screws. Connoisseurs identify the hand-wound movement among other things by the column wheel containing seven columns that controls the chronograph mechanism. There aren't many more of these old calibers, which were manufactured until 1966, left on the market. For this reason, Maurice Lacroix will manufacture only 250 pieces of the Vénus Chronograph: 150 pieces in rose gold and 100 in white.

Masterpiece Venus

Reference number: MP7038-PG101-120
Movement: manual winding, ML 36 (base Venus 175); ø 31.25 mm, height 5.7 mm; 23 jewels; 18,000 vph, hand-decorated and finished with swan-neck fine adjustment
Functions: hours, minutes, subsidiary seconds; chronograph
Case: rose gold, ø 43.5 mm; guilloché bezel; sapphire crystal; transparent case back
Band: reptile skin, buckle
Remarks: limited to 150 pieces
Price: $21,000

Masterpiece Venus

Reference number: MP7038-WG101-120
Movement: manual winding, ML 36 (base Venus 175); ø 31.25 mm, height 5.7 mm; 23 jewels; 18,000 vph, hand-decorated and finished with swan-neck fine adjustment
Functions: hours, minutes, subsidiary seconds; chronograph
Case: white gold, ø 43.5 mm; guilloché bezel; sapphire crystal; transparent case back
Band: reptile skin, buckle
Remarks: limited to 100 pieces
Price: $22,500

Masterpiece Jours Rétrogrades

Reference number: MP6119-SS001-11E
Movement: automatic, ML 102 (base ETA 2892-A2); ø 25.6 mm, height 3.6 mm (base movement); 22 jewels; 28,800 vph, hand-decorated
Functions: hours, minutes, sweep seconds; large date, day (retrograde)
Case: stainless steel, 39 x 41.5 mm; sapphire crystal; transparent case back; water-resistant to 50 m
Band: reptile skin, buckle
Price: $5,495
Variations: with black dial

Masterpiece Jours Rétrogrades

Reference number: MP6119-PS101-11E
Movement: automatic, ML 102 (base ETA 2892-A2); ø 25.6 mm, height 3.6 mm (base movement); 22 jewels; 28,800 vph, hand-decorated
Functions: hours, minutes, sweep seconds; large date, day (retrograde)
Case: stainless steel, 39 x 41.5 mm; bezel in rose gold; sapphire crystal; transparent case back; water-resistant to 50 m
Band: reptile skin, buckle
Price: $5,995
Variations: with black dial

Masterpiece Double Rétrograde Platinum Limited Edition

Reference number: MP7018-PL201-930
Movement: manual winding, ML 100 (base ETA 6498-2); ø 36.6 mm, height 6.3 mm; 50 jewels; 21,600 vph, hand-decorated
Functions: hours, minutes, subsidiary seconds; date (retrograde); 24-hour display (retrograde); power reserve display
Case: platinum, ø 43.5 mm, height 12 mm; guilloché bezel; sapphire crystal; transparent case back; water-resistant to 50 m
Band: reptile skin, buckle
Remarks: limited to 99 pieces
Price: $27,000

Masterpiece Double Rétrograde

Reference number: MP7018-PG101-930
Movement: manual winding, ML 100 (base ETA 6498-2); ø 36.6 mm, height 6.3 mm; 50 jewels; 21,600 vph, hand-decorated
Functions: hours, minutes, subsidiary seconds; date (retrograde); 24-hour display (second time zone) (retrograde); power reserve display
Case: rose gold, ø 43.5 mm, height 12 mm; sapphire crystal; transparent case back; water-resistant to 50 m
Band: reptile skin, buckle
Price: $15,000

Masterpiece Double Rétrograde

Reference number: MP7018-SS001-110
Movement: manual winding, ML 100 (base ETA 6498-2); ø 36.6 mm, height 6.3 mm; 50 jewels; 21,600 vph, hand-decorated
Functions: hours, minutes, subsidiary seconds; date (retrograde); 24-hour display (second time zone) (retrograde); power reserve display
Case: stainless steel, ø 43.5 mm, height 12 mm; sapphire crystal; transparent case back; water-resistant to 50 m
Band: reptile skin, buckle
Price: $6,495

Masterpiece Calendrier Rétrograde

Reference number: MP6198-SS001-191
Movement: manual winding, ML 76 (base ETA 6498-2); ø 37 mm; height 6.3 mm; 33 jewels; 18,000 vph, hand-decorated
Functions: hours, minutes, subsidiary seconds; date (retrograde); power reserve display
Case: stainless steel, ø 43 mm, height 11.5 mm; sapphire crystal; transparent case back; water-resistant to 50 m
Band: reptile skin, folding clasp
Price: $4,500
Variations: in stainless steel/rose gold; in rose gold; with black dial

Masterpiece Grand Guichet Dame

Reference number: MP6016-SD501-170
Movement: automatic, ML 58 (base ETA 2892-2); ø 25.6 mm, height 5.1 mm; 26 jewels; 28,800 vph, hand-decorated
Functions: hours, minutes, subsidiary seconds; large date
Case: stainless steel, ø 40 mm, height 9.6 mm; bezel set with diamonds; sapphire crystal; transparent case back; crown and lugs set with total of five sapphire cabochons; water-resistant to 50 m
Band: reptile skin, buckle
Remarks: dial with diamond markers
Price: $6,195
Variations: without diamonds

Masterpiece Grand Guichet Dame

Reference number: MP6016-YS101-110
Movement: automatic, ML 58 (base ETA 2892-2); ø 25.6 mm, height 5.1 mm; 26 jewels; 28,800 vph, hand-decorated
Functions: hours, minutes, subsidiary seconds; large date
Case: stainless steel, ø 40 mm, height 9.6 mm; bezel in yellow gold; sapphire crystal; transparent case back; water-resistant to 50 m
Band: reptile skin, buckle
Price: upon request
Variations: with diamonds

Masterpiece Phase de Lune Dame

Reference number: MP6066-SD501-37E
Movement: automatic, ML 37 (base ETA 2824-2); ø 26 mm, height 6.3 mm; 25 jewels; 28,800 vph, hand-decorated
Functions: hours, minutes, sweep seconds; date, day, month, moon phase
Case: stainless steel, ø 34.9 mm, height 12.2 mm; bezel set with diamonds; sapphire crystal; transparent case back; crown and lugs set with 5 sapphire cabochons; water-resistant to 50 m
Band: reptile skin, buckle
Remarks: mother-of-pearl dial with diamond markers
Price: $4,500
Variations: in stainless steel/yellow gold

Masterpiece Flyback Chronograph Annuaire

Reference number: MP6098-SS001-39G
Movement: automatic, ML 15 (base ETA 2892-2); ø 30 mm; height 7.5 mm; 49 jewels; 28,800 vph, hand-decorated
Functions: hours, minutes, subsidiary seconds; chronograph with flyback function; annual calendar with large date, month
Case: stainless steel, ø 40 mm, height 13.5 mm; sapphire crystal; transparent case back; water-resistant to 50 m
Band: reptile skin, buckle
Price: $5,850
Variations: in stainless steel/rose gold; with silver dial

Masterpiece Phase de Lune Tonneau

Reference number: MP6439-SS001-31G
Movement: automatic, ML 37 (base ETA 2824-2); ø 26 mm, height 6.3 mm; 25 jewels; 28,800 vph, hand-decorated
Functions: hours, minutes, sweep seconds; date, day, month, moon phase
Case: stainless steel, 38.7 x 51.6 mm, height 13.65 mm; sapphire crystal; transparent case back; water-resistant to 50 m
Band: reptile skin, folding clasp
Price: $4,500
Variations: in stainless steel/yellow gold, with stainless steel bracelet; different dial variations

Masterpiece Réveil Globe

Reference number: MP6388-SS001-330
Movement: automatic, ML 06 (base AS 5008); ø 30 mm, height 7.75 mm; 31 jewels; 28,800 vph, hand-decorated
Functions: hours, minutes, sweep seconds; date; 24-hour display (second time zone); alarm
Case: stainless steel, ø 43 mm, height 16 mm; bidirectionally rotating bezel under crystal with 12-hour scale, settable via crown; sapphire crystal; transparent case back; water-resistant to 50 m
Band: reptile skin, folding clasp
Price: $4,995
Variations: with bracelet; in stainless steel/rose gold

Pontos Small Seconds

Reference number: PT7518-SS001-130
Movement: manual winding, ETA 6498-1, ø 36.6 mm, height 4.5 mm; 17 jewels; 21,600 vph
Functions: hours, minutes, subsidiary seconds
Case: stainless steel, ø 43 mm, height 10.1 mm; sapphire crystal; transparent case back; water-resistant to 50 m
Band: leather, folding clasp
Price: $1,350
Variations: with black dial; in stainless steel/rose gold

Pontos GMT

Reference number: PT6068-SS001-320
Movement: automatic, ETA 2893-2, ø 25.6 mm, height 4.1 mm; 21 jewels; 28,800 vph
Functions: hours, minutes, sweep seconds; date; 24-hour display (second time zone)
Case: stainless steel, ø 40 mm, height 10.1 mm; sapphire crystal; transparent case back; water-resistant to 50 m
Band: leather, folding clasp
Price: $1,395
Variations: with black dial; in stainless steel/rose gold

Pontos Automatic Lady Size

Reference number: PT6044-PS101-110
Movement: automatic, ETA 2681, ø 19.4 mm, height 4.8 mm; 25 jewels; 28,800 vph
Functions: hours, minutes, sweep seconds; date
Case: stainless steel, ø 32 mm, height 10 mm; bezel in rose gold; sapphire crystal; transparent case back; water-resistant to 50 m
Band: leather, buckle
Price: $1,250
Variations: with black dial; in stainless steel; also in men's size

Pontos Day Date Limited Edition 2004

Reference number: PT6078-SS001-11G
Movement: automatic, ETA 2836-2, ø 25.6 mm, height 5.05 mm; 25 jewels; 28,800 vph, rotor engraved "Limited Edition 2004"
Functions: hours, minutes, sweep seconds; date, day
Case: stainless steel, ø 40 mm, height 10.5 mm; sapphire crystal; transparent case back; water-resistant to 50 m
Band: leather, folding clasp
Remarks: limited to 2004 pieces
Price: upon request

A. Lange & Söhne

In the 1930s Richard Lange invented the Nivarox balance spring for watches. Ten years after its refounding, the noble Saxon watch brand A. Lange & Söhne is once again in position to manufacture this delicate component, one that contributes heavily to the rate precision of a watch. The domination of this technology is a success that is in no way an everyday occurrence; it is the key to the complete independence of a *manufacture*.

This is something that hardly a soul would have expected of the Saxons — just as little as they would have expected the Lange euphoria that has meanwhile lasted for ten years. It certainly didn't take a fortune-teller to predict that from the ruins of the born-again German luxury brand, at least in Germany, a successful beginning would arise. But the extent of the enthusiasm for the newcomers from the East that has gripped not only impassioned Lange pocket watch collectors and homesick Saxons, but also ambitious watch collectors from every discipline and, above all, from every social stratum, who had never before wasted a thought on buying themselves a special (or expensive) watch is truly noteworthy.

Least expected in Glashütte was the positive resonance from international circles, especially Switzerland, the generally accredited home of luxury wristwatches. Italians, who are rightfully said to have a special feel for horological refinements and collectible exclusivities, welcomed the descendants of Ferdinand Adolph Lange with open arms. And in the country possessing the largest number of watch collectors and enthusiasts worldwide, the good ole U. S. of A., those in the know dashed to scoop up these mechanical gems made in Germany. Winners prefer to be in the company of winners, or so the saying goes.

There were four models in the starting collection from 1994: Lange 1; Arkade; Saxonia; and the tourbillon Pour le Mérite, no longer in production. The remaining three are now accompanied by numerous new classics. The successive ranges have produced models such as 1815, Cabaret, and Langematik, which have also garnered a loyal following with their individual character strengths.

In its inimitable way, the Datograph, introduced in 1999, combines the technical and aesthetic values of column-wheel control, flyback function, Lange large date, and a precisely jumping minute counter in one fascinatingly clean and unmistakable package. The newly introduced model Double Split takes this concept a step further. It additionally disposes of two rattrapante functions for stopping both seconds and minutes. In this way, intermediate times of up to thirty minutes are possible.

Not quite as sporty, and even more unassuming, is the second introduction of the year. The 1815 Chronograph definitely wins in elegance by the precise avoidance of many additional displays, making it far more than just the "little brother" of the Datograph.

Double Split

Reference number: 404.035
Movement: manual winding, Lange L001.1, ø 30.6 mm, height 9.45 mm; 40 jewels; 21,600 vph, two column wheels for control of the chronograph, double split seconds functions; precisely jumping minute counter
Functions: hours, minutes, subsidiary seconds; chronograph with flyback function, rattrapante for second and minute hands; power reserve display
Case: platinum, ø 43 mm, height 15.3 mm; sapphire crystal; transparent case back
Band: reptile skin, buckle in platinum
Price: $97,800

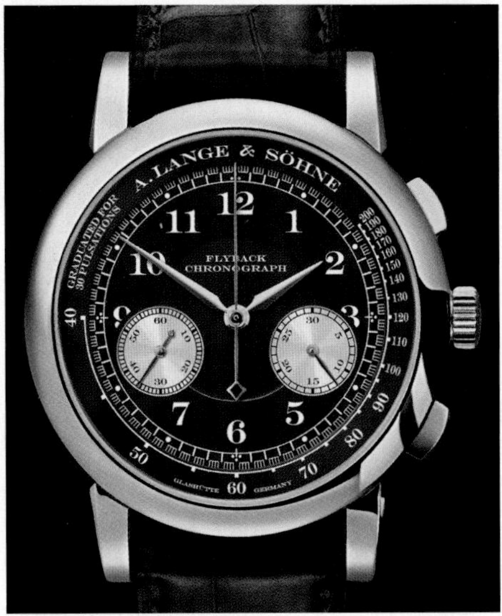

1815 Chronograph

Reference number: 401.031
Movement: manual winding, Lange L951.0, ø 30.6 mm, height 6.1 mm; 40 jewels; 18,000 vph, column-wheel control of the chronograph functions, precisely jumping minute counter
Functions: hours, minutes, subsidiary seconds; chronograph with flyback function
Case: red gold, ø 39.5 mm, height 10.8 mm; sapphire crystal; transparent case back
Band: reptile skin, buckle in red gold
Remarks: solid silver dial
Price: $33,600
Variations: in white gold

1815 Chronograph

Reference number: 401026.0
Movement: manual winding, Lange L951.0, ø 30.6 mm, height 6.1 mm; 40 jewels; 18,000 vph, column-wheel control of the chronograph functions, precisely jumping minute counter
Functions: hours, minutes, subsidiary seconds; chronograph with flyback function
Case: white gold, ø 39.5 mm, height 10.8 mm; sapphire crystal; transparent case back
Band: reptile skin, buckle in white gold
Remarks: solid silver dial
Price: $33,600
Variations: in red gold

1815 Automatic

Reference number: 303025.0
Movement: automatic, Lange L921.2, ø 30.4 mm, height 3.8 mm; 36 jewels; 21,600 vph, hand-setting device with zero-reset
Functions: hours, minutes, subsidiary seconds
Case: platinum, ø 37 mm, height 8.2 mm; sapphire crystal; transparent case back
Band: reptile skin, buckle in platinum
Remarks: solid silver dial
Price: $33,600
Variations: in yellow gold or red gold

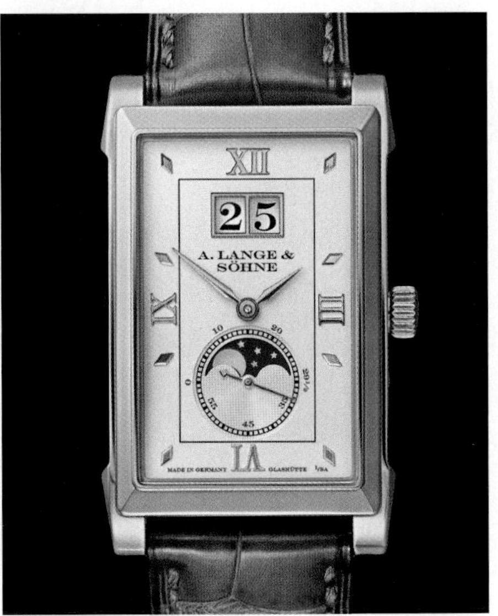

Cabaret Moon Phase

Reference number: 118021.0
Movement: manual winding, Lange L931.5, 25.6 x 17.6 mm, height 5.05 mm; 31 jewels; 21,600 vph
Functions: hours, minutes, subsidiary seconds; large date (patented); moon phase
Case: yellow gold, 36.3 x 25.5 mm, height 9.1 mm; sapphire crystal; transparent case back
Band: reptile skin, buckle in yellow gold
Remarks: solid silver dial
Price: $20,500
Variations: in red gold

Large Lange 1 Luminous

Reference number: 115029.0
Movement: manual winding, Lange L901.2, ø 30.4 mm, height 5.9 mm; 53 jewels; 21,600 vph; 72 h power reserve, twin spring barrels
Functions: hours, minutes, subsidiary seconds; large date (patented); power reserve display
Case: white gold, ø 41.9 mm, height 11 mm; sapphire crystal; transparent case back
Band: calfskin, buckle in white gold
Remarks: solid silver dial; hands and applied elements are luminous
Price: $22,500

Lange 1

Reference number: 101021.0
Movement: manual winding, Lange L 901.0, ø 30.4 mm, height 5.9 mm; 53 jewels; 21,600 vph; 72 h power reserve, twin spring barrels
Functions: hours, minutes, subsidiary seconds; large date (patented); power reserve display
Case: yellow gold, ø 38.5 mm, height 10 mm; sapphire crystal; transparent case back
Band: reptile skin, buckle in yellow gold
Remarks: solid silver dial
Price: $21,100
Variations: in white or red gold, in platinum

Lange 1 Soirée

Reference number: 110.030
Movement: manual winding, Lange L 901.4, ø 30.4 mm, height 5.9 mm; 53 jewels; 21,600 vph; 72 h power reserve, twin spring barrels
Functions: hours, minutes, subsidiary seconds; large date (patented); power reserve display
Case: white gold, ø 38.5 mm, height 10.4 mm; sapphire crystal; transparent case back
Band: reptile skin, buckle in white gold
Remarks: mother-of-pearl, guilloché dial
Price: $24,400

Large Lange 1

Reference number: 115031.0
Movement: manual winding, Lange L901.2, ø 30.4 mm, height 5.9 mm; 53 jewels; 21,600 vph; 72 h power reserve, twin spring barrels
Functions: hours, minutes, subsidiary seconds; large date (patented); power reserve display
Case: red gold, ø 41.9 mm, height 11 mm; sapphire crystal; transparent case back
Band: reptile skin, buckle in red gold
Remarks: solid silver dial
Price: $22,500
Variations: in yellow gold or platinum

Lange 1 Moon Phase

Reference number: 109.032
Movement: manual winding, Lange L 901.5, ø 30.4 mm, height 5.9 mm; 54 jewels; 21,600 vph; 72 h power reserve, twin spring barrels; moon phase display with continous drive via hour wheel; button for quick date correction
Functions: hours, minutes, subsidiary seconds; large date (patented); moon phase; power reserve display
Case: red gold, ø 38.5 mm, height 10.4 mm; sapphire crystal; transparent case back
Band: reptile skin, buckle in red gold
Remarks: solid silver dial
Price: $24,600

1815

Reference number: 206.021
Movement: manual winding, Lange L 941.1, ø 25.6 mm, height 3.2 mm; 21 jewels; 21,600 vph
Functions: hours, minutes, subsidiary seconds
Case: yellow gold, ø 35.9 mm, height 7.5 mm; sapphire crystal; transparent case back
Band: reptile skin, buckle in yellow gold
Remarks: solid silver dial
Price: $9,900
Variations: In white or red gold; in platinum

1815 AUF und AB

Reference number: 221.032
Movement: manual winding, Lange L 942.1, ø 25.6 mm, height 3.7 mm; 27 jewels; 21,600 vph
Functions: hours, minutes, subsidiary seconds; power reserve display
Case: red gold, ø 35.9 mm, height 7.9 mm; sapphire crystal; transparent case back
Band: reptile skin, buckle in red gold
Remarks: solid silver dial
Price: $13,600
Variations: in yellow or white gold; in platinum

Langematik Perpetual

Reference number: 310.021

Movement: automatic, Lange L 922.1 SAX-O-MAT, ø 30.4 mm, height 5.4 mm; 43 jewels; 21,600 vph, hand-setting device with zero-reset; main button for synchronized correction of all calendar functions, three individual buttons

Functions: hours, minutes, subsidiary seconds; perpetual calendar with large date (patented), day, month, moon phase, leap year; 24-hour display

Case: yellow gold, ø 38.5 mm, height 10.2 mm; sapphire crystal; transparent case back

Band: reptile skin, buckle in yellow gold

Price: $47,800

Langematik Perpetual

Reference number: 310025.0

Movement: automatic, Lange L 922.1 SAX-O-MAT, ø 30.4 mm, height 5.4 mm; 43 jewels; 21,600 vph, hand-setting device with zero-reset; main button for synchronized correction of all calendar functions, three individual buttons

Functions: hours, minutes, subsidiary seconds; perpetual calendar with large date (patented), day, month, moon phase, leap year; 24-hour display

Case: platinum, ø 38.5 mm, height 10.2 mm; sapphire crystal; transparent case back

Band: reptile skin, buckle in platinum

Price: $58,000

Langematik with Large Date

Reference number: 308.021

Movement: automatic, Lange L 921.4 SAX-O-MAT, ø 30.4 mm, height 5.55 mm; 45 jewels; 21,600 vph, hand-setting device with zero-reset

Functions: hours, minutes, subsidiary seconds; large date (patented)

Case: yellow gold, ø 37 mm, height 9.7 mm; sapphire crystal; transparent case back

Band: reptile skin, buckle in yellow gold

Remarks: solid silver dial

Price: $19,800

Variations: in white or red gold; in platinum

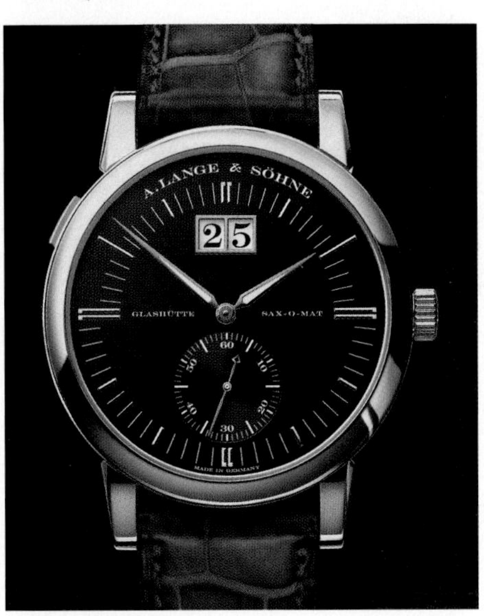

Large Langematik

Reference number: 309031.0

Movement: automatic, Lange L 921.4 SAX-O-MAT, ø 30.4 mm, height 5.55 mm; 45 jewels; 21,600 vph, hand-setting device with zero-reset

Functions: hours, minutes, subsidiary seconds; large date (patented)

Case: red gold, ø 40 mm, height 10.7 mm; sapphire crystal; transparent case back

Band: reptile skin, buckle in red gold

Remarks: solid silver dial, luminous hands

Price: $21,200

Variations: in yellow gold or platinum

Datograph

Reference number: 403031.0

Movement: manual winding, Lange L 951.1, ø 30.6 mm, height 7.5 mm; 40 jewels; 18,000 vph, column-wheel control of the chronograph functions, precisely jumping minute counter

Functions: hours, minutes, subsidiary seconds; chronograph with flyback function; large date (patented)

Case: red gold, ø 39 mm, height 12.8 mm; sapphire crystal; transparent case back

Band: reptile skin, buckle in red gold

Remarks: solid silver dial, luminous hands

Price: $38,900

Variations: in platinum

Datograph

Reference number: 403.035

Movement: manual winding, Lange L 951.1, ø 30.6 mm, height 7.5 mm; 40 jewels; 18,000 vph, column-wheel control of the chronograph functions, exactly jumping minute counter

Functions: hours, minutes, subsidiary seconds; chronograph with flyback function; large date (patented)

Case: platinum, ø 39 mm, height 12.8 mm; sapphire crystal; transparent case back

Band: reptile skin, buckle in platinum

Remarks: two-part dial, solid silver

Price: $49,300

Variations: in red gold

Saxonia

Reference number: 105.022
Movement: manual winding, Lange L 941.3, ø 25.6 mm, height 4.95 mm; 30 jewels; 21,600 vph
Functions: hours, minutes, subsidiary seconds; large date (patented)
Case: yellow gold, ø 33.9 mm, height 9.1 mm; sapphire crystal; transparent case back
Band: reptile skin, buckle in yellow gold
Remarks: solid silver dial
Price: $13,700
Variations: in platinum or white gold

Cabaret

Reference number: 808.033
Movement: manual winding, Lange L 931.2, 25.6 x 17.6 mm, height 4.95 mm; 30 jewels; 21,600 vph
Functions: hours, minutes; large date (patented)
Case: white gold, 36.3 x 25.5 mm, height 9.1 mm; case set with 244 brilliant-cut diamonds; sapphire crystal; transparent case back
Band: reptile skin, buckle in white gold
Remarks: onyx on solid gold dial, set with 146 diamonds
Price: $62,200
Variations: further jeweled versions

Cabaret

Reference number: 107.021
Movement: manual winding, Lange L 931.3, 25.6 x 17.6 mm, height 4.95 mm; 30 jewels; 21,600 vph
Functions: hours, minutes, subsidiary seconds; large date (patented)
Case: yellow gold, 36.3 x 25.5 mm, height 9.1 mm; sapphire crystal; transparent case back
Band: reptile skin, buckle in yellow gold
Remarks: solid silver dial
Price: $17,100
Variations: in white or red gold; in platinum

Arkade

Reference number: 861031
Movement: manual winding, Lange L 911.4, 25.6 x 17.6 mm, height 4.95 mm; 30 jewels; 21,600 vph
Functions: hours, minutes; large date (patented)
Case: white gold, 31.5 x 24.9 mm, height 8.2 mm; case set with 219 brilliant-cut diamonds; sapphire crystal; transparent case back
Band: white gold, set with 264 brilliant-cut diamonds, buckle
Remarks: solid silver dial
Price: $168,400
Variations: further jeweled versions

Arkade

Reference number: 103.021
Movement: manual winding, Lange L 911.4, 25.6 x 17.6 mm, height 4.95 mm; 30 jewels; 21,600 vph
Functions: hours, minutes; large date (patented)
Case: yellow gold, 29 x 22.2 mm, height 8.4 mm; sapphire crystal; transparent case back
Band: reptile skin, buckle in yellow gold
Remarks: solid silver dial
Price: $13,700
Variations: in white gold or platinum

Large Arkade

Reference number: 812021
Movement: manual winding, Lange L 911.4, 25.6 x 17.6 mm, height 4.95 mm; 30 jewels; 21,600 vph
Functions: hours, minutes; large date (patented)
Case: yellow gold, 38 x 29.5 mm, height 9 mm; case set with 62 brilliant-cut diamonds; sapphire crystal; transparent case back
Band: reptile skin, buckle in yellow gold
Remarks: dial solid silver
Price: $26,200
Variations: further jeweled versions

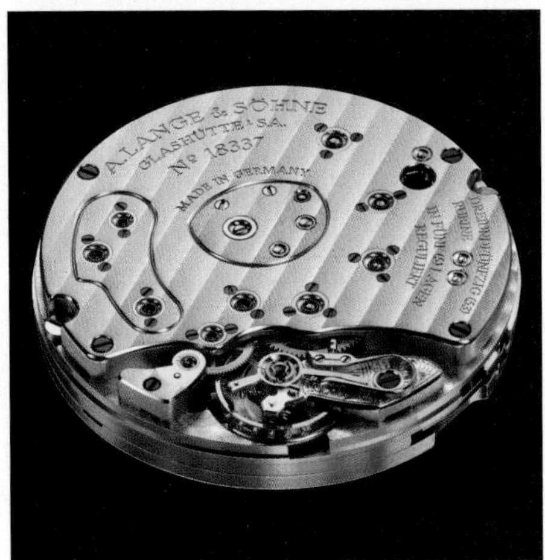

Caliber L 901.0 (Lange 1)

Mechanical with manual winding; twin serially operating spring barrels, power reserve 72 hours, stop-seconds
Functions: hours, minutes, subsidiary seconds; large date; power reserve indicator
Diameter: 30.4 mm; **Height:** 5.9 mm
Jewels: 53, including 9 screw-mounted gold chatons
Balance: glucydur with weighted screws
Frequency: 21,600 vph
Balance spring: Nivarox 1 with special terminal curve and swan-neck fine adjustment; beat adjustment via regulating screw
Shock protection: Incabloc
Remarks: chiefly manufactured, assembled, and decorated by hand according to highest quality criteria

Caliber L 901.5 (dial side)

Mechanical with manual winding; twin serially operating spring barrels, power reserve 72 hours, stop-seconds
Functions: hours, minutes, subsidiary seconds; large date; moon phase
Diameter: 30.4 mm; **Height:** 5.9 mm
Jewels: 54, including 9 screw-mounted gold chatons
Balance: glucydur with weighted screws
Frequency: 21,600 vph
Balance spring: Nivarox 1 with special terminal curve and swan-neck fine adjustment; beat adjustment via regulating screw
Remarks: chiefly manufactured, assembled, and decorated by hand according to highest quality criteria; moon phase driven by hour wheel, thus continuously in motion; precise dial train with deviation of only one day in 122.6 years

Caliber L 921.4 (Langematik)

Mechanical with automatic winding, bidirectionally winding three-quarter rotor in 21-karat gold and platinum, winding mechanism with four micro-ball bearings; power reserve 46 hours, stop-seconds with automatic return to zero ("zero reset")
Functions: hours, minutes, subsidiary seconds; large date
Diameter: 30.4 mm; **Height:** 5.55 mm; **Jewels:** 45
Balance: glucydur with weighted screws
Frequency: 21,600 vph
Balance spring: Nivarox 1 with swan-neck fine adjustment; beat adjustment via regulating screw
Shock protection: Incabloc
Remarks: chiefly manufactured, assembled, and decorated by hand according to highest quality criteria
Related calibers: L 921.2 (SAX-O-MAT without date, 36 jewels)

Caliber L 922.1 (Langematik Perpetual)

Mechanical with automatic winding, bidirectionally winding three-quarter rotor in 21-karat gold and platinum; power reserve 46 hours, stop-seconds with automatic return to zero ("zero reset")
Functions: hours, minutes, subsidiary seconds; perpetual calendar (large date, day, month, moon phase, leap year); 24-hour display with day/night indication
Diameter: 30.4 mm; **Height:** 5.4 mm; **Jewels:** 43
Balance: glucydur with weighted screws
Frequency: 21,600 vph
Balance spring: Nivarox 1 with swan-neck fine adjustment; beat adjustment via regulating screw
Shock protection: Incabloc
Remarks: synchronized/ind. setting of calendar functions

Caliber L 001.1 (Lange Double Split)

Mechanical with manual winding; power reserve 36 hours, stop-seconds; isolator mechanis; two column wheels for chrono
Functions: hours, minutes, subsidiary seconds; large date; chronograph with flyback function and double rattrapante for seconds and minutes
Diameter: 30.6 mm; **Height:** 9.54 mm
Jewels: 40 including 4 screw-mounted gold chatons
Balance: glucydur with eccentric regulating screws
Frequency: 21,600 vph
Balance spring: on-premises manufacture with collet (patent pending), swan-neck fine adjustment
Shock protection: Incabloc
Remarks: chiefly manufactured, assembled, and decorated by hand according to highest quality criteria

Caliber L 951.1 (Datograph)

Mechanical with manual winding; power reserve 36 hours, stop-seconds; column wheel for chronograph functions
Functions: hours, minutes, subsidiary seconds; large date; chronograph with flyback mechanism and exactly jumping minute counter
Diameter: 30.6 mm; **Height:** 7.5 mm
Jewels: 40, including 4 screw-mounted gold chatons
Balance: glucydur with weighted screws
Frequency: 18,000 vph
Balance spring: Nivarox 1 with special terminal curve and swan-neck fine adjustment; beat adjustment via regulating screw
Remarks: chiefly manufactured, assembled, and decorated by hand according to highest quality criteria

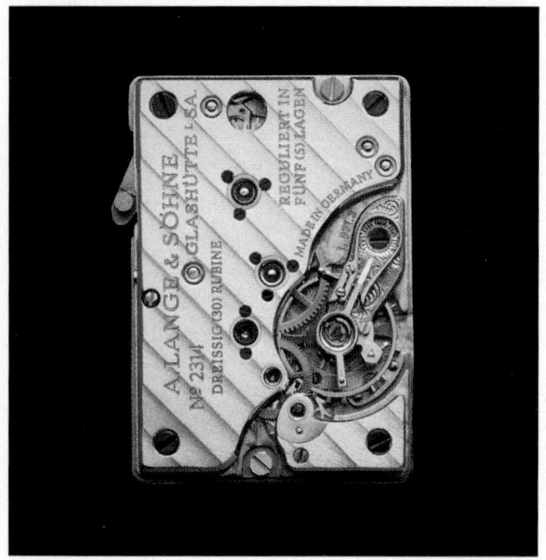

Caliber L 931.3 (Cabaret)

Mechanical with manual winding, power reserve 42 hours, stop-seconds
Functions: hours, minutes, subsidiary seconds; large date
Dimensions: 25.6 x 17.6 mm
Height: 4.95 mm
Jewels: 30, including 3 screw-mounted gold chatons
Balance: glucydur with weighted screws
Frequency: 21,600 vph
Balance spring: Nivarox 1 with swan-neck fine adjustment; beat adjustment via regulating screw
Shock protection: Incabloc
Remarks: chiefly manufactured, assembled, and decorated by hand according to highest quality criteria

Caliber L 931.3 (Cabaret Moon Phase)

Mechanical with manual winding, power reserve 42 hours, stop-seconds
Functions: hours, minutes, subsidiary seconds; large date; moon phase
Dimensions: 25.6 x 17.6 mm
Height: 5.05 mm
Jewels: 31, including 3 screw-mounted gold chatons
Balance: glucydur with weighted screws
Frequency: 21,600 vph
Balance spring: Nivarox 1 with swan-neck fine adjustment; beat adjustment via regulating screw
Shock protection: Incabloc
Remarks: chiefly manufactured, assembled, and decorated by hand according to highest quality criteria

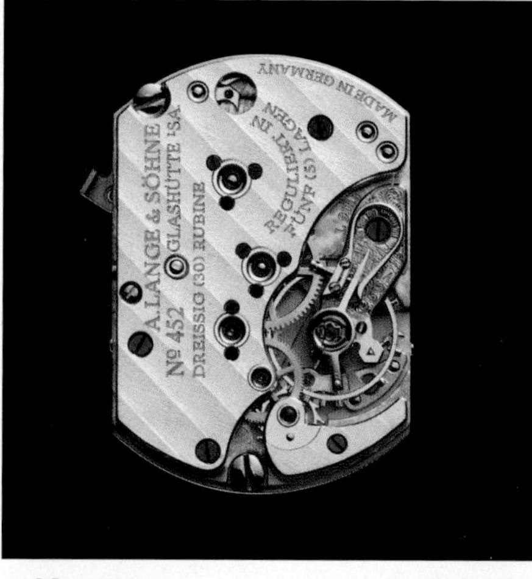

Caliber L 911.4 (Arkade)

Mechanical with manual winding, power reserve 42 hours, stop-seconds
Functions: hours, minutes, subsidiary seconds; large date
Dimensions: 25.6 x 17.6 mm
Height: 4.95 mm
Jewels: 30, including 3 screw-mounted gold chatons
Balance: glucydur with weighted screws
Frequency: 21,600 vph
Balance spring: Nivarox 1 with swan-neck fine adjustment; beat adjustment via regulating screw
Shock protection: Incabloc
Remarks: chiefly manufactured, assembled, and decorated by hand according to highest quality criteria

Caliber L 911.4 (dial side)

Caliber L 911.4, which has the same shape as the Arkade, including the rounded corners, is also outfitted with the patented Lange large date. The shape played an important role in the development of the large date for this model, which was included in the starting collection from 1994. Its final dimensions were actually based on the minimum size dictated by the date indicator. The unveiling of the secret of how it is at all possible to accommodate this large date indicator into such a petite watch was celebrated with justifiable pride some time after the original presentation of the model.

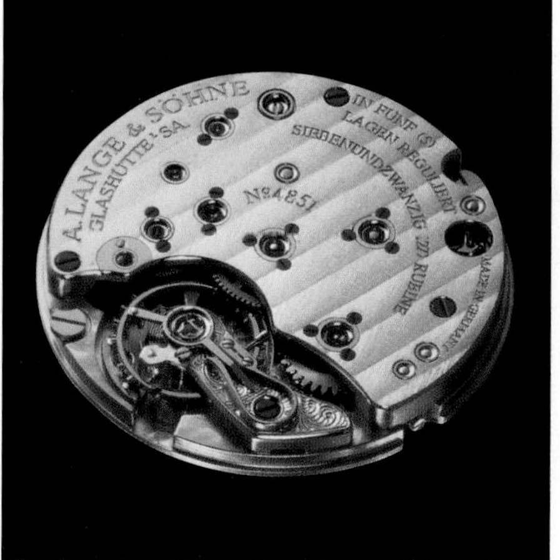

Caliber L 942.1 (1815 Up and Down)

Mechanical with manual winding, power reserve 45 hours, stop-seconds
Functions: hours, minutes, subsidiary seconds; power reserve display
Diameter: 25.6 mm
Height: 3.7 mm
Jewels: 27, including 6 screw-mounted gold chatons
Balance: glucydur with weighted screws
Frequency: 21,600 vph
Balance spring: Nivarox 1 with swan-neck fine adjustment; beat adjustment via regulating screw
Shock protection: Incabloc
Remarks: chiefly manufactured, assembled, and decorated by hand according to highest quality criteria

Caliber L 941.3 (Saxonia)

Mechanical with manual winding, power reserve 42 hours, stop-seconds
Functions: hours, minutes, subsidiary seconds; large date
Diameter: 25.6 mm
Height: 4.95 mm
Jewels: 30, including 3 screw-mounted gold chatons
Balance: glucydur with weighted screws
Frequency: 21,600 vph
Balance spring: Nivarox 1 with swan-neck fine adjustment; beat adjustment via regulating screw
Shock protection: Incabloc
Remarks: chiefly manufactured, assembled, and decorated by hand according to highest quality criteria

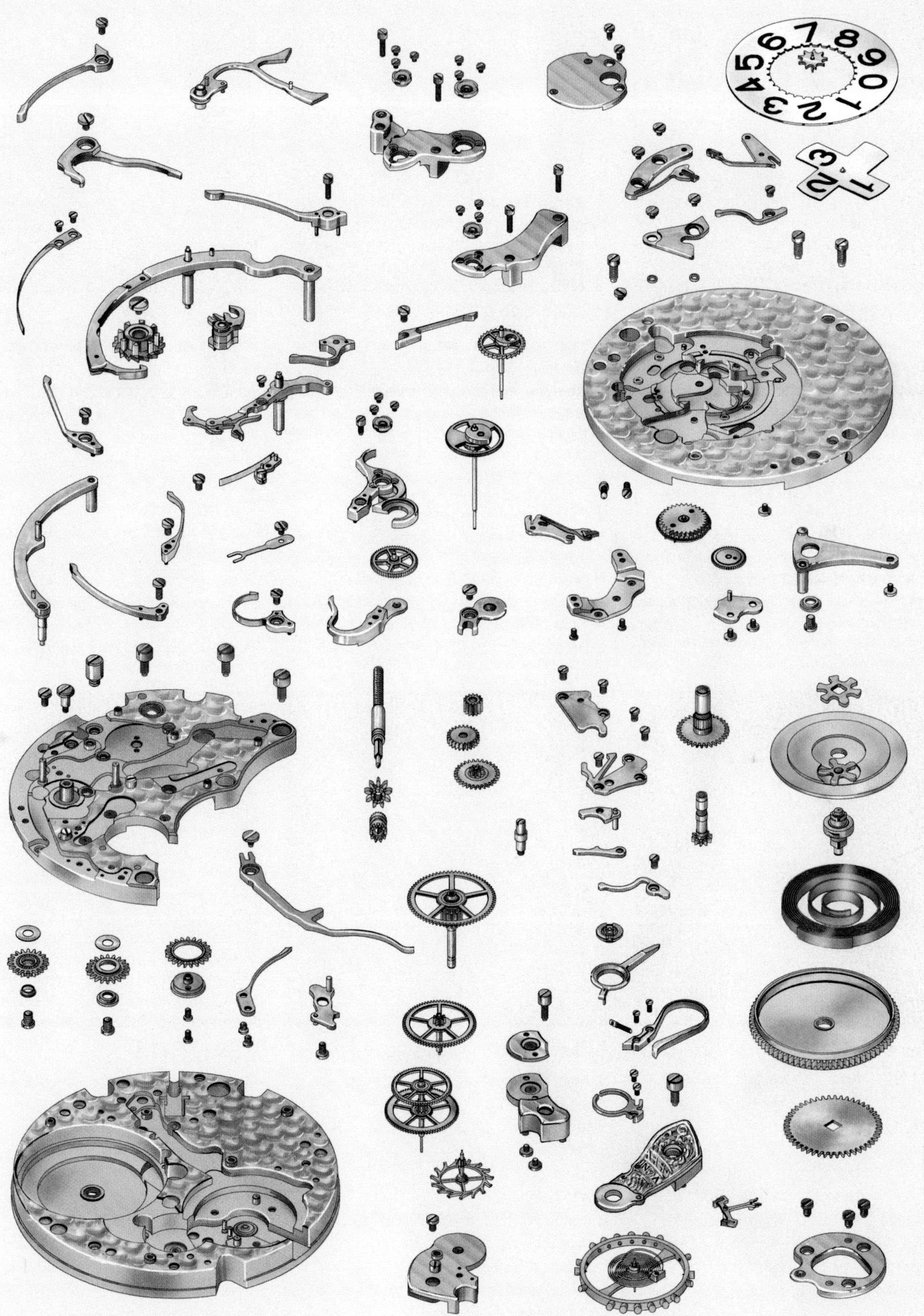

Limes

Watches by the Pforzheim manufacturer Limes are popular among watch fans because they transmit the fascination of mechanics at such a remarkable price. They are packed in cases that have been beautifully manufactured and are classic in design. No wonder, for the company was originally a pure case manufacturer.

Ickler GmbH was founded in 1924 by Karl Ickler, a trained chain maker who worked as a production foreman in foreign companies at the beginning of his career. He founded the watch case manufacturing company after returning to Pforzheim. After World War II, the company was rebuilt by the founder's sons, Heinz and Kurt. Today the company is managed by a third-generation Ickler, Thomas, an industrial engineer who at the end of the 1990s decided not only to manufacture high-quality cases, but also complete watches. This is how the watch brand Limes came into being.

The Ickler case manufacturer produces above all high-quality watch cases for internationally renowned customers using strict quality codes so that they are "made in Germany." The different case parts are manufactured by highly qualified employees who work on the most modern of CNC machines. Both the treatment of the case surfaces and the assembly of the watches require a large amount of talent and training.

In 1990 the company began manufacturing private label watches. Decades-long experience in the watch industry, a high level of quality, the already established production ability, and above all the desire to create something of his own led Thomas Ickler to the planning of the watch brand Limes a few years later. The concept was clear: high-quality Swiss movements in lavish *manufacture* cases by Ickler.

The lion's share of the Limes collection, in stainless steel and titanium, can be purchased for between $500 and $2,500. Watches in 18-karat rose or white gold can cost up to the $5,500 mark. For this amount of money, the customer gets high-quality, well-outfitted, and stylistically attractive watches, which cultivate their own aesthetic apart from short-lived fashion trends and need not fear any comparison to products from the established competition.

Beautiful back: The Pharo Power Reserve with finely finished movement.

The new the Pharo full calendar chronograph with moon phase is certainly a highlight of the Limes collection and combines technology and elegance at an elevated level. The flat and very elegant watch — although it is a chronograph — has a larger case than its predecessor as well as a newly designed dial. The decorated chronograph movement Valjoux 7751 can be seen through the sapphire crystal covering the screwed-down case back. The Ickler case possesses a domed and anti-reflective sapphire crystal. The top ring is decorated with a fine sunburst pattern and harmonizes with the finely guilloché dial and the applied, faceted markers. The lance hands complete the elegant, high-quality appearance of this timekeeper.

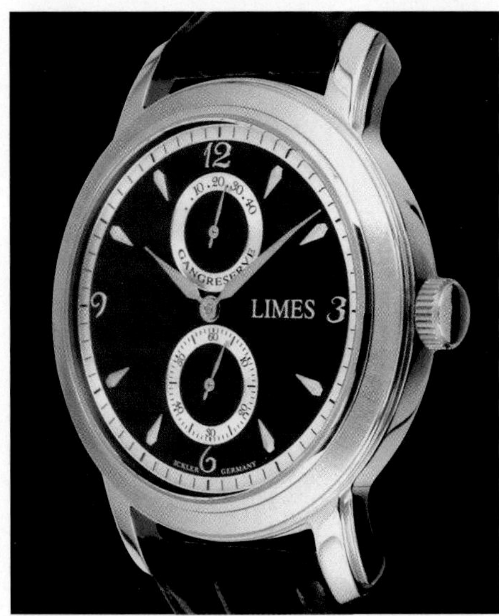

Pharo Power Reserve

Reference number: U6258-LHR1.3E
Movement: manual winding, ETA 7001 with module by Soprod, ø 23.3 mm, height 2.5 mm (base movement); 17 jewels; 21,600 vph
Functions: hours, minutes, subsidiary seconds; power reserve display
Case: stainless steel, ø 40 mm, height 9.4 mm; sapphire crystal; transparent case back; water-resistant to 50 m
Band: leather, buckle
Price: $1,745
Variations: dials in black/silver and silver/gold-plated, case in stainless steel/gold

Pharo Skeleton

Reference number: U6366-LASK2.2GR
Movement: automatic, ETA 2892, ø 25.6 mm, height 3.75 mm; 21 jewels; 28,800 vph, completely skeletonized
Functions: hours, minutes, sweep seconds
Case: rose gold, ø 37 mm, height 8.3 mm; sapphire crystal; transparent case back; water-resistant to 50 m
Band: leather, buckle
Price: $4,995
Variations: in stainless steel with leather strap or link bracelet; in stainless steel/yellow gold; in white gold

112

Reference number: U9427-LA3.1E
Movement: automatic, ETA 2892, ø 25.6 mm, height 3.75 mm; 21 jewels; 28,800 vph
Functions: hours, minutes
Case: stainless steel, ø 36.7 mm, height 7 mm; sapphire crystal; transparent case back; water-resistant to 50 m
Band: leather, buckle
Price: $995
Variations: different dial variations

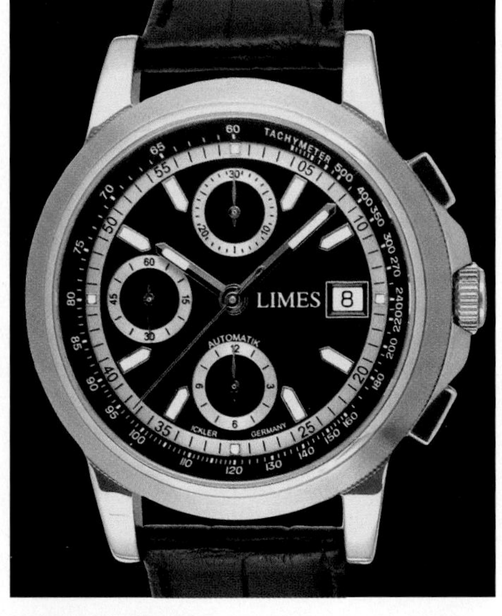

Principio Chrono

Reference number: U8715R-LC2.1
Movement: automatic, ETA 7750, ø 30 mm, height 7.9 mm; 25 jewels; 28,800 vph
Functions: hours, minutes, subsidiary seconds; chronograph; date
Case: stainless steel, ø 41 mm, height 13.5 mm; sapphire crystal; transparent case back; water-resistant to 100 m
Band: leather, buckle
Price: $1,725
Variations: with silver-colored dial; with stainless steel bracelet; as three-hand watch (ETA 2824)

1Thousand Chrono

Reference number: U8757-LC1.2
Movement: automatic, ETA 7750, ø 30 mm, height 7.9 mm; 25 jewels; 28,800 vph
Functions: hours, minutes, subsidiary seconds; chronograph; date
Case: stainless steel, ø 40 mm, height 15.5 mm; sapphire crystal; screw-in crown and buttons; water-resistant to 1000 m
Band: leather/rubber, buckle
Price: $1,795
Variations: black dial, as three-hand watch (2824), with stainless steel bracelet

Integral Chrono

Reference number: U8484B-LC4.2
Movement: automatic, ETA 7750, ø 30 mm, height 7.9 mm; 25 jewels; 28,800 vph
Functions: hours, minutes, subsidiary seconds; chronograph; date
Case: stainless steel, 38.5 x 41.3 mm, height 13.3 mm; sapphire crystal; transparent case back; water-resistant to 50 m
Band: stainless steel, double folding clasp
Price: $2,495
Variations: silver-colored dial; as three-hand watch (2824), with leather strap

Longines

Longines is one of the few brands in recent years that has truly understood how to retain traditional values and classic watch design in its product palette while balancing them with a model policy dominated by the newest in watch technology and contemporary shapes.
Shortly after the beginning of the new century, Longines celebrated the manufacture of a total of 30 million watches since its founding in 1832, but a company history that can be proud of a lot more than just high production hides behind this gigantic number of timepieces. Above all, what comes to light is that this old brand could occupy a much more prominent place within the brand hierarchy of the Swatch Group due to its immense history. Longines has outfitted polar researchers such as Amundsen and pioneers in aviation such as Lindbergh and von Weems with its products, later reaping an excellent reputation for board watches for airplanes.

Fans of the classic line will greet the new Master Collection with joy. This is a collection that mirrors the glorious '40s at the Longines *manufacture* — in a beautifully shaped chronograph as well as various attractive men's watches, including a version displaying world time. In such successful remakes the pride of the brand is manifested time and again by highlighting its own achievements, something that the other Swatch Group brands usually don't underscore. Longines has understood very well how to fulfill its position within the group at the upper end of the middle segment without compulsively feeling the need to cling to its tradition with nostalgic flashbacks. Seeing how modern, youthful, and full of élan the traditional brand's models such as DolceVita, Conquest, opposition, and Evidenza are today, it is certainly hard to believe that this is a company with a more than 170-year history.
A visit to the company's own museum, however, quickly makes clear what a grand history this brand has enjoyed and with how much imagination and spirit of invention the company's employees have worked in the immense production building located on the outskirts of the small Jura town St. Imier. Here, in the museum located on the uppermost floor of the old factory building, it becomes apparent that Longines has been involved in just about every area of watch technology, often playing the role of pioneer and trendsetter in the industry.

This is, in fact, the case with the original Evidenza model family, released last year and styled after a Longines watch from the year 1925, which bullseyed consumers' taste during a time that was dominated by social upheaval and multilayered reorientation. Capturing such currents and turning them into product ideas is one of the most elementary demands on a designer, and those employed by Longines have always mastered this perfectly.
Even Longines was caught up in the general euphoria caused by the 2004 Summer Olympic Games. This is no wonder given the large amount of sponsoring the brand has garnered in sports timekeeping at the new-era Olympics: In 1952 Longines entered the history of the Olympic Games as the official timekeeper and has been at almost every set of games until Atlanta. For this reason, two watches from the Olympic Collection stick out among the plethora of new products introduced at Baselworld 2004. One is a quartz chronograph; the other, automatic, which seems to go better with the nostalgic appearance of the rectangular buttons and curved Arabic numerals on the dial, including the missing hour counter at 6 o'clock that was left off to maintain contemporary visuals. Both chronographs are available with a black or silver-colored dial, and are delivered in a magnificent special packaging that includes a book about the merits of the brand in the world of sports timekeeping.

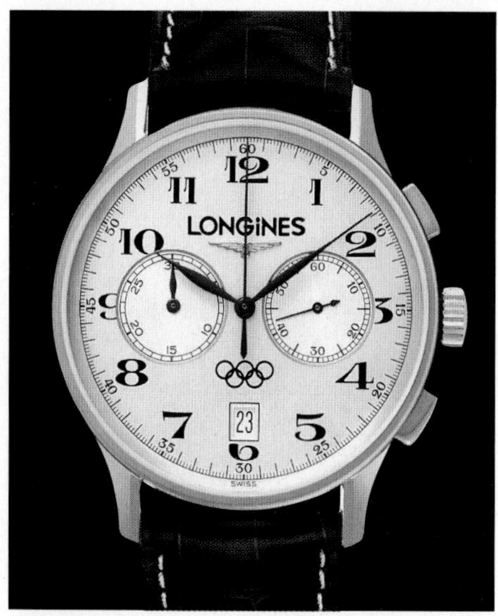

Olympic Collection Chronograph

Reference number: L2.650.4.73.2
Movement: automatic, Longines L651 (base ETA 2894-2); ø 28.6 mm, height 6.1 mm; 37 jewels; 28,800 vph
Functions: hours, minutes, subsidiary seconds; chronograph; date
Case: stainless steel, ø 40 mm, height 11.95 mm; sapphire crystal; transparent case back
Band: reptile skin, buckle
Price: $1,850
Variations: with metal bracelet

Master Collection Automatic

Reference number: L2.628.4.78.3
Movement: automatic, Longines L619 (base ETA 2892-A2); ø 25.6 mm, height 3.6 mm; 21 jewels; 28,800 vph
Functions: hours, minutes, sweep seconds; date
Case: stainless steel, ø 38.5 mm, height 9.1 mm; sapphire crystal; transparent case back
Band: reptile skin, double folding clasp
Price: upon request
Variations: with metal bracelet

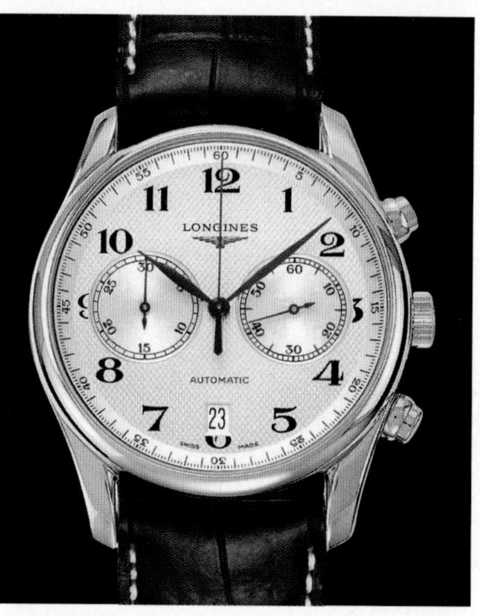

Master Collection Chronograph

Reference number: L2.629.4.78.3
Movement: automatic, Longines L651 (base ETA 2894-2); ø 28.6 mm, height 6.1 mm; 37 jewels; 28,800 vph
Functions: hours, minutes, subsidiary seconds; chronograph; date
Case: stainless steel, ø 40 mm, height 11.6 mm; sapphire crystal; transparent case back
Band: reptile skin, double folding clasp
Price: $2,100
Variations: with metal bracelet

Master Collection GMT

Reference number: L2.631.4.78.3
Movement: automatic, Longines L635 (base ETA 2824-2); ø 25.6 mm, height 4.6 mm; 25 jewels; 28,800 vph
Functions: hours, minutes, sweep seconds; date; 24-hour display disk with world time reference cities (second time zone)
Case: stainless steel, ø 38.5 mm, height 10.95 mm; sapphire crystal; transparent case back
Band: reptile skin, double folding clasp
Price: $2,000
Variations: with metal bracelet

Master Collection Maxi

Reference number: L2.640.4.78.3
Movement: manual winding, Longines L512 (base ETA 6498-2); ø 36.6 mm, height 4.5 mm; 17 jewels; 21,600 vph
Functions: hours, minutes, subsidiary seconds
Case: stainless steel, ø 47.5 mm, height 13.95 mm; sapphire crystal; transparent case back
Band: reptile skin, double folding clasp
Price: upon request

Master Collection Big Date

Reference number: L2.648.4.78.3
Movement: automatic, Longines L607 (base ETA 2896); ø 25.6 mm, height 4.85 mm; 21 jewels; 28,800 vph
Functions: hours, minutes, sweep seconds; large date
Case: stainless steel, ø 40 mm, height 11.06 mm; sapphire crystal; transparent case back
Band: reptile skin, double folding clasp
Price: $1,850
Variations: with metal bracelet

Evidenza

Reference number: L2.142.6.73.2
Movement: automatic, Longines L595 (base ETA 2000/1); ø 19.4 mm, height 3.6 mm; 20 jewels; 28,800 vph
Functions: hours, minutes, sweep seconds; date
Case: yellow gold, 26 x 30.6 mm, height 8.1 mm; sapphire crystal
Band: reptile skin, buckle
Price: $2,600
Variations: in red gold

Evidenza Lady Chronograph

Reference number: L2.156.0.73.4
Movement: automatic, Longines L652 (base ETA 2094); ø 23.30 mm, height 5.50 mm; 33 jewels; 28,800 vph
Functions: hours, minutes, subsidiary seconds; chronograph; date
Case: stainless steel, 30.5 x 35.6 mm, height 9.8 mm; case set with 160 diamonds; sapphire crystal
Band: reptile skin, double folding clasp
Price: $6,050
Variations: with black dial

Evidenza

Reference number: L2.642.4.51.4
Movement: automatic, Longines L615 (base ETA 2895/1); ø 25.6 mm, height 4.35 mm; 30 jewels; 28,800 vph
Functions: hours, minutes, subsidiary seconds; date
Case: stainless steel, 33.1 x 38.75 mm, height 10.45 mm; sapphire crystal
Band: reptile skin, double folding clasp
Price: $1,600
Variations: with silver-plated dial

Evidenza Chronograph

Reference number: L2.643.8.73.2
Movement: automatic, Longines L650 (base ETA 2894-2); ø 28.6 mm, height 6.1 mm; 37 jewels; 28,800 vph
Functions: hours, minutes, subsidiary seconds; chronograph; date
Case: rose gold, 34.9 x 40 mm, height 12.45 mm; sapphire crystal
Band: reptile skin, buckle
Price: $5,650
Variations: in yellow gold

Flagship Chronograph with Moon Phase

Reference number: L4.750.4.13.3
Movement: automatic, Longines L678 (base ETA 7751); ø 30 mm, height 7.9 mm; 25 jewels; 28,800 vph
Functions: hours, minutes, subsidiary seconds; chronograph; date, day, month, moon phase; 24-hour display
Case: stainless steel, ø 39 mm, height 13.4 mm; sapphire crystal; transparent case back
Band: reptile skin, buckle
Price: $2,200
Variations: with metal bracelet

Flagship Chronograph

Reference number: L4.718.6.22.0
Movement: automatic, Longines L650 (base ETA 2894-2); ø 28.6 mm, height 6.1 mm; 37 jewels; 28,800 vph
Functions: hours, minutes, subsidiary seconds; chronograph, date
Case: yellow gold, ø 39 mm, height 10.35 mm; sapphire crystal; transparent case back
Band: reptile skin, buckle
Price: $3,850
Variations: in stainless steel

Conquest 1958

Reference number: L1.611.4.52.2
Movement: automatic, Longines L633 (base ETA 2824-2); ø 25.6 mm, height 4.6 mm; 25 jewels; 28,800 vph
Functions: hours, minutes, sweep seconds; date
Case: stainless steel, ø 35.1 mm, height 9.75 mm; Hesalite crystal
Band: leather, buckle
Price: $1,000
Variations: in yellow or red gold

Conquest Replica Chronograph

Reference number: L1.641.8.72.2
Movement: automatic, Longines L650 (base ETA 2894/2); ø 28.6 mm, height 6.1 mm; 37 jewels; 28,800 vph
Functions: hours, minutes, subsidiary seconds; chronograph; date
Case: rose gold, ø 38.5 mm, height 12.05 mm; Hesalite crystal
Band: reptile skin, buckle
Price: $4,350
Variations: in yellow gold

Conquest Replica Chronograph Moon Phase

Reference number: L1.642.4.76.3
Movement: automatic, Longines L678.2 (base ETA 7751); ø 30 mm, height 7.9 mm; 25 jewels; 28,800 vph
Functions: hours, minutes, subsidiary seconds; chronograph; date, day, month, moon phase; 24-hour display
Case: stainless steel, ø 38.5 mm, height 13.8 mm; Hesalite crystal
Band: reptile skin, buckle
Price: $2,250

Conquest Replica Lady Chronograph

Reference number: L1.141.0.87.3
Movement: automatic, Longines L650.2 (base ETA 2894-2); ø 28.6 mm, height 6.1 mm; 37 jewels; 28,800 vph
Functions: hours, minutes, subsidiary seconds; chronograph; date
Case: stainless steel, ø 35 mm, height 10.75 mm; bezel set with 60 diamonds; Hesalite crystal
Band: calfskin, buckle
Price: $3,750

Flagship Replica

Reference number: L4.746.8.72.0
Movement: automatic, Longines L609 (base ETA 2895-1); ø 25.6 mm, height 4.35 mm; 30 jewels; 28,800 vph
Functions: hours, minutes, subsidiary seconds
Case: rose gold, ø 35 mm, height 10.3 mm; Hesalite crystal
Band: reptile skin, buckle
Price: $2,600
Variations: in yellow gold

Flagship Replica Chronograph

Reference number: L4.756.6.72.2
Movement: automatic, Longines L651 (base ETA 2894-A2); ø 28.6 mm, height 6.1 mm; 37 jewels; 28,800 vph
Functions: hours, minutes, subsidiary seconds; chronograph; date
Case: yellow gold, ø 37.8 mm, height 12.1 mm; Hesalite crystal
Band: reptile skin, buckle
Price: $4,350
Variations: in rose gold

Marcello C.

One year after the ten-year anniversary of this watch brand with the Italian-sounding name, Marcello C. continues to gather wind. Obviously, fans of beautiful mechanical watches reward the principle, declared by company founder Marcell Kainz, of offering watches with the best workmanship at exceptionally well-calculated prices with continuingly rising turnover numbers.

This friendly German goes shopping at only the best addresses in Switzerland, where he has movements, cases, crystals, and dials assembled according to his wishes at small, special workshops.

His current collection is clearly dominated, as in years past, by sporty automatic watches and chronographs in admirably robust versions. Pilot's watches and diver's watches with rotating bezels and screwed-in activating elements, classic models with somewhat nostalgic tendencies, and some pocket watches with skeletonized movements complete the program. Even the few women's watches he offers fit harmoniously into the overarching concept of solid watches for everyday use.

Meanwhile, Kainz has opened his own workshops in which he employs five watchmakers to assemble the Marcello C. models and also to care for after-sales service in a qualified manner. The continuing trend toward this brand will probably result in Kainz needing all the help that he can get.

Classic GMT

Reference number: 2013.3
Movement: automatic, ETA 2893-2, ø 25.6 mm, height 3.6 mm; 21 jewels; 28,800 vph
Functions: hours, minutes, sweep seconds; date; 24-hour display (second time zone)
Case: stainless steel, ø 42 mm, height 10.9 mm; sapphire crystal; transparent case back; water-resistant to 100 m
Band: reptile skin, double folding clasp
Price: $849
Variations: with black dial

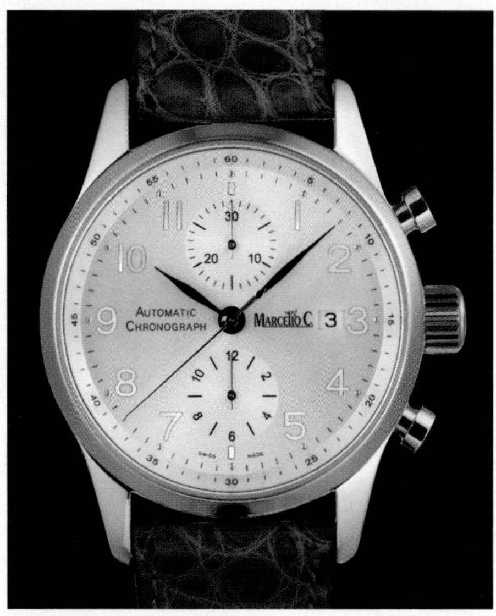

Classic Chronograph

Reference number: 2014.1
Movement: automatic, ETA 7750, ø 30 mm, height 7.9 mm; 25 jewels; 28,800 vph, finely finished with blued screws and côtes de Genève
Functions: hours, minutes, subsidiary seconds; chronograph; date
Case: stainless steel, ø 42 mm, height 14.6 mm; sapphire crystal; transparent case back; water-resistant to 100 m
Band: reptile skin, double folding clasp
Price: $1,229
Variations: with black dial

Pegasus Chronograph

Reference number: 2015.1
Movement: automatic, ETA 7750, ø 30 mm, height 7.9 mm; 25 jewels; 28,800 vph, finely finished with blued screws and côtes de Genève
Functions: hours, minutes, subsidiary seconds; chronograph; date
Case: stainless steel, ø 42 mm, height 14.6 mm; sapphire crystal; transparent case back; water-resistant to 100 m
Band: reptile skin, double folding clasp
Remarks: dial completely inlaid with luminous substance
Price: $1,229
Variations: with black dial

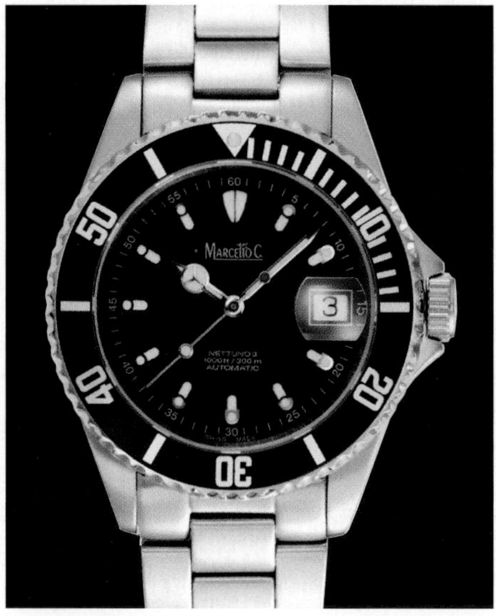

Nettuno 3

Reference number: 2007.2
Movement: automatic, ETA 2824-2, ø 25.6 mm, height 4.6 mm; 25 jewels; 28,800 vph
Functions: hours, minutes, sweep seconds; date
Case: stainless steel, ø 40 mm, height 12 mm; unidirectionally rotating bezel with 60-minute scale; sapphire crystal with magnifying lens above the date display; screw-in crown; water-resistant to 300 m
Band: stainless steel, folding clasp
Price: $489
Variations: with blue or silver-colored dial

Tridente Chronograph

Reference number: 2010.1
Movement: automatic, ETA 7750, ø 30 mm, height 7.9 mm; 25 jewels; 28,800 vph, finely finished with blued screws and côtes de Genève
Functions: hours, minutes, subsidiary seconds; chronograph; date
Case: stainless steel, ø 44.2 mm, height 16,8 mm; unidirectionally rotating bezel with 60-minute scale; sapphire crystal; screw-in crown; water-resistant to 500 m
Band: stainless steel, folding clasp
Price: $1,855
Variations: with silver or black dial

Scala Chronograph

Reference number: 2009
Movement: automatic, ETA 7750, ø 30 mm, height 7.9 mm; 25 jewels; 28,800 vph, finely finished with blued screws and côtes de Genève
Functions: hours, minutes, subsidiary seconds; chronograph; date
Case: stainless steel, ø 48 mm, height 15.8 mm; bidirectionally rotating rotating bezel under crystal, settable via crown, with 60-minute scale; sapphire crystal; transparent case back; water-resistant to 100 m
Band: leather, double folding clasp
Price: $1,355

Meistersinger

At first glance it would seem that something is not quite right with these watches. With their purposeful sobriety the dials seem somehow a bit, well, empty. Of course, watches don't always have to be chronographs or perpetual calendars, literally filled with scales and hands. But is one hand all by itself enough?

A good two hundred years after the introduction of the historical *montre à souscription* by Breguet — a type of "people's" pocket watch that was paid for in installments and which only possessed a simple movement without minute hand — Manfred Brassler has come up with the idea to once again manufacture a mechanical watch possessing only one single hand.

The designer chose a large case, 43 mm in diameter, with a relatively large dial area and made clear markings on the minute scale for the half and quarter hour as well as the five minute intervals. The very pointy (hour) hand is long enough to clearly move among the markings at the edge of the dial, and it actually becomes possible to rather accurately read the one-handed watch to within two or three minutes without trouble. No layperson alive needs a watch that is more precise than that.

Brassler had previously produced very successful watches (with Watch People), including extraordinarily modern and design-oriented timekeepers. The Scrypto models, which have, by the way, also been available right from the beginning as conventional two-handed watches, play with emotions located in the grey area situated between the Renaissance and the Space Age. In front, a purposefully sober dial whose numerals from 1 to 9 even carry an extra 0 (as if the human brain arranges the hours using a decimal program), while behind it a movement oscillating at the frequency of 18,000 or 28,800 vph ticks audibly.

Contrary to its more mundane siblings, the Scrypto Edition 1Z, introduced about a year ago, is powered by an Unitas manually wound movement, today produced by ETA and known under the caliber name of 6497, decorated to the nines. The fact that the 6497 is a rather largely dimensioned pocket watch movement with a diameter of 37 mm does not represent a problem for the large case of the Scrypto — to the contrary: Underneath the large sapphire crystal case back, the black-tie mechanism is visible without obstruction. The trouble the watchmakers went to becomes obvious: A screw balance, a beautifully finished swan-neck fine adjustment, côtes de Genève across all bridges, blued screws, gold-flushed engravings — there is hardly anything left to add to this simple, robust serial movement. And the dial does not languish in its shadow: Characteristic for the style of the house that plays with the contradictions between old and new, conservative and progressive, and traditional and avant-garde, the Scrypto Edition 1Z is outfitted with a genuine enamel dial. There are only a few workshops left in Switzerland's Jura region that understand this delicate craft of turning a small brass plate into a work of art needing up to thirty steps per piece. Today, the same tools and kilns are used that were used a hundred years ago — even though the typography of the dial is 100-percent Meistersinger.

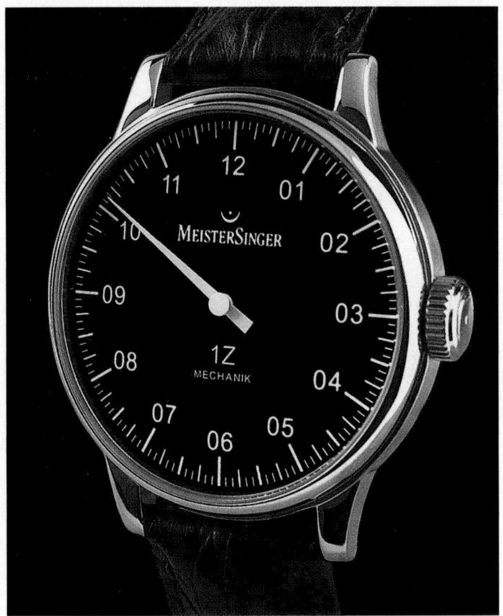

Scrypto 1Z

Reference number: AM3.03G
Movement: manual winding, ETA 2801-2, ø 25.6 mm, height 3.35 mm; 17 jewels; 28,800 vph
Functions: hours (every marker stands for 5 minutes)
Case: stainless steel, ø 43 mm, height 11.5 mm; mineral crystal; transparent case back
Band: leather, buckle
Price: $650
Variations: with silvery white dial; in 38 mm case diameter; starting in November 2004 also with ETA 6497

Scrypto 1Z

Reference number: AM3.02G
Movement: manual winding, ETA 2801-2, ø 25.6 mm, height 3.35 mm; 17 jewels; 28,800 vph
Functions: hours (every marker stands for 5 minutes)
Case: stainless steel, ø 43 mm, height 11.5 mm; mineral crystal; transparent case back
Band: leather, buckle
Price: $650
Variations: with silvery white dial; in 38 mm case diameter; starting in November 2004 also with ETA 6497

Scrypto Automatic

Reference number: AM2.03
Movement: automatic, ETA 2824-2, ø 25.6 mm, height 4.6 mm; 25 jewels; 28,800 vph
Functions: hours, minutes, sweep seconds; date
Case: stainless steel, ø 43 mm, height 11.5 mm; mineral crystal; transparent case back
Band: leather, buckle
Price: $750
Variations: with black or silvery white dial; with 38 mm case diameter

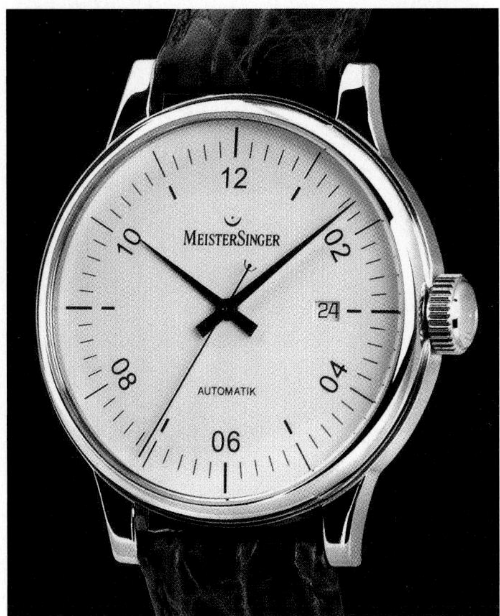

Scrypto Sport Automatic

Reference number: AM4.03
Movement: automatic, ETA 2824-2, ø 25.6 mm, height 4.6 mm; 25 jewels; 28,800 vph
Functions: hours, minutes, sweep seconds; date
Case: stainless steel, ø 43 mm, height 11.5 mm; mineral crystal; transparent case back
Band: leather, buckle
Price: $750
Variations: with black or silvery white dial

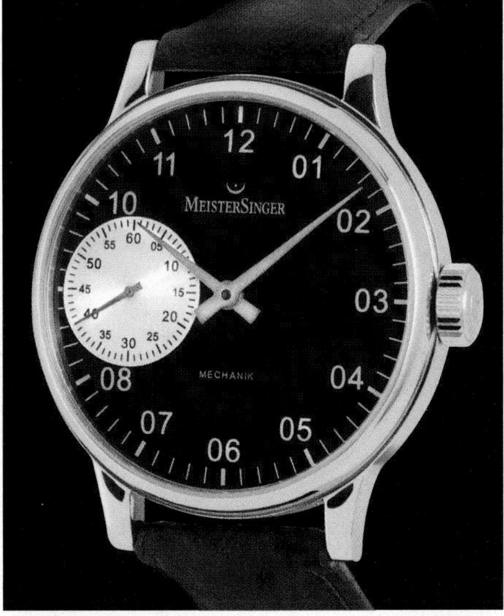

Scrypto Unitas

Reference number: AM5.05
Movement: manual winding, ETA 6497-1, ø 36.6 mm, height 4.5 mm; 17 jewels; 21,600 vph, finely finished with blued screws and côtes de Genève
Functions: hours, minutes, subsidiary seconds
Case: stainless steel, ø 43 mm, height 12.5 mm; mineral crystal; transparent case back
Band: leather, buckle
Price: $990
Variations: with beige dial

Scrypto GMT

Reference number: AM8.01
Movement: automatic, ETA 2893-2, ø 25.6 mm, height 4.1 mm; 23 jewels; 28,800 vph
Functions: hours, minutes, sweep seconds; 24-hour display (second time zone)
Case: stainless steel, ø 38 mm, height 11.2 mm; mineral crystal; transparent case back
Band: leather, buckle
Price: upon request
Variations: with beige or black dial

Mido

Within the brand conglomerate resulting in a gigantic number of watches available from the Swatch Group, Mido has seemed to live an unfortunate life in the shadows until only recently when it stepped out into the sunshine. This brand has shared a close relationship with sister brands Tissot and Certina regarding production, component purchasing, distribution, and logistics, and measured against the number of watches produced, this little brand has obviously had a hard time holding its own until now. Quite unjustly. Today's watches with their pleasing design, high practical value, and above all fair price/performance ratio represent a welcome alternative for watch fans whose timekeepers don't need to be displayed on the wrist of a celebrity "testimonial" or manufactured "by hand." This is especially true for the timepieces featuring mechanical movements that are more than suitable for watch fans with a shallow wallet: Mido timekeepers are welcome entry-level models for the average consumer enamored of cases and dials in simple, clean design.

The history of this brand began after its founding in 1918 with a few somewhat comical-looking models. Company founder Georges Schaeren was reacting to an era of increasing motorization and created the shape of his watches based on hoods of famous automobiles. From 1934 onward, Mido used the patented crown seal made of natural cork that was first used in the Multifort models (later known as the Aquadura) and has since been incorporated into the current Ocean Star and Commander models. These two historic watches brought Mido worldwide fame beginning in 1959.

The watches sealed in this way were tested extensively. They were placed in fresh and salt water for days on end, had to withstand simulated altitudes of more than 10 miles (16,600 meters), were subjected to water pressure of 13 bar, and were finally placed alternately in hot and cold chambers for environmental testing. Amazingly, virtually all of the watches survived this punishment, including even the torture of the manual winding simulator, which subjected the crown seal to an equivalent of thirty-four years of winding and time-setting, remaining 100 percent tight. The watches were accordingly robust and impervious to all types of stress encountered in daily use, and only very rarely did a watchmaker see a Mido again once it was sold. These quality standards still exist today, and there are still Mido watches bearing the names of Multifort and Commander that carry a small piece of natural cork fitted around their winding stems. Riding on the success of the little manually wound version of the Baroncelli model, the Swiss brand has introduced an only slightly larger version of this watch powered by an automatic movement this year. Featuring a guilloché dial and a transparent case back, the simple, yet elegant new watches have a great deal to offer the watch fan. Female connoisseurs can enjoy a well-designed new Multifort in a cushion-shaped stainless steel case powered by an automatic movement. Completely in the tradition of the classic everyday watch, this new women's watch is pleasantly unpretentious without denying its femininity.

Commander Chronometer

Reference number: M 8429.4.C1.1
Movement: automatic, ETA 2836-2, ø 25.6 mm, height 5.05 mm; 25 jewels; 28,800 vph, certified chronometer (C.O.S.C.)
Functions: hours, minutes, sweep seconds; date and day
Case: stainless steel, monocoque, ø 37 mm, height 10.2 mm; Hesalite crystal; Aquadura crown cork sealing system; water-resistant to 50 m
Band: stainless steel Milanaise-style bracelet, folding clasp
Price: $850
Variations: with leather strap, in yellow gold with Milanaise-style bracelet

Ocean Star Sport Diver

Reference number: M 8522.4.58.9
Movement: automatic, ETA 2836-2, ø 25.6 mm, height 5.05 mm; 25 jewels; 28,800 vph, finely decorated
Functions: hours, minutes, sweep seconds; date and day
Case: stainless steel, ø 40.3 mm, height 11 mm; unidirectionally rotating bezel with 60-minute scale; sapphire crystal; transparent case back; screw-in crown; water-resistant to 200 m
Band: rubber, folding clasp with diver's extension
Price: $695

All Dial Chrono Valjoux

Reference number: M 8360.4.B1.1
Movement: automatic, Mido 1320 (base ETA 7750); ø 30 mm, height 7.9 mm; 25 jewels; 28,800 vph, certified chronometer (C.O.S.C.), finely decorated with côtes de Genève and blued screws
Functions: hours, minutes, subsidiary seconds; chronograph; date, day
Case: stainless steel, ø 42.6 mm, height 13.6 mm; sapphire crystal; screw-in crown; water-resistant to 100 m
Band: stainless steel, folding clasp
Price: $1,895
Variations: with black dial; with rubber strap

Multifort Rectangular Chronograph

Reference number: M 8814.4.18.12
Movement: automatic, Mido 1320 (base ETA 7750); ø 30 mm, height 7.9 mm; 25 jewels; 28,800 vph, finely decorated
Functions: hours, minutes, subsidiary seconds, chronograph, date, day
Case: stainless steel, 44.5 x 39.5 mm, height 13.45 mm; sapphire crystal; transparent case back; screw-in crown; water-resistant to 100 m
Band: stainless steel, folding clasp
Price: upon request
Variations: with leather strap

Multifort Lady's

Reference number: M 7838.4.74.8
Movement: automatic, ETA 2671, ø 17.2 mm, height 4.8 mm; 25 jewels; 28,800 vph, finely decorated
Functions: hours, minutes, sweep seconds; date
Case: stainless steel, 27 x 29 mm, height 10.3 mm; sapphire crystal; transparent case back; Aquadura crown cork sealing system; water-resistant to 50 m
Band: leather, buckle
Price: upon request
Variations: with stainless steel bracelet; different dial variations

Baroncelli Automatic

Reference number: M 3890.4.21.8
Movement: automatic, Mido 1192 (base ETA 2892-A2); ø 25.6 mm, height 3.6 mm; 21 jewels; 28,800 vph, finely decorated with blued screws and côtes de Genève
Functions: hours, minutes, sweep seconds; date
Case: stainless steel, ø 39 mm, height 7.9 mm; sapphire crystal; transparent case back; Aquadura crown cork sealing system; water-resistant to 50 m
Band: leather, folding clasp
Price: upon request
Variations: with black dial

Daniel Mink

Daniel Mink may seem less celebrated than some other Swiss brands with long histories, despite the fact that it has been distributed here for years. Its low-key marketing and PR strategy does the brand an injustice, however, for the watches are wonderfully well designed and of very high quality.

The brand was founded at the height of the quartz craze in 1975 by Aaron and Rina Minkowitz, who originally introduced it to the world as Daniel Minx. The name was changed shortly thereafter to Daniel Mink. Aaron Minkowitz was a man who was thoroughly passionate about watches, and thus the brand manufactured both quartz and mechanical through the years, even though mechanical watches were only being bought by collectors at the time. Recognizing that mechanical watches were once again here to stay, the company – under new ownership since 1997 – ceased producing new quartz models completely in 2000. Daniel Mink Switzerland was bought by two young partners, also well versed in the ways of the mechanical watch. Mitchell Caplan is based in the United States and oversees the direction of the Montreux Group, Daniel Mink's fully owned U.S. subsidiary, which is also in charge of distribution. Davi Galvo makes his home in Switzerland and manages the Swiss office and assembly facility in Biel.

Daniel Mink has introduced a number of interesting collections over the years, such as the Radica, which featured unique bezels fashioned from rare Mediterranean woods and debuted in 1986. The Arx collection, launched in 1981, was a line of solid gold watches (the first made by the brand) and was characterized by a striking grid over the dial. The Monte Carlo line, premiering in 1978, bore the world's first rubber strap on a dress watch, which was integrated into the steel case.

Contemporary collections include 1999's Titus, Fusion-D and the complicated Rattrapante Collections, both from 2003, and the 1900 Collection, the first generation of which premiered in 1993. The 1900 Collection is particularly arresting with its *clous de Paris* décor on the bezel and bracelet. Furthermore: This is the first watch in stainless steel to ever be decorated with this detailed design. The pyramid-shaped *clous de Paris* pattern is applied by a machine, then hand-finished to a high polish. The men's bracelet features an excess of 2,340 individual cuts. The third generation of this outstanding collection will debut at Baselworld 2005, solely powered by mechanical movements.

And perhaps the most interesting timepiece this brand has brought forth is the Skeleton Gold. The main attraction of this watch is the hand-skeletonized and hand-engraved ETA 2892/2 that is totally visible due to the complete lack of a dial or case back, both being replaced by scratchproof sapphire crystals. The line's highlight is naturally the limited-edition model of fifty pieces worldwide housed in a warm 18-karat rose gold case. The 18-karat yellow gold model shown on this page is unlimited and retails for $5,495.

Tonneau Femme

Reference number: 4291DIAP
Movement: automatic, ETA 2681, ø 19.4 mm, height 4.8 mm; 25 jewels; 28,800 vph
Functions: hours, minutes, sweep seconds
Case: stainless steel, 36 x 27 mm, height 9 mm; bezel set with 58 diamonds; sapphire crystal; water-resistant to 30 m
Band: reptile skin, buckle
Remarks: mother-of-pearl dial
Price: $5,495
Variations: without diamonds ($1,395); choice of pink, fuschia, black, and red straps

Titus

Reference number: 7041WH
Movement: automatic, ETA 7750, ø 30 mm, height 7.9 mm; 25 jewels; 28,800 vph, rotor and bridges with perlage; rotor engraved with company name
Functions: hours, minutes, subsidiary seconds; date, day, month, moon phase; chronograph
Case: stainless steel, ø 38 mm, height 13 mm; bezel with tachymeter scale; sapphire crystal, anti-reflective; transparent case back; water-resistant to 50 m
Band: alligator skin, double folding clasp
Price: $2,795
Variations: with black dial

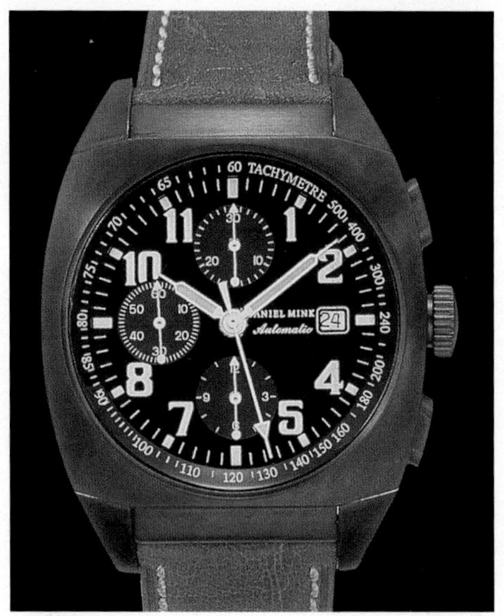

Tempus

Reference number: 61517BBKS
Movement: automatic, ETA 7750, ø 30 mm, height 7.9 mm; 25 jewels; 28,800 vph
Functions: hours, minutes, subsidiary seconds; chronograph
Case: stainless steel, 42 x 53 mm, height 13 mm; bezel with tachymeter scale; sapphire crystal; water-resistant to 30 m
Band: leather, buckle
Price: $2,150
Variations: with steel bracelet ($2,250); with black, beige or brown strap; with black or silver dial; with case in steel and black PVD

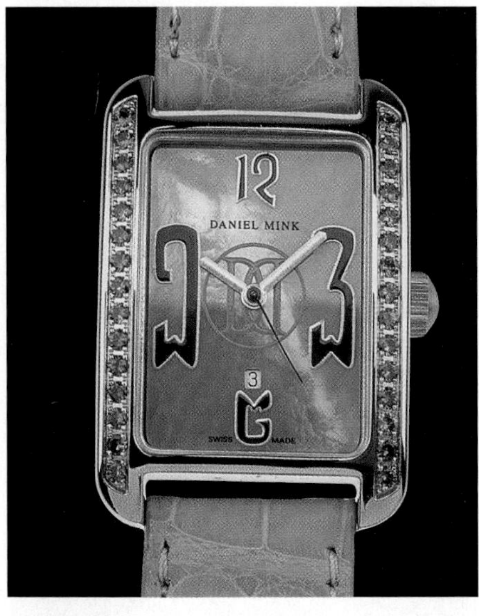

Fusion-D

Reference number: 3271
Movement: automatic, ETA 2671, ø 17.2 mm, height 4.8 mm; 25 jewels; 28,800 vph, rotor engraved with "Fusion-D"
Functions: hours, minutes, sweep seconds
Case: stainless steel, 38 x 27 mm, height 13 mm; case sides and lugs set with .80 carats of blue sapphires; sapphire crystal; transparent case back
Band: reptile skin, buckle
Remarks: mother-of-pearl dial
Price: $4,095
Variations: without gemstones ($1,395); with white diamonds ($4,595); with galuchat (stingray) strap

Tempus

Reference number: 61517SSVB
Movement: automatic, ETA 7750, ø 30 mm, height 7.9 mm; 25 jewels; 28,800 vph
Functions: hours, minutes, subsidiary seconds; chronograph
Case: stainless steel, 42 x 53 mm, height 13 mm; bezel with tachymeter scale; sapphire crystal; water-resistant to 50 m
Band: stainless steel, double folding clasp
Price: $2,250
Variations: with black dial

Skeleton

Reference number: 3323RW
Movement: automatic, ETA 2824, ø 25.6 mm, height 4.6 mm; 25 jewels; 28,800 vph
Functions: hours, minutes, sweep seconds
Case: stainless steel, ø 36 mm, height 9 mm; sapphire crystal; transparent case back; water-resistant to 30 m
Band: alligator skin, double folding clasp
Price: $1,050
Variations: with white or black dials with Roman or Arabic numerals; with black or brown straps

Montblanc

Montblanc, named for Europe's highest mountain and to be found at the summit of luxury writing instrument manufacturers for quite a while now, has been aiming to take on a protruding position among watch manufacturers for years — with increasing success. When the first watches from the Montblanc brand were introduced in 1997, this brand so rich in another tradition garnered a lot of head-shaking at first. The "sidestep" into a foreign industry was naturally accompanied by derisive comments.

But the success of the new watch brand issuing from a reputable, almost one-hundred-year-old company soon quieted even the skeptics, and the first collection launched eight years ago, of which the highest-quality component was doubtless its grand name, has been followed by models of an obviously much better quality. Today, Montblanc's watches don't need to fear comparison to other brands' models in this price class. The development of the design, originally thought to be too dainty, and its evolution including modern and sporty style elements find more recognition from year to year on the occasion of the S.I.H.H.

Writing instrument manufacturer Montblanc, like many watch brands, has its roots in craft and technology. Like the components of a movement, the most important parts of the brand's costly fountain pens are created in half-automated precision. In the modern production halls of the company headquarters near Hamburg's famous soccer stadium, automatic CNC machines stamp and form parts. The golden writing nibs are finely finished by hand, polished, then receive the narrow cut for the ink flow with the aid of a paper-thin diamond disk. Nibs, ink tank, and cartridge mechanics are strictly examined by quality control and must pass a great deal of testing very similar to the usual controls in watch production.

Montblanc Montre SA is at home in the little Jura town Le Locle, which, together with neighboring La Chaux-de-Fonds, is one of Switzerland's watch metropolises. This location was chosen purposefully, for the Swiss watch industry is concentrated in the western part of the country, or to be more specific in the region around Geneva and the Jura. Most suppliers of cases, bands, and dials are at home here.

The old art deco-style villa housing the watch company was renovated from 1997 until 1999 and care was taken to maintain old style elements, restoring windows, parquet wood floors, stairway, and ceilings decorated with gold leaf to their original states as far as possible. A new one-story glass building was annexed underneath the mansion's wide terrace, increasing the original work area from 200 square meters to about 1,000 — enough room for forty employees.

Star Platinum Chrono GMT Automatic

Reference number: 09632
Movement: automatic, ETA 7754, ø 30 mm, height 7.9 mm; 25 jewels; 28,800 vph
Functions: hours, minutes, subsidiary seconds; chronograph; date; 24-hour display (second time zone)
Case: stainless steel, PVD platinum-coated, ø 42 mm; sapphire crystal
Band: reptile skin, folding clasp
Price: $2,700

Sport Lady Jewels

Reference number: 09650
Movement: quartz, ETA 955112.0
Functions: hours, minutes, sweep seconds; date
Case: stainless steel, ø 32 mm; bezel set with 136 black diamonds; sapphire crystal
Band: rubber, double folding clasp
Remarks: mother-of-pearl dial with black diamond markers
Price: $6,700
Variations: with black dial and white diamonds

Time Walker Chrono Automatic

Reference number: 09671
Movement: automatic, ETA 7753, ø 30 mm, height 7.9 mm; 25 jewels; 28,800 vph
Functions: hours, minutes, subsidiary seconds; chronograph; date
Case: stainless steel, ø 43 mm, height 15.2 mm; sapphire crystal
Band: reptile skin, buckle
Price: $3,100
Variations: with black dial; with stainless steel bracelet

Sport Gold GMT Automatic

Reference number: 09644
Movement: automatic, ETA 2893-2, ø 25.6 mm, height 4.1 mm; 21 jewels; 28,800 vph, certified chronometer (C.O.S.C.)
Functions: hours, minutes, sweep seconds; date; 24-hour display (second time zone)
Case: yellow gold, ø 41.5 mm; bidirectionally rotating bezel with 24-hour scale; sapphire crystal with magnifying lens above the date display; water-resistant to 200 m
Band: reptile skin, buckle
Price: $10,000
Variations: with gold link bracelet

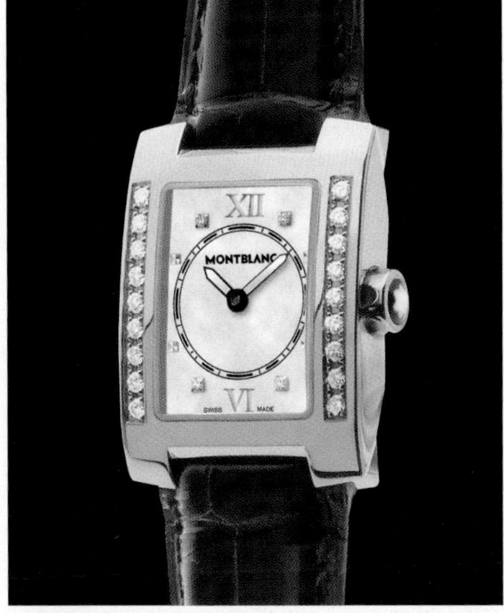

Profile Lady Gold Jewellery

Reference number: 08561
Movement: quartz, ETA 976001
Functions: hours, minutes
Case: yellow gold, 30.8 x 23.2 mm; case sides set with 18 diamonds; sapphire crystal
Band: reptile skin, buckle
Remarks: mother-of-pearl dial with diamond markers
Price: $5,400
Variations: different bands

Star Collection Platinum Réveil

Reference number: 08562
Movement: automatic, Jaquet AS 5008, ø 30 mm, height 7.6 mm; 31 jewels; 28,800 vph
Functions: hours, minutes, sweep seconds; date, day; alarm
Case: stainless steel, PVD platinum-coated, ø 38 mm; sapphire crystal
Band: reptile skin, folding clasp
Price: $3,900

Movado

This company's name originates in the synthetic world language Esperanto and means "constantly in motion." It's an aphorism that not only fits the internal workings of a watch, but also stands for the Ditesheim family's restless spirit of invention when founding the brand in 1881 in Switzerland's La Chaux-de-Fonds. In the first one hundred years of its existence, this company registered close to one hundred patents.

The brand earned worldwide respect for itself with the legendary Museum Watch, whose nearly blank dial without numerals or markers was created by the American artist Nathan George Horwitt in 1947. The Museum Watch, whose dot at 12 o'clock symbolizes the midday sun, owes its name to the fact that it was quickly accepted into the permanent collections of reputable museums all over the world, such as the Museum of Modern Art in New York.

Today, the Museum Watch is offered in innumerable variations that are all characterized by Horwitt's clear, timeless design. Movado now offers a myriad of contemporary interpretations of this classic, including the Capelo model that features a crescent-shaped case.

It's not hard to imagine the conflict of interest that the designers and watchmakers of the small workshop must have felt when confronted with the task of making the Museum Watch into a tourbillon. Naturally, every watchmaker would like to present his or her tourbillon at the most prominent spot on the dial, but Horwitt's creation allows this special position to be filled by the dot alone.

Wisely, the design and watchmaking departments were cleanly separated, with the result that the Museum Tourbillon looks just like a normal Museum Watch at first glance — except that it is 42 mm in diameter and more than 13 mm in height, making it larger and far more stately than in its usual presentation. When the heavy platinum case is turned over, it becomes clear that this is something unique in every sense of the word: For the Museum Tourbillon is truly a unique piece — a type of proof of skill to strengthen the ambitions that the Movado Group harbors in the watch industry (in the meantime with Ebel as its second luxury brand).

Two days before Christmas 2003 a report spread like wildfire through the agencies that the Movado Group Inc., headquartered in Paramus, NJ, had reached an agreement with the Louis Vuitton, Moet & Hennessy group (LVMH) regarding the takeover of the watch brand Ebel. The Movado Group hopes for better reception on the European markets with its takeover of the Swiss luxury brand and has certainly purchased a complementary marque to add to the group's watch portfolio (Movado, Concord, ESQ, Coach, and Tommy Hilfiger) in the higher price segment.

Capelo

Reference number: 0605012
Movement: quartz, ETA 956032
Functions: hours, minutes
Case: stainless steel, ø 32 mm, height 7.9 mm; sapphire crystal
Band: leather, buckle
Remarks: Nathan Horwitt's famous design trait: sun dot at 12 o'clock
Price: $550
Variations: with diamonds

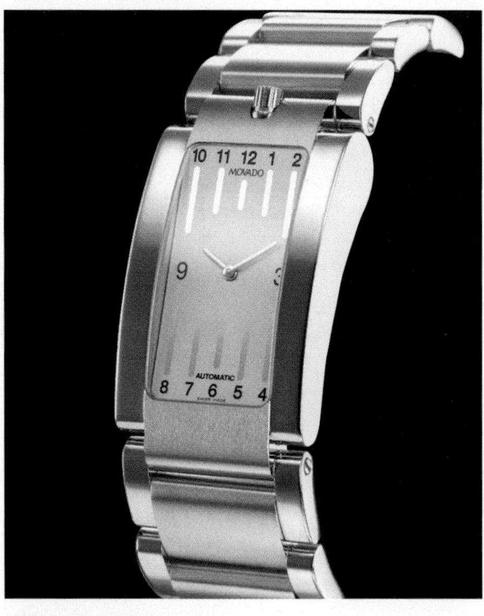

Elliptica Automatic

Reference number: 0604831
Movement: automatic, ETA 2000-1, ø 19.4 mm, height 3.6 mm; 20 jewels; 28,800 vph
Functions: hours, minutes
Case: stainless steel, domed, 25 x 47 mm, height 13.3 mm; sapphire crystal; crown between the upper lugs
Band: stainless steel, folding clasp
Price: $1,895
Variations: with reptile skin strap

Elliptica Réserve de Marche

Reference number: 0604893
Movement: automatic, ETA 2892-A2 modified with module by Jaquet, ø 25.6 mm, height 3.6 mm; 21 jewels; 28,800 vph, côtes de Genève
Functions: hours, minutes; date; 24-hour display (second time zone); power reserve display
Case: stainless steel, domed, ø 40 mm, height 13.25 mm; sapphire crystal; crown between the upper lugs
Band: reptile skin, buckle
Price: $4,095

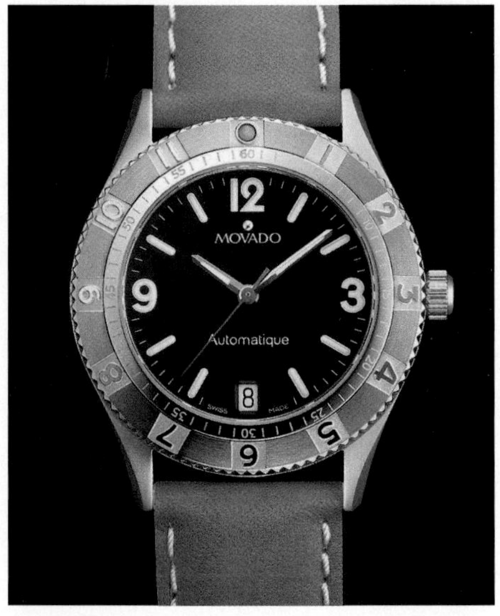

Gentry

Reference number: 0605069
Movement: automatic, ETA 2824-2, ø 25.6 mm, height 4.6 mm; 25 jewels; 28,800 vph
Functions: hours, minutes, sweep seconds; date
Case: stainless steel, ø 35.5 mm, height 8.7 mm; unidirectionally rotating, bezel with 12-hour scale; sapphire crystal
Band: leather, buckle
Price: $495
Variations: with stainless steel bracelet

Semi Moon

Reference number: 0605003
Movement: quartz, ETA 901000.0
Functions: hours, minutes
Case: stainless steel, 27 x 49 mm, height 7.1 mm; sapphire crystal
Band: reptile skin, buckle
Price: $1,095
Variations: with black band

Museum Watch Automatic

Reference number: 0605113
Movement: automatic, ETA 2892-A2, ø 25.6 mm, height 3.6 mm; 21 jewels; 28,800 vph
Functions: hours, minutes
Case: stainless steel, PVD-coated, ø 42 mm, height 7.5 mm; sapphire crystal
Band: reptile skin, buckle
Remarks: Nathan Horwitt's famous design trait: sun dot at 12 o'clock
Price: $895
Variations: in 37 mm case size; in stainless steel; with metal bracelet

Mühle

The history of Glashütte's watch industry has been tied for many decades to the family-owned company Mühle: 135 years ago Robert Mühle built, among other, things gauges for watchmakers, later also including clocks and tachometers for automobiles in the repertoire. For the last ten years the company, which is once again in the possession of the founding family, has manufactured marine clock systems and high-quality wristwatches.

On the occasion of the company's anniversary, the special edition Hommage to Robert Mühle was introduced in the spring of 2004. With this, company owner Hans-Jürgen Mühle honors his great-grandfather, the original founder.

The edition comprises five watches: two classic three-hand watches (one for men and one for women), another three-hand watch featuring a large date, a timekeeper displaying a second time zone, and a chronograph. The edition's watches differ from the regular collection by the addition of a special dial, among other things. The anniversary edition will probably be popular among collectors, since it is numbered and limited to 500 pieces worldwide.

The words "nautische Instrumente" in the company's official name (Mühle Glashütte GmbH Nautische Instrumente & Feinmechanik) also refer to watches, but to those which are able to fulfill professional demands, such as the S.A.R. Rescue-Timer. This especially robust automatic watch featuring a 4-mm thick sapphire crystal and exceptional legibility at night is the official timer on fifty-six rescue cruisers of the DGzRS (Deutsche Gesellschaft zur Rettung Schiffbrüchiger or the German Sea Rescue Service). Even under extreme conditions, this watch will survive anything that a person can. When developing and improving products, it is important for the company head to be involved. Hans-Jürgen Mühle is, and he recently developed a special fine adjustment device for the complicated models in his collection. One of the specialties of Glashütte watchmakers has always been the fine adjustment of a movement using an index and a spring that is bent to look like a swan's neck. But because Mühle didn't want to just copy the swan-neck fine adjustment developed by the old masters, the precision engineer designed a spring that looks more like the neck of a woodpecker. The design is called the woodpecker-neck fine adjustment and, in many of his complicated models, replaces the original adjustment system featuring an eccentric screw. The individual components of this subgroup, including the spring, index, and balance cock, are manufactured in the company's own workshop.

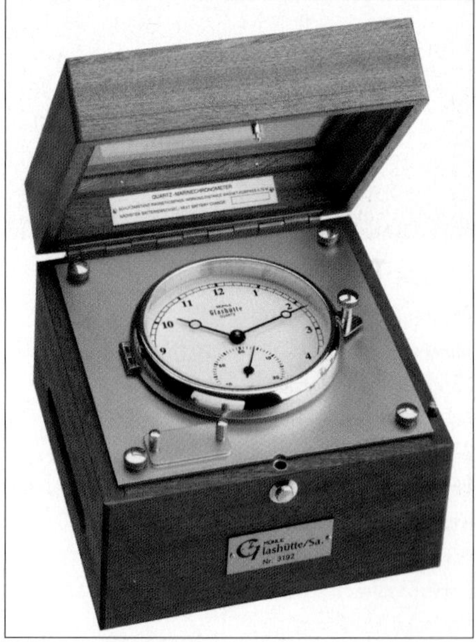

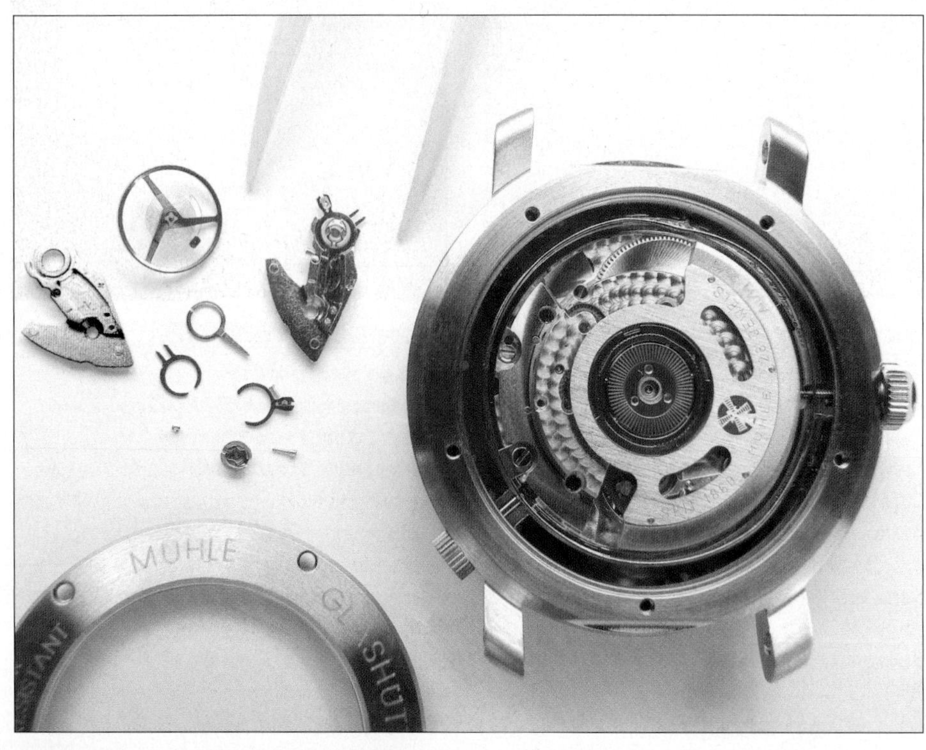

Global-Timer

Reference number: M1-41-13-LB
Movement: automatic, ETA 2893, ø 25.6 mm, height 4.1 mm; 23 jewels; 28,800 vph, Mühle woodpecker fine adjustment
Functions: hours, minutes, sweep seconds, date, 24-hour display, world time, countdown
Case: stainless steel, ø 42 mm, height 11 mm; bidirectionally rotating bezel under crystal with world times, outside bezel with countdown engraving (descending); sapphire crystal; transparent case back; screw-in crown; water-resistant to 50 m
Band: leather, buckle
Remarks: limited to 1,111 pieces
Price: 1,600 euros

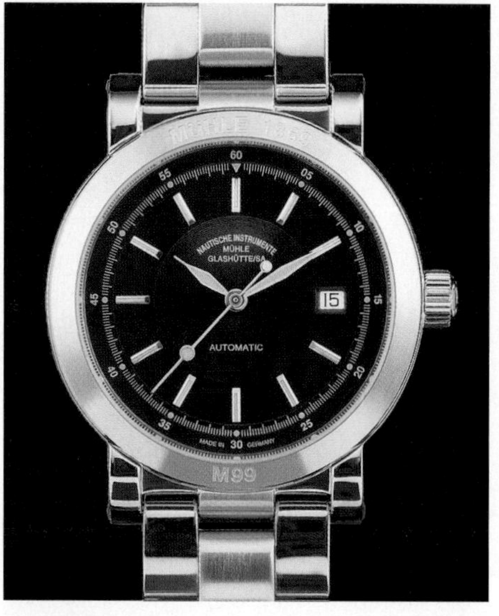

City 99

Reference number: M1-99-43-MB
Movement: automatic, ETA 2824-2, ø 25.6 mm, height 4.6 mm; 25 jewels; 28,800 vph, Mühle special finish
Functions: hours, minutes, sweep seconds; date
Case: stainless steel, ø 40 mm, height 10 mm; sapphire crystal; transparent case back; screw-in crown; water-resistant to 100 m
Band: stainless steel, folding clasp
Price: 800 euros
Variations: with leather strap; with white or blue dial

Robert Mühle I

Reference number: M1-10-15-5-LB
Movement: automatic, ETA/Valjoux 7750, ø 30 mm, height 7.9 mm; 25 jewels; 28,800 vph, Mühle special finish
Functions: hours, minutes, subsidiary seconds; chronograph; date, day
Case: stainless steel, ø 43 mm, height 14.5 mm; sapphire crystal; transparent case back; water-resistant to 100 m
Band: reptile skin, double folding clasp
Remarks: limited to 500 pieces
Price: 2,100 euros

Chronograph II

Reference number: M1-31-32-LB
Movement: automatic, ETA/Valjoux 7750, ø 30 mm, height 7.9 mm; 25 jewels; 28,800 vph, Mühle special finish
Functions: hours, minutes, subsidiary seconds; chronograph; date
Case: stainless steel, ø 37.4 mm, height 13 mm; sapphire crystal; transparent case back; water-resistant to 50 m
Band: leather
Price: 1,500 euros
Variations: with stainless steel bracelet; with white or black dial

S.A.R. Rescue-Timer

Reference number: M1-41-03-MB
Movement: automatic, ETA 2824-2, ø 25.6 mm, height 4.6 mm; 25 jewels; 28,800 vph, Mühle special finish
Functions: hours, minutes, sweep seconds; date
Case: stainless steel, ø 42 mm, height 13.5 mm; bezel with rubber coating; sapphire crystal, extra thick (4 mm); screw-in crown; water-resistant to 1000 m
Band: rubber, folding clasp with diver's extension
Price: 1,400 euros
Variations: with stainless steel bracelet with middle links in rubber and extension

Business-Timer 2000

Reference number: M1-30-65-LB
Movement: automatic, ETA 2892-A2 with module, ø 25.6 mm, height 3.6 mm; 21 jewels; 28,800 vph, Mühle special finish; company's own woodpecker-neck fine adjustment, module plate and gold/platinum rotor
Functions: hours, minutes, sweep seconds; date, day, calendar week, power reserve display
Case: stainless steel, ø 40.3 mm, height 10 mm; sapphire crystal; transparent case back; screw-in crown; water-resistant to 50 m
Band: reptile skin, folding clasp
Price: 2,300 euros

Franck Muller

The meteoric rise of the watch brand Franck Muller, founded a little more than ten years ago, is without equal in the world of Swiss watches. The brand's success is the result of a clever model policy paired with a feel for shapes, colors, and surfaces. The double-curved case shape of the Cintrée Curvex is incomparable in its characteristic 1920s gracefulness and has brought Franck Muller its commercial breakthrough. The models of this collection wonderfully document the creative conflict between "young" and "old" that has characterized the life and work of the Genevan watchmaker of the same name since his debut.
In recent months, the person who made it possible for even the young watchmaker Franck Muller to find his way into big business has stepped into the foreground: Vartan Sirmakes, who was the owner of a case factory back then and brave enough to take on the Franck Muller adventure.
Other things that have not been widely communicated until now are that the Franck Muller Group, founded in 1997, employs more than 500 people and owns outright or the majority of five companies. Technocase is Sirmakes's former main company and produces watch cases and crystals in Geneva's industrial suburb Plan-les-Ouates with 127 employees. Geco in Meyrin manufactures crowns, small parts, and metal link bracelets with forty-seven employees and is now building a department for production by hand. Dials come from Linder in Les Bois (fifty-one employees), and wheels, pinions, balances, and plates are supplied by Pignon Juracie SA in Lajoux with seventeen employees.

And then there's Watchland: a second manufacturing building has now been placed in the castle grounds surrounding the main building in Genthod, in which 280 employees finish parts, assemble movements, and mount complete watches — from the simple three-hand watches with supplied movements all the way to the breathtakingly complicated watches containing tourbillons. Additionally, the development and design departments are housed here, as well as the management and international distribution center that coordinates 545 points of sale worldwide, including sixteen of its own boutiques. But not only is the production of finished watches running at capacity: Plans for the production of two autonomous movement calibers — an automatic base movement by the name of Liberty and a column-wheel chronograph dubbed Freedom (both said to be on their feet without the help of supplied Swatch Group parts) are nearing perfection.
The "talking piece" of the year is the new tourbillon: After Tourbillon Revolution 2 that was presented last year, whose carriage rotates on two axes, it was almost an obligation for the company to present Tourbillon Revolution 3 this year, obviously revolving along three axes.
Like its predecessor, the new three-axis tourbillon of Caliber 2004 is housed in a large Cintrée Curvex case, and just like Caliber 2003, the cages revolve at varying speeds around the axes located at straight angles to one another: the inner cage every sixty seconds, the second cage every eight minutes, and the large, outer case once an hour. The complete movement comprises 289 components that are finely worked individually by hand and for the most part highly decorated. The model automatically limits itself due to the complicated and long manufacturing period.

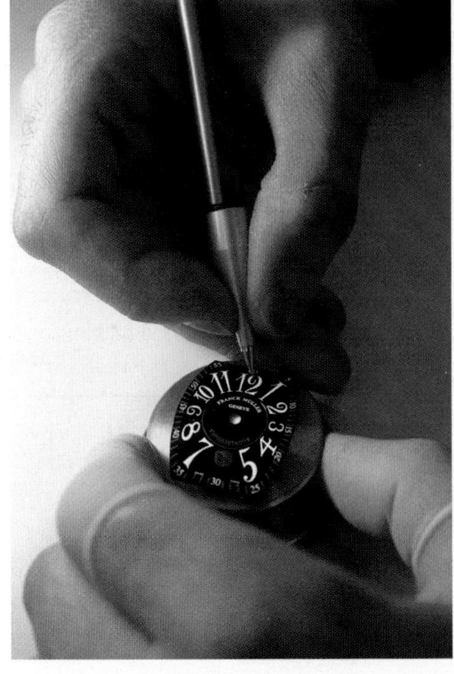

Long Island

Reference number: 1000 SC
Movement: automatic, FM 2800, ø 25.6 mm, height 3.6 mm; 21 jewels; 28,800 vph, with platinum rotor
Functions: hours, minutes
Case: white gold, 43 x 30.5 mm; sapphire crystal
Band: crocodile skin, buckle in white gold
Price: upon request
Variations: in rose, red or yellow gold; in platinum

Long Island Color Dreams

Reference number: 1200 SC
Movement: automatic, FM 2800, ø 25.6 mm, height 3.6 mm; 21 jewels; 28,800 vph, with platinum rotor
Functions: hours, minutes
Case: stainless steel, 43 x 30.5 mm; sapphire crystal
Band: crocodile skin, buckle
Price: upon request
Variations: in white, rose, red or yellow gold

Long Island Chronograph Monopulsant

Reference number: 1100 MP
Movement: automatic, FM 5000, ø 30 mm, height 7.9 mm; 25 jewels; 28,800 vph, one button for start-stop-reset
Functions: hours, minutes, subsidiary seconds; chronograph
Case: white gold, 45 x 32.4 mm; sapphire crystal
Band: crocodile skin, buckle in white gold
Price: upon request
Variations: in yellow gold or platinum

Long Island Master Calendar

Reference number: 1200 MCL
Movement: automatic, FM, ø 25.6 mm, height 3.6 mm; 21 jewels (base movement); 28,800 vph, module for complete calendar and moon phase
Functions: hours, minutes; date, day, month, moon phase
Case: white gold, 45 x 32.4 mm; sapphire crystal
Band: crocodile skin, buckle in white gold
Price: upon request
Variations: in yellow, rose or red gold; in platinum

Long Island Chronograph

Reference number: 1200 CC AT
Movement: automatic, FM, ø 30 mm, height 7.9 mm; 25 jewels; 28,800 vph, with platinum rotor
Functions: hours, minutes, subsidiary seconds; chronograph; date
Case: white gold, 45 x 32.4 mm; sapphire crystal
Band: crocodile skin, buckle in white gold
Price: upon request
Variations: in yellow, rose or red gold

Long Island Tourbillon

Reference number: 1200 T
Movement: manual winding, FM , one-minute tourbillon
Functions: hours, minutes, subsidiary seconds (on tourbillon cage)
Case: white gold, 45 x 32.4 mm; sapphire crystal
Band: crocodile skin, buckle in white gold
Price: upon request
Variations: in yellow, rose or red gold; in platinum

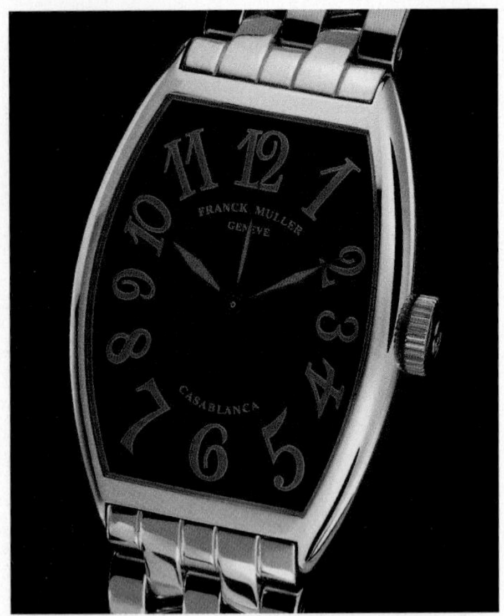

Cintrée Curvex Casablanca

Reference number: 2852 CASA O SAHARA
Movement: automatic, FM 2800, ø 25.6 mm, height 3.6 mm; 21 jewels; 28,800 vph, with platinum rotor
Functions: hours, minutes, sweep seconds
Case: stainless steel, 43 x 31 mm; sapphire crystal
Band: stainless steel, folding clasp
Price: upon request

Cintrée Curvex Grand Guichet

Reference number: 6850 S6 GG
Movement: automatic, FM, module construction for large date
Functions: hours, minutes, subsidiary seconds; large date
Case: stainless steel, 47 x 34 mm; sapphire crystal
Band: crocodile skin, buckle in yellow gold
Price: upon request
Variations: in rose, red, or yellow gold

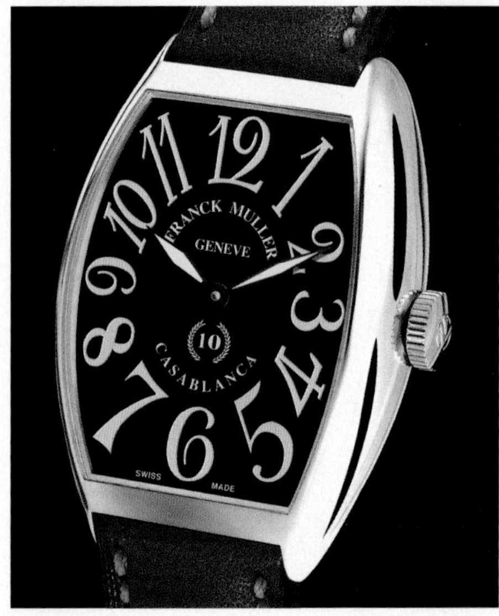

Cintrée Curvex Casablanca 10 Years

Reference number: 8880 SC C
Movement: automatic, FM 2800, ø 25.6 mm, height 3.6 mm; 21 jewels; 28,800 vph, with platinum rotor
Functions: hours, minutes, sweep seconds
Case: stainless steel, 43 x 31 mm, height 16 mm; sapphire crystal
Band: reptile skin, buckle
Price: upon request
Variations: as chronograph; with white or salmon-colored dial

Cintrée Curvex Chronograph Birétrograde

Reference number: 7850 CC B
Movement: automatic, FM 7000 B, ø 30 mm, height 7.9 mm; 25 jewels (base movement); 28,800 vph, module for retrograde seconds display and retrograde 30-minute counter
Functions: hours, minutes, seconds (retrograde); chronograph
Case: white gold, 48.7 x 35.3 mm; sapphire crystal
Band: crocodile skin, buckle in white gold
Price: upon request
Variations: in yellow, rose or red gold; in stainless steel

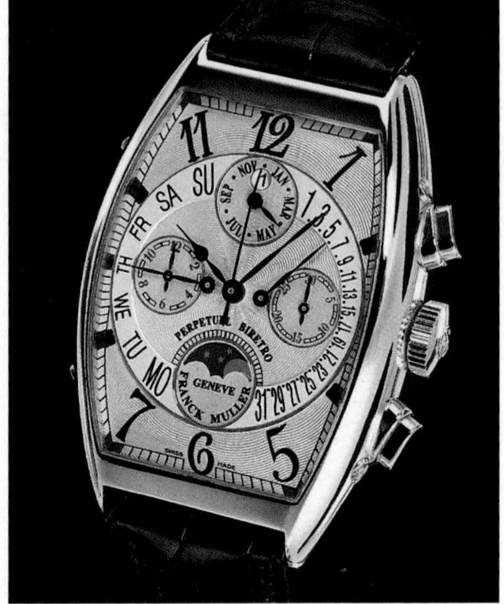

Cintrée Curvex Chrono QP Biretrograde

Reference number: 6850 CC QP B
Movement: automatic, FM 5888 BR, ø 30 mm, height 7.9 mm; 25 jewels (base movement); 28,800 vph, module for perpetual calendar with retrograde displays
Functions: hours, minutes; chronograph; perpetual calendar with date and day (retrograde), month, moon phase, leap year
Case: yellow gold, 47 x 34 mm, height 13 mm; sapphire crystal
Band: crocodile skin, buckle in yellow gold
Price: upon request
Variations: in white, rose or red gold; in platinum

Cintrée Curvex Quantième Perpétuel

Reference number: 7851 QPE
Movement: automatic, FM, module for perpetual calendar with retrograde displays
Functions: hours, minutes, sweep seconds; perpetual calendar with date, day, month (retrograde), moon phase, leap year; 24-hour display
Case: white gold, 48.7 x 35.3 mm, height 14 mm; sapphire crystal
Band: crocodile skin, buckle in white gold
Price: upon request
Variations: in white, rose or red gold; in platinum

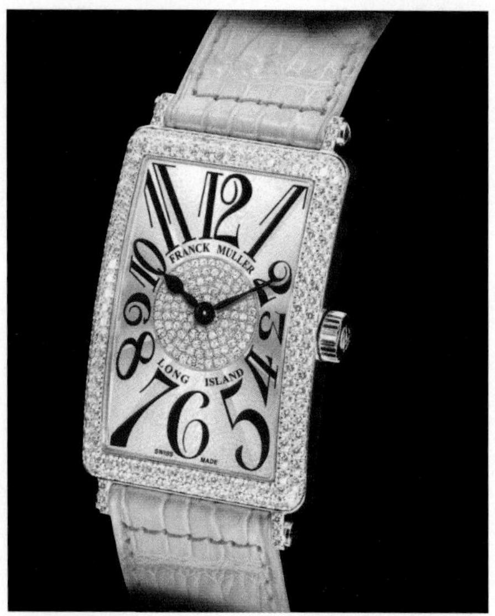

Long Island Lady

Reference number: 902 QZ D 1P
Movement: quartz, ETA 956032
Functions: hours, minutes
Case: white gold, 32.25 x 22.9 mm, height 8 mm; case and inner dial segment set with diamonds; sapphire crystal
Band: crocodile skin, buckle in white gold
Price: upon request
Variations: in yellow, rose or red gold

Long Island Lady

Reference number: 952 QZ D
Movement: quartz, ETA 956.032
Functions: hours, minutes
Case: white gold, 36.5 x 25.9 mm, height 8 mm; case set with 132 diamonds; sapphire crystal
Band: crocodile skin, buckle in white gold
Price: upon request
Variations: in rose, red or yellow gold; in platinum

Conquistador Cortez Chronograph

Reference number: 10000 CC KING
Movement: automatic, FM 2800 K, ø 30 mm, height 7.9 mm; 25 jewels; 28,800 vph
Functions: hours, minutes, subsidiary seconds; chronograph, date
Case: stainless steel, 45 x 45 mm, height 14.5 mm; sapphire crystal
Band: stainless steel, double folding clasp
Price: upon request
Variations: in white, rose or red gold; with sweep seconds and without chronograph, as Lady model

Conquistador Lady

Reference number: 8005 LSC O
Movement: automatic, FM 2600 (base ETA 2000/1); ø 19.4 mm, height 3.6 mm; 20 jewels; 28,800 vph, with platinum rotor
Functions: hours, minutes, sweep seconds; date
Case: stainless steel, 39 x 28 mm, height 11 mm; sapphire crystal
Band: stainless steel, folding clasp
Price: upon request
Variations: in rose, red, white or yellow gold with leather strap

Cintrée Curvex Ladies' Chronograph

Reference number: 2852 CC QZ D 1 PAST B
Movement: quartz, ETA 251.272
Functions: hours, minutes, subsidiary seconds; chronograph
Case: white gold, 43 x 31 mm, height 9 mm; case and bracelet links set with diamonds; sapphire crystal
Band: white gold, folding clasp in white gold
Remarks: inside dial segment with diamond pavé
Price: upon request
Variations: in yellow gold

Cintrée Curvex Joaillerie

Reference number: 6850 SC BAG CD
Movement: automatic, FM 2800, ø 25.6 mm, height 3.6 mm; 21 jewels; 28,800 vph, with platinum rotor
Functions: hours, minutes, sweep seconds
Case: white gold, 47 x 34 mm, height 11 mm; case set with baguette-cut diamonds; sapphire crystal
Band: crocodile skin, buckle
Remarks: dial with diamond pavé
Price: upon request
Variations: in rose, red or yellow gold

Ulysse Nardin

Ulysse Nardin founded his brand in 1846 and was soon able to make a name for himself by producing marine chronometers. There was a large demand for these big clocks in the wooden boxes in seafaring countries right into the first half of the twentieth century, as a ship's entire navigation was dependent upon precision timepieces on board. After the electronic quartz movement mowed down everything in its path, the company was no longer able to keep its head above water solely with the production of fine pocket and wristwatches for collectors.

When Rolf Schnyder purchased the company in 1983, the tide had taken most everything with it except a sonorous name. Schnyder himself knew little about watchmaking. Despite this, the man with the unconventional ideas led the washed-up company to new heights and found in Dr. Ludwig Oechslin the ideal collaborator to aid in fishing the company out of the water.

Oechslin's specialty is the astronomic timepiece, as he is learned not only in the complicated mechanics of celestial models, but in the actual cosmos in which we exist as well. He began his cooperation with Ulysse Nardin by creating the memorable Trilogy of Time: Tellurium Johannes Kepler, Astrolabium Galileo Galilei, and Planetarium Copernicus, three extraordinary wristwatches that display the positions of the heavenly bodies in the firmament.

Another milestone for the small brand was the Perpetual Calendar Ludwig GMT +/-, a timepiece that allows one not only to jump back and forth between time zones, but also to take the international dateline into account — both backward and forward. The base underdial work is meanwhile used in many models issuing from this house, even less complicated ones.

Before Oechslin took on his new job as curator of the watch museum in La Chaux-de-Fonds, he created one more exceptionally exciting timepiece for Ulysse Nardin: the Freak, presented at the Basel Fair 2002. This is a most unusual name for a most unusual watch, certainly the most unusual tourbillon ever created, and for which a brand-new escapement was also invented. The year 2003 presented the watch-buying public with another example of Oechslin's power of invention and the power of Ulysse Nardin's technicians to turn his ideas into a watch: The Sonata.

"Nothing shows more impressively than the Sonata itself where Ulysse Nardin stands today," explains the company president, not without a little pride. Schnyder is not only talking about the high technical level upon which the brand does its work, but also its economic success and resulting expansion.

Because space was getting tight in "downtown" Le Locle and didn't allow for another annex to the factory, Schnyder went ahead and bought a modern factory building in the industrial area of neighboring La Chaux-de-Fonds. Management, distribution headquarters, assembly, and high watchmaking remain at home in Le Locle, but all machine-driven departments moved to the adjacent town.

Two stories comprising 2,250 square meters of space provide a home not only to the production machines for every possible type of stamping, turning, and milling work, but also the development and design departments for *manufacture* movements and special complications. Under the direction of Pierre Gygax and Lucas Humair, the ideas which have poured from Dr. Oechslin are put into reality. The young *manufacture* currently employing about 150 people is well prepared for this considerable expansion of capacity: In the five years from 1998 to 2003, the brand's turnover has increased fourfold. Today, Ulysse Nardin sells about 14,000 watches per year — and it could soon sell a few more!

Maxi Marine Chronometer

Reference number: 266-66
Movement: automatic, Ulysse Nardin UN 26 (base ETA 2892); ø 25.6 mm, height 5.1 mm; 28 jewels; 28,800 vph, certified chronometer (C.O.S.C.)
Functions: hours, minutes, subsidiary seconds; date; power reserve display
Case: red gold, ø 41 mm, height 11.8 mm; sapphire crystal, anti-reflective; screw-in crown; water-resistant to 200 m
Band: reptile skin, folding clasp in 18-karat gold
Price: $12,900
Variations: with rubber strap/folding clasp

Maxi Marine Diver Chronometer

Reference number: 263-33-3
Movement: automatic, Ulysse Nardin UN 26 (base ETA 2892); ø 25.6 mm, height 5.1 mm; 28 jewels; 28,800 vph, certified chronometer (C.O.S.C.)
Functions: hours, minutes, subsidiary seconds; date; power reserve display
Case: stainless steel, ø 42.7 mm, height 12 mm; sapphire crystal, anti-reflective; screw-in crown; water-resistant to 300 m
Band: rubber/titanium, folding clasp in titanium
Price: $4,950
Variations: also available in 40 mm

Maxi Marine Diver Chronometer

Reference number: 263-33-7/92
Movement: automatic, Ulysse Nardin UN 26 (base ETA 2892); ø 25.6 mm, height 5.1 mm; 28 jewels; 28,800 vph, certified chronometer (C.O.S.C.)
Functions: hours, minutes, subsidiary seconds; date; power reserve display
Case: stainless steel, ø 42.7 mm, height 12 mm; sapphire crystal, anti-reflective; screw-in crown
Band: stainless steel, double folding clasp
Price: $5,650
Variations: also available in 40 mm

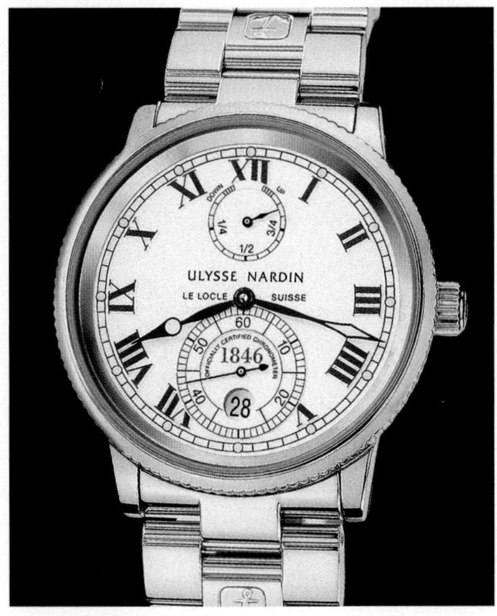

Marine Chronometer

Reference number: 263-22-7/30GR
Movement: automatic, Ulysse Nardin UN 26 (base ETA 2892); ø 25.6 mm, height 5.1 mm; 28 jewels; 28,800 vph, certified chronometer (C.O.S.C.)
Functions: hours, minutes, subsidiary seconds; date; power reserve display
Case: stainless steel, ø 38.5 mm, height 11 mm; sapphire crystal, anti-reflective; screw-in crown; water-resistant to 200 m
Band: stainless steel, double folding clasp
Price: $4,800
Variations: with leather strap; in different dial variations

GMT +/- Big Date Dual Time

Reference number: 226-87/61
Movement: automatic, Ulysse Nardin UN 22 (base ETA 2892); ø 25.6 mm, height 5.35 mm; 23 jewels; 28,800 vph, large date and patented quick-set mechanism for the hour hands
Functions: hours, minutes, sweep seconds; large date; second time zone
Case: red gold, ø 40 mm, height 11.8 mm; sapphire crystal, anti-reflective; transparent case back; screw-in crown; water-resistant to 100 m
Band: reptile skin, buckle in 18-karat gold
Price: $12,500
Variations: in different dial variations

GMT +/- Big Date Dual Time

Reference number: 223-88/60
Movement: automatic, Ulysse Nardin UN 22 (base ETA 2892); ø 25.6 mm, height 5.35 mm; 23 jewels; 28,800 vph, large date and patented quick-set mechanism for the hour hands
Functions: hours, minutes, sweep seconds; large date; second time zone
Case: stainless steel, ø 40 mm, height 11.8 mm; sapphire crystal, anti-reflective; transparent case back; screw-in crown; water-resistant to 100 m
Band: reptile skin, buckle
Price: $4,500
Variations: in different dial variations

NBY

No Barriers Yäeger

No barriers — this is a motto that is leading Black Forest-based master watchmaker Martin Braun down some brand-new paths. He has impressively proved he was already able to innovate for many years with his classically designed watches. Since 2004, Braun has also manufactured sports watches in pilot's dress, which, however, fit neither with the philosophy nor the price policies of his established Martin Braun brand. For this reason, he spontaneously created a new label.

"With our NBY brand, we have made it our goal to do something about boredom," Braun says. "There is a yawning chasm of unimaginativeness that exists most decidedly in the entry-level price class for mechanical watches." He would like to change this fact with his new brand, something that he has already set in motion with its name: NBY is both unusual and not necessarily self-explanatory.

It stands for No Barriers Yäeger. This proper name reminds one vaguely of Chuck Yeager, the pilot who was the first to break the sound barrier. However, Braun didn't want to name his brand for any one person. He just wanted a simple, catchy moniker.

The logo itself is presented rather unassumingly underneath the 12 on the dial of the first two new models Braun created to launch the new brand. One of them is a relatively simple three-hand watch with a date by the name of Delta; the other, a chronograph dubbed Charlie. The dial visuals of both watches are positively individual, characterized as they are by large double-digit hour numerals. The NBY 12 is marked throughout the line by a double zero instead of a one and a two.

The hour numerals and baton markers are generously inlaid with luminous material, making the three-hand watch especially legible. This is also true of the chronograph, which is designed in a very unique way for a stopper. The chronograph's totalizers are very distinctive: The scales near 06 and 00 are only half circles and outfitted with hands that look similar to propellers, painted half white and half blue. A second glance at the subsidiary dials reveals that the scale's markers are decorated with a white and a blue numeral each. Concentrate on the totalizers, and they become clearer and easier to read. And since no scales are overlapping, the legibility of the main function — reading the time — is always clear. Although this model is outfitted with the ETA 7750 movement, a widely used standard caliber, Braun has achieved highly unique dial visuals with it.

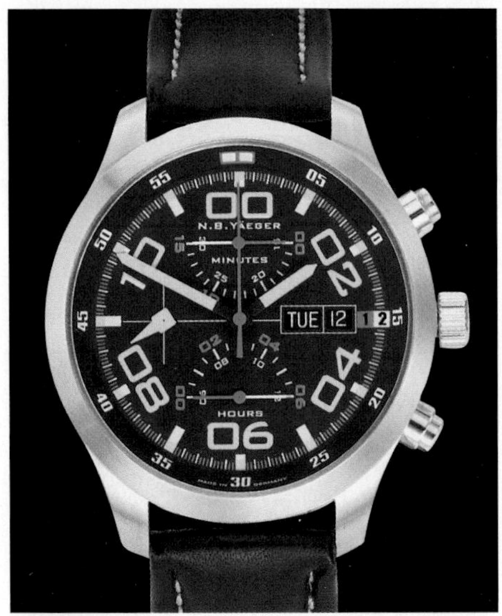

Charlie

Movement: automatic, ETA 7750, ø 30 mm, height 7.9 mm; 25 jewels; 28,800 vph
Functions: hours, minutes, subsidiary seconds; chronograph; date, day
Case: stainless steel, ø 42 mm, height 14 mm; sapphire crystal; screw-in crown; water-resistant to 100 m
Band: leather, additional rubber strap, buckle
Price: $1,695
Variations: with stainless steel bracelet

Delta

Movement: automatic, ETA 2824-2, ø 25.6 mm, height 4.6 mm; 25 jewels; 28,800 vph
Functions: hours, minutes, sweep seconds; date
Case: stainless steel, ø 40 mm, height 11 mm; sapphire crystal; screw-in crown; water-resistant to 100 m
Band: leather, additional rubber strap, buckle
Price: $695
Variations: with stainless steel bracelet

Short Flight

Movement: automatic, ETA 7750, ø 30 mm, height 7.9 mm; 25 jewels; 28,800 vph
Functions: hours, minutes, subsidiary seconds; chronograph; date
Case: stainless steel, ø 42 mm, height 14 mm; sapphire crystal; screw-in crown; water-resistant to 100 m
Band: leather, additional rubber strap, buckle
Remarks: crown and buttons on the left
Price: $1,695
Variations: with stainless steel bracelet

Delta Sector

Movement: automatic, ETA 2824-2, ø 25.6 mm, height 4.6 mm; 25 jewels; 28,800 vph
Functions: hours, minutes, sweep seconds; date
Case: stainless steel, ø 40 mm, height 11 mm; sapphire crystal; screw-in crown; water-resistant to 100 m
Band: leather, additional rubber strap, buckle
Price: $695
Variations: with stainless steel bracelet

Tango

Movement: automatic, ETA 2893-2, ø 25.6 mm, height 4.1 mm; 21 jewels; 28,800 vph
Functions: hours, minutes, sweep seconds; date; 24-hour display (second time zone)
Case: stainless steel, ø 40 mm, height 11 mm; sapphire crystal; screw-in crown; water-resistant to 100 m
Band: leather, additional rubber strap, buckle
Price: $1,350
Variations: with stainless steel bracelet

Turbulence

Movement: automatic, ETA 2824-2, ø 25.6 mm, height 4.6 mm; 25 jewels; 28,800 vph
Functions: hours, minutes, sweep seconds; date
Case: stainless steel, ø 40 mm, height 11 mm; sapphire crystal; screw-in crown; water-resistant to 100 m
Band: leather, additional rubber strap, buckle
Price: $850
Variations: with stainless steel bracelet

Armand Nicolet

Armand Nicolet was born in Tramelan, Switzerland, in 1884 as a member of a watchmaking dynasty. Tramelan was at the time an important horological city, and many members of his family were well-known for doing business there. It has been handed down that Armand opened his own workshop at the beginning of the twentieth century, but the first written records were registered when Nicolet Watch showed its wares at the World's Fair in 1939.

Armand Nicolet passed away in 1939, but he lives on as the namesake for a company of horological excellence that is still at home in the Jura region's Tramelan. Relaunched in 2001, modern-day Armand Nicolet timepieces utilize the best in contemporary technical reliability and traditional horological finesse.

The contemporary Nicolet collection comprises five main lines. The first four to be issued were based on a small set of models with purist cases and lots of juicy complications sure to please watch fans. M02 and Sloop Royal each comprise three classically designed models, with Sloop Royal appealing to the more sporty, yet elegant crowd. M02 is aimed at the individualist.

The Hunter collection is at home in classically proportioned, 38-mm, 18-karat yellow gold cases. This line includes most of the complications known to watchmaking at the current time, including a classic regulator, but not yet including a tourbillon. Sales manager Alessandro Braga once explained that he thought it was still too early for this type of complication.

Arc Royal features classically designed silvered dials that mark the passing of time with blued steel hands on roman numerals. The 39-mm gold case with movable lugs is classic, yet fresh as the new dawn. The complications include everything from subsidiary seconds to a chronograph with a complete calendar.

The latest addition to the collection, and without a doubt the most stunning yet, is a limited edition that will have collectors licking their lips in anticipation. Based upon a remnant movement of the original Nicolet stock from 1948, Caliber UT 176 experienced some modifications in 2003 to bring it up to today's speed. The revisions performed include the addition of an Incabloc shock protection device, the enhancement of the swan-neck fine adjustment, and the noble decoration of the surfaces with a beautiful *côtes de Genève* pattern to create a model of great simplicity and elegance. As there were only 135 pieces of this movement remaining intact, there is an automatic limitation on this timepiece. The dial comprises the underside of the base plate, naturally decorated with the abovementioned Geneva stripes, and a marker scale that features a striking guilloché subsidiary seconds dial following the shape of the stepped bezel. This masterpiece's transparent case back illustrates the complete beauty of the movement and its modifications, rendering the blued screws, decorated surfaces, and swan-neck fine adjustment especially visible. The edition comprises both white and rose gold models on either a black or brown strap with a gold buckle and retails for $10,800.

MO2 Complete Calendar

Reference number: 7142B NR P914NR2

Movement: automatic, AN 9200/2824-2 TND/TNK (base ETA 2824-2); ø 25.6 mm; 25 jewels; 28,800 vph; 40 hours power reserve, côtes de Genève on rotor, bridges finished with addouci pattern

Functions: hours, minutes, sweep seconds; date, day, month; moon phase

Case: rose gold, ø 43 mm, height 12 mm; sapphire crystal, anti-reflective; transparent case back; water-resistant to 50 m

Band: crocodile skin, buckle

Price: $8,400

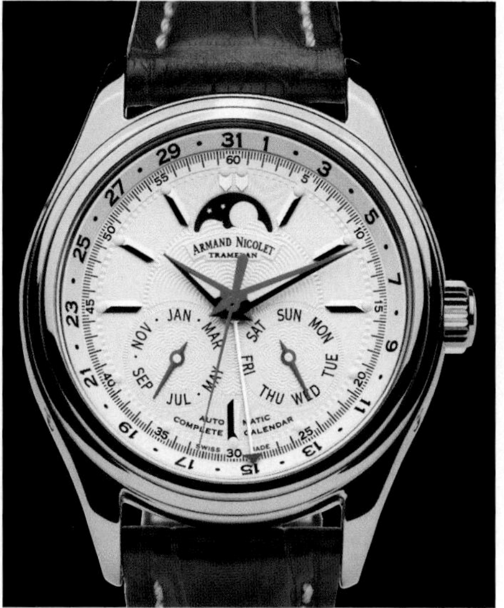

MO2 Complete Calendar

Reference number: 9142B AG P914MR2

Movement: automatic, AN 9200/2824-2 TND/TNK (base ETA 2824-2); ø 25.6 mm; 25 jewels; 28,800 vph; 40 hours power reserve, côtes de Genève on rotor, bridges finished with addouci pattern

Functions: hours, minutes, sweep seconds; date, day, month; moon phase

Case: stainless steel, ø 43 mm, height 12 mm; sapphire crystal, anti-reflective; transparent case back; water-resistant to 100 m

Band: crocodile skin, folding clasp

Price: $3,450

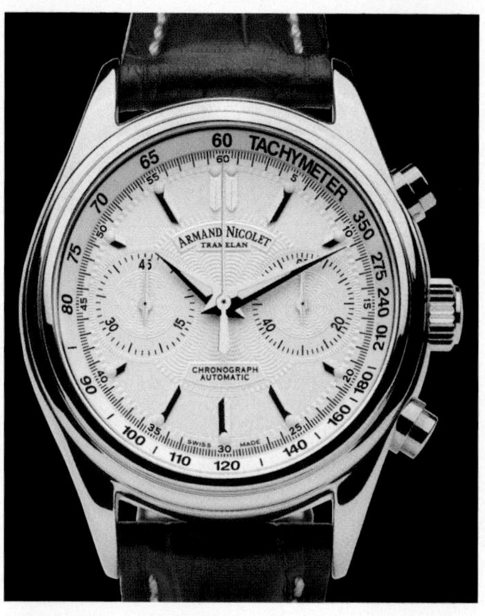

MO2 Chronograph

Reference number: 7144A AG P914MR2

Movement: automatic, AN 2045/2824-2 (base ETA 2824-2); ø 25.6 mm; 49 jewels; 28,800 vph; 40 hours power reserve, côtes de Genève on rotor, bridges finished with addouci pattern

Functions: hours, minutes, subsidiary seconds; chronograph

Case: rose gold, ø 43 mm, height 12 mm; tachymetric scale on flange; sapphire crystal, anti-reflective; transparent case back; water-resistant to 50 m

Band: crocodile skin, buckle

Price: $7,950

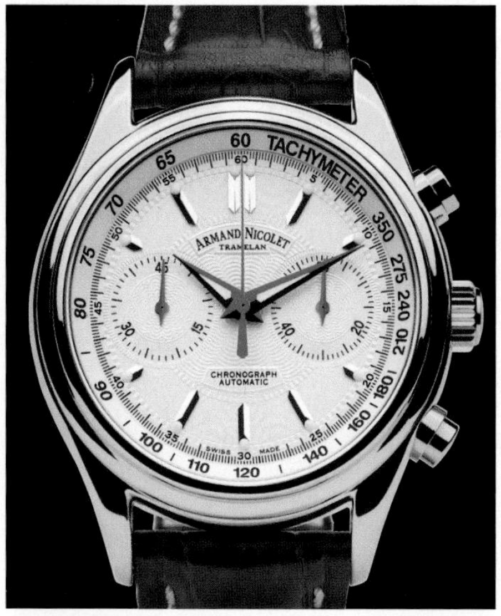

MO2 Chronograph

Reference number: 9144A AG P914MR2

Movement: automatic, AN 2045/2824-2 (base ETA 2824-2); ø 25.6 mm; 49 jewels; 28,800 vph; 40 hours power reserve, côtes de Genève on rotor, bridges finished with addouci pattern

Functions: hours, minutes, subsidiary seconds; chronograph

Case: stainless steel, ø 43 mm, height 12 mm; tachymetric scale on flange; sapphire crystal, anti-reflective; transparent case back; water-resistant to 100 m

Band: crocodile skin, folding clasp

Price: $3,200

MO2 Big Date and Small Seconds

Reference number: 7146A NR P914NR2

Movement: automatic, AN 14000/2824-2 (base ETA 2824-2); ø 25.6 mm; 30 jewels; 28,800 vph; 40 hours power reserve, côtes de Genève on rotor, bridges finished with addouci pattern

Functions: hours, minutes, subsidiary seconds; large date

Case: rose gold, ø 43 mm, height 12 mm; sapphire crystal, anti-reflective; transparent case back; water-resistant to 50 m

Band: crocodile skin, buckle

Price: $7,750

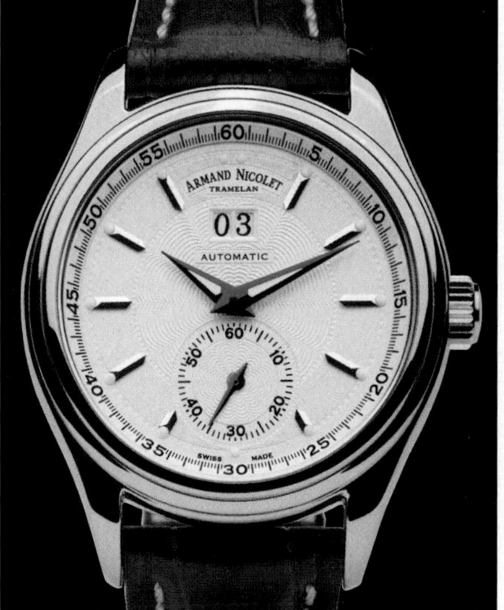

MO2 Big Date and Small Seconds

Reference number: 9146A AG P914MR2

Movement: automatic, AN 14000/2824-2 (base ETA 2824-2); ø 25.6 mm; 30 jewels; 28,800 vph; 40 hours power reserve, côtes de Genève on rotor, bridges finished with addouci pattern

Functions: hours, minutes, subsidiary seconds; large date

Case: stainless steel, ø 43 mm, height 12 mm; sapphire crystal, anti-reflective; transparent case back; water-resistant to 100 m

Band: crocodile skin, folding clasp

Price: $2,950

Nivrel

Nivrel is a brand that was originally founded in Switzerland in 1936. It later disappeared from the market, but was reactivated by the German businessman Gerd Hofer in 1993. This company's watches are a great example of how quickly a watch brand with an instantly recognizable look can create a good place for itself on the watch market. The timepieces' affordable prices certainly contributed to this as well. The latest example is a special automatic watch featuring a solid sterling silver dial at a particularly friendly price that Hofer is presenting his clientele on the occasion of the brand's tenth anniversary.
Hofer, who has added the tag line "since 1936" to his Nivrel label, explains quite frankly how he called the Fédération de l'Industrie Horlogère Suisse ten years ago during his search for a "good" brand name for his newly founded watch business, Time Art GmbH. Stored there "temporarily" are countless names of Swiss watchmakers that have disappeared from the market until an interested party acquires and reactivates them. Hofer resurrected the name Nivrel, plain and simple, without any history, without any sort of background information on the firm — without even a logo. This degree of openness and honesty is rather uncommon in the industry.
Nivrel's watches themselves are also crafted with openness and honesty: Everything that looks like gold actually is gold, usually 18 karat. The crystals are always made of synthetic sapphire, and if the hour indicators are raised, then they are most certainly applied to the dial — never just stamped. The watch movements are beautifully finished, and the rings that secure the movements to the cases, as one would expect, are made of metal instead of plastic. Hofer's credo: "Attention to quality in the details shouldn't drive up the costs so high that one could justify poorer craftsmanship."
This is quite a remarkable statement, as there are simpler mechanical watches by Nivrel that can be easily acquired for a small amount of money. And extras, such as large date, moon phase, and various other calendar features, can be had for a very moderate price. This is made possible, on the one hand, by a modular system, in which a relatively modest number of movements and case types are varied to produce a wide range of very attractive models. On the other hand, Hofer consistently works with first-class suppliers as opposed to maintaining expensive internal development and production departments. Here, too, there is no secretiveness. The movements come from ETA, and any additional mechanisms and complications are made by Soprod or Dubois-Dépraz. The watch designs, however, come from Hofer himself. "The idea is what counts," he says. And — as evidenced by the brand's current models — it's easy to see that Hofer is not only a good businessman.

Anniversary Watch

Reference number: N 125.010 CAAES
Movement: automatic, ETA 2824-2, ø 25.6 mm, height 4.6 mm; 25 jewels; 28,800 vph
Functions: hours, minutes, sweep seconds; date
Case: stainless steel, ø 40 mm, height 10.7 mm; sapphire crystal; transparent case back
Band: leather, buckle
Remarks: anniversary model with solid sterling silver dial in honor of the company's tenth year
Price: $450

Deep Sea

Reference number: N 140.001 CASMB
Movement: automatic, ETA 2824-2, ø 25.6 mm, height 4.6 mm; 25 jewels; 28,800 vph
Functions: hours, minutes, sweep seconds; date
Case: stainless steel, ø 41 mm, height 14.3 mm; unidirectionally rotating bezel with 60-minute scale; sapphire crystal; screw-in crown; water-resistant to 1000 m
Band: stainless steel, folding clasp
Price: $900

Diamond Moon

Reference number: N 437.001 CAPMK
Movement: automatic, Dubois-Dépraz 9310 (base ETA 2892-A2); ø 26.2 mm, height 5.2 mm; 21 jewels; 28,800 vph, movement finely finished, côtes de Genève
Functions: hours, minutes, sweep seconds; date, day, month, moon phase
Case: stainless steel, ø 36.9 x 35.5 mm, height 12 mm; sapphire crystal; transparent case back
Band: reptile skin, buckle
Remarks: mother-of-pearl dial with diamond markers
Price: $5,200

Five-Minute Repeater

Reference number: N 950.001.2 AAWEK
Movement: automatic, Dubois-Dépraz 87 (base ETA 2892-A2); ø 36.2 mm, height 7.35 mm; 21 jewels; 28,800 vph, repeater module and rotor hand-skeletonized and engraved
Functions: hours, minutes, sweep seconds; five-minute repeater
Case: stainless steel, ø 42 mm, height 13 mm; sapphire crystal; transparent case back
Band: reptile skin, buckle
Price: $6,500
Variations: in rose gold

Bell

Reference number: N 950.001.4 RAWEK
Movement: automatic, Dubois-Dépraz 87 (base ETA 2892-A2); ø 36.2 mm, height 7.35 mm; 21 jewels; 28,800 vph, repeater module and rotor hand-skeletonized and engraved
Functions: hours, minutes; five-minute repeater with moving automat
Case: rose gold, ø 42 mm, height 13 mm; sapphire crystal; transparent case back
Band: reptile skin, buckle
Price: $14,900
Variations: in stainless steel

Golf

Reference number: N 950.001.5 AAAMS
Movement: automatic, Dubois-Dépraz 87 (base ETA 2892-A2); ø 36.2 mm, height 7.35 mm; 21 jewels; 28,800 vph, repeater module and rotor hand-skeletonized and engraved
Functions: hours, minutes; five-minute repeater with moving automat
Case: stainless steel, ø 42 mm, height 13 mm; sapphire crystal; transparent case back
Band: reptile skin, buckle
Price: $9,800
Variations: in rose gold

Nomos

When a watch fan says Nomos, he or she usually means Tangente. It's easy to forget that these inventive Saxons have developed more than a dozen variations from one and the same base movement. Whether Tangente, Ludwig, Orion, or Tetra — Nomos watches are more than just timepieces for their loyal following. They acknowledge the traditions of German watchmaking history and the clear, functional language of good design. Prior to the Bauhaus movement, the philosophy that put its stamp on industrial design in the 1920s and '30s, it had been the German Manufacturer's Association that had formulated the fundamental principles of good design for German industry without ever uttering the phrase "form follows function." This association of artists, craftsmen, and industrialists that was formed in 1907 searched for an ideal compromise between beauty and functionality, and for a way of linking the craftsmanship of skilled workers to industrial production in a way that made good sense. That the principles propagated at that time are just as valid today can ultimately be seen in Nomos watches. With their clear, functional shape, they also embody a high level of aesthetic beauty.

The inventive watchmakers at Nomos have souped up the good little Peseux caliber (alias ETA 7001). The addition of a Triovis fine adjustment was followed by date display, stop-seconds, and last year's exchange of the traditional Swiss bridges for a nobly sandblasted three-quarter plate in best Glashütte tradition, complete with a Glashütte-style click (click spring and pawl) and a beautiful Glashütte sunburst decoration on the crown wheel.

The lavish manually wound movement, 1 TSDP (stands for **T**riovis fine adjustment, **s**top-seconds, **d**ate, and three-quarter **p**late), is not the last stop on the train of developments Nomos has in store for the Peseux movement: The company's developer, Thierry Albert, has also designed a power reserve into the mechanism.

Nomos's management is planning on investing about 2.3 million euros in the company over the next two years. Of this sum, about half will go into renovating the new headquarters and Glashütte's observatory as well as manufacturing machines, quite obviously increasing the company's depth of production. This small firm is flourishing, not in the least due to a continually growing clientele interested in design as well as quality-oriented consumers, and can now begin to turn its attention to new projects. Seeing as it is hardly possible to improve upon the design aspects of these timepieces, these new projects will surely have more to do with the inner values of Nomos timepieces.

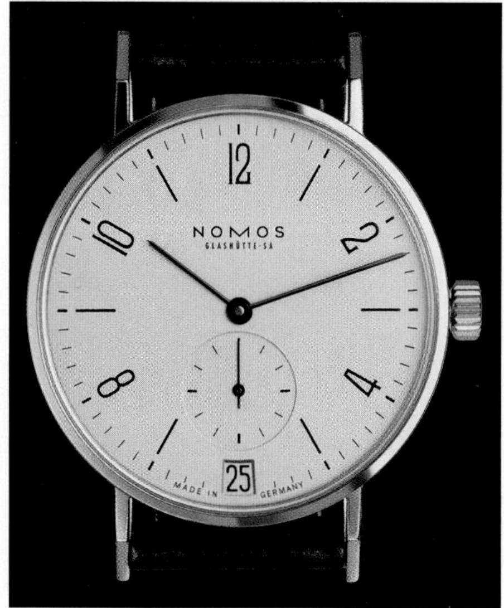

Tangente Date

Reference number: NM-TGDS
Movement: manual winding, Nomos Werk 1 TSDP, ø 32.15 mm, height 2.65 mm; 23 jewels; 21,600 vph, three-quarter plate, movement surfaces finely matte and gold-plated; Langeleist perlage; crown and ratchet wheels with Glashütte sunburst decoration
Functions: hours, minutes, subsidiary seconds; date
Case: stainless steel, ø 35 mm, height 6.05 mm; sapphire crystal; transparent case back
Band: Shell Cordovan, buckle
Price: $1,700
Variations: without date and sapphire crystal case back

Ludwig

Reference number: NM-LDSA
Movement: manual winding, Nomos Werk 1 TS, ø 23.3 mm, height 2.5 mm; 17 jewels; 21,600 vph, movement surfaces finely matte and gold-plated; Langeleist perlage; crown and ratchet wheels with Glashütte sunburst decoration
Functions: hours, minutes, subsidiary seconds
Case: stainless steel, ø 35 mm, height 6.25 mm; sapphire crystal; transparent case back
Band: Shell Cordovan, buckle
Price: $1,250
Variations: in gold case with sapphire crystal case back ($3,900)

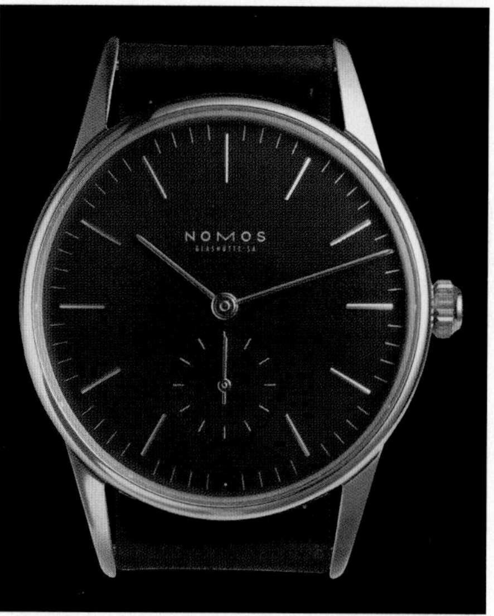

Orion

Reference number: NM-ORDG
Movement: manual winding, Nomos Werk 1 TSP, ø 23.3 mm, height 2.5 mm; 17 jewels; 21,600 vph, 3/4 plate, movement surfaces finely matte and gold-plated; Langeleist perlage; crown and ratchet wheels with Glashütte sunburst decoration
Functions: hours, minutes, subsidiary seconds
Case: stainless steel, ø 35 mm, height 8.77 mm; sapphire crystal, domed; transparent case back
Band: Shell Cordovan, buckle
Price: $1,500
Variations: with silver-colored dial ($1,500); with stainless steel case back ($1,200)

Tetra

Reference number: NM-TTRA
Movement: manual winding, Nomos Werk 1 TS, ø 23.3 mm, height 2.5 mm; 17 jewels; 21,600 vph, movement surfaces finely matte and gold-plated; Langeleist perlage; crown and ratchet wheels with Glashütte sunburst decoration
Functions: hours, minutes, subsidiary seconds
Case: stainless steel, 27.5 x 27.5 mm, height 6.05 mm; sapphire crystal
Band: Shell Cordovan, buckle
Price: $1,240
Variations: Tetra large, 29.5 x 29.5 mm ($1,300); in gold case ($3,800)

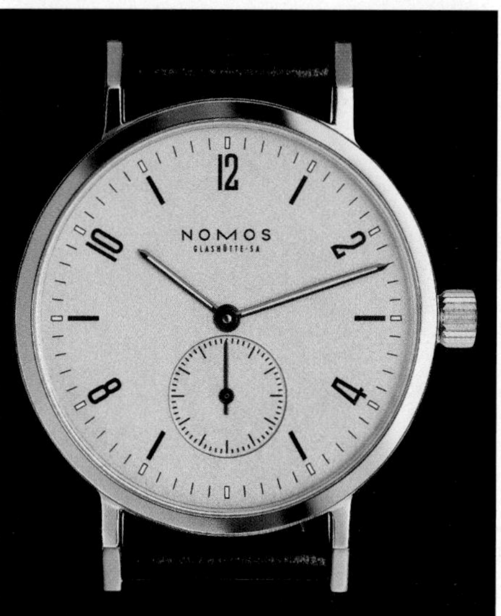

Tangente Sport

Reference number: NM-TGSP
Movement: manual winding, Nomos Werk 1 TS, ø 23.3 mm, height 2.5 mm; 17 jewels; 21,600 vph, movement surfaces finely matte and gold-plated; Langeleist perlage; crown and ratchet wheels with Glashütte sunburst decoration
Functions: hours, minutes, subsidiary seconds
Case: stainless steel, ø 36.5 mm, height 7.5 mm; sapphire crystal; water-resistant to 100 m
Band: Shell Cordovan, buckle
Price: $1,250
Variations: with date ($1,700)

Tangente Date Power Reserve

Reference number: NM-TGDP
Movement: manual winding, Nomos Werk 1 TSDPG, ø 32.15 mm, height 2.65 mm; 23 jewels; 21,600 vph, 3/4 plate, movement surfaces finely matte and gold-plated; Langeleist perlage; crown and ratchet wheels with Glashütte sunburst decoration
Functions: hours, minutes, subsidiary seconds; date, power reserve display
Case: stainless steel, ø 35 mm, height 6.2 mm; sapphire crystal; transparent case back
Band: Shell Cordovan, buckle
Price: $2,600

Omega

Precision and superlatives — this could also describe the rare golf stroke double eagle for which the new Omega Constellation is named. The men's watch Double Eagle is the first model of the Constellation line whose movement is outfitted with the coaxial escapement. This technology was at first only used in selected watches of the De Ville model family. However, in the meantime, the company has not only developed a chronograph movement making use of the exclusive escapement, but also systematically extended the use of the new technology. First, the Seamaster Aqua Terra was outfitted with coaxial movements, and now it's the Constellation's turn.

Thus, Omega — after a somewhat longer orientation phase in the 1970s and '80s — remains on course, placing its emphasis completely on horological competence. The industrial manufacture of the coaxial escapement invented by England's George Daniels may of course be viewed as the initial complication to jump-start the concept. This escapement, whose serial realization represented a very difficult task for watch engineers, was a challenging piece of micromechanics. Since this new escapement gets along almost entirely without lubrication, its individual parts must be manufactured within an extremely small measure of tolerance. For this reason, Omega is especially proud to also present watches whose coaxial movements pass the strict testing criteria of the C.O.S.C., the official Swiss testing institute for chronometers. The good reputation of the brand in recent history has not only been characterized by the Constellation, a line that celebrated its fiftieth birthday last year, but also by the Speedmaster, a model in the spotlight in 2004. The occasion is "one small step for man, one giant leap for mankind," as someone famous once said: When, on July 21, 1969, at 2:56 UT, the American astronaut Neil Armstrong was the first human ever to set foot on the surface of the moon, he was wearing an Omega Speedmaster Professional on his wrist.

This chronograph has been known as the "moon watch" ever since. This legend and its timeless design have made the Speedmaster Professional a top seller, and it is now being offered in a special edition in honor of the 35th anniversary of the first moon landing. This is made visible on the watch by an inscription on the dial and case back: The back's bezel bears the successive number of limitation (a total of 3,500 pieces) and the engraving "Apollo 35th anniversary limited edition," while on the transparent case back a colorful depiction of the flight path of the Apollo 11 mission can be seen.

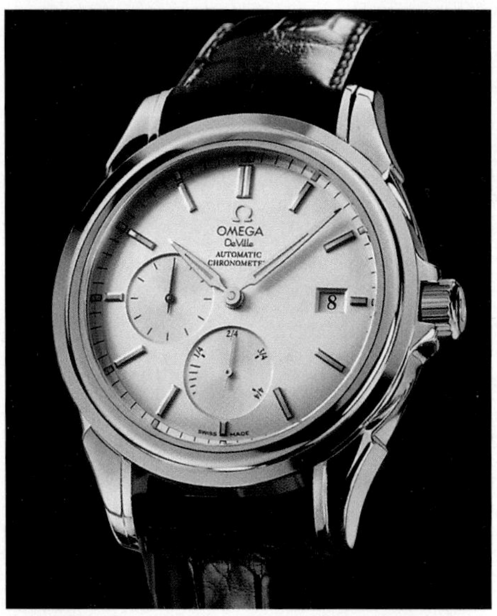

De Ville Co-Axial Réserve de Marche

Reference number: 4632.31.31
Movement: automatic, Omega 2627, ø 25.6 mm, height 5.35 mm; 29 jewels; 28,800 vph, coaxial escapement; certified chronometer (C.O.S.C.)
Functions: hours, minutes, subsidiary seconds; date; power reserve display
Case: yellow gold, ø 38.7 mm, height 11.05 mm; sapphire crystal; water-resistant to 100 m
Band: reptile skin, folding clasp in yellow gold
Price: $7,695
Variations: with dark blue dial; with yellow gold bracelet; in stainless steel

De Ville Co-Axial GMT

Reference number: 4533.51.00
Movement: automatic, Omega 2628, ø 25.6 mm, height 5.2 mm; 27 jewels; 28,800 vph, coaxial escapement; certified chronometer (C.O.S.C.)
Functions: hours, minutes, sweep seconds; date; second time zone
Case: stainless steel, ø 38.7 mm, height 11.6 mm; sapphire crystal; water-resistant to 100 m
Band: stainless steel, folding clasp
Price: $4,295
Variations: with ruthenium-grey dial; with leather strap; in yellow gold

De Ville Co-Axial Automatic

Reference number: 4831.31.32
Movement: automatic, Omega 2500, ø 25.6 mm, height 3.9 mm; 27 jewels; 28,800 vph, coaxial escapement; certified chronometer (C.O.S.C.)
Functions: hours, minutes, sweep seconds; date
Case: stainless steel, ø 37.5 mm, height 10 mm; sapphire crystal; water-resistant to 100 m
Band: reptile skin, folding clasp
Price: $2,995
Variations: with black dial; with stainless steel bracelet

De Ville Co-Axial Big Date

Reference number: 4644.30.32
Movement: automatic, Omega 2610, ø 25.6 mm, height 3.9 mm; 27 jewels; 28,800 vph, coaxial escapement; certified chronometer (C.O.S.C.)
Functions: hours, minutes, sweep seconds; large date
Case: rose gold, ø 38.7 mm, height 11.6 mm; sapphire crystal; transparent case back; water-resistant to 100 m
Band: reptile skin, folding clasp
Remarks: limited to 699 pieces
Price: $9,295
Variations: in yellow or white gold

De Ville Co-Axial Chronograph

Reference number: 4841.31.32
Movement: automatic, Omega 3313, ø 27 mm, height 6.85 mm; 37 jewels; 28,800 vph, coaxial escapement; column-wheel control of the chronograph functions; certified chronometer (C.O.S.C.)
Functions: hours, minutes, subsidiary seconds; chronograph; date
Case: stainless steel, ø 41 mm, height 12.9 mm; sapphire crystal; transparent case back
Band: reptile skin, folding clasp
Price: $4,495
Variations: with stainless steel bracelet; with black dial

De Ville Co-Axial Ladies

Reference number: 4586.75.00
Movement: automatic, Omega 2500, ø 25.6 mm, height 4.1 mm; 27 jewels; 28,800 vph, coaxial escapement; certified chronometer (C.O.S.C.)
Functions: hours, minutes, sweep seconds; date
Case: stainless steel, ø 31 mm, height 9.75 mm; bezel set with 40 brilliant-cut diamonds; sapphire crystal; water-resistant to 100 m
Band: stainless steel, folding clasp
Remarks: mother-of-pearl dial with 8 diamond markers
Price: $7,995
Variations: without diamonds; with reptile skin strap

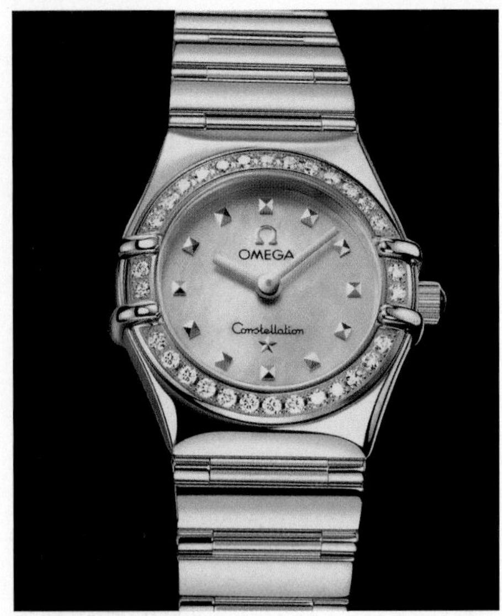

Constellation My Choice

Reference number: 1376.71.00
Movement: quartz, Omega 1456 (base ETA 976.001)
Functions: hours, minutes
Case: stainless steel, ø 25.5 mm, height 9 mm; bezel set with 38 brilliant-cut diamonds; sapphire crystal
Band: stainless steel/gold, folding clasp
Price: $3,895
Variations: without diamond bezel

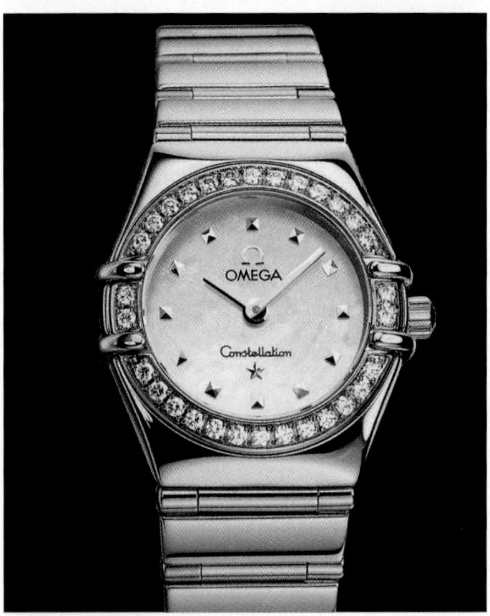

Constellation My Choice

Reference number: 1465.71.00
Movement: quartz, Omega 1456 (base ETA 976.001)
Functions: hours, minutes
Case: stainless steel, ø 22.5 mm, height 9 mm; bezel set with 30 brilliant-cut diamonds; sapphire crystal
Band: stainless steel, folding clasp
Price: $2,795
Variations: in stainless steel/yellow gold

Constellation

Reference number: 1272.30.00
Movement: quartz, Omega 1456 (base ETA 976.001)
Functions: hours, minutes
Case: stainless steel, ø 25.5 mm, height 9 mm; bezel in yellow gold, engraved with Roman hour markers; sapphire crystal
Band: stainless steel/yellow gold, folding clasp
Price: $2,495
Variations: in stainless steel or yellow gold

Constellation Double Eagle

Reference number: 1503.30.00
Movement: automatic, Omega 2500, ø 25.6 mm, height 4.1 mm; 27 jewels; 28,800 vph, coaxial escapement; certified chronometer (C.O.S.C.)
Functions: hours, minutes, sweep seconds; date
Case: stainless steel, ø 38 mm; sapphire crystal; transparent case back; water-resistant to 100 m
Band: stainless steel, folding clasp
Price: $3,095
Variations: in stainless steel/yellow gold

Constellation Double Eagle Chronograph

Reference number: 1514.51.00
Movement: automatic, Omega 3313, ø 27 mm, height 6.85 mm; 37 jewels; 28,800 vph, coaxial escapement; column-wheel control of the chronograph functions; C.O.S.C. certified
Functions: hours, minutes, subsidiary seconds; chronograph; date
Case: stainless steel, ø 41 mm; sapphire crystal; transparent case back
Band: stainless steel, folding clasp
Price: $4,395
Variations: with white dial

Seamaster Railmaster XXL Chronometer

Reference number: 2806.52.37
Movement: manual winding, Omega 2201 (base ETA 6498); ø 36.6 mm, height 4.5 mm; 17 jewels; 21,600 vph, certified chronometer (C.O.S.C.)
Functions: hours, minutes, subsidiary seconds
Case: stainless steel, ø 49.2 mm; sapphire crystal; transparent case back; water-resistant to 150 m
Band: reptile skin, folding clasp
Price: $2,995

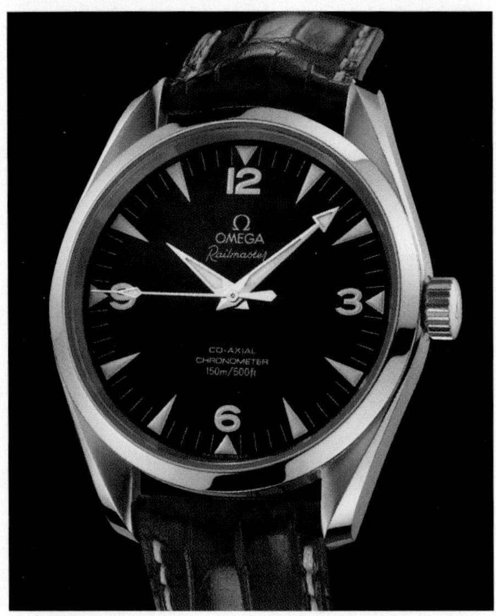

Seamaster Aqua Terra Railmaster

Reference number: 2802.52.37
Movement: automatic, Omega 2403A, ø 25.6 mm, height 4.1 mm; 27 jewels; 28,800 vph, coaxial escapement; certified chronometer (C.O.S.C.)
Functions: hours, minutes, sweep seconds
Case: stainless steel, ø 41 mm, height 11.5 mm; sapphire crystal; water-resistant to 150 m
Band: reptile skin, folding clasp
Price: $2,695
Variations: in 38 mm case size; with stainless steel bracelet

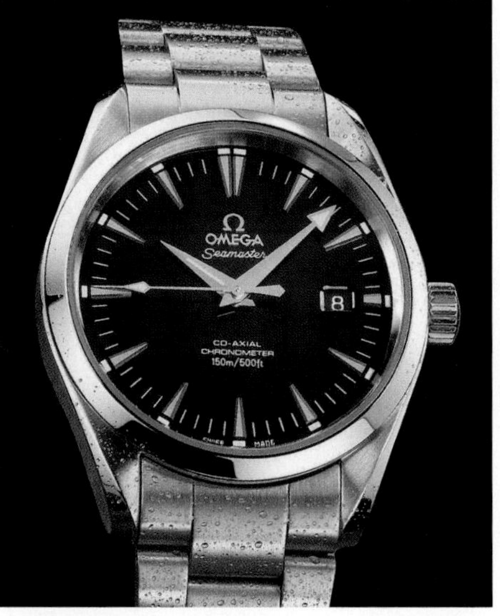

Seamaster Aqua Terra

Reference number: 2503.50.00
Movement: automatic, Omega 2500B, ø 25.6 mm, height 3.9 mm; 27 jewels; 28,800 vph, coaxial escapement; certified chronometer (C.O.S.C.)
Functions: hours, minutes, sweep seconds; date
Case: stainless steel, ø 38 mm, height 11.5 mm; sapphire crystal; transparent case back; water-resistant to 150 m
Band: stainless steel, folding clasp
Price: $2,695
Variations: in 35 and 41 mm case sizes; with reptile skin strap

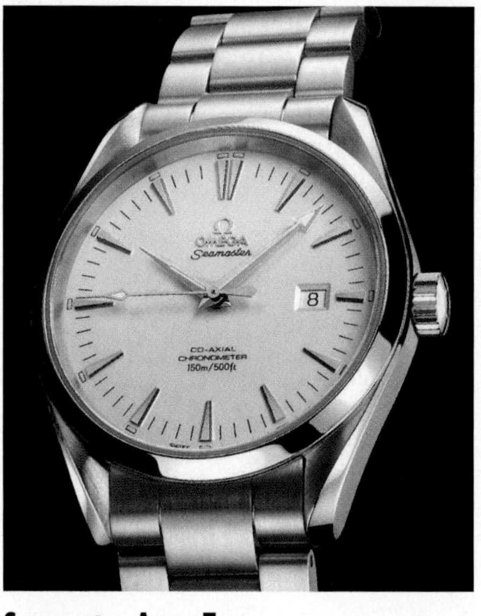

Seamaster Aqua Terra

Reference number: 2502.34.00
Movement: automatic, Omega 2500B, ø 25.6 mm, height 3.9 mm; 27 jewels; 28,800 vph, coaxial escapement; certified chronometer (C.O.S.C.)
Functions: hours, minutes, sweep seconds; date
Case: stainless steel, ø 41 mm, height 11.5 mm; sapphire crystal; transparent case back; water-resistant to 150 m
Band: stainless steel, folding clasp
Price: $2,795
Variations: in 35 and 38 mm case sizes; with reptile skin strap

Seamaster Aqua Terra Chronograph

Reference number: 2512.30.00
Movement: automatic, Omega 3301, ø 27 mm, height 6.85 mm; 33 jewels; 28,800 vph, column-wheel control of the chronograph functions, officially certified chronometer (C.O.S.C.)
Functions: hours, minutes, subsidiary seconds; chronograph; date
Case: stainless steel, ø 42.2 mm; sapphire crystal
Band: stainless steel, folding clasp
Price: $3,695
Variations: with leather strap

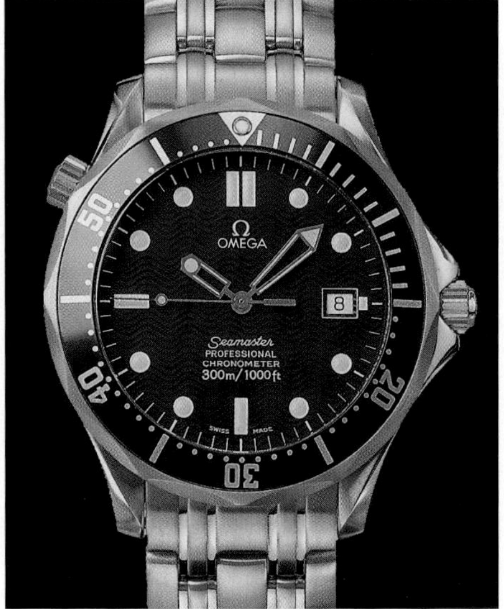

Seamaster Diver 300m

Reference number: 2531.80.00
Movement: automatic, Omega 1120 (base ETA 2892-A2); ø 25.6 mm, height 3.6 mm; 21 jewels; 28,800 vph, certified chronometer (C.O.S.C.)
Functions: hours, minutes, sweep seconds; date
Case: stainless steel, ø 39.9 mm, height 12 mm; unidirectionally rotating bezel with 60-minute scale; sapphire crystal, anti-reflective; screw-in crown; water-resistant to 300 m
Band: stainless steel, folding clasp with extension
Remarks: helium valve
Price: $1,895
Variations: with quartz movement

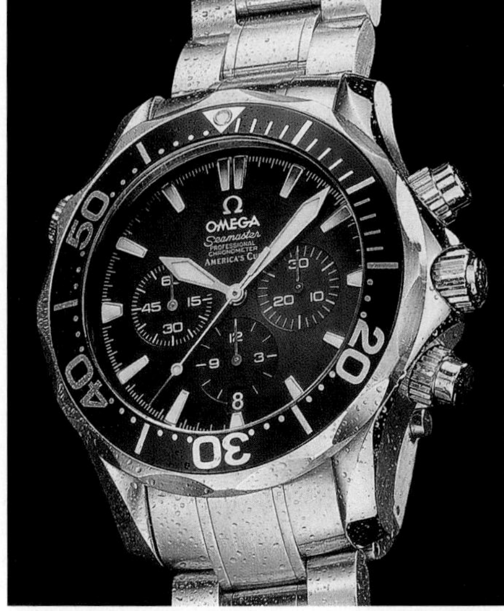

Seamaster America's Cup Chronograph

Reference number: 2594.52.00
Movement: automatic, Omega 3303, ø 27 mm, height 6.85 mm; 33 jewels; 28,800 vph, column-wheel control of the chronograph functions, certified chronometer (C.O.S.C.)
Functions: hours, minutes, subsidiary seconds; chronograph; date
Case: stainless steel, ø 41.5 mm, height 15.2 mm; unidirectionally rotating bezel with 60-minute scale; sapphire crystal; screw-in crown and buttons; water-resistant to 300 m
Band: stainless steel, folding clasp
Remarks: helium valve
Price: $3,495

Speedmaster Professional Moonwatch 35 Years

Reference number: 3569.31.00
Movement: manual winding, Omega 1861, ø 27.5 mm, height 6.85 mm; 18 jewels; 21,600 vph
Functions: hours, minutes, subsidiary seconds; chronograph
Case: stainless steel, ø 40 mm, height 14 mm; bezel with tachymeter scale; Hesalite crystal; transparent case back
Band: stainless steel, folding clasp
Remarks: anniversary edition "35 Years Moon Landing," limited to 3,500 pieces
Price: $3,195

Speedmaster Date

Reference number: 3513.50.00
Movement: automatic, Omega 1152 (base ETA 7750); ø 30 mm, height 7.9 mm; 25 jewels; 28,800 vph
Functions: hours, minutes, subsidiary seconds; chronograph; date
Case: stainless steel, ø 37 mm, height 13.7 mm; bezel with tachymeter scale; sapphire crystal, anti-reflective
Band: stainless steel, folding clasp
Price: $2,095
Variations: with leather strap/folding clasp

Speedmaster Broad Arrow

Reference number: 3551.50.00
Movement: automatic, Omega 3303, ø 27 mm, height 6.85 mm; 33 jewels; 28,800 vph, column-wheel control of the chronograph functions, certified chronometer (C.O.S.C.)
Functions: hours, minutes, subsidiary seconds; chronograph; date
Case: stainless steel, ø 38.8 mm, height 13.8 mm; bezel with tachymeter scale; sapphire crystal, anti-reflective
Band: stainless steel, folding clasp
Price: $4,495
Variations: with leather strap

Speedmaster Professional Moon Phase

Reference number: 3876.50.31
Movement: manual winding, Omega 1866 (base Nouvelle Lémania 1874); ø 27.5 mm, height 6.85 mm; 18 jewels; 21,600 vph
Functions: hours, minutes, subsidiary seconds; chronograph; date, moon phase
Case: stainless steel, ø 38.8 mm, height 14.3 mm; bezel with tachymeter scale; sapphire crystal, anti-reflective
Band: reptile skin, folding clasp
Price: $3,995

Speedmaster Professional Moonwatch

Reference number: 3570.50.00
Movement: manual winding, Omega 1861 (base Nouvelle Lémania 1873); ø 27.5 mm, height 6.85 mm; 18 jewels; 21,600 vph
Functions: hours, minutes, subsidiary seconds; chronograph
Case: stainless steel, ø 40 mm, height 14 mm; bezel with tachymeter scale; Hesalite crystal
Band: stainless steel, folding clasp
Price: $2,795
Variations: with leather strap

Speedmaster Ladies Automatic

Reference number: 3815.79.40
Movement: automatic, Omega 3220 (base ETA 2892-A2 with module 2020 by Dubois-Dépraz); ø 30 mm, height 6.5 mm; 47 jewels; 28,800 vph
Functions: hours, minutes, subsidiary seconds; chronograph
Case: stainless steel, ø 35.5 mm, height 11.9 mm; bezel set with brilliant-cut diamonds; sapphire crystal
Band: reptile skin, folding clasp
Price: $6,495

Caliber 2201

Base caliber: ETA 6498
Mechanical with manual winding, power reserve 60 hours
Functions: hours, minutes, subsidiary seconds
Diameter: 36.6 mm (16 3/4''')
Height: 4.5 mm
Jewels: 17
Balance: glucydur, three-legged
Frequency: 21,600 vph
Balance spring: Nivarox I flat hairspring
Shock protection: Incabloc
Remarks: base plate with perlage, bridges and cocks with côtes de Genève; officially certified C.O.S.C. chronometer

Caliber 2500

Mechanical with automatic winding, coaxial escapement; power reserve 44 hours
Functions: hours, minutes, sweep seconds; date
Diameter: 25.6 mm (11 1/2''')
Height: 3.9 mm
Jewels: 27
Balance: glucydur, four-legged, with gold regulating screws
Frequency: 28,800 vph
Balance spring: freely swinging
Remarks: base plate with perlage, bridges and rotor with côtes de Genève, rhodium-plated; officially certified C.O.S.C. chronometer

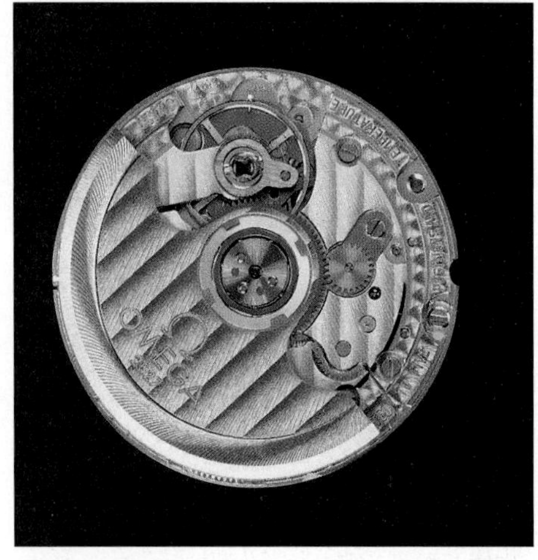

Caliber 2627

Base caliber: 2500
Mechanical with automatic winding, coaxial escapement; power reserve 44 hours
Functions: hours, minutes, subsidiary seconds; date; power reserve display
Diameter: 25.6 mm (11 1/2''')
Height: 5.35 mm
Jewels: 29
Balance: glucydur, four-legged, with gold regulating screws
Frequency: 28,800 vph
Balance spring: freely swinging
Related caliber: 2628 (hours, minutes, sweep seconds; date; 24-hour display/second time zone), height 5.2 mm, 27 jewels

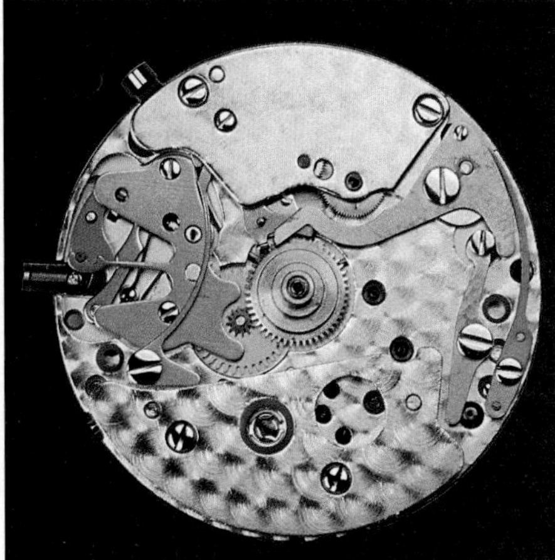

Caliber 1863 (dial side)

Base caliber: Nouvelle Lémania 1873
Mechanical with manual winding, power reserve 45 hours
Functions: hours, minutes, subsidiary seconds at 9 o'clock; chronograph with 3 counters (sweep seconds, minutes at 3, and hours at 6 o'clock)
Diameter: 27 mm (12'''); **Height:** 6.87 mm; **Jewels:** 18
Balance: glucydur, four-legged; **Frequency:** 21,600 vph
Balance spring: Nivarox I flat hairspring with fine adjustment
Remarks: base plate with perlage, beveled bridges with côtes de Genève; rhodium-plated; polished levers with beveled and polished edges
Related calibers: 1861 (with no additional finishing); 1866 (with date and moon phase)

Caliber 1866

Base caliber: Nouvelle Lémania 1874
Mechanical with manual winding, power reserve 45 hours
Functions: hours, minutes, subsidiary seconds at 9 o'clock; date at 12 o'clock; moon phase window at 12 o'clock; chronograph with 3 counters (sweep seconds, minutes at 3, and hours at 6 o'clock)
Diameter: 27 mm (12'''); **Height:** 6.87 mm, **Jewels:** 18
Balance: glucydur, four-legged
Frequency: 21,600 vph
Balance spring: Nivarox I flat hairspring with fine adjustment
Remarks: base plate with perlage, beveled bridges with côtes de Genève; rhodium-plated; polished levers with beveled and polished edges

Caliber 3313

Base caliber: Frédéric Piguet 1185
Mechanical with automatic winding; coaxial escapement; power reserve 55 hours; stop-seconds
Functions: hours, minutes, subsidiary seconds; date; chronograph with 3 counters (sweep seconds, minutes at 3, hours at 6 o'clock)
Diameter: 27 mm (12'''); **Height:** 6.85 mm; **Jewels:** 33
Balance: glucydur, four-legged, with two gold regulating screws
Frequency: 28,800 vph; **Balance spring:** freely swinging
Remarks: column-wheel control of chronograph functions; base plate with perlage, beveled bridges with côtes de Genève; rhodium-plated; officially certified C.O.S.C. chronometer
Related caliber: 3303 (without coaxial escapement)

Oris

A large anniversary for a small brand, that is actually not so small after all: Oris is celebrating its 100th birthday, taking the opportunity to show that one can assert oneself in a contested price segment by use of clever model policies and consistent love of the mechanical watch. Watch fans associate the name Oris not only with the slogan "It's High Mech," but also and above all with a mechanical watch at a reasonable price.

From 1910 until 1982, Oris was a genuine *manufacture* with a large degree of autonomy. All of the company's movements, their parts, and their finishing were produced in Oris's own ateliers, with the exception of mainsprings, balance springs, and jewels. In the 1950s Oris employed around 600 people and produced one to two million wristwatches and more than 100,000 alarm clocks per year.

Since its founding year of 1904, Oris has striven to bring high-quality mechanical watches of the company's own design outfitted with interesting movements to the market. Today there is hardly another company that can offer mechanical watches of comparable quality at these very competitive prices.

Fortunately, Oris has been able to call upon a rich fund of historical models that all seemed to have that *je ne sais quoi* about them. One need only think about the hand-winding alarm watch outfitted with the AS Caliber 1730 and its carefully modernized 1950s design, which was obviously so much to the taste of an entire generation of mechanical watch consumers with its moderate price that, for a while, the demand for it seemed almost hysterical.

That sparked, in a manner of speaking, the beginning of Oris's career. Strongly fueled by the above-mentioned catchy slogan and with just the right feel for consumer taste, the brand has presented models full of character such as the XXL Pointer, outfitted with an unusual sweep calendar hand, and the Complication. The XXL Worldtimer model, sporting a dial train developed exclusively for Oris, proves that the company also has the technical competence to profoundly and exclusively modify ETA base movements.

And let's not forget the overly large crown on some models, a characteristic that has practically become Oris's trademark over the last decade. In keeping with this, the company named an entire line Big Crown, now known in its abbreviated form BC. Oris's participation in Formula 1 racing as a sponsor of the BMW Williams team has inspired the technicians and designers to launch a racing collection. These sporty models magically recreate the glamour and excitement of Grand Prix races on the wrist: Take for example the Williams F1 Team Chronograph, limited to 2,000 pieces, in a titanium case with a carbon fiber dial and a rubber strap sporting racing tire tracks. And because Oris has also secured the services of race driver Ralf Schumacher, a special model dedicated to him has also been created. The Ralf Schumacher Limited Edition is immediately recognizable due to Ralf's number (4), which shines out as a blue numeral among the white markers surrounding it.

XXL Worldtimer

Reference number: 690 7513 40 61 LS
Movement: automatic, Oris 690 (base ETA 2836-2); ø 25.6 mm, height 5.05 mm; 25 jewels; 28,800 vph, hour hand settable backward and forward via button, coupled to the date
Functions: hours, minutes, subsidiary seconds; date, day/night display; second time zone
Case: stainless steel, ø 40 mm, height 11.55 mm; sapphire crystal; transparent case back
Band: leather, folding clasp
Price: $1,995
Variations: with rubber strap; with stainless steel bracelet

Ralf Schumacher Chronograph Limited Edition

Reference number: 673 7561 70 64 RS
Movement: automatic, Oris 673 (base ETA 7750); ø 30 mm, height 7.9 mm; 25 jewels; 28,800 vph
Functions: hours, minutes; chronograph; date
Case: titanium, ø 45 mm, height 14 mm; bezel engraved with tachymeter scale; sapphire crystal; transparent case back; Quick-Lock crown; water-resistant to 50 m
Band: rubber, folding clasp
Remarks: carbon fiber dial with blue four (Schumacher's number)
Price: $2,575

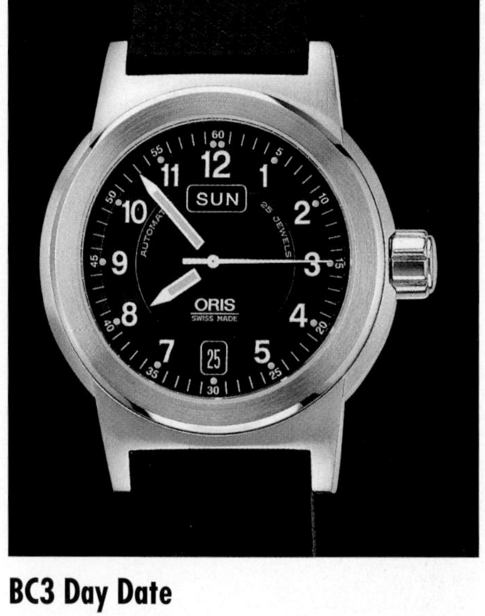

BC3 Day Date

Reference number: 635 7500 41 64 RS
Movement: automatic, Oris 635 (base ETA 2836-2); ø 25.6 mm, height 5.05 mm; 25 jewels; 28,800 vph
Functions: hours, minutes, sweep seconds; date and day
Case: stainless steel, ø 40 mm, height 11 mm; sapphire crystal; transparent case back; crown extra large; water-resistant to 50 m
Band: rubber, folding clasp
Price: $725
Variations: with stainless steel bracelet

Williams Chronograph

Reference number: 673 7563 41 84 RS
Movement: automatic, Oris 673 (base ETA 7750); ø 30 mm, height 7.9 mm; 25 jewels; 28,800 vph
Functions: hours, minutes; chronograph; date
Case: stainless steel, ø 45 mm, height 14 mm; bezel with tachymeter scale; sapphire crystal; transparent case back; water-resistant to 50 m
Band: rubber, folding clasp
Remarks: carbon fiber dial
Price: $2,125
Variations: with stainless steel bracelet

Williams Day Date

Reference number: 635 7560 41 64 RS
Movement: automatic, Oris 635 (base ETA 2836-2); ø 25.6 mm, height 5.05 mm; 25 jewels; 28,800 vph
Functions: hours, minutes, sweep seconds; date
Case: stainless steel, ø 40.5 mm, height 11 mm; sapphire crystal; transparent case back; water-resistant to 50 m
Band: rubber, folding clasp
Price: $895
Variations: with stainless steel bracelet

Miles Tonneau Chronograph

Reference number: 675 7532 40 64 LS
Movement: automatic, Oris 675 (base ETA 7750); ø 30 mm, height 7.9 mm; 25 jewels; 28,800 vph
Functions: hours, minutes, subsidiary seconds; chronograph; date and day
Case: stainless steel, 41 x 51.5 mm, height 14.7 mm; sapphire crystal; transparent case back
Band: leather, folding clasp
Price: $2,225
Variations: with stainless steel bracelet

TT1 Chronograph

Reference number: 674 7521 44 64 RS
Movement: automatic, Oris 674 (base ETA 7750); ø 30 mm, height 7.9 mm; 25 jewels; 28,800 vph
Functions: hours, minutes, subsidiary seconds; chronograph; date
Case: stainless steel, ø 42.5 mm, height 14.75 mm; ubber-coated bezel; sapphire crystal; transparent case back; screw-in crown; water-resistant to 100 m
Band: rubber, folding clasp
Price: $2,150
Variations: with stainless steel bracelet

TT1 Master Diver Regulateur

Reference number: 649 7541 70 64
Movement: automatic, Oris 649 (base ETA 2836-2); ø 25.6 mm, height 4.6 mm; 27 jewels; 28,800 vph
Functions: hours (off-center), minutes, subsidiary seconds; date
Case: titanium, ø 44 mm, height 13.2 mm; unidirectionally rotating bezel with 60-minute scale; sapphire crystal; screw-in crown; water-resistant to 1000 m
Band: rubber, folding clasp with diver's extension
Remarks: helium valve; delivered with additional titanium bracelet
Price: $1,850

TT1 Divers Chronograph

Reference number: 674 7542 70 54 RS
Movement: automatic, Oris 674 (base ETA 7750); ø 30 mm, height 7.9 mm; 25 jewels; 28,800 vph
Functions: hours, minutes, seconds; chronograph; date
Case: titanium, ø 44 mm, height 14.75 mm; unidirectionally rotating bezel with 60-minute scale; sapphire crystal; transparent case back; screw-in crown; water-resistant to 300 m
Band: rubber, folding clasp with diver's extension
Remarks: helium valve
Price: $2,195
Variations: with titanium bracelet

Artelier Date

Reference number: 561 7548 40 51 MB
Movement: automatic, Oris 561 (base ETA 2671); ø 17.2 mm; 25 jewels; 28,800 vph
Functions: hours, minutes, sweep seconds; date
Case: stainless steel, ø 31 mm; sapphire crystal; transparent case back
Band: stainless steel, folding clasp
Price: $925
Variations: with leather strap

Artelier Complication

Reference number: 581 7546 40 51 LS
Movement: automatic, Oris 581 (base ETA 2688/2671); ø 23.6 mm, height 5.6 mm; 17 jewels; 28,800 vph, modified movement diameter
Functions: hours, minutes, sweep seconds; date, day, moon phase; 24-hour display (second time zone)
Case: stainless steel, ø 40.5 mm, height 11.45 mm; sapphire crystal; transparent case back
Band: leather, folding clasp
Price: $1,350
Variations: with stainless steel bracelet

Artelier Date

Reference number: 633 7544 40 51 LS
Movement: automatic, Oris 633 (base ETA 2824-2); ø 25.6 mm, height 4.6 mm; 25 jewels; 28,800 vph
Functions: hours, minutes, sweep seconds; date
Case: stainless steel, ø 40.5 mm, height 10 mm; sapphire crystal; transparent case back
Band: leather, folding clasp
Price: $925
Variations: with stainless steel bracelet

Panerai

Guido Panerai & Figlio, founded in 1860 in Florence, originally specialized in precision mechanics and quickly advanced to become the official supplier of the Italian navy. Panerai provided this government organization with especially progressive and precise instruments such as compasses, depth measuring devices, and torpedo fuses. The company, which had in the meantime become Officine Panerai, manufactured its first timekeeper in 1936 — a diver's watch for combat swimmers called the Radiomir. Throughout the decades, the company's highly specialized product palette made the name Panerai synonymous with measuring maritime space and time, surely forming the base of Officine Panerai's good reputation among international watch collectors. This Italian cult brand has managed to garner quite a following stateside. Panerai's business has been brilliant since it was taken over by the Richemont group seven years ago, and the constant investment is now certainly bearing fruit. Just recently, Panerai Manufacture was opened in the former cantonal police prefect building of Neuchâtel, Switzerland, to modify existing movements. A current example of this updating process is the Radiomir 8 Days. The eight-day movement acquired from Richemont

sister company Jaeger-LeCoultre was lavishly redesigned, with its power reserve display having been placed on the back side of the movement. The re-forming of the plain Unitas hand-wound caliber has already taken on an impressive shape, and the Valjoux movement with subsidiary seconds that is the base for Panerai's watches is also being changed around. As if that weren't enough, the watch world can expect to see a completely autonomous movement soon. Although the company has moved its residence to Switzerland, it has not forgotten its roots. The Bottega d'Arte Panerai in the heart of Florence was one of the best addresses for fine Swiss watches in the year 1900. A good one hundred years later the small retail shop on Piazza San Giovanni has reopened, but not before the Italian military gave it their blessing: Wristwatches and measuring instruments that used to be manufactured on the second floor of this workshop are still top secret according to the law. Some of the historical instruments and tools that Guido Panerai and his son handled can be seen today in the altered workshop, including conventional table and grandfather clocks and numerous documents, blueprints, and sketches.

Luminor Marina

Reference number: PAM 00111
Movement: manual winding, Panerai OP XI (base ETA 6497); ø 36.6 mm, height 4.5 mm; 17 jewels; 21,600 vph, certified chronometer (C.O.S.C.); special movement finish
Functions: hours, minutes, subsidiary seconds
Case: stainless steel, ø 44 mm, height 16.8 mm; sapphire crystal; transparent case back; crown with security brake lever lock; water-resistant to 300 m
Band: leather, buckle
Remarks: additional rubber strap
Price: $3,650
Variations: in titanium

Luminor Base

Reference number: PAM 00176
Movement: manual winding, Panerai OP X (base ETA 6497); ø 36.6 mm, height 4.5 mm; 17 jewels; 21,600 vph, special movement finish
Functions: hours, minutes
Case: stainless steel, ø 44 mm, height 16.8 mm; sapphire crystal; crown with security brake lever lock; water-resistant to 300 m
Band: reptile skin, buckle
Remarks: additional rubber strap
Price: $3,750
Variations: with subsidiary seconds; in titanium

Radiomir Blackseal

Reference number: PAM 00183
Movement: manual winding, Panerai OP XI (base ETA 6497); ø 36.6 mm, height 4.5 mm; 17 jewels; 21,600 vph, certified chronometer (C.O.S.C.); special movement finish
Functions: hours, minutes, subsidiary seconds
Case: stainless steel, ø 45 mm; sapphire crystal; transparent case back; water-resistant to 100 m
Band: leather, buckle
Price: $4,000

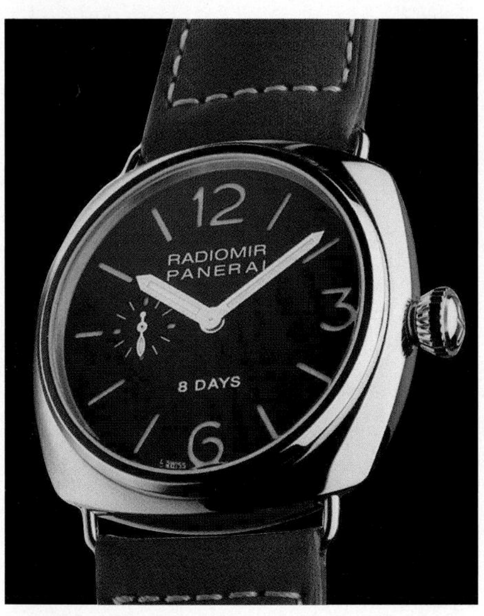

Radiomir 8 Days

Reference number: PAM 00190
Movement: manual winding, Panerai OP XIV (base JLC 1877); ø 32 mm, height 5.3 mm; 33 jewels; 28,800 vph, 8 days power reserve; special movement finish
Functions: hours, minutes, subsidiary seconds; power reserve display (on the back)
Case: stainless steel, ø 45 mm; sapphire crystal; transparent case back; water-resistant to 100 m
Band: leather, buckle
Price: $7,400

Luminor Marina Automatic 44 mm

Reference number: PAM 00104
Movement: automatic, Panerai OP III (base ETA 7750); ø 30 mm, height 7.9 mm; 21 jewels; 28,800 vph, certified chronometer (C.O.S.C.); special movement finish
Functions: hours, minutes, subsidiary seconds; date
Case: stainless steel, ø 44 mm, height 16.8 mm; sapphire crystal; crown with security brake lever lock; water-resistant to 300 m
Band: reptile skin, buckle
Remarks: additional rubber strap
Price: $4,000

Luminor GMT 44 mm

Reference number: PAM 00088
Movement: automatic, Panerai OP VIII (base ETA 7750); ø 30 mm, height 7.9 mm; 21 jewels; 28,800 vph, certified chronometer (C.O.S.C.); special movement finish
Functions: hours, minutes, subsidiary seconds; date; 24-hour display (second time zone)
Case: stainless steel, ø 44 mm, height 16.8 mm; sapphire crystal; crown with security brake lever lock; water-resistant to 300 m
Band: reptile skin, folding clasp
Remarks: additional rubber strap
Price: $4,600

Luminor Power Reserve

Reference number: PAM 00171
Movement: automatic, Panerai OP IX (base ETA 7750); ø 30 mm, height 7.9 mm; 21 jewels; 28,800 vph, certified chronometer (C.O.S.C.); special movement finish
Functions: hours, minutes, subsidiary seconds; date; power reserve display
Case: titanium, ø 44 mm, height 16.8 mm; sapphire crystal; crown with security brake lever lock; water-resistant to 300 m
Band: stainless steel/titanium, folding clasp
Price: $6,600

Luminor GMT 40 mm

Reference number: PAM 00159
Movement: automatic, Panerai OP VIII (base ETA 7750); ø 30 mm, height 7.9 mm; 21 jewels; 28,800 vph, certified chronometer (C.O.S.C.); special movement finish
Functions: hours, minutes, subsidiary seconds; date; 24-hour display (second time zone)
Case: stainless steel, ø 40 mm, height 16.8 mm; sapphire crystal; crown with security brake lever lock; water-resistant to 300 m
Band: reptile skin, folding clasp
Price: $4,600
Variations: with stainless steel bracelet

Luminor Power Reserve 40 mm

Reference number: PAM 00126
Movement: automatic, Panerai OP IX (base ETA 7750); ø 30 mm, height 7.9 mm; 21 jewels; 28,800 vph, certified chronometer (C.O.S.C.); special movement finish
Functions: hours, minutes, subsidiary seconds; date; power reserve display
Case: stainless steel, ø 40 mm, height 16.8 mm; sapphire crystal; crown with security brake lever lock; water-resistant to 300 m
Band: stainless steel, folding clasp
Price: $6,100
Variations: with leather strap

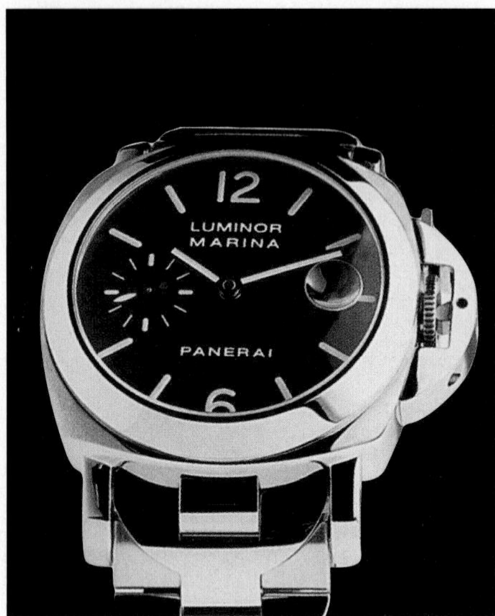

Luminor Marina Automatic 40 mm

Reference number: PAM 00050
Movement: automatic, Panerai OP III (base ETA 7750); ø 30 mm, height 7.9 mm; 21 jewels; 28,800 vph, certified chronometer (C.O.S.C.); special movement finish
Functions: hours, minutes, subsidiary seconds; date
Case: stainless steel, ø 40 mm, height 14.5 mm; sapphire crystal; crown with security brake lever lock; water-resistant to 300 m
Band: stainless steel, folding clasp
Price: $5,100
Variations: with leather strap

Luminor Daylight Chrono 44 mm

Reference number: PAM 00196
Movement: automatic, Panerai OP VII (base ETA 7753); ø 30 mm, height 7.9 mm; 27 jewels; 28,800 vph, certified chronometer (C.O.S.C.)
Functions: hours, minutes, subsidiary seconds; chronograph; date
Case: stainless steel, ø 44 mm, height 16.8 mm; bezel engraved with tachymeter scale; sapphire crystal; crown with security brake lever lock; water-resistant to 100 m
Band: reptile skin, folding clasp
Price: $5,900
Variations: with white dial

Radiomir GMT

Reference number: PAM 00184
Movement: automatic, Panerai OP XIII (base JLC 897); ø 25.6 mm, height 5.35 mm; 35 jewels; 28,800 vph, certified chronometer (C.O.S.C.); special movement finish
Functions: hours, minutes, subsidiary seconds; date; 24-hour display (second time zone)
Case: stainless steel, ø 42 mm, height 15 mm; sapphire crystal; transparent case back; water-resistant to 100 m
Band: reptile skin, folding clasp
Price: $6,600
Variations: in white gold

Parmigiani

Michel Parmigiani, a trained watch restorer of Italian descent, was for a long time unknown in the watch business. His skills, on the other hand, were very well known to famous European museums, where he achieved prominence for his talented reparation work on watches that had been judged irreparable by other experts in the field. With the complete refurbishment of the famous Montre Sympathique by Abraham-Louis Breguet, a task that no one else had even dared to attempt, Parmigiani's name became known to the rest of the horological world overnight. Soon after this, Parmigiani began developing and producing his own calibers, although he stayed with the sizes familiar to him from his clock and pocket watch "patients." When, in May 1996, on the initiative of the Sandoz Foundation, which subsequently acquired a 51 percent stake in his company, he launched his own collection of wristwatches, it didn't take long before he created his first "small" watch movement. The tonneau-shaped Caliber P110 from 1997 was Parmigiani's first movement, and two years ago, after a long period of trial and error, Caliber 331 joined the family. The strong motor of this automatic movement, constructed in an exceptionally modern fashion, lays the foundation for a complete *manufacture* collection. The classically beautiful movement is neither especially flat nor especially small in diameter, but it does contain two serially operating barrels that guarantee a power reserve of about fifty-five hours. This still very young luxury brand has been industrious in developing its model palette further, filling each collection with life. The confidently designed Forma features — along with its own movement from the Parmigiani *manufacture* — an unmistakable appearance and speaks to a clientele that can self-assuredly wear a statement on the wrist. This is something that women tend to find a little easier with this model than fully grown men who have more problems with the refined proportions of the watch. The latter seem to prefer the round Toric models, which radiate a somewhat more masculine aura in the appropriate color and material variations. Since the company is located in Fleurier, somewhat remote in the Val de Travers, the activities of the brand are not under continuous observation like those of other companies up in the Vallée de Joux, where literally no screwdriver can be dropped without a competitor finding out about it. Michel Parmigiani has been busy in the last few years buying buildings and machines upon which larger amounts of watch movements are manufactured under the new company name of Vaucher Manufacture — for example, for the aspiring watch collection by Hermès.

Of course, Parmigiani's own brand will benefit the most from the new developments. A small preview of the new complicated models can already be recognized in the new 30-second tourbillon that can chime on two gongs the hours, quarter hours, and minutes that have passed since midnight or noon at the will of the wearer.

Forma XL Automatique

Reference number: PF008625
Movement: automatic, Parmigiani 331, ø 25.95 mm, height 3.5 mm; 32 jewels; 28,800 vph, autonomous *manufacture* caliber
Functions: hours, minutes, sweep seconds; date
Case: rose gold, 41 x 34 mm, height 9 mm; sapphire crystal; transparent case back
Band: Hermès reptile skin, folding clasp
Price: $16,500
Variations: in white gold

Forma XL Minute Repeater

Reference number: PF008622
Movement: manual winding, Parmigiani 350, ø 24.85 mm, height 5 mm; 33 jewels; 21,600 vph, autonomous *manufacture* caliber
Functions: hours, minutes, subsidiary seconds; hour, quarter hour, and minute repeater
Case: rose gold, 41 x 34 mm, height 11 mm; sapphire crystal
Band: reptile skin, folding clasp
Price: $196,000
Variations: in platinum

Forma XL Tourbillon

Reference number: PF008644
Movement: manual winding, Parmigiani 500, 29.3 x 23.6 mm, 5.5 mm; 29 jewels; 21,600 vph, 30-second tourbillon; autonomous *manufacture* caliber; eight days power reserve
Functions: hours, minutes, sweep seconds; power reserve display
Case: white gold, 41 x 34 mm, height 12 mm; sapphire crystal; transparent case back
Band: Hermès reptile skin, folding clasp
Price: $180,000
Variations: in red gold

Toric Perpetual Calendar

Reference number: PF000474
Movement: automatic, Parmigiani 332, ø 25.95 mm, height 3.5 mm; 32 jewels (base movement); 28,800 vph, autonomous *manufacture* caliber, autonomous calendar module
Functions: hours, minutes, sweep seconds; perpetual calendar with date (retrograde), day, month, moon phase, leap year
Case: white gold, ø 40 mm; sapphire crystal; transparent case back; crown with sapphire cabochon
Band: reptile skin, buckle
Price: $48,900
Variations: in yellow or rose gold

Forma XL Hebdomadaire

Reference number: PF006804
Movement: manually wound, Parmigiani 110, 29.3 x 23.6 mm; height 4.90 mm; 28 jewels; 21,600 vph, autonomous *manufacture* caliber
Functions: hours, minutes, subsidiary seconds; date
Case: stainless steel, 53 x 37.2 mm, height 11.2 mm; sapphire crystal; transparent case back; water-resistant to 30 m
Band: stainless steel, folding clasp
Price: $18,300

Toric Chronograph

Reference number: PF006480
Movement: automatic, Parmigiani 190, ø 29.3 mm; 31 jewels; 36,000 vph, hand-beveled parts, côtes de Genève; 22-karat gold oscillating weight
Functions: hours, minutes; date; chronograph
Case: rose gold, ø 40 mm, height 12.40 mm; sapphire crystal; transparent case back; water-resistant to 30 m
Band: reptile skin, folding clasp
Price: $23,100

Patek Philippe

Patek Philippe built the most complicated portable mechanical watch in the world; Patek Philippe's watches always bring in the highest prices at auction; Patek Philippe possesses the most complete collection of portable watches. Superlatives such as these often make an important fact less obvious: This Genevan *manufacture* continues to contribute to the progression of technical details that make up the art of watchmaking.

The goal of this detailed work is usually to improve rate precision. For this reason, Patek Philippe patented the Gyromax balance in 1949, a component that was improved upon this past year. The new Gyromax now possesses four spokes instead of two, making it clearly more stable during both production and finishing. At the same time, the number of adjustable poising screws, or so-called masselottes, was reduced from eight to four. Together with the balance spring chosen to accompany it, it achieves an extremely precise and stable rate.

Also for this reason, Patek Philippe has changed the shape of the toothed wheels used in the gear train. The classic shape with rounded flanks has been replaced by wheels with an almost triangular shape.

These technical innovations are going to be used first in the astronomic complete calendar from the Gondolo collection. The new model, Reference 5135, possesses calendar mechanics that only need to be corrected manually once a year — on March 1 — and also displays day, date, and month in three windows on the upper part of the dial. The calendar is accompanied by moon phase and 24-hour displays on the bottom half of the dial. The functions are all powered by the new automatic Caliber 324/205, which may be admired through the timepiece's sapphire crystal case back.

And just as openly as this case back does, Philippe Stern displays his treasures for all to see: The company head fulfilled a lifelong dream for himself by opening a museum in the Genevan quarter Plainpalais. The Patek Philippe Museum is much more than a dusty room where the exhibits of a 160-year-old watch *manufacture* are kept. On the contrary: It is the most complete collection of wearable timekeeping there is and spans more than five centuries of horological history.

Since November 2001, house number 7 on rue des Vieux-Grenadiers is home to several thousand chiefly irreplaceable pieces of the comprehensive private collection of the Patek Philippe proprietary family Stern and presents it in an interesting manner to the general public on four stories comprising 700 square yards each. The collection of watches, tools, and literature, which has been compiled for decades by Philippe Stern and his father Henri, leaves everything else that could be seen publicly until now in its dust, including large national museum collections and thematic traveling exhibitions. Naturally, the presentation of 160 years of Patek Philippe watches alone is already a sensation for watch fans, as hardly one of the breathtaking "record watches" of the last few auction years is missing from this collection. A visit to the Patek Philippe Museum, located near the city center, is an absolute must for visitors to Geneva with a free afternoon.

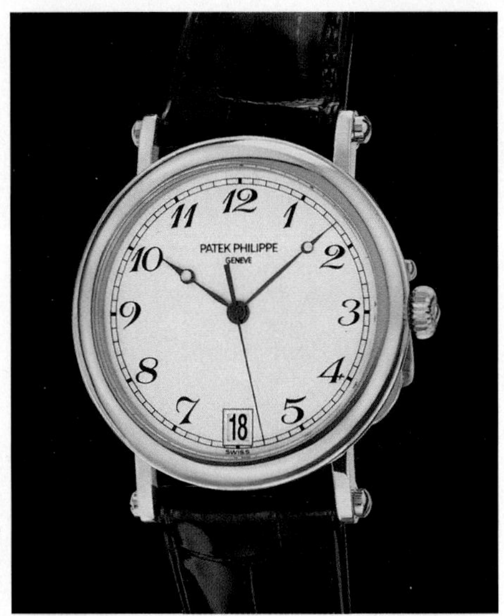

Calatrava

Reference number: 5053
Movement: automatic, Patek Philippe 315 SC, ø 27 mm, height 3.22 mm; 30 jewels; 21,600 vph, Seal of Geneva
Functions: hours, minutes, sweep seconds; date
Case: white gold, ø 35.6 mm, height 9.8 mm; sapphire crystal; transparent case back
Band: reptile skin, buckle
Price: $17,800
Variations: in rose gold ($17,800), in yellow gold ($16,750)

Calatrava Grande Taille

Reference number: 5107
Movement: automatic, Patek Philippe 315 SC, ø 27 mm, height 3.22 mm; 30 jewels; 21,600 vph, Seal of Geneva
Functions: hours, minutes, sweep seconds; date
Case: white gold, ø 37 mm, height 8.5 mm; sapphire crystal; transparent case back; screw-in crown
Band: reptile skin, buckle
Price: $15,200
Variations: in rose gold ($15,200), in yellow gold ($13,950), in platinum ($25,900)

Calatrava

Reference number: 5196
Movement: manual winding, Patek Philippe 215 PS (base 215); ø 21.9 mm, height 2.55 mm; 18 jewels; 28,800 vph, Seal of Geneva
Functions: hours, minutes, subsidiary seconds
Case: rose gold, ø 37 mm, height 6.8 mm; sapphire crystal
Band: reptile skin, buckle
Price: $13,000
Variations: in white gold ($13,000), in yellow gold ($11,850), in platinum ($21,000)

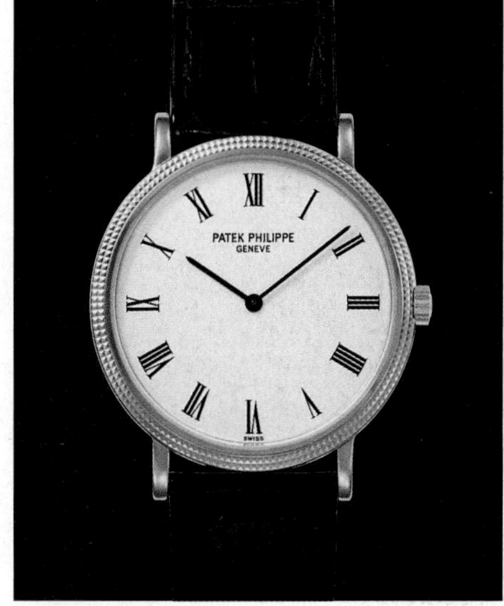

Calatrava Travel Time

Reference number: 5134
Movement: manual winding, Patek Philippe 215 PS FUS 24 H, ø 21.9 mm, height 3.35 mm; 18 jewels; 28,800 vph, Seal of Geneva; hour hand settable backward and forward by button
Functions: hours, minutes, subsidiary seconds; second time zone; 24-hour display
Case: platinum, ø 37 mm, height 9.8 mm; sapphire crystal; transparent case back
Band: reptile skin, folding clasp
Price: $29,800
Variations: in rose gold and white gold ($18,800), in yellow gold ($17,500)

Moon Phase

Reference number: 5054
Movement: automatic, Patek Philippe 240 PS IRM C LU, ø 31 mm, height 3.98 mm; 29 jewels; 21,600 vph, Seal of Geneva; microrotor in gold
Functions: hours, minutes, subsidiary seconds; date, moon phase; power reserve display
Case: yellow gold, ø 35.4 mm, height 9.54 mm; sapphire crystal; transparent case back and hinged lid
Band: reptile skin, folding clasp
Price: $24,800
Variations: in white gold or rose gold ($26,000), in platinum ($36,100)

Calatrava

Reference number: 5120
Movement: automatic, Patek Philippe 240, ø 27.5 mm, height 2.53 mm; 27 jewels; 21,600 vph, Seal of Geneva
Functions: hours, minutes
Case: white gold, ø 35 mm, height 6.7 mm; bezel decorated with clous de Paris; sapphire crystal; transparent case back
Band: reptile skin, buckle
Price: $15,000
Variations: in yellow gold ($13,850)

Gondolo

Reference number: 5109
Movement: manual winding, Patek Philippe 215 PS, ø 21.9 mm, height 2.55 mm; 18 jewels; 28,800 vph, Seal of Geneva
Functions: hours, minutes, subsidiary seconds
Case: white gold, 43 x 30 mm, height 7.22 mm; sapphire crystal
Band: reptile skin, buckle
Remarks: gold-plated dials in case colors
Price: $14,900
Variations: in yellow gold ($13,700), in rose gold ($14,900), in platinum ($23,700)

Nautilus

Reference number: 3711/1 G
Movement: automatic, Patek Philippe 315 SC, ø 28 mm, height 3.22 mm; 30 jewels; 21,600 vph, Seal of Geneva
Functions: hours, minutes, sweep seconds; date
Case: white gold, ø 42.5 mm; sapphire crystal; transparent case back; water-resistant to 120 m
Band: white gold, folding clasp
Price: $34,200

Perpetual Calendar

Reference number: 5136/1
Movement: automatic, Patek Philippe 240 Q, ø 27.5 mm, height 3.88 mm; 27 jewels; 21,600 vph, Seal of Geneva
Functions: hours, minutes; perpetual calendar with date, month, day, moon phase, leap year, AM/PM display
Case: yellow gold, ø 37 mm; sapphire crystal; transparent case back
Band: yellow gold, folding clasp with integrated button to correct date
Remarks: delivered with additional solid gold case back
Price: $60,300
Variations: in white gold ($63,200)

Annual Calendar

Reference number: 5035
Movement: automatic, Patek Philippe 315 S QA, ø 30 mm, height 5.22 mm; 35 jewels; 21,600 vph, Seal of Geneva
Functions: hours, minutes, sweep seconds; date, day, month (programmed for one year); 24-hour display
Case: rose gold, ø 37 mm, height 10.67 mm; sapphire crystal; transparent case back
Band: reptile skin, buckle
Price: $22,650
Variations: in rose gold ($22,650), in yellow gold ($21,500), in platinum ($32,600)

Chronograph, Perpetual Calendar

Reference number: 5970 R
Movement: manual winding, Patek Philippe CH 27-70 Q, ø 30 mm, height 7.2 mm; 24 jewels; 18,000 vph, Seal of Geneva
Functions: hours, minutes, subsidiary seconds; AM/PM display; chronograph; perpetual calendar with date, day, month, moon phase, leap year
Case: rose gold, ø 40 mm; sapphire crystal; transparent case back
Band: reptile skin, folding clasp
Price: $84,200
Variations: in white gold ($84,200)

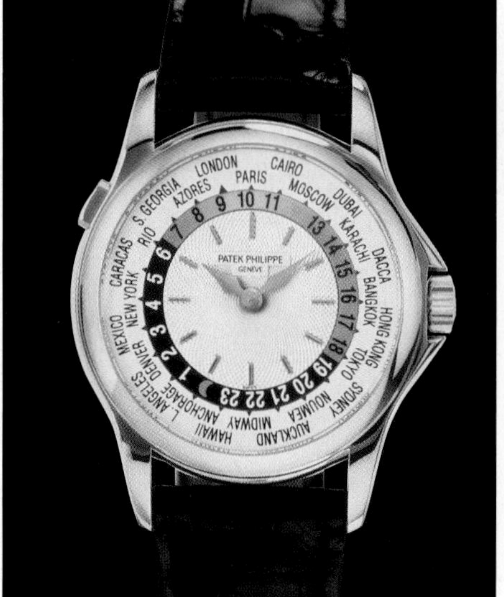

World Time Watch

Reference number: 5110
Movement: automatic, Patek Philippe 240 HU, ø 27.5 mm, height 3.88 mm; 33 jewels; 21,600 vph, Seal of Geneva; counterclockwise 24-hour chapter with names of reference cities, synchronized via button; microrotor in gold
Functions: hours, minutes; world time (24 hours/second time zone)
Case: rose gold, ø 37 mm, height 9.4 mm; sapphire crystal; transparent case back
Band: reptile skin, buckle
Price: $24,800
Variations: yellow gold, white gold, platinum ($34,900)

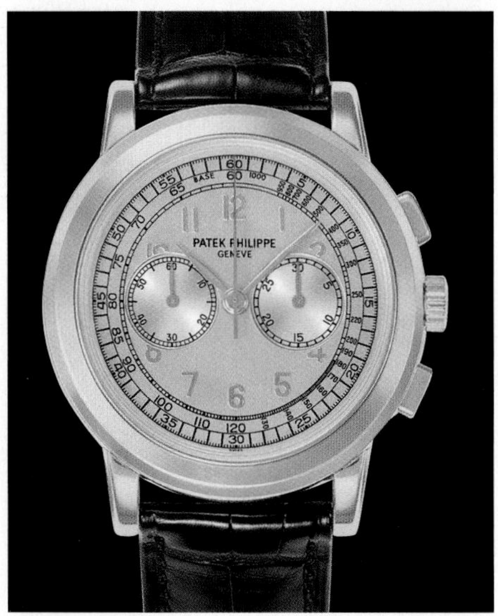

Chronograph

Reference number: 5070
Movement: manual winding, Patek Philippe CH 27-70 Q, ø 27.5 mm, height 5.57 mm; 24 jewels; 18,000 vph, Seal of Geneva; column-wheel control of the chronograph functions
Functions: hours, minutes, subsidiary seconds; chronograph
Case: rose gold, ø 42 mm, height 13 mm; sapphire crystal; transparent case back
Band: reptile skin, folding clasp
Price: $37,500
Variations: in white gold ($37,500), in yellow gold ($35,600)

Calatrava

Reference number: 5107 P
Movement: automatic, Patek Philippe 315 SC, ø 28 mm, height 3.22 mm; 30 jewels; 21,600 vph, Seal of Geneva
Functions: hours, minutes, sweep seconds; date
Case: white gold, ø 37 mm, height 8.5 mm; sapphire crystal; transparent case back
Band: reptile skin, buckle
Price: $15,200
Variations: in yellow gold ($13,950), in rose gold ($15,200)

Sky Moon

Reference number: 5102
Movement: automatic, Patek Philippe 240 LU CL, ø 38 mm, height 6.26 mm; 45 jewels; 21,600 vph, Seal of Geneva
Functions: hours, minutes; moon phase and moon descension; celestial chart
Case: white gold, ø 43.1 mm, height 9.78 mm; sapphire crystal; transparent case back
Band: reptile skin, buckle
Price: upon request

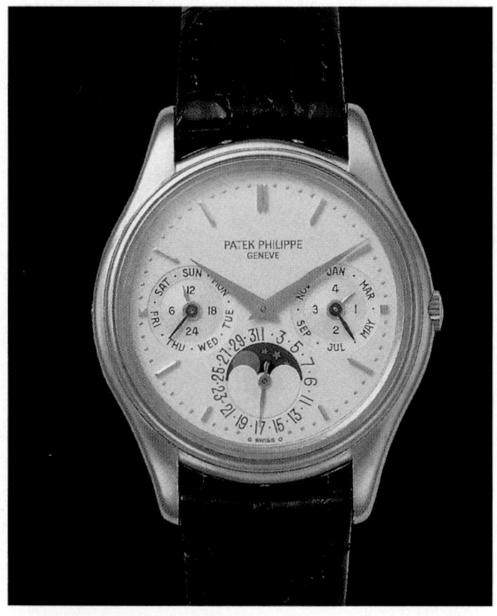

Perpetual Calendar

Reference number: 3940
Movement: automatic, Patek Philippe 240 Q, ø 27.5 mm, height 3.88 mm; 27 jewels; 21,600 vph, Seal of Geneva; microrotor in gold
Functions: hours, minutes; perpetual calendar with date, day, month, moon phase, leap year; 24-hour display
Case: yellow gold, ø 35.95 mm, height 9 mm; sapphire crystal
Band: reptile skin, buckle
Price: $81,750
Variations: in white gold and rose gold ($83,700), in platinum ($95,350)

10 Jours Tourbillon

Reference number: 5101 P
Movement: manual winding, Patek Philippe 28-20 REC10 PS IRM, 28 x 20 mm, height 6.3 mm; 29 jewels; 21,600 vph, Seal of Geneva; one-minute tourbillon; 10 days power reserve; certified chronometer (C.O.S.C.)
Functions: hours, minutes, subsidiary seconds; power reserve display
Case: platinum, 51.7 x 29.6 mm, height 12.2 mm; sapphire crystal; transparent case back
Band: platinum, buckle
Remarks: dial with black oxidized gold numerals
Price: upon request

Gondolo Calendario

Reference number: 5135
Movement: automatic, Patek Philippe 324 S QA LU 24 H, ø 31.4 mm, height 5.78 mm; 34 jewels; 28,800 vph, Seal of Geneva; new Gyromax balance with four spokes
Functions: hours, minutes, sweep seconds; annual calendar with date, day, month, moon phase; 24-hour display
Case: white gold, 51 x 40.33 mm, height 11.7 mm; sapphire crystal
Band: reptile skin, buckle
Price: $28,500
Variations: in yellow gold ($27,200), in rose gold ($28,500)

Calatrava Women

Reference number: 4905
Movement: manual winding, Patek Philippe 16-250, ø 19.4 mm, height 2.5 mm; 7 jewels, Seal of Geneva
Functions: hours, minutes
Case: rose gold, ø 28 mm, height 7.4 mm; sapphire crystal; transparent case back
Band: reptile skin, buckle
Price: $9,250
Variations: in white gold ($9,250), in yellow gold ($8,150)

Gondolo

Reference number: 4824
Movement: quartz, Patek Philippe E 15
Functions: hours, minutes
Case: yellow gold, 22.6 x 29 mm, height 6.8 mm; sapphire crystal
Band: reptile skin, buckle
Price: $8,600
Variations: with gold bracelet (ref.: 4824/1), in white gold ($9,600)

Twenty-4

Reference number: 4910/10A
Movement: quartz, Patek Philippe E 15
Functions: hours, minutes
Case: stainless steel, 25.1 x 30 mm, height 6.8 mm; case sides set with diamonds; sapphire crystal
Band: stainless steel, folding clasp
Price: $7,800

Twenty-4

Reference number: 4920
Movement: quartz, Patek Philippe E 15
Functions: hours, minutes
Case: rose gold, 25 x 30 mm, height 6.83 mm; case sides set with diamonds; sapphire crystal; crown with brilliant-cut solitaire
Band: satin, buckle
Remarks: dial with eight diamond markers
Price: $13,200
Variations: in white gold with grey or opal-white dial and rose gold with opal-white dial ($13,200)

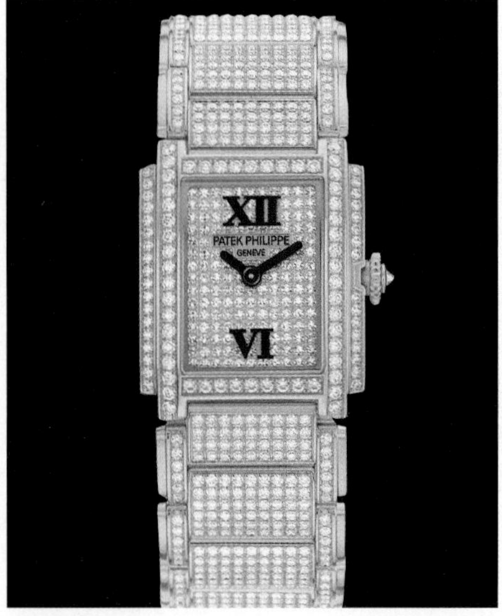

Twenty-4

Reference number: 4909/50 R
Movement: manual winding, Patek Philippe 16-250, ø 16.3 mm, height 2.5 mm; 18 jewels; 28,800 vph, Seal of Geneva
Functions: hours, minutes
Case: rose gold, 22 x 26.3 mm, height 6.94 mm; case sides set with diamonds; sapphire crystal; transparent case back; crown with diamond cabochon
Band: rose gold set with 1128 diamonds, folding clasp
Remarks: dial with diamond pavé
Price: $81,500
Variations: in white gold ($85,000)

Moon Phase

Reference number: 4858
Movement: manual winding, Patek Philippe 16-250 PS LU, ø 16.3 mm, height 2.5 mm; 18 jewels; 28,800 vph, Seal of Geneva
Functions: hours, minutes, subsidiary seconds; moon phase
Case: white gold, ø 29 mm, height 7.57 mm; bezel set with 60 diamonds; sapphire crystal; crown with diamond cabochon
Band: satin, buckle
Remarks: dial with diamond markers
Price: $15,800
Variations: in yellow gold ($14,700)

Caliber 27-70/150

Mechanical with manual winding, power reserve 58 hours
Functions: hours, minutes, subsidiary seconds, perpetual calendar (date, day, month, leap year, moon phase); 24-hour display; chronograph (minutes, seconds, split-seconds)
Diameter: 30 mm (13 1/2''')
Height: 8.86 mm
Jewels: 28 (escape wheel with endstone)
Balance: Gyromax, with eight masselotte regulating weights
Frequency: 18,000 vph
Balance spring: Breguet
Shock protection: Kif
Remarks: base plate with perlage, Seal of Geneva, 404 individual parts

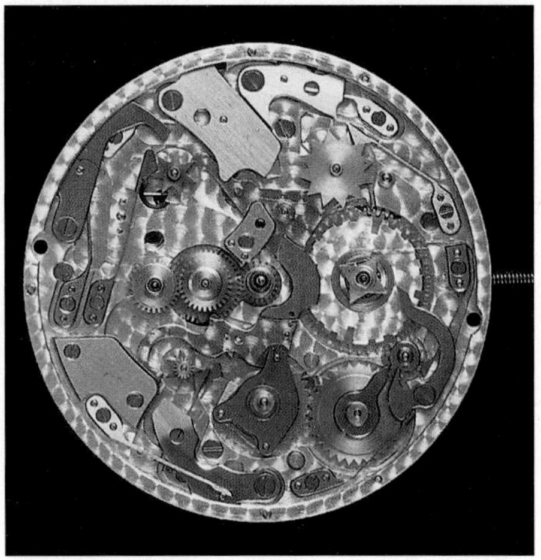

Caliber 27-70/150

Caliber 27-70/150 from the dial side.

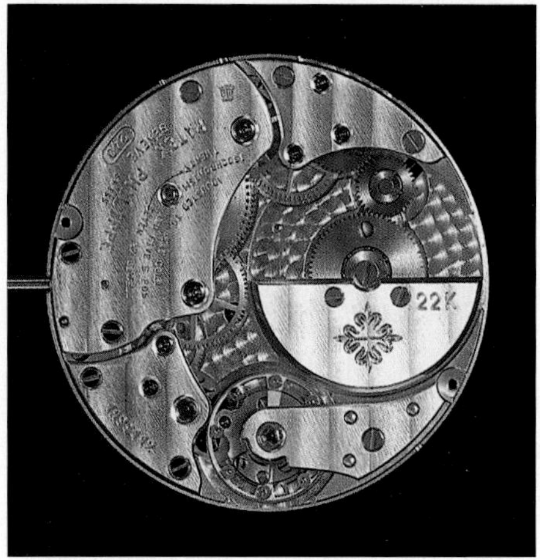

Caliber 240 PS

Base caliber: 240
Mechanical with automatic winding, power reserve 46 hours, off-center ball bearing micro-rotor in 22-karat gold, unidirectionally winding and integrated into the movement
Functions: hours, minutes, subsidiary seconds at 4 o'clock
Diameter: 27.5 mm (12 1/4''')
Height: ultra flat, 2.4 mm
Jewels: 27 (escape wheel with endstone)
Balance: Gyromax, with eight masselotte regulating weights
Frequency: 21,600 vph
Balance spring: flat hairspring
Shock protection: Kif
Remarks: base plate with perlage, beveled bridges and micro-rotor with côtes de Genève, 161 individual parts

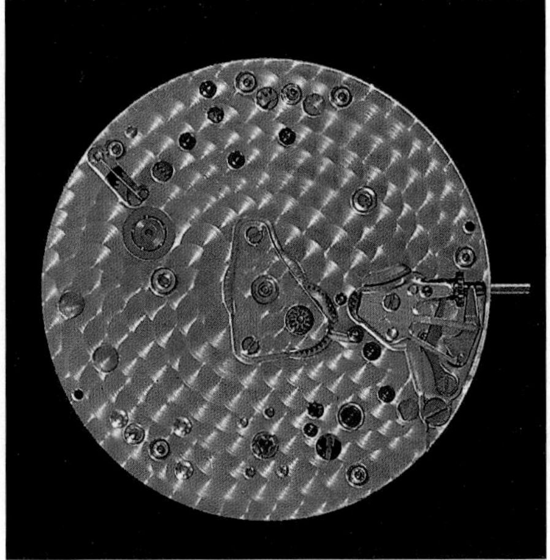

Caliber 240 PS

Caliber 240 from the dial side. The large surface of the micro-rotor recessed in the movement, which reduces the height of the construction greatly, can be clearly seen.
Related calibers: Base caliber 240 differs from Caliber 240 PS in the absence of a second hand; 240 Q (240 with perpetual calendar and 24-hour indication); 240/154 (240 PS with power reserve indicator and moon phase, diameter 31 mm, height 3.85 mm)

Caliber 315/136

Mechanical with automatic winding, power reserve 46 hours, central ball-bearing rotor in 21-karat gold, unidirectionally winding
Functions: hours, minutes, sweep seconds, perpetual calendar (retrograde date, day, month, leap year, moon phase)
Diameter: 28 mm (12 1/2''')
Height: 5.25 mm
Jewels: 31 (escape wheel with endstone)
Balance: Gyromax, with eight masselotte regulating weights
Frequency: 21,600 vph
Balance spring: flat hairspring
Shock protection: Kif

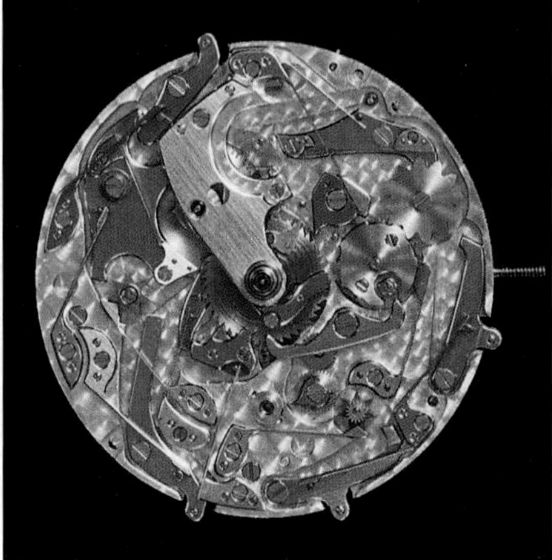

Caliber 315/136

Caliber 315/136 from the dial side.
Remarks: base plate with perlage, beveled bridges with côtes de Genève, rotor with côtes circulaires and an engraved cross of the Order of Calatrava, 368 individual parts
Related calibers: 330 SC (315 SC with date disk positioned closer to the center, height 3.5 mm)

Caliber 315/198

Mechanical with automatic winding, power reserve 46 hours, central ball-bearing rotor in 21-karat gold, unidirectionally winding
Functions: hours, minutes, sweep seconds, annual calendar (date, day, month); 24-hour indication
Diameter: 30 mm (13 1/4'''); **Height:** 5.22 mm
Jewels: 35 (escape wheel with endstone)
Balance: Gyromax, with eight masselotte regulating weights
Frequency: 21,600 vph
Balance spring: flat hairspring
Shock protection: Kif
Remarks: base plate with perlage, beveled bridges with côtes de Genève, rotor with côtes circulaires and an engraved cross of the Order of Calatrava, 316 individual parts

Caliber 324

Mechanical with automatic winding, power reserve 46 hours, central ball-bearing rotor in 21-karat gold, unidirectionally winding
Functions: hours, minutes, sweep seconds, annual calendar with three window displays (date, day, month) and moon phase; 24-hour indication
Diameter: 31.4 mm; **Height:** 5.78 mm; **Jewels:** 34
Balance: Gyromax, with four masselotte regulating weights
Frequency: 28,800 vph
Balance spring: flat hairspring
Shock protection: Kif
Remarks: Seal of Geneva; base plate with perlage, beveled bridges with côtes de Genève, rotor with côtes circulaires and an engraved cross of the Order of Calatrava

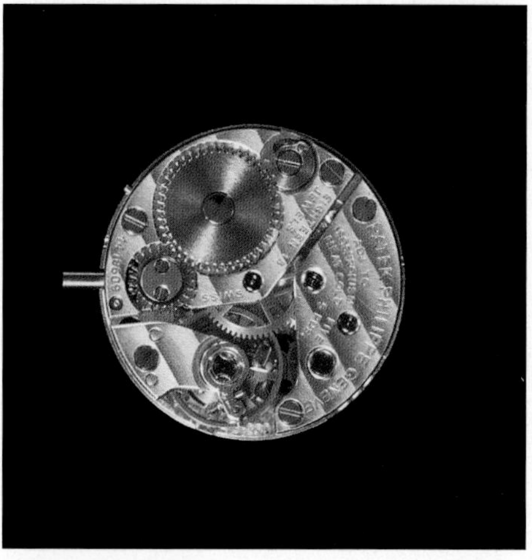

Caliber 16-250

Mechanical with manual winding, power reserve 36 hours
Functions: hours, minutes
Diameter: 16.3 mm (7''')
Height: 2.5 mm
Jewels: 18 (escape wheel with endstone)
Balance: ring, monometallic
Frequency: 28,800 vph
Balance spring: flat hairspring, with Triovis regulation and fine adjustment via micrometer screw
Shock protection: Incabloc
Remarks: base plate with perlage, beveled bridges with côtes de Genève, 99 individual parts

Caliber 16-250

Caliber 16-250 from the dial side.

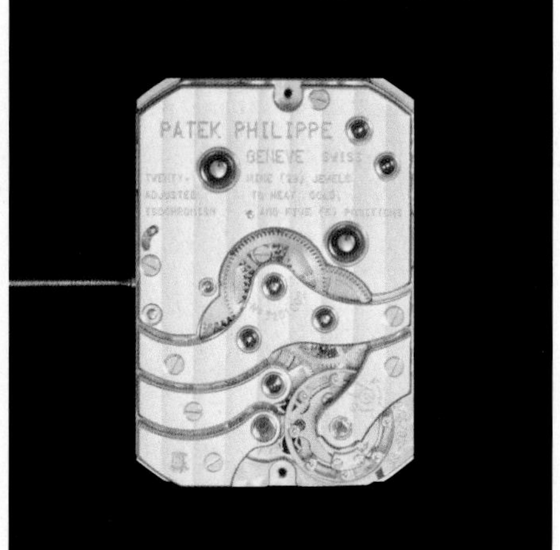

Caliber 28-20/220

Mechanical with manual winding, twin serially operating spring barrels, power reserve 10 days (240 hours)
Functions: hours, minutes, subsidiary seconds; power reserve display
Dimensions: 28 x 20 mm
Height: 5.05 mm
Jewels: 29 (escape wheel with endstone)
Balance: Gyromax in beryllium bronze with eight masselotte regulating weights
Frequency: 21,600 vph
Balance spring: flat hairspring
Shock protection: Kif
Remarks: base plate with perlage, beveled bridges with côtes de Genève, Seal of Geneva

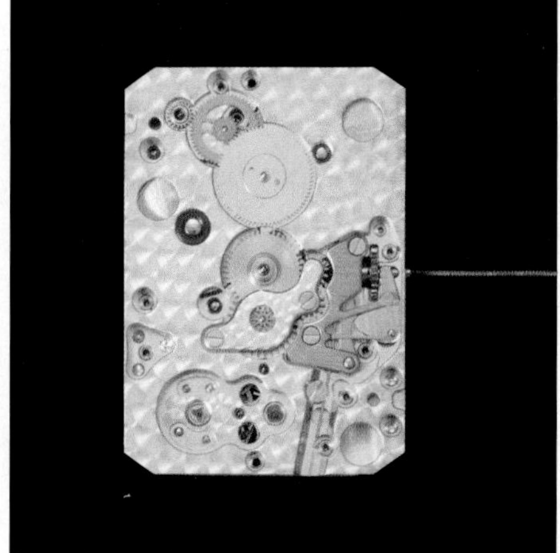

Caliber 28-20/220

Caliber 28-20/220 as seen from the dial side. All steel parts such as springs, levers, and bars are beveled and polished according to the regulations for the Seal of Geneva, and their surfaces are brushed by hand. The holes for the screws in the steel parts are also polished. In addition, each and every tooth on the toothed wheels and pinions are polished by hand with a hard-wood disk. This is, by the way, the case for all Patek Philippe movements that bear the Seal of Geneva.

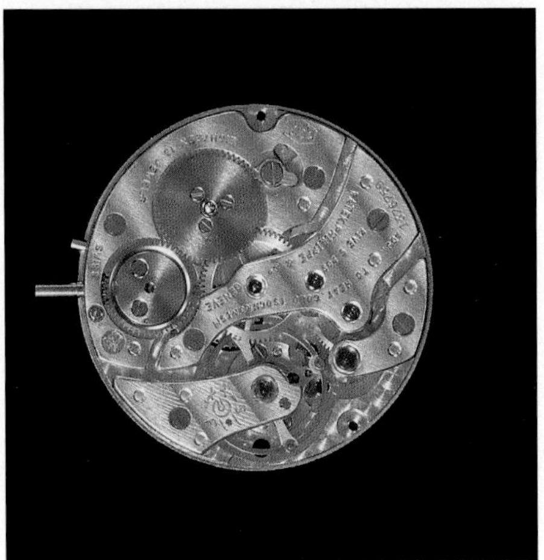

Caliber 177

Mechanical with manual winding, power reserve 41 hours
Functions: hours, minutes
Diameter: 20.8 mm (9 1/4''')
Height: ultra flat, 1.77 mm
Jewels: 18 (escape wheel with endstone)
Balance: Gyromax, diameter 7.4 mm, in beryllium bronze, with four masselotte regulating weights
Frequency: 21,600 vph
Balance spring: flat hairspring
Shock protection: Kif
Remarks: base plate with perlage, beveled bridges with côtes de Genève, Seal of Geneva, 112 individual parts

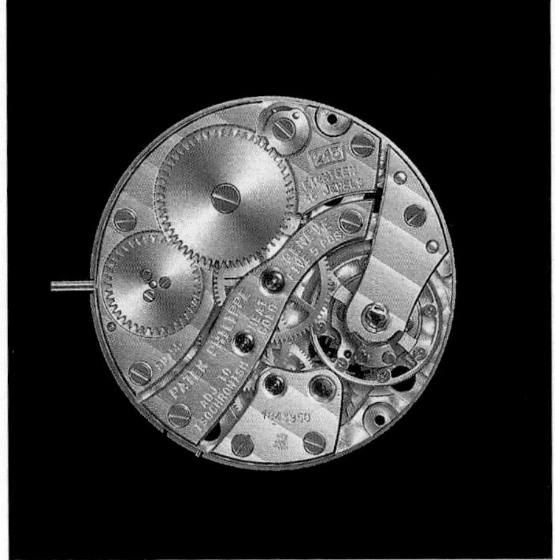

Caliber 215

Mechanical with manual winding, power reserve 43 hours
Functions: hours, minutes, subsidiary seconds at 6 o'clock
Diameter: 21.9 mm (9 3/4''')
Height: 2.55 mm
Jewels: 18 (escape wheel with endstone)
Balance: Gyromax, with eight masselotte regulating weights
Frequency: 28,800 vph
Balance spring: flat hairspring
Shock protection: Kif
Remarks: base plate with perlage, beveled bridges with côtes de Genève, Seal of Geneva, 130 individual parts

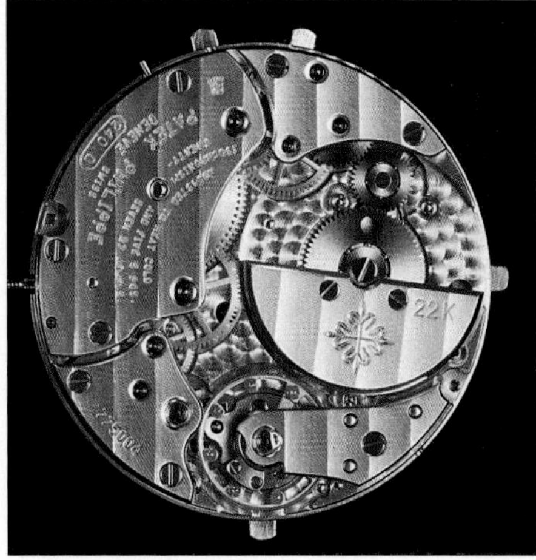

Caliber 240 Q

Mechanical with automatic winding, power reserve 46 hours, off-center ball-bearing micro-rotor in 22-karat gold, unidirectionally winding and integrated into movement
Functions: hours, minutes, perpetual calendar (date, day, month, leap year, moon phase) with 4 correction buttons; 24-hour display
Diameter: 30 mm (13 1/2'''); **Height:** 3.75 mm
Jewels: 27 (escape wheel with endstone)
Balance: Gyromax, with eight masselotte regulating weights
Frequency: 21,600 vph; **Balance spring:** flat hairspring
Shock protection: Kif
Remarks: module plate and stepped disk of the four-year cycle with perlage, bridges and levers beveled and satin-finished, base plate with perlage, beveled micro-rotor with côtes de Genève, Seal of Geneva, 275 individual parts

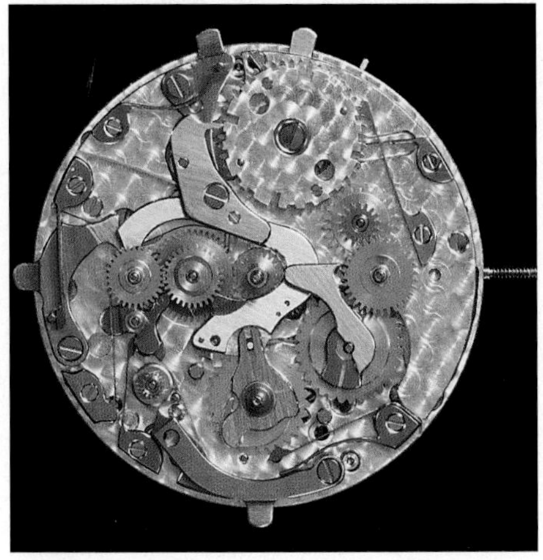

Caliber 240 Q

The illustration shows Caliber 240 Q from the dial side.

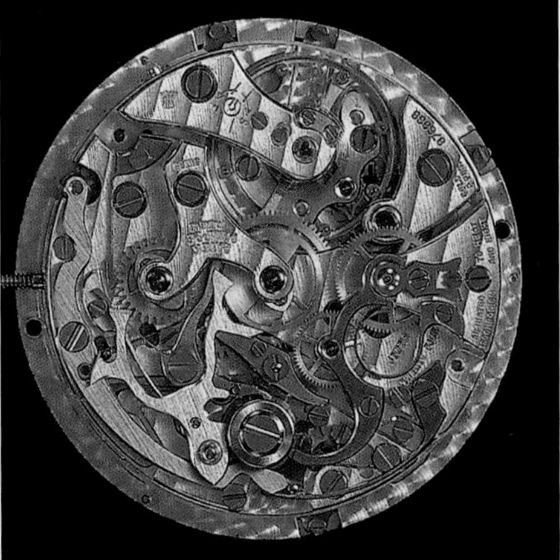

Caliber CH 27-70 Q

Mechanical with manual winding, power reserve 58 hours
Functions: hours, minutes, subsidiary seconds, perpetual calendar (date, day, month, leap year, moon phase) with 4 correction buttons; 24-hour display; chronograph with two counters (sweep seconds, minutes)
Diameter: 30 mm (13 1/2'''); **Height:** 7.2 mm
Jewels: 24 (escape wheel with endstone)
Balance: Gyromax, with eight masselotte regulating weights
Frequency: 18,000 vph; **Balance spring:** Breguet
Shock protection: Kif
Remarks: base plate with perlage, beveled bridges with côtes de Genève, Seal of Geneva, 350 individual parts
Related caliber: 27-70/150 (CH 27-70 Q with split-seconds chronograph)

Caliber CH 27-70 Q

Caliber CH 27-70 Q viewed from the dial side. In addition to the crown, the tiered disk for the leap year indication, divided in four cycles of 12 months each, is visible. A closer look reveals the pattern for the month of February in a leap year, which only has 28 days. The moon phase disk, which provides very accurate indication, can be seen at 6 o'clock - within a period of one year, the mean deviation is just 11 minutes 47 seconds, in other words after a period of 122 years, the moon phase indication shows a deviation of only one day!

Piaget

Piaget is known to a wider audience as a brand that manufactures jeweled timepieces. One of the lesser known facts in today's industry, however, is that Piaget has been one of the most important Swiss producers of *ébauches* and movement parts for more than one hundred years, supplying some of the industry's most renowned companies. In comparison to the other genuine watch *manufactures*, this company has communicated less of its illustrious history to a broad audience, something that may be founded in the fact that Piaget has only concentrated on producing watches under its own name since the 1950s.

As an homage to its eminent *manufacture* tradition, and almost seeming to form a counterpoint to the opulent jeweled pieces it is now famous for, Piaget has presented a new, round Altiplano XL to complement the successful square model already featured in the collection. The company's Genevan designers have created a minimalized watch that even goes along well with the Bauhaus motto "form follows function." This timepiece's elegant overall appearance is additionally underscored by its case, as its height comprises a svelte 4.3 mm. This ultra-flat construction was made possible by the company's own manually wound Caliber 430 P, which itself is only 2.1 mm high.

A lot has happened over the last few years at this exclusive watchmaker in remote La Côte-aux-Fées. The company has managed to break away from its image of being a pure jewelry watch brand, partly as a result of being responsible for designing and supplying movements for the Richemont watch group and its leading brand, Cartier. The 400/500P caliber family that has emerged is, of course, also now being used in diverse models of Piaget's continually growing collection, which has included a tourbillon since last year.

The elegant square Emperador Tourbillon is powered by *manufacture* Caliber 600, a shaped, manually wound movement containing a flying one-minute tourbillon at 12 o'clock. The real showstopper is the incredibly flat construction height of only 3.5 mm, made possible by a tourbillon cage that juts out from the surface of the dial a bit. This cage is an exceptionally complex structure comprising forty-two individual components and weighing only 0.2 grams thanks to its conservative dimensions (the balance's diameter is only 7.5 mm). The three main components making up the tourbillon cage are constructed of feather-light titanium, connected to one another by miniscule screws and taps.

By decorating the circle around the center of the tourbillon cage with *côtes de Genève*, Piaget is going down an unusual path in terms of the finishing of the movement's back. This is also evident in the numerous retracted corners (*angles rentrants*), making the use of machine tools impossible on them, and speaks for the remarkably lavish amount of detail work: A master beveler (*maître angleur*) needs an entire week before the individual parts of Piaget Caliber 600P live up to the expectations of its constructor.

The watch family that Piaget is perhaps best known for currently celebrates its 25th anniversary. The Polo was originally a timepiece favored by the rich and famous, earning a reputation as a "jet-set" watch. Currently, two new models — a men's watch powered by an automatic movement and a smaller women's watch that runs on quartz, both of which are *manufacture* calibers, by the way – are now gracing refined wrists. These two new Polos in white gold are available either fully or semi-paved with high-quality diamonds.

Piaget rightfully presents itself today as a *manufacture* of the finest quality, dedicated to traditional watchmaking skills and technical innovation. This is also documented by the completely modern factory building in Plan-les-Ouates, a Genevan industrial area jokingly referred to as the "watch suburb" by locals due to the growing settlement of watch companies there. The manufacture of cases and bracelets and the accompanying tasks of polishing, rhodium-plating, and jewel-setting are performed on the just about 4,000 m^2 of contemporary premises. The movement *manufacture* will, however, remain in the peace and tranquility of the mountainous Jura town La Côte-aux-Fées.

Emperador Tourbillon Skeleton

Reference number: GOA 29108
Movement: manual winding, Piaget 600P skeleton, 22.4 x 28.7 mm, height 3.5 mm (without tourbillon cage); 24 jewels; 21,600 vph, flying one-minute tourbillon, skeletonized
Functions: hours, minutes; power reserve display
Case: white gold, 32 x 41 mm, height 10 mm; sapphire crystal; transparent case back; water-resistant to 30 m
Band: leather, folding clasp
Price: $108,000

Emperador Tourbillon

Reference number: GOA 28073
Movement: manual winding, Piaget 600P, 22.4 x 28.7 mm, height 3.5 mm (without tourbillon cage); 24 jewels; 21,600 vph, flying one-minute tourbillon
Functions: hours, minutes, subsidiary seconds (on tourbillon cage); power reserve display
Case: rose gold, 32 x 41 mm, height 10 mm; sapphire crystal; transparent case back
Band: reptile skin, buckle
Remarks: limited to nine pieces
Price: $91,000

Emperador Retrograde Seconds

Reference number: GOA 28072
Movement: automatic, Piaget 560P, ø 20.5 mm (base movement); 21,600 vph
Functions: hours, minutes, subsidiary seconds (retrograde); date
Case: white gold, 32 x 41 mm, height 10 mm; sapphire crystal; transparent case back
Band: reptile skin, buckle
Price: $13,800

Altiplano Ultra Thin

Reference number: GOA 29112
Movement: manual winding, Piaget 430P, ø 20.5 mm, height 2.1 mm; 18 jewels; 21,600 vph
Functions: hours, minutes
Case: white gold, ø 38 mm, height 8 mm; sapphire crystal
Band: reptile skin, buckle
Price: $8,700
Variations: in yellow gold

Altiplano Ultra Thin XL

Reference number: GOA 28064
Movement: manual winding, Piaget 430P, ø 20.5 mm, height 2.1 mm; 18 jewels; 21,600 vph, côtes de Genève, beveled bridges, blued screws
Functions: hours, minutes
Case: white gold, 33 x 33 mm; sapphire crystal; water-resistant to 30 m
Band: reptile skin, buckle
Price: $8,900

Rectangle XL Retrograde Seconds

Reference number: GOA 28061
Movement: automatic, Piaget 561P, ø 20.5 mm (base movement); 21,600 vph
Functions: hours, minutes, subsidiary seconds (retrograde); date; power reserve display
Case: rose gold, 31 x 46 mm, height 9.5 mm; sapphire crystal
Band: reptile skin, buckle
Price: $13,700

Polo

Reference number: GOA 28050
Movement: quartz, Piaget 690P, ø 18.4 mm, height 2.15 mm; 7 jewels côtes de Genève, beveled bridges, blued screws
Functions: hours, minutes
Case: white gold, ø 28 mm, height 9 mm; sapphire crystal
Band: white gold, folding clasp
Remarks: meteorite dial
Price: $20,900

Polo

Reference number: GOA 28047
Movement: quartz, Piaget 690P, ø 18.4 mm, height 2.15 mm; 7 jewels, côtes de Genève, beveled bridges, blued screws
Functions: hours, minutes
Case: white gold, ø 28 mm, height 9 mm, diamond bezel; sapphire crystal; water-resistant to 30 m
Band: white gold, double folding clasp
Remarks: onyx dial
Price: $20,900

Polo

Reference number: GOA 28045
Movement: automatic, Piaget 504P (base Piaget 500P); ø 24.6 mm, height 3.4 mm; 26 jewels; 21,600 vph, côtes de Genève, beveled bridges, blued screws
Functions: hours, minutes, sweep seconds; day
Case: white gold, ø 38 mm; sapphire crystal; water-resistant to 30 m
Band: white gold, double folding clasp
Remarks: onyx dial
Price: $23,500

25th Anniversary Polo

Reference number: GOA 29037
Movement: automatic, Piaget 430P (base Piaget 500P); ø 24.6 mm, height 3.4 mm; 26 jewels; 21,600 vph, côtes de Genève, beveled bridges, blued screws
Functions: hours, minutes
Case: white gold, ø 38 mm; sapphire crystal; water-resistant to 30 m
Band: white gold, folding clasp
Remarks: fully paved with diamonds
Price: $75,000

25th Anniversary Polo

Reference number: GOA 29038
Movement: quartz, Piaget 690P, ø 18.4 mm, height 2.15 mm; 7 jewels, côtes de Genève, beveled bridges, blued screws
Functions: hours, minutes
Case: white gold, ø 28 mm; sapphire crystal; water-resistant to 30 m
Band: white gold, folding clasp
Remarks: fully paved with diamonds
Price: $59,000

Polo

Reference number: GOA 28504
Movement: quartz, Piaget 690P, ø 18.4 mm, height 2.15 mm; 7 jewels, côtes de Genève, beveled bridges, blued screws
Functions: hours, minutes
Case: yellow gold, ø 28 mm; sapphire crystal; water-resistant to 30 m
Band: yellow gold, double folding clasp
Price: $31,900

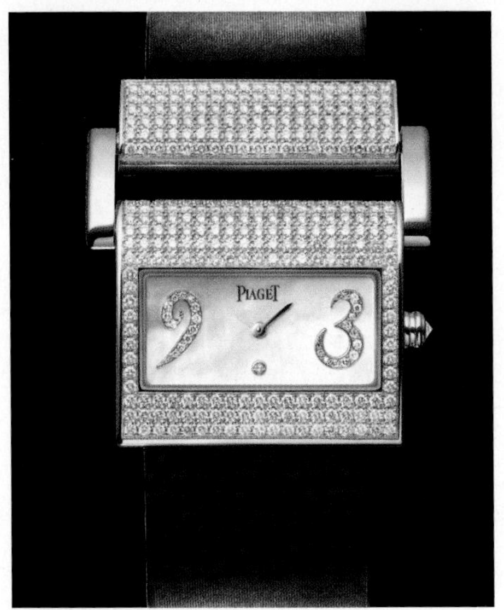

Miss Protocole XL

Reference number: GOA 29020
Movement: quartz, Piaget 157P, ø 15.3 mm, height 2.1 mm; 4 jewels
Functions: hours, minutes
Case: white gold, 36 x 40 mm; sapphire crystal; water-resistant to 30 m
Band: satin, integrated gem-set clasp
Remarks: paved with diamonds
Price: $33,000
Variations: with fully paved diamond bracelet

Tonneau

Reference number: GOA 26054
Movement: quartz,Piaget 59P, ø 11 mm, height 2.5 mm; 5 jewels
Functions: hours, minutes
Case: white gold,18 x 33.6 mm, height 8mm; sapphire crystal; water-resistant to 30 m
Band: white gold, integraed clasp
Remarks: fully paved with diamonds
Price: $54,900

Tonneau Joaillerie

Reference number: GOA 27063
Movement: quartz,Piaget 59P, ø 11 mm, height 2.5 mm; 5 jewels
Functions: hours, minutes
Case: white gold,18 x 33.6 mm, height 8 mm, case sides completely set with diamonds; sapphire crystal; water-resistant to 30 m
Band: satin, integrated gem-set clasp
Remarks: genuine mother-of-pearl dial
Price: $17,800
Variations: in white gold, with reptile skin strap

Protocole XLS

Reference number: GOA 28020
Movement: quartz, Piaget 690P, ø 18.4 mm, height 2.15 mm; 7 jewels
Functions: hours, minutes
Case: white gold, 25.8 x 31 mm; sapphire crystal; water-resistant to 30 m
Band: satin, integrated gem-set clasp
Remarks: paved with diamonds
Price: $23,900

Altiplano

Reference number: GOA 29106
Movement: quartz, Piaget 690P, ø 18.4 mm, height 2.15 mm; 7 jewels
Functions: hours, minutes
Case: white gold, 30 x 30 mm; sapphire crystal; water-resistant to 30 m
Band: satin, buckle
Remarks: case and dial diamond-paved
Price: $19,900

Limelight

Reference number: GOA 29103
Movement: quartz, Piaget 57P (base Piaget 157P); 15.3 x 13 mm, height 2.1 mm; 4 jewels
Functions: hours, minutes
Case: white gold, 28 x 22 mm, diamond bezel; sapphire crystal; water-resistant to 30 m
Band: white gold, integrated clasp
Remarks: white mother-of-pearl dial
Price: $23,900

Caliber 9P2

Mechanical with manual winding, power reserve 36 hours
Functions: hours, minutes
Diameter: 20.8 mm
Height: 2.15 mm
Jewels: 18
Balance: with smooth wheel, three-legged
Frequency: 19,800 vph
Balance spring: flat hairspring with fine adjustment via micrometer screw
Shock protection: Incabloc
Remarks: base plate with perlage, beveled bridges with côtes de Genève

Caliber 551P

Mechanical with automatic winding, stop-seconds, power reserve 40 hours
Functions: hours, minutes, subsidiary seconds; power reserve display
Diameter: 20.5 mm
Height: 3.9 mm
Jewels: 27
Balance: glucydur
Frequency: 21,600 vph
Balance spring: flat hairspring with fine adjustment via index
Shock protection: Incabloc
Remarks: modular winding mechanism

Caliber 441P

Base caliber: 430P
Mechanical with manual winding, stop-seconds, power reserve 40 hours
Functions: hours, minutes, subsidiary seconds; date, power reserve display
Diameter: 20.5 mm; **Height:** 3.6 mm; **Jewels:** 20
Balance: glucydur; **Frequency:** 21,600 vph
Balance spring: flat hairspring with fine adjustment via index
Shock protection: Incabloc
Related calibers: 430P (hours, minutes); 420P (430P with date window); 410P (430P with sweep seconds/stop-seconds); 400P (430P with date window and sweep seconds/stop-seconds)

Caliber 500P

Mechanical with automatic winding, stop-seconds, power reserve 40 hours
Functions: hours, minutes, sweep seconds; date
Diameter: 20.5 mm
Height: 3.4 mm
Jewels: 26
Balance: glucydur
Frequency: 21,600 vph
Balance spring: flat hairspring with fine adjustment via index
Shock protection: Incabloc
Remarks: modular winding mechanism
Related Calibers: 510P (with sweep seconds only); 520P (with date window only); 530P (hours and minutes only)

Caliber 600P

Mechanical with manual winding, one-minute tourbillon, power reserve 40 hours
Functions: hours, minutes, subsidiary seconds (on tourbillon cage); power reserve display
Dimensions: 22.4 x 28.7 mm
Height: 3.5 mm (without tourbillon cage)
Jewels: 24
Balance: glucydur, diameter 7.5 mm
Frequency: 21,600 vph
Remarks: flying tourbillon with cage made of titanium

PIAGET

Paul Picot

Paul Picot is more than just a great name in horological art. It stands for the philosophy under which the work in the company's Le Noirmont workshops is performed. A clear sense of aesthetics and perfection, the mastery of watchmaking technology, and schooled eyes and hands: These are some of the secrets that combine to create the uniqueness of Paul Picot watches.
In 1976, during the middle of the toughest crisis the Swiss watch industry ever had to face, when many historic names went under, one of the newest companies in *haute horlogerie* was created. This firm was born of the will to save the rich tradition of the Swiss watch industry and let its true values once again come to light. The conventional customs of watchmaking were threatening to fall into disrepair; qualified masters of the craft were disappearing from the workplace, and the once-fascinating atmosphere of watchmakers' workshops had given way to the industrial hustle and bustle of anonymous trade names.
For company founder and president Mario Boiocchi, the only chance for the survival of European watch culture was to rediscover quality and precision. While Japanese and American competitors forced the Swiss watch industry to make compromises in order to meet the demands of mass consumption, Paul Picot chose to walk a different path.
Although the market was calling for futuristic design and electronic technology, Paul Picot entered it with fine gold cases and mechanical watch movements. In the years to follow, it was sporty, elegant collections such as the unique Méditerranée and the first chronographs 4888 and 4889 that opened the market for them. The models U-Boot, Plongeur No. 1, and Le Chronographe sealed Boiocchi's success, and the Atelier, Technicum, and Firshire collections have already begun to write chapters of watch history all their own.
The diver's watch Le Plongeur has developed into an evergreen for Paul Picot. Featuring a unidirectionally rotating bezel outfitted with polished, angular numerals in relief on a granular background and an additional gripping edge, this powerful watch is just as elegant as it is practical, and just as attractive as it is robust—not every functional diver's watch needs to look like an iron lung. The middle ring made of hardened plastic that had originally served to reduce friction between the bezel and the case now serves an aesthetic purpose with its yellow signal coloring. In this way the Plongeur C-Type has evolved into a yacht club cult classic.
The somewhat neglected product family Gentleman has been defined anew for the 2004/2005 season and has, above all, been given larger dimensions. The first introduction of the line's new era is the Gentleman Chronograph GMT with a 42-mm case diameter. Based on the reliable ETA Valjoux 7750 caliber, a stylishly designed and not too nostalgic chronograph was created that, along with symmetrically arranged totalizers, displays a discrete 24-hour sweep hand. To display a second time zone, this hand can be set independently of the main hands in increments of one hour.

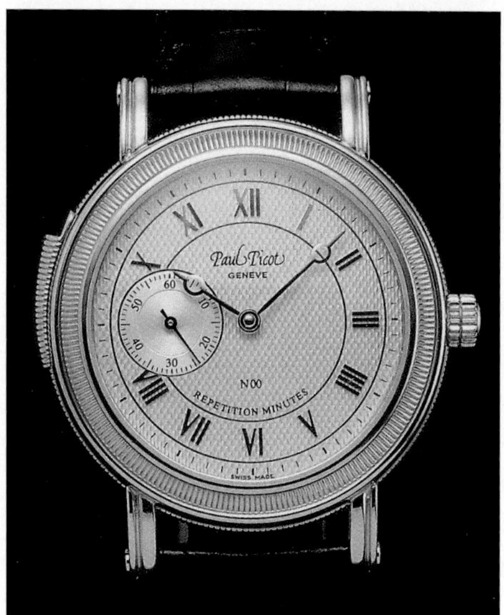

Atelier 818 Minute Repeater

Reference number: 153
Movement: manual winding, PP 818, ø 27.60 mm, height 5.70 mm; 32 jewels; 18.000 vph
Functions: hours, minutes, subsidiary seconds; hour, quarter hour, and minute repeater
Case: rose gold, ø 39.5 mm, height 10.2 mm; sapphire crystal; transparent case back
Band: reptile skin, buckle
Remarks: numbered edition
Price: $177,990

Atelier Chronograph Rattrapante

Reference number: 100
Movement: manual winding, PP 310 (base Venus 179); vintage *manufacture* caliber from the 1940s, reworked to include calendar cadrature
Functions: hours, minutes, subsidiary seconds; split-seconds chronograph; date, day, month, moon phase
Case: yellow gold, ø 42 mm, height 14.9 mm; sapphire crystal; transparent case back; water-resistant to 50 m
Band: reptile skin, buckle
Price: $105,990
Variations: in platinum

Atelier Technicum

Reference number: 102
Movement: automatic, PP 8888 (base ETA 7750); ø 30 mm, height 8.4 mm; 28 jewels; 28,800 vph, certified chronometer (C.O.S.C.); solid gold rotor
Functions: hours, minutes, subsidiary seconds; split-seconds chronograph; date, day; power reserve display
Case: rose gold, ø 40 mm, height 15 mm; sapphire crystal; transparent case back; screw-in crown; water-resistant to 50 m
Band: reptile skin, buckle
Price: $32,000
Variations: in yellow gold; in stainless steel

Majestic Chrono Rattrapante

Reference number: 0521 R
Movement: automatic, PP 1290 (base Jaquet 8932); ø 30 mm, height 7.9 mm; 25 jewels; 28,800 vph, certified chronometer (C.O.S.C.); solid gold rotor
Functions: hours, minutes, subsidiary seconds; split-seconds chronograph
Case: rose gold, 50.5 x 44.5 mm, height 14.50 mm; sapphire crystal; transparent case back; water-resistant to 50 m
Band: reptile skin, buckle
Price: $34,500
Variations: in yellow gold; in white gold; in stainless steel

Majestic Chronograph

Reference number: 0533 Y
Movement: automatic, ETA 7751, ø 30 mm, height 7.9 mm; 25 jewels; 28,800 vph, certified chronometer (C.O.S.C.); solid gold rotor
Functions: hours, minutes, subsidiary seconds; chronograph; date, day, month, moon phase; 24-hour display
Case: yellow gold, 50.5 x 44.5 mm, height 14.40 mm; sapphire crystal; transparent case back; water-resistant to 50 m
Band: reptile skin, buckle
Price: $25,890
Variations: in rose gold; in white gold; in stainless steel

Firshire Tonneau 3000 Regulateur

Reference number: 0740
Movement: automatic, PP 1100 (base ETA 2892-A2); ø 25.6 mm, height 3.6 mm (base movement); 30 jewels; 28,800 vph, certified chronometer (C.O.S.C.)
Functions: hours, (off-center) minutes, subsidiary seconds; date; power reserve display
Case: stainless steel, 52 x 40.5 mm, height 12.40 mm; sapphire crystal
Band: reptile skin, buckle
Price: $8,300

Firshire Tonneau 3000 Retrograde

Reference number: 0773
Movement: automatic, PP 1300 (base ETA 2892-A2); ø 25.6 mm, height 3.6 mm (base movement); 34 jewels; 28,800 vph, certified chronometer (C.O.S.C.)
Functions: hours, minutes, subsidiary seconds (retrograde, 30 seconds)
Case: stainless steel, 52 x 40.5 mm, height 12.20 mm; sapphire crystal
Band: reptile skin, buckle
Price: $6,600

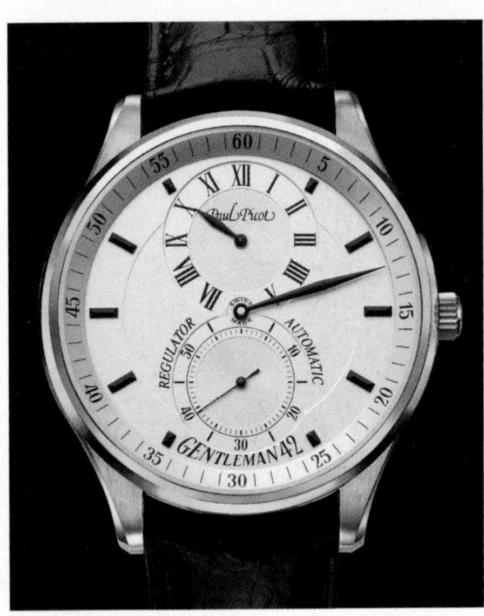

Gentleman Regulator

Reference number: 4114
Movement: automatic, PP 1000 (base ETA 2892 with module 3305); ø 25.6 mm, height 3.6 mm; 21 jewels (base movement); 28,800 vph
Functions: hours, (off-center) minutes, subsidiary seconds
Case: stainless steel, ø 42 mm, height 9.7 mm; sapphire crystal; water-resistant to 50 m
Band: reptile skin, buckle
Price: $4,400
Variations: with stainless steel bracelet

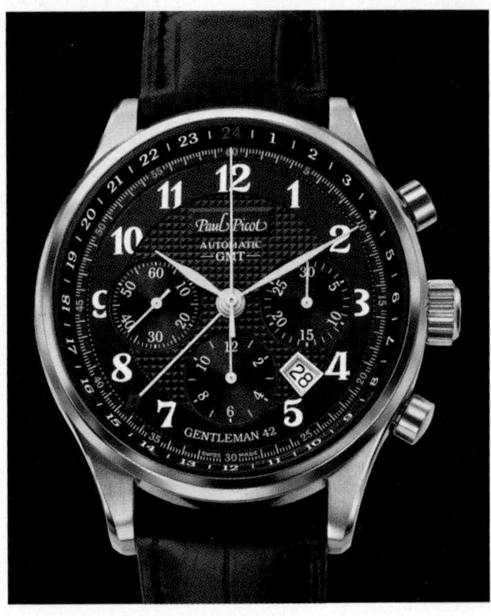

Gentleman Chrono GMT

Reference number: 2031 S
Movement: automatic, PP 8104 (base ETA 7750); ø 30 mm, height 7.9 mm; 25 jewels; 28,800 vph, with Tricompax dial train modification
Functions: hours, minutes, subsidiary seconds; chronograph; date; 24-hour display (second time zone)
Case: stainless steel, ø 42 mm, height 14.65 mm; sapphire crystal; screw-in crown; water-resistant to 50 m
Band: reptile skin, buckle
Price: $5,600
Variations: with stainless steel bracelet; in rose gold

Gentleman Chronographe

Reference number: 4109
Movement: automatic, ETA 7750 modified, ø 30 mm, height 7.9 mm; 25 jewels; 28,800 vph, with Bicompax dial train modification
Functions: hours, minutes, subsidiary seconds; chronograph
Case: stainless steel, ø 42 mm, height 14.8 mm; sapphire crystal; screw-in crown; water-resistant to 50 m
Band: reptile skin, buckle
Price: $4,500
Variations: with stainless steel bracelet

Le Plongeur C-Type Date

Reference number: 4117
Movement: automatic, ETA 2824-2, ø 25.6 mm, height 4.6 mm; 25 jewels; 28,800 vph, certified chronometer (C.O.S.C.)
Functions: hours, minutes, sweep seconds; date
Case: stainless steel, ø 43 mm, height 13.3 mm; unidirectionally rotating bezel with 60-minute scale; sapphire crystal; screw-in crown; water-resistant to 300 m
Band: rubber, folding clasp with wetsuit extension
Price: $4,000
Variations: with stainless steel bracelet

Le Plongeur C-Type Chronograph

Reference number: 4116
Movement: automatic, ETA 7750, ø 30 mm, height 7.9 mm; 25 jewels; 28,800 vph, certified chronometer (C.O.S.C.)
Functions: hours, minutes, subsidiary seconds; chronograph; date
Case: stainless steel, ø 43 mm, height 16.3 mm; unidirectionally rotating bezel with 60-minute scale; sapphire crystal; screw-in crown and buttons; water-resistant to 300 m
Band: rubber, folding clasp with wetsuit extension
Price: $7,000
Variations: with stainless steel bracelet

A PRACTICAL GUIDE

PRUNING

How and when to prune for better shrubs, trees, fruit, and climbers

PETER McHOY
Foreword by Elvin McDonald

This invaluable guide illustrates how to prune hundreds of shrubs, trees, and climbers, enhancing the beauty, health, and productivity of plants.

"Indispensible. Indeed, it is the best book I have ever seen on this vital subject. . . . If you don't own an easy-to-follow pruning guide, this book is highly recommended."
—Horticulture

By Peter McHoy
Foreword by Elvin McDonald
300 full-color illustrations
240 pages · 7½ × 9¾ in. · Cloth
ISBN 1-55859-634-8 · $35.00

Published by ABBEVILLE PRESS
116 West 23rd Street, New York, N.Y. 10011
1-800-ARTBOOK (in U.S. only)
Also available wherever fine books are sold
Visit us at www.abbeville.com

Poljot-International

There is hardly a private watch collection in Europe that does not include at least a Buran chronograph or a Poljot alarm watch. Following the political upheaval in Eastern Europe, huge numbers of somewhat exotic-looking watches appeared on the black market, and few could resist the temptation to buy a robust mechanical watch with a Swiss family tree for comparatively little outlay.
The great appeal of watches produced by the First Moscow Watch Factory to collectors is the fact that various Swiss mechanical movements were able to survive in exile in Russia following the quartz boom of the 1970s. In addition to alarm movements by A. Schild SA, the Poljot watchmakers also acquired complete production facilities from the Swiss in the mid seventies, including design blueprints for Venus Caliber 188, the successor of which, following the merger, was manufactured under the name of Valjoux Caliber 7734. In the meantime the original automatic Caliber 2416 designed by the Second Moscow Watch Factory has gotten some stiff competition from Switzerland: Since 1998 the company has been purchasing large quantities of the ETA Caliber 2671.
The First Moscow Watch Factory is at the forefront of the many privatized Russian companies now entering the global business community and the free-market economy. It is not difficult to imagine the powers of persuasion needed to convince factory workers used to seeing millions of simple watches designed to meet their basic needs to suddenly accept western quality standards for luxury goods. With the foundation of Poljot Uhrenvertrieb GmbH in Germany, the partially privatized watch factory, in which the city of Moscow also has a share, has created a first export outlet. In Germany's Alzenau, five watchmakers monitor the quality of the movements and cases supplied from Russia. Following a visual inspection and a rate test, each individual watch is provided with an international guarantee certificate as well as a hand-written rate certificate complete with serial number and the signature of the watchmaker who carried out the test. "Good quality at a fair price," says Alexander Schorochov, managing director of the German Poljot Uhrenvertrieb GmbH, "is the only way of surviving long-term in the international marketplace."

Alexander Schorochov presents the first Mikhail chronograph to its namesake, former Soviet president Mikhail Gorbachev.

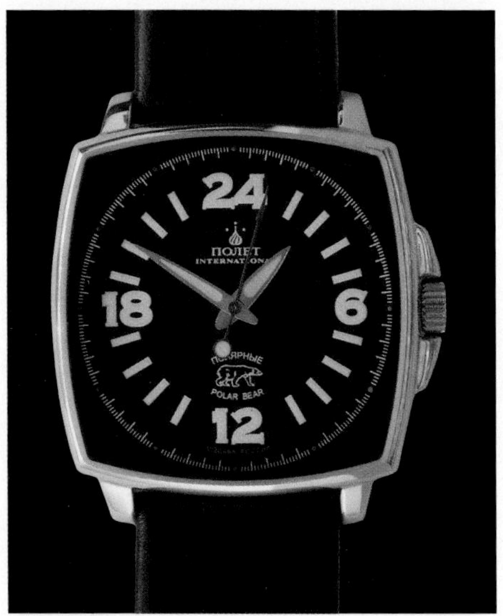

Polar Bear

Reference number: 2423.2004792
Movement: manual winding, Vostok 2423, ø 24 mm, height 3.95 mm; 17 jewels; 19,800 vph, finished with decoration and blued screws
Functions: hours (24-hour display), minutes, sweep seconds
Case: stainless steel, 36 x 36 mm, height 8 mm; mineral crystal; transparent case back
Band: leather, buckle
Price: 260 euros
Variations: different dial variations

Arktika Automatic

Reference number: 2416.2004906
Movement: automatic, Vostok 2416.B, ø 24 mm, height 6.87 mm; 31 jewels; 19,800 vph, decorated with blued screws
Functions: hours, minutes, sweep seconds; date
Case: stainless steel, 36 x 36 mm, height 10 mm; mineral crystal; transparent case back
Band: leather, buckle
Price: 370 euros
Variations: different dial variations; with stainless steel bracelet

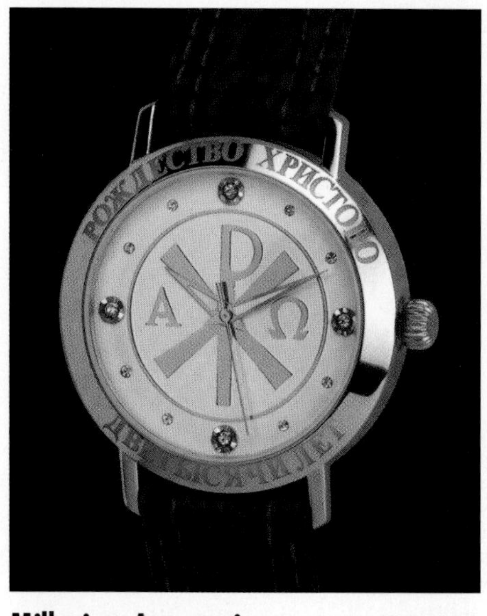

Millenium Automatic

Reference number: 2416.1926010
Movement: automatic, Slava 2416, ø 24 mm, height 6.5 mm; 21 jewels; 18,000 vph
Functions: hours, minutes, sweep seconds
Case: red gold, ø 35.6 mm, height 12.15 mm; engraved bezel; mineral crystal
Band: leather, folding clasp
Remarks: dial with zirconia markers
Price: 1,200 euros
Variations: in women's size with Tschaika Caliber 1601

Volga 2

Reference number: 31681.6441611
Movement: manual winding, Poljot 31681, ø 31 mm, height 7.38 mm; 23 jewels; 21,600 vph, finished with decoration and blued screws
Functions: hours, minutes, subsidiary seconds; chronograph; date; 24-hour display
Case: stainless steel, 38 x 35 mm, height 14 mm; sapphire crystal; transparent case back
Band: leather, folding clasp
Price: 479 euros
Variations: different dial colors

Chronograph Nikolai II

Reference number: 3133.1956612
Movement: manual winding, Poljot 3133, ø 31 mm, height 7.38 mm; 23 jewels; 21,600 vph
Functions: hours, minutes, subsidiary seconds; chronograph; date
Case: yellow gold, ø 37 mm, height 12 mm; mineral crystal; transparent case back
Band: leather, folding clasp
Price: 2,600 euros
Variations: in white gold (2,900 euros); with hand-engraved and gold-plated movement (surcharge 540 euros)

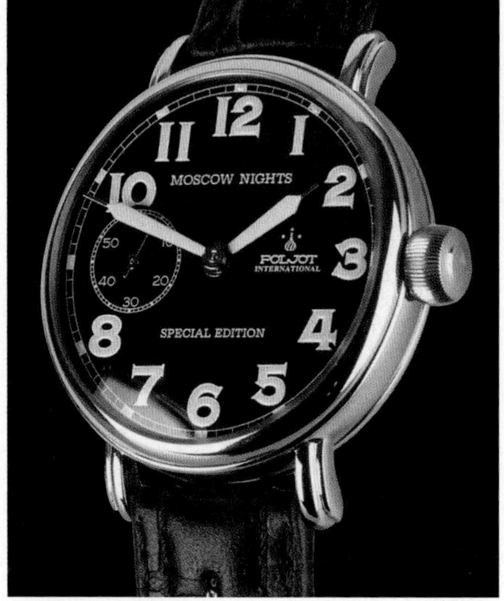

Moscow Nights

Reference number: 36022.1940862
Movement: manual winding, Molnija 3602, ø 36 mm, height 4.6 mm; 18 jewels; 18,000 vph
Functions: hours, minutes, subsidiary seconds
Case: stainless steel, ø 43 mm, height 13.5 mm; mineral crystal; transparent case back
Band: leather, buckle
Price: 450 euros
Variations: with black, blue or white dial; surcharge for gold-plated movement 40 euros

Porsche Design

An absolute world innovation surprised visitors to Baselworld 2004: Porsche Design's Indicator, the first chronograph to display the hours and minutes of stopped time stopped digitally — but in a purely mechanical manner, of course. First-class legibility was the primary goal of the chronograph's design as Eterna's managing director and the project's initiator, Ernst F. Seyr, explains: "The most important demand on the Indicator was to give people as little room as possible to misinterpret." The project as a whole leaves absolutely no room for misinterpretation: The Indicator is proof of horological skill of a special kind, simultaneously waking the brands Porsche Design and Eterna, which are both created under one roof in the Swiss watch town Grenchen, out of their Sleeping Beauty-like sleep.

The Porsche Design brand has always had its finger on the pulse of time regarding design, for it is Professor Ferdinand Alexander Porsche who is responsible for it. "The greatest thing that can happen to a designer is to have complete control of the production of his idea, from the beginning sketch to the finished product," the master of German product design is on record as saying. "But it can quickly turn into a nightmare."

To have complete responsibility for material, production quality, marketing, distribution, and after-sales service does require a few virtues foreign to most designers, and actually even goes against the grain in most cases. It entails compromising at the right time and the right place, not only accepting the hated red pencil but even using it oneself, exercising a measure of discipline and objectivity unheard-of in artistic circles, and the ability to let the head of production or distribution have a say.

With this in mind, it is easy to see that Porsche Design AG's takeover of the established watch company Eterna was a very professional move, and the quality of the new products sporting the label Porsche Design speaks a very lucid language. First-class and excellently worked materials, classic yet modern cases, and clean design completely resisting superficial decoration constitute the characteristics of watches by Porsche Design. These are products that homogeneously fit into the line of other items created by F. A. Porsche's design studio. The company's style includes material combinations that may seem unusual at first glance, but appear quite harmonious when the product is looked at more closely. There is, for example, the PGC (**P**orsche **G**old **C**hronograph) with gold case and rubber strap as well as the PAT (**P**orsche **A**luminum **T**itanium) with a black anodized aluminum case and a bezel and folding clasp made of titanium.

The complete case of the Indicator is fittingly made of titanium, and it was also designed by F. A. Porsche. Every year, about fifty pieces at a price of around $85,000 will be manufactured — which makes the Indicator not only one of the most complicated wristwatches in the world, but also one of the most exclusive.

PTR Titanium Rattrapante

Reference number: 6613.10.50
Movement: automatic, ETA 7750 with rattrapante module, ø 30 mm, 7.9 mm; 25 jewels; 28,800 vph, rotor in titanium with heavy metal weight
Functions: hours, minutes, subsidiary seconds; split-seconds chronograph; date
Case: titanium, ø 42 mm, height 16.2 mm; sapphire crystal; transparent case back; screw-in crown; water-resistant to 100 m
Band: titanium, folding clasp
Price: $10,150

PTC Titanium Chronograph

Reference number: 6612.10.50
Movement: automatic, ETA 2894, ø 28.6 mm, height 6.1 mm; 37 jewels; 28,800 vph, rotor in titanium with heavy metal weight
Functions: hours, minutes, subsidiary seconds; chronograph; date
Case: titanium, ø 42 mm, height 14.85 mm; sapphire crystal; transparent case back; water-resistant to 100 m
Band: rubber, folding clasp
Price: $5,070
Variations: with titanium link bracelet ($5,750)

PGC Gold Chronograph

Reference number: 6612.69.50
Movement: automatic, ETA 2894, ø 28.6 mm, height 6.1 mm; 37 jewels; 28,800 vph, rotor in titanium with heavy metal weight
Functions: hours, minutes, subsidiary seconds; chronograph; date
Case: rose gold, ø 42 mm, height 14.85 mm; sapphire crystal; transparent case back; screw-in crown; water-resistant to 100 m
Band: rubber, buckle
Price: $13,310
Variations: in white gold

Aluminum Titanium Chronograph

Reference number: 6612.14.50
Movement: automatic, ETA 2894, ø 28.6 mm, height 6.1 mm; 37 jewels; 28,800 vph, rotor in titanium with heavy metal weight
Functions: hours, minutes, subsidiary seconds; chronograph; date
Case: titanium/aluminum, ø 42 mm, height 14.8 mm; sapphire crystal; transparent case back; screw-in crown; water-resistant to 100 m
Band: rubber, buckle
Price: $5,070
Variations: with black titanium link bracelet ($5,750)

PO11 Titanium

Reference number: 6625.10
Movement: automatic, ETA 7750, ø 30 mm, 7.9 mm; 25 jewels; 28,800 vph
Functions: hours, minutes, subsidiary seconds; chronograph; date, day
Case: titanium, ø 40.5 mm, height 14.2 mm; sapphire crystal; screw-in crown; water-resistant to 120 m
Band: rubber, folding clasp
Price: $3,320
Variations: with titanium link bracelet; in stainless steel

PAT Aluminum Titanium Chronograph Quartz

Reference number: 6610.14.50.1085
Movement: quartz, ETA 251.272
Functions: hours, minutes, subsidiary seconds; chronograph; date
Case: aluminum, matte black anodized, ø 39.5 mm, height 11.7 mm; bezel with tachymeter scale; sapphire crystal; screw-in crown; water-resistant to 100 m
Band: rubber, folding clasp
Price: $2,530
Variations: with titanium link bracelet

Rado

With their watch cases made of hard metal and ceramic in distinct designs, Rado watches have been able to capture a special position for themselves on the watch scene, easily spotted at big events. Rado is a brand that has been active in tennis for twenty years, even sponsoring the French Open for more than ten years. Rado has now honored this partnership with the model Sintra Chrono Roland Garros. This special model is recognizable by its Roland Garros logo, above which the second hand makes its rounds, and a special bezel marked with the numbers 0, 15, 30, and 40 — the numbers that count the points in a game of tennis. Additionally, every watch is numbered on its case back. This special model is available either with a matte black rubber strap or a platinum-colored ceramic bracelet. Bracelets and watch cases made of hard metal and ceramic are just as characteristic of Rado as the classic logo comprising the company's name in capital letters.

The history of this brand began in the year 1957 when the first watches bearing the name Rado were produced. The cornerstone for its international success story was, however, laid by Rado in 1962. At that time, the Swiss watch company surprised the world with a revolutionary invention: the Rado DiaStar, the first truly scratch-resistant watch ever, sporting a case made of sintered tungsten carbide. In 1985 the parent company, the Swatch Group, decided to utilize Rado's know-how and its extensive experience in developing materials. From then on the brand intensified its research activities at its home in Lengnau, Switzerland, and continued to produce only watches with extremely hard cases.

Although the DiaStar case was manufactured by mixing tungsten or titanium carbide powder with a binding agent, subjecting it to pressure equal to 1,000 bar, and sintering it at 1,450°C, modern Rado models are made of ceramic. This is the same type of material that serves the space shuttle as heat protection, that keeps modern water faucets functioning perfectly, and without which bone surgery would be unthinkable. Engineers at this watch brand still have to continually break new ground, taking on the role of industry pioneers. The company already holds more than thirty patents for material development. When producing ceramic cases, various powders, already mixed together with binding agents and additives to later create the desired color, are pressed into molds to make the cases, which are then fired and finally polished with diamond powder.

Within the Swatch Group, Rado is the most successful individual brand in the upper price segment. The watches, whose ultra-hard, high-gloss cases in characteristic design have become their own trademark, are distributed worldwide at more than 8,000 points of sale. This brand image was coined most strongly by the Ceramica model, which among others won the Red Dot award for high design quality given by German state North Rhine-Westphalia's Design Center in the 1990s.

Sintra Automatic

Reference number: R 13 598 10 2
Movement: automatic, ETA 2892-A2, ø 25.6 mm, height 3.6 mm; 21 jewels; 28,800 vph
Functions: hours, minutes, sweep seconds; date
Case: ceramic, 44.2 x 34.6 mm, height 11.4 mm; sapphire crystal
Band: ceramic, double folding clasp in titanium
Price: $2,400
Variations: different dial variations; with black rubber strap; also with quartz movement

Integral Chronograph

Reference number: R 20 591 10 2
Movement: quartz, ETA 251471.0
Functions: hours, minutes, subsidiary seconds; chronograph; date
Case: stainless steel, 36.2 x 30.2 mm, height 9.9 mm; sapphire crystal
Band: stainless steel/ceramic, folding clasp
Price: $2,200
Variations: with blue dial; also in black

Sintra Chronograph

Reference number: R 13 434 11 2
Movement: quartz, ETA 251471.0
Functions: hours, minutes, subsidiary seconds; chronograph; date
Case: ceramic, 44.5 x 34 mm, height 11 mm; sapphire crystal
Band: ceramic, double folding clasp in titanium
Price: $2,500
Variations: with blue dial; also in black

Ceramica Multi

Reference number: R 21 386 15 2
Movement: quartz, ETA 988332
Functions: hours, minutes; eight additional digital functions (chronograph, perpetual calendar, second time zone, alarm, countdown)
Case: ceramic, 33 x 28 mm, height 7.5 mm; sapphire crystal
Band: ceramic, double folding clasp in titanium
Price: $1,790
Variations: in two sizes, also in black

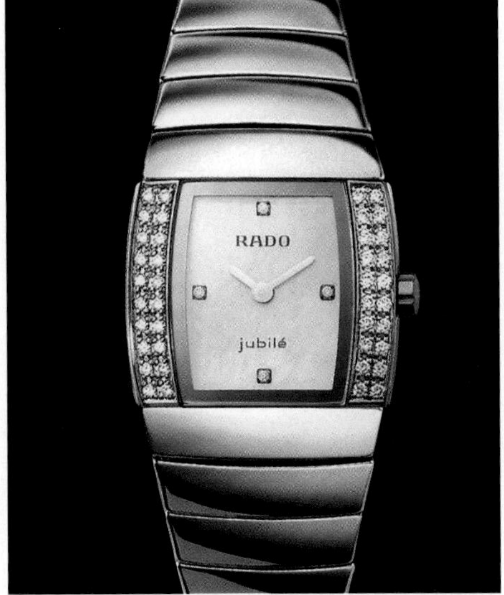

Sintra Superjubilé

Reference number: R 13 578 90 2
Movement: quartz, ETA 976001
Functions: hours, minutes
Case: ceramic, 28 x 21.5 mm, height 7.5 mm; case sides set with diamonds; sapphire crystal
Band: ceramic, double folding clasp in titanium
Price: $3,200
Variations: in two sizes, also with black, blue and pink dials

Integral

Reference number: R 20 282 19 2
Movement: quartz, ETA 256041
Functions: hours, minutes
Case: stainless steel, PVD-coated, 32 x 27 mm, height 7 mm; sapphire crystal
Band: stainless steel/ceramic, folding clasp
Price: $1,690
Variations: in three sizes, also in platinum color with blue dial

Auguste Reymond

The company Auguste Reymond, hailing from Tramelan in the Swiss Jura, has had a rather turbulent history, in some aspects absolutely typical of many smaller Swiss watch producers. Founded in 1898 by the twenty-seven-year-old Auguste Reymond, the company lost its independence to a large holding company along with many other brands in 1932 when Switzerland began its gigantic restructuring of the watch industry.
At the beginning, Auguste Reymond belonged to ASUAG, where it was in charge of distributing the brands ARSA and UNITAS. Later it changed hands to SSIH, and finally, to the SMH (today's Swatch Group). In 1984 the mayor of the village of Tramelan, James Choffat, bought back "his" watch factory and gave it its independence.
Only when the factory was put up for sale again in 1989 due to old age did Norbert and Thomas Loosli grab the opportunity to awaken Auguste Reymond to a new life with new models.
The young Thomas put his money on unconventional ideas, but ones of uncommonly good sense. He strives for a fresh, young image for the brand and concentrates on both mechanical movements and the fact that his watches remain financially reasonable for the consumer. This was how the collection Jazz came into being, so successful that it is continually being expanded. Through the years, a stately model palette has emerged consisting of mech-anical watches with musical names such as Ragtime, Charleston, and Dixieland. Even so-called day-to-day complications are offered. A GMT indicator, a large decentral "doctor's" seconds subdial, a power reserve, a full calendar, and of course, various chronographs are all available.
Since the motto"tradition et qualité" has been carried in the company's logo for the last hundred years, a few specialties outfitted with vintage Unitas and ARSA calibers, which have slept for the last sixty years in Auguste Reymond's storeroom, now completely restored and newly decorated, have been created as an homage to the Auguste Reymond "of old."

Memphis

Reference number: 712003,0
Movement: automatic, ETA/Valjoux 7751, ø 30 mm, height 7.9 mm; 21 jewels; 28,800 vph, finely decorated; côtes de Genève; gold-plated rotor
Functions: hours, minutes, subsidiary seconds; chronograph; date, day, month, moon phase; 24-hour display
Case: stainless steel, ø 38.5 mm, height 13.3 mm; bezel in 18-karat yellow gold; sapphire crystal; transparent case back
Band: leather, buckle
Price: $3,000
Variations: in stainless steel; without moon phases and calendar

Boston

Reference number: 69170-56
Movement: automatic, ETA 2824-2, ø 25.6 mm, height 4.6 mm; 25 jewels; 28,800 vph, finely finished
Functions: hours, minutes, sweep seconds; date
Case: stainless steel, 42 x 31 mm, height 11 mm; sapphire crystal; transparent case back
Band: leather, buckle
Price: $750
Variations: in women's size 37.5 x 25.5 mm/Caliber ETA 2671; with steel bracelet ($825)

Pittsburgh

Reference number: 69180
Movement: automatic, AR 14000, (base ETA 2892-A2); ø 26 mm, height 5.2 mm; 21 jewels; 28,800 vph, finely decorated; côtes de Genève; gold-plated rotor
Functions: hours, minutes, subsidiary seconds; large date
Case: stainless steel, 39 x 39 mm, height 13.3 mm; sapphire crystal; transparent case back
Band: leather, buckle
Price: $3,000
Variations: as chronograph (Caliber ETA 7750 and 7751); as automatic alarm (AS 5008)

Mobile

Reference number: 69104
Movement: automatic, AR 9000, (base ETA 2892-A2 with Kalendermodule von Dubois-Dépraz); ø 26 mm, height 6 mm; 25 jewels (base caliber); 28,800 vph, finely decorated; côtes de Genève; gold-plated rotor; blued screws
Functions: hours, minutes, sweep seconds; date, day, month, moon phase
Case: stainless steel, ø 36.5 mm, height 11 mm; sapphire crystal; transparent case back
Band: leather, buckle
Price: $1,700
Variations: with power reserve display; as chronograph

Ballad

Reference number: 66100-50
Movement: manual winding, Unitas 6580, ø 19.6 mm, height 3.95 mm; 17 jewels; 18,000 vph, original movement from the A. Reymond *manufacture* from 1960, completely restored and newly decorated; 999 pieces
Functions: hours, minutes, subsidiary seconds; date
Case: stainless steel, 43.5 x 28 mm, height 8.2 mm; sapphire crystal; transparent case back
Band: leather, buckle
Price: $800

The Gentlemen's Watch

Reference number: 211100
Movement: manual winding, Unitas 6425, ø 29.4 mm, height 4 mm; 17 jewels; 18,000 vph, original movement from the A. Reymond *manufacture* from 1960, completely restored and newly decorated; 999 pieces
Functions: hours, minutes, subsidiary seconds; date
Case: rose gold, ø 35 mm, height 10.3 mm; sapphire crystal; transparent case back
Band: ostrich leather strap, buckle
Remarks: limited to 50 pieces
Price: $7,500
Variations: with anthracite-colored dial; in steel ($1,100)

RGM

The United States isn't exactly a hotbed of watchmaking. Granted, there are always exceptions, but in general one would be hard-pressed to count American watch companies on two hands. And of those that could be named, the management offices might be located in the States though the watches themselves are invariably produced in the Far East or are "Swiss made." A proud moniker for a watch to wear, to be sure, but there is something very courageous about starting a luxury watch company in the United States and not falling back on this certain sign of quality as it is seen today.

Roland Murphy is certainly courageous. Originally hailing from Maryland, he discovered at a fairly early age that he has a natural talent with his hands. From woodworking at a vocational school he then began to make cabinets at a clock company, finally moving on to constructing his own clocks. At this point his proclivity for watch and clock movements became apparent, and he went to Lancaster, Pennsylvania's Bowman Technical School and then to Neuchâtel, Switzerland, to graduate from the famed Wostep program. A few years with one of the industry's biggest names, the SMH (now the Swatch Group), taught him the rest of what he needed to know about the watch business. Here he learned the important features of design, marketing, and business.

In the early 1990s he took that final step and started his own company, his collection soon freely disposing of almost all complications known today. Murphy's rectangular beveled case, first introduced in 1994 and unique to the RGM brand, has become the identifying trait of his William Penn collection, a series of watches created to honor the memory of William Penn and the state of Pennsylvania.

Expansion is the order of the day at RGM. Recently moving into new premises in Mount Joy, Pennsylvania, the company now employs three full-time watchmakers alongside Murphy as well as an in-house art director for all of the non-horological creative work that any watch company must be able to complete well in addition to its chief task of making watches. The historical building, from the 1930s era, now housing RGM was originally a bank, providing more than enough space for these watchmakers to breathe life into mechanical parts made of precious metals. One big advantage of being in a former bank is the huge safe still located on the premises, which has been duly decorated by the company's art director. Murphy has financed such expansion projects by becoming the U.S. service center for such top-quality brands as Girard-Perregaux and JeanRichard.

Custom-made watches can also be ordered from RGM, completely according to the specifications of the customer, a rarity in the United States, and in fact anywhere else, in this quality. While the predicate "Swiss made" might be worth its weight in gold for most watch companies, Roland Murphy displays the only predicate he needs on his dials: "RGM."

William Penn Power Reserve-Moon Phase

Reference number: 121M
Movement: manually wound, RGM caliber (base Jaquet); shaped movement; 22 jewels, bridges and plates with perlage and côtes de Genève
Functions: hours, minutes; power reserve, moon phase
Case: rose gold, 40 x 28 mm, height 7.9 mm; sapphire crystal; sapphire crystal case back
Band: leather, folding clasp
Remarks: solid gold, silvered dial
Price: $12,500
Variations: in stainless steel ($6,495)

Grande Pilot's

Reference number: 150
Movement: manually wound, modified Unitas 6498, 17 jewels, screw balance, bridges and plates with perlage and côtes de Genève
Functions: hours, minutes, subsidiary seconds
Case: stainless steel, ø 42 mm, height 10.5 mm; sapphire crystal; sapphire crystal case back
Band: leather, buckle
Price: $2,300
Variations: with blue dial; on stainless steel bracelet ($2,600)

Pilot's Professional Automatic

Reference number: 151P
Movement: automatic, modified ETA 2892-A2, 21 jewels, bridges and plates with perlage and côtes de Genève
Functions: hours, minutes, sweep seconds
Case: stainless steel, ø 38.5 mm, height 10 mm; sapphire crystal; sapphire crystal case back
Band: leather, buckle
Price: $1,995
Variations: with black Carbon Sport or ostrich leather strap; with stainless steel bracelet ($2,395)

Classic Automatic

Reference number: 151EB
Movement: automatic, modified ETA 2892-A2, 21 jewels, bridges and plates with perlage and côtes de Genève
Functions: hours, minutes, sweep seconds; date
Case: stainless steel, ø 38.5 mm, height 10 mm; sapphire crystal; sapphire crystal case back
Band: stainles steel, folding clasp
Remarks: solid silver dial hand-guilloché
Price: $5,200
Variations: on strap ($4,800); dial also available in copper or all silver; in 18-karat rose gold

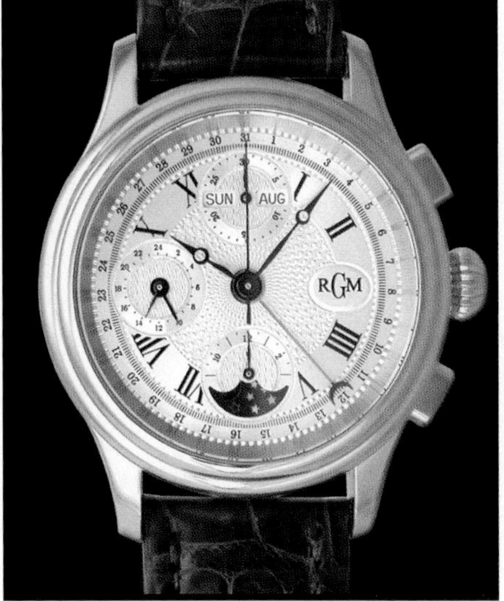

Automatic Moonphase Chronograph

Reference number: 160M
Movement: automatic, ETA/Valjoux 7751, bridges and plates with perlage and côtes de Genève
Functions: hours, minutes, subsidiary seconds; date, day; chronograph; month, moon phase, 24-hour display
Case: stainless steel, ø 38.2 mm, height 13 mm; sapphire crystal; sapphire crystal case back
Band: leather, folding clasp
Remarks: solid silver dial hand-guilloché
Price: $5,900

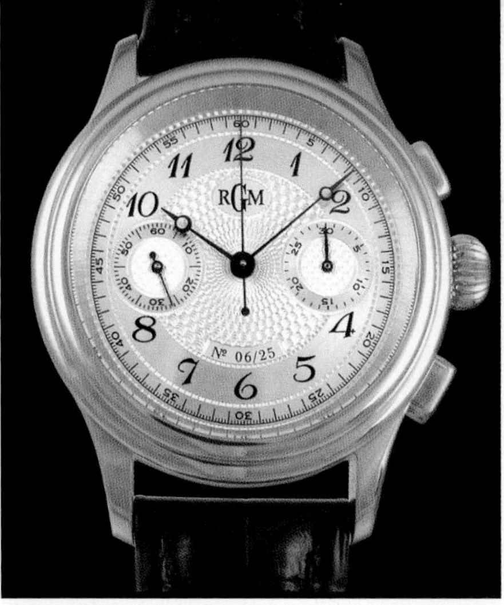

Master Chronograph

Reference number: 161
Movement: manually wound, Valjoux 23, 17 jewels, bridges and plates with perlage and hand-engraved
Functions: hours, minutes, subsidiary seconds; chronograph
Case: rose gold, ø 38.5 mm, height 12.6 mm; sapphire crystal; sapphire crystal case back
Band: leather, rose gold buckle
Remarks: solid silver dial hand-guilloché
Price: $26,000

Rolex

So many legends begin with the words, "Once upon a time ..." And this is how the legendary story of a company that revolutionized the watch industry in the twentieth century also begins. Once upon a time in the year 1905, the then-twenty-four-year-old German Hans Wilsdorf founded Wilsdorf & Davis Co. in London. This was a company specializing in the distribution of watches, and Wilsdorf rechristened it Rolex three years later. After the ambitious Wilsdorf moved the company to Switzerland, he registered Montres Rolex S.A. in 1920. At a time when men wore pocket watches almost exclusively, the far-sighted entrepreneur put his money on the wristwatch. Not in the least thanks to Hans Wilsdorf and his fundamental inventions concerning water-resistant, shockproof watches with automatic winding as well as the unheard-of precision of Rolex watch movements, the wristwatch began its unstoppable path to glory in the first decades of the past century.

Time flies, and a Rolex continues to run tirelessly. Today, almost a century later, this watch brand is still setting standards — both in prestige and elegance. A Rolex is a watch that will last a lifetime: timelessly beautiful, unmistakable, and keeping its value.

Also a long time ago, in the year 1878, another success story began its run. Master watchmaker Gerhard D. Wempe laid the cornerstone for his reputable jewelry and watch store chain. In the 1960s, Rolex's first wristwatches were sold in Germany, where Wempe's headquarters are located. Hellmut Wempe, grandson of the company's founder, discovered the elegant and robust wristwatches in London. "Deciding what is a short-lived trend and what could become a classic is not always an easy job. These watches had the stuff of classics, however," he remembers. "My father Herbert didn't believe in these unknown watches, but he trusted my feeling for them. And their success proved us right." Rolex watches are still sold by Wempe, a branch of which can be found on Fifth Avenue in New York City, along with many other interesting finds, proving Wempe's feel for interesting timekeepers has not dwindled over the years.

Cellini Cellinium

Reference number: 5241/6
Movement: manual winding, Rolex 1240, ø 23.8 mm, height 3.77 mm; 17 jewels, glucydur balance with Microstella regulating screws
Functions: hours, minutes, subsidiary seconds
Case: platinum, ø 38 mm, height 6.3 mm; sapphire crystal
Band: reptile skin, folding clasp in platinum
Price: $12,850
Variations: with platinum buckle instead of deployant clasp ($10,600); different dial variations

Cellini Classic

Reference number: 5116/8
Movement: manual winding, Rolex 1602, ø 20.8 mm, height 2.35 mm; 20 jewels, glucydur balance with Microstella regulating screws
Functions: hours, minutes
Case: yellow gold, ø 32 mm, height 6.3 mm; sapphire crystal
Band: reptile skin, buckle
Price: $3,650
Variations: different dial variations

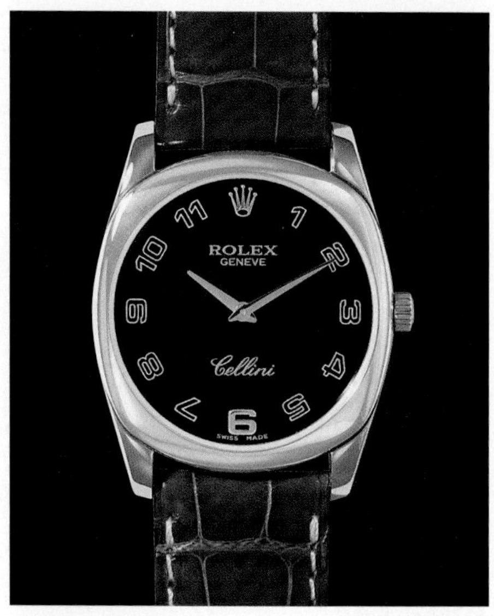

Cellini Danaos

Reference number: 4233/9
Movement: manual winding, Rolex 1602, ø 20.8 mm; height 2.35 mm; 20 jewels, glucydur balance with Microstella regulating screws
Functions: hours, minutes
Case: white gold, ø 32 mm, height 6.3 mm; sapphire crystal
Band: reptile skin, folding clasp
Price: $4,800
Variations: different dial variations

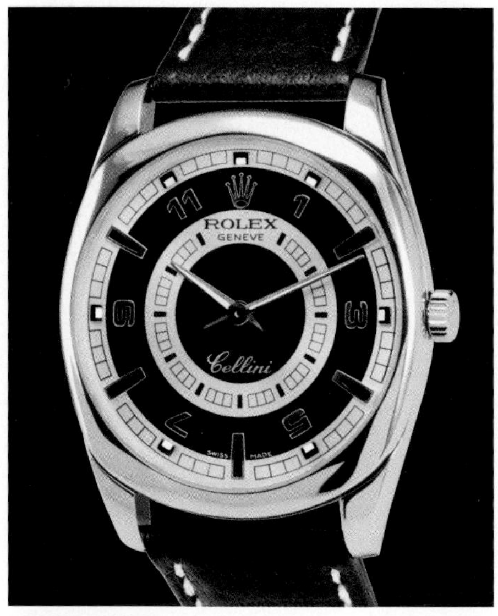

Cellini Danaos

Reference number: 4243/9
Movement: manual winding, Rolex 1602, ø 20.8 mm; height 2.35 mm; 20 jewels, glucydur balance with Microstella regulating screws
Functions: hours, minutes
Case: white gold, ø 38 mm, height 6.3 mm; sapphire crystal
Band: leather, folding clasp
Price: $5,700
Variations: different dial variations

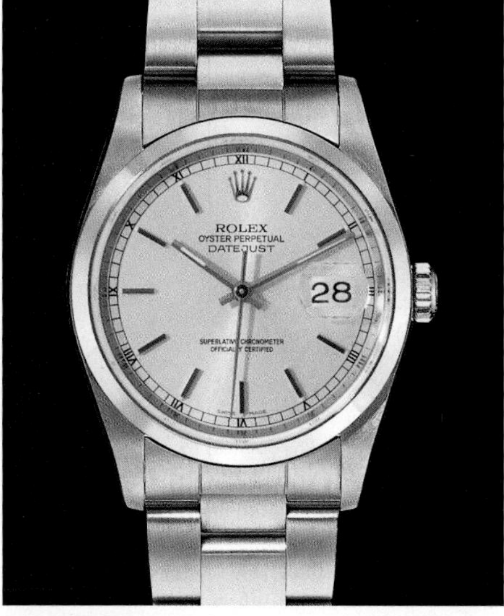

Oyster Perpetual Datejust

Reference number: 16200
Movement: automatic, Rolex 3155 (base Rolex 3135); ø 28.5 mm, height 6 mm; 31 jewels, Breguet balance spring, glucydur balance with Microstella regulating screws; certified chronometer (C.O.S.C.)
Functions: hours, minutes, sweep seconds; date
Case: stainless steel, ø 36 mm, height 11.8 mm; sapphire crystal with magnifying lens above the date display; screw-in crown; water-resistant to 100 m
Band: Oyster stainless steel, folding clasp
Price: $3,575
Variations: with Jubilé bracelet; different dial variations

Oyster Perpetual

Reference number: 14203M
Movement: automatic, Rolex 3130 (base Rolex 3135); ø 28.5 mm, height 5.85 mm; 31 jewels, Breguet balance spring, glucydur balance with Microstella regulating screws; certified chronometer (C.O.S.C.)
Functions: hours, minutes, sweep seconds
Case: stainless steel, ø 34 mm, height 11.1 mm; bezel in yellow gold; sapphire crystal; screw-in crown; water-resistant to 100 m
Band: Oyster stainless steel/yellow gold, folding clasp
Price: $5,000
Variations: different dial variations

Oyster Perpetual Date

Reference number: 15210
Movement: automatic, Rolex 3135, ø 28.5 mm, height 6 mm; 31 jewels, Breguet balance spring, glucydur balance with Microstella regulating screws; certified chronometer (C.O.S.C.)
Functions: hours, minutes, sweep seconds; date
Case: stainless steel, ø 34 mm, height 11.8 mm; bezel with hour reference scale; sapphire crystal with magnifying lens above the date display; screw-in crown; water-resistant to 100 m
Band: Oyster stainless steel, folding clasp
Price: $3,450
Variations: different dial variations

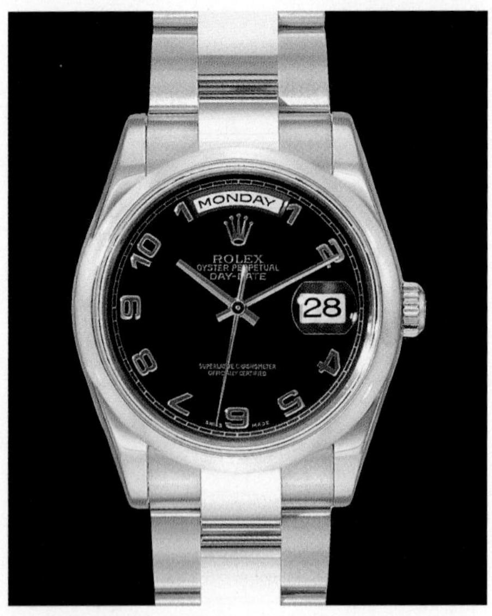

Oyster Perpetual Day-Date

Reference number: 118205
Movement: automatic, Rolex 3155 (base Rolex 3135); ø 29.3 mm, height 6.45 mm; 31 jewels, Breguet balance spring, glucydur balance with Microstella regulating screws; certified chronometer (C.O.S.C.)
Functions: hours, minutes, sweep seconds; date and day
Case: rose gold, ø 36 mm, height 11.9 mm; sapphire crystal with magnifying lens above the date display; screw-in crown; water-resistant to 100 m
Band: Oyster rose gold, folding clasp
Price: $17,850
Variations: with President bracelet; diverse dial variations

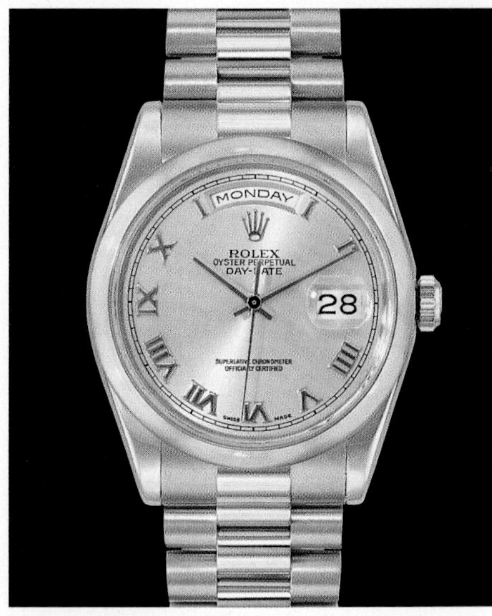

Oyster Perpetual Day-Date

Reference number: 118206
Movement: automatic, Rolex 3155 (base Rolex 3135); ø 29.3 mm, height 6.45 mm; 31 jewels, Breguet balance spring, glucydur balance with Microstella regulating screws; certified chronometer (C.O.S.C.)
Functions: hours, minutes, sweep seconds; date and day
Case: platinum, ø 36 mm, height 11.9 mm; sapphire crystal with magnifying lens above the date display; screw-in crown; water-resistant to 100 m
Band: President platinum, folding clasp
Price: $35,750
Variations: different dial variations

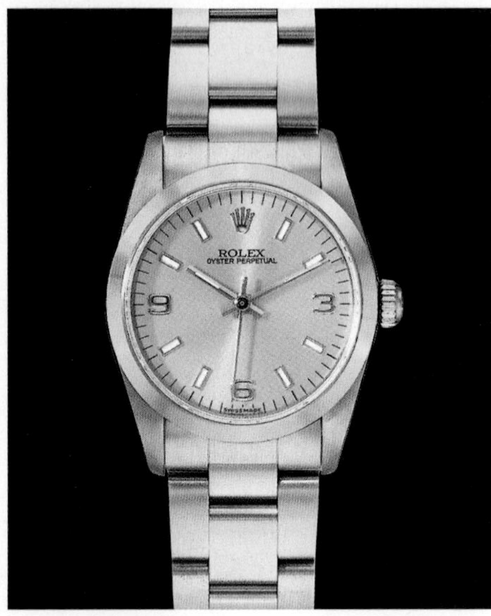

Oyster Perpetual

Reference number: 77080
Movement: automatic, Rolex 2230, ø 20 mm, height 5.4 mm; 31 jewels, Breguet balance spring, glucydur balance with Microstella regulating screws
Functions: hours, minutes, sweep seconds
Case: stainless steel, ø 31 mm, height 11.8 mm; sapphire crystal; screw-in crown; water-resistant to 100 m
Band: Oyster stainless steel, folding clasp
Price: $2,950
Variations: different dial variations

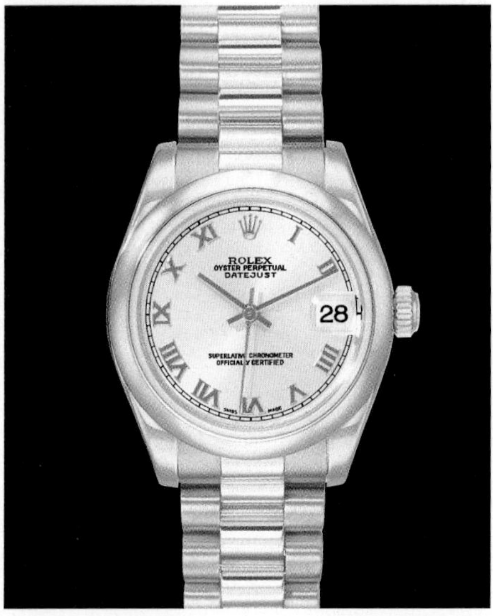

Oyster Perpetual Datejust

Reference number: 178245
Movement: automatic, Rolex 2235 (base Rolex 2230); ø 20 mm, height 5.95 mm; 31 jewels, Breguet balance spring, glucydur balance with Microstella regulating screws; certified chronometer (C.O.S.C.)
Functions: hours, minutes, sweep seconds; date
Case: rose gold, ø 31 mm, height 10.5 mm; sapphire crystal; screw-in crown; water-resistant to 100 m
Band: President rose gold, folding clasp
Price: $16,000
Variations: different dial variations

Oyster Perpetual Lady-Datejust

Reference number: 179165
Movement: automatic, Rolex 2235 (base Rolex 2230); ø 20 mm, height 5.95 mm; 31 jewels, Breguet balance spring, glucydur balance with Microstella regulating screws; certified chronometer (C.O.S.C.)
Functions: hours, minutes, sweep seconds; date
Case: rose gold, ø 26 mm, height 10.5 mm; sapphire crystal; screw-in crown; water-resistant to 100 m
Band: Oyster rose gold, folding clasp
Price: $17,500
Variations: different dial variations

Oyster Perpetual Lady-Datejust Pearlmaster

Reference number: 80319
Movement: automatic, Rolex 2235 (base Rolex 2230); ø 20 mm, height 5.95 mm; 31 jewels, Breguet balance spring, glucydur balance with Microstella regulating screws; certified chronometer (C.O.S.C.)
Functions: hours, minutes, sweep seconds; date
Case: white gold, ø 29 mm, height 10.3 mm; bezel set with 12 diamonds; sapphire crystal with magnifying lens above the date display; screw-in crown; water-resistant to 100 m
Band: Pearlmaster white gold, folding clasp
Price: $17,250

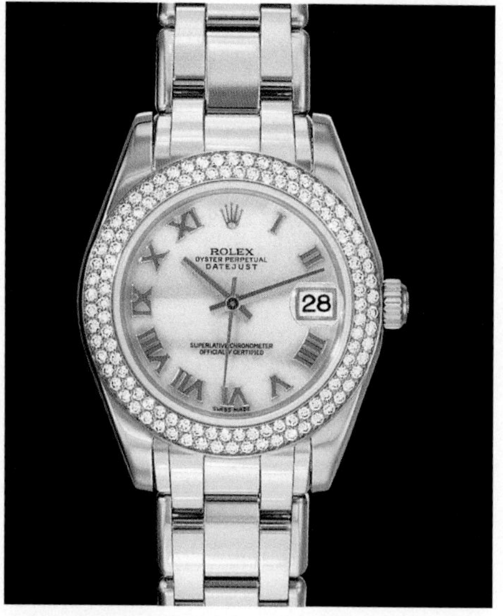

Oyster Perpetual Datejust

Reference number: 81339
Movement: automatic, Rolex 2235 (base Rolex 2230); ø 20 mm, height 5.95 mm; 31 jewels, Breguet balance spring, glucydur balance with Microstella regulating screws; certified chronometer (C.O.S.C.)
Functions: hours, minutes, sweep seconds; date
Case: white gold, ø 34 mm; bezel set with two rows of diamonds; sapphire crystal with magnifying lens above the date display; screw-in crown; water-resistant to 100 m
Band: Oyster white gold, folding clasp
Price: $31,050
Variations: different dial variations

Oyster Perpetual Explorer II

Reference number: 16570
Movement: automatic, Rolex 3185 (base Rolex 3135); ø 28.5 mm, height 6.4 mm; 31 jewels, Breguet balance spring, glucydur balance with Microstella regulating screws; certified chronometer (C.O.S.C.)
Functions: hours, minutes, sweep seconds; date; 24-hour hand (second time zone)
Case: stainless steel, ø 40 mm, height 12.1 mm; bidirectionally rotating bezel with 24-hour scale; sapphire crystal with magnifying lens; screw-in crown; water-resistant to 100 m
Band: Oysterlock stainless steel, folding clasp w/security device
Price: $4,175

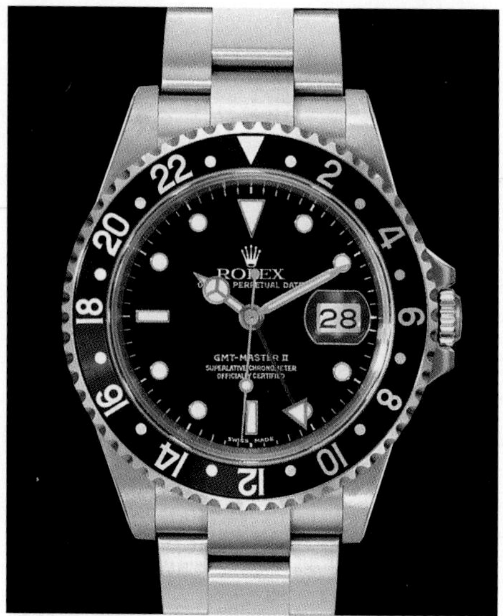

Oyster Perpetual GMT-Master II

Reference number: 16710 LN
Movement: automatic, Rolex 3185 (base Rolex 3135); ø 28.5 mm, height 6.4 mm; 31 jewels, Breguet balance spring, glucydur balance with Microstella regulating screws; certified chronometer (C.O.S.C.)
Functions: hours, minutes, sweep seconds; date; 24-hour hand (second time zone)
Case: stainless steel, ø 40 mm, height 12.1 mm; bidirectionally rotating bezel with 24-hour scale; sapphire crystal with magnifying lens; screw-in crown; water-resistant to 100 m
Band: Oysterlock stainless steel, folding clasp w/security device
Price: $4,250

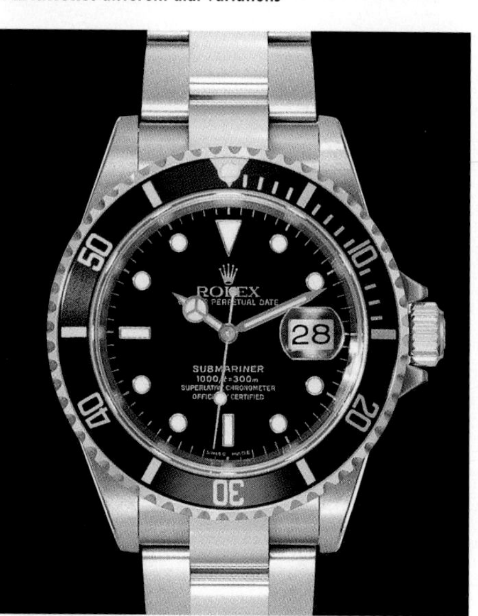

Oyster Perpetual Submariner Date

Reference number: 16613LN
Movement: automatic, Rolex 3135, ø 28.5 mm, height 6 mm; 31 jewels, Breguet balance spring, glucydur balance with Microstella regulating screws; certified chronometer (C.O.S.C.)
Functions: hours, minutes, sweep seconds; date
Case: stainless steel, ø 40 mm, height 12.8 mm; unidirectionally rotating gold bezel with 60-minute scale; sapphire crystal; Triplock screw-in crown; water-resistant to 300 m
Band: Oyster Fliplock stainless steel/yellow gold, folding clasp with security device and extension link
Price: $6,675
Variations: different dial variations; with blue bezel

Oyster Perpetual Cosmograph Daytona

Reference number: 116528
Movement: automatic, Rolex 4130, ø 30.5 mm, height 6.5 mm; 44 jewels, Breguet balance spring, glucydur balance with Microstella regulating screws; power reserve appx. 72 hours; certified chronometer (C.O.S.C.)
Functions: hours, minutes, subsidiary seconds; chronograph
Case: yellow gold, ø 40 mm, height 12.8 mm; bezel engraved with tachymeter scale; sapphire crystal; Triplock screw-in crown and buttons; water-resistant to 100 m
Band: Oysterlock yellow gold, folding clasp with security device
Price: $21,950
Variations: different dial variations

Oyster Perpetual Cosmograph Daytona

Reference number: 116509
Movement: automatic, Rolex 4130, ø 30.5 mm, height 6.5 mm; 44 jewels, Breguet balance spring, glucydur balance with Microstella regulating screws; power reserve appx. 72 hours; certified chronometer (C.O.S.C.)
Functions: hours, minutes, subsidiary seconds; chronograph
Case: white gold, ø 40 mm, height 12.8 mm; bezel engraved with tachymeter scale; sapphire crystal; Triplock screw-in crown and buttons; water-resistant to 100 m
Band: Oysterlock white gold, folding clasp with security device and extension link
Price: $23,950

Oyster Perpetual Datejust

Reference number: 116138
Movement: automatic, Rolex 3135, ø 28.5 mm, height 6 mm; 31 jewels, Breguet balance spring, glucydur balance with Microstella regulating screws; certified chronometer (C.O.S.C.)
Functions: hours, minutes, sweep seconds; date
Case: yellow gold, ø 36 mm, height 11.8 mm; finely fluted bezel; sapphire crystal with magnifying lens above the date display; screw-in crown; water-resistant to 100 m
Band: reptile skin, folding clasp
Price: $12,800
Variations: different dial variations

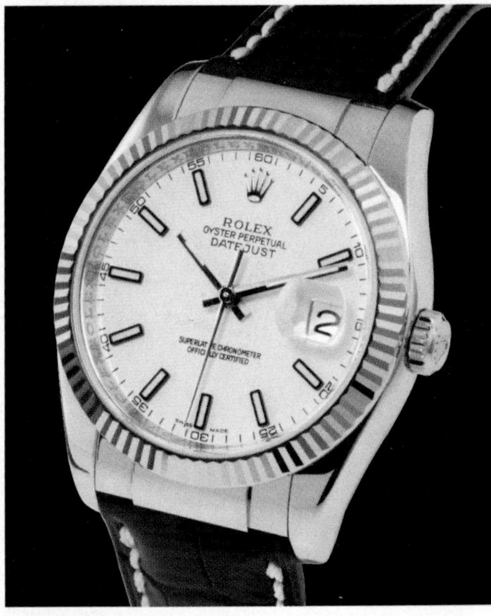

Oyster Perpetual Datejust

Reference number: 116139
Movement: automatic, Rolex 3135, ø 28.5 mm, height 6 mm; 31 jewels, Breguet balance spring, glucydur balance with Microstella regulating screws; certified chronometer (C.O.S.C.)
Functions: hours, minutes, sweep seconds; date
Case: white gold, ø 36 mm, height 11.8 mm; finely fluted bezel; sapphire crystal with magnifying lens above the date display; screw-in crown; water-resistant to 100 m
Band: reptile skin, folding clasp
Price: $14,000
Variations: different dial variations

Oyster Perpetual Turn-O-Graph

Reference number: 116261
Movement: automatic, Rolex 3135, ø 28.5 mm, height 6 mm; 31 jewels, Breguet balance spring, glucydur balance with Microstella regulating screws; certified chronometer (C.O.S.C.)
Functions: hours, minutes, sweep seconds; date
Case: stainless steel, ø 36 mm, height 11.7 mm; bidirectionally rotating, faceted rose gold bezel with five-minute divisions; sapphire crystal with magnifying lens above the date display; screw-in crown; water-resistant to 100 m
Band: Oyster stainless steel/rose gold, folding clasp
Price: $7,075

Oyster Perpetual Turn-O-Graph

Reference number: 116263
Movement: automatic, Rolex 3135, ø 28.5 mm, height 6 mm; 31 jewels, Breguet balance spring, glucydur balance with Microstella regulating screws; certified chronometer (C.O.S.C.)
Functions: hours, minutes, sweep seconds; date
Case: stainless steel, ø 36 mm, height 11.7 mm; bidirectionally rotating, faceted yellow gold bezel with five-minute divisions; sapphire crystal with magnifying lens above the date display; screw-in crown; water-resistant to 100 m
Band: Oyster stainless steel/yellow gold, folding clasp
Price: $7,075

Oyster Perpetual Turn-O-Graph

Reference number: 116264
Movement: automatic, Rolex 3135, ø 28.5 mm, height 6 mm; 31 jewels, Breguet balance spring, glucydur balance with Microstella regulating screws; certified chronometer (C.O.S.C.)
Functions: hours, minutes, sweep seconds; date
Case: stainless steel, ø 36 mm, height 11.7 mm; bidirectionally rotating, faceted white gold bezel with five-minute divisions; sapphire crystal with magnifying lens above the date display; screw-in crown; water-resistant to 100 m
Band: Jubilé stainless steel, folding clasp
Price: $5,425
Variations: with Oyster bracelet; diverse dial variations

Daniel Roth

There are products whose shapes are just so strikingly obvious at first glance that they don't even need a logo on them. Their silhouettes are enough for the consumer to be able to associate them with the brand. The unmistakable Coca-Cola bottle is one of these objects. The VW Beetle was most certainly one as well. And anyone who has ever been to Spain and seen the outline of a giant tin bull along the hills of the highway will know that Osborne brandy is being advertised.

In the world of luxury watches there is a man who has also achieved having his products directly recognized by their shape: Daniel Roth. Ever since this master watchmaker brought his first watch onto the market in 1990, he has been one of the greats to grace the luxury industry. Master watchmakers had been constructing complicated watches long before Roth decided to make his own timepieces. However, industry insiders were quickly impressed not only by the fact that Roth's watches contained movements of excellent quality with original complications and extra displays created especially by the master, but also by the fact that all cases emanating from his production — both for women's and men's models — bore an interesting standard shape, a shape with no equal up to that point, a true innovation, the creation of which took about two years.

Today it is easy to see that all that work was worth it. The Bvlgari group bought the small *manufacture* four years ago and has since invested a great deal of money in the technical and personnel aspects of the brand.

Because a portion of the movements used by Daniel Roth bear the sought-after Seal of Geneva, something only extended to watches that are manufactured in the Swiss city itself, the production of these movements takes place there. Alongside management and after-sales service, a small production area is located in the sober office building on the edge of the city. The heart of the brand beats, however, in the Vallée de Joux's Le Sentier. Truly, nowhere else in the world is there a larger accumulation of watch companies and horological potential than in the Vallée de Joux, a place located about 1,000 meters above sea level that is not called Switzerland's Watch Valley for no reason.

Today at Daniel Roth, it is possible to make proprietary watch movements. Two modern CNC machines utilizing forty-eight different tools, produce the base plates, bridges, and cocks developed by two specialists in the company's design office. The necessary production software for the manufacture of the individual components is also developed in the old house in Le Sentier. This know-how and these technical devices naturally benefit sister brands Gérald Genta and Bvlgari as well — as their fast-growing collections filled with horological specialties can attest.

Company founder and namesake Daniel Roth has completely left the day-to-day business for personal reasons. However, the brand that bears his name still embodies the spirit of the world-famous watchmaker. And that is surely not only due to the unique silhouette of the watches.

Tourbillon 200 Hours Power Reserve

Reference number: 197.X.40.161.CN.BA
Movement: manual winding, Daniel Roth DR 720, 34.5 x 31.5 mm, height 6.3 mm; 25 jewels; 21,600 vph, one-minute tourbillon; power reserve 200 hours
Functions: hours and minutes (off-center), subsidiary seconds (on tourbillon cage); date and power reserve display (back)
Case: rose gold, 40.35 x 43.35 mm, height 12.9 mm; sapphire crystal; case back with lid
Band: reptile skin, buckle
Price: $121,850
Variations: in white gold; in platinum

Tourbillon Retrograde Date

Reference number: 196.X.40.168.CN.BA
Movement: manual winding, Daniel Roth DR 730, 25 x 28 mm, height 4.68 mm; 34 jewels; 18,000 vph, one-minute tourbillon
Functions: hours and minutes (off-center), subsidiary seconds (on tourbillon cage); date (retrograde)
Case: rose gold, 38 x 41 mm, height 9.5 mm; sapphire crystal; transparent case back
Band: reptile skin, buckle
Price: $100,700
Variations: in white gold; in platinum

Tourbillon Perpetual Calendar Retro Date

Reference number: 199.Y.40.165.CN.BD
Movement: automatic, Daniel Roth DR 740 (base M 070); 26.5 x 29.5 mm, height 5.1 mm; 43 jewels. 21,600 vph; power reserve 64 h, tourbillon, perpetual calendar with retrograde displays
Functions: hours, minutes, subsidiary seconds; perpetual calendar with date (retrograde), day, month, year (retrograde)
Case: rose gold, 44 x 41 mm, height 14.9 mm; sapphire crystal; transparent case back
Band: reptile skin, folding clasp
Price: $134,050

Perpetual Calendar Moon Phase

Reference number: 118.L.60.161.CN.BA
Movement: automatic, Daniel Roth DR 114 (base GP 3100); 27 x 30 mm, height 5.28 mm; 27 jewels; 28,800 vph
Functions: hours, minutes; perpetual calendar with date, day, month, moon phase, leap year
Case: white gold, 35 x 38 mm, height 9.8 mm; sapphire crystal; transparent case back
Band: reptile skin, buckle
Price: $47,700
Variations: in rose gold; in 38 x 41 mm case size; in platinum

Perpetual Calendar Time Equation

Reference number: 121.Y.60.168.CN.BD
Movement: automatic, Daniel Roth DR 114 (base GP 3100); 26.5 x 29.5 mm, height 2.98 mm; 27 jewels; 28,800 vph, finely finished with côtes de Genève
Functions: hours, minutes; perpetual calendar with date, day, month, leap year, moon phase; display of the length of the month; equation of time
Case: white gold, 44 x 41 mm, height 13 mm; sapphire crystal; transparent case back
Band: reptile skin, folding clasp
Price: $83,650
Variations: in rose gold; in platinum

Instantaneous Perpetual Calendar

Reference number: 119.X.40.161.CN.BA
Movement: automatic, Daniel Roth DR 114 (base GP 3100); 27 x 30 mm, height 5.28 mm; 27 jewels; 28,800 vph, movement partially skeletonized; simultaneous and spontaneous change of all calendar displays at midnight
Functions: hours, minutes, perpetual calendar with date, day, month, moon phase, leap year
Case: rose gold, 38 x 41 mm, height 9.8 mm; sapphire crystal; transparent case back
Band: reptile skin, buckle
Price: $68,850
Variations: in white gold; in platinum

Ellipsocurvex Moon Phase

Reference number: 368.X.60.161.CN.BA
Movement: manual winding, Daniel Roth DR 904, 17.5 x 25 mm, height 3.85 mm; 19 jewels; 28,800 vph, movement gold-plated and finely decorated, with côtes de Genève
Functions: hours, minutes, subsidiary seconds; date, moon phase; power reserve display
Case: white gold, 38 x 41 mm, height 9.45 mm; sapphire crystal; transparent case back
Band: reptile skin, buckle
Price: $23,850
Variations: in rose gold; in platinum; with diamonds

Grande Sonnerie

Reference number: 607.X.60.166.CN.BD
Movement: automatic, Daniel Roth DR 760 (base Gérald Genta 31000); ø 31.5 mm, height 8.75 mm; 82 jewels; 21,600 vph, minute repeater with large and small strike train, 4 gongs, Westminster gong; tourbillon; finely finished with côtes de Genève
Functions: hours, minutes; two power reserve displays (movement and strike train)
Case: white gold, 43 x 40 mm, height 13 mm; sapphire crystal; transparent case back; limited edition of 7 pieces
Band: reptile skin, folding clasp
Price: $695,650

Datomax

Reference number: 208.L.40.011.CN.BA
Movement: automatic, Daniel Roth DR 130, ø 25.6 mm and module 30 x 27 mm, height 4.9 mm; 32 jewels; 28,800 vph
Functions: hours, minutes, subsidiary seconds; large date
Case: rose gold, 35 x 38 mm, height 9.45 mm; sapphire crystal; transparent case back
Band: reptile skin, buckle
Price: $17,500
Variations: in white gold; in platinum; in 38 x 41 mm case size; with diamonds

Chronomax

Reference number: 347.Y.60.170.CN.BD
Movement: automatic, Daniel Roth DR 210 (base FP 4085); ø 25.6 mm, height 6.6 mm; 38 jewels; 21,600 vph, finely finished with côtes de Genève
Functions: hours, minutes, subsidiary seconds; chronograph; date; Optimax display (torque reserve)
Case: white gold, 44 x 41 mm, height 14.9 mm; sapphire crystal; transparent case back
Band: reptile skin, folding clasp
Price: $26,150
Variations: in rose gold; in platinum

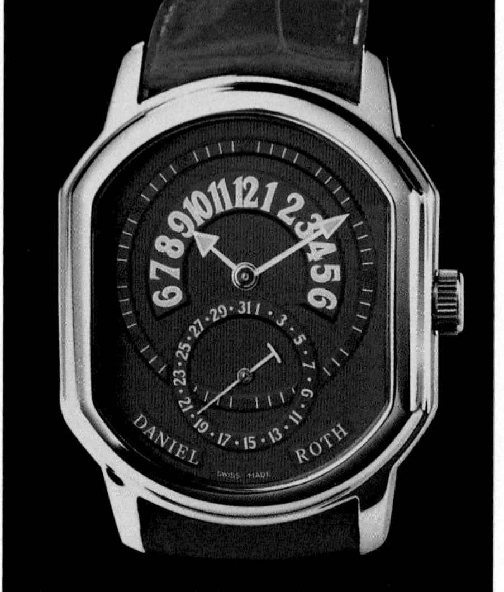

Premier

Reference number: 807.L.10.609.CM.BD
Movement: automatic, Daniel Roth DR 700/10, ø 26 mm, height 5.15 mm; 27 jewels; 28,800 vph
Functions: hours (retrograde), minutes; date
Case: stainless steel, 35 x 41 mm, height 10.4 mm; sapphire crystal; transparent case back
Band: reptile skin, folding clasp
Price: $7,750
Variations: with stainless steel bracelet; with diamonds; in red or white gold

Metropolitan

Reference number: 857.X.60.189.CN.BA
Movement: automatic, Daniel Roth DR 700/21, 31.4 x 34.8 mm, height 6.35 mm; 26 jewels; 28,800 vph, power reserve 42 h
Functions: hours, minutes; world time (second time zone) with day/night indication
Case: white gold, 38 x 41 mm, height 11.4 mm; sapphire crystal; transparent case back
Band: reptile skin, buckle
Price: $22,350
Variations: in rose gold; in stainless steel

The only full-color, illustrated guide to the history, the subtle varieties of style and flavor, and the culture surrounding one of the world's favorite beverages. Winner of the 2004 Glenfiddich Drink Book of the Year Award.

"Rum has been a forgotten drink for some decades now. Just why it fell from favor isn't entirely clear, but now, more or less all of a sudden, it's back. And it comes with this handsome book—a real lapful of pleasure—to do it justice."
—Bill Marsano, wine and spirits writer

Text by Dave Broom
Photography by Jason Lowe
80 full-color illustrations
176 pages · 9½ × 11 in. · Cloth
ISBN 0-7892-0802-4 · $35.00

Scalfaro

Scalfaro represents contemporary luxury and is the result of the creative cooperation between two brothers who let their Mediterranean feel for life and their ideas of luxury flow into a distinct form. Alexander and Dominik Kuhnle needed several years until they were finally able to formulate the dream of their own watch collection and translate it into wearable three-dimensionality.
Growing up in a family that can look back on a long tradition in the production and international distribution of precious jewelry, the meaning of creativity and the art of the craft were transmitted early on to the brothers, who developed a great amount of respect for these elements.
In order to distribute their exclusive creations, they traveled the world early on and forged close ties to the best jewelers. "Travel feeds all creativity," seems to be the apothegm of these brothers, and their watches represent the essence of design styles and lifestyles influenced by varying peoples around the globe. The new interpretation of luxury stands for quality without compromise, passionate design, and high demands on design and production. Scalfaro outfits its exclusive timekeepers, which are assembled in the workshops of experienced master watchmakers, wholly with highly refined Swiss automatic movements that have been decorated by hand. Every element of a Scalfaro is created with great attention to detail and bears the signature of the brand's two founders.

Building on a solidly dimensioned case, two different bezel shapes and dial cutaways determine the character of the two model families. Cap Ferrat presents itself with playful and elegant, baroquely curving contours despite the imposing stature of the watches. The Cap Ferrat Grand Tour only differs in a rotating bezel located underneath the crystal, which is set by an additional crown found at 10 o'clock. The Porto Cervo model, whose striking feature is an individualistic, flowing hexagon formed by the bezel and dial, comes across a bit more sporty. The quality of the case, dial, and bands' workmanship is obvious. Both of the large model families are available on link bracelets or leather straps. The striking center link element that extends from the upper and lower parts of the watch case is continued all the way around the bracelet, while at that point on the leather strap there is a slim, padded track running the length of the material.
Great care was taken in the proportioning of the hands, the profile of the crown, and the design of the subsidiary seconds scale. The red 12, whether represented by a numeral or double marker, the solid crown protection, the screwed-in crown, and the screwed-on strap lugs are wonderful details — but it is the screws that stand out most especially. These are special screws that were developed just for Scalfaro. The heads of these ScalfaScrews are reminiscent of Torx screws, but feature only five points.
With their clear, harmoniously structured, and well-outfitted Scalfaro collection, the Kuhnle brothers have a good chance of breaking into the luxury watch markets currently dominated by men's watches, most especially since the brand's price level has been chosen so that demanding interested parties will have a hard time finding much comparison.

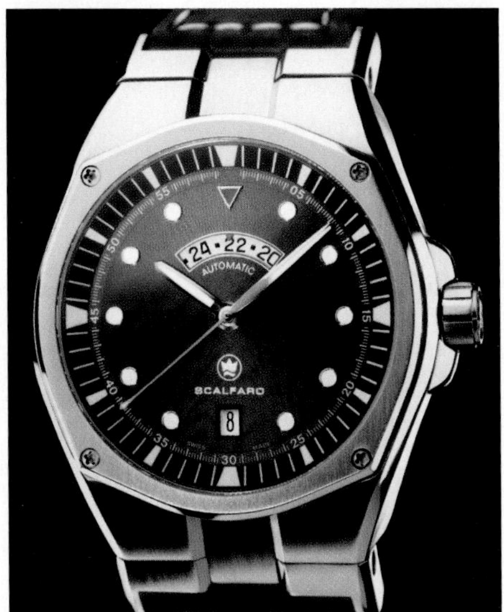

Cap Ferrat Second Time Zone

Reference number: A01A.02.01.1.12.L01.10
Movement: automatic, ADK 148 (base ETA 2892-2); ø 25.6 mm, height 4.1 mm; 21 jewels; 28,800 vph, côtes de Genève, perlage, blued screws
Functions: hours, minutes, sweep seconds; date; 24-hour display (second time zone)
Case: stainless steel, ø 43 mm, height 10.8 mm; sapphire crystal (anti-reflective); transparent case back; screw-in crown; water-resistant to 100 m
Band: leather, buckle
Price: $3,550
Variations: diverse dial variations; with rubber strap

Cap Ferrat Grand Tour Chronograph Flyback Large Date

Reference number: A02A.05.01.2.12.Q01.20
Movement: automatic, ADK 151 (base ETA 7750); ø 30 mm, height 8.85 mm; 28 jewels; 28,800 vph, côtes de Genève, perlage, blued screws
Functions: hours, minutes, subsidiary seconds; chronograph with flyback function; large date
Case: stainless steel, ø 43 mm, height 15.9 mm; bidirectionally rotating flange with 60-minute scale; sapphire crystal; transparent case back; screw-in crown; water-resistant to 100 m
Band: reptile skin, folding clasp
Price: $6,925

Cap Ferrat Grand Tour Chronograph

Reference number: A02A.04.02.2.12.Q16.20
Movement: automatic, ADK 150 (base ETA 7750); ø 30 mm, height 8.4 mm; 28 jewels; 28,800 vph, côtes de Genève, perlage, blued screws
Functions: hours, minutes, subsidiary seconds; chronograph; date
Case: stainless steel, ø 43 mm, height 14.9 mm; bidirectionally rotating flange with 60-minute scale, settable via crown; sapphire crystal; transparent case back; screw-in crown; water-resistant to 100 m
Band: reptile skin, folding clasp
Price: $5,675

Cap Ferrat Grand Tour Chronograph

Reference number: A02A.03.01.2.12.A00.31
Movement: automatic, ADK 149 (base ETA 7750); ø 30 mm, height 8.4 mm; 28 jewels; 28,800 vph, côtes de Genève, perlage, blued screws
Functions: hours, minutes, subsidiary seconds; chronograph; date
Case: stainless steel, ø 43 mm, height 14.8 mm; bidirectionally rotating flange with 60-minute scale, settable via crown; sapphire crystal; transparent case back; screw-in crown; water-resistant to 100 m
Band: stainless steel, folding clasp
Price: $6,000

Porto Cervo Chronograph Flyback

Reference number: A03A.05.06.1.12.Q16.20
Movement: automatic, ADK 151 (base ETA 7750); ø 30 mm, height 8.85 mm; 28 jewels; 28,800 vph, côtes de Genève, perlage, blued screws
Functions: hours, minutes, subsidiary seconds; chronograph with flyback function; large date
Case: stainless steel, ø 42 mm, height 15.7 mm; sapphire crystal; transparent case back; screw-in crown; water-resistant to 100 m
Band: reptile skin, folding clasp
Price: $7,100
Variations: with stainless steel bracelet; with diamond bezel

Porto Cervo Chronograph TriCompax

Reference number: A03A.04.01.1.12.Q01.20
Movement: automatic, ADK 150 (base ETA 7750); ø 30 mm, height 8.4 mm; 28 jewels; 28,800 vph, côtes de Genève, perlage, blued screws
Functions: hours, minutes, subsidiary seconds; chronograph; date
Case: stainless steel, ø 42 mm, height 14.8 mm; sapphire crystal; transparent case back; screw-in crown; water-resistant to 100 m
Band: reptile skin, folding clasp
Price: $5,900
Variations: with stainless steel bracelet, with diamond bezel

Jörg Schauer

Jörg Schauer calls himself a "watch builder." And this is a precise description, for Schauer's watches are not put together by just anyone: Each and every one of the 800 watches that are annually issued from his workshop lands on Schauer's own bench before it goes. The lion's share of these watches comprises models from the current collection.

However, Schauer also makes customers' wishes outside of the current collection come true. Such clients have to be patient when waiting for their dream watches, though, for each serial model is worked and scheduled individually, causing Schauer's small team to run permanently at capacity. Although the cases received from the supplier are of the best quality, each one is polished yet again in Schauer's workshop. "My standards are just too high," Schauer says with a grin. "I touch absolutely everything up!" When looking at these unconventional timepieces more closely, a quality of workmanship is discovered that deserves anyone's respect.

The design of Schauer's watches is not exactly of mass consumer taste: Relinquishing obvious decoration, the sheer weight of the case and the working of the cases' matte, unpolished surfaces lead one to believe that a "typical" watchmaker (if there is such a thing) is not at work here. Schauer has a different take on watches. For him, design, material, surface, and working of the details are most important. This is the goldsmith in him coming out.

He creates functional, edgy cases with a visibly screwed-on bezel, and sober dials in simple black or white characterize the strict design. There will never be models that follow fashion trends in Schauer's workshop, for he only makes watches that he himself likes. A good example is the extraordinary Digital 2, featuring a jump hour display that has allowed him to realize his wish of "building a crazy watch."

Digital 2 is crazy because it has the appearance of a quartz watch, behind whose simple black dial is hidden a disk mechanism powered by a historical *manufacture* caliber: PUW Caliber 560 D made by the former Pforzheimer Uhrenrohwerke. Schauer always finds rarities such as these from Pforzheim's history and makes modern watches from them — delicacies for collectors.

Schauer's latest creation, Sportstopp, also leaves the beaten mainstream design path. It realizes the measurement of sports timing not with a chronograph movement, but with a very special case construction: By synchronizing the hour and minute hands, two rotating bezels mark the starting time of the event — making a relatively precise ascertainment of the time that has passed at the end possible. Here, the watch builder from Engelsbrand has once again thought a tick further.

Kleine Schauer

Reference number: KLSCH/WAL
Movement: automatic, ETA 2824, ø 26 mm, height 4.6 mm; 25 jewels; 28,800 vph, finished with decoration and blued screws, exclusive Schauer rotor with engraving
Functions: hours, minutes, sweep seconds
Case: stainless steel, ø 37 mm, height 9.2 mm; bezel secured with 12 screws; sapphire crystal; transparent case back; water-resistant to 50 m
Band: leather, buckle
Price: $1,200
Variations: with stainless steel Milanaise-style bracelet/double folding clasp ($1,350); dials in different colors; with date

Automatic Day-Date

Reference number: Auto 2836-42WGL
Movement: automatic, ETA 2836, ø 26 mm, height 5.3 mm; 25 jewels; 28,800 vph, finished with decoration and blued screws, exclusive Schauer rotor with engraving
Functions: hours, minutes, sweep seconds; date and day
Case: stainless steel, ø 42 mm, height 11 mm; bezel secured with 12 screws; sapphire crystal; transparent case back; water-resistant to 50 m
Band: rubber, folding clasp
Price: $1,900
Variations: with stainless steel Artus-style bracelet/double folding clasp ($2,300); dials in black or white, in 41 mm case

Chronograph Kulisse

Reference number: Edition 10
Movement: automatic, ETA 7750, ø 30 mm, height 7.9 mm; 28 jewels; 28,800 vph, finished with decoration and blued screws, exclusive Schauer rotor with engraving
Functions: hours, minutes, subsidiary seconds; chronograph
Case: stainless steel, ø 42 mm, height 15 mm; bezel secured with 12 screws; sapphire crystal; transparent case back; water-resistant to 50 m
Band: buffalo leather, buckle
Price: $3,100
Variations: with stainless steel Artus-style bracelet/double folding clasp ($3,500); dials in black or white

Chronograph Kulisse

Reference number: Edition 12
Movement: automatic, ETA 7753 (base ETA 7750); ø 30 mm, height 7.9 mm; 28 jewels; 28,800 vph, finished with decoration and blued screws, exclusive Schauer rotor with engraving
Functions: hours, minutes, subsidiary seconds; chronograph
Case: stainless steel, ø 41 mm, height 15 mm; bezel secured with 12 screws; sapphire crystal; transparent case back; water-resistant to 50 m
Band: crocodile skin, buckle
Price: $3,100
Variations: with stainless steel Artus-style bracelet/double folding clasp ($3,500)

Quarada

Reference number: Quarada SL
Movement: automatic, ETA 7750, ø 30 mm, height 7.9 mm; 28 jewels; 28,800 vph, finished with decoration and blued screws, exclusive Schauer rotor with engraving
Functions: hours, minutes, subsidiary seconds; chronograph
Case: stainless steel, 35 x 35 mm, height 14 mm; bezel secured with 12 screws; sapphire crystal; transparent case back
Band: leather, buckle
Price: $4,900
Variations: with reptile skin strap

Sportstop

Reference number: Sportstop S
Movement: automatic, ETA 2824, ø 26 mm, height 4.6 mm; 25 jewels; 28,800 vph, finished with decoration and blued screws, exclusive Schauer rotor with engraving
Functions: hours, minutes, sweep seconds
Case: titanium, ø 41 mm, height 12.9 mm; two rotating bezels; with scales to time periods of up to 12 hours; sapphire crystal (3 mm); solid case back; water-resistant to 200 m
Band: rubber, folding clasp
Price: $1,700
Variations: different dials

Alain Silberstein

"This year I am not introducing any new watches." With this sentence, Alain Silberstein welcomed customers and interested parties to his booth at Baselworld 2004. In answer to the incredulous astonishment this statement aroused, he continued with a mischievous grin, "I am putting on a parade." Sometimes it's difficult to know whether one should take him seriously or not. Silberstein just loves to play the part of the *enfant terrible* of the watchmaking scene, and he does it well. Reveling in the confused faces of those across from him, he sends his new collection out on the runway: A series of sixteen new watches, divided into four groups of matching color themes. "Life is not black and white either." Neither is time, apparently. Nor are these timekeepers.

These are tourbillons. In the eyes of Silberstein, they display the highest concentration of movement mechanics possible. "And they are so superfluous that they once again become indispensable." Silberstein's play with fashion juggles up to seven different color tones in one and the same watch. While others struggle with the fine tuning of watch movements, this architect and designer celebrates the fine adjustment of color. And any means of achieving this is all right by him: enamel, galvanic, oxidation, PVD, paint, oil under crystal. Sometimes he completely does without the dial or sets fine, organically shimmering mother-of-pearl as a contrast to sandblasted or machined perlage surfaces.

The new tourbillon collection represents the ultimate consequence of Silberstein's watch design theory. The colorful, graphically shaped hands of his watches have become true trademarks. The designer's mischievous humor jumps out at the casual observer from every detail of the dial, from every hand, and from every triangular crown, making a sober discussion about beauty, value, and wearability completely impossible. Silberstein, a designer — actually architect — who lives and works in Besancon, France, often has his fun at the cost of functionality, but never at the cost of a function.

The official chronometer certificate is just as important to him as the careful finishing of the movement, even if the latter is carried out according to Silberstein's own unorthodox standard. "I have no problems with being laughed at, but those who don't have the sense of humor to see beyond the facade are not the people I'm interested in," says the designer in his self-assured manner, then turns serious. "They have to realize that the humorous visual aspect conceals traditional challenges. Skeleton work on the watch movements, the use of enamel as a weatherproof way of adding color, and cases set with diamonds have always been part of the tradition of watchmaking. All I have done is to change the final result, but not the quality of what is actually flawless craftsmanship."

Tourbillon Galuchat Caviar

Reference number: TAT5-001
Movement: automatic, ASC 1.2, ø 31 mm, height 6.5 mm; 26 jewels; 28,800 vph, flying one-minute tourbillon; black PVD movement finish
Functions: hours, minutes; date
Case: titanium, PVD black, ø 40 mm, height 12.8 mm; sapphire crystal; transparent case back; water-resistant to 100 m
Band: stingray, folding clasp; delivered with extra rubber strap
Remarks: dial with inlaid with stingray; limited to 500 pieces, numbered
Price: 50,000 euros

Tourbillon Black Sea

Reference number: MTT2-004L
Movement: automatic, ASC 1.2, ø 31 mm, height 6.5 mm; 26 jewels; 28,800 vph, flying one-minute tourbillon
Functions: hours, minutes; date
Case: titanium, PVD black, ø 40 mm, height 14 mm; sapphire crystal; transparent case back; water-resistant to 200 m
Band: rubber, folding clasp
Remarks: limited to 500 pieces, numbered
Price: 50,000 euros
Variations: with painted or mother-of-pearl dial

Tourbillon Blue Hope

Reference number: TAA1-003N
Movement: automatic, ASC 1.2, ø 31 mm, height 6.5 mm; 26 jewels; 28,800 vph, flying one-minute tourbillon; blue PVD movement finish
Functions: hours, minutes; date
Case: stainless steel, ø 40 mm, height 12.7 mm; sapphire crystal; transparent case back; water-resistant to 100 m
Band: reptile skin, folding clasp; delivered with extra rubber strap
Remarks: limited to 500 pieces, numbered
Price: 50,000 euros
Variations: in titanium

Tourbillon African Summer

Reference number: TMT2-002
Movement: manual winding, ASC 1.1, ø 31 mm, height 5.4 mm; 26 jewels; 28,800 vph, flying one-minute tourbillon; PVD bronze movement finish
Functions: hours, minutes; date
Case: titanium, PVD bronze, ø 40 mm, height 11 mm; sapphire crystal; transparent case back; water-resistant to 100 m
Band: reptile skin, folding clasp; delivered with extra rubber strap
Remarks: limited to 500 pieces, numbered
Price: 33,000 euros

Tourbillon Indian Summer

Reference number: TMT2-003
Movement: manual winding, ASC 1.1, ø 31 mm, height 5.4 mm; 26 jewels; 28,800 vph, flying one-minute tourbillon; PVD gold movement finish
Functions: hours, minutes; date
Case: titanium, PVD gold, ø 40 mm, height 11 mm; sapphire crystal; transparent case back; water-resistant to 100 m
Band: reptile skin, folding clasp; delivered with extra rubber strap
Remarks: limited to 500 pieces, numbered
Price: 33,000 euros

Tourbillon Leather Pink

Reference number: TMA3-002
Movement: manual winding, ASC 1.1, ø 31 mm, height 5.4 mm; 26 jewels; 28,800 vph, flying one-minute tourbillon; violet PVD movement finish
Functions: hours, minutes; date
Case: stainless steel, completely covered with alligator skin, ø 40.7 mm, height 11.8 mm; sapphire crystal; transparent case back
Band: reptile skin, folding clasp
Remarks: limited to 500 pieces, numbered
Price: 35,000 euros
Variations: available in different colors

Bolido Krono Carbon Fiber

Reference number: BK 84
Movement: automatic, Frédéric Piguet 1185, ø 25.6 mm, height 5.4 mm; 37 jewels; 21,600 vph, modified by Silberstein
Functions: hours, minutes, subsidiary seconds; chronograph; date
Case: stainless steel, 48 x 36 mm, height 13.5 mm; cylindrical movable lugs made of carbon fiber; sapphire crystal; transparent case back; water-resistant to 100 m
Band: rubber, folding clasp; delivered with extra stainless steel bracelet
Remarks: limited to 250 pieces, numbered
Price: 9,500 euros

Bolido Krono Titanium

Reference number: BK 73
Movement: automatic, Frédéric Piguet 1185, ø 25.6 mm, height 5.4 mm; 37 jewels; 21,600 vph, modified by Silberstein
Functions: hours, minutes, subsidiary seconds; chronograph; date
Case: titanium, 48 x 36 mm, height 13.5 mm; cylindrical movable lugs; sapphire crystal; transparent case back; water-resistant to 100 m
Band: rubber, folding clasp; delivered with extra stainless steel bracelet
Remarks: limited to 250 pieces, numbered
Price: 9,300 euros

Jumbo Krono

Reference number: JK 11
Movement: automatic, Nouvelle Lémania 5100, ø 31 mm, height 8.25 mm; 17 jewels; 28,800 vph, modified by Silberstein
Functions: hours, minutes, subsidiary seconds; chronograph; date, day; 24-hour display
Case: stainless steel, 44 x 40 mm, height 17 mm; sapphire crystal; transparent case back; water-resistant to 100 m
Band: rubber, folding clasp; delivered with extra stainless steel bracelet
Remarks: limited to 500 pieces, numbered
Price: 6,500 euros

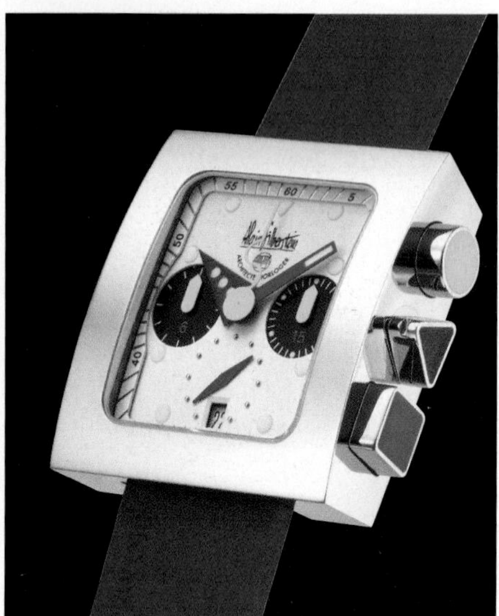

Pavé Krono

Reference number: VK 12
Movement: automatic, Frédéric Piguet 1185, ø 25.6 mm, height 5.4 mm; 37 jewels; 21,600 vph, modified by Silberstein
Functions: hours, minutes, subsidiary seconds; chronograph; date
Case: stainless steel, 37.6 x 37.4 mm, height 11.5 mm; sapphire crystal; transparent case back; water-resistant to 100 m
Band: rubber, folding clasp; delivered with extra stainless steel bracelet
Remarks: limited to 500 pieces, numbered
Price: 9,200 euros

Pavé GMT

Reference number: VG 11
Movement: automatic, ETA 2893-2, ø 25.6 mm, height 4.1 mm; 21 jewels; 28,800 vph, modified by Alain Silberstein
Functions: hours, minutes, sweep seconds; date; 12-hour hand (second time zone or "home time")
Case: stainless steel, 37.6 x 37.4 mm, height 12 mm; sapphire crystal; transparent case back; water-resistant to 100 m
Band: rubber, folding clasp; delivered with extra stainless steel bracelet
Remarks: limited to 500 pieces, numbered
Price: 3,600 euros

Pavé Smileday

Reference number: VS 11
Movement: automatic, ETA 2836-2, ø 25.6 mm, height 5.05 mm; 25 jewels; 28,800 vph
Functions: hours, minutes, sweep seconds; date; "Smileday"
Case: stainless steel, 37.6 x 37.4 mm, height 11.5 mm; sapphire crystal; transparent case back; water-resistant to 100 m
Band: rubber, folding clasp; delivered with extra stainless steel bracelet
Remarks: limited to 500 pieces, numbered
Price: 3,600 euros

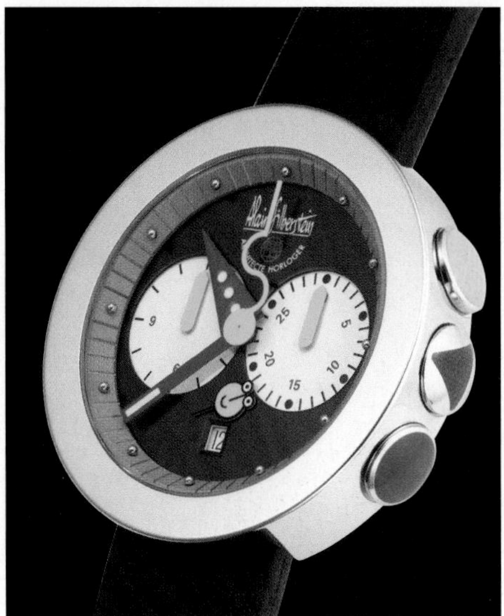

Rondo Krono Steel

Reference number: OK 11
Movement: automatic, Frédéric Piguet 1185, ø 25.6 mm, height 5.4 mm; 37 jewels; 21,600 vph, modified by Silberstein
Functions: hours, minutes, subsidiary seconds; chronograph; date
Case: stainless steel, ø 42 mm, height 11.8 mm; sapphire crystal; transparent case back; recessed crown and buttons; water-resistant to 100 m
Band: rubber, folding clasp; delivered with extra stainless steel bracelet
Remarks: limited to 500 pieces, numbered
Price: 9,000 euros

Rondo GMT

Reference number: OG 12
Movement: automatic, ETA 2893-2, ø 25.6 mm, height 4.1 mm; 21 jewels; 28,800 vph, modified by Alain Silberstein
Functions: hours, minutes, sweep seconds; date; 12-hour hand (second time zone or "home time")
Case: stainless steel, ø 42 mm, height 12 mm; sapphire crystal; transparent case back; recessed crown; water-resistant to 100 m
Band: rubber, folding clasp; delivered with extra stainless steel bracelet
Remarks: limited to 500 pieces, numbered
Price: 3,600 euros

Rondo Smileday

Reference number: OS 11
Movement: automatic, ETA 2836-2, ø 25.6 mm, height 5.05 mm; 25 jewels; 28,800 vph
Functions: hours, minutes, sweep seconds; date; "Smileday"
Case: stainless steel, ø 42 mm, height 12 mm; sapphire crystal; transparent case back; recessed crown; water-resistant to 100 m
Band: rubber, folding clasp; delivered with extra stainless steel bracelet
Remarks: limited to 500 pieces, numbered
Price: 3,600 euros

Krono B Titanium

Reference number: KB 123
Movement: automatic, Nouvelle Lémania 5100, ø 31 mm, height 8.25 mm; 17 jewels; 28,800 vph, modified by Silberstein
Functions: hours, minutes, subsidiary seconds; chronograph; date, day; 24-hour display
Case: titanium, ø 39.6 mm, height 15 mm; sapphire crystal; transparent case back; water-resistant to 100 m
Band: rubber, folding clasp; delivered with extra stainless steel bracelet
Remarks: limited to 500 pieces, numbered
Price: 5,600 euros

Krono B Alligator

Reference number: KB 1010B
Movement: automatic, Nouvelle Lémania 5100, ø 31 mm, height 8.25 mm; 17 jewels; 28,800 vph, modified by Silberstein
Functions: hours, minutes, subsidiary seconds; chronograph; date, day; 24-hour display
Case: stainless steel, completely covered with alligator skin, ø 39.6 mm, height 15 mm; sapphire crystal; transparent case back; water-resistant to 50 m
Band: reptile skin, folding clasp
Remarks: limited to 250 pieces, numbered
Price: 7,000 euros

Krono B Diamonds

Reference number: KB 81
Movement: automatic, Nouvelle Lémania 5100, ø 31 mm, height 8.25 mm; 17 jewels; 28,800 vph, modified by Silberstein
Functions: hours, minutes, subsidiary seconds; chronograph; date, day; 24-hour display
Case: stainless steel, ø 39.6 mm, height 15 mm; case set with 297 diamonds; sapphire crystal; transparent case back; water-resistant to 100 m
Band: rubber, folding clasp; delivered with extra stainless steel bracelet
Remarks: limited to 250 pieces, numbered
Price: 36,000 euros

Sinn

At Sinn in Frankfurt yet another anniversary is making waves. In 2001, the 40th anniversary of the company's founding was celebrated, while in September 2004, Lothar Schmidt can festively observe ten years of his own "special watchmaking." The current owner of the company understands the philosophy of the "instrument watch" conceived by company founder Helmut Sinn all too well, maintaining it with his own innovative ideas and continuing in the newest state of technology. Mechanical engineer Schmidt has convinced his continually growing clientele of this with his ideas of "sin(n)fully" good innovation.
The best example of this high-tech watch technology is the Duochronograph 756 Diapal. Here Schmidt presents the hardest steel watch case available on the market today, created with what Sinn has dubbed the Tegiment technology. Tegiment is a specialized process of treating steel developed for surgical instruments so that the surface is protectively coated (Latin *tegimentum* means covering) and reaches a hardness of 1,200 Vickers. That is five to six times harder than the conventional steel used for watch cases. In addition, the watch is outfitted with a special gasket system for crown and pushers, protection against magnetic fields up to 80,000 A/m, and a dehumidifying capsule filled with copper sulphate. A patent pending for Schmidt's Diapal tech-

nology, also included in Model 756, documents that Sinn is not only on the technological cutting edge where case construction is concerned. Diapal literally stands for "**dia**mond **pal**lets" and describes an escapement system that does completely without lubrication. The pallet and escapement wheel materials were chosen so that they hardly produce friction, thus functioning more lightly than those of a classic, freshly lubricated Swiss pallet escapement.
The backbone of the Sinn collection is still formed by exceptionally technical pilot's chronographs as well as military-styled diver's and sports watches. The high-tech substance titanium also plays a large part in the product philosophy as the case material, chiefly attracting technically oriented customers or those in technical positions such as pilots, race car drivers, and extreme athletes.
In addition, an opening in the direction of elegant sporty can be noticed of late in the model palette, embodied above all by the watches of the Frankfurt series and featuring glossy, high-polished cases: Finance Watch, Time Zone Watch, and Finance Alarm. Important for the appearance of this line are the galvanically blackened, shiny dials with their polished applied elements. The otherwise unchanged, simple Sinn cases are now almost impossible to recognize.
Sinn customers are price-conscious watch lovers, who demand a lot of watch for their money. This is helped along by the Frankfurt company with its distribution system, among other points. In Europe, the direct sale of the watches from the showroom in Germany's financial metropolis or from so-called depots helps Sinn to calculate its prices more precisely than if they were to adhere to conventional methods of sales through dealers. The central service station in Frankfurt also helps to save time and money. This concept is to be continued by Sinn's new distribution in the United States, which plans on using the Internet as its chief sales channel.

The Multifunction Chronograph

Reference number: 900

Movement: automatic, ETA 7750 modified, ø 30 mm, height 7.9 mm; 26 jewels; 28,800 vph, magnetic field protection to 80,000 A/m; shockproof and antimagnetic

Functions: hours, minutes, subsidiary seconds; chronograph; date; 24-hour display (second time zone)

Case: stainless steel, tegimented (1200 Vickers), ø 44 mm, height 15.5 mm; bidirectionally rotating flange with 24-hour scale; sapphire crystal; screw-in crown; water-resistant to 200 m

Band: calfskin, buckle

Remarks: tachymeter, telemeter, pulsometer; dehumidifyer

Price: $2,490

The Automatic Navigational Chronograph

Reference number: 903 St Schwarz

Movement: automatic, ETA 7750 modified, ø 30 mm, height 7.9 mm; 25 jewels; 28,800 vph, finely finished with blued screws; shockproof and antimagnetic according to DIN

Functions: hours, minutes, sub. seconds; chronograph; date

Case: stainless steel, ø 41 mm, height 14.5 mm; bidirectionally rotating flange with logarithmic scale; sapphire crystal; transparent case back; screw-in crown; water-resistant to 100 m

Band: stainless steel, folding claspl

Price: $2,090

Variations: with leather strap ($1,990); with silver dial

The Rallye Chronograph

Reference number: 956 KLASSIK

Movement: automatic, ETA 7750, ø 30 mm, height 7.9 mm; 25 jewels; 28,800 vph, finely finished with blued screws; shockproof and antimagnetic according to DIN

Functions: hours, minutes, subsidiary seconds; chronograph; date; power reserve display

Case: stainless steel, ø 41.5 mm, height 15 mm; sapphire crystal; transparent case back; screw-in crown; water-resistant to 100 m

Band: leather, buckle

Price: $2,340

Variations: stainless steel bracelet ($2,540); with black dial

The Space Chronograph

Reference number: 142 St

Movement: automatic, Nouvelle Lémania 5100, ø 31 mm, height 8.25 mm; 17 jewels; 28,800 vph, shockproof and antimagnetic according to DIN

Functions: hours, minutes, subsidiary seconds; chronograph; date, day; 24-hour display

Case: stainless steel, sandblasted, ø 44 mm, height 15 mm; bidirectionally rotating flange with 60-minute scale; sapphire crystal; screw-in crown; water-resistant to 100 m

Band: stainless steel, folding clasp with wetsuit extension

Remarks: new stainless steel bracelet integrated into case

Price: $1,590

The Pilot's Chronograph

Reference number: 356 FLIEGER

Movement: automatic, ETA 7750, ø 30 mm, height 7.9 mm; 25 jewels; 28,800 vph, shockproof and antimagnetic according to DIN

Functions: hours, minutes, subsidiary seconds; chronograph; date, day

Case: stainless steel, sandblasted, ø 38.5 mm, height 14 mm; sapphire crystal; screw-in crown; water-resistant to 100 m

Band: leather, buckle

Price: $1,340

Variations: with stainless steel bracelet ($1,440); as UTC; with copper-colored dial

The Sporty Chronograph

Reference number: 303 Silber 12

Movement: automatic, ETA 7750, ø 30 mm, height 7.9 mm; 25 jewels; 28,800 vph, shockproof and antimagnetic according to DIN

Functions: hours, minutes, subsidiary seconds; chronograph; date, day

Case: stainless steel, ø 41 mm, height 16.5 mm; bezel engraved with 12-hour scale; sapphire crystal; screw-in crown; water-resistant to 200 m

Band: leather, buckle

Price: $1,240

Variations: stainless steel bracelet ($1,340); tachymeter bezel

The Frankfurt Finance Watch

Reference number: 6000
Movement: automatic, ETA 7750 modified, ø 30 mm, height 8.4 mm; 25 jewels; 28,800 vph, finely finished with blued screws and engraved rotor; shockproof and antimagnetic according to DIN
Functions: hours, minutes, subsidiary seconds; chronograph; date; 12-hour hand (second time zone)
Case: stainless steel, ø 38.5 mm, height 16.5 mm; bidirectionally rotating flange with 12-hour scale (3rd time zone); sapphire crystal; transparent case back; water-resistant to 100 m
Band: stainless steel, double folding clasp
Price: $2,990

The Frankfurt World Time Watch

Reference number: 6060
Movement: automatic, ETA 2893-2, ø 25.6 mm, height 4.1 mm; 21 jewels; 28,800 vph, finely finished with blued screws and engraved rotor; DIN shockproof and antimagnetic
Functions: hours, minutes, sweep seconds; date; 24-hour display (second time zone)
Case: stainless steel, ø 38.5 mm, height 12 mm; bidirectionally rotating flange with 12-hour scale (3rd time zone); sapphire crystal; transparent case back; water-resistant to 100 m
Band: calfskin, buckle
Remarks: delivered with maintenance set incl. steel bracelet
Price: $2,090

The Frankfurt Finance Alarm

Reference number: 6066
Movement: automatic, Jaquet 5900 (base AS Caliber 5008); ø 30.4 m. height 7.75 mm; 31 jewels; 28,800 vph, finely finished with blued screws and engraved rotor; shockproof and antimagnetic according to DIN
Functions: hours, minutes, sweep seconds; date; 24-hour display (second time zone); alarm
Case: stainless steel, ø 38.5 mm, height 15 mm; bidirectionally rotating flange with 12-hour scale (3rd time zone); sapphire crystal; transparent case back; water-resistant to 100 m
Band: stainless steel, double folding clasp
Price: $3,990

The Classic Pilot's Chronograph

Reference number: 103 Ti Ar UTC
Movement: automatic, ETA 7750 modified, ø 30 mm, height 7.9 mm; 25 jewels; 28,800 vph, shockproof and antimagnetic according to DIN
Functions: hours, minutes, subsidiary seconds; chronograph; date; 12-hour hand (second time zone)
Case: titanium, sandblasted, ø 41 mm, height 16.5 mm; bidirectionally rotating bezel with 60-minute scale; sapphire crystal; transparent case back; screw-in crown; water-resistant to 200 m
Band: leather, buckle
Price: $1,890

The Diver's Chronograph ARKTIS

Reference number: 203 ARKTIS
Movement: automatic, ETA 7750, ø 30 mm, height 7.9 mm; 25 jewels; 28,800 vph, shockproof and antimagnetic; use of special oil (for use in temperatures between -45 °C and +80 °C)
Functions: hours, minutes, subsidiary seconds; chronograph; date, day
Case: stainless steel, ø 41 mm, height 16 mm; unidirectionally rotating bezel with 60-minute scale; sapphire crystal; screw-in crown and buttons; water-resistant to 300 m
Band: shark skin, folding clasp with wetsuit extension
Remarks: case filled with Argon and dehumidifying capsule
Price: $1,670

The World Time Chronograph

Reference number: 144 GMT Ti
Movement: automatic, ETA 7750 modified, ø 30 mm, height 7.9 mm; 25 jewels; 28,800 vph, shockproof and antimagnetic according to DIN
Functions: hours, minutes, subsidiary seconds; chronograph; date; 12-hour hand (second time zone)
Case: titanium, sandblasted, ø 41 mm, height 14.5 mm; sapphire crystal; transparent case back; screw-in crown; water-resistant to 200 m
Band: titanium, folding clasp with wetsuit extension
Price: $1,690
Variations: leather strap; without second time zone; in steel

EZM 1 (Official German Border Police Watch)

Reference number: EZM 1

Movement: automatic, Nouvelle Lémania 5100, ø 31 mm, height 8.25 mm; 17 jewels; 28,800 vph, shockproof and antimagnetic according to DIN

Functions: hours, minutes, chronograph; date

Case: titanium, sandblasted, ø 40 mm, height 16.5 mm; bidirectionally rotating bezel with 60-minute scale count-down; sapphire crystal; screw-in crown; water-resistant to 300 m

Band: leather, buckle

Price: $1,990

Variations: with titanium bracelet ($2,190)

EZM 2 (Official GSG9 Diver's Watch)

Reference number: EZM 2

Movement: quartz, ETA 955.612, case completely filled with oil, thus pressure-proof to every reachable diving depth and legible under water from every angle

Functions: hours, minutes, sweep seconds; date

Case: stainless steel, sandblasted, ø 41 mm, height 11.4 mm; unidirectionally rotating bezel with 60-minute scale; sapphire crystal; screw-in crown; water-resistant without limit

Band: rubber, buckle

Price: $890

Variations: with leather or velcro strap; with stainless steel bracelet ($990)

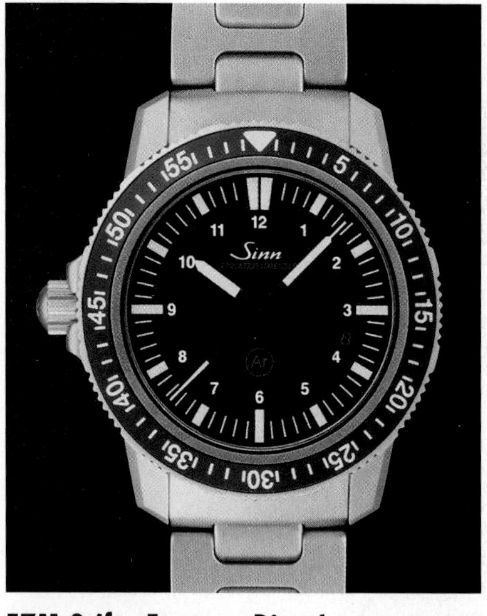

EZM 3 (for Extreme Dives)

Reference number: EZM 3

Movement: automatic, ETA 2824-2, ø 25.6 mm, height 4.6 mm; 25 jewels; 28,800 vph, magnetic field protection to 80,000 A/m; special oil

Functions: hours, minutes, sweep seconds; date

Case: stainless steel, sandblasted, ø 40 mm, height 13 mm; unidirectionally rotating bezel with 60-minute scale; sapphire crystal; screw-in crown; water-resistant to 500 m

Band: stainless steel, folding clasp

Remarks: case filled with Argon and dehumidifying capsule

Price: $1,390

Variations: with leather, rubber or shark skin strap ($1,290)

The Pilot's Chronograph with Second Time Zone

Reference number: 856 S

Movement: automatic, ETA 2893-2, ø 25.6 mm, height 4.1 mm; 21 jewels; 28,800 vph, shockproof and antimagnetic

Functions: hours, minutes, sweep seconds; date; 24-hour display (second time zone)

Case: stainless steel, tegimented black, ø 40 mm, height 10.7 mm; sapphire crystal; screw-in crown; water-resistant to 200 m

Band: leather, buckle

Price: $1,130

Variations: with tegimented black bracelet ($1,290)

The Pilot's Chronograph with Magnetic Field Protection

Reference number: 656

Movement: automatic, ETA 2824-2, ø 25.6 mm, height 4.6 mm; 25 jewels; 28,800 vph, magnetic field protection to 80,000 A/m

Functions: hours, minutes, sweep seconds; date

Case: stainless steel, sandblasted, ø 38.5 mm, height 10.1 mm; sapphire crystal; screw-in crown; water-resistant to 100 m

Band: leather, buckle

Price: $890

Variations: with stainless steel bracelet ($990); black chrome-plated

The Duochronograph with Diapal Technology and Second Time Zone

Reference number: 756 DIAPAL

Movement: automatic, ETA 7750 modified, ø 30 mm, height 7.9 mm; 25 jewels; 28,800 vph, escapement with Diapal technology; magnetic field protection to 80,000 A/m; shockproof and antimagnetic according to DIN

Functions: hours, minutes, chronograph; date

Case: stainless steel, tegimented (1,200 Vickers), ø 40 mm, height 13.7 mm; sapphire crystal; screw-in crown; water-resistant to 200 m

Band: leather, buckle

Price: $1,890

Sothis

For the last eight years, Sothis has supplied the whole world with high-quality mechanical watches.
The brand name is derived from ancient Egyptian mythology and the embodiment of the star Sirius. According to stories handed down through the ages, the appearance of this star in the winter sky was a harbinger of the Nile flood, thus symbolizing that nothing would stand in the way of a good harvest.
For the designer and founder of Sothis, the naming of his company is just as important as the design and quality of each and every watch. Wolfgang Steinkrüger places great value on details, and no watch leaves the workshop without his personal examination.
Tri-fluting is a typical characteristic of the striking case housing each Sothis watch. Because of the modification of the moon phase of Caliber ETA 7751 (from the Valjoux line), the Spirit of Moon model has developed into a sought-after collector's object. This model is already available in four different variations, and another is in planning for 2005.
The current collection, now comprising fourteen models, has been added on to year after year. Every model is available with different dial versions, and, additionally, Steinkrüger does his best to comply with every possible customer wish in that respect.
In the new models that were introduced at Baselworld 2004, Sothis has created two new chronographs of simple elegance: Libra and Janus. Both models focus on the functions of the chronograph itself. The subsidiary dials were kept as large as possible, and the massive lance hands guarantee clear and quick reading of the stopped times. The complete design of the dial, reduced to only that which is necessary, with Super LumiNova-coated hour markers and matching hands, make quick and clear reading of the time possible, both day and night.
Also new in the family are the models Triga, housed in a mid-sized case (39 mm in diameter), and Big Bridge II, whose new chronograph face harmonizes perfectly with the cornered dial shape and lends it an even more striking appearance in conjunction with the case. The cases are quite typical of Sothis's corporate identity and are, of course, limited.

Chronograph Big Brigde II

Reference number: 024001.
Movement: automatic, ETA 2892-A2 with chronograph module 2025 by Dubois-Dépraz, ø 30 mm, height 6.9 mm; 57 jewels; 28,800 vph
Functions: hours, minutes, subsidiary seconds; chronograph; date
Case: stainless steel, 50 x 37 mm, height 12.7 mm; sapphire crystal; transparent case back; water-resistant to 50 m
Band: leather, folding clasp
Remarks: limited to 200 pieces
Price: $5,250
Variations: with black dial

Chronograph Triga

Reference number: 024002.
Movement: automatic, ETA 7753 Tricompax, ø 30 mm, height 7.9 mm; 25 jewels; 28,800 vph
Functions: hours, minutes, subsidiary seconds; chronograph; date
Case: stainless steel, ø 39 mm, height 13.9 mm; sapphire crystal; transparent case back; water-resistant to 50 m
Band: leather, folding clasp
Remarks: limited to 500 pieces
Price: $3,550
Variations: with white dial; with stainless steel bracelet ($4,190); as set

Chronograph Janus

Reference number: 024003.
Movement: automatic, ETA 7750, ø 30 mm, height 7.9 mm; 25 jewels; 28,800 vph
Functions: hours, minutes, subsidiary seconds; chronograph; date and day
Case: stainless steel, ø 42.5 mm, height 13.9 mm; sapphire crystal; transparent case back; water-resistant to 50 m
Band: leather, folding clasp
Remarks: limited to 500 pieces
Price: $3,400
Variations: with black dial; with stainless steel bracelet ($4,040); as set

Chronograph Stardust

Reference number: 020001.
Movement: automatic, ETA 7750, ø 30 mm, height 7.9 mm; 25 jewels; 28,800 vph
Functions: hours, minutes, subsidiary seconds; chronograph; date and day
Case: stainless steel, ø 42.5 mm, height 13.9 mm; sapphire crystal; transparent case back; water-resistant to 50 m
Band: leather, folding clasp
Remarks: limited to 500 pieces
Price: $3,050
Variations: with black dial; with stainless steel bracelet ($3,690); as set

Chronograph Spirit of Moon

Reference number: 098003.
Movement: automatic, ETA 7751 modified, ø 30 mm, height 7.9 mm; 25 jewels; 28,800 vph
Functions: hours, minutes, subsidiary seconds; chronograph; date, day, month, moon phase
Case: stainless steel, ø 42.5 mm, height 13.9 mm; sapphire crystal; transparent case back; water-resistant to 50 m
Band: stainless steel, folding clasp
Remarks: limited to 500 pieces
Price: $4,190
Variations: with black dial; in case size 39 mm, in different dial variations; with leather strap ($3,550); as set

Quantième Spirit of Moon

Reference number: 098008.
Movement: automatic, ETA 2824-2 with calendar module 9000 by Dubois-Dépraz,
Functions: hours, minutes, sweep seconds; date, day, month, moon phase
Case: stainless steel, ø 37 mm, height 10.6 mm; sapphire crystal; transparent case back; water-resistant to 50 m
Band: leather, folding clasp
Remarks: limited to 500 pieces
Price: $2,800
Variations: with silver-colored dial

Stowa

Stowa was founded in 1927 in Hornberg, Germany by Walter Storz. In the 1930s and '40s, the company situated in the Black Forest produced especially high-quality, reliable watches. The degree of excellence achieved by their watches brought Stowa a good reputation, and their pilot's and observation watches were of special note. These watches had to be completely precise and trustworthy as they were used in ways that demanded 100-percent accuracy. The pilot in his cockpit had to be just as sure as the officer on the deck of his ship that his watch was correct. In the 1940s Stowa was one of the five most famous German manufacturers of pilot's and marine watches. These and other historic Stowa models can be admired in the Stowa watch museum maintained by the current owner of the brand, Jörg Schauer.

"Stowa — the German Quality Watch." This is how the traditional Pforzheim brand advertised during its heyday. This elementary concept is being carried on in this day and age: The watches are as striking in their visuals as in their absolute functionality. In this way the old pilot's watches, their designs unfailingly adapted, have today become luxury wristwatches, and their technical straightforwardness and uncomplicated clarity have also been kept. Alongside the pilot's series, a new marine series — also historical in nature — is being produced. In keeping with the motto, "Characteristically original — the details of a Stowa," all Stowa watches are striking in their attention to detail. Nearly every piece of every serial watch undergoes its own individual revision and checking. That the watches are "made in Germany" and thus labeled is enough reason for the new owners of the name to deliver the highest-quality products.

Tradition and modern marketing are united in the seventy-seven-year-old brand, for they are not to be found in the cases of any dealer: Stowa watches can only be purchased at the online shop www.stowa.de. This is equally true of the current model Antea, a remake of a Stowa model from the 1930s.

Antea

Reference number: Antea auto weiss 12 Z LE
Movement: automatic, ETA 2824, ø 25.6 mm, height 4.6 mm; 25 jewels; 28,800 vph, exclusive STOWA rotor
Functions: hours, minutes, sweep seconds
Case: stainless steel, ø 39 mm, height 9.5 mm; sapphire crystal; transparent case back; water-resistant to 50 m
Band: leather, buckle
Price: 299 euros
Variations: with stainless steel bracelet/double folding clasp; with date display

Antea

Reference number: Antea auto schwarz 12ZD LE
Movement: automatic, ETA 2824, ø 25.6 mm, height 4.6 mm; 25 jewels; 28,800 vph, exclusive STOWA rotor
Functions: hours, minutes, sweep seconds; date
Case: stainless steel, ø 39 mm, height 9.5 mm; sapphire crystal; transparent case back; water-resistant to 50 m
Band: leather, buckle
Price: 299 euros
Variations: with stainless steel bracelet/double folding clasp; without date display

Antea

Reference number: Antea auto weiss 12 R LE
Movement: automatic, ETA 2824, ø 25.6 mm, height 4.6 mm; 25 jewels; 28,800 vph, exclusive STOWA rotor
Functions: hours, minutes, sweep seconds
Case: stainless steel, ø 39 mm, height 9.5 mm; sapphire crystal; transparent case back; water-resistant to 50 m
Band: leather, buckle
Price: 299 euros
Variations: with stainless steel bracelet/double folding clasp; with date display

Seatime

Reference number: Seatime orange
Movement: automatic, ETA 2824, ø 25.6 mm, height 4.6 mm; 25 jewels; 28,800 vph, exclusive STOWA rotor
Functions: hours, minutes, sweep seconds
Case: stainless steel, ø 42 mm, height 13 mm; unidirectionally rotating bezel with 60-minute scale; sapphire crystal (3 mm); water-resistant to 300 m
Band: rubber, folding clasp
Price: upon request
Variations: with stainless steel bracelet/double folding clasp; with date display

Airman 47040

Reference number: Flieger 47040 mN
Movement: automatic, ETA 2824, ø 25.6 mm, height 4.6 mm; 25 jewels; 28,800 vph, exclusive STOWA rotor
Functions: hours, minutes, sweep seconds
Case: stainless steel, ø 40 mm, height 10.5 mm; sapphire crystal; transparent case back; water-resistant to 50 m
Band: leather, buckle
Price: 470 euros
Variations: with stainless steel bracelet/double folding clasp

Marine 45040

Reference number: Marine 45040
Movement: automatic, ETA 2824, ø 25.6 mm, height 4.6 mm; 25 jewels; 28,800 vph, exclusive STOWA rotor
Functions: hours, minutes, sweep seconds
Case: stainless steel, ø 40 mm, height 10.5 mm; sapphire crystal; transparent case back; water-resistant to 50 m
Band: leather, buckle
Price: 450 euros
Variations: with stainless steel bracelet/double folding clasp

Swiss Army

Swiss traditions are well cared for, and not only in the world of watches are 100-year and longer anniversaries celebrated. In 1884 Karl Elsener founded his knife cutlery in Ibach, near Schwyz, which is close to Lake Lucerne and the street that will take you to the infamous Gotthard Tunnel. He was soon the official supplier to the Swiss army.

At the beginning, he mainly manufactured simple and robust soldier's pocketknives, but in 1897 he patented his vision of a variable pocketknife containing several blades and tools. From then on, Elsener supplied the Swiss military with this "officer's knife" that has today become a national symbol.

In 1909 he created the brand name Victoria for his inventions, in honor of his mother, and after rustproof steel (called Inox, derived from inoxidable) was invented, the family business was renamed Victorinox in 1921.

Today, Carl Elsener senior and his son Carl junior employ about 1,000 people who manufacture 25 million knives annually. In 1989 father and son Elsener decided to strategically extend the product palette with a collection of sporty and robust wristwatches, which were at first mainly sold in the U.S. — and that with incredible success — under the brand name Swiss Army. Right from the beginning, the Swiss cross in the brand's emblem didn't stand for Victorinox or the officer's knife, but for "Swiss made" and legendary Swiss quality.

Now the Swiss Army brand has moved into its next phase, and the red-and-white cross can be found on leisure clothing and outdoor accessories. And, something even more important for the watch fan, the watch collection is being clearly moved upmarket.

While the Swiss Army watch collections were mainly characterized by sporty quartz watches with a touch of military about them, including different additional functions and in varying case materials, the brand is now clearly going for a slightly different customer. Above all, it is the Professional collection that has become the big winner.

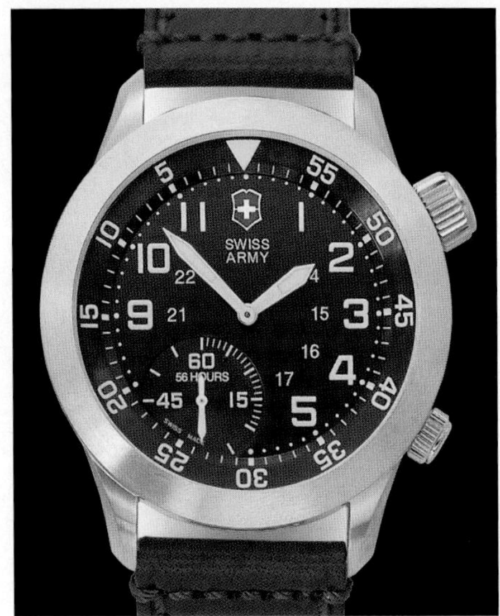

Airboss Mach 4

Reference number: V.25044
Movement: manual winding, ETA 6498-2, ø 37.2 mm, height 4.5 mm; 17 jewels; 21,600 vph
Functions: hours, minutes, subsidiary seconds
Case: stainless steel, ø 45 mm, height 12.1 mm; bidirectionally rotating rotating bezel under crysta with 60-minute scale, settable via crown; sapphire crystal; transparent case back
Band: leather, buckle
Price: $650
Variations: with stainless steel bracelet

Infantry XL

Reference number: V.25053
Movement: automatic, ETA 2895-1, ø 26.2 mm, height 4.5 mm; 30 jewels; 28,800 vph
Functions: hours, minutes, subsidiary seconds; date
Case: stainless steel, ø 43 mm, height 10.2 mm; sapphire crystal; transparent case back
Band: leather, buckle
Price: $595

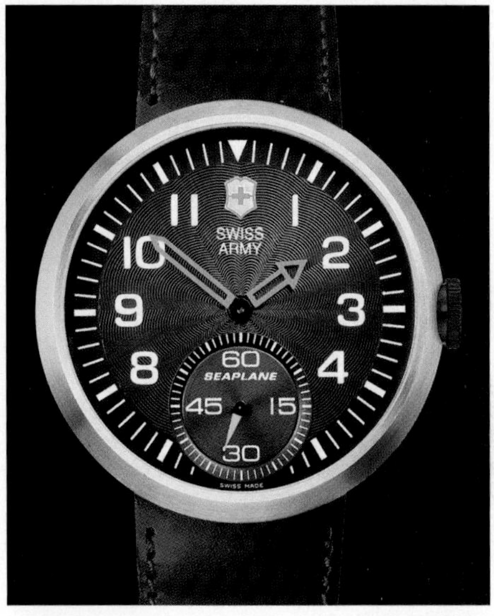

Seaplane XL

Reference number: V.25076
Movement: manual winding, ETA 6498-1, ø 36.6 mm, height 4.5 mm; 17 jewels; 18,000 vph
Functions: hours, minutes, subsidiary seconds
Case: stainless steel, ø 45 mm, height 12.75 mm; mineral crystal; transparent case back
Band: leather, buckle
Remarks: patented band changing system with bayonet catch; delivered with additional stainless steel bracelet
Price: $650
Variations: with black leather strap

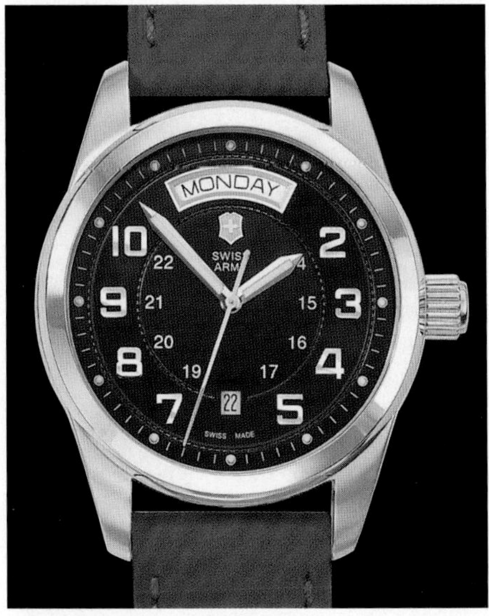

Ambassador Day & Date

Reference number: V.25147
Movement: automatic, ETA 2834-2, ø 29.6 mm, height 5.05 mm; 25 jewels; 28,800 vph
Functions: hours, minutes, sweep seconds; date and day
Case: stainless steel, ø 41 mm, height 11.15 mm; sapphire crystal; transparent case back
Band: leather, buckle
Price: $525
Variations: with silver dial; with stainless steel bracelet

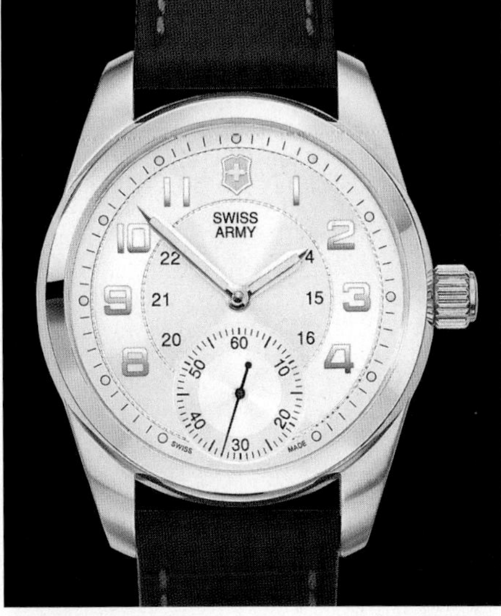

Ambassador XL

Reference number: V.25152
Movement: manual winding, ETA 6498-2, ø 36.6 mm, height 4.5 mm; 17 jewels; 18,000 vph
Functions: hours, minutes, subsidiary seconds
Case: stainless steel, ø 45 mm, height 11.75 mm; sapphire crystal; transparent case back
Band: leather, buckle
Price: $550

Chronopro

Reference number: V.25162
Movement: automatic, ETA 7750, ø 30 mm, height 7.9 mm; 25 jewels; 28,800 vph
Functions: hours, minutes, subsidiary seconds; chronograph; date
Case: stainless steel, ø 42 mm, height 15.2 mm; sapphire crystal; transparent case back; screw-in crown and buttons
Band: stainless steel, double folding clasp with security button
Price: $1,195
Variations: with leather strap

TAG Heuer

During its 144-year-long history, this prestigious Swiss manufacturer with a special reputation for chronographs has given itself the job of measuring sports' best performances of the twentieth and twenty-first centuries with the highest precision watch-making has to offer. The mastering of time always motivated the Heuer family, but, simultaneously, the brand was always interested in being somewhat more avant-garde than other Swiss manufacturers. Thus, it was in 1916 that Charles-Auguste Heuer, son of the company's founder, developed the first mechanical timekeeping instrument capable of measuring hundredths of a second.

Jack W. Heuer, great-grandson of the company's founder and from 1958 its head for twenty years, added a further highlight to the company's history in 1966: The patented Microtimer was the first compact, electronic timekeeper possessing precision to one-thousandth of a second.

This company treasures its proximity to the world of automobiles and racing and has recently done more than just name watches for its stars and premier events. The presentation of a watch movement design not dissimilar to that of an automobile motor surprised the watch world at Baselworld 2004. Not only that, but it broke all the accepted laws of watchmaking. Energy transmission in the winding mechanism, for example, is not done as usual via toothed wheels in this movement, but rather by use of thirteen miniature toothed belts. The lion's share of the usual synthetic rubies used in a normal movement to reduce friction were exchanged for micro ball bearings. The oscillating weight, which generally rotates around its own axis in order to wind the mainspring, was exchanged for a linear weight that bounces back and forth. This new oscillating weight, a bar of platinum, winds the contents of four spring barrels placed in a v-shaped pair of rows, strongly reminiscent of the cylinders found in an automobile's motor. This

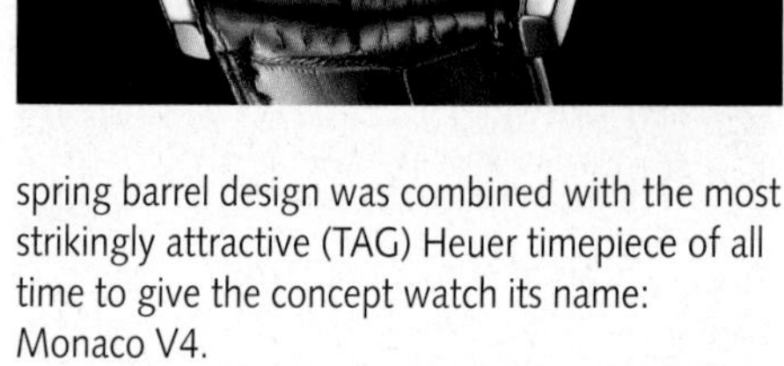

spring barrel design was combined with the most strikingly attractive (TAG) Heuer timepiece of all time to give the concept watch its name: Monaco V4.

Alongside such technical highlights, TAG Heuer also possesses a large portfolio filled with conventional watches and chronographs. The collection includes the three sports watch lines Series 2000, Kirium, and Link as well as the alter ego (Latin for "the other me"), a line developed especially for women. Particularly in Europe, models from the Classic line such as Monza, Carrera, Targa Florio, Monaco, and Autavia are exceptionally popular.

Another new product also symbolizes the relationship TAG Heuer has with fast cars: the SLR Chronograph with its regulator dial. This unusual watch displays the fundamental design elements of the super sports car Mercedes Benz SLR McLaren. Unfortunately, not everyone can buy this watch: In order to gain the right to acquire the timepiece, one must first purchase the larger, four-wheeled model made by the car manufacturer.

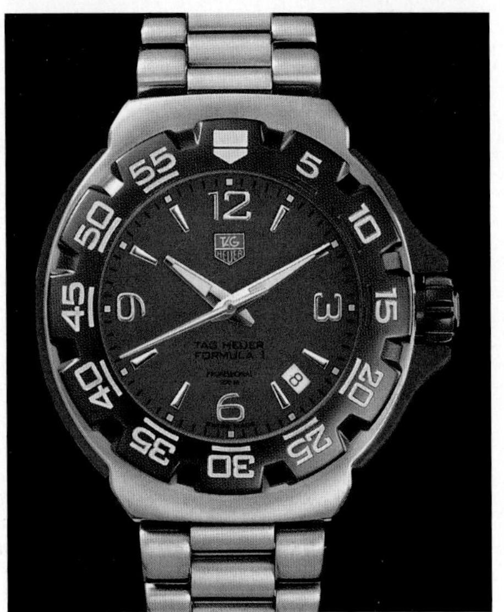

New Formula 1

Reference number: WAC1113.BA0850
Movement: quartz, ETA 955.112
Functions: hours, minutes, sweep seconds; date
Case: stainless steel with plastic elements, ø 40 mm, height 11.6 mm; unidirectionally rotating bezel with 60-minute scale; sapphire crystal; screw-in crown; water-resistant to 200 m
Band: stainless steel, folding clasp
Price: $650
Variations: with rubber strap ($595); different dial colors

New Formula 1 Chronograph

Reference number: CAC1111.BA0850
Movement: quartz, ETA G10.711
Functions: hours, minutes, subsidiary seconds; chronograph; date
Case: stainless steel with plastic elements, ø 40 mm, height 11.6 mm; unidirectionally rotating bezel with 60-minute scale; sapphire crystal; screw-in crown; water-resistant to 200 m
Band: stainless steel, folding clasp
Price: $850
Variations: with rubber strap; with black dial

2000 Classic Quartz

Reference number: WK1110.FT8002
Movement: quartz, ETA 955.112
Functions: hours, minutes, sweep seconds; date
Case: stainless steel, ø 37 mm, height 9 mm; unidirectionally rotating bezel with 60-minute scale; sapphire crystal; screw-in crown; water-resistant to 200 m
Band: stainless steel, folding clasp
Price: $995
Variations: with rubber strap ($850); different dial colors; in stainless steel/yellow gold with two-tone bracelet ($1,250)

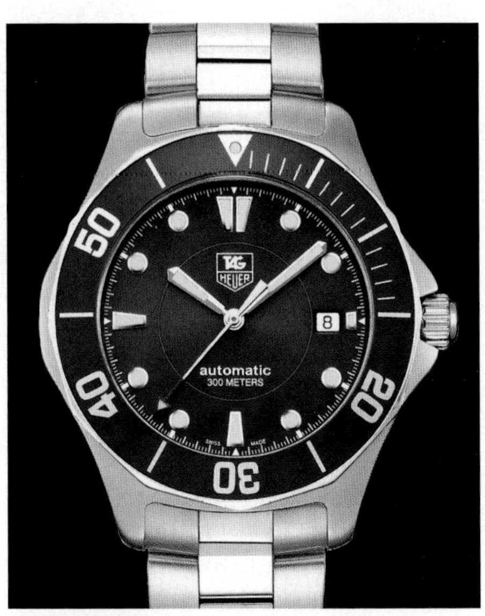

2000 AQUARACER Automatic

Reference number: WAB2011.BA0803
Movement: automatic, TAG Heuer 5 (base ETA 2824); ø 25.6 mm, height 4.6 mm; 25 jewels; 28,800 vph
Functions: hours, minutes, sweep seconds; date
Case: stainless steel, ø 41 mm, height 10 mm; unidirectionally rotating bezel with 60-minute scale; sapphire crystal; screw-in crown; water-resistant to 300 m
Band: stainless steel, folding clasp
Price: $1,250
Variations: with black dial; with quartz movement

2000 Exclusive Automatic Chronograph

Reference number: CN2110.BA0361
Movement: automatic, TAG Heuer 16 (base ETA 7750); ø 30 mm, height 7.9 mm; 25 jewels; 28,800 vph
Functions: hours, minutes, subsidiary seconds; chronograph; date
Case: stainless steel, ø 39 mm, height 15 mm; unidirectionally rotating bezel with 60-minute scale; sapphire crystal; screw-in crown; water-resistant to 200 m
Band: stainless steel, folding clasp
Price: $1,995
Variations: different dial colors

2000 Aquagraph Automatic

Reference number: CN211A.BA0353
Movement: automatic, TAG Heuer 60 (base Dubois-Dépraz 2073); ø 25.6 mm, height 7.4 mm; 46 jewels; 28,800 vph
Functions: hours, minutes, subsidiary seconds; chronograph; date; automatic helium valve
Case: stainless steel, ø 43 mm, height 14 mm; unidirectionally rotating bezel with 60-minute scale and patented protection against accidental turning; sapphire crystal; screw-in crown with security indicator; buttons functional & water-resistant to 500 m
Band: stainless steel, security folding clasp with wetsuit extension
Price: $2,800

Kirium Chronograph Formula 1

Reference number: CL111A.BA0700
Movement: quartz, ETA E20.321, multifunctional electronic module with LCD-Display integrated into dial
Functions: hours, minutes, sweep seconds; chronograph, perpetual calendar with date, day, calendar week, month, leap year, second time zone, alarm, countdown in LCD display
Case: stainless steel, ø 39 mm, height 14.5 mm; unidirectionally rotating bezel with 60-minute scale; sapphire crystal; water-resistant to 200 m
Band: stainless steel, folding clasp
Price: $1,995
Variations: with rubber strap

Link Quartz

Reference number: WJ1111.BA0570
Movement: quartz, ETA 905.112
Functions: hours, minutes, sweep seconds; date
Case: stainless steel, ø 39 mm, height 11 mm; unidirectionally rotating bezel with 60-minute scale; sapphire crystal; screw-in crown; water-resistant to 200 m
Band: stainless steel, folding clasp
Price: $1,595
Variations: different dial colors

Link Automatic Limited Edition Tiger Woods 2004

Reference number: WJF2113.BA0570
Movement: automatic, TAG Heuer 7 (base ETA 2892-A2); ø 25.6 mm, height 3.6 mm; 21 jewels; 28,800 vph
Functions: hours, minutes, sweep seconds; date
Case: stainless steel, ø 39 mm, height 10.5 mm; sapphire crystal; case back with engraved signature of Tiger Woods; screw-in crown; water-resistant to 200 m
Band: stainless steel, folding clasp
Remarks: special edition model; limited to 5,500 pieces
Price: $2,295

Link Automatic Chronograph

Reference number: CJF2110.BA0576
Movement: automatic, TAG Heuer 16 (base ETA 7750); ø 30 mm, height 7.9 mm; 25 jewels; 28,800 vph
Functions: hours, minutes, subsidiary seconds; chronograph; date
Case: stainless steel, ø 41 mm, height 16 mm; flange with tachymeter scale; sapphire crystal; screw-in crown; water-resistant to 200 m
Band: stainless steel, folding clasp
Price: $2,495
Variations: different dial colors

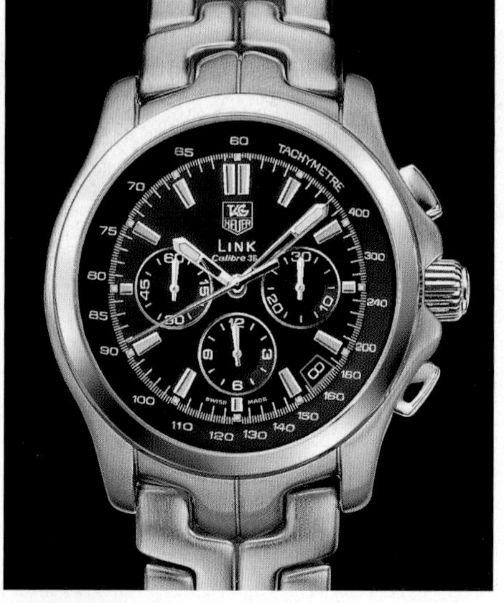

Link Calibre 36 Chronograph

Reference number: CT511A.BA0564
Movement: automatic, TAG Heuer 36 (base Zenith El Primero 400); ø 30 mm, height 6.5 mm; 31 jewels; 36,600 vph, certified chronometer (C.O.S.C.)
Functions: hours, minutes, subsidiary seconds; chronograph; date
Case: stainless steel, ø 42 mm, height 14.5 mm; flange with tachymeter scale; sapphire crystal; transparent case back; screw-in crown; water-resistant to 200 m
Band: stainless steel, folding clasp
Price: $2,595
Variations: with silver-colored dial

Microtimer

Reference number: CS111C.FT6003
Movement: quartz, TAG Heuer HR 03, multifunctional movement developed by TAG Heuer
Functions: hours, minutes, date; chronograph (with 1/1000 display precision), alarm; second time zone; stop-timing; lap time memory (80 laps)
Case: stainless steel, 38 x 52 mm, height 10 mm; sapphire crystal
Band: rubber, folding clasp
Price: $1,850
Variations: with diamonds

Carrera Automatic Twin-Time

Reference number: WV2115.FC6180
Movement: automatic, TAG Heuer 7 (base ETA 2893-2); ø 25.6 mm, height 4.6 mm; 25 jewels; 28,800 vph
Functions: hours, minutes, sweep seconds; date; 24-hour display (second time zone)
Case: stainless steel, ø 39 mm, height 12 mm; flange with 24-hour scale; sapphire crystal; water-resistant to 50 m
Band: reptile skin, folding clasp
Price: $1,695
Variations: with silver-colored dial; with leather strap designed to look like a driving glove

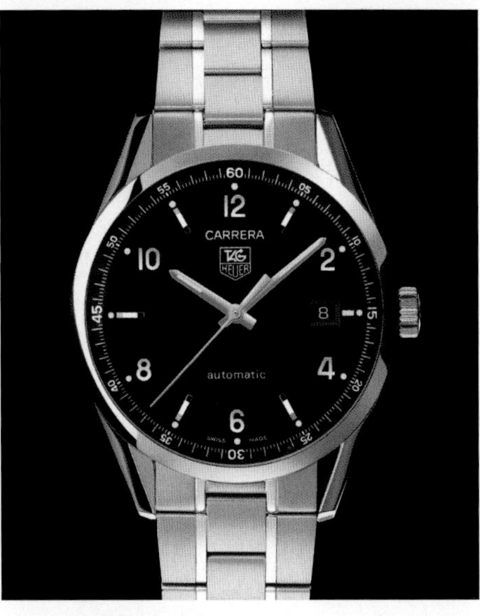

Carrera Automatic

Reference number: WV211B.BA0787
Movement: automatic, TAG Heuer 5 (base ETA 2824); ø 25.6 mm, height 4.6 mm; 25 jewels; 28,800 vph
Functions: hours, minutes, sweep seconds; date
Case: stainless steel, ø 39 mm, height 11 mm; sapphire crystal; transparent case back; water-resistant to 50 m
Band: stainless steel, folding clasp
Price: $2,350
Variations: with silver-colored dial

Carrera Chronograph Racing

Reference number: CV2113.FC6182
Movement: automatic, TAG Heuer 17 (base ETA 2894-2); ø 28.6 mm, height 6.1 mm; 37 jewels; 28,800 vph
Functions: hours, minutes, subsidiary seconds; chronograph; date
Case: stainless steel, ø 39 mm, height 14 mm; sapphire crystal; water-resistant to 50 m
Band: leather, gelocht, folding clasp
Price: $2,650
Variations: with silver-colored dial

Carrera Chronograph Limited Ed. 1964

Reference number: CV2117.FC6182
Movement: automatic, TAG Heuer 17 (base ETA 2894-2); ø 28.6 mm, height 6.1 mm; 37 jewels; 28,800 vph
Functions: hours, minutes, subsidiary seconds; chronograph; date
Case: stainless steel, ø 39 mm, height 14 mm; sapphire crystal; case back with engraved signature of Jack W. Heuer; water-resistant to 50 m
Band: leather with holes, folding clasp
Remarks: limited to 1,964 pieces
Price: $2,650

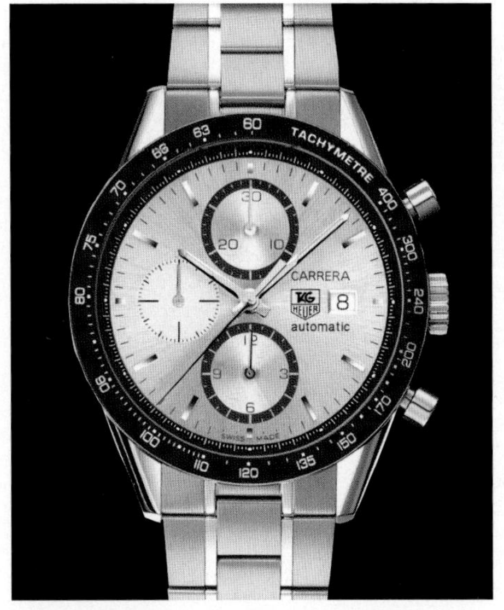

Carrera Chronograph Tachymeter

Reference number: CV2011.BA0786
Movement: automatic, TAG Heuer 16 (base ETA 7750); ø 30 mm, height 7.9 mm; 25 jewels; 28,800 vph
Functions: hours, minutes, subsidiary seconds; chronograph; date
Case: stainless steel, ø 41 mm, height 16 mm; aluminum bezel with tachymeter scale; sapphire crystal; transparent case back; water-resistant to 50 m
Band: stainless steel, folding clasp
Price: $2,095
Variations: different dial variations

Monaco Chronograph Python

Reference number: CW2114.EB0017
Movement: automatic, TAG Heuer 17 (base ETA 2894-2); ø 28.6 mm, height 6.1 mm; 37 jewels; 28,800 vph
Functions: hours, minutes, subsidiary seconds; chronograph; date
Case: stainless steel, 40 x 40 mm, height 13.5 mm; Plexiglas
Band: python skin, folding clasp
Remarks: delivered with brown crocodile skin strap
Price: $2,995

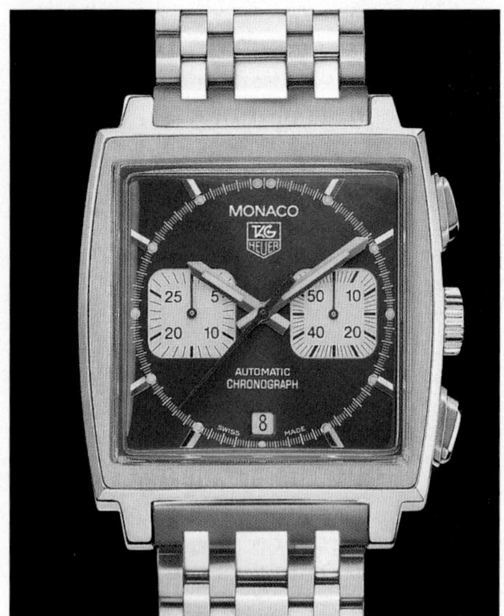

Monaco Chronograph Steve McQueen Edition

Reference number: CW2113.BA0780
Movement: automatic, TAG Heuer 17 (base ETA 2894-2); ø 28.6 mm, height 6.1 mm; 37 jewels; 28,800 vph
Functions: hours, minutes, subsidiary seconds; chronograph; date
Case: stainless steel, 40 x 40 mm, height 13.5 mm; Plexiglas
Band: stainless steel, folding clasp
Price: $2,895
Variations: with reptile skin strap

Monaco Sixty Nine

Reference number: CW9110.FC6177
Movement: manual winding, TAG Heuer 2 (base ETA 7001); additionally TAG Heuer Caliber HR 03 (quartz)
Functions: hours, minutes, subsidiary seconds (front); chronograph (with 1/1000 display precision), alarm; second time zone; stop timing; lap time memory (back)
Case: stainless steel, ø 40 x 41 mm, height 18 mm; case can be turned and rotated 180°; sapphire crystal; water-resistant to 50 m
Band: reptile skin, folding clasp
Price: $5,900

Autavia Chronograph

Reference number: CY2111.BA0775
Movement: automatic, TAG Heuer 11 (base Dubois-Dépraz Caliber 2022); ø 30 mm; 55 jewels; 28,800 vph
Functions: hours, minutes, subsidiary seconds; chronograph; date
Case: stainless steel, ø 42 mm, height 14 mm; bezel with tachymeter scale; sapphire crystal; water-resistant to 50 m
Band: stainless steel, folding clasp
Price: $3,095
Variations: different dial versions; with leather strap

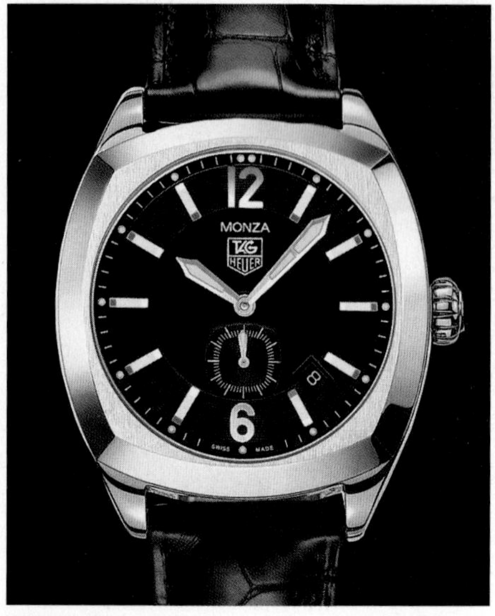

Monza Automatic

Reference number: WR2110.FC6164
Movement: automatic, TAG Heuer 6 (base ETA 2895-1); ø 25.6 mm, height 4.35 mm; 30 jewels; 28,800 vph
Functions: hours, minutes, subsidiary seconds; date
Case: stainless steel, ø 39.5 mm, height 9 mm; sapphire crystal; water-resistant to 50 m
Band: reptile skin, folding clasp
Price: $1,695
Variations: with brown crocodile skin strap

Monza Automatic Chronograph

Reference number: CR2113.FC6165
Movement: automatic, TAG Heuer 17 (base ETA 2894-2); ø 28.6 mm, height 6.1 mm; 37 jewels; 28,800 vph
Functions: hours, minutes, subsidiary seconds; chronograph; date
Case: stainless steel, ø 39.5 mm, height 13.5 mm; sapphire crystal; water-resistant to 50 m
Band: reptile skin, folding clasp
Price: $2,950
Variations: with silver-colored dial

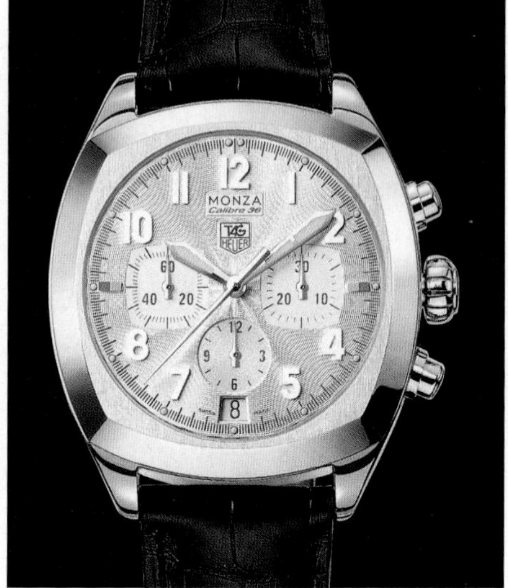

Monza Calibre 36 Chronograph

Reference number: CR5110.FC6175
Movement: automatic, TAG Heuer 36 (base Zenith El Primero 400); ø 30 mm, height 6.5 mm; 31 jewels; 36,000 vph, certified chronometer (C.O.S.C.)
Functions: hours, minutes, subsidiary seconds; chronograph; date
Case: stainless steel, ø 39.5 mm, height 14 mm; sapphire crystal; transparent case back; water-resistant to 50 m
Band: reptile skin, folding clasp
Price: $4,495
Variations: with black dial

Temption

The brand's name already shows what company founder Klaus Ulbrich is all about: Temption is a word that he invented, combining *tempus* and *function*, thus intending it to mean functional timekeeping. Ulbrich has also kept the design of the watch subservient to the function. He says that he "does not want to re-warm things from the past, but rather find inspiration in the present, in order to anticipate the future."

Regardless of this, Ulbrich has researched the past, occupying himself for a long time with the reasons why some things created by humans easily last decades, even centuries, and remain contemporary, while others hardly make it a season. Ancient cave drawings, for example, represent animals with a stylistic elegance and grace that is still fascinating today. The talented painter succeeded in perfectly capturing the character of the animals, as well as the kinetics and charm of their movements, with minimalistic lines. These cave drawings have stood firm against the test of time due to the level of their artistry — they truly represent the meaning of the word "timeless." And this is also Ulbrich's demand on timekeepers: "My watches should hold for an entire lifetime and more." Without a doubt there is a rule that lurks behind the reasons for "timelessness," to whose elementary characteristics using only what is necessary, clear functionality, and originality all belong.

It is Ulbrich's goal to transfer this "law" to his watch design by use of the ideals typical of design schools such as the Moderns and Wabi Sabi. Components such as the overall simplicity of shapes come from the Bauhaus movement; the attention to materials and simple warmth, from Wabi Sabi. From both philosophical schools comes the idea of reducing to only that which is necessary — as well as the conclusion that less is often more.

The focal point of Temption's design character is a model that Ulbrich likes to call the "information pyramid." At the top of this pyramid are located the central hour and minute indicators; other functions follow underneath in order to give these main functions a visual priority. For this reason, the most contrast within the dial visuals can be found between the dial and hands. The date window is the same color as the dial and not framed (so the dial remains calm); the totalizers and stop functions are not encircled, and the stop hands are not outfitted with arbors for the same reason. At the low end of this information pyramid is situated the brand's logo, most unimportant to reading the time, and for this reason it is printed in shiny black on a matte black background, where it may only be seen — and then quite clearly — when light shines on it from the side.

At a time when most smaller German watch manufacturers — including Temption itself — are producing relatively large watches, Temption has introduced a chronograph with a surprisingly small case diameter of 29.2 mm (and 9.6 mm height), striking in its delicateness. The Cora model may even be the smallest automatic wrist chronograph in current production.

Automatic with Second Time Zone

Reference number: Olympic
Movement: automatic, Temption T16.1 (base ETA 2893-2); ø 25.6 mm, height 4.1 mm; 21 jewels; 28,800 vph, finished, perlage bridges, côtes de Genève
Functions: hours, minutes, sweep seconds; date; 24-hour hand (second time zone)
Case: stainless steel, ø 42 mm, height 9.8 mm; sapphire crystal; transparent case back; screw-in crown; water-resistant to 100 m
Band: stainless steel, double folding clasp
Price: $1,770
Variations: with leather strap

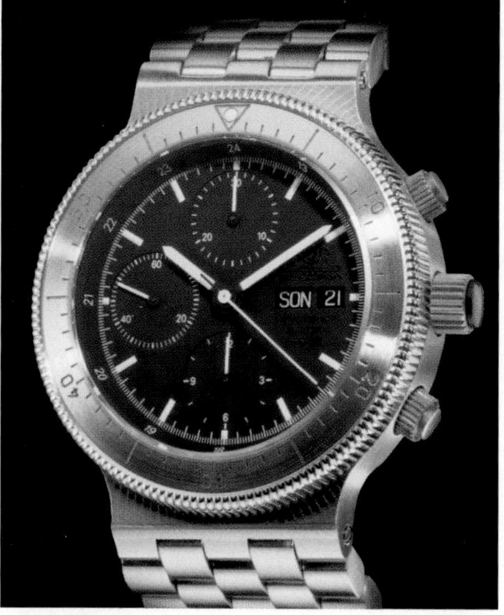

Chronograph

Reference number: CG103
Movement: automatic, Temption T17.2 (base ETA 7750); ø 30 mm, height 7.8 mm; 25 jewels; 28,800 vph, finished, movement gold-plated, bridges with perlage, côtes de Genève
Functions: hours, minutes, subsidiary seconds; chronograph; date
Case: stainless steel, ø 42 mm, height 14.8 mm; unidirectionally rotating bezel with 60-minute scale; sapphire crystal; transparent case back; screw-in crown and buttons; water-resistant to 100 m
Band: stainless steel, double folding clasp
Price: $2,635

Chronograph with Complication

Reference number: CGK203
Movement: automatic, Temption T18.2 (base ETA 7751); ø 30 mm, height 7.8 mm; 25 jewels; 28,800 vph, finished, movement gold-plated, bridges with perlage, côtes de Genève
Functions: hours, minutes, subsidiary seconds; chronograph; date, day, month, moon phase; 24-hour display
Case: stainless steel, ø 42 mm, height 14.8 mm; unidirectionally rotating bezel with 60-minute scale; sapphire crystal; transparent case back; screw-in crown and buttons; water-resistant to 100 m
Band: stainless steel, double folding clasp
Price: $3,300

Chronograph Rattrapante

Reference number: Cherubin-R
Movement: automatic, Temption T19.1 (base Soprod VAL7750-SORA (ETA 7750)); ø 30 mm, height 8.3 mm; 28 jewels; 28,800 vph, finished, bridges with perlage, côtes de Genève; certified chronometer (C.O.S.C.)
Functions: hours, minutes, subsidiary seconds; split seconds chronograph; date
Case: stainless steel, ø 42 mm, height 15.3 mm; sapphire crystal; transparent case back; screw-in crown and buttons; water-resistant to 100 m
Band: stainless steel, double folding clasp
Price: $6,760

Chronograph Cora

Reference number: CORA
Movement: automatic, Temption T22.1 (base ETA 2094); ø 23.9 mm, height 5.5 mm; 33 jewels; 28,800 vph, finished, movement gold-plated, bridges with perlage, côtes de Genève
Functions: hours, minutes, subsidiary seconds; chronograph; date
Case: stainless steel, ø 29.2 mm, height 9.6 mm; sapphire crystal; transparent case back; water-resistant to 60 m
Band: leather, buckle
Remarks: smallest mechanical chronograph on the market
Price: $3,960
Variations: different dial versions

Chronograph Cora Diamond

Reference number: CORA
Movement: automatic, Temption T22.1 (base ETA 2094); ø 23.9 mm, height 5.5 mm; 33 jewels; 28,800 vph, finished, movement gold-plated, bridges with perlage, côtes de Genève
Functions: hours, minutes, subsidiary seconds; chronograph; date
Case: stainless steel, ø 29.2 mm, height 9.6 mm; bezel and lugs set with diamonds; sapphire crystal; transparent case back; water-resistant to 60 m
Band: stingray, buckle
Remarks: smallest mechanical chronograph on the market
Price: $8,770

Tissot

Times change, but there is hardly another watch brand that has literally contributed to the worldwide fame of the Swiss watch industry as Tissot has. Along with entrepreneurial vision and good fortune in business dealings, one of the strongest characteristics of company presidents bearing the name Tissot for many generations was a propensity for travel.

The wild and woolly adventures experienced by Charles-Emile Tissot as he journeyed by sled and troika across Russia at the end of the nineteenth century are legend. Russia and North America then became the markets in which Tissot expanded and prospered.

Back home in Switzerland, the respective managers also knew what they were doing. A liaison with the Brandt company, which owned the Omega brand, led to the foundation of the Société Suisse pour l'Industrie Horlogère S.A. (S.S.I.H.), a forerunner of the SMH, today's Swatch Group, under whose umbrella Tissot still operates. Even then the areas of responsibility were very clearly defined and assigned: Omega was to handle the lower end of the luxury segment, and Tissot was to focus on the mid-priced watch category. One of the results of this was that Tissot began to use a sophisticated modular system at a very early stage, so that with just five cases, for example, a total of forty different models were created.

Another effect of this division was that Tissot was also responsible for promoting innovation and technical development. As early as the beginning of the 1930s, Tissot produced the first antimagnetic watch; in 1960 the idea of a standard caliber was developed, a concept later adopted by the entire watchmaking industry; and in 1971 Tissot launched a new watch with a plastic mechanical movement. With the manufacture of these plastic watch movements, it was Tissot who actually cleared the path for injected plastic in watch production, a process that just a mere decade later would make the greatest success in the history of the watch-making industry possible: Swatch. Additionally, both the first autoquartz caliber and T-Touch technology, featuring sensors in the crystal that are sensitive to touch, debuted in Tissot watches. Tissot's recently chosen tagline, "Innovators by Tradition," sums it up nicely: For 151 years, Tissot has stood for innovation, unusual ideas, and an inventive spirit.

Another burst of popularity is being experienced by the brand since it has been especially active in sports timekeeping. The dynamic sports the company sponsors include cycling and motorcycling (track, street, and classic) and also team sports such as ice hockey and fencing, where Tissot functions as the official timekeeper.

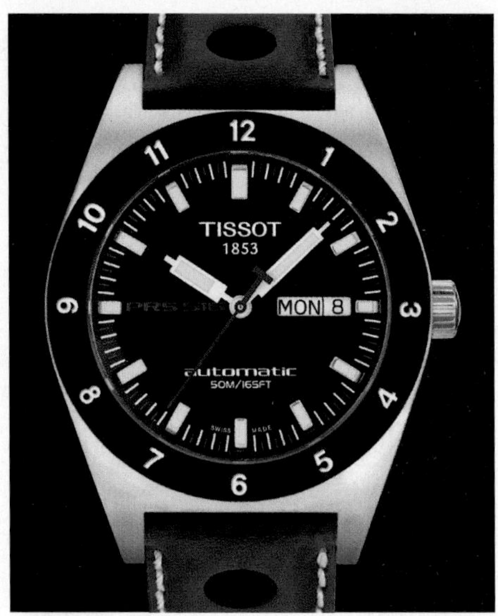

PRS 516

Reference number: T91.1.413.51
Movement: automatic, ETA 2836-2, ø 25.6 mm, height 5.05 mm; 25 jewels; 28,800 vph
Functions: hours, minutes, sweep seconds; date and day
Case: stainless steel, ø 40 mm, height 12.3 mm; sapphire crystal; transparent case back; water-resistant to 50 m
Band: leather, folding clasp
Remarks: dial with "hanging markers," meaning the hands pass underneath under the markers
Price: $350
Variations: with silver-colored dial; stainless steel bracelet

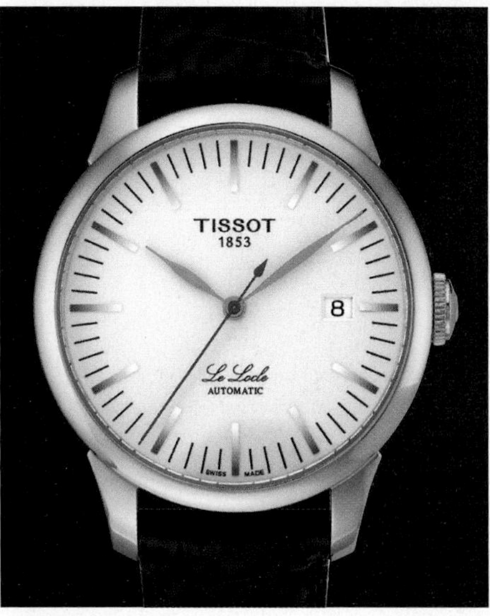

Le Locle

Reference number: T41.1.423.71
Movement: automatic, ETA 2824-2, ø 25.6 mm, height 4.6 mm; 25 jewels; 28,800 vph, movement finely decorated
Functions: hours, minutes, sweep seconds; date
Case: stainless steel, ø 39.3 mm, height 9.2 mm; sapphire crystal; transparent case back
Band: leather, folding clasp
Price: $350
Variations: with PVD-coated case

Le Locle Automatic Chronograph

Reference number: T41.1.317.31
Movement: automatic, ETA 7750, ø 30 mm, height 7.9 mm; 25 jewels; 28,800 vph, movement finely decorated
Functions: hours, minutes, subsidiary seconds; chronograph; date and day
Case: stainless steel, ø 42.3 mm, height 13 mm; sapphire crystal; transparent case back
Band: leather, double folding clasp
Price: $795
Variations: with stainless steel bracelet and black dial

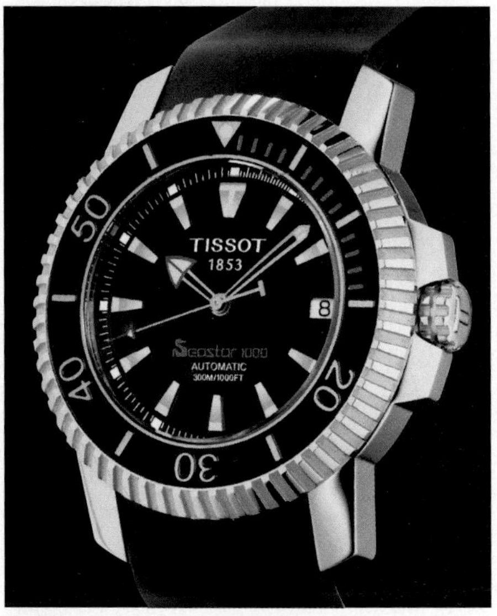

Diver Seastar 1000 Automatic

Reference number: T19.1.593.51
Movement: automatic, ETA 2824-2, ø 25.6 mm, height 4.6 mm; 25 jewels; 28,800 vph, movement finely decorated
Functions: hours, minutes, sweep seconds; date
Case: stainless steel, ø 44 mm, height 15.4 mm; unidirectionally rotating bezel with 60-minute scale; sapphire crystal; transparent case back; screw-in crown; water-resistant to 300 m
Band: rubber, folding clasp with wetsuit extension
Price: $495
Variations: with stainless steel bracelet and different dial variations

T-Race

Reference number: T90.4.496.51
Movement: quartz, ETA G10.211
Functions: hours, minutes, subsidiary seconds; chronograph; date
Case: stainless steel and carbon fiber, ø 39.6 mm, height 11.85 mm; sapphire crystal; water-resistant to 50 m
Band: rubber, folding clasp
Price: $350
Variations: with blue dial and blue rubber strap

BellflHour

Reference number: T11.1.425.51
Movement: quartz, ETA 901001
Functions: hours, minutes
Case: stainless steel, 19.5 x 38 mm, height 8.8 mm; bezel and lugs set with brilliant-cut diamonds; sapphire crystal; water-resistant to 50 m
Band: leather, folding clasp
Price: $1,095
Variations: with fewer diamonds

Tudor

Those who decide to buy a Tudor prove that they possess taste and a sense of quality that is not influenced from the outside. Wristwatches by Tudor stand for excellent workmanship and absolute reliability, combined with timeless elegance. They offer individual variety thanks to a large selection of dials, bands, and bezels, depending on the model, and are available in different sizes. The models Prince Date and Princess Date as well as the Prince chrono-graphs are water-resistant to 100 meters, with the Hydronauts water-resistant to even 200 meters. The best sales argument for Tudor watches has always been their direct relation to Rolex. Conceived right from the beginning as the company's "second" brand, to attract customers in a financial class below the typical Rolex customer, Tudor watches possessed all of the same ingredients a Rolex did — at least on the outside. The most important difference to the mother brand was already inherent in the 1940s when the first Tudor Oyster reached the market: Nestled in the watertight screwed-down Oyster case, well protected from prying eyes, there ticked not a Rolex *manufacture* caliber, but a standard movement supplied by Ébauches SA, today's ETA. "Standard" is certainly a word to be careful with, as Tudor watches outfitted thusly are absolutely precise.

Today, the company still places value on the fact that the modified automatic and quartz calibers by ETA are "especially made for Tudor," and the movements' rates certainly do speak for careful adjustment.

It is qualities such as the water- and pressure-resistant screwed-in case back, the thick crystal (some varieties of which bear a magnifying lens over the date window), the doubly sealed and screwed-in crown, and the extravagant, high-quality construction of the unidirectional rotating diver's bezel (depending on the model) that are talked about just as much as the comparatively reasonable price of the "little sisters." In this way the Tudor brand has been able to establish itself in watch enthusiast circles as a genuine insider tip for quality-conscious collectors without branding preference. The sum of the financial advantages outweigh the missing *manufacture* caliber after all.

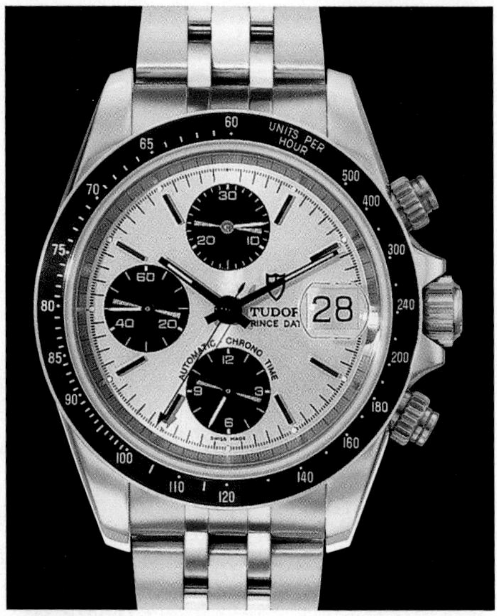

Prince Date Chronograph

Reference number: 79260 P
Movement: automatic, ETA 7750-1, ø 30.4 mm, height 7.9 mm; 25 jewels; 28,800 vph, especially manufactured for Tudor
Functions: hours, minutes, subsidiary seconds; chronograph; date
Case: stainless steel, ø 39 mm, height 15.3 mm; bezel with tachymeter scale; sapphire crystal with magnifying lens; screw-in crown and buttons; water-resistant to 100 m
Band: stainless steel, folding clasp
Price: upon request
Variations: with leather strap/folding clasp; different dials

Chronautic Chronograph

Reference number: 79380 P
Movement: automatic, ETA 7750-1, ø 30.4 mm, height 7.9 mm; 25 jewels; 28,800 vph, especially manufactured for Tudor
Functions: hours, minutes, subsidiary seconds; chronograph; date
Case: stainless steel, ø 41 mm, height 13.8 mm; bezel with tachymeter scale; sapphire crystal; screw-in crown; water-resistant to 100 m
Band: stainless steel, folding clasp with security device
Price: upon request
Variations: different dial variations

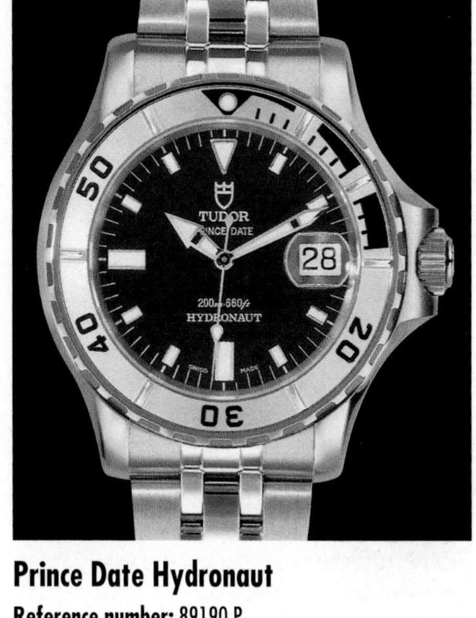

Prince Date Hydronaut

Reference number: 89190 P
Movement: automatic, ETA 2824-2, ø 25.6 mm, height 4.6 mm; 25 jewels; 28,800 vph, especially manufactured for Tudor
Functions: hours, minutes, sweep seconds; date
Case: stainless steel, ø 39 mm, height 12.5 mm; unidirectionally rotating bezel with 60-minute scale; sapphire crystal with magnifying lens above the date display; screw-in crown; water-resistant to 200 m
Band: stainless steel, folding clasp with security device
Price: upon request
Variations: different dial variations

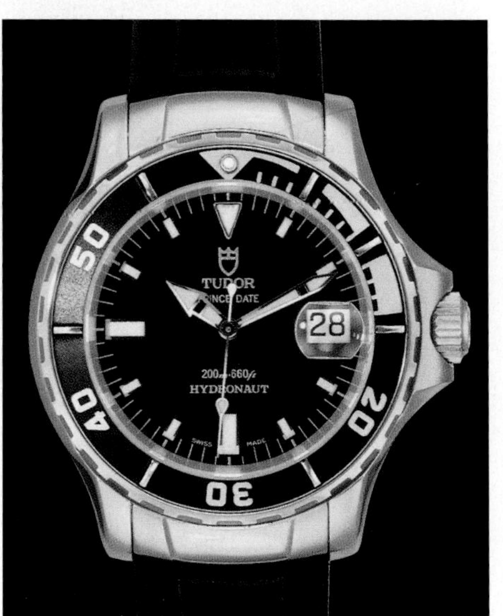

Prince Date Hydronaut

Reference number: 89190 PN
Movement: automatic, ETA 2824-2, ø 25.6 mm, height 4.6 mm; 25 jewels; 28,800 vph, especially manufactured for Tudor
Functions: hours, minutes, sweep seconds; date
Case: stainless steel, ø 39 mm, height 12.5 mm; unidirectionally rotating bezel with 60-minute scale; sapphire crystal with magnifying lens above the date display; screw-in crown; water-resistant to 200 m
Band: rubber, folding clasp
Price: upon request
Variations: different dial variations

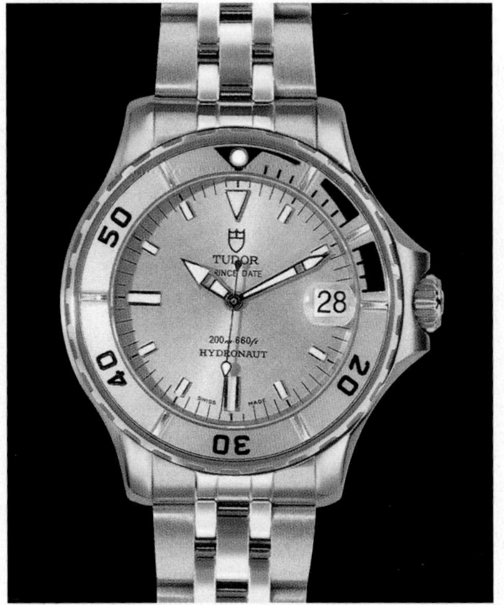

Prince Date Hydronaut

Reference number: 85190 P
Movement: automatic, ETA 2824-2, ø 25.6 mm, height 4.6 mm; 25 jewels; 28,800 vph, especially manufactured for Tudor
Functions: hours, minutes, sweep seconds; date
Case: stainless steel, ø 35 mm, height 12.5 mm; unidirectionally rotating bezel with 60-minute scale; sapphire crystal with magnifying lens above the date display; screw-in crown; water-resistant to 200 m
Band: stainless steel, folding clasp with security device
Price: upon request
Variations: different dial variations

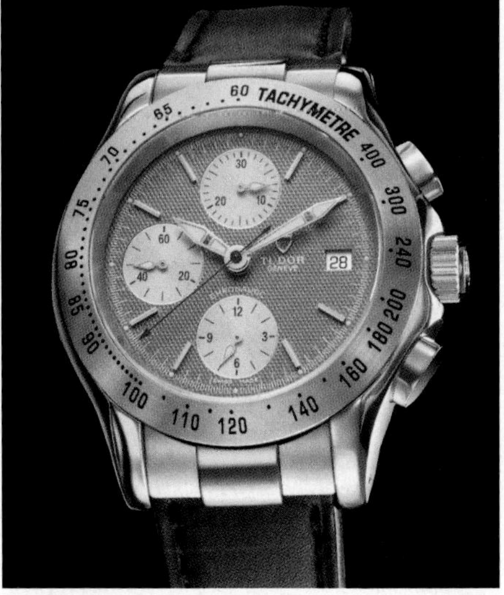

Chronautic Chronograph

Reference number: 79390 P
Movement: automatic, ETA 7750-1, ø 30.4 mm, height 7.9 mm; 25 jewels; 28,800 vph, especially manufactured for Tudor
Functions: hours, minutes, subsidiary seconds; chronograph; date
Case: stainless steel, ø 39 mm, height 15.3 mm; bezel with tachymeter scale; sapphire crystal; screw-in crown; water-resistant to 100 m
Band: leather, folding clasp
Remarks: dial in ruthenium
Price: upon request

Tutima

Tutima watches have been around for more than seventy years now. The company's beginnings were in Saxony's Glashütte, one of the most important centers of German watch-making until World War II. The best products of the Glashütter Uhren-Rohwerke-Fabrik (UROFA), managed by Dr. Ernst Kurtz, were distributed under the name Tutima, a word that is derived from the Latin word *tutus* (meaning secure, protected).

Dr. Kurtz left Glashütte just before the end of the war, saved the brand name from the fall of the iron curtain, and in the same year founded a new watch production in southern West Germany. In the year 1951 he moved Watch Factory Kurtz to a very northern region of Germany. When he set up his company again, Dr. Kurtz did not forget Glashütte's high-quality standards and ensured that the production of his watch movements was based strictly upon them. The brand name he chose, Kurtz Glashütter Tradition, also indicated this high level of quality for all to see on the dials. In Ganderkesee he created Nurofa, Norddeutsche Uhren-Rohwerke-Fabrik, for the production of *ébauches*, and next to it the company sales and marketing offices of Tutima-Uhren. In 1959 lack of profitability forced him to stop production of his watch movements.

The fortunes of the Tutima-Uhren brand then passed to a young businessman and former associate of Kurtz, Dieter Delecate. What Delecate had inherited with the Tutima brand, however, was not going to be easy to continue. Nobody was interested in tradition in those days; instead the demand called for large amounts of inexpensive watches. The tiny watch factory on Germany's northern coast nevertheless managed to survive the great plague that was killing off watch brands at the time of the quartz shock and became popular again during the renaissance of the mechanical watch in the late '80s with high-quality instrument watches that were manufactured exclusively in Germany with movements from Switzerland.

The current model palette has long since outgrown its humble beginnings when the military chronograph designed for tender and issued by the German armed forces in 1985 ruled the collection. Functional pilot's watches are still the center of attention, but the range now runs from a detailed remake of the Tutima pilot's chronograph 1941 to the modernly styled FX model in cool steel.

The small watch factory in Ganderkesee employs around fifty people. An active troop of field representatives ensures that the watches from Lower Saxony are available in 150 selected outlets in Germany. In the U.S., Tutima has made quite a name for itself with spectacular actions such as being the official timekeeper at the San Francisco Fleet Week, the most impressive air show in the United States, keeping its image close to that of aviation.

Flieger Chronograph F2 UTC

Reference number: 780-81
Movement: automatic, ETA 7750 modified, ø 30 mm, height 7.9 mm; 25 jewels; 28,800 vph
Functions: hours, minutes, subsidiary seconds; chronograph; date; power reserve display
Case: stainless steel, ø 38.7 mm, height 15.8 mm; bidirectionally rotating bezel with reference marker; sapphire crystal; transparent case back; screw-in crown; water-resistant to 100 m
Band: reptile skin, folding clasp
Price: $3,800
Variations: with stainless steel bracelet; with blue dial

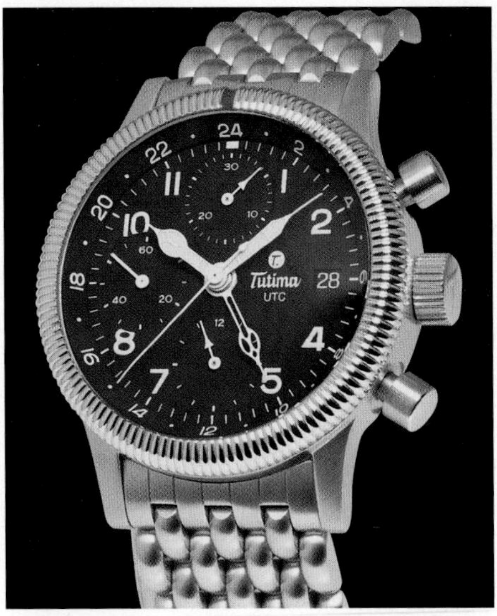

Flieger Chronograph F2 UTC

Reference number: 780-52
Movement: automatic, ETA 7750 modified, ø 30 mm, height 7.9 mm; 25 jewels; 28,800 vph
Functions: hours, minutes, subsidiary seconds; chronograph; date; 24-hour display (second time zone)
Case: stainless steel, ø 38.7 mm, height 15.8 mm; bidirectionally rotating bezel with reference marker; sapphire crystal; screw-in crown; water-resistant to 100 m
Band: stainless steel, folding clasp
Price: $3,400
Variations: with leather strap

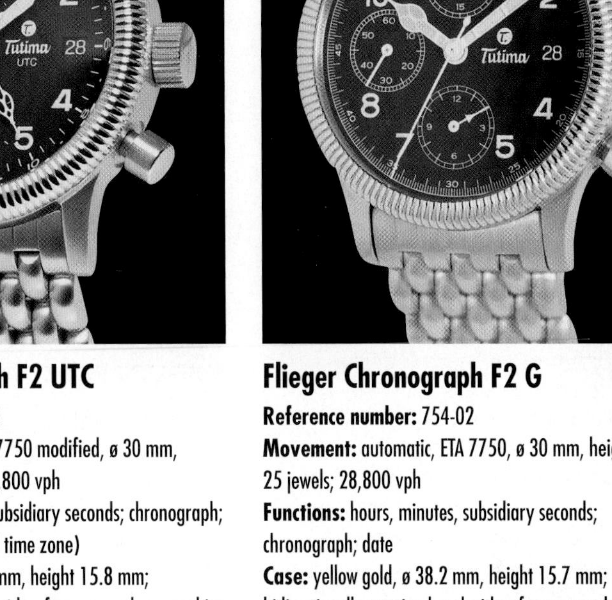

Flieger Chronograph F2 G

Reference number: 754-02
Movement: automatic, ETA 7750, ø 30 mm, height 7.9 mm; 25 jewels; 28,800 vph
Functions: hours, minutes, subsidiary seconds; chronograph; date
Case: yellow gold, ø 38.2 mm, height 15.7 mm; bidirectionally rotating bezel with reference marker; sapphire crystal; transparent case back; screw-in crown; water-resistant to 100 m
Band: yellow gold, folding clasp
Price: $18,900
Variations: with reptile skin strap

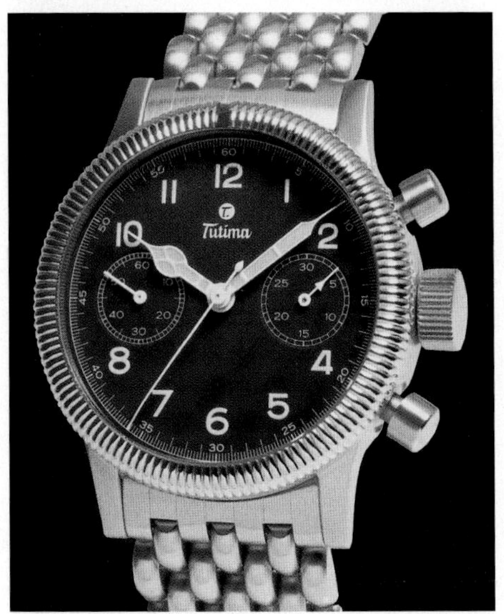

Classic Flieger Chronograph

Reference number: 783-02
Movement: manual winding, ETA 7760 modified, ø 30 mm, height 7 mm; 21 jewels; 28,800 vph
Functions: hours, minutes, subsidiary seconds; chronograph
Case: stainless steel, ø 38.7 mm, height 14.7 mm; bidirectionally rotating bezel with reference marker; sapphire crystal; water-resistant to 100 m
Band: stainless steel, folding clasp
Price: $2,900
Variations: with leather strap

Chronograph FX UTC

Reference number: 740-54
Movement: automatic, ETA 7750 modified, ø 30 mm, height 7.9 mm; 25 jewels; 28,800 vph
Functions: hours, minutes, subsidiary seconds; chronograph; date; 24-hour display (second time zone)
Case: stainless steel, ø 38.7 mm, height 15.13 mm; bidirectionally rotating bezel with 24-hour scale; sapphire crystal; transparent case back; screw-in crown; water-resistant to 100 m
Band: stainless steel, folding clasp
Price: $3,400
Variations: with leather strap; bezel with 60-minute scale or satin-finished

Chronograph FX

Reference number: 788-01
Movement: automatic, ETA 7750, ø 30 mm, height 7.9 mm; 25 jewels; 28,800 vph
Functions: hours, minutes, subsidiary seconds; chronograph; date
Case: stainless steel, ø 38.5 mm, height 15.5 mm; sapphire crystal; screw-in crown; water-resistant to 100 m
Band: leather, buckle
Price: $2,100
Variations: with stainless steel bracelet; with rotating bezel including 60-minute scale

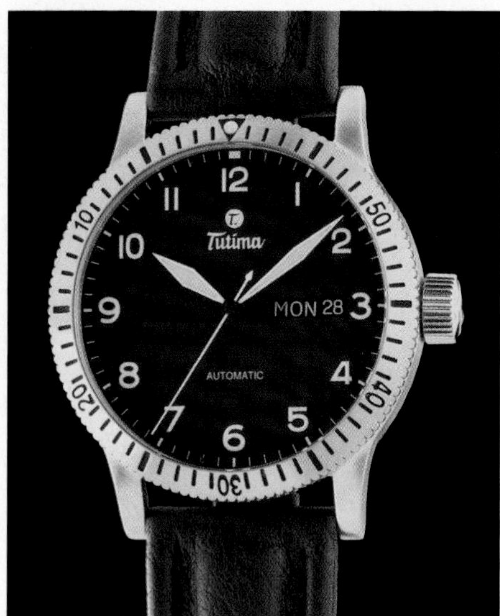

Automatic FX

Reference number: 631-01
Movement: automatic, ETA 2836-2, ø 26 mm, height 5.05 mm; 25 jewels; 28,800 vph
Functions: hours, minutes, sweep seconds; date and day
Case: stainless steel, ø 38.5 mm, height 12.4 mm; bidirectionally rotating bezel with 60-minute scale; sapphire crystal; screw-in crown; water-resistant to 100 m
Band: leather, buckle
Price: $1,100
Variations: with stainless steel bracelet

Automatic FX UTC

Reference number: 632-24
Movement: automatic, ETA 2893-2, ø 26 mm, height 4.1 mm; 21 jewels; 28,800 vph
Functions: hours, minutes, sweep seconds; date; 24-hour display (second time zone)
Case: stainless steel, ø 38.5 mm, height 11.4 mm; sapphire crystal; transparent case back; screw-in crown; water-resistant to 100 m
Band: stainless steel, folding clasp
Price: $1,600
Variations: with leather strap, with black dial

Military Flieger Chronograph TL

Reference number: 750-02
Movement: automatic, Nouvelle Lémania 5100, ø 31 mm, height 8.25 mm; 17 jewels; 28,800 vph
Functions: hours, minutes, subsidiary seconds; chronograph; date and day; 24-hour display
Case: titanium, ø 43 mm, height 14.6 mm; bidirectionally rotating bezel with 60-minute scale; sapphire crystal; screw-in crown; water-resistant to 200 m
Band: titanium, folding clasp with wetsuit extension
Price: $2,900
Variations: with leather strap

Military Airforce Chronograph TLG

Reference number: 738-02
Movement: automatic, Nouvelle Lémania 5100, ø 31 mm, height 8.25 mm; 17 jewels; 28,800 vph
Functions: hours, minutes, subsidiary seconds; chronograph; date and day; 24-hour display
Case: titanium, ø 43 mm, height 14.6 mm; bidirectionally rotating bezel in yellow gold with 60-minute scale; sapphire crystal; screw-in crown; water-resistant to 200 m
Band: titanium/gold, folding clasp with wetsuit extension
Price: $7,600
Variations: with leather strap

Commando II

Reference number: 760-42
Movement: automatic, Nouvelle Lémania 5100, ø 31 mm, height 8.25 mm; 17 jewels; 28,800 vph
Functions: hours, minutes; chronograph; date
Case: titanium, ø 43.2 mm, height 14.5 mm; sapphire crystal; screw-in crown; water-resistant to 200 m
Band: titanium, folding clasp with wetsuit extension
Price: $2,700
Variations: with tachymeter scale; with leather strap

DI 300

Reference number: 629-12
Movement: automatic, ETA 2836-2, ø 26 mm, height 5.05 mm; 25 jewels; 28,800 vph
Functions: hours, minutes, sweep seconds; date and day
Case: titanium, ø 43.8 mm, height 12.5 mm; unidirectionally rotating bezel with 60-minute scale; sapphire crystal; screw-in crown; water-resistant to 300 m
Band: titanium, folding clasp with wetsuit extension
Price: $1,250,
Variations: with black dial

Tutima
28

Union

The business idea of the Union watch *manufacture* in the tranquil city of Glashütte in Germany's Saxony is today more current than ever: The best in quality at a comparatively good price is something that everyone wants. Thus, Union watches are incredibly popular among connoisseurs, as this brand is quite an insider tip.

At the end of the nineteenth century, due to an era of great economic distress, few people could afford to buy the very good, but also expensive, original Glashütte watches. For this reason, Dresden watch wholesaler Johannes Dürrstein wanted to offer a less expensive variation. After his idea for such a watch fell on deaf ears in the established Glashütte companies, he quickly founded his own watch factory, the Präzisions-Taschenuhrenfabrik UNION Glashütte, on January 1, 1893.

For 111 years the name Union has stood for functional, but inexpensive precision watches that incorporate the classic characteristics of Glashütte quality. On the occasion of this special anniversary, the watchmakers at Union have developed an edition of purist automatic watches, each limited to 111 pieces. In functionality and technical know-how, these anniversary models are presented completely in the tradition of the old masters. In design and aesthetics, they are clearly modern contemporaries, which do justice to today's demands on legibility and comfort.

The watch lover will find a modern interpretation of classic complications in the anniversary edition. The models respectively featuring subsidiary seconds and a date hand celebrate the premiere of automatic winding in this limited special edition. The trusty Union Caliber 26 used here and in the accompanying chronograph model represents a special guarantee for reliability and the highest in rate precision "made in Germany." Produced in the Glashütte *manufacture*, this movement is striking in its precision and fine finish. The watches' purist case made of stainless steel and the strikingly black galvanized dial with white printed railroad minute scales characterize the modern appearance of the anniversary edition. The hand-sewn leather straps made of black calfskin are available with a classic white seam or with a more obvious red one, lending the watches an individual appearance.

Johannes Dürrstein 3

Reference number: 45.01.01.01.09
Movement: manual winding, Union 45-01, ø 26.2 mm, height 4.3 mm; 18 jewels and two diamonds; 21,600 vph, flying one-minute tourbillon
Functions: hours, minutes; (off-center), subsidiary seconds (on tourbillon cage)
Case: rose gold, 36.5 x 36.5 mm, height 11.8 mm; sapphire crystal; transparent case back
Band: reptile skin, buckle in rose gold
Remarks: limited to 50 pieces
Price: $46,560

Johannes Dürrstein 2

Reference number: 40.02.01.01.09
Movement: manual winding, Union 40-02, ø 26.2 mm, height 5.9 mm; 18 jewels; 28,800 vph
Functions: hours, minutes; perpetual calendar with date, day, month, moon phase, leap year
Case: rose gold, 36.5 x 36.5 mm, height 11.2 mm; sapphire crystal; transparent case back
Band: reptile skin, buckle in rose gold
Remarks: limited to 50 pieces
Price: $11,900

Johannes Dürrstein 1

Reference number: 40.01.01.01.09
Movement: manual winding, Union 40-01, ø 26.2 mm, height 5.9 mm; 23 jewels; 28,800 vph
Functions: hours, minutes, subsidiary seconds
Case: rose gold, 34.5 x 34.5 mm, height 11.8 mm; sapphire crystal; transparent case back
Band: reptile skin, buckle in rose gold
Remarks: limited to 50 pieces
Price: $7,910

Anniversary Edition Chronograph

Reference number: 26.31.02.02.10
Movement: automatic, Union 26-03, ø 32.2 mm, height 7.2 mm; 50 jewels; 28,800 vph, finely finished, polished screws, wheels with sunburst decoration, skeletonized rotor
Functions: hours, minutes, subsidiary seconds; chronograph
Case: stainless steel, ø 39.8 mm, height 13.3 mm; sapphire crystal; transparent case back; water-resistant to 50 m
Band: Nappa leather, buckle
Price: $3,360
Variations: Nappa leather strap with red stitching

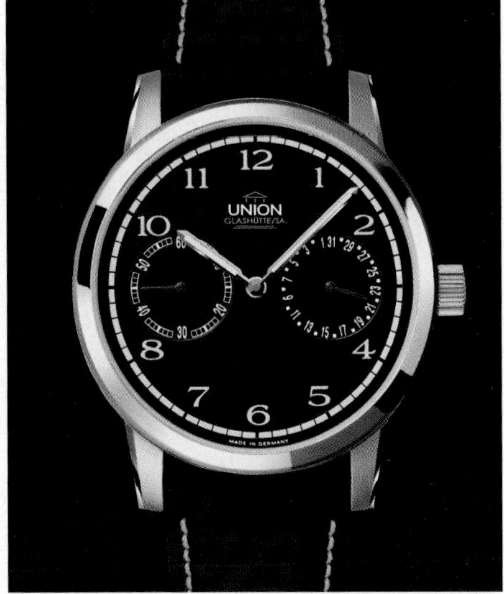

Anniversary Edition Date Hand

Reference number: 26.02.02.02.10
Movement: automatic, Union 26-02, ø 30.95 mm, height 5.9 mm; 36 jewels; 28,800 vph, finely finished, polished screws, wheels with sunburst decoration, skeletonized rotor
Functions: hours, minutes, subsidiary seconds; date
Case: stainless steel, ø 37.8 mm, height 9.9 mm; sapphire crystal; transparent case back; water-resistant to 50 m
Band: Nappa leather, buckle
Price: $3,160
Variations: Nappa leather strap with red stitching

Anniversary Edition Small Seconds

Reference number: 26.05.02.02.10
Movement: automatic, Union 26-05, ø 26.2 mm, height 4.3 mm; 30 jewels; 28,800 vph, finely finished, polished screws, wheels with sunburst decoration, skeletonized rotor
Functions: hours, minutes, subsidiary seconds
Case: stainless steel, ø 37.8 mm, height 9.9 mm; sapphire crystal; transparent case back; water-resistant to 50 m
Band: Nappa leather, buckle
Price: $2,950
Variations: Nappa leather strap with red stitching

Diplomat Perpetual Calendar

Reference number: 26.53.16.02.10
Movement: automatic, Union 26-53, ø 31.15 mm, height 5.9 mm; 48 jewels; 28,800 vph, finely finished, polished screws, wheels with sunburst decoration, skeletonized rotor
Functions: hours, minutes, sweep seconds; perpetual calendar with panorama date, day, month, moon phase, leap year
Case: stainless steel, ø 39.8 mm, height 13.8 mm; sapphire crystal; transparent case back; water-resistant to 50 m
Band: reptile skin, double folding clasp
Price: $8,380
Variations: with stainless steel bracelet

Diplomat Panorama Date

Reference number: 26.45.16.01.10
Movement: automatic, Union 26-45, ø 30.95 mm, height 5.9 mm; 39 jewels; 28,800 vph, finely finished, polished screws, wheels with sunburst decoration, skeletonized rotor
Functions: hours, minutes, sweep seconds; panorama date
Case: stainless steel, ø 39.8 mm, height 11.8 mm; sapphire crystal; transparent case back; water-resistant to 50 m
Band: reptile skin, double folding clasp
Price: $3,480
Variations: with stainless steel bracelet

Diplomat Chronograph

Reference number: 26.32.16.05.10
Movement: automatic, Union 26-32, ø 32.2 mm, height 7.2 mm; 51 jewels; 28,800 vph, finely finished, polished screws, wheels with sunburst decoration, skeletonized rotor
Functions: hours, minutes, subsidiary seconds; chronograph; date
Case: stainless steel, ø 39.8 mm, height 13.3 mm; sapphire crystal; transparent case back; water-resistant to 50 m
Band: reptile skin, double folding clasp
Price: $2,930
Variations: with stainless steel bracelet

Klassik Automatic

Reference number: 26.11.15.02.10
Movement: automatic, Union 26-11, ø 26.2 mm, height 4.3 mm; 25 jewels; 28,800 vph, finely finished, polished screws, wheels with sunburst decoration, skeletonized rotor
Functions: hours, minutes, sweep seconds; date
Case: stainless steel, ø 37.8 mm, height 9.9 mm; sapphire crystal; transparent case back; water-resistant to 50 m
Band: reptile skin, double folding clasp
Price: $1,730
Variations: with stainless steel bracelet

Klassik Power Reserve

Reference number: 26.44.15.02.10
Movement: automatic, Union 26-44, ø 30.95 mm, height 5.9 mm; 36 jewels; 28,800 vph, finely finished, polished screws, wheels with sunburst decoration, skeletonized rotor
Functions: hours, minutes, sweep seconds; date; power reserve display
Case: stainless steel, ø 39.8 mm, height 11.8 mm; sapphire crystal; transparent case back; water-resistant to 50 m
Band: reptile skin, double folding clasp
Price: $2,380
Variations: with stainless steel bracelet

Klassik Pilot's Chronograph

Reference number: 26.32.09.05.10
Movement: automatic, Union 26-32, ø 32.2 mm, height 7.2 mm; 51 jewels; 28,800 vph, finely finished, polished screws, wheels with sunburst decoration, skeletonized rotor
Functions: hours, minutes, subsidiary seconds; chronograph; date
Case: stainless steel, ø 39.8 mm, height 13.3 mm; sapphire crystal; transparent case back; water-resistant to 50 m
Band: Nappa leather, buckle
Price: $2,710
Variations: with stainless steel bracelet

Caliber 45

Mechanical with manual winding, flying one-minute tourbillon on the dial side; power reserve 48 hours
Functions: hours, minutes, subsidiary seconds (on tourbillon cage)
Diameter: 26.2 mm
Height: 4.35 mm (without tourbillon carriage)
Jewels: 18, plus two diamond endstones
Balance: screw balance with 18 gold weighted screws
Frequency: 21,600 vph
Balance spring: Breguet
Remarks: beautifully finished movement, rose gold-plated, screw-mounted gold chatons, blued screws, winding wheels with double sunburst pattern

Caliber 40

Mechanical with manual winding, power reserve 40 hours
Functions: hours, minutes (base caliber)
Diameter: 26.2 mm
Height: 5.9 mm
Jewels: 23 (Caliber 40-01, subsidiary seconds)
18 (Caliber 40-02, perpetual calendar)
Balance: screw balance
Frequency: 28,800 vph
Balance spring: flat hairspring, swan-neck fine adjustment
Remarks: beautifully finished movement, rose gold-plated, screw-mounted gold chatons, steel parts beveled and polished, blued screws, winding wheels with double sunburst pattern

Caliber 30

Mechanical with manual winding, power reserve 40 hours
Functions: hours, minutes (base caliber)
Diameter: 26.2 mm; **Height:** 5.9 mm
Jewels: 19 (Caliber 30-01, perpetual calendar)
29 (Caliber 30-02, date hand)
35 (Caliber 30-03, power reserve display)
26 (Caliber 30-04, regulator)
24 (Caliber 30-05, subsidiary seconds)
45 (Caliber 30-0, chronograph)
Balance: screw balance with 18 gold weighted screws
Frequency: 28,800 vph; Shock protection: Incabloc
Balance spring: flat hairspring, swan-neck fine adjustment
Remarks: Glashütte ribbing, screw-mounted gold chatons, steel parts beveled/polished, blued screws, sunburst on wheels

Caliber 26

Mechanical with automatic winding, unidirectionally winding rotor, power reserve 40 hours, stop-seconds
Functions: hours, minutes, sweep seconds; date (base caliber)
Diameter: 26.2 mm
Height: 4.3 mm
Jewels: 25 (Caliber 26-11, automatic)
51 (Caliber 26-32, chronograph with date)
36 (Caliber 26-44, power reserve display)
39 (Caliber 26-45, panorama date)
48 (Caliber 26-53, perpetual calendar)
Balance spring: flat hairspring
Frequency: 28,800 vph; **Shock protection:** Incabloc
Remarks: beautifully finished movement with decorations, polished screws, and a skeletonized rotor

Vacheron Constantin

In the remaining months before its 250th birthday, the Genevan brand Vacheron Constantin has returned to the tried and true — these models continue in the tradition of the *manufacture*. In 1914, as watches were finding their way out of vest pockets, Vacheron Constantin built its first chronograph for the wrist. It had one button with which the three functions start/stop/reset were controlled. At the beginning of the 1930s, a chronograph was launched that possessed two buttons, a style that is still characteristic today. This is also what the new chronograph from the Malte line is outfitted with, and its column-wheel chronograph move-ment can measure events lasting up to thirty minutes.
The beginnings of the oldest watch *manufacture* date back into the year 1755 when the twenty-four-year-old Jean-Marc Vacheron opened a workshop in Geneva. Since then, the company has built highly complicated and precise timepieces encased in especially decorous and costly shells. It is no surprise that the Genevan *manufacture* Vacheron et Constantin has been one of the most popular watchmakers to royalty for centuries. The Vacheron Constantin museum, exhibiting more than four hundred unusual and rare pieces, tells quite a story about the glorious history of the company, and the showcased pieces also illustrate how easy it was for the Genevans to leave pocket watches behind in favor of wristwatches at the beginning of the twentieth century.
After a long period of prosperity, which reached into the 1950s and '60s, not much was heard from the brand whose emblem comprises the cross of the Maltese knights. However, since the middle of the 1990s, when Vacheron Constantin went over to the Vendôme Luxury Group (today Richemont SA), the world's oldest uninterruptedly active watch brand has been dancing between luxury sports watches (such as the current Overseas model) and *haute horlogerie*. In the last few years a new collection has grown, advantageously orienting itself to modern forms as well as traditional patterns, and extravagant creations such as the Assymetrique have found room, a watch that originally delighted European jet-setters in the early 1970s.
The presentation of the Malte watch line — French for the small rocky Mediterranean island of Malta — represents not only a new model family, but also the reintroduction of Vacheron Constantin's technical competence in the form of a fully new, hand-wound caliber. Caliber 1400 is produced in a subsidiary plant of the Genevan brand in the "watch valley" Vallée de Joux. The traditional construction allows the ancient brand to celebrate its 250th anniversary in 2005 knowing it once again belongs to the illustrious group of true Swiss watch *manufactures* with its own movements.
Alongside extending the collection, a spatial expansion of the company is also in the works. Starting in the fall of 2004, the brand has had most reputable neighbors such as Patek Philippe and Piaget as the new Vacheron Constantin manufacture took up residence in Geneva's industrial suburb Plan-les-Ouates. Both the company's management and large parts of the production find room here, making the production facilities in the Les Acacias district unnecessary. The above-mentioned workshop in the Vallée de Joux will be occupied more with developmental work, design, and prototypes. The company's famous building housing the museum and boutique on the Rhône island in the Genevan old city center will remain as is.

Égerie

Reference number: X25G5697
Movement: quartz, Vacheron Constantin 1202, finely finished
Functions: hours, minutes
Case: white gold, 27.5 x 39 mm, height 9.53 mm; bezel set with 48 brilliant-cut diamonds; sapphire crystal
Band: satin, buckle
Price: $15,900
Variations: in yellow gold

Égerie

Reference number: X25G5704
Movement: quartz, Vacheron Constantin 1202, finely finished
Functions: hours, minutes
Case: white gold, 27.5 x 39 mm, height 9.53 mm; case completely set with 312 brilliant-cut diamonds; sapphire crystal
Band: satin, buckle set with 21 brilliant-cut diamonds
Price: $21,200
Variations: with pavé case

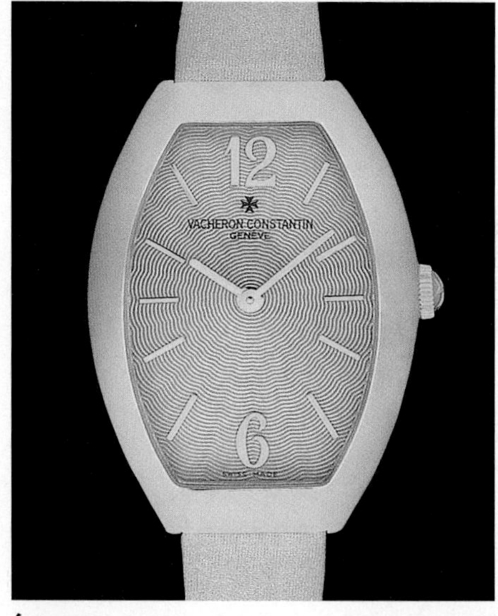

Égerie

Reference number: X25J5698
Movement: quartz, Vacheron Constantin 1202, finely finished
Functions: hours, minutes
Case: yellow gold, 27.5 x 39 mm, height 9.53 mm; sapphire crystal
Band: satin, buckle
Price: $8,000
Variations: in different size, movement, and case versions

Malte Ladies Pavé

Reference number: X25G4977
Movement: quartz, Vacheron Constantin 1207, finely finished
Functions: hours, minutes; date
Case: white gold, ø 30.5 mm, height 8.55 mm; case, lugs, and crown set with 185 brilliant-cut diamonds; sapphire crystal
Band: reptile skin, folding clasp
Price: $17,500
Variations: with gold link bracelet; different model variations

1972

Reference number: X25J6982
Movement: quartz, Vacheron Constantin 1202, finely finished
Functions: hours, minutes
Case: yellow gold, 23.4 x 34 mm, height 6.62 mm; bezel set with 46 brilliant-cut diamonds; sapphire crystal
Band: reptile skin, buckle
Remarks: dial made of mother-of-pearl
Price: $12,100
Variations: in different variations

1972

Reference number: X25G6983
Movement: quartz, Vacheron Constantin 1202, finely finished
Functions: hours, minutes
Case: white gold, 23.4 x 34 mm, height 6.62 mm; sapphire crystal
Band: reptile skin, buckle
Remarks: dial made of mother-of-pearl
Price: $8,900
Variations: in different variations

1972 Grand Modèle Cambré

Reference number: X25R6990
Movement: quartz, Vacheron Constantin 1202, finely finished
Functions: hours, minutes
Case: rose gold, 22.8 x 45 mm, height 7.25 mm; sapphire crystal
Band: reptile skin, buckle
Remarks: mirror-polished markers
Price: $10,900
Variations: with pink dial

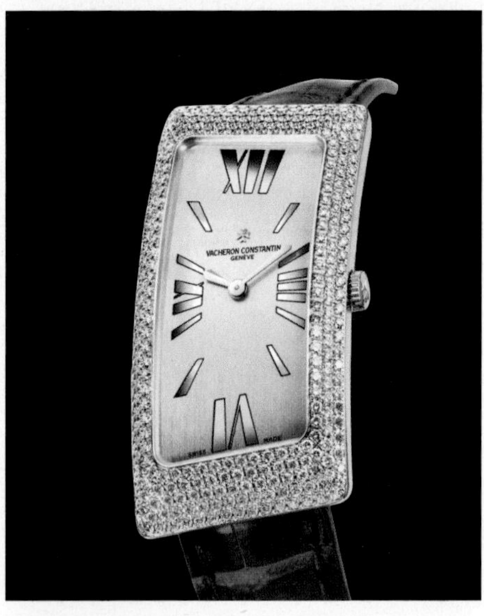

1972 Grand Modèle Cambré

Reference number: X25G6988
Movement: quartz, Vacheron Constantin 1202, finely finished
Functions: hours, minutes
Case: white gold, 22.8 x 45 mm, height 7.25 mm; bezel completely set with 308 brilliant-cut diamonds; sapphire crystal
Band: reptile skin, buckle set with 25 brilliant-cut diamonds
Remarks: mirror-polished markers
Price: $25,000
Variations: with dark blue dial

Patrimony Small Seconds Rosé

Reference number: X81R6964
Movement: manual winding, Vacheron Constantin 1400, ø 20.35 mm, height 2.6 mm; 20 jewels; 28,800 vph, finely finished with Seal of Geneva
Functions: hours, minutes, subsidiary seconds
Case: rose gold, ø 35 mm, height 6.5 mm; sapphire crystal; transparent case back
Band: reptile skin, buckle
Price: $9,900
Variations: in yellow gold; in white gold

Patrimony 40 mm

Reference number: X81J6986
Movement: manual winding, Vacheron Constantin 1400, ø 20.35 mm, height 2.6 mm; 20 jewels; 28,800 vph, finely finished with Seal of Geneva
Functions: hours, minutes
Case: yellow gold, ø 40 mm, height 6.7 mm; sapphire crystal
Band: reptile skin, buckle
Price: $10,500
Variations: in white gold

Malte Grande Classique

Reference number: X81G6970
Movement: manual winding, Vacheron Constantin 1400, ø 20.35 mm, height 2.6 mm; 20 jewels; 28,800 vph, finely finished with Seal of Geneva
Functions: hours, minutes, subsidiary seconds
Case: white gold, ø 37 mm, height 7.3 mm; sapphire crystal; transparent case back
Band: reptile skin, buckle
Price: $11,300
Variations: in different variations

Toledo 1952

Reference number: X47G5709
Movement: automatic, Vacheron Constantin 1125, ø 26 mm, height 5.53 mm; 36 jewels; 28,800 vph, finely finished with côtes de Genève
Functions: hours, minutes, subsidiary seconds; date, day, month, moon phase
Case: white gold, 35.7 x 41 mm, height 12.7 mm; sapphire crystal
Band: reptile skin, buckle
Price: $24,500
Variations: in yellow gold

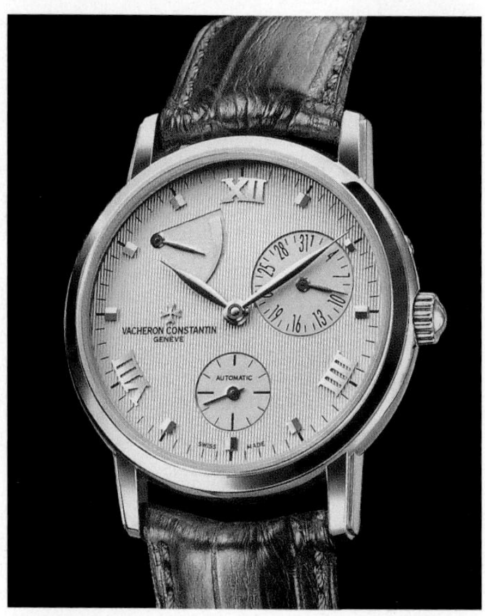

Les Complications Power Reserve

Reference number: X47J5351
Movement: automatic, Vacheron Constantin 1127, ø 26 mm, height 4.85 mm; 45 jewels; 28,800 vph, finely finished with côtes de Genève
Functions: hours, minutes, subsidiary seconds; date; power reserve display
Case: yellow gold, ø 36 mm, height 9.26 mm; sapphire crystal; transparent case back
Band: reptile skin, buckle
Price: $14,400
Variations: in white gold

Royal Eagle

Reference number: X42G5718
Movement: automatic, Vacheron Constantin 1206, ø 25.6 mm, height 4.92 mm; 31 jewels; 28,800 vph, finely finished with côtes de Genève
Functions: hours, minutes, subsidiary seconds; date, day
Case: white gold, 35.6 x 48.5 mm, height 12 mm; sapphire crystal
Band: reptile skin, buckle
Price: $19,900
Variations: with diamonds; in yellow gold

Royal Eagle Chronograph

Reference number: X49R5715
Movement: automatic, Vacheron Constantin 1137, ø 25.6 mm, height 6.6 mm; 37 jewels; 21,600 vph, finely finished with côtes de Genève
Functions: hours, minutes, subsidiary seconds; chronograph; large date
Case: rose gold, 36.8 x 50.2 mm, height 14 mm; sapphire crystal; water-resistant to 50 m
Band: reptile skin, folding clasp
Price: $26,500
Variations: in different stainless steel variations

Malte Dual Time

Reference number: X42R5725
Movement: automatic, Vacheron Constantin 1206 RDT, ø 25.6 mm, height 4.92 mm; 31 jewels; 28,800 vph, finely finished with côtes de Genève; C.O.S.C. certified chronometer
Functions: hours (off-center), minutes, subsidiary seconds; date; 24-hour display (second time zone)
Case: rose gold, ø 38.5 mm, height 11 mm; sapphire crystal; transparent case back and hinged lid
Band: reptile skin, buckle
Price: $21,500
Variations: in yellow gold; in white gold

Malte Chronograph

Reference number: X47R6957
Movement: manual winding, Vacheron Constantin 1141, ø 27 mm, height 5.57 mm; 21 jewels; 18,000 vph, swan-neck fine adjustment, finely finished with côtes de Genève
Functions: hours, minutes, subsidiary seconds; chronograph
Case: rose gold, ø 41.5 mm, height 10.9 mm; sapphire crystal; transparent case back
Band: reptile skin, buckle
Price: $27,500
Variations: in white gold

Malte Retrograde Perpetual Calendar

Reference number: X47P5214
Movement: automatic, Vacheron Constantin 1126 QPR, ø 26 mm, height 5.05 mm; 36 jewels; 28,800 vph, finely finished with côtes de Genève
Functions: hours, minutes; perpetual calendar with date (retrograde), day, month, year, leap year
Case: platinum, ø 38.5 mm, height 11.3 mm; sapphire crystal; transparent case back and hinged lid
Band: reptile skin, buckle
Price: $65,000
Variations: in rose gold

Malte Retrograde 245

Reference number: X47G4793
Movement: automatic, Vacheron Constantin 1126 R31, ø 26 mm, height 3.25 mm; 36 jewels; 21,600 vph, finely finished with côtes de Genève
Functions: hours, minutes; date (retrograde), day
Case: white gold, ø 37 mm, height 10 mm; sapphire crystal; transparent case back
Band: reptile skin, buckle
Price: $20,900
Variations: in rose gold; in platinum with black dial

Malte Chronograph Perpetual Calendar

Reference number: X47J4954
Movement: manual winding, Vacheron Constantin 1141 QP, ø 27 mm, height 7.37 mm; 21 jewels; 18,000 vph, finely finished with côtes de Genève
Functions: hours, minutes, subsidiary seconds; chronograph; perpetual calendar with date, day, month, moon phase, leap year
Case: yellow gold, ø 39 mm, height 13.75 mm; sapphire crystal; transparent case back and hinged lid
Band: reptile skin, buckle
Price: $77,000
Variations: in platinum

Overseas Ladies

Reference number: X25A7033
Movement: quartz, Vacheron Constantin 1207, finely finished
Functions: hours, minutes; date
Case: stainless steel, ø 34 mm, height 7.66 mm; sapphire crystal; water-resistant to 50 m
Band: stainless steel, folding clasp
Price: $6,600
Variations: different stainless steel variations, also with brilliant-cut diamonds

Overseas Ladies

Reference number: X25A6949
Movement: quartz, Vacheron Constantin 1207, finely finished
Functions: hours, minutes; date
Case: stainless steel, ø 34 mm, height 7.66 mm; sapphire crystal; water-resistant to 50 m
Band: stainless steel, folding clasp
Remarks: mother-of-pearl dial with 12 diamond markers
Price: $7,600
Variations: different stainless steel variations, also with brilliant-cut diamonds

Overseas

Reference number: X47A6953
Movement: automatic, Vacheron Constantin 1126, ø 26 mm, height 3.25 mm; 36 jewels; 28,800 vph, finely finished with côtes de Genève
Functions: hours, minutes, seconds; date
Case: stainless steel, ø 42 mm, height 9.7 mm; sapphire crystal; water-resistant to 150 m
Band: stainless steel, folding clasp
Price: $9,900
Variations: with white dial

Overseas Chronograph

Reference number: X49A6954
Movement: automatic, Vacheron Constantin 1137, ø 25.6 mm, height 6.6 mm; 37 jewels; 21,600 vph, finely finished with côtes de Genève
Functions: hours, minutes, subsidiary seconds; chronograph; date
Case: stainless steel, ø 42 mm, height 12.45 mm; sapphire crystal; water-resistant to 150 m
Band: stainless steel, folding clasp
Price: $14,000
Variations: with black dial

Caliber 1400

Mechanical with manual winding, power reserve appx. 40 hours

Functions: hours, minutes, subsidiary seconds

Diameter: 20.3 mm (9''')

Height: 2.6 mm

Jewels: 20

Balance: glucydur

Frequency: 28,800 vph

Balance spring: flat hairspring with fine adjustment via index

Shock protection: Kif

Remarks: base plate with perlage, edges beveled, bridges with côtes de Genève; polished steel parts; Seal of Geneva

Caliber 1410

Mechanical with manual winding, power reserve appx. 40 hours

Functions: hours, minutes; moon phase; power reserve display

Diameter: 20.35 mm (9''')

Height: 4.2 mm

Jewels: 20

Balance: glucydur

Frequency: 28,800 vph

Balance spring: flat hairspring with fine adjustment via index

Shock protection: Kif

Remarks: base plate with perlage, edges beveled, bridges with côtes de Genève; polished steel parts; Seal of Geneva

Caliber 1003

Mechanical with manual winding, power reserve appx. 35 hours

Functions: hours, minutes

Diameter: 20.8 mm (9''')

Height: 1.64 mm

Jewels: 18

Balance: glucydur

Frequency: 18,000 vph

Balance spring: flat hairspring with fine adjustment via index

Shock protection: Kif

Remarks: base plate with perlage, edges beveled, bridges with côtes de Genève; Seal of Geneva

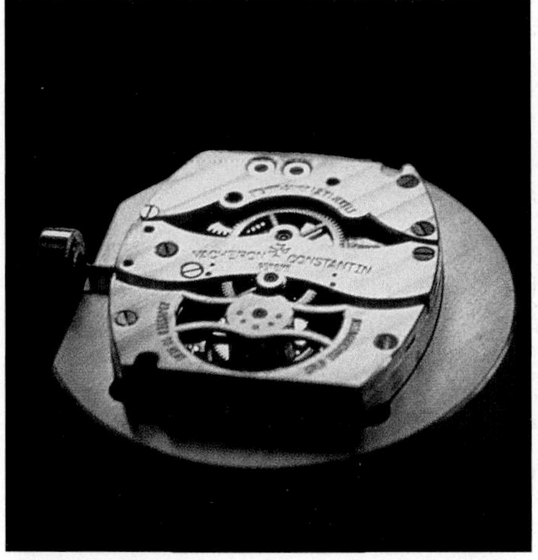

Caliber 1790

Mechanical with manual winding, one-minute tourbillon; power reserve appx. 40 hours

Functions: hours, minutes, subsidiary seconds (on tourbillon cage); date; power reserve display

Dimensions: 28.5 x 26.9 mm

Height: 6.1 mm

Jewels: 27

Balance: screw balance in tourbillon cage

Frequency: 18,000 vph

Remarks: base plate with perlage, edges beveled, bridges with côtes de Genève; polished steel parts; Seal of Geneva

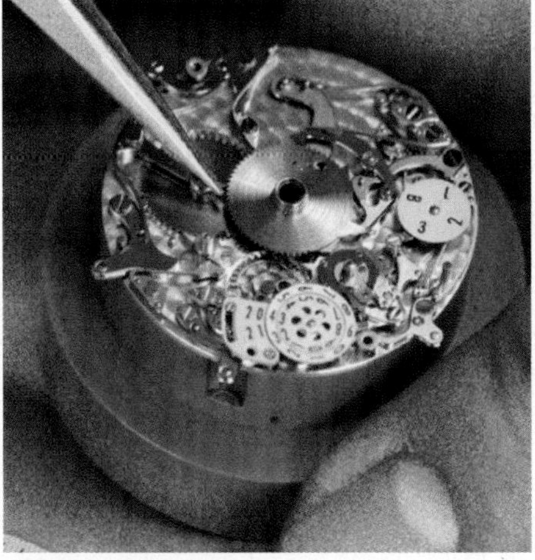

Caliber 1126 QPR

Mechanical with automatic winding, power reserve appx. 38 hours

Base movement: Jaeger-LeCoultre

Functions: hours, minutes; perpetual calendar with date (retrograde); day, month, leap year indication

Diameter: 26mm

Height: 5.05 mm

Jewels: 36

Balance: glucydur

Frequency: 28,800 vph

Remarks: base plate with perlage, edges beveled, bridges with côtes de Genève; polished steel parts; Seal of Geneva

Ventura

"When competing with numerous world-famous brands that can claim a long tradition — or at least pretend they can — as a young, barely fourteen-year-old company we are able to allow ourselves the somewhat ironic remark that Ventura has no past, only a future." Company founder Pierre Nobs can barely keep a grin under control when uttering these words.

The ever-present omission of a past also has advantages: Ventura watches do not need to keep up the pretense of a pseudo-tradition, and so they can dare to include the never-heard-of. The frontier bordering on short-lived, "trendy" fashion is almost naturally recognized by the likes of Hannes Wettstein, who is in charge of design at Ventura, and a close cooperation with leading figures of Swiss design and architecture guarantees a unique understanding of shapes, forms, and identity. Also when designing new dials, professional font developers such as Adrian Frutiger are sometimes asked to come on board. In order to be able to forge such strategic alliances, Ventura needed to achieve an uncompromising attitude toward quality. That is quite an extensive mandate, for not only are individual series subjected to the stringent testing of the C.O.S.C. to become certified chronometers, so is the company's entire range of mechanical watches.

"At Ventura, design is never created empirically. It is always the result of extensive research in the areas of functionality and ergonomics," says Nobs. The numerous international design prizes and awards are proof positive of this statement. So that this remains the case in the future, Ventura is constantly investing in technical innovation. Cases and bracelets made of Titanox, the scratchproof, hardened version of pure titanium, and Durinox, the same in stainless steel, lend the products a unique longevity.

With the development of the world's first — and still only — batteryless LCD watch (the models SPARC fx and px utilize autoquartz technology) as well as the patented EasySkroll operating system of the v-tec Alpha, Ventura has become a leader in digital watch technology: These high-quality products come from the company's own electronic *manufacture*.

The past isn't everything. It's just as important to have an eye to the future.

v-tec Alpha

Reference number: W15 S
Movement: quartz, Ventura VEN_03, multifunctional quartz movement with scroll wheel for menu ("EasySkroll")
Functions: hours, minutes, seconds; chronograph; perpetual calendar with date, day, month, year; second time zone; alarm and countdown
Case: stainless steel (Durinox), 33.5 x 39 mm, height 8.5 mm; sapphire crystal
Band: stainless steel (Durinox), folding clasp
Price: $1,490
Variations: with leather strap ($1,290)

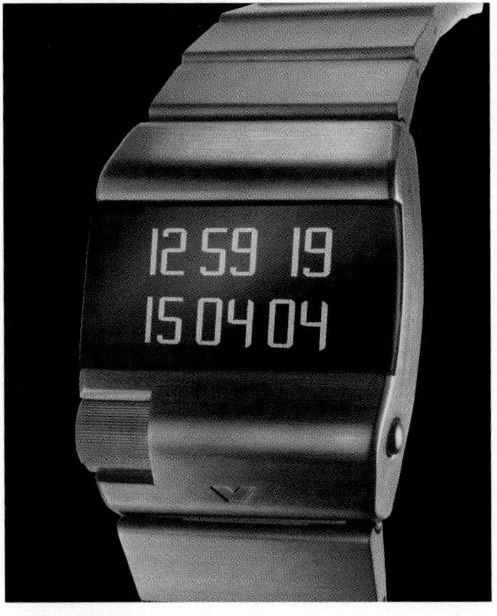

v-tec Delta

Reference number: W21.01S
Movement: quartz, Ventura VEN_04, multifunctional quartz movement with scroll wheel for menu ("EasySkroll")
Functions: hours, minutes, seconds; chronograph; perpetual calendar with date, day, month, year; second time zone; alarm and countdown
Case: stainless steel (Durinox), black, 35 x 40.6 mm, height 8.5 mm; sapphire crystal
Band: stainless steel (Durinox), blackened, folding clasp
Price: $1,490
Variations: with leather strap ($1,190)

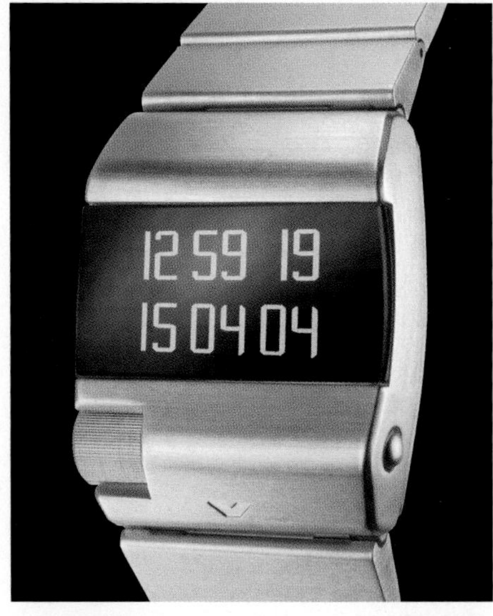

v-tec Delta

Reference number: W20.01.S
Movement: quartz, Ventura VEN_04, multifunctional quartz movement with scroll wheel for menu ("EasySkroll")
Functions: hours, minutes, seconds; chronograph; perpetual calendar with date, day, month, year; second time zone; alarm and countdown
Case: stainless steel (Durinox), 35 x 40.6 mm, height 8.5 mm; sapphire crystal
Band: stainless steel (Durinox), folding clasp
Price: $1,390
Variations: with leather strap ($1,190)

v-matic LOGA

Reference number: VM6.11 T
Movement: automatic, ETA 7750, ø 30 mm, height 7.9 mm; 25 jewels; 28,800 vph, certified chronometer (C.O.S.C.); shockproof and antimagnetic according to DIN
Functions: hours, minutes, subsidiary seconds; chronograph; date
Case: titaniumox, ø 40.25 mm, height 14.7 mm; rotating flange with 60-minute scale under crystal; sapphire crystal; transparent case back; screw-in crown; water-resistant to 100 m
Band: leather, folding clasp
Price: $4,000
Variations: Titanox bracelet ($4,400); stainless steel

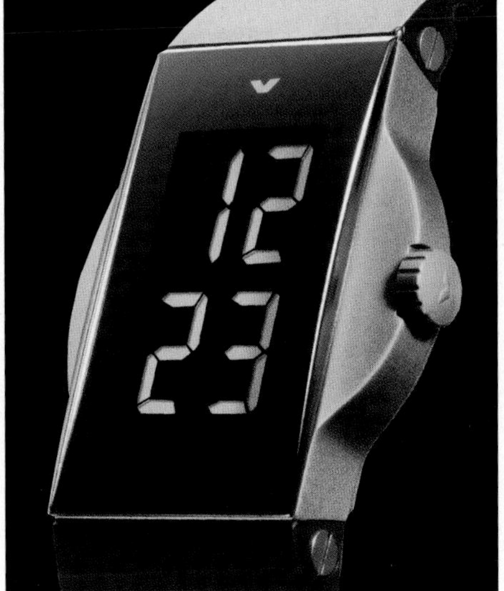

SPARC fx

Reference number: W10 R
Movement: quartz, Ventura 99, autonomous energy supply via rotor and microgenerator; turns off automatically
Functions: hours, minutes; date, month
Case: titaniumox, ø 35 mm, height 10.9 mm; sapphire crystal; transparent case back
Band: rubber, double folding clasp
Price: $2,200
Variations: with Titanox bracelet ($2,600)

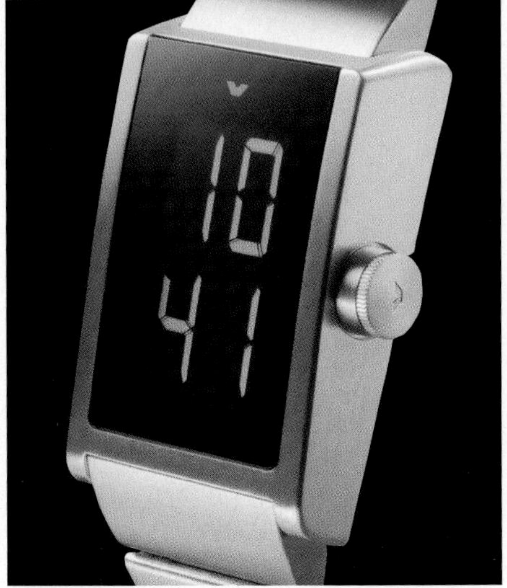

SPARC px

Reference number: W11 S
Movement: quartz, Ventura 99, autonomous energy supply via rotor and microgenerator; turns off automatically
Functions: hours, minutes; date, month
Case: stainless steel, 42.4 x 32.5 mm, height 8.4 /11.7 mm; sapphire crystal; transparent case back
Band: stainless steel, double folding clasp
Price: $1,900
Variations: with leather strap ($1,700); with white diamonds and stingray strap ($8,600); with black diamonds and stingray strap ($11,000)

my EGO Frutiger

Reference number: VM21.07 S
Movement: manual winding, ETA 6498-2, ø 36.6 mm, height 4.5 mm; 17 jewels; 21,600 vph, certified chronometer (C.O.S.C.); movement finely finished with côtes de Genève
Functions: hours, minutes, subsidiary seconds
Case: stainless steel, ø 43 mm, height 11.7 mm; sapphire crystal; transparent case back; screw-in crown
Band: stainless steel, folding clasp
Remarks: dial design exclusively by Adrian Frutiger
Price: $3,400
Variations: with leather strap ($3,100); in yellow or rose gold ($11,600); in white gold ($13,400)

EGO Chrono Square

Reference number: VM25.05 S
Movement: automatic, ETA 2894-2, ø 28.6 mm, height 6.1 mm; 37 jewels; 28,800 vph, certified chronometer (C.O.S.C.)
Functions: hours, minutes, subsidiary seconds; chronograph; date
Case: stainless steel (Durinox), 37 x 37 mm, height 13.5mm; sapphire crystal; transparent case back
Band: leather, double folding clasp
Price: $4,700

EGO Chrono Square

Reference number: VM25.06 L
Movement: automatic, ETA 2894-2, ø 28.6 mm, height 6.1 mm; 37 jewels; 28,800 vph
Functions: hours, minutes, subsidiary seconds; chronograph; date
Case: stainless steel (Durinox), 37 x 37 mm, height 13.5mm; sapphire crystal; transparent case back
Band: stainless steel (Durinox), double folding clasp
Price: $4,300

EGO Square

Reference number: VM26.06 L
Movement: automatic, ETA 2892-A2, ø 25.6 mm, height 3.6 mm; 21 jewels; 28,800 vph, C.O.S.C. certified chronometer
Functions: hours, minutes, sweep seconds; date
Case: stainless steel (Durinox), 37 x 37 mm, height 13.5mm; sapphire crystal; transparent case back
Band: leather, folding clasp
Price: $2,700
Variations: with Durinox bracelet ($3,100)

v-matic II Chrono

Reference number: VM30.01 T
Movement: automatic, ETA 7750, ø 30 mm, height 7.9 mm; 27 jewels; 28,800 vph, certified chronometer (C.O.S.C.)
Functions: hours, minutes, subsidiary seconds; chronograph; date
Case: Titanox, ø 42 mm, height 15mm; sapphire crystal; transparent case back
Band: Titanox, double folding clasp
Price: $4,100

v-matic II SUB

Reference number: VM31.01 T
Movement: automatic, ETA 7750, ø 30 mm, height 7.9 mm; 27 jewels; 28,800 vph, certified chronometer (C.O.S.C.)
Functions: hours, minutes, subsidiary seconds; chronograph; date
Case: Titanox, ø 46.8 mm, height 15.5mm; unidirectionally rotating bezel with 60-minute scale; sapphire crystal; transparent case back; screw-in crown
Band: Titanox, double folding clasp
Price: $4,400

George J von Burg

With a cleanly structured collection of classic chronographs, George J von Burg is competing for the attention of America's watch-loving audience.
Even though one might assume this is a new brand, in all reality it isn't: As the son of a watchmaker, George Josef von Burg (1914-1986) had already learned about the manufacture of watches at a rather young age, acquiring all the necessary knowledge and skills. When he was barely twenty years old, he had already manufactured and sold his first timekeepers under the registered name of Geo Automatic. In the 1950s, von Burg immigrated with his family to the United States, where he founded a company for watch accessories. During this time, he purchased a watch factory in Switzerland, which he directed under the name Semag after returning from the U.S. His company expanded, and von Burg opened another branch of the factory in Claro (in the Swiss canton Tessin) where he — one of the first of his guild to do this — manufactured mechanical watch movements for reputable watch brands on modern production machines. Claro Watch SA was founded in 1961 for the production of mechanical pallet escapement movements.
Semag and Claro developed into two of the largest manufacturers of mechanical movements and wristwatches, which were sold under various brand names all over the world. These companies are still owned by the von Burg family today and are managed by von Burg's son, George J. von Burg II, and his grandson, George J. von Burg III.
The individual components of the chronographs come from various suppliers. They are, however, of the best quality, from the carefully finished cases and valuable leather straps to the very finely finished Valjoux chronograph movements and finely structured dials. At first glance, the sweep chronograph hands inlaid with a luminous substance seem a bit surprising, but they are an important style element that is incorporated into all three model families.
The current collection of George J. von Burg III comprises three product lines: Collectors Series, Chronograph Series, and Prestige Series. The Collectors Series is based on pure, undecorated shapes and communicates in fine details. Alongside a bicompax chronograph and a GMT chronograph with flyback function, the highlight of the company is also found in this series: a split-seconds chronograph called The Roman Rattrapante. The designated collector's pieces from the Collectors Series come in a very fine wood box together with a watch winder.
The latest model, introduced at Baselworld 2004, is also at home in the Collectors Series: Perpetual Calendar.

Roman Rattrapante

Reference number: 70021 C
Movement: automatic, GJVB 8721 (base ETA 7750); ø 30 mm, height 7.9 mm; 27 jewels; 28,800 vph, finely finished with côtes de Genève
Functions: hours, minutes, subsidiary seconds; split-seconds chronograph; date
Case: stainless steel, ø 42 mm, height 16 mm; sapphire crystal; transparent case back; screw-in crown
Band: reptile skin, buckle
Remarks: limited to 50 pieces
Price: upon request
Variations: in yellow, rose, or white gold

GMT Flyback

Reference number: 80021 C
Movement: automatic, GJVB 8107 (base ETA 7750); ø 30 mm, height 7.9 mm; 27 jewels; 28,800 vph, finely finished with côtes de Genève
Functions: hours, minutes, subsidiary seconds; chronograph with flyback function; date; 24-hour display (second time zone)
Case: stainless steel, ø 42 mm, height 16 mm; sapphire crystal; transparent case back; screw-in crown; water-resistant to 50 m
Band: reptile skin, buckle
Remarks: limited to 50 pieces
Price: upon request

Classic Aviator

Reference number: 90021 C
Movement: automatic, GJVB 8147 (base ETA 7750); ø 30 mm, height 7.9 mm; 27 jewels; 28,800 vph, finely finished with côtes de Genève
Functions: hours, minutes, subsidiary seconds, chronograph; date
Case: stainless steel, ø 42 mm, height 16 mm; sapphire crystal; transparent case back; screw-in crown
Band: reptile skin, buckle
Remarks: limited to 50 pieces
Price: upon request
Variations: in yellow, rose, or white gold

Classic Collection

Reference number: 20012 C
Movement: automatic, ETA 7750, ø 30 mm, height 7.9 mm; 27 jewels; 28,800 vph
Functions: hours, minutes, subsidiary seconds; chronograph; date and day
Case: stainless steel, gold-plated, ø 40 mm, height 15 mm; sapphire crystal; screw-in crown; water-resistant to 100 m
Band: reptile skin, buckle
Price: $1,795
Variations: with gold-plated stainless steel bracelet; in polished stainless steel

Sport Collection

Reference number: 30021 C
Movement: automatic, ETA 7750, ø 30 mm, height 7.9 mm; 27 jewels; 28,800 vph
Functions: hours, minutes, subsidiary seconds; chronograph; date and day
Case: stainless steel, ø 40 mm, height 15 mm; sapphire crystal; screw-in crown; water-resistant to 100 m
Band: reptile skin, buckle
Price: $1,695
Variations: with stainless steel bracelet; in gold-plated stainless steel

Modern Collection

Reference number: 10021 B
Movement: automatic, ETA 7750, ø 30 mm, height 7.9 mm; 27 jewels; 28,800 vph
Functions: hours, minutes, subsidiary seconds; chronograph; date and day
Case: stainless steel, ø 40 mm, height 15 mm; sapphire crystal; screw-in crown; water-resistant to 100 m
Band: stainless steel, folding clasp
Price: $1,425
Variations: with reptile skin strap; in gold-plated stainless steel

Harry Winston

The Genevan company Harry Winston Rare Timepieces is part of a fine jewelry institution with a reputation like no other. It is trying to recreate this reputation in the fine watch sector, successfully doing justice to its great name with a current production palette that includes an interesting new launch. Only fifty new Avenue C Jumping Hours, a timepiece that combines extravagance of shape with a fine watch movement, will be available. A square case houses a shaped movement that displays hours, minutes, and seconds, but in a rather unique way. The dial comprises two unequally sized large circles which together form the number eight. The second hand does its laps on the bottom circle, while the minute hand revolves around its axis in the circle above it. Where the 12 would normally be placed, there is instead a trapezoidal window in which a digital numeral jumps at the beginning of every hour. Although as a jeweler this company enjoys a worldwide reputation as a producer of costly timepieces set extravagantly with diamonds, its management is continually and increasingly stressing the brand's technical competence. In following this strategy, the company has called a wonderful new tradition to life. Harry Winston initiates collaborations with exceptional, independent watchmakers, always very well regarded in the field for their special talents. These artists exclusively design one or more new watches that are realized together with Harry Winston and — completely in line with the predicate "rare" in the brand's name — are introduced to the market in strictly limited editions called Opus.

After Opus One by Francois-Paul Journe in 2001, Opus Two by Antoine Preziuso the following year, and Opus 3 by Vianney Halter in 2003, the company presented a watch designed by Christophe Claret at 2004's Baselworld called Opus 4. Opus 4 combines the classic high complications of tourbillon, minute repeater, and an eye-catching moon phase display. When compared with the usual windows for the lunar display, this one is gigantic and takes up nearly the entire upper half of the dial — although, as the Opus 4 actually contains two dials, this is only half true. Thanks to the rotating platinum case, the observer can decide, as the mood strikes him, to have the "moon side" or the "technical side" facing up. The technical side allows one to admire the little hammers of the repeater movement in action alongside the fascinating tourbillon. The Opus 4, limited to eighteen pieces, respectfully and fittingly continues Harry Winston's tried-and-tested concept of combining costliness, watch technology, and exclusivity.

Z1

Reference number: 400/MCRA44ZCA
Movement: automatic, Frédéric Piguet 1185 with module HW 2831 A, ø 32 mm, height 7.2 mm; 49 jewels; 21,600 vph
Functions: hours, minutes (off-center), subsidiary seconds (retrograde); chronograph with retrograde counters
Case: zalium, ø 44 mm, height 12.5 mm; sapphire crystal; transparent case back; screw-in crown
Band: rubber, buckle
Remarks: limited to 100 pieces
Price: $17,400

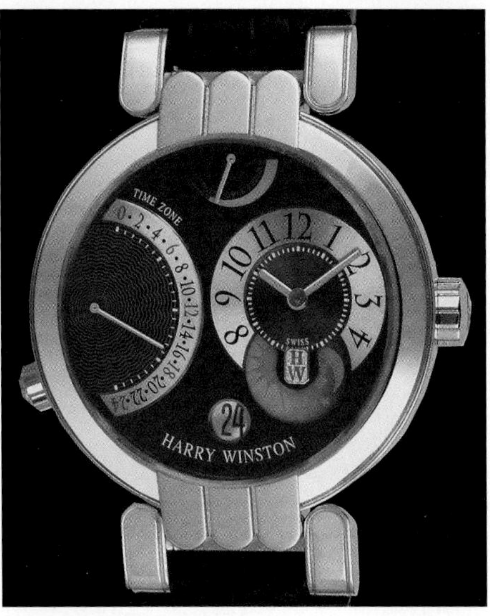

Excenter Timezone

Reference number: 200/MMTZ39WL.A
Movement: manual winding, Jaquet 7060 with module HW 2821, ø 32 mm, height 6 mm; 28 jewels; 21,600 vph
Functions: hours, minutes; date, moon phase; retrograde 24-hour display (second time zone); power reserve display
Case: white gold, ø 39 mm, height 11.1 mm; sapphire crystal
Band: reptile skin, folding clasp
Price: $22,850

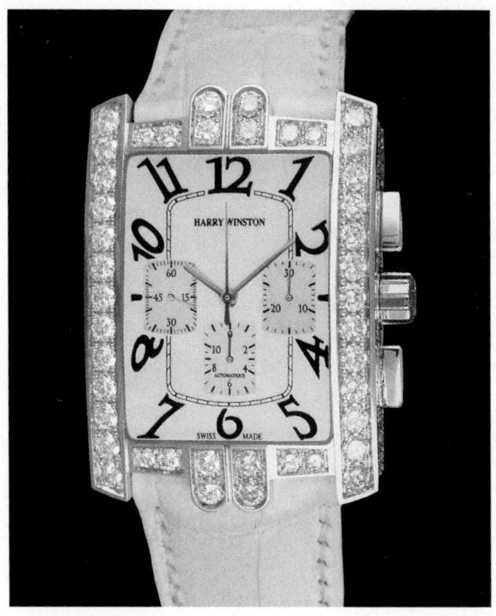

Avenue C Chronograph

Reference number: 330/MCAWL.M/D3.1
Movement: automatic, ETA 2094, ø 24 mm, height 5.5 mm; 33 jewels; 28,800 vph
Functions: hours, minutes, subsidiary seconds; chronograph
Case: white gold, 32 x 44.3 mm, height 12.1 mm; bezel and lugs set with diamonds; sapphire crystal
Band: reptile skin, buckle
Price: $38,050
Variations: in red gold

Lady Premier Chronograph

Reference number: 200/UCQ32WW1.MD/D3.1/D2.1
Movement: quartz, Frédéric Piguet 1270
Functions: hours, minutes, subsidiary seconds; chronograph
Case: white gold, ø 32 mm, height 9.65 mm; bezel and lugs set with diamonds; sapphire crystal; crown with diamond cabochon
Band: white gold and white rubber, set with diamonds, folding clasp
Price: $58,400
Variations: in yellow gold with black rubber

Avenue C Jump Hours

Reference number: 330/UMJPL.T
Movement: manual winding, HW 315, 21 x 27 mm, height 8.35 mm; 20 jewels; 21,600 vph
Functions: hours (jump), minutes (off-center), subsidiary seconds
Case: platinum, 26 x 46 mm, height 10.85 mm; sapphire crystal; transparent case back
Band: reptile skin, folding clasp
Remarks: limited to 2 x 25 pieces
Price: $22,800

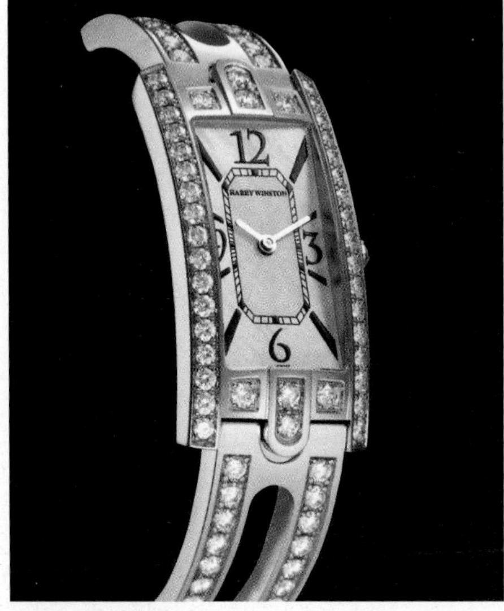

Avenue C Captive

Reference number: 330/LQWW31.M/D3.1/D2.1
Movement: quartz, ETA 901.001
Functions: hours, minutes
Case: white gold, 19 x 39.5 mm, height 9.4 mm; bezel and lugs set with diamonds; sapphire crystal
Band: white gold bangle with spring mechanism, set with diamonds
Price: $40,600
Variations: in yellow gold

Xemex

The rare feat of adding a fully new chapter to the big book of watch design was achieved in the middle of the 1990s by the Xemex brand. Literally, right from the beginning in 1996, Xemex's hands have permanently been set to success. From its modest beginnings as an insider tip for watch lovers, it has developed into a watch brand with Swiss tradition and unmistakable design in just a short amount of time, successfully creating a place for itself on the market. The unique, clean shapes of all of the brand's timekeepers are created in-house and embody pure perfection and harmony down to the smallest detail according to the apothegm "the power of simplicity."

And it all starts with the name of this brand. Xemex: short, to the point, without an arrogant attitude, easy to remember, same both forward and backward, and pronounced the same way in most languages.

Watches of this name feature steel cases with movable strap lugs, and that is only one of the special features. All of the watches have black or white dials with clear minute and hour markers and very conspicuous hands. These are characteristics that don't change Ruedi Külling's fundamental concept of "simplify, objectify, clarify." They support it. As they should, for Külling, who made the original sketches, is someone who can look back on more than forty years of successful work in the field of design. His artistic signature places him as a contemporary representative of the beginning of the German Bauhaus movement, although he is often — usually out of sheer frustration — placed in the group "form follows function." The brand's actual creative concern placed more emphasis on developing an alternative without just creating a fashion gag, to create a timeless counterpart to more traditional watch shapes. Last year Xemex Swiss Watch AG committed to a new strategic partnership with Designfactory AG Schweiz. The brothers Axel and Marc Schlund, long loyal to the watch world of Xemex, are part of a watchmaking tradition that reaches back several generations and are pleased to be able to lend their great amount of experience and ambition to the successful and long-term development of the brand as partners and co-owners.

The common goal of the strengthened team is to continue winning worldwide friends and customers for the unique, fascinating world of Xemex wristwatches.

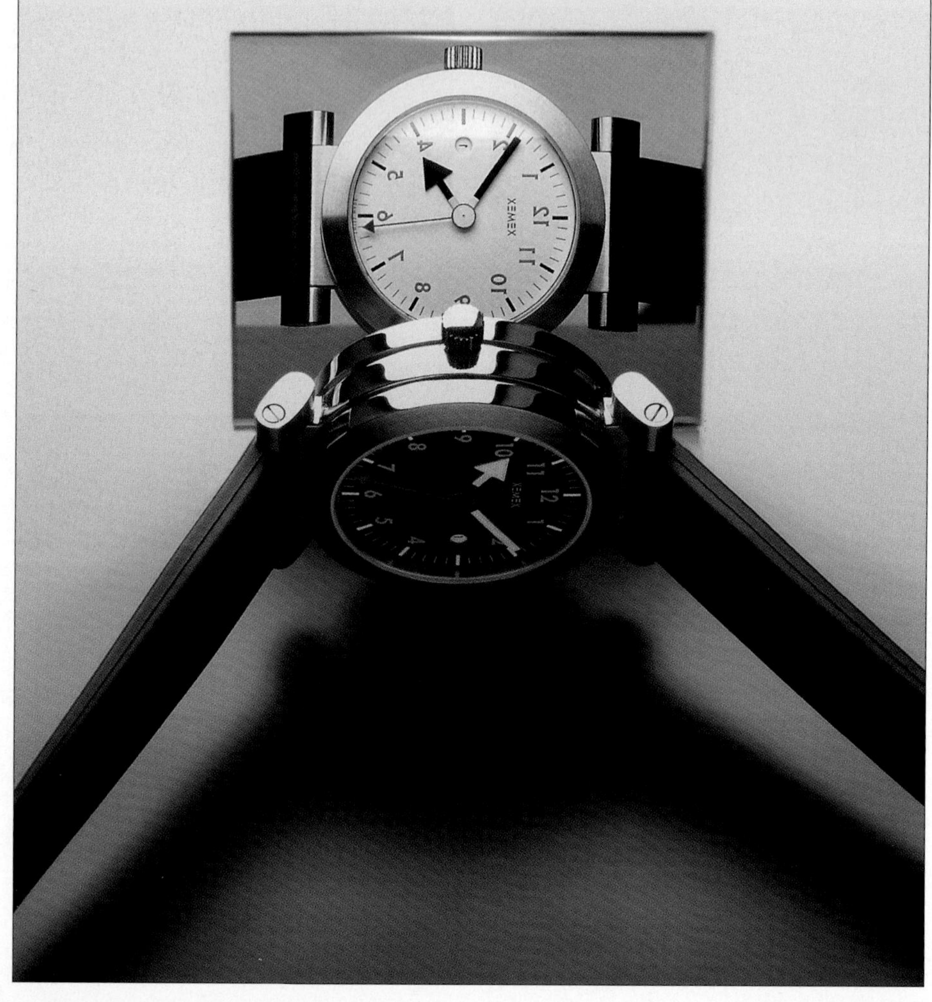

Avenue Chronograph

Reference number: 2350
Movement: automatic, ETA 2894-2, ø 28.6 mm, height 6.1 mm; 37 jewels; 28,800 vph
Functions: hours, minutes, subsidiary seconds, chronograph; date
Case: stainless steel, movable lugs, 33 x 37 mm, height 15 mm; sapphire crystal; transparent case back; screw-in crown; water-resistant to 50 m
Band: reptile skin, folding clasp
Price: $4,950
Variations: with stainless steel bracelet

Avenue Petite Seconde

Reference number: 2800
Movement: automatic, ETA 2895-2, ø 25.6 mm, height 4.35 mm; 30 jewels; 28,800 vph
Functions: hours, minutes, subsidiary seconds; date
Case: stainless steel, movable lugs, 33 x 37 mm, height 9.9 mm; sapphire crystal; transparent case back; screw-in crown; water-resistant to 50 m
Band: leather, folding clasp
Price: $2,595
Variations: with white dial

Offroad Nr. 1

Reference number: 215
Movement: automatic, ETA 2824-2, ø 25.6 mm, height 4.6 mm; 25 jewels; 28,800 vph
Functions: hours, minutes, sweep seconds; date
Case: stainless steel, movable lugs, ø 38 mm, height 9.75 mm; sapphire crystal; transparent case back; screw-in crown; water-resistant to 50 m
Band: leather, buckle
Price: $1,395
Variations: with rubber strap; with stainless steel bracelet

Offroad Chronograph

Reference number: 1000
Movement: automatic, ETA 2894-2, ø 28.6 mm, height 6.1 mm; 37 jewels; 28,800 vph
Functions: hours, minutes, subsidiary seconds; chronograph; date
Case: stainless steel, movable lugs, ø 40 mm, height 14 mm; bezel with tachymeter scale; sapphire crystal; transparent case back; screw-in crown; water-resistant to 100 m
Band: stainless steel, double folding clasp
Price: $4,895
Variations: with leather strap ($4,495)

Speedway Chronograph

Reference number: 5501
Movement: automatic, ETA 7750, ø 30 mm, height 7.9 mm; 25 jewels; 28,800 vph
Functions: hours, minutes, subsidiary seconds; chronograph; date
Case: stainless steel, movable lugs, ø 44 mm, height 14.75 mm; sapphire crystal; transparent case back; recessed crown; water-resistant to 100 m
Band: rubber, double folding clasp
Price: $3,950
Variations: with stainless steel bracelet

Piccadilly Big Date

Reference number: 810
Movement: automatic, ETA 2896, ø 25.6 mm, height 4.85 mm; 22 jewels; 28,800 vph
Functions: hours, minutes, sweep seconds; large date
Case: stainless steel, movable lugs, ø 40 mm, height 10.8 mm; sapphire crystal; transparent case back; screw-in crown; water-resistant to 50 m
Band: calfskin, buckle
Price: $2,895
Variations: with white dial

Zenith

The watch *manufacture* Zenith, very rich in tradition, belongs to the watch and jewelry division of the Louis Vuitton, Moet & Hennessy (LVMH) concern, a department that was called to life in November 1999.
Current Zenith president, Thierry Nataf, was transferred from Paris to the Swiss Jura — some say this is a "punishment," but the stylishly perfect gentlemen disagrees profusely. "I am tempted by the challenge of waking this Sleeping Beauty. I understood right from the beginning what type of potential this brand has. And it hurt my soul to see how others have adorned themselves with the values of this *manufacture*. Zenith is something very special and deserves much more respect."
The modernization of the outdated machines at Zenith was a top priority for the engineer. He invested millions in the extension of the R&D department, hired vector graphic specialists foreign to the industry, and sat them down at a table together with classically trained movement designers. That "modern watchmaking is a mixture of craft and futuristic music" is something Nataf is convinced of. "We are once again looking at the beginning of a revolution." The extensive reworking of the El Primero caliber family bears witness not only to new caliber numbers, but also to a thoroughly improved finish on all components.
Nataf's second priority was to "get back to the Zenith style." That the *manufacture*'s products were sold at ruinously under-valued prices in comparison to those of the competition was only one side of the coin. A larger handicap was the missing glamour and shine according to Nataf. "It is so easy to combine technology and glamour in such a fascinating product as the mechanical wristwatch." — but he had to prove this.
At Baselworld 2004, Zenith presented the first tourbillon ever to run at a frequency of 36,000 vph. And as if that weren't enough: It is built into an automatic chronograph movement and encircled by a date ring that moves counterclockwise. The designers at the venerable *manufacture* worked for three years on this technical act of power. In comparison, last year's Open chronograph seems as if it appeared magically with a flick of the wrist.

Next to such a sensational world premiere, every other new watch seems practically overshadowed. But it would be a shame to overlook the return to classic sizes represented by the reduction of the case diameter on the smaller-sized Open model — especially after it was Zenith who propagated the XXL case in recent years. The new Baby Star for women also possesses a slimmer 32-mm case and can be dressed to appear more sporty or more elegant, depending on the dial and strap, but certainly always feminine.

Grande ChronoMaster XXT Tourbillon

Reference number: 18.1260.4005/01.C505
Movement: automatic, Zenith 4005 El Primero, ø 35 mm, height 7.55 mm; 35 jewels; 36,000 vph, one-minute tourbillon; counterclockwise date ring between bridge and cage
Functions: hours, minutes; chronograph; date
Case: rose gold, ø 45 mm; sapphire crystal; transparent case back
Band: reptile skin, threefold folding clasp
Remarks: limited series
Price: $104,000
Variations: in white gold

ChronoMaster XXT Open

Reference number: 03.1260.4021/02.C505
Movement: automatic, Zenith 4021 El Primero, ø 30 mm, height 7.75 mm; 39 jewels; 36,000 vph, movement partially skeletonized under cutaway in dial above escapement
Functions: hours, minutes, subsidiary seconds; chronograph; power reserve display
Case: stainless steel, ø 45 mm, height 14.1 mm; sapphire crystal; transparent case back
Band: reptile skin, threefold folding clasp
Price: $6,900
Variations: with stainless steel or rubber strap; different dial variations

ChronoMaster T Open

Reference number: 18.0240.4021/01.C495
Movement: automatic, Zenith 4021 El Primero, ø 30 mm, height 7.75 mm; 39 jewels; 36,000 vph, movement partially skeletonized under cutaway in dial above escapement
Functions: hours, minutes, subsidiary seconds; chronograph; power reserve display
Case: rose gold, ø 40 mm, height 14.1 mm; sapphire crystal; transparent case back
Band: reptile skin, threefold folding clasp
Price: $13,800
Variations: in stainless steel with white, black or cobalt-colored dial; with stainless steel bracelet

ChronoMaster T Open

Reference number: 03.0240.4021/73.C495
Movement: automatic, Zenith 4021 El Primero, ø 30 mm, height 7.75 mm; 39 jewels; 36,000 vph, movement partially skeletonized under cutaway in dial above escapement
Functions: hours, minutes, subsidiary seconds; chronograph; power reserve display
Case: stainless steel, ø 40 mm, height 14.1 mm; sapphire crystal; transparent case back
Band: leather, threefold folding clasp
Price: $6,200
Variations: with white or black dial

Grande Class Grande Date

Reference number: 03.0520.4010/21.C492
Movement: automatic, Zenith 4010 El Primero, ø 30 mm, height 7.65 mm; 31 jewels; 36,000 vph
Functions: hours, minutes, subsidiary seconds; chronograph; large date
Case: stainless steel, ø 44 mm; sapphire crystal; transparent case back
Band: reptile skin, threefold folding clasp
Price: upon request
Variations: with stainless steel /rubber bracelet

Grande Class Rattrapante Grande Date

Reference number: 65.0520.4026/73.C492
Movement: automatic, Zenith 4026 El Primero, ø 30 mm, height 9.35 mm; 32 jewels; 36,000 vph, certified chronometer (C.O.S.C.)
Functions: hours, minutes, subsidiary seconds; split-seconds chronograph; large date
Case: white gold, ø 44 mm; sapphire crystal; transparent case back
Band: reptile skin, threefold folding clasp
Price: $34,000

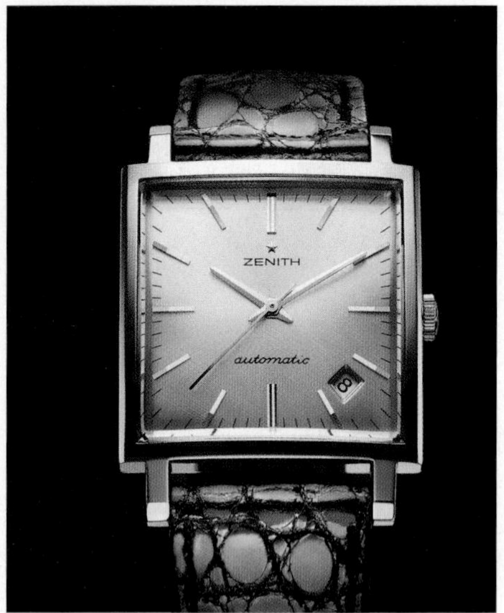

New Vintage 1965

Reference number: 35.1965.6
Movement: automatic, Zenith Elite 670, ø 25.6 mm, height 3.28 mm; 27 jewels; 28,800 vph
Functions: hours, minutes, sweep seconds; date
Case: yellow gold, 33 x 33 mm; sapphire crystal; transparent case back
Band: reptile skin, buckle
Remarks: after a model from 1965
Price: $9,500
Variations: in rose gold

ChronoMaster Star

Reference number: 03.1230.4002./21.R527
Movement: automatic, Zenith 4002 El Primero, ø 30 mm, height 6.5 mm; 31 jewels; 36,000 vph, C.O.S.C certified chronometer
Functions: hours, minutes, subsidiary seconds; chronograph; date
Case: stainless steel, ø 37.5 mm; sapphire crystal; transparent case back
Band: rubber, threefold folding clasp
Price: $4,800
Variations: with colorful dials and matching leather straps; with stainless steel bracelet

ChronoMaster Star Open

Reference number: 03.1230.4021/21.C545
Movement: automatic, Zenith 4021 El Primero, ø 30 mm, height 7.75 mm; 39 jewels; 36,000 vph, movement partially skeletonized under heart-shaped cutaway in dial above escapement
Functions: hours, minutes, subsidiary seconds; chronograph; power reserve display
Case: stainless steel, ø 37.5 mm; sapphire crystal; transparent case back
Band: satin, threefold folding clasp
Price: $5,800
Variations: with colorful dials and matching bands

ChronoMaster Baby Star

Reference number: 35.1220.67/41.C519
Movement: automatic, Zenith Elite 67, ø 25.6 mm, height 3.81 mm; 27 jewels; 28,800 vph
Functions: hours, minutes, sweep seconds
Case: yellow gold, ø 32 mm; sapphire crystal; transparent case back
Band: reptile skin, buckle
Price: $7,900
Variations: with colorful dials and matching bands; in stainless steel and in rose gold

ChronoMaster Baby Star Diamonds

Reference number: 16.1220.67/61.C534
Movement: automatic, Zenith Elite 67, ø 25.6 mm, height 3.81 mm; 27 jewels; 28,800 vph
Functions: hours, minutes, sweep seconds
Case: stainless steel, ø 32 mm; bezel set with diamonds; sapphire crystal; transparent case back
Band: reptile skin, buckle
Price: $5,200
Variations: with colorful dials and matching bands; in yellow or rose gold

Grande Class El Primero

Reference number: 03.0520.4002/01.C492
Movement: automatic, Zenith 4002 El Primero, ø 30 mm, height 6.5 mm; 31 jewels; 36,000 vph, certified chronometer (C.O.S.C.)
Functions: hours, minutes, subsidiary seconds; chronograph; date
Case: stainless steel, ø 44 mm, height 13.9 mm; sapphire crystal; transparent case back
Band: reptile skin, threefold folding clasp
Remarks: Star Collection, numbered edition
Price: $7,700
Variations: with white or black dial; stainless steel bracelet

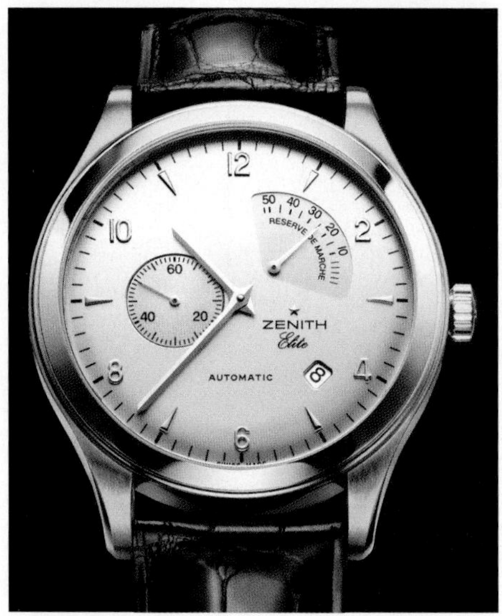

Grande Class Elite Power Reserve

Reference number: 03.0520.685/21.C492
Movement: automatic, Zenith Elite 685, ø 25.6 mm, height 4.48 mm; 38 jewels; 28,800 vph
Functions: hours, minutes, subsidiary seconds; date; power reserve display
Case: stainless steel, ø 44 mm; sapphire crystal; transparent case back
Band: reptile skin, threefold folding clasp
Remarks: Star Collection, numbered edition
Price: upon request
Variations: with white dial; with stainless steel bracelet

Grande Class Elite Power Reserve Dual Time

Reference number: 18.0520.683/01.C492
Movement: automatic, Zenith Elite 683, ø 25.6 mm, height 4.95 mm; 36 jewels; 28,800 vph
Functions: hours, minutes, subsidiary seconds; date; power reserve display; 24-hour display (second time zone)
Case: rose gold, ø 44 mm; sapphire crystal; transparent case back
Band: reptile skin, threefold folding clasp
Remarks: Star Collection, numbered edition
Price: $12,000
Variations: stainless steel, yellow and white gold; bracelet

Port Royal Rectangle Elite

Reference number: 01.0251.684/02.C504
Movement: automatic, Zenith Elite 684, ø 25.6 mm, height 3.28 mm; 26 jewels; 28,800 vph
Functions: hours, minutes, subsidiary seconds; date
Case: stainless steel, 31 x 44 mm; sapphire crystal
Band: reptile skin, threefold folding clasp
Price: $3,400
Variations: with black dial; with stainless steel bracelet

Port Royal Elite Dual Time

Reference number: 01.0451.682/02.C491
Movement: automatic, Zenith Elite 682, ø 25.6 mm, height 3.75 mm; 26 jewels; 28,800 vph
Functions: hours, minutes, subsidiary seconds; date; 24-hour display (second time zone)
Case: stainless steel, ø 38.5 mm; sapphire crystal; transparent case back
Band: reptile skin, threefold folding clasp
Price: $3,400
Variations: with black dial; with stainless steel bracelet

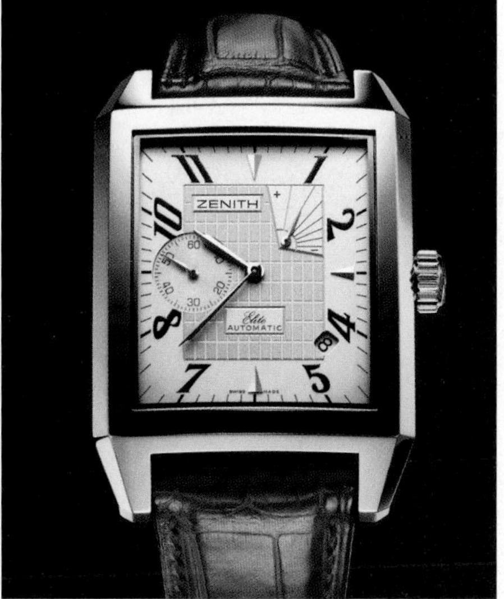

Grande Port Royal Elite Power Reserve

Reference number: 03.0550.685/01.C507
Movement: automatic, Zenith Elite 685, ø 25.6 mm, height 4.48 mm; 38 jewels; 28,800 vph
Functions: hours, minutes, subsidiary seconds; date; power reserve display
Case: stainless steel, 36 x 51 mm, height 10.2 mm; sapphire crystal; transparent case back
Band: reptile skin, threefold folding clasp
Price: $5,200
Variations: with black dial; with stainless steel bracelet or rubber strap

Port Royal El Primero

Reference number: 02.0451.400/22.M451
Movement: automatic, Zenith 400 El Primero, ø 30 mm, height 6.5 mm; 31 jewels; 36,000 vph
Functions: hours, minutes, subsidiary seconds; chronograph; date
Case: stainless steel, ø 40 mm, height 13 mm; sapphire crystal; transparent case back
Band: stainless steel, threefold folding clasp
Price: $4,800
Variations: with white dial; with reptile skin strap

El Primero 4001

Base caliber: El Primero 410
Mechanical with automatic winding, power reserve more than 50 hours, ball-bearing rotor; column-wheel control of chronograph functions
Functions: hours, minutes, subsidiary seconds; complete calendar date, day, month, moon phase); chronograph with flyback function
Diameter: 30 mm (13'''); **Height:** 7.55 mm; **Jewels:** 31
Balance: glucydur
Frequency: 36,000 vph
Balance spring: self-compensating flat hairspring with fine adjustment
Shock protection: Kif
Remarks: 355 components; quick-set date and moon phase

El Primero 4002

Base caliber: El Primero 400
Mechanical with automatic winding, power reserve more than 50 hours, ball-bearing rotor; column-wheel control of chronograph functions
Functions: hours, minutes, subsidiary seconds; date; chronograph
Diameter: 30 mm (13'''); **Height:** 6.5 mm
Jewels: 31
Balance: glucydur
Frequency: 36,000 vph
Balance spring: self-compensating flat hairspring with fine adjustment
Shock protection: Kif
Remarks: 266 components; quick-set date

El Primero 4003

Base caliber: El Primero 410
Mechanical with automatic winding, power reserve more than 50 hours, ball-bearing rotor; column-wheel control of chronograph functions
Functions: hours, minutes, subsidiary seconds; perpetual calendar (date, day, month, moon phase); chronograph with flyback function
Diameter: 30 mm (13'''); **Height:** 8.1 mm; **Jewels:** 31
Balance: glucydur; **Frequency:** 36,000 vph
Balance spring: self-compensating flat hairspring with fine adjustment
Shock protection: Kif
Remarks: moon phase with disk display; quick-set date and moon phase

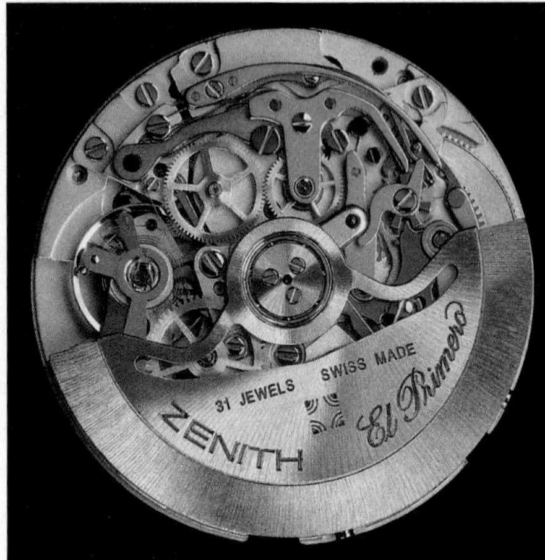

El Primero 400

Mechanical with automatic winding, power reserve more than 50 hours, ball-bearing rotor; column-wheel control of chronograph functions
Functions: hours, minutes, subsidiary seconds; date; chronograph
Diameter: 30 mm (13'''); **Height:** 6.5 mm; **Jewels:** 31
Balance: glucydur
Frequency: 36,000 vph
Balance spring: self-compensating flat hairspring with fine adjustment
Shock protection: Kif
Remarks: 280 components; quick-set date
Related calibers: 410 (additional indicators: day, month, moon phase), 354 components

Caliber 4021 «Open»

Mechanical with automatic winding, power reserve more than 50 hours; ball-bearing rotor; column-wheel control of chronograph functions
Functions: hours, minutes, subsidiary seconds; chronograph; power reserve display
Diameter: 30 mm (13'''); **Height:** 6.5 mm; **Jewels:** 39
Balance: glucydur
Frequency: 36,000 vph
Balance spring: self-compensating flat hairspring with fine adjustment
Shock protection: Kif
Remarks: base plate in the area of the escapement is open and the flat parts are skeletonized

Elite 685

Mechanical with automatic winding, power reserve more than 50 hours, ball-bearing rotor, unidirectionally winding; stop-seconds
Functions: hours, minutes, subsidiary seconds; date; power reserve indicator
Diameter: 26.2 mm (11 1/2'''); **Height:** 4.28 mm
Jewels: 38
Frequency: 28,800 vph
Balance spring: self-compensating flat hairspring with fine adjustment via micrometer screw
Shock protection: Kif
Options: without date/seconds (661), date/sweep seconds (670), date/sweep seconds/24h (672), date/subsidiary seconds (680), date/subsidiary seconds/24h (682)

ZENITH
ZENITH
Love

Zeno

Among the most important towns on Switzerland's watchmaking map has always been La-Chaux-de-Fonds, where in 1868 Jules Godat founded a small pocket watch manufacturing company called Godat & Co., producing fine pocket watches with solid silver cases and women's pendant watches in small quantities. The small factory he built was taken over by the company of A. Eigeldinger & Fils in 1920.

The Eigeldinger family business specialized in military wristwatches, producing pieces encased in stainless steel, silver, gold, and platinum that featured mechanical movements with diameters of up to 43 mm. The owner's son, André-Charles Eigeldinger, introduced the Zeno brand, the name of which is derived from the Greek word *zenodopolus*, meaning "gift of Zeus" or "divine offering."

The first watches carrying the Zeno brand name were manufactured in 1922, and in 1949 Zeno watches were first exhibited at the Basel Watch Fair. In the '60s, watches were also produced under the name of FHB (Felix Huber Basel) and Aida.

Felix W. Huber bought the rights to the Zeno name in 1963. The brand attracted international attention with 1969's futuristic Spaceman model, made of the then absolutely novel material fiberglass; the vacuum-compressed, hermetically sealed diver's watch Compressor, manufactured from 1970 until 1973; and the acquisition of other Swiss watch factories such as Josmar, Jupiter, Corona, Dalil, Fleuron, Penelope, Le Clip, Helveco, Imhof, and Jean Roulet.

Today Zeno, a Swiss company that has managed to remain independent, is now called Zeno Watch Basel, honoring the city it has called home since its acquisition, and is still headed up by Felix W. Huber. Further workshops are to be found in the Jura near Neuchâtel and in the Italian-language Swiss canton of Tessin.

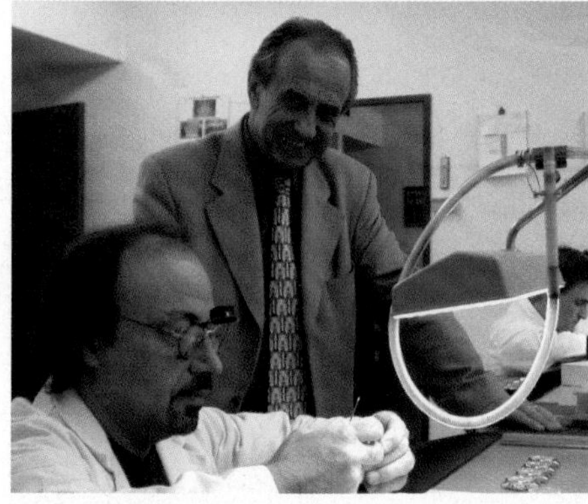

The company prides itself on offering the most quality and design innovation available for a reasonable price. In recent years Zeno has made a name for itself in the growing arena of oversized watches. Although the company's growing palette (featuring more than 1,500 models, including variations) comprises both men's and women's watches in almost every variation imaginable (mechanical and quartz, pocket watches, military watches, diver's watches, and sports watches) in every combination of materials, it is the extra-large format of the Pilot family that has given Zeno its characteristic look. These leading models are based on Zeno pilot's watches that were produced in 1965, at that time measuring 37 mm in diameter. In comparison, the con-temporary Pilot Oversized measures 47.5 mm in diameter, surely one of the largest wristwatches made today, and is available as an automatic or manually wound model and with chronograph and GMT complications as well as C.O.S.C. certification.

Pilot OS Chronograph

Reference number: 855J TVDD
Movement: automatic, ETA 7750, ø 30 mm, height 7.9 mm; 25 jewels; 28,800 vph
Functions: hours, minutes, subsidiary seconds; chronograph; date and day
Case: stainless steel, ø 47.5 mm, height 17 mm; mineral crystal; transparent case back
Band: leather, buckle
Price: $1,490
Variations: with sapphire crystal; with stainless steel bracelet; different dial variations

Pilot Classic Chronograph

Reference number: 655J TVD
Movement: automatic, ETA 7750, ø 30 mm, height 7.9 mm; 25 jewels; 28,800 vph
Functions: hours, minutes, subsidiary seconds; chronograph; date and day
Case: stainless steel, ø 40.5 mm, height 15.5 mm; mineral crystal; transparent case back
Band: leather, buckle
Price: $1,285
Variations: with sapphire crystal; with stainless steel bracelet; different dial variations

Pilot OS Chronograph Power Reserve

Reference number: 8557/2 TVD-PR
Movement: automatic, ETA 7750, ø 30 mm, height 7.9 mm; 25 jewels; 28,800 vph
Functions: hours, minutes, subsidiary seconds; chronograph; date; power reserve display
Case: stainless steel, ø 47.5 mm, height 17 mm; mineral crystal; transparent case back
Band: leather, buckle
Price: $2,250
Variations: with sapphire crystal; with stainless steel bracelet; different dial variations

Pilot OS Pointer

Reference number: 8554 Z D-SV
Movement: automatic, ETA 2824-2, ø 25.6 mm, height 4.6 mm; 25 jewels; 28,800 vph
Functions: hours, minutes, sweep seconds; date
Case: stainless steel, ø 47.5 mm, height 15 mm; mineral crystal; transparent case back
Band: leather, buckle
Price: $675
Variations: with sapphire crystal; with stainless steel bracelet; different dial variations

Pilot OS Manual Winding

Reference number: 8558 9
Movement: manual winding, ETA 6497, ø 36.6 mm, height 4.5 mm; 17 jewels; 21,600 vph
Functions: hours, minutes, subsidiary seconds
Case: stainless steel, ø 47.5 mm, height 15 mm; mineral crystal; transparent case back
Band: leather, buckle
Price: $650
Variations: small seconds at 6 o'clock; with stainless steel bracelet

Pilot Classic

Reference number: 6554 SW
Movement: automatic, ETA 2824-2, ø 25.6 mm, height 4.6 mm; 25 jewels; 28,800 vph
Functions: hours, minutes, sweep seconds; date
Case: stainless steel, ø 40.5 mm, height 12.5 mm; mineral crystal; transparent case back
Band: leather, buckle
Price: $470
Variations: with silver dial; with sapphire crystal; with stainless steel bracelet

ETA

This Swatch Group movement manufacturer produces more than five million movements a year. And after the withdrawal of Richemont's Jaeger-LeCoultre as well as Swatch Group sisters Nouvelle Lémania and Frédéric Piguet from the business of selling movements on the free market, most watch brands can hardly help but beat down the door of this full service manufacturer. ETA offers a broad spectrum of automatic movements in various dimensions with different functions, chronograph movements in varying configurations, as well as pocket watch classics (Calibers 6497 and 98) and manually wound calibers of days gone by (Calibers 1727 and 7001) – this company offers everything that a manufacturer's heart could desire. That's not to mention the sheer variety of quartz technology: from inexpensive three-hand mechanisms to highly complicated multifunctional movements and futuristic Etaquartz featuring autonomous energy creation using a rotor and generator.
The almost stereotypical accusation of ETA being "mass goods," however, might just sound like praise in the ears of new ETA director Thomas Meier: He knows only too well how difficult it is to consistently manufacture high-quality filigreed micromechanical technology. This is certainly one of the reasons why there are no (longer) any other movement factories today in Europe that can compete with ETA, or that would want to.
Since the success of Swatch – a pure ETA product – millions of Swiss francs have been invested in new development and manufacturing technologies. ETA today owns more than twenty production locales in Switzerland, France, Germany, Malaysia, and Thailand.

ETA, which was created from an amalgamation of several independent *ébauche* manufacturers called Ebauches SA, still delivers some of its movements as half-done "kits" to be reassembled, rebuilt, and/or decorated. These go to specialized workshops such as Soprod, Sellita, Jaquet, and Dubois-Dépraz as Swiss watch tradition has dictated for decades. This practice is supposed to come to an end soon: The Swatch Group's concern management is no longer interested in leaving the lion's share of movement upscaling to others, but will only deliver complete movements in the future, ready for encasing, with personalization and individualization already done as the client wishes.

Caliber 2660

Mechanical with manual winding, power reserve 42 hours
Functions: hours, minutes, sweep seconds
Diameter: 17.2 mm (7 3/4''')
Height: 3.5 mm
Jewels: 17
Frequency: 28,800 vph
Fine adjustment system:
ETACHRON

Caliber 1727

Mechanical with manual winding, power reserve 50 hours
Functions: hours, minutes, subsidiary seconds at 6 o'clock
Diameter: 19.4 mm (8 3/4''')
Height: 3.5 mm
Jewels: 19
Frequency: 21,600 vph
Fine adjustment system:
ETACHRON
Remark: Movement based on prototype AS 1727

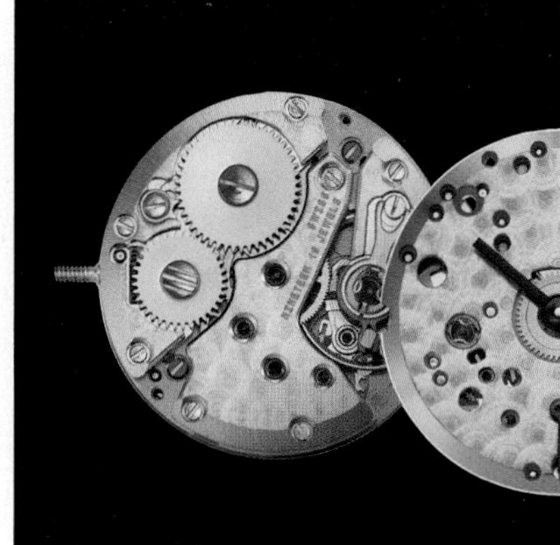

Caliber 7001

Mechanical with manual winding, ultraflat, power reserve 42 hours
Functions: hours, minutes, subsidiary seconds at 6 o'clock
Diameter: 23.3 mm (10 1/2''')
Height: 2.5 mm
Jewels: 17
Frequency: 21,600 vph
Fine adjustment system:
ETACHRON

Caliber 2801-2

Mechanical with manual winding, power reserve 42 hours
Functions: hours, minutes, sweep seconds
Diameter: 25.6 mm (11 1/2''')
Height: 3.35 mm
Jewels: 17
Frequency: 28,800 vph
Fine adjustment system:
ETACHRON
Related caliber: 2804-2
(with date window and quick-set)

Caliber 7765

Mechanical with manual winding, stop-seconds, power reserve 42 hours
Functions: hours, minutes, subsidiary seconds at 9 o'clock; chronograph (30-minute counter at 12 o'clock, sweep stop second hand); date window with quick-set at 3 o'clock
Diameter: 30 mm (13 1/4''')
Height: 6.35 mm
Jewels: 17
Frequency: 28,800 vph
Fine adjustment system:
ETACHRON with index
Related calibers: 7760 (with additional 12-hour counter at 6 o'clock and day window at 3 o'clock; height 7 mm); 7750 and 7751 (automatic versions)

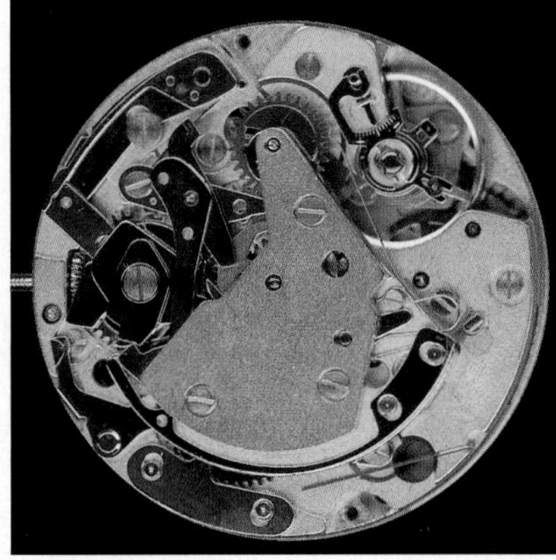

Caliber 6497/6498

Only a few watch fans know that ETA still manufactures two pure pocket watch movements. Caliber 6497 (a so-called Lépine movement, subsidiary seconds located on the lengthened winding stem) and 6498 (a so-called hunter, subsidiary seconds in a right angle to the winding stem) are available in two qualities: as 6497-1 and 6498-1 (rather sober, undecorated version); 6497-2 and 6498-2 (with off-center stripe decoration on bridges and cocks as well as beveled and striped crown and ratchet wheels). The photograph shows Lépine Caliber 6497-2.
Functions: hours, minutes, subsidiary seconds
Diameter: 36.6 mm (16 1/2''')
Height: 4.5 mm
Jewels: 17
Frequency: 21,600 vph
Fine adjustment system:
ETACHRON with index

Caliber 2671

Mechanical with automatic winding, ball-bearing rotor, stop-seconds, power reserve 38 hours
Functions: hours, minutes, sweep seconds; date window with quick-set at 3 o'clock
Diameter: 17.2 mm (7 3/4''')
Height: 4.8 mm
Jewels: 25
Frequency: 28,800 vph
Fine adjustment system: ETACHRON with index
Related calibers: 2678 (additional day window at 3 o'clock, height 5.35 mm)

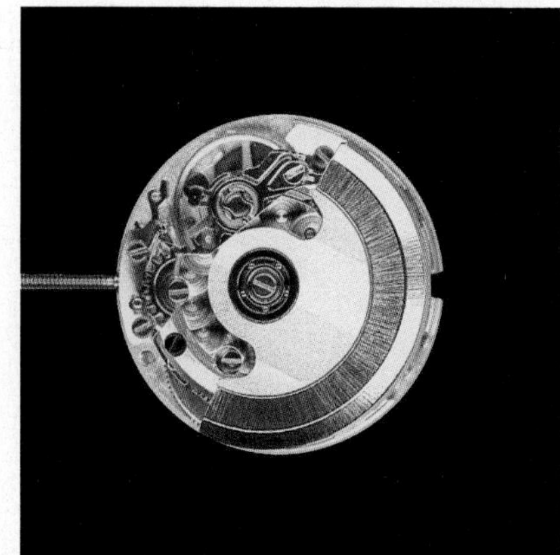

Caliber 2681

Mechanical with automatic winding, ball-bearing rotor, stop-seconds, power reserve 38 hours
Functions: hours, minutes, sweep seconds; day/date window with quick-set at 3 o'clock
Diameter: 19.4 mm (8 3/4''')
Height: 4.8 mm
Jewels: 25
Frequency: 28,800 vph
Fine adjustment system: ETACHRON with index
Related calibers: 2685 (sweep date hand and moon phase at 6 o'clock)

Caliber 2000

Mechanical with automatic winding, ball-bearing rotor, stop-seconds, power reserve 40 hours
Functions: hours, minutes, sweep seconds; date window with quick-set at 3 o'clock
Diameter: 19.4 mm (8 3/4''')
Height: 3.6 mm
Jewels: 20
Frequency: 28,800 vph
Fine adjustment system: ETACHRON with index

Caliber 2004

Mechanical with automatic winding, ball-bearing rotor, stop-seconds, power reserve 40 hours
Functions: hours, minutes, sweep seconds; date window with quick-set at 3 o'clock
Diameter: 23.3 mm (10 1/2''')
Height: 3.6 mm
Jewels: 20
Frequency: 28,800 vph
Fine adjustment system: ETACHRON with index

Caliber 2824-2

Mechanical with automatic winding, ball-bearing rotor, stop-seconds, power reserve 38 hours
Functions: hours, minutes, sweep seconds; date window with quick-set at 3 o'clock
Diameter: 25.6 mm (11 1/2''')
Height: 4.6 mm
Jewels: 25
Frequency: 28,800 vph
Fine adjustment system: ETACHRON with index
Related Calibers: 2836-2 (additional day window at 3 o'clock, height 5.05 mm)

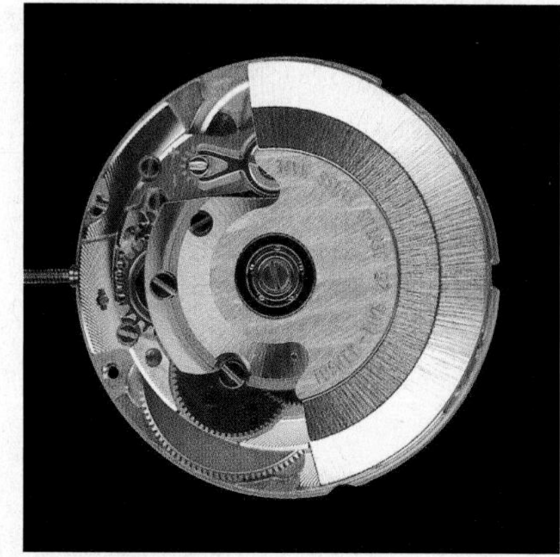

Caliber 2834-2

Mechanical with automatic winding, ball-bearing rotor, stop-seconds, power reserve 38 hours
Functions: hours, minutes, sweep seconds; date window with quick-set at 3 o'clock and day display with quick-set at 12 o'clock
Diameter: 29 mm (13''')
Height: 5.05 mm
Jewels: 25
Frequency: 28,800 vph
Fine adjustment system: ETACHRON with index

Caliber 2891-A9

Mechanical with automatic winding (base caliber 2892-A2), ball-bearing rotor, stop-seconds, power reserve 42 hours
Functions: hours, minutes, sweep seconds; perpetual calendar (date, day, month hands), moon phase disk, leap year indication
Diameter: 25.6 mm (11 1/2 "')
Height: 5.2 mm
Jewels: 21
Frequency: 28,800 vph
Fine adjustment system:
ETACHRON with index
Related Calibers: 2890-A9 (without second hand and stop-seconds)

Caliber 2892-A2

Mechanical with automatic winding, ball-bearing rotor, stop-seconds, power reserve 42 hours
Functions: hours, minutes, sweep seconds; date window with quick-set at 3 o'clock
Diameter: 25.6 mm (11 1/2''')
Height: 3.6 mm
Jewels: 21
Frequency: 28,800 vph
Fine adjustment system:
ETACHRON with index

Caliber 2893-1

Mechanical with automatic winding, ball-bearing rotor, stop-seconds, power reserve 42 hours
Functions: hours, minutes, sweep seconds; date window with quick-set at 3 o'clock; world time with central disk
Diameter: 25.6 mm (11 1/2''')
Height: 4.1 mm
Jewels: 21
Frequency: 28,800 vph
Fine adjustment system:
ETACHRON with index
Related Calibers: 2893-2 (24-hour hand/second time zone instead of world time disk); 2893-3 (only world time disk without date window)

Caliber 2895-1

Mechanical with automatic winding, ball-bearing rotor, stop-seconds, power reserve 42 hours
Functions: hours, minutes, subsidiary seconds at 6 o'clock; date window with quick-set at 3 o'clock
Diameter: 25.6 mm (11 1/2''')
Height: 4.35 mm
Jewels: 30
Frequency: 28,800 vph
Fine adjustment system:
ETACHRON with index

Caliber 2896

Mechanical with automatic winding, ball-bearing rotor, stop-seconds, power reserve 42 hours
Functions: hours, minutes, sweep seconds; large date window (double digits) at 3 o'clock
Diameter: 25.6 mm (11 1/2''')
Height: 4.85 mm
Jewels: 22
Frequency: 28,800 vph
Fine adjustment system:
ETACHRON with index

Caliber 2897

Mechanical with automatic winding, ball-bearing rotor, stop-seconds, power reserve 42 hours
Functions: hours, minutes, sweep seconds; power reserve display at 7 o'clock
Diameter: 25.6 mm (11 1/2''')
Height: 4.85 mm
Jewels: 21
Frequency: 28,800 vph
Fine adjustment system:
ETACHRON with index

Caliber 2894-2

Mechanical with automatic winding, ball-bearing rotor, stop-seconds, power reserve 42 hours
Functions: hours, minutes, subsidiary seconds at 3 o'clock; chronograph (30-minute counter at 9 o'clock, 12-hour counter at 6 o'clock, sweep stop second hand); date window with quick-set at 4 o'clock
Diameter: 28.6 mm (12 1/2''')
Height: 6.1 mm
Jewels: 37
Frequency: 28,800 vph
Fine adjustment system: ETACHRON with index
Remarks: Module construction

Caliber 2094

Mechanical with automatic winding, ball-bearing rotor, stop-seconds, power reserve 40 hours
Functions: hours, minutes, subsidiary seconds at 9 o'clock; chronograph (30-minute counter at 3 o'clock, 12-hour counter at 6 o'clock, sweep stop second hand); date window with quick-set at 3 o'clock
Diameter: 23.3 mm (10 1/2''')
Height: 5.5 mm
Jewels: 33
Frequency: 28,800 vph
Fine adjustment system: ETACHRON with index

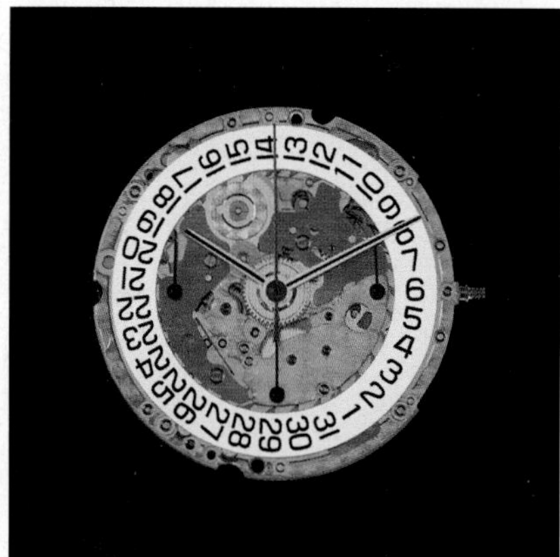

Caliber 7750

Mechanical with automatic winding, ball-bearing rotor, stop-seconds, power reserve 42 hours
Functions: hours, minutes, subsidiary seconds at 9 o'clock; chronograph (30-minute counter at 12 o'clock, 12-hour counter at 6 o'clock, sweep stop second hand); day/date window with quick-set at 3 o'clock
Diameter: 30 mm (13 1/4''')
Height: 7.9 mm
Jewels: 25
Frequency: 28,800 vph
Fine adjustment system: ETACHRON with index
Related calibers: 7751 (with sweep date hand, windows for day and month below the 12, moon phase at 6 o'clock, 24-hour hand at 9 o'clock); 7765 and 7760 (manually wound versions)

Caliber 7751 (dial side)

Based on chronograph Caliber 7750, Caliber 7751 differs in having 24-hour hand, moon phase indication, sweep date hand, and windows for day and month placed prominently below the 12. All calendar functions, including moon phase, can be quick set.

Caliber 7754

Mechanical with automatic winding, ball-bearing rotor, stop-seconds, power reserve 42 hours
Functions: hours, minutes, subsidiary seconds at 9 o'clock; chronograph (30-minute counter at 12 o'clock, 12-hour counter at 6 o'clock, sweep stop second hand); date window with quick-set at 3 o'clock; settable sweep 24-hour hand (second time zone)
Diameter: 30 mm (13 1/4''')
Height: 7.9 mm
Jewels: 25
Frequency: 28,800 vph
Fine adjustment system: ETACHRON with index

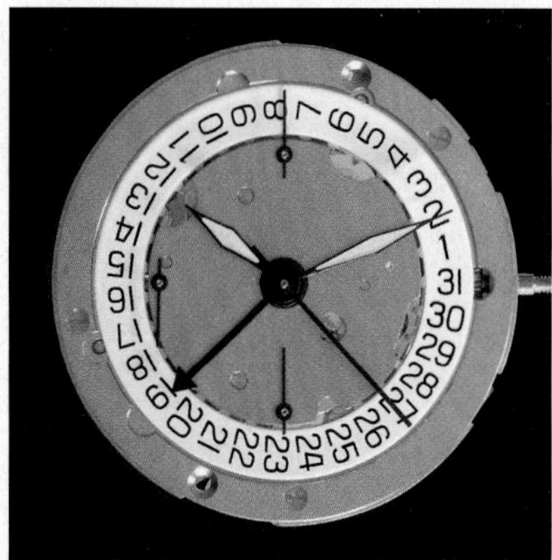

Caliber A07.111

Mechanical with automatic winding, ball-bearing rotor, stop-seconds, power reserve 42 hours
Functions: hours, minutes, subsidiary seconds at 9 o'clock; chronograph (30-minute counter at 12 o'clock, 12-hour counter at 6 o'clock, sweep stop second hand); date window with quick-set at 3 o'clock
Diameter: 36.6 mm (16 3/4''')
Height: 7.9 mm
Jewels: 24
Frequency: 28,800 vph
Fine adjustment system: ETACHRON with index
Remarks: Based on Caliber 7750, this movement is also available in a manually wound version

Revised and
Updated Edition
TEQUILA
The Spirit of Mexico
PREFACE
Carlos Monsiváis
PHOTOGRAPHY
Michael Calderwood
TEXT
Enrique Martínez Limón

De Bethune

Watchmaking for the Twenty-first Century

by Elizabeth Doerr

Switzerland is full of specialists. This may not be news to the avid watch fan, but it is something that easily slips the mind. These specialists are tucked away in every nook and cranny of the craggy, picturesque country, their names rarely coming to light.
This was not a fate David Zanetta was ready to share. For many, many years Zanetta has helped to form some of the industry's most creative pieces, never taking credit, always remaining a behind-the-scenes figure with his team of horological specialists.
But now Zanetta has branched out. Founding a new watch brand, he is ready to show everyone what he is capable of and take full responsibility for it. The results, quiet as they have been until now, are remarkable. When setting up this new company, he did it right. He acquired all of the necessary machines right off the bat to allow De Bethune to design and manufacture its own movements. And he started right off with complications – no fooling around here. This brand means business.
Currently, the collection comprises twelve different models, both of the automatic and manually wound varieties. The watches range from the sober DB2, an elegant two-handed timepiece, to a veritable feast of complications

David Zanetta

Baselworld 2004's striking introduction: DB15.

extending through the rest of the collection. These specialties include a single-button chronograph simply called DB1 that follows a vintage horological tradition: all of the column-wheel controlled chronograph functions (start-stop-reset) are activated by one single button that is found on the elegant case's crown. DB3 is a GMT model with seven entire days of power reserve. The power reserve indicator is represented by a gold moon upon a blue disk that moves back and forth between "maximum" and "minimum." The crown and its three positions are used to set all of the functions and wind the manual movement.
DB5 and DB10 are "simple" automatic watches with sweep seconds, while DB4 is a complicated piece whose highlight is formed by a minute repeater on two gongs. The repeater slide, located at 9 o'clock on the 42-mm case, activates the mechanism as well as a look of pure joy on the face of the listener.
DB9 might look simpler than the others, but this timepiece displaying hours and minutes also indicates the remaining power reserve – 168 hours of it (seven days). The movement is the one developed for DB2 with an added original up-and-down mechanism integrated into the base caliber. DB8, on the other hand, goes back to the single-button chronograph theme. While DB1 has a 30-minute counter and a small seconds dial, DB8 features a 45-minute counter at 6 o'clock, also controlled by a column wheel. DB12 features a chronograph that is more traditional in appearance and function according to today's standards. In addition, it is outfitted with a large date and a month display as well. DB12's chronograph is controlled by a column wheel, and the functions are turned on and off by the conventional buttons located above and below the crown on the right side of the case. The date is set by a small button located at 10 o'clock, while the month is set by one at 3:30. And from here on out, it gets more and more complicated. DB CS1 is a split-seconds chronograph with perpetual calendar and large date,

making it the first timepiece ever to combine these characteristics. Control of the split-seconds function is found on the crown, while the chronograph buttons are in the regular spot as on DB12.
DB CS2 gets even more complicated: minute repeater, equation of time, perpetual calendar, and tourbillon all in one. In keeping with the overall low-key, traditional appearance of these watches, however, the tourbillon can only be seen through the sapphire crystal case back. The equation of time is displayed by a discrete rose gold hand that moves along a scale positioned inside the *minuterie* that goes from -17 to +17 to show the difference between mean and solar time.
DB CS3, housed in a platinum case, features a minute-repeater, a perpetual calendar, and a moon phase display, while DB CS4 is a mono-pusher minute repeater. The repeater is not activated as it usually would be by a slide, but by a button located on the crown.
The highlight of Baselworld 2004 was, of course, DB 15, a perpetual calendar with a three-dimensional moon phase display. This timepiece's unusual focal point is formed by the sphere made of platinum and stainless steel that rotates upon its own axis on the dial. The steel half of the sphere is blued to represent the dark side of the moon. This timepiece's movement is manufactured entirely in De Bethune's workshops, as is its perpetual calendar mechanism. The regulating system is outfitted with a number of new characteristics such as a balance made of titanium and platinum and stabilizing bars made of blued titanium.
The appearance of each of these timepieces is very obviously cut from the same cloth. The elegant case design is understated and classic as hardly another brand. The dials are made of silver-plated solid gold and are very often guilloché à main, with hands of blued steel. The cases are manufactured only in the finest precious metals – yellow gold, rose gold, white gold, and platinum. But perhaps the most striking element on the cases is their so-called ogival lugs, a brand-new lug shape that is only utilized by this company.

DB8 is a single-button chronograph with a 45-minute counter.

This chronograph with a large date display is called DB12.

Svend Andersen
Krone
1275 Busch Parkway
Buffalo Grove, IL 60089
Tel.: 847-215-0011
Fax: 847-215-7146
www.andersen-geneve.ch

Angular Momentum USA
11006 N. Port Washington Road
Mequon, WI 53092
Tel: 414-379-3880
info@angularmomentum.us
www.angularmomentum.us

Anonimo Firenze USA
85 Hazel Road
Berkeley, CA 94705
Tel.: 510-649-0450
Fax: 510-649-0460
anonimofirenzeus@aol.com
www.anonimousa.com

Arnold & Sons
British Masters, LLC
444 Madison Avenue, Suite 601
New York, NY 10022
Tel.: 212-688-4500
Fax: 212-888-5025
www.thebritishmasters.biz

Audemars Piguet (North America) Inc.
40 East 57th Street
New York, NY 10022
Tel.: 212-758-8400
Fax: 212-758-8538
www.audemarspiguet.com

Ball Watch Company, Inc.
1131 4th Street North
St. Petersburg, FL 33701
Tel.: 800-922-HESS
www.ballwatch.com

Baume & Mercier
Richemont North America
Fifth Avenue and 52nd Street
New York, NY 10022
Tel.: 212-753-0111
Fax: 212-753-7250
www.baume-et-mercier.com

Bell & Ross, Inc.
1688 Meridian Ave., Suite 504
Miami Beach, FL 33139
Tel.: 305-674-9464
Fax: 305-672-3840
information@bellrossusa.com
www.bellross.com

Ernst Benz
6740 Netherlands Drive
Wilmington, NC 28405
Tel.: 910-792-9802
Fax: 910-792-0523
info@ernstbenz.com
www.ernstbenz.com

Blancpain
The Swatch Group (U.S.), Inc.
1200 Harbor Boulevard
Weehawken, NJ 07087
Tel.: 201-271-1400
Fax: 201-271-4633
www.blancpain.com

blu – source du temps
PK Time Group LLC
30 West 57th Street, 2nd Floor
New York, NY 10019
Tel.: 888-919-TIME
Fax: 212-397-0960
info@pktime.com
www.pktime.com

Rainer Brand
WatchBuys
Tel.: 888-333-4895
www.watchbuys.com

Martin Braun USA
1717 West 6th St., Suite 212
Austin, TX 78703
Tel.: 512-499-0123
Fax: 512-499-8112
info@time-central.com
www.martinbraunusa.com

Breguet
The Swatch Group (U.S.), Inc.
1200 Harbor Boulevard
Weehawken, NJ 07087
Tel.: 201-271-1400
Fax: 201-271-4633
www.breguet.com

Breitling U.S.A. Inc.
206 Danbury Road
Stamford, CT 06897
Tel.: 800-641-7343
Fax: 203-327-2537
www.breitling.com

Carl F. Bucherer
1805 South Metro Parkway
Dayton, OH 45459
Tel.: 800-395-4300
info@cfbnorthamerica.com
www.carl-f-bucherer.com

Bvlgari Corporation of America
730 Fifth Avenue
New York, NY 10019
Tel.: 212-315-9700

Cartier Inc.
Fifth Avenue and 52nd Street
New York, NY 10022
Tel.: 1-800-CARTIER
Fax: 212-753-7250
www.cartier.com

Chase-Durer
270 N. Canon Drive
Beverly Hills, CA 90210
Tel.: 310-550-7280
Fax: 310-550-0830
www.chase-durer.com

Chopard
630 Fifth Avenue
Suite 3410
New York, NY 10111
Tel.: 212-247-0545
Fax: 212-397-0197
www.chopard.com

Chronoswiss
Bellport Time Group, LLC
112 South Country Road, Suite 101
Bellport, NY 11713
Tel.: 631-776-1135
Fax: 631-776-1136
www.chronoswiss.com

Frédérique Constant
International Time Group
7700 Congress Avenue, Suite 1115
Boca Raton, FL 33487
Tel.: 561-241-3509
Fax: 561-241-3574
www.frederique-constant.com

Corum USA, LLC
3 Mason
Irvine, CA 92618
Tel.: 949-458-4200
Fax: 949-458-1258
www.corum.ch

d.freemont, Inc.
P.O. Box 1344
Wickenburg, AZ 85358
Tel.: 877-236-9248
dfreemont@earthlink.net
www.dfreemontwatches.com

Davosa
d.freemont, Inc.
P.O. Box 1344
Wickenburg, AZ 85358
Tel.: 877-236-9248
dfreemont@earthlink.net
www.dfreemontwatches.com

De Bethune
Wings of Time
530 Lincoln Road, Suite 200
Miami Beach, FL 33139
Tel.: 305-531-2600
Fax: 305-531-6002
www.debethune.ch

De Grisogono, Inc.
21 East 63rd Street, 5th Floor
New York, NY 10021
Tel.: 212-821-0280
Fax: 212-821-0281
www.degrisogono.com

Doxa S.A.
Ferdinand-Frey-Weg 36/6
1140 Vienna, Austria
Tel.: (011-43) 1-577 26 44
Fax: (011-43) 1-577 26 27
info@doxawatches.com
www.doxawatches.com

Dubey & Schaldenbrand
PK Time Group LLC
30 West 57th Street, 2nd Floor
New York, NY 10019
Tel.: 888-919-TIME
Fax: 212-397-0960
info@pktime.com
www.pktime.com

Roger Dubuis
Helvetia Time Co., Inc.
100 N. Wilkes-Barre Boulevard, Suite 303
Wilkes-Barre, PA 18702
Tel.: 717-822-1900
Fax: 717-822-4699

Alfred Dunhill (North America) Limited
450 Park Avenue
New York, NY 10022
Tel.: 800-541-0738
Fax: 212-750-8841
www.dunhill.com

Ebel U.S.A. Inc.
750 Lexington Avenue
New York, NY 10022
Tel.: 212-888-3235
Fax: 212-888-6719
www.ebel.ch

Eberhard, LLC
444 Madison Avenue, Suite 601
New York, NY 10022
Tel.: 212-688-4500
Fax: 212-888-5025
www.eberhard-co-watches.ch

Epos
GNT Incorporated
P.O. Box 6724
Providence, RI 02940
Tel.: 1-800-689-2225
www.gntwatches.com

Eterna
Porsche Design of America
3001 Red Hill Avenue
Building 6, Suite 109
Costa Mesa, CA 92626
Tel.: 800-512-5152
Fax: 714-556-2239
www.eterna.ch

Jacques Etoile
DECHUSA Watches
1210 N. Cherokee Avenue 225
Los Angeles, CA 90038
Tel.: 323-461-7230
jetoile-usa@comcast.net
www.jacquesetoile.com

Carlo Ferrara
Ferret S.r.l.
Via Fulvio Palmieri, 6
00151 Rome, Italy
Tel.: (011-39) 06-657 950 97
Fax: (011-39) 06-653 78 73
info@carloferrara.it
www.carloferrara.it

Fortis
LWR Time Ltd.
15 South Franklin Street, Suite 214
Wilkes-Barre, PA 18711
Tel.: 570-408-1640
Fax: 570-408-1657
www.fortis-watch.com

Gérald Genta
730 Fifth Avenue
New York, NY 10019
Tel.: 1-866-DrandGG

Gevril
23 Dover Terrace
Monsey, NY 10952
Tel.: 866-425-9882
Fax: 845-425-9897
info@gevril.net
www.gevril.net

Girard-Perregaux
Tradema of America, Inc.
201 Route 17 North
Rutherford, NJ 07070
Tel.: 1-877-846-3447
Fax: 201-507-1553
gpwebmaster@girard-perregaux-usa.com
www.girard-perregaux-usa.com

Glashütte Original
The Swatch Group (U.S.), Inc.
1200 Harbor Boulevard
Weehawken, NJ 07087
Tel.: 201-271-1400
Fax: 201-271-4633
www.glashuette-original.com

Glycine, LLC
444 Madison Avenue, Suite 601
New York, NY 10022
Tel.: 212-688-4500
Fax: 212-888-5025
www.glycine-watch.ch

Graham
British Masters, LLC
444 Madison Avenue, Suite 601
New York, NY 10022
Tel.: 212-688-4500
Fax: 212-888-5025
www.thebritishmasters.biz

Hanhart
Eric Armin, Inc.
Fine Watch Division
567 Commerce Street – P.O. Box 644
Franklin Lakes, NJ 07417-0644
Tel.: 800-853-5486
Fax: 201-891-5689
www.hanhartusa.com

Harwood
LWR Time Ltd.
15 South Franklin Street, Suite 214
Wilkes-Barre, PA 18711
Tel.: 570-408-1640
Fax: 570-408-1657
www.harwood-watch.com

Hermès of Paris, Inc.
55 East 59th Street
New York, NY 10022
Tel.: 800-441-4488
Fax: 212-835-6460
www.hermes.com

Hublot
MDM of America, Inc.
500 Cypress Creek Road West, Suite 430
Fort Lauderdale, FL 33309
Tel.: 800-536-0636
Fax: 954-568-6337
www.hublot.ch

IWC North America
645 Fifth Avenue, 6th Floor
New York, NY 10022
Tel.: 1-800-432-9330
Fax: 212-872-1312
www.iwc.ch

Jacob & Co. Watches, Inc.
1196 Avenue of the Americas
New York, NY 10039
Tel.: 1-866-522-6210
Fax: 212-719-0074
contact@jacobandco.com
www.jacobandco.com

Jaeger-LeCoultre
645 Fifth Avenue
New York, NY 10022
Tel.: 800-JLC-TIME
www.jaeger-lecoultre.com

Montres Jaquet Droz SA
Rue Jaquet Droz 5
2300 La Chaux-de-Fonds, Switzerland
Tel.: 011-49-32-911 28 88
Fax: 011-49-32-911 28 85
jd@jaquet-droz.com
www.jaquet-droz.com

JeanRichard
Tradema of America, Inc.
201 Route 17 North, 8th Floor
Rutherford, NJ 07070
Tel.: 1-877-357-8463
Fax: 201-507-1553
webmaster@djr-usa.com
www.djr-usa.com

F.P. Journe
Wings of Time
530 Lincoln Road, Suite 200
Miami Beach, FL 33139
Tel.: 305-531-2600
Fax: 305-531-6002
www.fpjourne.com

Kobold Instruments Inc.
1801 Parkway View Drive
Pittsburgh, PA 15205
Tel.: 412-788-2830
Fax: 412-788-4890
info@koboldusa.com
www.koboldusa.com

Maurice Lacroix USA
17835 Ventura Boulevard, Suite 301
Encino, CA 91316-3629
Tel.: 1-800-794-7736
Fax: 818-609-7079
www.mauricelacroixusa.com

Lange Uhren GmbH
Altenberger Str. 15
01768 Glashütte, Germany
Tel.: 011-49-35053-44 0
Fax: 011-49-35053-44 100
info@lange-soehne.com
www.lange-soehne.com

Limes
DECHUSA Watches
1210 N. Cherokee Avenue 225
Los Angeles, CA 90038
Tel.: 323-461-7230
www.limes-watches.com

Longines
The Swatch Group (U.S.), Inc.
1200 Harbor Boulevard
Weehawken, NJ 07087
Tel.: 201-271-1400
Fax: 201-271-4633
www.longines.com

Marcello C. Watches
Matt van Doorn
8674 Chanhassen Hills Drive
Chanhassen, MN 55317
Tel.: 952-949-0315
Fax: 952-949-0315
sales@MarcelloC-watches.com
www.MarcelloC-watches.com

Meistersinger
WatchBuys
Tel.: 888-333-4895
www.watchbuys.com

Mido
Swiss Watches
800 South Pacific Coast Highway, Suite 8-202
Redondo Beach, CA 90277
Tel.: 310-212-6436
Fax: 310-212-5764
www.midowatches.com

Daniel Mink
560 Main Street, Suite 2A
Allenhurst, NJ 07711
Tel.: 732-663-9950
Fax: 732-663-9952
www.danielmink.com

Montblanc International
26 Main Street
Chatham, NJ 07928
Tel.: 908-508-2301
www.montblanc.com

Nautische Instrumente Mühle GmbH
Müglitztalstr. 7
01768 Glashuette, Germany
sales@muehle-glashutte.info
www.muehle-uhren.com

Montres Franck Muller USA, Inc.
207 W. 25th Street, 8th Floor
New York, NY 10001
Tel.: 212-463-8898
Fax: 212-463-7082
www.franckmullerusa.com

Movado Group Inc.
650 From Road
Paramus, NJ 07652
Tel.: 201-267-8115
Fax: 201-267-8020
www.movado.com

Ulysse Nardin Inc.
6001 Broken Sound Parkway, Suite 504
Boca Raton, FL 33487
Tel.: 561-988-6400
Fax: 561-988-0123
usa@ulysse-nardin.com
www.ulysse-nardin.com

NBY
1717 West 6th St., Suite 212
Austin, TX 78703
Tel.: 512-499-0123
Fax: 512-499-8112
info@time-central.com
www.martinbraunusa.com

Armand Nicolet
Fifth Avenue Luxury Group
590 Fifth Avenue, 2nd Floor
New York, NY 10036
Tel.: 212-398-4440
Fax: 212-398-2179
www.armandnicolet.com

Nivrel
WatchBuys
Tel.: 888-333-4895
www.watchbuys.com

Nomos USA
AMEICO
1 Church Street
New Milford, CT 06776
Tel.: 860-354-8765
Fax: 860-354-8620
info@ameico.com
www.glashuette.com

Officine Panerai
645 Fifth Avenue
New York, NY 10022
Tel.: 1-877-PANERAI
Fax: 212-891-2315
www.panerai.com

Omega
The Swatch Group (U.S.), Inc.
1200 Harbor Boulevard
Weehawken, NJ 07087
Tel.: 201-271-1400
Fax: 201-271-4633
www.omegawatches.com

Orbita Corporation
1205 Culbreth Drive
Wilmington, NC 28405
Tel.: 910-256-5300
Fax: 910-256-5356
info@orbita.net
www.orbita.net

Oris USA, Inc.
2 Skyline Drive
Hawthorne, NY 10532
Tel.: 914-347-6747
Fax: 914-347-4782
sales@orisusa.com
www.oris-watch.com

Parmigiani Fleurier USA
33552 Valle Road
San Juan Capistrano, CA 92675
Tel.: 949-489-2885
Fax: 949-488-0116
www.parmigiani.ch

Patek Philippe
1 Rockefeller Plaza, #930
New York, NY 10020
Tel.: 212-581-0870
Fax: 212-956-6399
info@patek.com
www.patek.com

Piaget
663 Fifth Avenue, 7th Floor
New York, NY 10022
Tel.: 212-355-6444
Fax: 212-909-4332

Paul Picot of America Inc.
International Time Group
7700 Congress Avenue, Suite 1115
Boca Raton, FL 33487
Tel.: 561-241-3509
Fax: 561-241-3574
www.paulpicot.ch

Poljot-V Uhrenvertriebs GmbH
Hanauer Str. 25
63755 Alzenau, Germany
Tel.: (011-49) 6023-91 99 3
Fax: (011-49) 6023-91 99 49
Poljot-International@t-online.de
www.poljot-international.com

Porsche Design of America
3001 Red Hill Avenue
Building 6, Suite 109
Costa Mesa, CA 92626
Tel.: 800-512-5152
Fax: 714-556-2239
www.americanporschedesign.com

Rado
The Swatch Group (U.S.), Inc.
1200 Harbor Boulevard
Weehawken, NJ 07087
Tel.: 201-271-1400
Fax: 201-271-4633
www.rado.com

Auguste Reymond USA
2221 Justin Road, Suite 119-330
Flower Mound, TX 75028
Tel.: 940-484-4976
Fax: 940-484-4699
info@augustereymond.com
www.augustereymond.ch

RGM Watch Company
PMB #130, 590 Centerville Road
Lancaster, PA 17601-1306
Tel.: 717-653-9799
Fax: 717-653-9700
rgmwatches@aol.com

Rolex Watch U.S.A., Inc.
Rolex Building, 665 Fifth Avenue
New York, NY 10022-5358
Tel.: 212-758-7700
Fax: 212-826-8617
www.rolex.com

Daniel Roth
730 Fifth Avenue
New York, NY 10019
Tel.: 1-866-DrandGG

Scalfaro USA
4600 Lusk Lane
Flower Mound, TX 7528
Tel.: 877-688-1560
Fax: 817-491-1341
www.scalfarousa.com

Scatola del Tempo
Fifth Avenue Luxury Group
590 Fifth Avenue, 2nd Floor
New York, NY 10036
Tel.: 212-398-4440
Fax: 212-398-2179

Jörg Schauer
WatchBuys
Tel.: 888-333-4895
www.watchbuys.com

Galerie Alain Silberstein
200 Boulevard Saint-Germain
75007 Paris, France
Tel.: (011-33) 1-45 44 10 10
Fax: (011-33) 1-45 44 53 53
www.a-silberstein.fr

Sinn
WatchBuys
Tel.: 888-333-4895
www.watchbuys.com

Sothis Fine Watches
WatchBuys
Tel.: 888-333-4895
www.watchbuys.com

Stowa
Salmbacher Weg 52
75331 Engelsbrand, Germany
Tel.: (011-49) 7082-930 60
Fax.: (011-49) 7082-930 62
info1@stowa.de
www.stowa.de

Swiss Army Brands, Inc.
One Research Drive, P.O. Box 874
Shelton, CT 06484-0874
Tel.: 203-944-2334
Fax: 203-944-2105
www.swissarmy.com

TAG Heuer
LVMH Watch & Jewelry USA
960 S. Springfield Avenue
Springfield, NJ 07081
Tel.: 973-467-1890
www.tagheuer.com

Temption GmbH
Raistinger Str. 53
71083 Herrenberg, Germany
Tel.: (011-49) 7032-97 79 54
Fax: (011-49) 7032-97 79 55
ftemption@aol.com

Tissot
The Swatch Group (U.S.), Inc.
1200 Harbor Boulevard
Weehawken, NJ 07087
Tel.: 201-271-1400
Fax: 201-271-4633
www.tissot.ch

Tudor
Rolex Watch U.S.A., Inc.
Rolex Building, 665 Fifth Avenue
New York, NY 10022-5358
Tel.: 212-758-7700
Fax: 212-826-8617

Tutima USA, Inc.
20710 Manhattan Place
Torrance, CA 90501
Tel.: 1-TUTIMA-USA-1
Fax: 310-381-2930
www.tutima.com

Union Uhrenfabrik GmbH
Altenberger Str. 1
01768 Glashütte, Germany
Tel.: (011-49) 35053-46 476
Fax: (011-49) 35053-46 222
www.union-glashuette.com

Vacheron Constantin
Richemont North America
Fifth Avenue and 52nd Street
New York, NY 10022
Tel.: 212-753-0111
Fax: 212-753-7250
www.vacheron-constantin.com

Ventura USA, Inc.
540 West Boston Post Road 252
Mamaroneck, NY 10543
Tel.: 866-USA-1116
Fax: 914-835-4622
ventura@ventura.ch
www.ventura.ch

George J von Burg
Von Burg USA
Tel.: 1-866-635-9460
www.vonburgusa.com

Harry Winston, Inc.
718 Fifth Avenue
New York, NY 10019
Tel.: 1-800-848-3948
Fax: 212-582-4605
www.hwtimepieces.com

Xemex
Universal Watch Co., Inc.
5016 Schuster Street
Las Vegas, NV 89118
Tel.: 1-800-360-2568
info@silverprince.com
www.xemex.com

Zenith
LVMH Watch & Jewelry USA
960 S. Springfield Avenue
Springfield, NJ 07081
Tel.: 973-467-1890
Fax: 973-467-5495
www.zenith-watches.com

Zeno USA, LLC
12900 Preston Road, Suite 1035
Dallas, TX 75230
Tel.: 972-404-ZENO
Fax: 972-404-4660
sales@zenowatchbasel.com
www.zenowatchbasel.com

Editor-in-Chief: Peter Braun
Senior Editor: Elizabeth Doerr
Production and Layout: Collibri Prepress GmbH
Printed by: Schnitzer Druck GmbH

For more information about editorial content and advertising,
please contact:
Elizabeth Doerr
Wehlauer Str. 25a, 76139 Karlsruhe, Germany,
Fax: +49 / 721 / 680 29 72, DoerrElizabeth@aol.com

For more information about book sales, please contact:
Abbeville Press, 116 West 23rd Street, New York, NY 10011, 1-800-ARTBOOK,
www.abbeville.com

ISBN 0-7892-0839-3

Seventh Edition

2 4 6 8 10 9 7 5 3 1

Library of Congress Cataloging-in-Publication Data available upon request.

For further information about this title please contact Abbeville Press.

ISBN 0-7892-0839-3 U.S. $35.00
53500
EAN
9 780789 208392